Test Theory:

A Unified Treatment

Test Theory:
A Unified Treatment

Roderick P. McDonald
University of Illinois at Urbana–Champaign

 LAWRENCE ERLBAUM ASSOCIATES, PUBLISHERS
1999   Mahwah, New Jersey   London

Lawrence Erlbaum Associates, Inc., Publishers
10 Industrial Avenue
Mahwah, New Jersey 07430

Library of Congress Cataloging-in-Publication Data

McDonald, Roderick P.
　　Test theory : a unified treatment / Roderick P. McDonald.
　　　　p.　　cm.
　　Includes bibliographical references (p.　　　) and index.
　　ISBN 0-8058-3075-8 (c : alk. paper)
　　1. Psychology—Statistical methods.　2. Psychometrics.　3. Social
sciences—Statistical methods.　I. Title.
BF39.M175　　1999
150′.28′7—dc21　　　　　　　　　　　　　　　99-24196
　　　　　　　　　　　　　　　　　　　　　　　　CIP

Books published by Lawrence Erlbaum Associates are printed on acid-free paper,
and their bindings are chosen for strength and durability.

Printed in the United States of America
10　9　8　7　6　5　4　3　2

Contents

Preface

This text is an outcome of my experience in teaching a laboratory course on test theory in the Department of Psychology, University of Illinois at Urbana-Champaign, to a number of classes, typically containing approximately equal numbers of juniors, seniors, and graduate students. These students have generally not been specialists in mathematics, statistics, or quantitative psychology, but they have been sufficiently motivated to work with the necessary mathematical concepts.

The object of such a course on test theory is to introduce students to the main quantitative concepts, methods, and computational techniques needed for the development, evaluation, and application of tests in the behavioral/social sciences, including, of course, educational tests. In an account of the theory of test construction and use, actual tests and test items have a place as context, and as material for practical exercises. It is my view, as I hope the following chapters show, that test development and analysis should at every point be grounded in, and guided by, substantive knowledge and sound, substantively based concepts, and not treated as a set of statistical exercises. Even so, the field of test theory can be separated from that of psychological testing and assessment, much as texts on psychological statistics and research methods can be separated from texts on substantive psychological research topics. With this in mind, I have carried just two main empirical examples—small-scale but genuine applications—throughout the text, reused where possible to illustrate alternative methods, and a handful of other data sets for special illustrations. My students have not wished for more, but instructors will likely have favorite cases to add.

Books on test theory have generally consisted of collections of not very closely related topics. Partly because my research and teaching interests have included structural models—factor models and structural equation models—I have long believed that a very general version of the common factor model supplies a rigorous and unified treatment of the major concepts and techniques of test theory. The implicit unifying principle throughout the following pages is a general nonlinear common factor model, which includes item response models as special cases, and includes also the (linear) common factor model as an approximation. The account of the field in this text is developed from that unifying perspective, while giving appropriate coverage of the conventional topics. Instructors, more than students, may be troubled initially by some of the expository developments that follow from the logic of my position: for example, the derivation of coefficient alpha from the linear common factor model, or the use of item factor analysis to arrive at item response theory. It is my hope that they will be able to see the logic of this approach and find it both congenial and useful.

This book is intended primarily for students of psychology, including, of course, educational psychology, and any other fields of social science where tests are constructed and used. Experience with classes of students ranging from junior to graduate, and ranging even more widely in their quantitative skills, has led me to believe that an account of test theory should treat at least some parts of the mathematics of the subject as "optional extras"—proofs or technical explanations that can be omitted without loss of continuity. With the help of their instructors, students can tailor the course to their own needs and abilities. Some will bypass the optional remarks, proofs, and sections, given the approval of their instructor. Some, possessing good formal training in mathematical statistics, are asked to excuse a degree of informality in the proofs, which are designed to be accessible to well-motivated students of intermediate mathematical ability. The essential prerequisite is the typical undergraduate course or courses in statistics for the behavioral/social sciences.

In a one-semester course based on the draft chapters, I found it possible to teach the first 13 chapters as material to be tested. For this I used exercises, examinations, and a major individual test-construction project developed out of each student's research interests. To fit the material into one semester it is sufficient to give introductory lectures on the central concepts of the remaining chapters, which can then be regarded as resource materials rather than topics that must be covered in detail. I have chosen not to include exercises in the text (such as those developed by or with my teaching assistants). This seems to be a place where instructors rightly prefer to create their own exercises as a flexible response to the needs of their students. Although the intention was certainly to develop a teaching text, this book may also supply resource materials for a substantive course on testing and assessment. The unified treatment offered will also be of interest to researchers, including specialists in this field.

In a laboratory course on test theory, minor computations can be done by pocket calculator, but the main technologies require computer programs. Some instructors may wish to choose a statistical package providing confirmatory and possibly exploratory factor analysis and a method for fitting and using item response models from the available commercial products. A diskette with self-contained programs for these purposes is available upon request by contacting Lawrence Erlbaum Associates, 10 Industrial Ave., Mahwah, NJ 07430, or by e-mail, orders@erlbaum.com. It is deliberately left as a separate instructional device. The instructor or reader can treat the programs as a direct way into these methods. A computer program, TESTCOMP, kindly supplied by Brad Crouch, has been used for most of the computations in Chapter 13. All other computer analyses use programs developed for me by Colin Fraser, to whom I owe a permanent debt of gratitude. These are the programs supplied on the diskette.

Helpful comments on chapters have been kindly supplied by Martha Stocking, Linda Hynan, Larry Hubert, Roger Millsap, Tim Johnson, Dan Bolt, Don Dulany, Mark Gierl, Mike Butler, Ringo Ho, and other colleagues and students, whose forgiveness for not naming them I now beg. Remaining errors are my own responsibility. I acknowledge a particular debt of gratitude to my wife Avis for her patient acceptance of my long disappearances into the study.

Roderick P. McDonald

General Introduction

Test theory is an abbreviated expression for *theory of psychological tests and measurements*, which can in turn be abbreviated back to *psychometric theory* (psychological measurement). Test theory provides a general collection of techniques for evaluating the development and use, in assessment, of specific psychological tests. It has the same relation to the practice of testing as statistical and experimental design principles have to actual programs of experimental research in behavioral science. There are courses and corresponding textbooks available on *assessment*—the evaluation of characteristics of individuals through the use of tests, interviews, and so on.[1] There are also more specialized courses and textbooks—on tests used to measure educational abilities and achievements, tests used to assess personality characteristics, and tests developed for the measurement of social attitudes. Test theory is both more general and much narrower in scope, just as the topic of experimental design and statistical analysis is more general and narrower than any survey of actual experimental studies in an area of psychology.

The objectives of this chapter are, first, to indicate the kinds of problem that motivate study of the topic known as test theory; second, to give a general orientation to it, including an outline of key historical developments; and, third, to give, as far as possible, a preview of the chapters to follow, with suggestions about the approaches that can be taken to them.

As a way to get started, let us consider three practical problems of measurement. These serve as concrete examples of the types of question answered by test theory:

1. A teacher constructs 20 items for a mathematics test. The answer to each item can be checked very easily as *pass* or *fail.* The teacher gives the examination to a number of students, and adds up the number of passes to make a score for mathematics for each of them. The teacher wonders about several problems: (a) Should there be one score for mathematics or two scores, one for items that on the face of it are about geometry, and one for items that appear to be about algebra? (b) And what about items that require both geometry and algebra? (c) Are all the items good measures of mathematical ability or are some better than others? (d) If one score is sufficient, how accurate is it as a measure of mathematics knowledge? (e) Are 20 items sufficient to give a reasonably accurate determination of each student's knowledge? Should more be used? Could fewer have been used, with a saving of time and effort? (f) If different items had been written, would they have measured the same thing? Equally well? In particular, can two tests be made, with different items, whose scores are completely interchangeable? Perhaps the teacher would like to put the items in a computer and have the students respond at the keyboard. A computer program could decide which items each student should be tested on. (g) Are students at the lower end of the scale measured as accurately as students in the middle or at the high end? If some students score 0 or 20, the test seems respectively too difficult or too easy for them, so perhaps easier and/or more difficult items should be added? (h) Are the items free from bias, when given to students of different backgrounds? Could some students have irrelevant problems with certain items because of differences in their background and experience? How would we know?

2. A clinical psychologist writes a set of items such as:

I have difficulty sleeping: True/False

I am afraid of heights: True/False

I get tired easily: True/False

I often have bad dreams: True/False . . .

(Readers are invited to consider how they would write more items "of the same kind.") The intention here is to use a score obtained from a subject's responses to these items to determine whether the subject suffers from a neurotic disorder. The clinical psychologist wonders about the following: Should there be one score for neurosis, or should there be several for, say, phobias, endogenous anxiety, . . . ? How accurate are the score(s) as measures of neurotic conditions? And further questions follow along the lines of (a) through (h) for the first problem.

3. A survey researcher wants to study attitudes to gun control. She starts writing a series of items, with a typical survey format, such as:

(a) Assault weapons do not belong in private hands—

Strongly agrcc (SA)
Agree (A)
Neither agree nor disagree (nAD)
Disagree (D)
Strongly disagree (SD)

(b) All hand-guns should be licensed—

SA   A   nAD   D   SD

(c) Government interference with the right to bear arms is an infringement of liberties—

SA   A   nAD   D   SD

(The reader is invited to consider writing a few more items "of the same kind.") The survey researcher wonders: Is there a good way to score the items, separately or together? [We notice that item (c) seems to measure in the opposite direction from (a) and (b), and we might believe that "strongly agree" should carry more "weight" than just "agree."] Do the item scores add up to make a general score for approval of gun control, or do different items measure different aspects of the question? Again, how accurately is the attitude measured? How many items are needed to cover the attitude and measure it well enough? And so on.

Test theory consists of the use of mathematical concepts that have been developed in order to refine questions such as these into more precise forms and to provide answers to them. The student may need an immediate assurance that it is possible to acquire knowledge of the essential concepts of test theory, and the skill to apply these concepts to practical problems, without understanding all of the mathematical technicalities—foundations and proofs. But it is necessary to recognize from the beginning that test theory is essentially applied mathematics, overlapping with statistics.

The development of test theory has generally been motivated by the need to solve problems in psychology, including educational psychology and educational measurement. It has largely taken place at the hands of psychologists, who in many cases had to struggle to acquire the mathematics and, in particular, the statistical knowledge they needed to solve their problems. Until recent decades it was generally difficult (although there have been notable exceptions) to get mathematicians to recognize that problems of great urgency in psychological research could be interesting, and not without challenge, to the mathematicians. This fact has some good and some bad consequences for the student entering this field of work. On the good side, a great deal of the theory that has been developed was originally expressed in fairly straightforward formulas. By now, mathematicians have taught the field to express these concepts much more formally, rigorously, pedantically, and incomprehensibly, but behavioral science students and researchers can work on a principle of not demanding a higher level of formality and rigor in test theory than is needed for the comprehension and application of a particular piece of theory. We do not need to set an unnecessarily high level of aspiration in mathematical credentials. On the bad side, the development of psychometric theory has tended to be a piecemeal and rather confused process. In some ways, the field has been slow to recognize mathematical and conceptual equivalences among different developments.

Another problem with the development of test theory is that a major part of it took place before the computer revolution of the late 1950s. Yet much of psychometric theory was and is far more computationally intensive than most of the comparable developments in statistics in the earlier era. Consequently, the pioneers were forced to invent short-cut numerical devices, which sometimes made the theory itself look rather crude to mathematicians. Some of these devices have not been removed to a museum of psychometric theory, but remain in operation alongside more efficient computer methods. Sometimes these older methods provide the main defaults in computer packages. This can be very confusing for the user.

So that these last remarks can take a more concrete form, we turn in the next section to a sketchy contextual and historical introduction, mainly referring to key theoretical developments. The following section describes the approach taken in this book, as well as various ways the text can be used by different readers. The chapter concludes with an outline of the contents. Like all such outlines, this can be understood better on a second reading, after the book itself has been not merely read but worked through.

CONTEXTUAL AND HISTORICAL

It has often been remarked that psychology has a long past and a short history, traceable as past to ancient Greece at least, and as history to its splitting off from philosophy about the middle of the 19th century. Similarly, if we include educational testing within the field of psychological measurement, the practice of testing has a past traceable to ancient China, but psychometric theory has a history that begins about the mid-19th century in the psychophysical laboratory. Within that short history, there are some key developments that form the foundations of modern test theory. Chronological order is not used in this sketch. Instead, several branches of development are outlined.

In 1904, Charles Spearman published two seminal papers, which included alternative analyses of the same data.[2] The first paper showed how to recognize, from test data, that the tests measure just one psychological attribute in common—a "common factor." The second showed how to estimate the amount of error in test scores. To do this, it was supposed that what the tests measure in common is a "true score," each being subject to "error of measurement." Over decades, by further elaborations, the first paper gave rise to common factor theory (chaps. 6 and 9), and the other gave rise to classical true-score theory (chaps. 5 and 7). These theories have tended to be treated as separate and unrelated branches of psychometrics, but they need not be.

Spearman thought of his work as supporting a psychological theory—that cognitive performances depend on a unitary psychological function, general intelligence. In his initial work he used ordinary examination results in academic subjects as measures of intelligence.

The very first functioning intelligence test was produced by Alfred Binet and Victor Henri in 1895, with an improved version following in 1905 from Binet and Simon. This test was based on the simple but effective device of choosing items for which the percentage of correct answers increased with (chronological) age, and identifying a "mental age" as the chronological age of subjects who typically passed those items. In 1914, Stern introduced the concept of an *intelligence quotient*, defined as the ratio of mental age to chronological age multiplied by 100. Lewis Terman developed the Stanford–Binet tests of intelligence out of Binet's work, and used Stern's age-based IQ. David Wechsler developed intelligence tests in which the mean and standard deviation of the group of examinees used to develop the test gave an IQ based on individual deviation from others of the same age. He chose a mean of 100 and a standard deviation of 15 for the resulting deviation IQ, which makes it appear comparable to the age-based IQ of Stern. This deviation IQ points toward the need to consider the choice of scale of a psychological test.[3]

Following Spearman's initial work, psychologists made increasingly careful attempts to develop items considered to measure intelligence, with related attempts to define the meaning of the concept more precisely. These attempts provided the main context for the development of test theory. A major question for several decades was whether intelligence was a unitary function, or whether it was necessary to recognize a number of distinct scholastic aptitudes—verbal versus nonverbal intelligence, or major "group factors" of intelligence. L. L. Thurstone in the 1930s elaborated Spearman's model into a "multiple factor" model.[4] This was conceived as a method of data analysis by which the psychologist could discover how many distinct kinds of ability "exist," and what their nature is. This ambitious program required the development of increasingly elaborate mathematical and numerical devices. As already mentioned, these were complicated by the need to reduce computational effort when human operators, not electronic computers, had to perform these functions. Work in the framework given by Thurstone tended to eliminate any notion of a general intelligence or scholastic aptitude in favor of an ever-increasing number of specialized but related aptitudes—numerical ability, verbal ability, spatial ability, and so on.

The prototype of personality self-report questionnaires was developed by Woodworth, about 1920, derived from psychiatric descriptions of symptoms of neurotic patients. The four items in example 2 can be taken as representative of Woodworth's Personal Data Sheet, as it was called, and of other personality inventories developed since. Perhaps the most widely used self-report personality inventory up to the time of writing is the Minnesota Multiphasic Personality Inventory (MMPI). Items were chosen from a large initial collection on the basis of contrasting responses of psychiatrically diagnosed groups of subjects—such as depressives, hysterics, psychopaths, paranoids, schizophrenics—to create subtests measuring tendencies toward these pathologies.[5]

Eventually, factor analysis methods were applied to personality tests. A degree of consensus seems to have emerged, through the work of Eysenck, Norman, and others,[6] that there are probably five main personality traits, with corresponding scales to measure them. These are:

1. Emotional stability—calm versus anxious, nonhypochondriac versus hypochondriac, and so on.
2. Extraversion—talkative versus silent, sociable versus reclusive, and so on.
3. Agreeableness—goodnatured versus irritable, mild versus headstrong, cooperative versus negativistic, and so on.
4. Conscientiousness—fussy versus careless, responsible versus undependable, and so on.
5. Culture—artistically sensitive versus insensitive, intellectual versus unreflective, imaginative versus unimaginative, and so on.

The reader may note that these dimensions of personality, or at least their descriptive adjectives, selected here to fill out their meaning, belong to the natural language. It seems as though we recognize the general meanings of these terms without, as in the case of the MMPI, criterion groups to determine appropriate subtests, and we could hope to develop self-report items to measure these attributes simply on the basis of a common language. As shown later, psychometric methods can be used to test the adequacy of the items we write as measures of such attributes.

Some researchers still use factor theory ambitiously as a method that they hope will lead to discovery of the fundamental components of cognition, of personality, and so on. Later we consider how this technique can be used more cautiously and perhaps more safely in test development, as a check on the extent to which the items of the test have been developed to measure the psychological attribute or attributes they are designed to measure.

In the 1940s and 1950s, Louis Guttman showed in a series of papers the necessity for behavioral scientists to have a clear prior conception of the domain of measurements that they aimed to study by factor analysis of the tests they were inventing.[7] He made it clear that factor analysis (and test development) was essentially about generalizing from measures we have created to more measures of the same kind. The question of the extent to which the dimensions of cognition or of personality are discovered or created by the invention of tests is still with us.

Lawley in 1940 gave a rigorous foundation for the statistical treatment of common factor analysis—estimation and hypothesis-testing. However, the method was so computationally demanding that it had to wait for the computer revolution of the 1950s before it could be applied. Work by Howe and by Bargmann in 1955 showed the way, and Jöreskog in 1967 successfully completed this development.[8]

As conceived by Thurstone, factor analysis was essentially an exploratory technique, allowing the test data to suggest how many abilities there were to be "discovered," and what these appeared to be. Lawley in 1952 showed how a common factor model could be set up to confirm a very detailed hypothesis about the abilities measured by each one of a set of tests. This, also, had to wait for the computer revolution and for further important contributions by Jöreskog in the 1970s.[9] The confirmatory form of the factor model, as shown in Chapter 9, is an important technique for checking how well we design tests to measure prespecified attributes.

Spearman's second paper of 1904 showed how the correlation between just two alternative forms of the same test, or possibly two sets of scores from a test taken at a suitable time interval, could be used to determine test reliability—an index of the precision with which the test measures (chap. 5). Guttman in 1945 showed how this reliability could be obtained from the relations between the items of a test. Further work by Cronbach on Guttman's index led to its popular identification in the literature as "Cronbach's alpha."[10] It also led to the further elaboration of this work into theory for the measurement of generalizability from the measurements we have made to other measurements of the same kind (see chap. 6).

The concepts introduced by these major figures in the history of psychometric theory make up the main elements of what is regarded here as *classical test theory*. Some writers would conceive of classical test theory more narrowly, as not including factor analysis. In this account, however, factor analysis becomes the key concept for a unified treatment of test theory, as will be seen.

A fundamental problem with the methods mentioned so far is that they do not strictly apply to "two-valued"—binary—items (e.g., the pass/fail items or true/false items mentioned at the beginning of this chapter). Lazarsfeld in 1950, recognizing this difficulty, introduced a related but distinct theory called *latent structure analysis*.[11] Most of his central concepts have become part of what is now most widely known as *item response theory*.

The commonly used item response models combine the basic idea of factor analysis (as in chaps. 6 and 9) with one of the oldest laws in psychology, the *phi–gamma law*. As early as 1878 it became known that if an observer is shown a series of stimuli—say, a light stimulus—controlled to range from zero intensity to sufficiently high intensity, measured in physical units (lumens), the probability that the observer detects the stimulus increases from zero to unity along a smooth curve that can be represented by the cumulative normal distribution (chap. 12).[12] This *observer response function*, the functional relationship between the probability of signal detection and stimulus intensity, became conventionally known as the phi–gamma law. The combination of a version of the phi–gamma law with a version of Spearman's common factor model produced what has variously been called *item factor analysis, latent trait theory,* and now, most commonly, *item response theory*. A key development here was Frederic Lord's demonstration in 1952 that a form of Spearman's single factor model can be applied to binary item scores. This was followed by major mathematical contributions from Birnbaum in the 1960s.[13] Lord's further studies of item response theory constitute an important series of contributions to this area.

Historically, the development of classical test theory preceded that of item response theory. There is a sense in which item response theory was a quite revolutionary departure from the classical theory, and yet there is also a sense in which the latter is a reasonable first approximation to the former. Of course, many names and many important contributions have been left out of this sketch. These are properly reserved for the following chapters and their end notes.

Item response theory (chaps. 12 through 16), as now available, gives precise answers to the questions that were set out at the beginning of the introduction section for the first two problems in test construction—the mathematics test with pass/fail responses, and the personality test with true/false responses. Does the test measure just one thing? (Chapter 12.) How should it be scored? (Chapters 13 and 14.) How precisely does it measure? (Chapter 13.) How does the precision vary over the scale? (Chapter 13.) Are the items biased? (Chapter 15.) Can we make alternative, equivalent tests, or adapt the test to the examinee by computer? (Chapter

16.) Common factor theory gives fairly precise answers to the corresponding questions when the items can be scored over a range of numbers, as would be the case for the third example—attitude to gun control. Common factor theory also gives a generally crude but often acceptable approximation to the treatment of binary items. The closeness of the connection between common factor theory and item response theory has not always been recognized, and receives some attention in the following chapters.

The unified treatment of test theory offered in the following chapters stems from a recognition of three fundamental points:

1. Classical test theory can largely be developed from the common factor model—originated by Spearman, elaborated by Thurstone, formalized by Lawley, and made practical by Jöreskog.
2. Item response theory for binary data—originating, in a sense, in the phi–gamma law, and developed primarily by Lord and Birnbaum—is essentially a nonlinear common factor model.
3. When applied to binary data, the common factor model is a linear approximation, sometimes satisfactory, sometimes poor, to the appropriate item response model.

Some accounts of item response theory make it sound like a revolutionary and very modern development, in part replacing, in part disconnected from, classical concepts. A unifying treatment of the main topics of test theory makes it as coherent as possible. It is hoped that this will also make it easier to learn and easier to operate well.

HOW TO USE THIS TEXT

A point deserving repetition is that test theory is essentially the collection of mathematical concepts that formalize and clarify certain questions about constructing and using tests, and then provide methods for answering them. A book on test theory is not coextensive with a book on tests. Both real and invented data are analyzed extensively in the following chapters, to illustrate theory and put flesh on the conceptual bones. Two main sets of real data, one with quantitative responses—the Satisfaction with Life Scale—and one with pass/fail scoring—the LSAT6—are subjected to repeated analyses of various kinds through the following chapters. By going through these analyses in sufficient detail, the student can learn to handle data of the same kind.

A natural prerequisite for any reader of this book is the typical undergraduate course or courses in statistics for behavioral science. Such a course includes the basic concepts of probability, statistical distributions, means, variances, correlations, regression, and a first introduction to analysis of variance. This in turn presupposes at least high school mathematics, as something retained, not merely gone through and forgotten. Students who complete an undergraduate statistics course with satisfactory grades still vary widely in their motivation for mathematics, their appreciation of the pleasures of mathematical thinking, their understanding of mathematical concepts, and their skill in applying mathematics. There are students who do not feel they understand a topic until they have worked through the mathematical proofs. There are also students who would like—not entirely unreasonably—to be given a set of cookbook recipes that will enable them to construct or use tests without making serious mistakes, and allow them to escape from a confrontation with mathematical concepts.

Given this range of conditions on the readers, there is a range of options for the writer. These require decisions that cannot be without risk. I have rejected the cookbook option. It is not possible to learn cookbook methods and operate these without the constant danger of serious mistakes. (Also, the field changes with time, and the student needs to know how to read accounts of further developments.) I have also tried to avoid the opposite extreme of writing a very mathematical text.

The student is warned, however, that I have followed some of the specialized conventions of mathematical discourse. The reader is invited to become accustomed to these. For example, all definitions are introduced *functionally*—that is, *contextually*—by embedding the new term, italicized, in a context of statements that give it its meaning. Note how the method is illustrated in the last sentence, which could have stated that "a functional or contextual definition is one in which the term is embedded in a sentence from which its meaning may be inferred." In fact, much language is learned contextually in this way. We cannot use a dictionary to learn the meaning of words unless, by luck, the meaning of the synonymous word or phrase is already known. In the glossary, definitions are listed in a more dictionary-like format, and the reader can cross-check with these. Other minor features of mathematical style include the method of writing the equations. These are either *displayed*, that is, set off from the text and numbered, or they are embedded in the text. In either case they are part of a grammatical sentence in which the reader interprets the "=" sign in one of two ways—either as "equals" or as "which is equal to," according to the context. If the sentence takes a form such as "$Y = f(X)$ measures . . . ," then this is read as "Y which is equal to $f(X)$ measures . . .". If it takes a form such as "the expression needed is $Y = f(X)$," then it is read as "the expression needed is Y equals $f(X)$." Other conventions of mathematical writing may strike some readers as novel or odd, from such simple things as the use of the mathematicians' preferred word "unity" rather than "one" for the number 1, to the use in many places of uppercase italics, such as X, for a variable (commonly a random variable), and lowercase, such as x, for some particular numerical value it is supposed to be taking. Sometimes I make statements that may carry a deeper or more precise meaning for a reader with a formal background in mathematical statistics, yet intended to carry a sufficiently clear intuitive meaning for the student with the previously assumed background.

In looking for a middle way between a cookbook and a fully formal account, I have deliberately written the chapters in a continuous style, in which "we" implies a dialogue with my reader. (This also follows a common mathematical convention—the author as "we.") This style of presentation allows successive discovery of further ideas building on preceding ones, rather than the presentation of chunks of information. Some flexibility is available here for students (and instructors) in the treatment of proofs. Short proofs and optional comments are embedded in the main text, but marked off by an opening *** and a closing $$$. Sometimes the interpolated proofs are as short as a single line. This method of presentation is more flexible than mathematical appendices. All users are encouraged to read through the optional proofs and comments, to see what they might add to a conceptual grasp of the material. Students (and/or instructors) can decide what knowledge of these is necessary to establish that the goals of the work are attained. A sufficient appreciation of all the concepts, operative formulas, and methods is possible without the marked-off sections.

Undergraduate courses in statistics vary widely. It is possible to design a course in which distinctions between a random variable and sample observations, between probability and relative frequency, between parameters and sample statistics, and so on, are very clear, and a course in which they are not as clear as might be desired. I have not attempted to review these topics, as student backgrounds are so different that a short review could be either superfluous or insufficient. Because a large number of the interpolated proofs are applications of the algebra of expected values—population means—Appendix A is added to give the basic rules of this algebra. Again, this is optional work for the student, but may prove helpful.

The review sections at the ends of the chapters are intended to supply guidance to the main concepts developed and the main skills that can be operated after reading the chapter. There is very little use of direct references, by author and date, in the main text. Instead, the reader is referred to footnotes within the end notes. These are intended to give guidance about the technical level of the references, and their degree of appropriateness for further reading. The end notes also occasionally add brief indications of specialized topics not covered in this text, with pointers to further reading.

PREVIEW OF REMAINING CHAPTERS

Chapter 2 gives an account of nine main types of item that compose objective tests. Simple methods for coding and scoring responses to single items are described. A distinction is drawn between binary item scores, as from pass/fail, true/false items, and quantitative item scores, as from items that can be individually scored with a range of numbers. Already at this point we can see how the question of combining item scores to make a measure of a psychological attribute—a property of individual persons—requires a conceptual analysis and a mathematical treatment.

Chapter 3 treats some fairly basic statistical properties of item scores, with emphasis on the concept of covariances. This concept tends to be neglected in undergraduate statistics courses for behavioral science students, but item covariances are fundamental to classical models in test theory. From the basic item statistics we derive some equally basic statistics of simple test scores. This material just supplies necessary preparation for the models and methods that follow.

Chapter 4 is a deliberately brief and oversimplified account of the notion of measurement as the assignment of a numerical value to an attribute on the basis of observations of responses to items. The discussion of measurement scales is left elementary and incomplete, although sufficient as a basis for the following chapters. This makes it possible to leave the topics that usually fall under the rubric of "scaling" to Chapter 18, where it is easier to develop them effectively.

An introduction to true-score theory in its classical form, based on the relationship between two appropriately chosen test scores, is given in Chapter 5. The theory, which is very simple, is carefully separated from procedures for applying it to actual data, where serious problems arise. This provides the basis for a first answer to the question: How shall we measure a psychological attribute, and how accurately have we measured it?

Chapter 6 applies the concepts of true-score theory to relationships between the item scores of a test. It immediately extends the theory so that it becomes the general factor model of Spearman's first 1904 paper. This model gives a good overall approximation to the behavior of a set of items that are all designed to measure the same thing.

A special case of the Spearman model gives the widely used coefficient of reliability given by Guttman and commonly referred to as Cronbach's alpha. A further specialization of the Spearman factor model gives a measure of reliability known as the Spearman–Brown "prophecy" formula. The measures of reliability obtained from the factor model and its special cases give generally better answers than those in Chapter 5 to the questions: How shall we measure the attribute, and how accurately can we measure it? The last section of the chapter deals with two ways to treat the problem of indexing generalizability from the items we have written to items of the same kind that might be added.

In Chapter 7, the coefficients of reliability developed in Chapters 5 and 6 are applied to a number of problems. The first of these is the effect of adding or dropping items on the precision with which a test measures an attribute, and answers the question: Should more or fewer items be used? Discussion of choices of scale for a test leads to an account of the error variance of a test score. This gives us a procedure for estimating an examinee's score and putting confidence limits on it. A classical problem in test theory is then dealt with. This is the effect of errors of measurement on relationships between different tests, the possibility of "correcting" correlations for this effect, and the conditions under which this is justifiable and safe. The final topic of this chapter is that of error in the difference between two scores as a result of errors of measurement in each of them.

Chapter 8 deals broadly with the prediction of a criterion measure from one or more independent variables. It is primarily a review of the basic concept of regression of one variable on another, and an elementary account of the extension to multiple regression. Some attention is given to indexing the effectiveness of prediction and to selection of predictor variables from a large initial set. A brief review of partial correlation is included. The material of this chapter provides concepts that are used in Chapters 9 and 10.

In Chapter 6, the simple Spearman factor model is treated as a slight extension of true-score theory and a way to find out if a set of items forms a homogeneous test—measuring just one attribute. Chapter 9 builds on Chapter 6 to show how the more general multiple-factor model can be used to group items into subsets measuring different attributes. This treats the questions: How many things are measured by the items in the test, and how can they be grouped to form a number of subtests, each deserving a separate score? The emphasis is on what is known as confirmatory factor analysis, whereby we check very precise notions as to what each item in a mixed set of items is measuring. Some attention is also given to the older exploratory form of factor analysis, stemming from Thurstone's work. In exploratory factor analysis we allow the data, with a bit of luck, to reveal its structure. Chapter 9 sets out some alternative forms of the model— higher order and hierarchical solutions—which have important functions in later chapters (10 and 14), on the question of validity.

The topic of validity then follows in Chapter 10. Approximately, this concerns the extent to which a test score measures the psychological attribute it was designed or is used to measure. The emphasis in this account is on the role of the prior conceptualization of the attribute to be measured—so-called *content validity*—and the closely related use of factor models to check so-called *construct validity*—the theoretical basis of the attribute.

The methods of Chapter 8 are recalled in a discussion of predictive utility—the construction and use of tests to predict a criterion performance.

A survey of the collection of statistical indices and devices that traditionally come under the heading of classical item analysis occupies Chapter 11. These devices are classified into sections of the chapter respectively as indexes relating items to a test score, further statistics of test scores, and relationships between items. It is a transitional chapter. Most of the material in it follows on naturally from Chapter 3, but it is placed here so that traditional item analysis can be related to the use of classical factor theory in Chapters 6, 9, and 10, and to provide a direct link to the models of Chapters 12 through 16 that provide a more rigorous treatment of binary responses. Traditional methods of item analysis provide answers to the question: How shall we choose good sets of items out of a very large set of items we are trying out?

Chapter 12 introduces item response models by acknowledging the limits of true-score and common-factor theory as used in Chapters 6 through 9 when applied to binary responses. It presents the appropriate way to relate the probability of an item response to the attribute measured—such as the probability of passing the item related to examinee ability. More precise answers are thus provided to the question: Do the items measure just one attribute? Fairly simple forms of "item factor analysis" are used to estimate the parameters of item response models.

Several forms of item response model are treated in Chapter 13, which shows how they can be used to answer a number of the questions in the introduction to this chapter: questions about obtaining a score for an attribute, choosing a scale, determining how precisely the attribute is measured at different points on the scale, and so on.

The theory of Chapters 12 and 13 is then extended, in Chapter 14, from homogeneous to mixed sets of items that require a multidimensional item response model. It thereby answers the questions: How many things do the binary items measure, and how should we group them to make subtest scores? It also gives a rigorous counterpart for binary items of the measurement of validity in Chapter 10.

Chapter 15 discusses the use of tests to compare subjects from different populations—classified by gender, by ethnicity, by culture, or by one of an indefinite number of ways in which individuals get classified, for sociopolitical or other reasons. The central question of our time in the context of population comparisons has become that of detecting whether some of the items in a test measure differently in distinct populations of interest. Differential item functioning can produce socially, legally, or politically significant bias affecting one group. A more general question also arises: Does the test measure the same attribute in the different populations? For example, responses to items could be gender specific, corresponding to distinct perceptions of the "meaning" of the item by males and females.

Chapter 16 deals with the need to construct two or more tests designed to measure the same attribute—most commonly the same ability or achievement—and to be equitably exchangeable, so that if two examinees take different tests neither can feel disadvantaged. We face two difficult and pressing questions: Can two tests be made to measure the same thing? And can one be equitably substituted for the other?

Chapter 17 would follow naturally from Chapter 10 on validity, because it deals with a topic variously known as path analysis, causal analysis, or structural equation modeling. The object of this technology is to trace out paths of causal influence in a network of variables. It is commonly believed that one way to establish the validity of a test is to verify predictions about its cause–effect relations with other measures. The topic has been left to a late, optional chapter for two reasons. It is technically rather difficult, and in its present stage of development it appears to me that it is not in fact a very safe strategy for validity studies.

The last substantive chapter, Chapter 18, is a deliberately postponed elaboration of Chapter 4. It introduces a set of models and methods that are conventionally regarded as usable for "scaling" an attribute. This chapter is also technical. It has been relegated to a position suited to an optional extra in the belief, as the chapter itself explains, that sophisticated scaling methods are not necessary components of test-construction technology. However, an understanding of the foundations of scaling theory will feed back into a deeper understanding of test theory on the part of those students who read it.

The closing chapter does not contain an overview in the obvious sense. Instead I examine my claim to offer a unified treatment of the field, acknowledge some of the consequent limitations, and discuss some of the choices to be made between alternative methods of analysis.

REVIEW GUIDE

The student can be satisfied to take from this introduction just a general sense of the scope of the text—the topic of test theory as a collection of models and methods for the analysis of test results, as distinguished from a text reviewing the range and variety of instruments and methods for psychological and educational assessment. At this point the topic is identified by the questions asked. Later chapters turn these into more precise forms, and provide answers.

The outline history of the field should be worth rereading later. It is desirable, if not essential knowledge, to be able to attach the names of the major theorists to their contributions to this field.

Advice on the use of the text can be summarized in the following points:

1. Conventions of mathematical writing are followed, such as the use of functional definition (by context) and embedding equations in the text to make grammatical sentences. The student should consciously adjust to these conventions if not already used to them.
2. Proofs and other sections marked off from the text should be looked at on first reading for the possible help they offer to understanding. However, they can be omitted without loss of continuity, and perhaps without much loss of understanding.
3. The chapters are written to encourage learning by discovery and conceptualization. The object of a review guide such as this is to identify the central concepts in a chapter, and the material on how to apply the concepts and computational procedures.

END NOTES

1. Commendable books on the field of tests available for assessment of cognition, personality, and so on would include Cohen, Swerdlik, and Smith (1992) and Anastasi (1982).
2. A primary source is Spearman (1927).
3. See Thorndike and Lohman (1990) for a good account of this history.
4. Again, see Thorndike and Lohman (1990).
5. See Cohen et al. (1992, chap. 12).
6. See McCrae and Costa (1985).
7. There is no nontechnical account of Guttman's treatment of behavior domains. A primary source is Guttman (1957) and references therein.
8. See McDonald (1985, chaps. 2 and 3).
9. See McDonald (1985, chap. 4).
10. Original sources are Guttman (1945) and Cronbach (1951).
11. A good original source is Lazarsfeld (1960).
12. A classical, and very good, account is in Guilford (1954).
13. Lord and Novick's text (1968) gave an account of Lord's earlier work, and contained chapters by Birnbaum on the latter's contribution. Most of Lord's later work was surveyed in Lord (1980).

Items and Item Scores

It is hardly likely that any reader of these pages could have missed experiencing the items of an "objective test," if only as a respondent—selecting appropriate answers to questions and submitting these to be scored and interpreted. Most likely you have experienced, in this sense, tests of your scholastic aptitude or educational achievements. Possibly you have responded to an attitude test or marketing survey. Possibly you have completed an inventory designed to measure your interests, beliefs, personal preferences, personal traits, or emotional state. In the case of an aptitude or achievement test it may have seemed obvious to you that several different abilities or areas of knowledge were tested. You might then expect to receive a set of scores from the test, one for each ability or area. In some cases it may not seem possible for you as a respondent to guess which or how many "things"—abilities, values, personality traits—are being measured by the items comprising the test.

As a statement of what is meant by an *objective test,* it is sufficient to say that the test is objective if the items in it do not leave any room for judgment in the scoring of the responses. Of course, it may be that the original construction of the test items involved some "subjectivity" of judgment. But it is objectivity of scoring that marks the objective test. The most common form of objective item is the multiple-choice cognitive item. This has just one correct answer and two or more incorrect answers for the respondent to choose from. You may have experienced such a test in a paper-and-pencil form, which needs a human examiner, at least to code the responses for a computer. In that case you expect that the only way two examiners can disagree is if one makes a procedural error. The test may have been machine readable, eliminating such examiner errors. It may have been computer interactive, again allowing scoring without human intervention. (This is a rapidly growing trend.) You might feel pleased that the objectivity of the process eliminated examiner bias. Or you might feel irritated that the rigid form of the response categories did not allow you to express yourself precisely or creatively, as you might in an expository paragraph or essay.

Some test theory is applicable to examiners' ratings of such products as expository paragraphs or essays, creative works, or performances—music, dance, figure skating, diving, and so forth. But we concentrate here on tests composed of objectively scorable items, with some recognition of wider applications of parts of the theory. In the next section of this chapter we examine the main *formats* or logical structures of the items of an objective test, and we consider the question of assigning an item score to the examinee's response. The following section contains a preliminary account of some of the fundamental questions to which test theory seeks to give answers: How should we create test scores out of the item responses? What does the test measure? How many "things" does it measure? How precisely does it measure them?

ITEM TYPES

Although much of test theory has been developed for the measurement of abilities, we take a wider view of its applicability. The typical item consists of an *item stem*, which contains the stimulus materials to which the examinees are to respond, and a system of *response options*—a means for the examinees to record their (variable) responses. For each item type we require a method of assigning numbers to the item responses—item scores—which can then be combined to give test scores. At least the following nine item types can be usefully distinguished:

1. A *completion* or *constituted-response* item contains a blank space for a response to be constructed and entered by the examinee to complete the item statement. A paradigm case would be a simple arithmetic item, of the form: $2 + 2 =$ _____? Obviously, for such an item to be objective, the test constructor must be confident that the only acceptable responses to the item are clearly known. The strictness of this requirement would tend to limit this format to items from the most well-established and well-delimited areas of knowledge. Even trials of such items on a large sample of respondents might not reveal all acceptable answers. There may be acceptable responses that are idiosyncratic and perhaps creative, and have not been listed in a scoring manual. Consider, for example, the question: What

do air and water have in common? Possible answers might include: "They are both fluids"; "they both contain oxygen"; and others. The possibility remains that there are more correct answers, and someone will construct one of them. I am not aware of any noncognitive applications of completion items that do not require judgment on the part of a scorer. In the past, completion items would normally have required human agency to score them, but machine-readable and computer-interactive versions become increasingly feasible with advances in technology.

A completion item can be scored simply by assigning the number unity (1) to an acceptable completion and the number zero (0) to any other response. The advantage that can be claimed for a (cognitive) completion item is that generally it does not allow the examinee to supply the correct answer by guessing. However, we can imagine that partial knowledge, or the structure of the item, may limit the set of possible completions to just a few, with uncertainty in the final choice.

2. A *multiple-choice item* supplies three or more response *options*, of which one is *keyed* as the acceptable answer and the remainder are unacceptable answers. The unacceptable answers are typically written to have some plausibility for an examinee who does not recognize the appropriateness of the keyed answer, so that they have some chance of being chosen. It is very difficult to imagine noncognitive applications of multiple-choice items. In cognitive applications the keyed option is (hopefully) the correct answer. The remainder are plausible incorrect answers, referred to as *distractors* or *foils*.

Note that conventional test theory does not attempt to provide a theory of what the mental process is whereby the examinee "guesses." Yet, clearly, an examinee who does not "know" the right answer may choose it as if by a lucky chance. It might seem that if the examinee is in a state of total ignorance, the options have equal probability of being chosen. But test theorists do not necessarily make such an assumption.

Consider the example (taken from test theory itself):

> If items on an achievement test are scored 0 (incorrect) and 1 (correct) then the mean score on each item is
>
> A. equal to the item difficulty
> B. equal to (1-item difficulty)
> C. equal to item difficulty divided by sample size
> D. none of the above.

Supposing you do not yet have the knowledge base to answer this question, you might ask yourself: Do these answers appear equally plausible? Do you feel that if you choose one without relevant knowledge there is one chance in four that you will choose a specific option?

The common method of scoring a multiple-choice item is to assign the number unity to the keyed (correct) answer and the number zero to every distractor. It is possible to create scores for distractors, but we do not consider such procedures in these pages (except for a brief account in Chap. 18).

3. A *two-choice—dichotomous—item* has just two response options. Some examples are:

    (i)   The mode is a measure of central tendency. TRUE/FALSE   (Circle the correct answer.)
   (ii)   Compared to water, the density of ice is GREATER/LESS
  (iii)   I often suffer from sleeplessness. TRUE/FALSE
   (iv)   I am generally HAPPY/UNHAPPY
    (v)   Assault weapons do not belong in private hands. AGREE/DISAGREE
   (vi)   I feel anxious right now. TRUE/FALSE

Again, we may score the keyed answer unity and the nonkeyed answer zero. An obvious problem with dichotomous cognitive items such as (i) and (ii) is that the examinee has a high probability—on the order of 50%—of giving the right answer by "guessing." In a self-report item such as (iii), where TRUE/FALSE has a different meaning, the question of guessing does not arise.

4. A possible format for a cognitive item is one with three or more response options, each of which can be keyed as correct or incorrect. Consider the example:

Which of the following is/are measures of central tendency?

    A. mean
    B. median
    C. 50th centile
    D. Student's t
    E. SD
    F. all of the above
    G. none of the above

Clearly each of the options can be scored unity for correct and zero for incorrect answers. The response options behave like a group of two-choice items attached to a common root, except for options such as the last two (which need not be included in such an item). A reasonable item score would be the number of correct answers. If either of "all of the above" or "none of the above" is included and is correct, it can be assigned the equivalent number of individually correct/incorrect options. The fact that each option allows a "guessing" strategy and the observation that examinees commonly experience this type of item as "unfair" may explain the fact that it does not seem to be a commonly used format and does not seem to possess an accepted name.

A somewhat similar format for noncognitive items is exemplified by:

Which of the following emotions have you experienced within the last few days?

    A. sadness   B. shame   C. fear . . .

Note that these are all negative emotions, so a simple count of those reported could constitute an item score for "negative affect." We might not wish to give each of them equal value, but it is unlikely that we can improve on this scoring scheme.

As another example, consider:

In which of the following activities have you participated?

    A. signed a petition
    B. written my Congressperson
    C. written the President
    D. participated in a legal demonstration
    E. participated in an illegal demonstration
    F. been arrested for demonstrating

Again, a simple count of activities reported might serve as a score for, say, "political activism." And again we might hesitate to give these activities equal value.

It will suffice for us to describe items such as these as *checklists* and the simple item score suggested as a *frequency count.* (This may seem a strange use of language in the case of cognitive items, but there is no accepted alternative, it seems.)

5. In a *matching* item, a number of objects/concepts/stimuli in one list are to be matched by a stated principle to objects/concepts/stimuli in another. For example:

For each person named in the left column, record the letter from the right column that identifies the field with which the name is associated:

	Person	Field
____	1. Marie Curie	A. Linguistics
____	2. Margaret Mead	B. Psychiatry
____	3. Sigmund Freud	C. Anthropology
____	4. Noam Chomsky	D. Palinology
		E. Physics

We can score the item simply by counting the correct matches. (We might also subtract the number of incorrect matches.)

6. In an *ordered-category item,* there are at least three response options (categories) that have a natural order. Some examples are:

(i)   Assault weapons do not belong in private hands.
       strongly agree
       agree   _____
       neither agree nor disagree   _____
       disagree   _____
       strongly disagree   _____
                                                                  _____

(ii) I suffer from sleeplessness:
       very often
       fairly often   _____
       seldom   _____
       never   _____
                                                                  _____

(iii) I am generally:
       very optimistic
       fairly optimistic   _____
       fairly pessimistic   _____
       very pessimistic   _____
                                                                  _____

A middle or neutral option expressed as "no opinion" is problematic, as it does not necessarily represent a strictly neutral position between "agree" and "disagree." Some item writers prefer to omit a neutral option and force the respondent's choice, but this can have a negative effect on motivation to respond carefully. The use of "neither agree nor disagree" is reasonable, although it might not be used by all respondents to express a clear intermediate opinion.

Through a common misreading of the literature, ordered-category items are sometimes attributed to a paper by Likert, written in 1932, and referred to as *Likert items* or *Likert scales*. Likert introduced a very sophisticated scaling method for assigning scores to the response categories of items with ordered categories. He then showed that his method was not a clear improvement on just assigning integers, as in:

Strongly agree	5	Very often	4
Agree	4	Often	3
Neither agree nor disagree	3	Seldom	2
Disagree	2	Never	1
Strongly disagree	1		

Scoring the items using integers is so commonly referred to as *Likert scaling* that it is virtually impossible to correct the misunderstanding. It seems inevitable that we follow the accepted usage and refer to an integer score for an ordered-category item as a *Likert score*.

Ordered-category items can also be described as *graded response items*. There are several alternative ways to present this type of item. In a *numerical rating item* the respondent is presented with the numerical values assigned to each of a set of ordered categories. A classical example[1] is a rating scale for affective values of a stimulus:

10 Most pleasant imaginable
 9 Most pleasant
 8 Extremely pleasant
 7 Moderately pleasant
 6 Mildly pleasant
 5 Indifferent
 4 Mildly unpleasant
 3 Moderately unpleasant
 2 Extremely unpleasant
 1 Most unpleasant
 0 Most unpleasant imaginable

It should be noted that the values represented here are, in an intuitively obvious sense, *bipolar*—lying between two opposite poles. It might therefore seem natural to use the numbers 5 4 3 2 1 for positive affects, 0 for indifference, and −1 −2 −3 −4 −5 for increasingly negative affects. This is not common practice, perhaps because mathematically unsophisticated respondents might find this confusing. *Graphic rating scales (items)* can be illustrated by:

In social conversation, how have you behaved?

talkative |
an easy talker |
talk when necessary |
prefer listening |
refrain from talking |

The respondent marks one of the segments on the right of the response options, or possibly the segments are replaced by a continuous line, and the respondent marks a point on it. The first version can obviously be scored on a Likert scale. The second might seem to have the advantage that it can be scored more accurately by physical measurement of the marked length. There is evidence that in typical cases the respondent cannot effectively use more than about seven to nine categories in an ordered-category item or numerical rating item. Correspondingly, the accuracy of any finely graduated measurements from a graphic rating scale is largely specious if it goes much beyond the integers up to 10. We can regard all of these variants as ordered-category items yielding graded responses.

7. A *forced-choice* item requires the respondent to express a preference for one of two alternative options. The most obvious applications of this item format are to the expression of preferences, such as:

I prefer

strawberry ice cream   vanilla ice cream

The forced-choice item can be used to require the respondents to express a preference between two descriptions of themselves or of others (peers, significant persons), such as:

Which adjective more closely fits you (or, possibly, him/her)?

(1) easy-going vs. demanding   (2) serious-minded vs. energetic

Such alternative-description forms have been suggested to avoid halo effects in ratings of others, or biasing toward lenient judgments (of oneself or others) or toward socially desirable responses. *Halo effect* is a term used to describe a tendency for judgments of one rated characteristic to influence judgments of other characteristics in a positive or negative direction.

Assigning scale values to forced-choice item responses is a generally complex problem. Preference is not equivalent to choosing an option by some criterion as in Type 3 items. The respondent might wish to choose neither, but is forced to express a preference. There is no simple rational way to assign an integer value to a given forced choice. Further, consider a complete set of preferences obtained by the forced-choice method, such as the following:

The respondent is asked to record preferences among four ice cream flavors, say: (V)anilla, (S)trawberry, (R)um and raisin, and (P)istachio, responding to all six pairs, yielding

$$S > V; \quad R > V; \quad P > V$$
$$R > S; \quad P > S$$
$$P > R$$

(where > symbolizes "is preferred to"). Notice that we can summarize these results in the simple rank order:

$$P > R > S > V$$

from most to least preferred. Suppose instead of P > R we had R > P, with the other five choices as already shown. The pairwise choices are then inconsistent, and cannot be summarized in a single rank order. Such inconsistencies can be interesting and informative, or a nuisance for the investigation. Because of their special characteristics, forced-choice items are not considered further in these pages until a brief account is given in Chapter 18.

8. In *rankings*, respondents may be presented with three or more stimuli and asked directly to rank them in order of personal preference—for example, ice cream flavors, TV programs, or other commodities—or to rank them in order of applicability to themselves or to a known other, or with respect to a named attribute, such as aesthetic appeal. In particular, an examiner might rank expository essays in terms of overall quality instead of grading them. Examples are:

(1) Rank the following ice creams according to your order of preference, using 1 for your "most preferred" and 4 for your "least preferred"

vanilla   _____
strawberry   _____
rum & raisin   _____
pistachio   _____

(2) Rank the following TV programs according to your order of preference, where 1 represents your "most preferred" and 5 represents your "least preferred"

Program X   _____
Program XX   _____
Program Y   _____
Program UV   _____

(Television programs are far too ephemeral and culture bound for it to be worthwhile to give actual names. Perhaps ice creams are human universals?) Notice that a respondent could give the same rank order for the ice creams, loving them all, as would also be given by an ice cream hater, and could regard all the TV shows as unacceptable, yet give the same rank order as would be given by someone who has the ability to enjoy watching them.

As in the case of forced-choice items, rankings possess the inherent difficulty that there is no simple way to assign scores—scale values—to the rankings given by the respondents, and there is no simple statistical treatment of the rank numbers themselves, to give a test score to a respondent. We do not consider them further until Chapter 18.

9. An *unordered categorical item* provides three or more response options or categories that do not possess a natural order, for example:

(i) Which of the following colors do you like the best?

(A) red   (B) yellow   (C) blue   (D) green

Generally, the categories will be mutually exclusive, and commonly, exhaustive of possible responses. Note that a multiple-choice item is a particular case of an unordered categorical item, in which one option is the keyed correct answer. In the general case there is no simple rational way to score the item. A response can be numerically coded by entering the number unity for the category checked and zeros for the remaining categories, but the code cannot be treated as a score. Sophisticated methods can be employed for giving values to the categories to yield a score for the item equal to the value of the category chosen. (See Chap. 18 for the topic of optimal scaling.)

Item writing in a particular field of behavioral science may need to be learned by experience, including immersion in the existing literature of tests and measurements for that field. Here it will have to suffice to offer some general guidelines—rules for which exceptions would need specific justification. Item stems (a) should be short, (b) should be unambiguous, (c) should be definite, avoiding generalities that may create one type of ambiguity, (d) should be simple, containing one proposition, not several combined, (e) should avoid negatives, especially double negatives, (f) should use simple vocabulary, and (g) should use conventional vocabulary. The student is left to test these principles in action in a chosen field.

ITEM SCORES AND TEST SCORES

The listing just given of nine types of item to be found in objective tests is not exhaustive, but does capture the main ones. A review of the remarks made in connection with these varieties shows that some item formats are generally appropriate for cognitive items, some for items measuring noncognitive attributes, and some for either. The cognitive–noncognitive distinction appears to have some importance later when we consider the problem of guessing.

A number assigned to an item response can serve as a code, or, in addition, as a score. It is at least a *code* when its assignment serves to distinguish between response categories, and it serves as an item score when arithmetic is performed on it as a numerical quantity. For most of the following material, distinctions between types of item score are more important than distinctions between item formats. Following usual practice, it was proposed earlier that for completion items, multiple-choice items, and dichotomous items, the respondent be assigned an item score of unity for giving the keyed answer, and zero for a nonkeyed answer. We refer to an item given just the two alternative scoring values zero and unity as a *binary* (two-valued) item. A binary item can have a two-choice, multiple-choice, or completion format. The simple scoring schemes generally adopted for matching items, frequency-count items, and ordered-category/rating scale items all yield an item score taking a limited range of integer values. We refer to an item score taking more than two values as a *quantitative* item score. Quantitative item scores virtually never take a sufficiently wide range of values to allow them to be modeled as continuous, possibly normally distributed, variables. However, in a number of methods of analysis treated in this book, we choose to regard the normal distribution assumption as an acceptable approximation.

Table 2.1 gives a summary of the item types and the usual method of coding or scoring them. Two or more items taken together form a test, and we expect to combine the item scores in some reasonable way (almost always simply adding them) to form a *test score*. The test score is generally intended to measure a *psychological attribute*, such as an ability, a personality trait, an emotional state, or an attitude. The set of items forming a test can sometimes comprise subsets, measuring distinct attributes. Each subset forms a *subtest*, and its item scores can be combined (summed) to form a subtest score. One form of "subtest" is an *item bundle* or *testlet*—terminology is unsettled—a set of questions about a common "object," such as a paragraph requiring interpretation. A number of tests—a *test battery*—may be administered to an examinee and a *profile* of test scores—a list of scores from each test—computed and reported. The distinction between a test comprising subtests—including item bundles or testlets—and a test battery comprising tests is, obviously, somewhat arbitrary. Generally, the item is the ultimate, "atomic" subtest (where *a-tomic*, from the Greek, means uncuttable). It should be noted, however, that matching items, frequency-count items, and what we have provisionally called item bundles could in principle be divided into

TABLE 2.1
Item Types

Item Type	Score/Code
1. Completion: Respondent constructs answer	1 for accepted answer 0 others
2. Multiple-choice: A keyed option and distractors	1 for keyed answer 0 others
3. Two-choice (dichotomous): A keyed and nonkeyed option	1 for keyed answer 0 for nonkeyed
4. Checklist: Three or more options, each keyed or not.	Number of keyed options
5. Matching: Stimuli in one list to match stimuli in another	Number of correct matches
6. Ordered-category: Response options with natural order (includes numerical ratings, graphic ratings)	Integer assigned to category
7. Forced choice: Prefer one of two options	?
8. Rankings: Order a set of stimuli on an attribute	Assign integer (representing only order)
9. Unordered category: Choose an option	?

more elementary units if we wish. The following remarks are intended to illustrate some preliminary notions about the problems arising when we want to make subtest and test scores out of item scores.

The investigator seldom stops short at the invention of a single item. Exceptions would include opinion polls, such as approval ratings for a government or president. Consider the single item:

(1)   I am satisfied with my life.

   A. Strongly agree   B. Agree   C. Slightly agree   D. Neither agree
   nor disagree   E. Slightly disagree   F. Disagree
   G. Strongly disagree

It would be possible to take a Likert score on this item 7, 6, 5, 4, 3, 2, 1—as a single, clear measure of how far "[I] am satisfied with [my] life," and use it as a dependent variable in a study of its determinants.

Intuitively (i.e., without the aid of test-theory concepts) we might feel that we would measure more accurately if we add further items, for example:

(2)   The conditions of my life are excellent.

   A. Strongly agree . . . G. Strongly disagree

Because the second item is worded somewhat differently from the first, the question then arises: If we add their two Likert scores together, to measure more accurately, just what are we measuring more accurately? On the face of it, the answer requires abstraction. We might claim that the two items are alternative, perhaps interchangeable, *indicators* of *satisfaction with [the conditions of] life.* Suppose now we add a third item:

(3)   In most ways my life is close to the ideal.

   A. Strongly agree . . . G. Strongly disagree

We may now add three (integer) Likert scores together to measure *satisfaction with life.* The reader might pause to consider whether this process of inventing items to measure satisfaction with life can continue indefinitely, by writing more items of "the same kind," and whether the attribute measured changes as we proceed. If we are satisfied to combine the scores on the items so far, this is essentially because in terms of content they form a *homogeneous test* (from the Greek—*homo* = same, *genos* = kind). Suppose now we add two more items, namely:

(4)   So far I have gotten the important things I want from life.

   A. Strongly agree . . . G. Strongly disagree

(5) If I could live my life over, I would change almost nothing.

A. Strongly agree ... G. Strongly disagree

This gives a five-item test, the Satisfaction with Life Scale (SWLS),[2] which is used in a number of illustrations in this book.

Direct examination of the wording of the items suggests that items (1), (2), and (3) are alternative indicators of *present satisfaction,* and items (4) and (5) are alternative indicators of *satisfaction with the past.* That is, without any further information beyond a natural-language judgment of the item content, we conjecture that items {(1), (2), (3)} and items {(4), (5)} form two distinct content-homogeneous subsets. Indeed, without collecting data from possible respondents, it is easy to imagine, for example, an ex-prisoner of war with an unpleasant past and a satisfying present, or a suddenly unemployed person in the opposite situation. These logical/semantic considerations do not prevent us from combining two subtest scores, from (1), (2), and (3), and from (4) and (5), into a total score of Satisfaction with Life (SWL) (present and past life), but such a total score represents a higher level of abstraction/generality than a score on the first three— satisfaction with one's present life—or a score on the last two—satisfaction with one's past life. Later we see what analysis of SWL data tells us about those conjectures.

SOME PHILOSOPHICAL CONSIDERATIONS

Just to establish some points of terminology, it is necessary to glance briefly at an awkward side issue in the philosophy of science. It should be clear by now that when we invent a set of items to form an objective test, the intention, generally, is to create items yielding a test score (or subtest scores) that will serve as a respondent's measure on an attribute that possesses some generality beyond that of a single item. In this book the word *attribute* is used in a sense that is close to its dictionary meaning. Webster gives, for attribute, "an inherent quality," "an accidental quality," and "a word ascribing a quality." Measurable attributes, such as intelligence, introversion, somatic anxiety, SWL, attitude toward gun control, and so forth, are abstract or conceptual, quantifiable properties of the respondents—conceptual variables, we might say. The items one writes are intended to elicit behaviors that are indicative of the respondent's value of such a conceptual variable—alternative "atomic" instances of the same concept.

Historically, method in the social sciences has been strongly influenced by attempts made by logical positivist philosophers to solve certain problems in the theory of knowledge (epistemology) by the principle that "meaning is verifiability"—that the meaning of a concept is, in some sense, the observations that verify statements containing the concept. The motivation of this movement in philosophy must be respected. The hope was to put scientific knowledge on a firm foundation in what is "observable."

The logical positivist position was seen by many philosophers to be untenable almost as soon as it was stated, but it appeared plausible to social-behavioral scientists when popularized for them in psychology journals from about the 1940s. In particular, it led to the notion that an abstract concept in psychology—a "psychological construct"—is a convenient construction by the psychological theorist, which is "given meaning" by a precise statement of the "operations" that an investigator puts forward as a measure of it. This process is referred to as "establishing an operational definition" of the—as yet undefined?—construct. For example, satisfaction with life will be (operationally) defined only when one has written down a series of items, such as (1)–(5) given earlier. This way of conceptualizing scientific method creates some difficulties. Any psychological concept—indeed, any concept—is logically prior to attempts to measure it. Its definition may be imprecise, and subject to revision. But logically, for example, "satisfaction with life" is a quantitative attribute before we invent items, or face questions such as: Shall we keep it general, or should we measure specific satisfactions with health, finances, relationships, and so on? If this were not the case, we would not be able to make any judgment—no matter how uncertain—of the appropriateness of items for inclusion in the scale.

Two investigators can disagree about the denotation of a concept. For example, Freud and Jung had overlapping but distinct concepts of "introversion." Freud saw it as a preneurotic condition, while Jung saw it as a generally healthy personality style, opposed to extraversion. It is also possible for two investigators to have essentially the same psychological concept and to create distinct sets of items to measure it. These appear sufficient reasons for avoiding the notion that finding indicators of a psychological concept amounts to (operationally) defining it. It seems reasonable to speak of the process of test construction as developing a measure of a (quantifiable) attribute. Although there is no harm in calling this "operationalizing" the attribute, except that the word is not euphonious, there is no need for it in the following pages.

REVIEW GUIDE

The main emphasis in this chapter is on objective tests. Nine main types of objective test item are described and illustrated here, and simple scoring methods are given for the first five of these. The student should be able to identify and to write examples of each type, and to state the appropriate scoring methods where applicable.

END NOTES

General: Further reading could include Sax (1980), Chapters 1–7, for a practical account of item and test construction. Kaufman (1990) is a good resource on cognitive testing. Maloney and Ward (1976) discussed tests in the context of clinical assessment.

1. See Guilford (1954, pp. 263–264). See also Guilford (1954, pp. 459–460) for a clear account of the origin of Likert scales.
2. See Diener et al. (1985) for an account of the Satisfaction with Life Scale.

Item and Test Statistics

In this chapter we consider some standard statistical concepts as applied in the context of item and test scores, and introduce some specialized concepts and terminology. We consider in turn the statistics of binary item scores, the statistics of quantitative item scores, and the statistics of test scores obtained from combining a number of item scores.

In virtually all analyses of test data, the usual condition of statistical surveys applies. We have administered the items to a necessarily finite sample of respondents and we wish to draw inferences about a population on the basis of the sample. In applications, the assumption that each respondent in the sample has been drawn independently and at random from the population of interest is generally suspect. Subjects may be undergraduate volunteers, or clustered in classes or schools, or obtained on some other nonrepresentative demographic basis. The usual rule applies: We hope—and *hope* is the operative notion—that the convenient sample obtained behaves sufficiently like a random sample not to invalidate statistical estimates.

BINARY ITEM STATISTICS

Suppose a single examinee is drawn at random from a well-defined population of interest. The examinee yields either a pass or a fail on just one cognitive item, which may be coded as 1 or 0. Imagine drawing further examinees at random, and coding their pass/fail responses as 1/0, recorded as in Table 3.1. In this table the observations have been grouped in successive sets of 20.

TABLE 3.1
A Constructed Binary Variable

Observations				Cumulative Proportion
01101	00001	01001	00110	8/20 = .40
00100	00010	01111	10111	18/40 = .45
00000	00100	00100	10000	21/60 = .35
00101	01100	00000	10000	26/80 = .325
00001	10101	00000	00000	30/100 = .30
00100	00000	00101	00001	34/120 = .283
11000	00011	00010	00011	41/140 = .293
00000	10000	10001	10010	46/160 = .287
00101	00000	00101	00001	51/180 = .283
00010	10000	00100	10110	57/200 = .285
. . .				

Population proportion = .3 (probability)

On the right the table shows a count of the number of passes—coded as unity—out of, successively, 20, 40, 60, . . . , examinees. These are converted into the proportion—relative frequency—of passes. The data were constructed using a table of random numbers, which gives a "population" in which the probability of a pass is known to be .3. Digits 0, 1, and 2 were scored *pass*, and digits 3 through 9 were scored *fail.* The data illustrate two relevant statistical principles: (a) As the sample size increases, the relative frequency of passes approaches the probability that a single examinee will pass the item. This is an application of the *law of large numbers,* which states that the relative frequency of a property (or event) in a sample approaches its probability as the sample size increases. (b) The relative frequency of passes, which is the number of passes divided by sample size, is the same as the sample mean item score (the sum of 0/1 scores divided by sample size).

There is a certain degree of necessary formality in these remarks. It is desirable to think of drawing one examinee as like the classical probability problem of drawing black and red balls from an urn (with replacement) and estimating the probability of drawing a red one. Sampling an examinee without replacement is analogous if the population is very large.

Now suppose we have some number m of cognitive binary items with pass/fail coding and zero/one scores. We write X_j for the jth item score and x_{ji} for the score—either 1 or 0—obtained by the ith examinee in a sample of n examinees. This notation follows the convention that upper case X_j represents the jth random variable and lower case x_{ji} represents the ith observed value of it, given by the ith sampled subject. We write π_j for the probability of passing item j, and n_j for the number of examinees in the sample that are observed to pass it. We write

$$p_j = n_j/n \tag{3.1}$$

for the relative frequency of passes in the sample, and

$$X_j = \sum_i x_{ji}/n \tag{3.2}$$

for the sample mean. Then principle (b) given earlier becomes: With binary scoring, in the sample

$$p_j = \bar{X}_j, \tag{3.3}$$

and in the population

$$\pi_j = \mu_j, \tag{3.4}$$

where μ_j is the population mean of X_j. Principle (a) becomes: As the sample size increases, p_j becomes an increasingly precise estimate of π_j, converging in probability on it in the limit.

Because p_j is a proportion and π_j a probability, they are confined within the range of values from zero to unity. It is intuitively obvious that an item that everyone in the population of interest passes ($\pi_j = 1$) is too easy, and an item that everyone fails ($\pi_j = 0$) is too difficult. Clearly also, it is natural to describe an item that 90% of the population passes as "easy" and, in comparison, to describe one that only 10% pass as "difficult." For this reason, in classical test theory, π_j, estimated by p_j, is known as the _item difficulty_. More precisely, we call π_j the _item difficulty parameter_ of item j. This partly solves the problem that π_j is an inverse—upside down—measure of item difficulty, because the difficulty "parameter" is logically permitted to be, itself, an inverse measure of "difficulty." As we have just seen, an item with a high difficulty parameter is "easy" and one with a low difficulty parameter is "difficult." A more rational term for π_j, _item easiness_, has been suggested, but never became generally adopted.

A further problem with terminology arises when we consider binary noncognitive items, such as personality items in format "true" or "false" (as statements applicable to the respondent), or attitude items in format "agree" or "disagree." Hopefully, the item "I often have hallucinations" would receive a "true" response with low probability in a general population. If "true" is the keyed response, scored unity as an indicator of "psychopathology," the item's π_j value is very low. If "false" is the keyed response, scored unity as an indicator of "mental health," the item's π_j value is very high. It seems to violate English usage to call the item easy or difficult, but in the following we conventionally extend the term *item difficulty parameter* to noncognitive items, always remembering that this is just a label for the mathematical quantity π_j.

Generally in statistics we need at least the mean and the variance (or *SD*) to characterize a distribution. In the case of a binary item, the variance is a function of the item mean—difficulty parameter—and contains no new information. The sample variance,

$$s_j^2 = \sum_{i=1}^{n} (x_{ji} - \bar{x}_j)^2 / n \tag{3.5}$$

or

$$s_j^2 = (\sum_{i=1}^{n} x_{ji}^2 / n) - \bar{x}_j^2, \tag{3.6}$$

reduces to

$$s_j^2 = p_j(1 - p_j) \tag{3.7}$$

and estimates the corresponding population variance

$$\sigma_j^2 = \pi(1 - \pi_j). \tag{3.8}$$

*** A proof of (3.8) assumes a basic understanding of a probability distribution. Because X_j has the distribution

X_j	$P\{X_j\}$	$X_j - \bar{X}_j$
1	π_j	$1 - \pi_j$
0	$1 - \pi_j$	$-\pi_j$

it follows that

$$\sigma_j^2 = \pi_j (1 - \pi_j)^2 + (1 - \pi_j)(-\pi_j)^2$$
$$= \pi_j (1 - \pi_j)[1 - \pi_j + \pi_j]$$
$$= \pi_j (1 - \pi_j). \; \$\$\$$$

It is easy to tabulate values of variance corresponding to a set of values of the probabilities, as in Table 3.2.

TABLE 3.2
Binary Item Variance and Difficulty

π_j	.0	.1	.2	.3	.4	.5	.6	.7	.8	.9	1.0
σ_j^2	.0	.09	.16	.21	.24	.25	.24	.21	.16	.09	.0

Thus, for the single item in Table 3.1, the sample of 200 gives us $\bar{X} = p = .285$, as our estimate of the item difficulty parameter—known to be .3—and (3.7) gives a sample variance equal to $.285(1 - .285) = .2038$. This estimates the population variance, known to be $.3(1 - .3) = .21$, according to (3.8).

We next consider the problem of measuring association between two binary items. Consider two cognitive items, j and k, yielding item scores in any of the four combinations

$$X_j = 0 \ (\text{fail}) \qquad X_k = 0 \ (\text{fail})$$
$$X_j = 1 \ (\text{pass}) \qquad X_k = 0 \ (\text{fail})$$
$$X_j = 0 \ (\text{fail}) \qquad X_k = 1 \ (\text{pass})$$
$$X_j = 1 \ (\text{pass}) \qquad X_k = 1 \ (\text{pass}).$$

We think of these scores equally as numerical codes for pass/fail or as numbers to be added (with scores from other items) to make a total test score.

From elementary probability theory, we recall that two events A and B are *independent in probability* if

$$P\{A \text{ and } B\} = P\{A\} \times P\{B\}$$

(where $P\{\ \}$ is to be read as "probability of"). For example, if event A is throwing a six with a die ($P\{6\} = 1/6$) and event B is throwing a head with a penny ($P\{H\} = 1/2$), then

$$P\{6 \text{ and } H\} = (1/6) \times (1/2).$$

Thus if we suppose that responses to items j and k are independent in probability, then

$$P\{\text{pass } j \text{ and pass } k\} = P\{\text{pass } j\} \times P\{\text{pass } k\}$$

or

$$P\{X_j = 1 \text{ and } X_k = 1\} = P\{X_j = 1\} \times P\{X_k = 1\}.$$

Writing π_{jk} for $P\{\text{pass } j \text{ and pass } k\}$, this becomes

$$\pi_{jk} = \pi_j \pi_k. \tag{3.9}$$

However, this seems an unlikely state of affairs if the items measure or depend on the same ability or area of knowledge. An examinee who knows the answer to item j seems more likely to know the answer to item k than one who does not. This suggests we take the difference

$$\pi_{jk} - \pi_j \pi_k,$$

that is,

$$P\{X_j = 1 \text{ and } X_k = 1\} - P\{X_j = 1\} \times P\{X_k = 1\}$$

as a measure of the extent to which the items are (positively) associated in probability—the extent to which $P\{X_j = 1 \text{ and } X_k = 1\}$ exceeds what we would expect if the events were independent.

Suppose, as in the construction of Table 3.1, we start drawing examinees randomly from a population, but now we record four more scores for each examinee. This gives, say, $m = 5$ binary items—pass/fail—as in Table 3.3. Here, again, the process can be imagined to continue until the population is exhausted, but we stop at $n = 10$, to make a simple illustrative sample.

We recall the formulas for the Pearson product–moment correlation coefficient for a sample of n pairs of observations x_i, y_i, as

TABLE 3.3
Set of Constructed Binary Variables

			Items			Total	Proportion
Examinees	1	2	3	4	5	Right	Right
1	1	1	1	1	1	5	1.0
2	1	0	1	1	1	4	.8
3	1	1	1	1	0	4	.8
4	0	1	0	1	1	3	.6
5	0	0	1	1	1	3	.6
6	1	0	1	1	1	4	.8
7	0	0	0	0	1	1	.2
8	0	0	0	1	1	2	.4
9	1	1	0	1	1	4	.8
10	0	0	0	0	1	1	.2
Sum	5	4	5	8	9		
Mean	.5	.4	.5	.8	.9		

$$r_{xy} = \frac{(1/n)\sum_{i=1}^{n}(x_i - \bar{x})(y_i - \bar{y})}{\left\{[(1/n)\sum_{i=1}^{n}(x_i - \bar{x})^2][(1/n)\sum_{i=1}^{n}(y_i - \bar{y})^2]\right\}^{1/2}} \tag{3.10}$$

or, in computational form, as

$$r_{xy} = \frac{(1/n)\sum_{i=1}^{n}x_iy_i - \overline{xy}}{\left\{[(1/n)\sum_{i=1}^{n}x_i^2 - \bar{x}^2][(1/n)\sum_{i=1}^{n}y_i^2 - \bar{y}^2]\right\}^{1/2}} \tag{3.11}$$

where $\bar{x}, \bar{y}$ are the respective means. Most students in the social sciences have been given a meaning or meanings for this coefficient, and for the population correlation coefficient ρ_{XY} that it estimates. We think of it as a "dimensionless" or "scale-free" measure of the extent to which the random variables X and Y are related. The numerator is the *sample covariance*, given by

$$s_{xy} = (1/n)\sum_{i=1}^{n}(x_i - \bar{x})(y_i - \bar{y}), \tag{3.12}$$

or

$$s_{xy} = (1/n)\sum_{i=1}^{n}x_iy_i - \overline{xy}. \tag{3.13}$$

This quantity is the average product of the deviations of x_i and y_i from their means, and is an estimate of the corresponding average product of X and Y in the population. The magnitude of a covariance depends on the units of measurement of X and Y and commonly does not have an interpretation. (It is easier to understand a correlation of, say, .7 between height and weight than a covariance of, say, 170 pound-inches.) Note that (3.13) includes an estimate of the variance of an item score as a special case when y_i is replaced by x_i. In small samples, the sample variance and covariance are biased estimates of the corresponding population values. The bias is corrected by replacing n by $n - 1$ in the computational expressions.[1]

If we apply the computational expression (3.13) (without correcting for bias) for a covariance to the binary scores in any two columns of Table 3.3, it turns out that it is equivalent to

$$s_{jk} = p_{jk} - p_j p_k \qquad (3.14a)$$

where p_{jk} is the relative frequency of the event {pass j and pass k} and p_j, p_k are relative frequencies of the events {pass j} and {pass k}. So the covariance of two binary item scores X_j, X_k is simply the sample estimate, $p_{jk} - p_j p_k$, of their (positive) association in probability,

$$\sigma_{jk} = \pi_{jk} - \pi_j \pi_k. \qquad (3.14b)$$

The student might find it helpful to study Table 3.4, to see how little difference there is in the two formulae when applied, say, to the first two items in Table 3.3.

Most users of statistics in the social sciences have learned—perhaps overlearned—to use and interpret the product–moment correlation coefficient as a measure of relatedness of two quantitative variables. In the example, it is not obvious how the covariance of .1, which is the difference between the joint probability .3 (as estimated) and the product of the separate probabilities, $.2 = .5 \times .4$, can possibly be judged to be "large" or "small." It will seem natural to most readers to complete the computation of the product–moment correlation by dividing by the product of the SD terms, estimated as $\{.5(1 - .5)\}^{1/2}$ and $\{.4(1 - .4)\}^{1/2}$. On using

TABLE 3.4
Computation of Binary Item Covariances

Ex.	Items 1	2	
			$\bar{x}_1 = 5/10 = .5$
			$\bar{x}_2 = 4/10 = .4$
1	1	1	$1/10(\Sigma\ x_{1i} x_{2i}) = 3/10 = .3$
2	1	0	$s_{12} = .3 - .5 \times .4 = .1$
3	1	1	
4	0	1	$p_{12} = \dfrac{\text{count of } (1,1) \text{ pairs}}{10} = .3$
5	0	0	
6	1	0	
7	0	0	$p_1 = \dfrac{\text{count of 1s in item 1}}{10} = .5$
8	0	0	
9	1	1	
10	0	0	$p_2 = \dfrac{\text{count of 1s in item 2}}{10} = .4$
			$p_{12} - p_1 p_2 = .3 - .5 \times .4 = s_{12}$

$$r_{jk} = s_{jk}/(s_j s_k), \tag{3.15}$$

we get

$$r_{12} = .1/\sqrt{.25 \times .24} = .408.$$

This step gives the impression that we now have a measure of association between the item responses.

To examine this impression more carefully, we rearrange the data and our notation. Still concentrating on items 1 and 2, we see that all the information about them can be gathered up in the conventional *fourfold*, or *2 by 2, contingency table*, as illustrated by Table 3.5.

Table 3.5(a) contains frequency counts, which in Table 3.5(b) become proportions. It will be convenient for the moment to pretend that those are also the population probabilities. In addition to the four cells of the table, with frequencies or proportions of the four pass/fail or 1/0 combinations, entered in the obvious way, *marginal* frequencies $n_{1\bullet}$, $n_{0\bullet}$, $n_{\bullet0}$, $n_{\bullet1}$, and corresponding proportions $p_{1\bullet}$, $p_{0\bullet}$, $p_{\bullet0}$, $p_{\bullet1}$ are shown. These use the convention that a dot represents a sum of cell entries, so that, for example, $n_{\bullet1} = n_{01} + n_{11}$ and $p_{\bullet1} = p_{01} + p_{11}$.

TABLE 3.5
Contingency Tables

Frequency counts
(a1)

		Item 1		
		1	0	
	0	n_{10}	n_{00}	$n_{\bullet0}$
Item 2	1	n_{11}	n_{01}	$n_{\bullet1}$
		$n_{1\bullet}$	$n_{0\bullet}$	n

Proportions
(b1)

		Item 1		
		1	0	
	0	p_{10}	p_{00}	$p_{\bullet0}$
Item 2	1	p_{11}	p_{01}	$p_{\bullet1}$
		$p_{1\bullet}$	$p_{0\bullet}$	1

(a2)
(Example)

	1	0	
0	3	4	6
1	3	1	4
	5	5	10

(b2)
(Example)

	1	0	
0	.2	.4	.6
1	.3	.1	.4
	.5	.5	1

There are two specialized, equivalent formulas for calculating the correlation of two binary items from proportions as in Table 3.5 (b1), namely,

$$r = \frac{p_{11} - p_{1\bullet}p_{\bullet 1}}{\sqrt{p_{1\bullet}p_{0\bullet}p_{\bullet 1}p_{\bullet 0}}}, \tag{3.16a}$$

or

$$r = \frac{p_{11}p_{00} - p_{01}p_{10}}{\sqrt{p_{1\bullet}p_{0\bullet}p_{\bullet 1}p_{\bullet 0}}}. \tag{3.16b}$$

Computation by (3.16a) gives

$$r = (.3 - .5 \times .4)/\sqrt{(.5 \times .5 \times .6 \times .4)} = .1/\sqrt{(.06)} = .408.$$

Computation by (3.16b) gives

$$r = (.12 - .02)/\sqrt{(.06)} = .408.$$

A common textbook formula corresponding to (3.16b), from the sample frequencies, is

$$r = \frac{n_{11}n_{00} - n_{01}n_{10}}{\sqrt{n_{1\bullet}n_{0\bullet}n_{\bullet 1}n_{\bullet 0}}}. \tag{3.17}$$

In the computer age, we do not need these specialized expressions. The only use we make of (3.16b) is to help understanding of perfect and maximum association.

*** Proof that $p_{11} - p_{1\bullet}p_{\bullet 1} = p_{11}p_{00} - p_{01}p_{10}$:

$$\begin{aligned} p_{11} - p_{1\bullet}p_{\bullet 1} &= p_{11} - (p_{10} + p_{11})(p_{01} + p_{11}) \\ &= p_{11} - p_{10}p_{01} - p_{11}p_{01} - p_{10}p_{11} - p_{11}^2 \\ &= (1 - p_{01} - p_{11} - p_{10})p_{11} - p_{01}p_{10} \\ &= p_{00}p_{11} - p_{01}p_{10}. \quad \$\$\$ \end{aligned}$$

Now consider extreme cases. If the item responses are independent,

$$\pi_{11} = \pi_{1\bullet}\pi_{\bullet 1}, \tag{3.18}$$

or equivalently,

$$\pi_{11}\pi_{00} = \pi_{01}\pi_{10}. \tag{3.19}$$

For example, if in the population we have the fourfold table:

	1	0	
0	.2	.2	.4
1	.3	.3	.6
	.5	.5	1

then (3.18) gives .3 = .5 × .6, and (3.19) gives .3 × .2 = .2 × .3. The first of these might appear more intuitively appealing as an expression of independence. But consider the opposite extreme, where the item responses are as closely associated as possible. One might then suppose we can find only

$$\text{Pass both: } X_j = 1 \text{ and } X_k = 1$$
$$\text{Fail both: } X_j = 0 \text{ and } X_k = 0.$$

This would certainly be perfect association and provide perfect prediction of either response from the other. However, it is easy to see that in this case we have

	1	0	
0	0	p_{00}	p_{00}
1	p_{11}	0	p_{11}
	p_{11}	p_{00}	1

In such a case the two items must have the same marginals, and—what is the same thing—the same difficulty parameters. That is, to have perfect prediction, each from the other, the items must be of equal difficulty.

If two items, j and k, have different difficulty parameters, with, say, $\pi_j > \pi_k$, the maximum possible covariance between them is

$$\sigma_{jk} = \pi_j(1 - \pi_k), \tag{3.20}$$

and the corresponding product–moment correlation is

$$\rho_{jk} = \sqrt{\frac{\pi_j(1-\pi_k)}{\pi_k(1-\pi_j)}} \qquad (3.21)$$

which is necessarily less than unity. This is because if π_k is smaller than π_j, the 2-by-2 table can have only one zero cell. Examinees who pass the more difficult item must pass the easier one. Those who pass the easier item may fail the harder one, and some examinees must do so. There is perfect prediction from the more difficult item to the easier one, but not conversely.[2] (No "perfect" correlation could express this fact.) To illustrate, the marginals

	1	0	
0	—	—	.4
1	—	—	.6
	.5	.5	1

allow

	1	0	
0	.0	.4	.4
1	.5	.1	.6
	.5	.5	1

with maximum correlation .82.

Table 3.6(a) gives the covariances of all five items from Table 3.3, arranged in the conventional form of a *symmetric matrix*. The sample covariance of X_j and X_k is entered in the jth row and kth column of the matrix. It is said to be the (j,k)th *element* of the matrix. It is repeated, as

TABLE 3.6
Binary Covariance and Correlation Matrices

(a) Covariance Matrix

	1	2	3	4	5
1	.25	.10	.15	.10	−.05
2	.10	.24	.00	.08	−.06
3	.15	.00	.25	.10	−.05
4	.10	.08	.10	.16	−.02
5	−.05	−.06	−.05	−.02	.09

(b) Correlation Matrix

	1	2	3	4	5
1	1	.408	.600	.500	−.333
2	.408	1	.000	.408	−.408
3	.600	.000	1	.500	−.333
4	.500	.408	.500	1	−.167
5	−.333	−.408	−.333	−.167	1

the covariance of X_k and X_j, in the kth row and jth column—as the (k,j)th element. [Note the convention that (j,k) names the row index first, then the column index.] The expression (3.14) for covariance includes the expression for variance.

*** This is because, if $j = k$, $p_{jk} = p_j$, and $p_j - p_j^2 = p_j(1 - p_j)$. $$$

When dealing with a matrix of variances and covariances it is therefore natural to write, instead of s_j^2,

$$s_{jj} = p_j(1 - p_j),$$
(3.22a)

estimating

$$\sigma_{jj} = \pi_j(1 - \pi_j).$$
(3.22b)

Accordingly, the (j,j)th entries in the matrix, running down the *main diagonal* (from top left to bottom right), are the item variances. They are, in fact, the "covariances" of the items with themselves. In further work we find both notations—σ_{jj} and σ_j^2—for variance useful, depending on the application. We say the matrix is *symmetric* about the diagonal, because $\sigma_{jk} = \sigma_{kj}$. Table 3.6(b) gives the corresponding correlation matrix.

We have already completed the computation of the covariance .10 and the correlation .408 between items 1 and 2. The student is encouraged to check one or two more of these values.

With experience, by inspecting such matrices, we can learn a good deal, especially if the items have been grouped on a reasonable basis, for example, into algebra and geometry items for the mathematics test envisaged in Chapter 1. (We would then go on to more technical analyses.) Thus, we can recognize pairs or clusters of items that seem most closely related— suggesting perhaps that they measure the same thing—or pairs or sets of items that appear mutually independent—suggesting perhaps that they measure different things.

One noticeable feature of Table 3.6 is that item 5 has negative covariances (and correlations, of course) with all four of the remaining items. If these were cognitive items, all scored unity for a correct answer and zero for incorrect, this would be very puzzling, as it is a very general finding in cognitive psychology that cognitive performances are positively correlated. If they are personality items, we immediately suspect that item five has been scored in the opposite direction from the other four. For example, if the items were measuring extraversion, the other four might be scored unity for the extravert response, whereas item 5 is scored unity for the introvert response. We can rescore 5 itself, switching ones and zeros, but do not have to do that at this stage. If we just change the signs of the covariances/correlations of item 5 with the other four items, this is equivalent to rescoring it with the opposite *polarity*. An attribute is *bipolar* if we can just as easily imagine measuring it in either direction of scoring—high for extraversion, or high for introversion, for example. Many attributes can have their polarity reversed. Even those appearing to have a "valued" or "important" direction that seems to deserve a high score are not unambiguous. A test for "neuroticism" could be scored for "adjustment," and a test for "anxiety" might be scored for "calmness/poise." The important point is that we can have a mixture of items measuring in opposite polarities. (It can be good testing technique to balance items with "positive" and "negative" connotations.) We should then either reverse score one set until they all measure in the same direction, or change the signs of their covariances with the other items. Care is needed. We change the signs of one item at a time, and need to be sure that there are no items with a mixture of positive and negative relationships that cannot be eliminated by choosing the scoring direction. Getting a consistent direction for the scores is essential for reliability measures in Chapter 6.

QUANTITATIVE ITEM STATISTICS

Suppose now we draw a respondent at random from a population of interest and administer just one attitude item—say, the gun-control example in Chapter 1, "assault weapons do not belong in private hands." The response options can be tabulated as shown:

Options	*Scores*
Strongly agree	5
Agree	4
Neither agree nor disagree	3
Disagree	2
Strongly disagree	1

The options and scores are in perfect correspondence, and the scores, like binary scores, can be thought of either as codes labeling the options or as item scores whose values could be used to make a test score on combining with further scores. With some probability, the respondent must give one of these options. Again we imagine drawing further respondents, yielding the scores in Table 3.7, in which the process has been stopped at sample size $n = 100$, but is imagined to continue indefinitely.

We draw up the distribution in Table 3.8, where n_c is the observed frequency of each category, p is the relative frequency, and π is the prob-

TABLE 3.7
Constructed Quantitative Variable

13433	24333	333213	22544
33533	33223	13243	43331
43315	33234	12322	32521
31222	43232	24433	44412
23453	35243	33342	22315
. . .			

TABLE 3.8
Distribution of Quantitative Variable

X	n_c	p	π	πx	πx^2
5	7	.07	.1	0.5	2.5
4	17	.17	.2	0.8	3.2
3	41	.41	.4	1.2	3.6
2	25	.25	.2	0.4	0.8
1	10	.10	.1	0.1	0.1
				$\mu = \Sigma\pi x = 3.0$	$\Sigma\pi x^2 = 10.2$

$$\sigma^2 = 10.2 - 3.0^2 = 1.2$$

ability or proportion in the "population" that was used to create these artificial data. (To make up the numbers in Table 3.7, I just took random digits 0 through 9 and assigned a score of 5 to digit 0, a score of 4 to digits 1 or 2, a score of 3 to digits 3, 4, 5, or 6, a score of 2 to digits 7 or 8, and a score of 1 to digit 9. This gives the probabilities in Table 3.8.)

Using the population values, we obtain a mean of 3.0 and variance of 1.2—$SD = \sqrt{1.2} = 1.095. \ldots$ The reader may wish to compute the corresponding sample estimates, by the standard formulas for frequency data. Suppose now the unlikely case occurs in which just half the respondents strongly agree, and half strongly disagree, with no one taking the three intermediate options. Then, by the same procedure, we obtain $\mu = 3.0$, but $\sigma^2 = 4.0$, and $SD = 2.0$. This is the maximum possible value for the variance of an item scored over five successive integers, and it will be reached only with the unlikely distribution described. The maximum possible variance for a score ranging over the numbers 1, 2, . . . , k is given by

$$\sigma_{max}^2 = [(k - 1)/2]^2 \qquad (3.23)$$

reached when the probability of each of the two extreme values is .5, and the probability of all intermediate values is zero. A tabulation for $k = 2$, . . . ,10 is given in Table 3.9.

Now, more generally, we suppose we have any item scored over integers 1,2, . . . ,k—possibly a cognitive item, matching, frequency count, or item

TABLE 3.9
Maximum Variance of Quantitative Item Score

k	2	3	4	5	6	7	8	9	10
σ_{max}	.25	1	2.25	4	6.25	9	12.25	16	20.25

bundle. If it is indeed a cognitive item, we naturally extend the idea of an item difficulty parameter from the probability of passing a binary item to the item mean score on a quantitative item. Already in the binary case the probability of passing is the same as the item mean, and generally, a low score is expected on a difficult item and a high score on an easy one. More generally, we expect a group of people to get a lower mean score on a difficult test than on an easy test. With the same linguistic hesitation as before, when the item is noncognitive we agree to call the item mean an item difficulty parameter also.

As soon as there are at least three integers, the item variance is no longer determined by its mean. In the case just given, with $\mu = 3$, we have a variance of 1.2 with the distribution in Table 3.8, and of 4.0 with the extreme distribution. By definition, the variance measures *diversity* of response, and in the case of an attitude item can be fairly described as measuring diversity of opinion. The mean and variance are still not independent. That is, it is still impossible to have the mean move toward an extreme value without the variance becoming smaller. Diversity prevents an average extreme view.

Consider now the data in Table 3.10. These are the responses of the first 10 subjects from a larger sample—treated later—to the SWLS, discussed in Chapter 2, namely:

TABLE 3.10
Satisfaction With Life Data

	Items						
Respondent	1	2	3	4	5	Total	Mean
1	2	4	3	5	2	16	3.2
2	5	7	7	7	6	32	6.4
3	3	5	5	4	1	18	3.6
4	6	6	6	6	5	29	5.8
5	7	7	6	2	2	24	4.8
6	5	2	6	7	2	22	4.4
7	2	3	3	3	1	12	2.4
8	4	3	6	3	3	19	3.8
9	3	5	5	5	1	19	3.8
10	4	4	5	6	4	23	4.6
Total	41	46	52	48	27		
Mean	4.1	4.6	5.2	4.8	2.7		

(1) I am satisfied with my life.
(2) The conditions of my life are excellent.
(3) In most ways my life is close to the ideal.
(4) So far I have gotten the important things I want from life.
(5) If I could live my life over, I would change almost nothing.

These response categories are scored:

Strongly agree	7
Agree	6
Slightly agree	5
Neither agree nor disagree	4
Slightly disagree	3
Disagree	2
Strongly disagree	1

Using the general expressions (3.13) and (3.11) for (estimated) covariance and correlation, we obtain the sample covariance matrix in Table 3.11(a). (This is an unbiased estimate, dividing by $n - 1 = 9$ in the terms of the expression for covariance.) Table 3.11(b) then gives the sample correlation matrix.

Again, and for the same reasons as in the binary case, two items scored over a limited range of integers cannot be perfectly correlated unless their separate probability distributions over the integers are the same, but the

TABLE 3.11
Satisfaction With Life Covariance/Correlations

(a) Covariance Matrix

	1	2	3	4	5
1	2.78	1.49	1.76	0.24	1.48
2	1.49	2.93	0.98	−0.09	1.31
3	1.76	0.98	1.73	0.71	1.40
4	0.24	−0.09	0.71	3.07	1.71
5	1.48	1.31	1.40	1.71	3.12

(b) Correlation Matrix

	1	2	3	4	5
1	1	.53	.80	.08	.50
2	.52	1	.43	−.03	.43
3	.80	.43	1	.31	.60
4	.08	−.03	.31	1	.55
5	.50	.43	.60	.55	1

effect can generally be safely neglected in most forms of analysis of the correlation matrix. We do most of our work with covariances.

TEST SCORES

For some purposes we might multiply item or subtest scores by numbers—*weights*—that give them different amounts of influence on the test score, but we suppose until indicated otherwise that a test score is formed either as a simple sum or as a simple average of the item scores. Tables 3.3 and 3.10 show on the right, for the ith examinee, the total sum of the item scores,

$$y_i = \sum_{j=1}^{m} x_{ji}. \qquad (3.24)$$

This is the *total test score* for examinee i. These tables also show on the right for the ith examinee, the mean of the item scores,

$$m_i = (\sum_{j=1}^{m} x_{ji})/m. \qquad (3.25)$$

This is the *relative test score* or *mean test score* for examinee i.

For a binary item, y_i is also the number of keyed responses given by the examinee, and in a cognitive item, it is the *number-right score*; m_i is the *proportion-keyed score*, and, in a cognitive item, the *proportion-right score*. For some purposes, these scores are immediately and clearly interpretable, at least at the extremes, which are often the regions of most concern. If we know that the examinee got most or few of the items right, or showed most or few of the symptoms of a specific personality disorder, we also know approximately what the typical responses were without reexamining the actual item responses. The raw test score can often be anchored in this way to "typical" behaviors, much as the temperature scale is anchored to the melting point and boiling point of water.

In the case of the item totals and item means for the five Likert items in Table 3.10, the total score does not easily lend itself to interpretation. But given that the five items correspond to *strongly agree–strongly disagree* on aspects of a common issue, it can be reasonable to refer the mean item score back to those categories. The extreme scores correspond to modal behaviors dominated respectively by agreeing or by disagreeing, on the set of items, again anchoring the test-score scale in typical behaviors. The modal response of examinee 2 is on the strong side of *agree*, so to speak. The modal response of examinee 7 is on the strong side of *disagree*. So we understand the difference in their degree of expressed satisfaction as a qualitative distinction, not merely a quantitative difference.

Given the 10 total test scores on the right in Tables 3.3 and 3.10 it is an easy task to compute their means and variances. From Table 3.3,

$$\bar{y} = 3.10 \qquad s_y^2 = 1.69,$$

and from Table 3.10,

$$\bar{y} = 21.4 \qquad s_y^2 = 35.6.$$

We notice that if we add the 25 elements in the covariance matrices in Tables 3.6(a) and 3.11(a)—the 20 item covariances s_{jk} and the 5 variances s_{jj}—the resulting sum is the same as the variances obtained from the 10 test scores. (This is a simple exercise for the student.)

Quite generally, one can compute the sample variance s_y^2 of a set of n total test scores y_i, $i = 1, \ldots, n$, either directly by the formula for variance

$$s_y^2 = (\sum_{i=1}^{n} y_i^2 / n) - \bar{y}^2, \tag{3.26}$$

or as the sum of the variances and covariances

$$s_y^2 = \sum_{j=1}^{m} \sum_{k=1}^{m} s_{jk}. \tag{3.27}$$

The sum is over all m^2—in the examples, 5^2—elements of the matrix.

*** Proof: By the algebra of expectations, as in Appendix A,

$$Y = X_1 + \cdots + X_m$$

gives

$$\mathrm{Var}\{Y\} = \mathrm{Var}\{X_1 + \cdots + X_m\}$$
$$= \sum \sum \mathrm{Cov}\{X_j, X_k\}. \qquad \$\$\$$$

For some purposes, we may separate the sum of the m diagonal elements, say,

$$D = \sum_{j=1}^{m} s_{jj} \qquad (3.28)$$

and the sum of the $m(m - 1)$ off-diagonal elements. We can write this either as

$$O_d = \sum\sum_{j \neq k} s_{jk} \qquad (3.29a)$$

(summed, that is, over all elements for which j is not equal to k) or as

$$O_d = 2\sum\sum_{j < k} s_{jk} \qquad (3.29b)$$

(summed, that is, over all elements for which j is less than k, then doubled). Thus, in the examples, from Table 3.6(a)

$$D = 1.00 \quad \text{and} \quad O_d = .70$$

and from Table 3.11(a)

$$D = 13.63 \quad \text{and} \quad O_d = 21.98.$$

There is no practical computational advantage in having this alternative method for calculating total test score variance as a sum of item variances and item covariances. We see later that it is possible to analyze the structure of the covariance matrix for what it tells us about the quality of the test and the appropriateness of forming a test score. Some intuitive notions about constructing good tests have rested on the basis of the distinction between contributions to test variance from the item variances and contributions from the item covariances. Suppose all the items have the same variance. Then if they are all uncorrelated—and if a correlation is zero the covariance is zero—the test variance is m times the item variance; but if they are all perfectly correlated, then all covariances equal the common value of the variance, so the test variance is m^2 times the item variance, which is much larger.

If we have a pool of items from which we are to choose just m items to make a test, it can be argued that we should choose the items that give the largest ratio of test variance to the sum of the m item variances, that is, to make

$$s_y^2 / (\sum_{j=1}^{m} s_j^2) = (D + O_d)/D \qquad (3.30)$$

large. For this purpose we would choose items with large (positive) covariances. A test whose items have large positive correlations—not quite the same thing—is sometimes called *internally consistent*. (See Chap. 6 and Chap. 18.)

It can also be argued that in adding further items to an existing set to make the test longer (and, hopefully, a better measure) we should choose items that make the greatest proportional contribution to total variance. This implies choosing further items with large variances and large positive covariance with existing items and with each other. This simple device—choosing items with high covariances—will actually tend to lead to the choice of items with similar content, and it may suffice to yield a homogeneous test with good measurement properties. The argument is sometimes carried to the point of claiming, in the case of binary items, that we should choose items of the same difficulty, to maximize possible item covariances, and choose them with difficulty parameter .5, to maximize item variance. These recommendations are not without merit, but can now be replaced by better procedures. Modern treatments of theory show that this last recommendation makes a test that will be good for middle-range examinees, but not good for diagnosing extreme cases. The methods of item response theory allow the test developer to choose to create a test for middle-range examinees or to create a test applicable to extreme examinees, according to what is needed. (See Chap. 13.)

For completeness, and for later use, we note that if we have one test of m_1 items, $X_{11}, \ldots, X_{1m_1}$, and a second test of m_2 items, $X_{21}, \ldots, X_{2m_2}$, then the covariance between Y_1, the total score on the first test, and Y_2, the score on the second, is given by the sum of the $m_1 m_2$ covariances between their items,

$$\text{Cov}\{Y_1, Y_2\} = \sum_j \sum_k \text{Cov}\{X_{1j}, X_{2k}\}. \qquad (3.31)$$

Consider, for example, from Table 3.11(a), the covariance between a sum score on the three items referring to satisfaction with the present, $Y_1 = X_1 + X_2 + X_3$ and a sum score on the two items referring to satisfaction with the past, $Y_2 = X_4 + X_5$. From the table, we pick out the six needed covariances, and add them, giving

$$\text{Cov}\ \{Y_1, Y_2\} = s_{41} + s_{42} + s_{43}$$
$$|\ s_{51} + s_{52} + s_{53}$$
$$= .24 - .09 + .71$$
$$+ 1.48 + 1.31 + 1.40 = 5.05.$$

Also using (3.27) with the necessary parts of Table 3.11(a) gives

$$\text{Var}\{Y_1\} = 2.78 + 1.49 + 1.76$$
$$+ 1.49 + 2.93 + .98$$
$$+ 1.76 + .98 + 1.73 = 15.9,$$

and

$$\text{Var}\{Y_2\} = 3.07 + 1.71$$
$$+ 1.71 + 3.12 = 9.61,$$

so the correlation between these sums is

$$5.05/\sqrt{(15.9 \times 9.61)} = .409.$$

REVIEW GUIDE

After a first reading of this chapter, students (perhaps guided by instructors) may see a need for supplementary review of statistics.[3] A minimum necessity is to have clear conceptions of sample versus population, of relative frequency as estimating and converging on a population probability, and, more generally, of a sample statistic estimating and converging on a population parameter as the sample size increases.

The central concepts in this chapter to be learned are as follows:

For binary item scores: (a) the difficulty parameter of an item, (b) the variance of an item score given by (3.8) and estimated by (3.7), (c) the covariance of two item scores given by (3.14b) and estimated by (3.14a), which is a measure of their association in probability, and (d) the fact that the correlation between two item scores is not generally a good measure of their association.

For quantitative item scores: (a) The difficulty parameter of an item is its population mean, estimated by the sample mean. (b) Estimates of the covariance and correlation of two item scores are given by (3.13) and (3.11).

For both kinds of item: The covariances and variances can be arranged in a symmetric covariance matrix as in Tables 3.6(a) and 3.11(a), and the correlations can similarly be arranged as in Tables 3.6(b) and 3.11(b).

For test scores: (a) Total and relative test scores (mean scores) are given respectively by (3.24) and (3.25). These include number-keyed or proportion-keyed scores and number-right or proportion-right scores. (b) The variance of a total test score is given by the sum of the item variances and covariances, that is, by (3.27), as well as by the regular formula for variance, (3.26). (c) The covariance of two item sums can be computed as the sum of the covariances between their items, by (3.31).

The student should also, of course, be able to operate these computational formulas as illustrated in the numerical examples.

END NOTES

1. For simplicity I have discussed sample variances in this chapter that are, in small samples, biased estimates of the corresponding population parameters. Most introductory statistics texts show that an unbiased estimate of variance is obtained by replacing n by $n - 1$ in (3.5), essentially because the variability of samples about their own sample means must be less than their variability about the population mean. The same is true for estimates of covariance in (3.12) and (3.13). In large samples—the usual case in test construction—the bias can be ignored. Where it matters, the corrected expressions replacing (3.5) and (3.12) will be used.

2. In the older literature the fact that the maximum possible correlation between two binary items is generally less than unity has sometimes been discussed as a defect of the coefficient. Attempts to "correct" this defect by, for example, dividing it by the maximum possible value—"phi over phi max"—have not generally been well motivated, and should be avoided. It has been shown that application of models such as the factor model to such a corrected coefficient does not solve the "problem" that was supposed to be created by differential item difficulty.

3. Moore and McCabe (1993) is representative of the knowledge assumed, and could serve for review, if the student does not have a preference.

The Concept of a Scale

This chapter contains a first treatment—somewhat informal and limited—of concepts to be more fully developed in Chapter 18. The intention is to set out enough material on notions about scales to support the following chapters, and to leave the rest of this quite deep topic to a position where nothing depends on it and it can be treated as optional by the instructor or student.

The purpose of measurement is to quantify an attribute. To do this, we find a rule that assigns a numerical value to the attribute in correspondence to the observations. *Measurement* is the assignment of numbers to an attribute according to a rule of correspondence. Sometimes the correspondence holds in both directions, as in the case of a single ordered-category item scored with integers. The response "strongly agree" receives a score of 5, and a score of 5 uniquely implies "strongly agree." More usually, the correspondence goes in one direction only, as in most cognitive tests, where one can get the same number-right score by passing different sets of items. We know the score from the set of items passed, but from the score we do not know which items were passed.

Consider an ordinary test of 10 cognitive pass–fail items designed to measure a specified ability—for example, a verbal test of scholastic aptitude. The simple number-right score fulfills the basic requirement of measurement. It assigns a numerical value to the ability by a clear rule of correspondence. Now suppose we administer the test to a large sample of examinees. In the sample distribution it may or may not happen that no examinee fails every item (scoring 0), and/or no examinee passes every item (scoring a perfect 10). However, there still may be examinees in the population who would score 0 or 10, and they would need easier or more difficult items to be written to prevent this. Thus, any test will have a *floor*—corresponding to the zero score—and a *ceiling*—corresponding to the perfect score. Below its floor and above its ceiling it cannot measure the attribute. Of course, whether the floor or ceiling will be reached depends on the population of interest. A test that is easy for university students may be just right for high school students and difficult for elementary school students.

Perhaps naively, we generally believe without hesitation that the rules of physical measurement—such as for length, mass, temperature—give us *equal intervals* in the sense that the difference in the physical attribute of length, mass, or temperature between objects measuring 2 or 3 units (centimeters, kilograms, degrees) and objects measuring 12 or 13 units is "the same." But notice that it is not obvious what it is in our observations that can assure us that the *interval* between 2°C and 3°C is the same as the interval between 12°C and 13°C or between 1002°C and 1003°C, in respect of what we believe we are measuring. Notice also that we unhesitatingly describe an object 2 m long as "twice as long" as an object 1 m long. The *ratio* of two lengths appears to have "meaning" for us. In contrast, we do not say that 20°C is "twice as hot" as 10°C, so the ratio of two temperatures does not appear to have "meaning." It looks as though some physical measurement units may have "interval" properties, and some may have "ratio" properties. A perhaps less familiar scale is the Mohs scale for hardness of minerals. This is based on a scratch test; if mineral A scratches mineral B, A is said to be harder than B. A set of minerals, from the hardest—diamond—down to the softest—talc—has been assigned numbers, and other minerals are judged relative to these on the scratch test. So it would seem that the only meaning in this case reflected in the numbers assigned is the order of the hardnesses. This is an example of an *ordinal* scale.

It should be clear intuitively that we would hesitate to say that the differences in ability between examinees with number-right scores of 0 versus 1, of 5 versus 6, or of 9 versus 10 are "the same." Similarly, we would hesitate to say that the difference in attitude toward gun control, measured by the item "assault weapons do not belong in private hands," between "strongly disagree" and "disagree" is the same as the difference between "agree" and "neither agree nor disagree." In effect, the scores we have considered so far appear to have at best *ordinal* properties, like the Mohs scale of hardness. The number-right scores (with some error) order the examinees in respect of ability. The Likert scores order respondents in respect of their attitude. But the differences between the numbers do not in any obvious sense measure "distances"—intervals—between the abilities or the attitudes. And the examinee who gets 10 passes cannot be called "twice as able" as the examinee with 5.

Suppose now we describe our basic observations of pass/fails in summary form as "passed k items." In Table 4.1, the first column represents such a summary. These are 11 occurrences. The second column gives a *scale value* to these 11 occurrences. The distinction is perhaps seemingly trivial, but it is crucial. The scores in the second column are merely one way to assign a scale value—a measurement—to the ability.

We are not forced to choose the number-right score. The scores in the columns headed Scale 2, Scale 3, and Scale 4 are equally acceptable scale values for the ability. They put the examinees in the same order. Indeed, any set of numbers with the order property will serve. Scale 2 contains the square of the number right score. Scale 3 contains the square root (rounded to two decimal places). Scale 4 was obtained by computing the ratio of the proportion of passes to the proportion of failures (known in gambling and in probability theory as the odds) and then taking its natural logarithm. We meet this *log-odds scale* again later. Its scale values stretch out on the number line from negative infinity to positive infinity, so that ability is unbounded. This may seem nice, but we might not wish to take the extremes seriously. Notice that we do not assign infinite values, as mathematically implied by the log-odds transformation, to the extreme scores. In applications it is not generally appropriate to do so, as we see later.

We describe the choice of a set of numbers to assign to the set of observations as a choice of *metric*. Table 4.1 illustrates the point that in the case of the observations listed in the first column, a wide range of choices of metric is available. These remarks apply with no change to binary noncognitive items, with keyed/nonkeyed replacing pass/fail, and a specified attribute, such as extraversion, replacing "ability." It should be obvious that we could assign ordered numbers to the ordered categories

TABLE 4.1
Alternative Scales

	Number Right Scale	Scale 2	Scale 3	Scale 4
Passed all items	10	100	3.16	(?)
Passed 9 items	9	81	3	2.18
Passed 8 items	8	64	2.83	1.39
Passed 7 items	7	49	2.65	0.85
Passed 6 items	6	36	2.45	0.41
Passed 5 items	5	25	2.24	0
Passed 4 itcms	4	16	2	−0.41
Passed 3 items	3	9	1.73	−0.85
Passed 2 items	2	4	1.14	−1.39
Passed 1 item	1	1	1	−2.18
Failed all items	0	0	0	(−?)

of an ordered-category item in a variety of ways. Integers are just one easy choice. Or, in a second step, we could transform the total or mean score, just as in Table 4.1.

Choosing a metric—a set of scale values for the observations—includes choosing an origin and a unit of measurement. We decide what observation should correspond to the number zero, and what difference between observations should correspond to the number unity. If this choice is made without use of a distribution of responses from actual examinees, seemingly "natural" choices are already made when we use raw sum scores or the proportion or mean—relative—scores that we dealt with in Chapter 3. In this case the origin corresponds to giving no keyed responses. In raw sum scores the unit corresponds to a single keyed response, whereas in a relative score the unit corresponds to giving all the keyed responses. As already seen, raw scores often have a clear and absolute reference to behavior. A score of 1 on "assault weapons do not belong in private hands" means "strongly disagree," and we know where the respondent stands, "absolutely." We do not need to relate that opinion to other opinions. Similarly, it is easy to see that if a student successfully answers a set of arithmetic items requiring comprehension of place value, the student has, in plain English, "mastered" place value. This requires no comparison with other students. For a long time this virtue of raw scores was neglected, but it has more recently been recognized that scores on a test can be used in this absolute way to see if an examinee meets a criterion of mastery of curricular materials, or a standard for selection to a program, say. Such use is referred to as *criterion-referenced measurement*.[1]

It has commonly been considered desirable to choose a metric—at least to choose an origin and scale unit—on the basis of the distribution of scores obtained from a population of interest. This is appropriate for some purposes of educational testing, when it becomes necessary to measure an aptitude for study, or an educational achievement following study, across large segments of a nation-state that is linguistically and culturally homogeneous. Choosing an origin and unit of measurement based on the population distribution yields a *norm-referenced measurement*.

It is not always clear that the setting of national or cultural standards—*norms*—is well motivated. The motivation rests on applications of the test. It is important to recognize that the same test can be referred to a criterion or to a norm. For example, the original motive for the first intelligence test of Binet and Simon (1895) was to identify children with cognitive disabilities who needed special education. This had nothing to do with national norms for intelligence. The same holds for the use of tests in selecting examinees for identifiable cognitive competencies. Similarly, detection of psychopathology should have little to do with its general incidence in the nation-state or culture in which the test is developed.

On the other hand, there are very good reasons for examining the distribution of raw test scores in the population of interest. The test may be too easy or difficult. Given this distribution, it can be reasonable to choose an origin and unit, and possibly to transform the raw-score metric to a preferable one, on the basis of the estimated population distribution. From a large sample of examinees drawn from the population of interest, we can estimate the mean and standard deviation (*SD*) of the total test score; we can graph the distribution in a histogram to inspect its shape; and we can do a statistical test for departure from a normal distribution. The effects of an active constraint due to the floor or ceiling of the test will be shown by the distribution.

If the distribution is normal to a good approximation, we can continue to work with the raw test score (total or mean). We may also turn it into a standard score,

$$Z = (Y - \mu_y)/\sigma_y.$$

$$z = \frac{score - mean}{std\ dev}$$

This simply refers the scale of measurement to the population mean μ_Y as its origin, and the *SD* of the distribution σ_Y as its unit of measurement. Then a "z score" is an individual's number of (population-of-interest) *SD* values above (if positive) or below (if negative) the (population-of-interest) mean. In applications, of course, large-sample estimates of μ_y, σ_y are substituted. A problem created by all choices of metric that use some population of interest to define the origin and unit is that there may be more than one population of interest (see Chap. 15).

Further transformations of origin and unit can be adopted arbitrarily, in the form

$$S = cZ + a,$$

where c and a are chosen constants. If Z is the standard score on an intelligence test, then

$$S = 15Z + 100$$

gives a score with mean 100 and *SD* 15. This is a *deviation IQ*, as used in the Wechsler intelligence scales. The constants are chosen to make it resemble the classical IQ, defined as

$$IQ = \frac{mental\ age}{chronological\ age} \times 100.$$

Rightly or wrongly, many people feel they have learned to attach a quite direct meaning to this measure of the human being.

If the distribution of raw scores appears to depart from normality, one may choose to assign values so that the rescaled scores are (approximately) normally distributed. One way to do this is to try to find a transformation rule—like the square-root transformation in Table 4.1—that happens to yield a normal distribution. A guaranteed way is to use normalized standard scores. These are calculated by converting each raw score in the large sample into a percentile rank, which is the proportion—estimated probability—of examinees scoring lower. We then use the table of the normal curve—the cumulative normal distribution function—to further convert the percentile rank into the standard score that has that proportion of scores below it. A suitable transformation rule is generally preferable to normalized standard scores, being less dependent on chance effects of sampling.

A normalized score does have an obviously desirable property. It satisfies a commonly desired distribution assumption for statistical tests. It also satisfies the requirement of defining a metric—of providing a clear rule for assigning numbers to the observations. (Note that it does not solve the problem of an active floor or ceiling.) It does not convert ordinal observations into numbers on an interval scale, such that equal differences correspond to equal changes in amount of the attribute being measured. It is not in general possible to arrive at a uniquely desirable scale by imposing a normal distribution. Thus, whether normalized or not, there is no reason to say, for example, that the difference in amount of intelligence between a person with IQ 160 and one with IQ 140 is the same as that between a person with IQ 110 and one with IQ 90. For most purposes this is not a problem.

It has been argued by Stevens (but see Chap. 18) that permissible statistical operations on scale values depend on whether or not we have an interval scale. For example, a test of a difference in means could require that equal differences in assigned scale values—160 – 140 versus 110 – 90—correspond to equal differences in amount of the attribute being scaled. (A few statistical operations appear to need a "natural" origin also.) Others have insisted that "statistics don't need permission," but merely need the relevant statistical assumptions. For example, statistical tests on a difference could require that the measures are normally distributed, but not require them to satisfy a scaling property also.[2]

Some statistical hypotheses are unaltered by transformations of the scale(s) of measurement. The example we already have is the hypothesis that the means of two populations are different. The *t* test for this hypothesis requires normally distributed scale values, but says nothing about equal interval properties. Other hypotheses are altered by changes of scale. An example is the hypothesis that the relationship between one test score and another is linear. If the mean of one variable—the dependent variable—increases with another—the independent variable—we could change the scale of one or both to make the relationship linear or nonlinear. More generally, it is possible to choose a scale of measurement to simplify the form of the mathematical relationship between variables, or to simplify a distribution—for example, by normalizing. This seems to be the real basis of most scaling methods (see Chap. 18).

In typical applications of testing, then, a measurement rule does not need to yield scale values corresponding to equal differences in the attribute, to satisfy the requirement of a scale. We can have number-right or number-keyed scores, or total or mean scores from quantitative items, or convenient transformations of these to origins and units based on some population of interest, or possibly nonlinear transformations of them. All of these serve to measure an attribute. Numbers are assigned to the observations according to a rule of correspondence, giving us scale values. Care is needed in statistical applications of these scale values, when the acceptance or rejection of the hypothesis tested could depend on the measurement scale chosen.

REVIEW GUIDE

Concepts to be learned include the floor and ceiling of a test, the meaning of measurement, and the possibility of choosing alternative metrics, including the choice of origin and unit for the measurement scale. An intuitive idea of ordinal, interval, and ratio scales will suffice. The general distinction between criterion-referenced measures, which are absolute measures based on raw scores, and norm-referenced measures, which are based on a population of interest, will suffice for our purposes.

END NOTES

1. The distinction between criterion-referenced and norm-referenced tests is due to Glaser (1963). For further information about mastery and criterion-referenced tests see Berk (1980).
2. This is a difficult and controversial matter, considered further in Chapter 18. See Guttman (1977).

Chapter 5

Reliability Theory for
Total Test Scores

The basic motivation for classical true-score theory is to provide a workable method for estimating the precision of measurement of a test score. Generically, this is the problem of *test reliability.* The mathematics of the theory is extremely simple. The application of the theory can be problematic.

Let us begin by considering the contrasting case of estimating the precision of a physical measurement—length. Given a graduated rule, if we wish to estimate the error of measurement of the length of an object, we will replicate the measurement operation a number of times. We take the mean of the measurements as our best estimate of its length, and their *SD* is our best estimate of the error in the measuring process. This procedure rests on the reasonable assumption that the replications are independent trials, so the errors are independent of each other, and therefore uncorrelated. There are, of course, further assumptions implicit in this process. Thus it is assumed that the graduated instrument contains no source of constant error, and that the length of the object does not change over the time period during which the repeated measurements are taken. (If, for example, we were measuring lengths of railroad track with a plastic tape, we might have to allow for expansion of the object with temperature.) But with appropriate precautions, such replicated measurements give us the amount of error with which the test instrument measures the specified property of the object, in the metric defined by the instrument—say, centimeters or inches. (This is the very simplest case in physical measurement. A deeper analysis would show that there are nontrivial problems to be found in all physical measurement, but these do not concern us here.)

As soon as we imagine a problem in psychological measurement, we see difficulties over replicating the measurement. If we propose to administer a psychological test a large number of times to a single examinee, we see how unlikely it is that the replications could constitute independent trials and yield uncorrelated errors. The closer together in time the retests are given, the more similar the test scores will be, due to factors such as memory of previous responses. After no more than, say, three replications of the test procedure, the motivation of the examinee will probably decline, stereotyped responses will ensue, and the results will not constitute independent trials. Further, few of the attributes we measure will be strictly constant over time. An extreme case is mood. We only have to consult personal experience of self or others to recognize that emotional states are characterized by lability, and some people are more labile than others. Thus a short time interval between retests will make the responses spuriously alike, while a long time interval will allow change in the attribute to be measured. And there is no clear way to choose an intermediate time interval at which the attribute is unchanged and the repeated measures are statistically independent. No trait is stable from the cradle to the grave. Some states are stable enough to be treated as though they are traits.

There is a further point of contrast with the simpler forms of physical measurement. In the case of length, it does not seem possible to question whether we are measuring the property of the object we wish to measure. Indeed, we may find it hard to distinguish conceptually between the graduation mark we read off the scale and the length of the object it has been laid against. In the case of a psychological attribute we can see a clear distinction between the concept—extraversion, intelligence, attitude toward gun control, positive affect—and the total score on a specific set of items selected to measure it. There have been three apparently distinct ways to conceive the relationship between the test score and the attribute:

1. It has been treated as the precision with which the test score measures the attribute—the *reliability* of the test as a composite indicator of the attribute.

2. It has been treated as the extent to which the test measures the attribute it was designed to measure—the *validity* of the test as a composite indicator of the attribute.

3. It has been treated as the extent to which the composite test score generalizes beyond the specific items chosen to form the composite, to the domain of further indicators that might have been used—the question of *generalizability*, from items we have to items we do not have.

These distinctions are generally hard to sustain in practice.

One conclusion that might seem to follow by now is that the problem in the opening statement—how to provide "a workable method for estimating the precision of measurement of a test score"—has no solution. Another is that the problem as stated contains ambiguities requiring analysis. We can postpone the conceptual issues by treating the classical true-score model as a piece of pure mathematics, and separating the question of whether it can be applied to empirical data, and under what conditions. For this purpose it can be illustrated with artificial, simulated data. The strategy adopted in this chapter is to describe the classical true-score model as a piece of mathematics, illustrated with random numbers, in the next section. The following section then provides an account of the necessary assumptions (and attendant problems) for the two main techniques for applying the theory—test–retest and alternate-form methods.

THE TRUE-SCORE MODEL FOR TEST SCORES

We simulate the process of drawing a single examinee at random from a population of interest, administering a test consisting of m items, and form a total number-right or number-keyed score Y. We suppose that Y consists of the sum of two parts—a random component T and a random component E, which is independent of T. We can call T a *true score* and E an *error*, but for the present these are just quantities in a mathematical equation. Thus we write simply

$$Y = T + E. \tag{5.1}$$

For the moment we do not interpret these variables. Table 5.1, row 1, presents a simulation of the process of drawing a series of random numbers T from a table and, for each T, adding independent random numbers E. The process was stopped at 10 random drawings, but is imagined to continue indefinitely.

I chose numbers T and numbers E with variances σ_T^2 and σ_E^2 known to me, of course, but not to you. From this information alone, even if you had the "population," because I have hidden the numbers making up Y,

TABLE 5.1
True-Score Model Simulation

| | | \multicolumn{11}{c}{"Subject"} |
		1	*2*	*3*	*4*	*5*	*6*	*7*	*8*	*9*	*10*	$\cdots$
P_1	Y	48	100	62	14	44	66	40	94	34	78	$\cdots$
	Y'	32	100	72	14	44	54	48	96	24	78	$\cdots$
P_2	Y	89	91	76	73	76	89	81	81	84	90	$\cdots$
	Y'	100	87	86	73	76	77	89	83	74	90	$\cdots$

you can draw up the distribution of Y, compute its mean and variance, and examine its shape, but that is about all. By their construction, you know some general properties of the components T and E. You know the following facts:

1. T and E are measured on the scale of Y and are bounded within the range of Y, having the same floor and ceiling.
2. T and E are uncorrelated, that is,

$$\rho_{TE} = 0, \tag{5.2}$$

because E is chosen independent of T.

3. The variance of Y is the sum of the variances of T and of E. That is, with σ_T^2, and σ_E^2 for the respective variances of T and of E, and σ_Y^2 for the total variance of Y,

$$\sigma_Y^2 = \sigma_T^2 + \sigma_E^2 \tag{5.3}$$

(because variances of uncorrelated variables add).

4. The variances of T and of E are both less than and at most equal to the variance of Y. That is,

$$\sigma_T^2 \le \sigma_Y^2 \quad \text{and} \quad \sigma_E^2 \le \sigma_Y^2.$$

5. The ratio of the variance of T to the variance of Y,

$$\rho_r = \sigma_T^2 / \sigma_Y^2 = \sigma_T^2 / (\sigma_T^2 + \sigma_E^2) \tag{5.4}$$

is bounded by zero and unity. That is,

$$0 \le \rho_r \le 1. \tag{5.5}$$

The variance ratio ρ_r is by definition the *reliability coefficient* of Y. This is a fundamental theoretical quantity in test theory.

But these properties are not very informative. Now suppose I give you a second total score Y', from each of the randomly drawn "examinees" where Y' (to be read as "Y prime") is the sum of the same T as before and an independent E', also with variance σ_E^2, and so we write

$$Y' = T + E'. \tag{5.6}$$

In row 2 of Table 5.1(a) I have simulated this process, drawing further numbers E' from a table of random numbers, and adding them to the same numbers T that were used to construct the first row. So Y and Y'' have the same randomly drawn T value, and independently drawn E and E' values. By construction, therefore, E and E' are uncorrelated with T and with each other. That is,

$$\rho_{TE} = \rho_{TE'} = \rho_{EE'} = 0. \tag{5.7}$$

Also by construction they have equal variances, i.e.,

$$\sigma_{E'}^2 = \sigma_E^2. \tag{5.8}$$

It follows that

$$\sigma_{Y'}^2 = \sigma_Y^2, \tag{5.9}$$

so Y' also yields properties 1–5 like Y.

A further property now follows, namely, that

$$\rho_{YY'} = \rho_r, \tag{5.10}$$

where

$$\rho_r = \sigma_T^2 / \sigma_Y^2, \tag{5.11}$$

and $\rho_{YY'}$ is the correlation between Y and Y'. The important consequence is that ρ_r can now be computed from observations, and estimated from a finite sample. That is, the correlation coefficient between Y and Y'' gives the reliability coefficient of Y (or, equally, of Y'). (We would not normally expect a variance ratio to equal a correlation coefficient. This will seem less strange when it is noted that

$$\rho_r = \rho_{YT}^2 = \rho_{Y'T}^2, \tag{5.12}$$

that is, the reliability coefficient is the square of the correlation between Y and T or Y' and T. The latter correlation is known as the *reliability index*. Although of interest to psychometricians, it is not commonly quoted by users of reliability theory.)

*** Proof of (5.10): By Appendix A,

$$Cov\{Y,Y'\} = Cov\{(T + E)(T + E')\}$$
$$= \sigma_{TT} + \sigma_{TE} + \sigma_{TE'} + \sigma_{EE'}$$
$$= \sigma_T^2,$$

and $Var\{Y\} = Var\{Y'\}$. $\$\$\$$

Note. The subscript r on ρ_r is preferred here because it draws attention to the facts that (a) ρ_r is, by definition, the reliability coefficient, and (b) it is, by definition, a ratio of variances. Some accounts use $\rho_{YY'}$ as representing both the variance ratio and the correlation from which it is obtained in applications. This is quite correct, given the mathematical equivalence, but it loses useful conceptual distinctions.

In the simulation in Table 5.1, you are still unable to derive the three component scores, T, E, and E', from just two numbers Y and Y'. Two knowns cannot give three unknowns. But you can estimate the correlation $\rho_{YY'}$, and this is an estimate of the variance ratio ρ_r. In fact, I chose numbers, with equal probability, from the 10 numbers 0,10,20, . . . ,90, for T and two sets of numbers, with equal probability, from 0,2,4,6, . . . ,18, for E and E', by multiplying random digits 0 through 9 by 10 and by 2 respectively. This means I know precisely that $\sigma_T^2 = 825$, $\sigma_E^2 = 33$, and so $\sigma_Y^2 = 825 + 33 = 858$, and $\rho_r = .9615$. If you estimate these quantities from the rather small sample in the first two rows of Table 5.1, you will find out how close it is to .96. You can also check the sample variances of Y and Y', using (3.6) and correcting for bias, to see how close they are to each other and to the population value 858.

The reliability coefficient is merely a means to an end. The ultimate object is to obtain an estimate of the variance of E in the metric of the test score. The expression for this,

$$\sigma_E^2 = \sigma_Y^2(1 - \rho_{YY'}), \tag{5.13a}$$

is just a rearrangement of (5.4). It gives us what generally is not known, σ_E^2, in terms of two quantities, σ_Y^2 and $\rho_{YY'}$, that can be estimated from samples. Using the population values—as though we had taken an infinite sample—we have

$$\sigma_E^2 = 858(1 - .9615) = 33.0.$$

Given data such as those in Table 5.1, we can compute estimates $s_Y^2, r_{YY'}$ of σ_Y^2 and $\rho_{YY'}$, as already suggested, and now we can get an estimate s_E^2 of σ_E^2 from these.

As a further step, we define the *standard error of measurement* of the test score Y, as

$$SEM\{Y\} = \sqrt{\sigma_E^2}. \tag{5.13b}$$

It is estimated by a sample counterpart

$$SEM\{Y\} = \sqrt{s_E^2}. \tag{5.13c}$$

In the artificial example, with known population values, we have $SEM\{Y\}$ = 5.74 (= $\sqrt{33}$). If the test score had understandable units—say number right out of a hundred—we could read the $SEM\{Y\}$ as approximately six correct answers.

In interpreting the true-score model we think of T as characteristic of the examinee, and E as characteristic of the test. Suppose now that in a second population of interest, variability of T is much smaller, but the variability of E is unaltered. In Table 5.1, we think of the first two rows as being from population P_1. To begin a simulation of a population P_2, with smaller σ_T^2, I took the previous values of T, divided them by 10, added 68, and added the same E and E' to get rows 3 and 4 in Table 5.1. This divides σ_T^2 by 100, to give 8.25, and it leaves σ_E^2 unaltered, giving $\sigma_Y^2 = 8.25 + 33$ = 41.25 and $\rho_{YY'} = .20$. But we still obtain $\sigma_E^2 = 41.25(1 - .2) = 33.0$. As an exercise, the student should estimate $\rho_{YY'}$, σ_Y^2, $\sigma_{Y'}^2$, and σ_E^2 from rows 3 and 4.

In applications of this model, we can usually expect that the reliability coefficient will vary according to the population sampled. This is because in practice the variance of T represents the variability in each population of the attribute we are measuring. Under reasonable assumptions the variance of E will remain approximately invariant, even though the reliability coefficient varies with the population sampled.

APPLICATIONS OF THE MODEL

To apply the simple model (5.1), we wish to interpret T as the true score of an examinee, and E as an error of measurement. A possible link to applications has been described by Lord and Novick[1]:

> The correlation between truly parallel measurements taken in such a way that the person's true score does not change between them is often called the *coefficient of precision*. For this coefficient, the only source contributing to error variance is the unreliability or imprecision of the measurement procedure. This is the variance ratio that would apply if a measurement

were taken twice and if no practice, fatigue, or memory factor affected repeated measurements. In most practical situations, other sources of error variation affect the reliability of measurement, and hence the coefficient of precision is not the appropriate measure of reliability.

The quoted remarks in effect permit two distinct views. One is that there is an ideal situation—"taking measurements" without practice, fatigue, memory, and other effects in which the correlation between the two measurements gives the precision of the test score. The other is that when other sources of "error" are possible, the coefficient of precision, and the resulting "error" variance, are not what is wanted. And we do not yet have a workable definition of "error."

The three main recognized methods for estimating the reliability coefficient of an objective test from real data are (a) test–retest methods, (b) parallel or alternate-form methods, and (c) internal analysis. The first two of these rest on the correlation between two total test scores, and directly apply the theory of the preceding section. The third requires theory concerning relations between the items constituting the test, and is dealt with in Chapter 6.

In retest methods, a test of m items is administered to a large sample of examinees at two points in time, yielding pairs of scores Y and Y'. It is proposed that we use these paired scores to estimate $\rho_{YY'}$ and equate this to ρ_r. We can then use (5.13) to estimate σ_E^2, and obtain the SE of measurement. This proposal might be justified in two ways. The first is to admit that we are making the strong assumption that the true values of the examinees' scores do not change between administrations. If so, the errors are independent, so the ideal situation yielding $\rho_{YY'}$ as the coefficient of precision has been closely approximated. A problem with this position is that nothing distinguishes a case where the assumption holds and a case where it does not. The second is to say that the *retest true score* is defined as the component of the observed score that does not change "between administrations." Some writers at least implicitly adopt this second option and actually define the resulting reliability coefficient as a *coefficient of stability*. (The danger of conflating this interpretation with the first must then be carefully watched. If an attribute is very unstable over time, and gives a low retest reliability, it may be a mistake, as we demonstrate later, to regard the retest coefficient as the precision with which the attribute is measured.)

The main problem with the second position is that what is observed is a small fraction of a possible larger and more informative study of the behavior of the test score over time. By retesting at a sequence of time intervals we could graph the stability coefficient, as just defined, as a function of time. (To do this, we can take a large cohort of examinees at an initial time and retest subsets of them once only at a series of time intervals.

This will avoid the effects of many replications.) Generally, the longer the time interval, the lower the coefficient. We might take into account the stability or otherwise of relevant environmental factors. We would certainly plot the scores against time for systematic changes—individual curves of growth or decay of the performance measured by the m items in the given test. Such a study can be very informative, especially if situational factors allow conclusions about causes of change. However, once this point is reached in the investigation we do not have a single "retest true score" and we do not have a single coefficient that we can call *the* retest reliability or coefficient of stability. Of course, retest correlations contain useful information about the stability or lability of an attribute. They tell us the extent to which it is traitlike or statelike, so to speak. This can be important information. But it is best to obtain a set of retest correlations, over a series of increasing time intervals, if we wish to study either the stability of the measurement or the course that it follows through time.

Accordingly, there are good reasons for conducting longitudinal studies involving repeated administrations of a test. But we do not yet have good reasons for relating such data to the ideal coefficient of precision. This is not to say that it is impossible, merely that it is generally difficult to motivate such a step. Lord and Novick (1968) stated that any coefficient of stability underestimates the coefficient of precision because the "error" variance includes unstable "true" variance. Certain physiological functions, certain sensory or motor tasks, may approximate the conditions for the ideal coefficient of precision. These may also be cases where we do not have a psychological attribute for which "test theory" is necessary or appropriate. Instead, it may become possible to estimate error by a large number of replications.

In *alternate form* methods, two tests—the alternate forms—contain disjoint, that is, nonoverlapping, sets of items, and these are administered, usually close together in time, to a large sample of examinees, to yield pairs of scores Y, and Y'. To treat them by the true-score model we must be able to suppose that their variances $\sigma_Y^2, \sigma_{Y'}^2$ are the same in the population of interest. At least they should not be significantly different as tested in the sample. This is not a very stringent condition. As in the case of test–retest data, we use the scores to estimate $\rho_{YY'}$, we interpret it as ρ_r, and we obtain an estimate of σ_E^2, and the SE of measurement, by the equations of the preceding section.

In making the transition from retest reliability to alternate-form reliability we should note that the retest reliability of the total score from m specific items has no necessary relation to the precision with which we measure the psychological attribute itself. The m items are just one set of indicators of it, and possibly not closely related to it. A set of items may have high stability and low alternate-form reliability, or low stability and high alternate-form reliability.

We might regard it as an assumption that each of two alternate forms equally measures the examinees' true scores and that they differ by independent errors of measurement. But then nothing defines the true score or the error, so as to distinguish a case where the assumption holds and a case where it does not. Instead we might define the *alternate-form true score* to be a component in the two total test scores that is common to the forms we have constructed. Then their errors are components of the total test scores that are unique to each form. (This statement should be intuitively understandable already. It should also become clearer after discussion of the common factor model in Chap. 6.) Writers who choose this option define the resulting reliability coefficient as a *coefficient of equivalence* of the alternate forms that have been constructed.

In terms of the mathematics of the model, a given test form can have as many alternate forms as there are tests of the same variance to correlate it with, and as many coefficients of equivalence. These correlations could be thought of as measuring how much the test measures in common with each other test. In applications, restrictions on content will be imposed in the construction of equivalent forms. The hope would be that the coefficient of equivalence will become a coefficient of precision—corresponding to a decomposition into "true" and "error" parts—because the alternate forms will then measure the same attribute. Thus, Lord and Novick (1968) stated that generally a coefficient of equivalence will be less than the (ideal) coefficient of precision because the "error" component will include true-score variability due to lack of parallelism of the tests, but "when conditions of the two administrations are equivalent and the intervening time is short," the alternate forms method produces "a coefficient of equivalence which is close to the coefficient of precision."[2] In the simple classical true-score model of this chapter, *parallel forms* are tests that give parallel measurements, and two parallel measurements are just two test scores with equal variance from which we choose to compute a coefficient of equivalence. We meet other, more stringent requirements for parallel forms later.[3]

In applications, we would expect that conditions will be placed on the substantive content of the items composing each form. We would expect to correlate the scores on two algebra tests to get a coefficient of equivalence, rather than correlating algebra with geometry or with English vocabulary. (But note that algebra and geometry measure mathematical ability in common, and algebra and vocabulary measure scholastic ability in common.) We could require the items in each form to be in some sense equivalent to the items in the other. We want them to be similar yet not identical. This is not a precise requirement. Consider a word-fluency test consisting of one frequency-count item, namely, "Write down as many words as you can think of beginning with the letter E" (time, 5 minutes). Similar items can be obtained by substituting other initial letters. Similar items can also be obtained by the format "Write down as many items as you can think of whose 2nd, 3rd, ..., last letter is E." Similarity is, in a sense, multidimensional; different principles of similarity will yield different coefficients of equivalence.

A distinction can be made between content-parallel test forms and content-equivalent test forms. *Content-parallel test forms* are two forms containing the same number of items, in which the items are paired to be similar in content, while distinct items within each form may be less similar. Consider, for example, a general test of intelligence in the forms:

Form L	Form M
(1) What day of the week is it?	(1) What month is it?
(2) If I buy 4 cents' worth of candy and pay 10 cents what change do I get?	(2) If I buy 12 cents' worth of candy and pay 15 cents what change do I get?
(3) Repeat in reverse order 6–5–2–8	(3) Repeat in reverse order 3–6–2–9

(These items are taken from an old version of the Stanford–Binet test, year 9.) The principle should be clear. Having written the first form to measure an attribute, the test constructor tries to write a closely similar but not identical alternate for each item. This requires judgment.

One reasonable conception of *content-equivalent test forms* would be two tests, whose items can be recognized as *content-homogeneous* when they are combined to make a test. Clearly the construction of such test forms requires judgment, and it involves an element of idealization. Consider the test in Table 5.2. Consulting nothing more than our experience of life and our understanding of the words of these statements, we can agree, I hope, that all 14 indicate or exemplify an attribute that could be called "satisfaction with life."[4] (Items 2, 8, and 12 are negative indicators, measuring in the direction of dissatisfaction.) We have met the items marked A–E already.

As will commonly happen, there are a number of ways to form subsets of these items that indicate something more specific than satisfaction with life, and more general than the meaning of any one item. Items 1, 4, 5, 7, 12, 13, and 14 seem to indicate satisfaction with one's present life. Items 2, 6, 9, and 11 seem to indicate satisfaction with one's past life. Items 3, 8, and 10 perhaps indicate emotional lability as opposed to items of a more purely evaluative character. The reader is free to debate these suggestions and to find other reasonable subsets in the same way. The fact that it can be debated does not deny that a set of items can be judged to be content-homogeneous—that judgments can be offered. Having made such a judgment, we can draw two subsets from it to make content-equivalent forms.

The important general point is this: In applications, it is reasonable to select alternate forms from a set of items that are indicators of a common

TABLE 5.2
Satisfaction With Life Items

You should agree or disagree with each item using the 1–7 scale below. Place a number from 1 to 7 next to each item on the answer sheet to indicate your degree of agreement with that item.

7. Strongly agree
6. Agree
5. Slightly agree
4. Neither agree nor disagree
3. Slightly disagree
2. Disagree
1. Strongly disagree

A 1. In most ways my life is close to my ideal.
   2. I frequently think about unhappy times or events of my past.
   3. I am a person who can feel happy very easily.
E 4. The conditions of my life are excellent.
   5. I am satisfied with the current state of affairs in my life.
   6. I like the life I have led.
C 7. I am satisfied with my life.
   8. I frequently experience intense negative emotions that make me unhappy.
D 9. So far I have gotten the important things I want in life.
   10. When something makes me happy, this emotion usually lasts a long time.
B 11. If I could live my life over, I would change almost nothing.
   12. My life does not live up to the standards I have for a good life.
   13. I am satisfied with my present life.
   14. If I imagine the most desirable life for myself (the ideal), my life is very close to that point.

attribute. A judgment of homogeneity of content, where possible, will be strong evidence that an item-set has this property. Statistical evidence requires the methods of Chapter 6.

Suppose we have tried to create alternate forms that are content-parallel or content-equivalent. We return to the question: In what sense, and to what extent, do two total test scores—from test- and retest forms, from content-equivalent forms, or from content-parallel forms—give information about the precision of measurement of a test?

Perhaps enough has been said to establish that a test–retest correlation—a coefficient of stability—generally bears no clear relation to anything we would regard as the precision of measurement of the test. Even if a test–retest correlation may approximate the coefficient of precision—the extent to which the responses to the given items are stable across replications in unrealizable conditions (no effects of previous responses, fatigue, etc.)—the coefficient of precision is commonly not of interest. In most cases the quantity of interest is the precision with which the attribute itself is measured. This is not the sum score on a particular set of items chosen to measure it. The study of stability as such may be very important in some applications of tests. Note that getting respondents to provide retest measures is generally an expensive research procedure, and may require a good research motive.

Intuitively, it can be seen that the correlation between alternate forms—their coefficient of equivalence—is a possible measure of the precision of measurement of the attribute itself. This requires the condition that all the items in the two forms are indicators of just that attribute. And it might be sufficient evidence for this condition that the items are judged content-homogeneous. Each form contains a distinct set of indicators, and the indicators are related to each other because they are related to their common attribute. In effect, the "true score" T is the common trait measured by all the indicators, measured in the same units as the raw scores Y and Y'. One limitation of this intuitive interpretation is that there are many ways we could assign $2m$ homogenous items to two test forms. The coefficient of equivalence would vary over different assignments. Given item data, we would use the methods of Chapter 6. We may accept published alternate-form reliabilities if these are the best figures made available to us, and if enough has been said to let us evaluate the choice of the alternate forms.

The case of content-parallel test forms is rather curious. It actually requires a complicated measurement model. Matched item pairs measure something in common across forms that they do not measure in common with other items in their own form. What they measure in common with their own set is an attribute of a higher level of abstraction from behavior than what is measured by each pair. In the example already given, pairs measure (a) understanding the calendar, (b) problem arithmetic, (c) digit span backward, and so on. Hopefully, following Binet and Terman, we may suppose they combine in either form as indicators of "general intelligence." In consequence, the coefficient of equivalence will be spuriously high as a measure of the ratio of variance due to the trait—in this case "intelligence"—represented by either form to total variance. This is because the numerator includes a sum of shared variances of the paired items. This effect rapidly becomes negligible as m becomes large, until content-parallel forms behave just like content-equivalent forms.

To continue, we need theory at the level of items, or at least of subtests. That is one topic of the next chapter. Classical true-score theory as we have considered it may seem too unsatisfactory to be worth our attention. It is introduced here because the basic true-score model does need to be understood, and can be considered the foundation of the treatment by internal analysis of the item relationships. We keep the model but improve the method. It is also necessary for the student to be aware that both retest and alternate form methods have had a large role in the history of psychological tests, and their use still continues.

REVIEW GUIDE

General problems in assessing precision of psychological measurements need to be understood. These include:

1. Repeated measures are not generally independent.
2. The attribute changes over time.
3. The attribute is not the same as the score from any given set of items used to measure it.

The classical true-score model (5.1) gives the reliability coefficient—a variance ratio—defined by (5.4). The reliability coefficient is equivalent to the correlation between two measurements satisfying the assumptions of the model. Given an acceptable reliability coefficient, we can compute the error variance of the test score using (5.13), and the *SE* of measurement using (5.13b) and (5.13c). Generally, the measurement error variance will be unaltered by a choice of population, whereas the reliability coefficient varies.

Both retest methods and parallel-form methods for estimating a reliability coefficient from a correlation between measures are problematic. They can be interpreted respectively as a measure of stability of the test score over time, and as a measure of the equivalence of the test forms.

END NOTES

General: See Lord and Novick (1968) for a more comprehensive, and more technical, account of classical reliability theory. Further resources for followup reading could include Feldt and Brennan (1989).

1. Lord and Novick (1968, p. 134).
2. Lord and Novick (1968, p. 137).
3. In the classical accounts of alternate form reliability, two tests are *parallel* if they have the same variance and the same covariances with every other test they might be correlated with. This second condition is untestable, and in practice it is not subjected even to limited testing.
4. Diener et al. (1985).

Test Homogeneity, Reliability, and Generalizability

If two variables are correlated, there are at least three ways we can "explain" the presence of a relationship between them.

1. It may be that one variable (partly) determines the other, in a sense that has no converse. We say that one is a cause of the other. For example, observing a rat in an activity cage, we say that hunger causes activity. And after a good workout we say activity causes hunger. But we do not say that activity and hunger are merely contingently associated. Both the meaning and the verification of causal claims are deep and controversial matters. It is to be hoped that the reader, like the writer, makes a distinction between "teaching causes learning" and "teaching and learning are activities often found together."

2. It may be that the two variables are related effects of a common cause. For example, distinct stock prices vary together from the impact of political events on the psyches of market "players."

3. It may be that the two variables are correlated because they measure, or indicate, something in common. This can be literally true. Some tests contain items that can be scored for more than one trait, and the correlation between scores for the traits comes from shared score components. This would generally be regarded as a spurious correlation. But by *measuring in common*, nothing quite so literal is intended. The notion is that the variables are indicators, "symptoms" or manifestations of the same state of affairs. For example, extraversion is an abstract concept whose instances are the recognized extravert behaviors, and it is therefore circular to say

that extraversion "causes" its manifestations. This explanation of related-ness has already been used earlier in a qualitative and intuitive way. At this point we use it to introduce a statistical model to refine our conception of homogeneous tests—of tests whose items are all of the same kind. This is a more general model, and the true-score model is just a special case of it. The model we need deals with relationships between the items, not just relationships between total test scores.

The next section shows how the Spearman single-factor model can be used to test the homogeneity of a set of items. The following section derives a measure of reliability from the parameters of the factor model, and the fourth gives two special cases. The fifth section gives results for binary data. The last section, which can be omitted without loss of continuity, gives an introduction to the theory of generalizability.

HOMOGENEITY AND THE SINGLE-FACTOR MODEL

In this chapter we do not need to distinguish between a test composed of m items that are not decomposable into smaller elements, and a test com-posed of m subtests—including *item bundles* or *testlets*, each of which are decomposable into their constituent items. We could also have a *test battery* composed of m tests, if there is any reason to form a total score over the entire set of tests. It is convenient to regard items and item scores here as including subtests and subtest scores. All of the results in this chapter apply to whatever measurements we regard as the basic sets of scores to be combined into a global test score.

Suppose m items $j = 1, \ldots, m$, with scores $X_1, \ldots, X_m$, have pairwise co-variances σ_{jk} in a population of interest. These can be estimated from a sample by the formulas (3.12) and (3.13), correcting for bias in small samples. We wish to give a statistical meaning to the idea that these co-variances are nonzero because the items measure just one attribute in common. This requires an extension of the idea in the alternate-forms treatment of true-score theory. In this version, the statements

$$Y = T + E \quad \text{and} \quad Y' = T + E'$$

mean that T is the attribute common to the test forms; that it is measured equally well by either; and that E and E' are due to unique or idiosyncratic properties of the particular items in the separate forms.

If we apply this principle to the m items, we might consider the model

$$X_j = T + E_j \tag{6.1}$$

for each of them. However, the model (6.1) is a special case of the one that is needed, and it will be studied later for its special properties. For more than two items the model needs to allow three possibilities in explaining the covariances by a common attribute. First, it must be possible that indicators of the common attribute have different means in the population of interest. Items of different difficulties can measure the same thing. Second, the items are not equally good indicators in general. Some items may measure the attribute more sensitively than others. They may discriminate more clearly between levels of the attribute. Third, the items may have different amounts of unique variance—of variation due to their idiosyncratic properties. We symbolize the quantity measured in common by F, and we call it the *common factor* that ties the items together. The appropriate model is the single general factor model of Charles Spearman, namely:

$$X_j = \mu_j + \lambda_j F + E_j \quad j = 1, \ldots, m. \tag{6.2}$$

In this model, X_j is a random examinee's score on the jth item, F is the examinee's measure of the common attribute, and E_j is the examinee's measure of the unique or idiosyncratic property of item j. More precisely, E_j is the amount by which the idiosyncratic property of item j shifts the response X_j, in a positive or negative direction, from the expected level of response to the attribute itself. The constants μ_j allow each item to have a distinct difficulty.

Following an old tradition, the coefficient λ_j is labeled the *factor loading* of item j. (Metaphorically, it is the extent to which the item is "loaded" with the attribute. Some "carry" more of it than others.) The factor loading measures how sensitively each item functions as an indicator of the common factor/attribute F. An item whose λ_j value is (relatively) large is a better indicator of F than one whose λ_j value is (relatively) small. It represents the amount of difference in the item score that corresponds to a unit difference in the attribute. It is therefore a measure of the ability of the item to discriminate between subjects with high and low values of F. It may be considered a measure of the *discriminating power* of the item. A (psychometrically) *homogeneous* test is one whose items measure just one attribute in common—a common factor. We can check on our judgment that the items are of the same kind—of homogeneous content—by seeing if the responses to them fit the single factor model.

As in the special case of alternate forms, the unique component E_j is independent of the common factor F (by definition), so it is uncorrelated with it. Also, any two unique components E_j, E_k are (by definition) independent of each other, so they are also uncorrelated. Equation (6.2) expresses the regression of X_j on F, in the usual meaning of regression theory.

Consequently, λ_j is the expected difference in X_j for a unit difference in F between subgroups of the population. An item with zero λ_j does not measure F at all.

Starting from the model (5.1), we were able to compute the variance of the true part and the variance of (either) error part, from the variances of the two measurements and their covariance using the derived equations. Now we need to generalize this. The conditions are that the common factor is uncorrelated with each unique component and the unique components are uncorrelated for all distinct items. (These conditions are not assumptions. They state what is meant by the *common factor F* and the *unique parts E_j.*) To determine a scale for F, we are free to consider it as a standard score, with mean zero and variance unity in the population studied. We use ψ_j^2 for the variance of E_j. This variance is referred to in the literature either as the *unique variance* of the item or as its *uniqueness*. In this model the covariance of any two item scores X_j, X_k is just the product of their factor loadings. That is,

$$\sigma_{jk} = \lambda_j \lambda_k. \tag{6.3}$$

Also, the variance σ_{jj} of the jth item is expressed as

$$\sigma_{jj} = \lambda_j^2 + \psi_j^2, \tag{6.4}$$

the sum of the squared loading of the item and its unique variance.

***Proof is by the algebra of expectations, with terms in $\text{Cov}\{F,E_j\}$ and $\text{Cov}\{E_j,E_k\}$ becoming zero because of the assumptions. $$$

The quantities $\lambda_1, \ldots, \lambda_m, \psi_1^2, \ldots, \psi_m^2$ are the parameters of this model for the population. In practice we need to estimate them from samples. For the moment, suppose we know the numerical values of the parameters. It is then easy to use an ordinary calculator to compute the resulting variances and covariances by (6.3). Consider, for example, Table 6.1. (The student should check one or two further values.)

In applications we need the reverse procedure. Given the 5 variances and 10 covariances in Table 6.1(b), is it possible to compute the 10 parameters—five loadings, and five unique variances? The answer is yes. The factor loadings can be obtained from any three items, j, k, and l, by using

$$\lambda_j = \sqrt{\sigma_{jk}\sigma_{jl}/\sigma_{kl}}. \tag{6.5}$$

TABLE 6.1
Computation of Item Covariances From Spearman Parameters

(a) Suppose $\sigma_F^2 = 1$

and	$\lambda_1 = 1.8$	$\psi_1^2 = 1.0$		$\sigma_{21} = 2.7$
	$\lambda_2 = 1.5$	$\psi_2^2 = 1.2$		(1.8×1.5)
	$\lambda_3 = 1.2$	$\psi_3^2 = 1.4$	then	$\sigma_{11} = 4.24$
	$\lambda_4 = 1.0$	$\psi_4^2 = 1.6$		$(1.8^2 + 1.0)$
	$\lambda_5 = 0.8$	$\psi_5^2 = 2.0$		and so on

giving

(b)

	1	2	3	4	5
$\Sigma = 1$	4.24	2.70	2.16	1.80	1.44
2	2.70	3.45	1.80	1.50	1.20
3	2.16	1.80	2.84	1.20	0.96
4	1.80	1.50	1.20	2.60	0.80
5	1.44	1.20	0.96	0.80	2.64

[If all the covariances are positive, all the loadings are positive. If some covariances are negative, a possible choice of the negative square root in (6.5) is resolved by consulting their signs. If we take λ_j positive and λ_k negative, σ_{jk} is negative—and so on.] Then to get ψ_j^2 we use

$$\psi_j^2 = \sigma_{jj} - \lambda_j^2. \tag{6.6}$$

The important result is that item covariances fitting the model determine the loadings, and then the item variances determine the uniquenesses.

*** Proof of (6.5) and (6.6): From any three items j, k, l, we have

$$\sigma_{jk} = \lambda_j\lambda_k \qquad \sigma_{jl} = \lambda_j\lambda_l \qquad \sigma_{kl} = \lambda_k\lambda_l.$$

Then

$$\lambda_j^2 = (\sigma_{jk}\sigma_{jl})/\sigma_{kl}$$

which gives (6.5). $$$

For example, in Table 6.1,

$$\sigma_{12} = 2.70 \qquad \sigma_{13} = 2.26 \qquad \sigma_{23} = 1.80,$$

so

$$\lambda_1 = \sqrt{(2.70 \times 2.16)/1.80} = 1.80$$

and

$$\psi_1^2 = 4.24 - 1.80^2 = 1.0.$$

(The student might check some more of these results.) Notice that we can compute each loading in a number of ways. Here we can get λ_1 in six ways, from

$$\sigma_{12}\sigma_{13}/\sigma_{23} =$$
$$\sigma_{12}\sigma_{14}/\sigma_{24} =$$
$$\sigma_{12}\sigma_{15}/\sigma_{25} =$$
$$\sigma_{13}\sigma_{14}/\sigma_{34} =$$
$$\sigma_{13}\sigma_{15}/\sigma_{35} =$$
$$\sigma_{14}\sigma_{15}/\sigma_{45} = .$$

These results must be consistent because Table 6.1—an artificial example—contains exactly fitting "population" values.

The object of this demonstration was to show that the parameters of the single-factor model are determined by the covariance matrix they generate. Formally, we say the parameters are *identified*—they have a unique identity as functions of the variances and covariances. That is, (6.3) and (6.4) have unique solutions (6.5) and (6.6). Some readers will know that a set of simultaneous linear equations may or may not have a consistent or a unique solution. Equations (6.3) and (6.4) are simultaneous nonlinear equations. More general common factor models—with more than one factor—can fail to have unique solutions. (See Chap. 9.) The Spearman model is a possibly false statistical hypothesis, which may or may not fit a given set of items. Table 6.2 contains a covariance matrix resembling the one in Table 6.1, which does not fit the model (6.2) for homogeneity. Using covariances of variables 1, 2, 3 gives

$$\lambda_1 = \sqrt{(2.70 \times 2.16)/1.80} = 1.8$$

as before, but using variables 1, 4, 5 gives

$$\lambda_1 = \sqrt{(.18 \times .144)/.96} = .164.$$

Table 6.2 corresponds to a case where items 1, 2, 3 are homogeneous, and items 4 and 5 are homogeneous, but each group measures different things, so jointly they need more than one common factor—more than one attribute—to explain the relations between the items. This is the topic of Chapter 9.

TABLE 6.2
Covariance Matrix—Nonhomogeneous Case

	1	2	3	4	5
1	4.24	2.70	2.16	0.18	0.144
2	2.70	3.45	1.80	0.15	0.12
3	2.16	1.80	2.84	0.12	0.96
4	0.18	0.15	0.12	2.60	0.80
5	0.144	0.12	0.96	0.80	2.64

For decades—from 1907 to 1967—there were only crude devices for estimating the parameters of a common factor model. Consider the covariance matrix in Table 6.3. This is a sample covariance matrix from items marked A, B, C, D, E in Table 5.1, scored 1–7 as indicated there (which explains the order of magnitude of the item variances). The sample size is $n = 215$. In an example like this, with a small number of items, we can use the earliest device for fitting the Spearman—one-factor—model. This device is due to Spearman himself. We apply the expression (6.5) for every k,l pair to the sample covariances, getting somewhat varying estimates of λ_j, and then average these estimates. For the estimated factor loading of item 1, the expressions listed

$$\hat{\lambda}_1 = [(1.560 \times 1.487)/1.283]^{1/2} = 1.345$$
$$\hat{\lambda}_1 = [(1.560 \times 1.195)/.845]^{1/2} = 1.485$$
$$\hat{\lambda}_1 = [(1.560 \times 1.425)/1.313]^{1/2} = 1.301$$
$$\hat{\lambda}_1 = [(1.487 \times 1.195)/1.127]^{1/2} = 1.256$$
$$\hat{\lambda}_1 = [(1.487 \times 1.425)/1.313]^{1/2} = 1.270$$
$$\hat{\lambda}_1 = [(1.195 \times 1.425)/1.323]^{1/2} = 1.135$$

give an averaged estimate 1.299. Then the estimate of ψ_1^2 is just the variance, 2.566, minus the squared loading, 1.299^2, giving .879. Similarly, we can get

TABLE 6.3
Covariance Matrix—Satisfaction With Life Scale

	1	2	3	4	5
1	2.566	1.560	1.487	1.195	1.425
2	1.560	2.493	1.283	0.845	1.313
3	1.487	1.283	2.462	1.127	1.313
4	1.195	0.845	1.127	2.769	1.323
5	1.425	1.313	1.313	1.323	3.356

the remaining parameters. The reader will find it easy but very tedious to do this for the remaining four loadings.

Modern methods of estimation use a computer program that systematically searches—quite literally—for a set of parameter values that make a *discrepancy function*—a function of the discrepancies, $s_{jk} - \sigma_{jk}$, between the unbiased sample covariances and the fitted covariances—as small as possible. A simple and intuitively natural discrepancy function is

$$q_u = (1/m^2) \sum_j \sum_k (s_{jk} - \sigma_{jk})^2, \qquad (6.7a)$$

the ordinary mean of the squared differences between sample and fitted values. (Other discrepancy functions are mentioned later.) This function is the unweighted least squares function—the ULS function. For the single-common-factor model, this discrepancy function can be broken down into two parts, one for the diagonal elements, $s_{jj} - \sigma_{jj}$, and one for the off-diagonal elements, $s_{jk} - \sigma_{jk}$, by writing *formula for variance σ_{jj} (fitted)*

$$q_u = (1/m^2) \left[\sum_{j \neq k} \sum (s_{jk} - \lambda_j \lambda_k)^2 + \sum_j (s_{jj} - \lambda_j^2 - \psi_j^2)^2 \right]. \qquad (6.7b)$$

fit statistic   *form. for covariance if meet assumpts of spearman*

Unweighted least squares is so called because the discrepancy function q_u *$\hat\sigma_{jk}$* gives equal "value" or "weight" to each discrepancy. The computer searches for values $\hat\lambda_j, \hat\psi_j^2$ of λ_j, ψ_j^2 that make this mean-square discrepancy as small *determines* as possible. It is not necessary for the general reader to know the systematic *when* process—the *algorithm* by which a computer finds the minimum. Having *that* found it, the computer program prints out the estimates and the entire *shld be* matrix of discrepancies, $s_{jk} - \hat\sigma_{jk}$, if the user asks for it. (This should always be examined by the program user.) Estimation using ULS does not give a statistical test of the hypothesis, and it does not tell us how accurately we have estimated the parameters. We can look at the discrepancies and judge that they are "negligible." A good measure of closeness of fit of the model takes into account the magnitude of the sample covariances themselves, by computing

$$c = (1/m^2) \sum_j \sum_k s_{jk}^2 \qquad (6.8)$$

and then defining the *goodness of fit index*

$$\text{GFI} = 1 - q_u/c. \qquad (6.9)$$

If the fit is good, the GFI is close to unity, which would be perfect fit. ULS makes no assumptions about the distribution of the item scores (although the results will be affected by that distribution).

Fitting the single-factor model to the covariance matrix of Table 6.3 by program CONFA[1] using the ULS function gives the fitted parameter values in Table 6.4(a) and the *fitted* matrix—reproduced from those values—in Table 6.4(b). The discrepancies $s_{jk} - \hat{\sigma}_{jk}$ are given in Table 6.4(c). We do not usually study the fitted covariances, as it is hard to judge how close they are to the sample values. We should always look at the discrepancies.

Using (6.8) we obtain for the mean of squares of the sample covariances calculated from Table 6.3, $c = 2.866$. For the mean of squares of the discrepancies in Table 6.4, we obtain $q_u = .00915$, so the goodness of fit index

$$GFI = .9968.$$

Experience suggests this is a very good fit. As a guide to the inexperienced user, but not a firm decision rule, I suggest that the fit is "good" when GFI is greater than .95, and "acceptable" when it is greater than .9. The discrepancy matrix will tell us if any misfit is due to just one or two large discrepancies, or a general spread of discrepancies over the matrix. Generally, the discrepancy matrix allows a much more informed judgment

TABLE 6.4
Satisfaction With Life Scale—Spearman Analysis

	(a)		(b)				
	λ	ψ^2	1	2	3	4	5
1	1.290	0.901	2.565	1.424	1.481	1.328	1.529
2	1.104	1.274	1.424	2.493	1.267	1.051	1.308
3	1.148	1.144	1.481	1.267	2.462	1.093	1.360
4	0.952	1.863	1.328	1.051	1.093	2.769	1.128
5	1.185	1.951	1.529	1.308	1.360	1.128	3.355

	(c)				
	1	2	3	4	5
1	.0	.135	.006	−.033	−.104
2	.135	.0	.015	−.206	.004
3	.006	.015	.0	.035	−.048
4	−.033	−.206	.035	.0	.195
5	−.104	.004	−.048	.195	.0

than any simple fit index. Unfortunately, most investigators appear to rely entirely on a fit index and a rule of thumb for its application.

Next we consider two special cases of the single-factor model, resembling (6.1). To repeat, the model for m homogeneous items is

$$X_j = \lambda_j F + E_j + \mu_j,$$

where F and E_j are uncorrelated for every item j, and E_j and E_k are uncorrelated for all distinct pairs. There are two important special cases of this model.

True-score equivalent items—also known as *essentially tau-equivalent* items—can be defined by the property

$$\lambda_1 = \lambda_2 = \cdots = \lambda_m = \lambda.$$

For then

$$X_j = \lambda F + E_j + \mu_j, \tag{6.10}$$

which becomes

$$X_j = T_x + E_j + \mu_j \tag{6.11}$$

if we write T_x for λF, that is, if we rescale the common attribute so that it is measured in the same units as the items. That is, the *item true-score* T_X is just the common factor multiplied by the factor loading. It then has variance λ^2. To describe the items as true-score equivalent is to declare that they measure the common property equally sensitively—with equal discrimination. Then the common factor can be rescaled so as to be considered the "true" part of each item score. Note that in this chapter we have a number of "true scores," which are distinguished by a subscript indicating the variable of which each is the "true part."

The *true-score equivalence* model (6.10) or (6.11) gives, for the elements of the covariance matrix,

$$\sigma_{jk} = \lambda^2 = \sigma_{T_x}^2 \tag{6.12}$$

for all j not equal to k, and

$$\sigma_{jj} = \lambda^2 + \psi_j^2 = \sigma_{T_x}^2 + \sigma_j^2 \tag{6.13}$$

for all j. This is a very restrictive hypothesis. The $m(m-1)/2$ covariances of distinct items must all be equal.

Parallel items can be defined by the property that $\lambda_1 = \lambda_2 = \cdots = \lambda_m = \lambda$, plus the property that $\psi_1^2 = \psi_2^2 = \cdots = \psi_m^2 = \psi^2$. Accordingly, the *parallel items* model is again written as (6.10) or (6.11), and gives (6.12) for the covariances, but it also restricts the item variances to

$$\sigma_{jj} = \lambda^2 + \psi^2 = \sigma_{Tx}^2 + \psi^2. \tag{6.14}$$

That is, all covariances are equal to each other, and all variances are equal to each other. Some writers define parallel items so that they must also have equal means. To make a distinction that we need in the present treatment, we call items with this further restriction *strictly parallel* items. (This is also consistent with the definition of strictly parallel items used in item response theory.) Equation (6.14) includes the basic breakdown of variance in Chapter 5 for test scores from two alternate forms, when $m = 2$. But then the hypothesis of parallelism is not restrictive and not testable/falsifiable. Using only information from total test scores in this way is generally unsafe because it is uninformative.

In the case of true-score equivalent and parallel items, the ULS estimators are precisely what intuition would guess them to be. They can easily be calculated from the sample covariance matrix, without using a computer search algorithm. (In practice we would still find it easier to use a computer program.) In the true-score equivalence model, the ULS estimate $\hat{\sigma}_T^2$ of σ_T^2 in (6.12) is the average of all covariances of distinct items, i.e.,

$$\hat{\sigma}_T^2 = [1/m(m-1)]\sum_{j \neq k}\sum s_{jk}, \tag{6.15}$$

and the estimate of ψ_j^2 in (6.13) is

$$\hat{\psi}_j^2 = s_{jj} - \hat{\sigma}_T^2, \tag{6.16a}$$

for each item. (In small samples, we would use unbiased estimates of the variances and covariances.) In the parallel-items model, the estimate of σ_T^2 is (still) (6.15), and the estimate of the constant ψ^2 is

$$\hat{\psi}^2 = (1/m)\sum_j s_{jj} - \hat{\sigma}_{Tx}^2. \tag{6.16b}$$

From Table 6.3, the reader may easily verify that

TABLE 6.5
Discrepancy Matrices—Restricted Models

	(a) True-Score Equivalence Model				
	1	*2*	*3*	*4*	*5*
1	.0	.273	.200	−.092	.138
2	.273	.0	−.004	−.442	.026
3	.200	−.004	.0	−.160	.026
4	−.092	−.442	−.160	.0	.036
5	.138	.026	.026	.036	.0

	(b) Parallel Items Model				
	1	*2*	*3*	*4*	*5*
1	−.163	.273	.200	−.092	.138
2	.273	−.236	−.004	−.442	.026
3	.200	−.004	−.268	−.160	.026
4	−.092	−.442	−.160	.040	.036
5	.138	.026	.026	.036	.627

$$\hat{\sigma}^2_{Tx} = 1.287,$$

which is the average of the elements below the diagonal. In the true-score-equivalence model, $\hat{\psi}^2_1 = 1.279$, $\hat{\psi}^2_2 = 1.206$, $\hat{\psi}^2_3 = 1.175$, $\hat{\psi}^2_4 = 1.482$, and $\hat{\psi}^2_5 = 2.069$. The parallel-items model gives the same estimate of true score variance, of course, and, from Table 6.3,

$$\hat{\psi}^2 = (1/5)(2.566 + \cdots + 3.356) - 1.287 = 1.442.$$

The true-score equivalence model gives the discrepancy matrix in Table 6.5(a), and GFI = .991. The parallel-items model gives the discrepancy matrix in Table 6.5(b), and GFI = .949. Both these models give acceptable approximations by the usually accepted criteria.

THE RELIABILITY OF A HOMOGENEOUS TEST

From the single-factor model (6.2) for homogeneous items, the total test score is

$$Y = \sum_j X_j = (\sum_j \lambda_j)F + \sum_j E_j + \sum_j \mu_j. \qquad (6.17a)$$

If we write $C = (\Sigma\ \lambda_j)F$ for the part of Y due to the common factor, and $U_j = \Sigma\ E_j$ for the part due to unique properties, then

$$Y = C + U + \mu_Y, \tag{6.17b}$$

which is the sum of the *common part* of Y and its *unique part* (plus the mean of Y). The common part C is the measure of the attribute given by Y, and the unique part is the error of measurement, so we are back to the decomposition into true and error parts, as in Chapter 5. But now we have a clear meaning for the decomposition and a clear method for estimating the variances of these. That is, the factor model gives us an interpretation of the total true score T_Y as the common part C of Y, and of the error E as the unique part U. So in another notation, (6.17) can be written as

$$Y = T_Y + E_Y + \mu_Y. \tag{6.17c}$$

By the algebra of expectations,

$$\sigma_Y^2 = \left(\sum \lambda_j\right)^2 + \sum \psi_j^2, \tag{6.18a}$$

or

$$\sigma_Y^2 = \sigma_C^2 + \sigma_U^2, \tag{6.18b}$$

that is,

$$\sigma_Y^2 = \sigma_{T_Y}^2 + \sigma_{E_Y}^2. \tag{6.18c}$$

The variance of the total score is made up of two parts. The part $\sigma_{T_Y}^2 = \sigma_C^2 = (\Sigma\ \lambda_j)^2$, the square of the sum of the factor loadings, is the true-score variance of the total test score—variance due to the attribute of which the items are indicators. The part $\sigma_{E_Y}^2 = \sigma_U^2 = \Sigma\ \psi_j^2$, the sum of the m unique variances of the indicators, is the error variance of the total test score—a sum of variances due to the individual, idiosyncratic properties of each of the m indicators. (The beginning student is warned to be careful about the difference between summing loadings and squaring the sum for estimating σ_C^2, and simply summing the unique variances for σ_U^2.)

On this interpretation, the reliability coefficient defined in (5.4) becomes

$$\rho_r = \sigma_C^2/(\sigma_C^2 + \sigma_U^2). \tag{6.19}$$

This gives us a reliability coefficient based on the factor model—coefficient omega.[2] The coefficient is defined by

$$\omega = \sigma_C^2/\sigma_Y^2 = (\sum \lambda_j)^2/\sigma_Y^2, \tag{6.20a}$$

or

$$\omega = (\sum \lambda_j)^2/[(\sum \lambda_j)^2 + \sum \psi_j^2]. \tag{6.20b}$$

Omega is the ratio of the true-score variance of Y to the total variance of Y. Here the true-score variance is interpreted as the variance due to the (common) attribute. The variance of Y is the sum of the true-score variance (i.e., common variance), and the error variance (i.e., unique variance). In a homogeneous set of items—with a single common factor—an equivalent expression is given by

$$\omega = 1 - (\sum \psi_j^2)/\sigma_Y^2. \tag{6.21}$$

The first form of the expression—(6.20)—has a version that applies to nonhomogeneous sets of items (see Chap. 9), whereas the second—(6.21)—requires homogeneity.

The coefficient omega—the reliability coefficient based on the parameters of the items in the factor model—can easily be estimated in applications. We just substitute estimates of the loadings $\lambda_1, \ldots, \lambda_m$ and the unique variances $\psi_1^2, \ldots, \psi_m^2$ in (6.20b). In estimating from a sample, the expressions (6.20a) and (6.21) will give identical results if σ_Y^2 is estimated from the fitted covariances. A (slightly) different answer will be obtained if the sample variance of Y—computed from the total scores or by summing the elements of the sample covariance matrix—is mixed in with the estimated parameters of the model. This is acceptable and more convenient unless the fit is poor, in which case we should not be using the coefficient anyway.

Coefficient omega has been defined as the ratio of the variance due to the common attribute to the total variance of Y. It may be shown also that:

1. Omega is the square of the correlation between Y and the common factor F, or between Y and T_Y (or C), which is just F rescaled to be in the same units as Y.

2. Omega is the correlation—not the squared correlation—between two test scores Y and Y' that have the same sum (or average) of their loadings and the same sum (or average) of their unique variances, and jointly fit the single common factor model, that is, are jointly homogeneous.

3. Omega is the square of the correlation between the total (or mean) score on the given m items and the mean score on an infinite set of items from a homogeneous domain of items of which the m items used in the test are a subset (see final section of this chapter).

Property 3 is consistent with a conception of the true score of the set of m items as the mean score on a test of infinite length. Some accounts assume that the m items, and the infinitely many more, are parallel or true-score equivalent.[3] This is not necessary. The conclusion at this point is that coefficient omega captures the notion of the reliability of a test score. It measures the precision with which a homogeneous test measures the common attribute of its items.

For the SWLS data, from Table 6.3, the ULS estimates in Table 6.4 give

$$\left(\sum \hat{\lambda}_j\right)^2 = 1.290 + 1.104 + 1.148 + .952 + 1.185)^2 = 32.251$$

and

$$\sum \hat{\psi}_j^2 = .901 + 1.274 + 1.144 + 1.863 + 1.951 = 7.133.$$

Then using (6.20b) gives

$$\hat{\omega} = 32.251/(32.25 + 7.133) = 32.25/39.383 = .8189.$$

The sum of the elements in Table 6.3 gives $s_Y^2 = 39.388$ for the sample variance of Y. This is hardly different from the fitted value 39.383 obtained by summing estimated common variance and unique variances, so (6.20a) gives

$$\hat{\omega} = 32.251/39.388 = .8188.$$

COEFFICIENT ALPHA AND THE SPEARMAN–BROWN FORMULA

In the case in which the m items satisfy the true-score equivalence model, (6.2) becomes (6.11), on rescaling the common factor so that it has variance λ^2. This gives the simple decomposition of item variance into true variance and error variance in (6.13)—with distinct error variances σ_{Ej}^2 for the items. The reliability coefficient can then be written as a function of the covariance between any two items and the variance of the total score. That is, when σ_{jk} has a single value $\lambda^2 = \sigma_T^2$, or, equivalently, all items have equal factor loadings, omega in (6.20a) takes the simple form

$$\omega = m^2\lambda^2/\sigma_Y^2. \tag{6.22}$$

This can be expressed as

$$\omega = \sigma_{Ty}^2/\sigma_Y^2 = m^2\sigma_T^2/\sigma_y^2. \tag{6.23}$$

We can estimate it by substituting $\hat{\sigma}_{Tx}^2, \hat{\sigma}_Y^2$ in (6.23). In the SWLS example in the last section, $\hat{\sigma}_{Tx}^2 = 1.287$, $\hat{\sigma}_Y^2 = 39.382$, so

$$\hat{\omega} = 25 \times 1.287/39.382 = .8170,$$

which is slightly lower than the value—.8189—estimated under the more general hypothesis of homogeneity.

If we use the ULS estimator of σ_{Tx}^2, and use s_y^2 as the estimator of σ_y^2, then

$$\hat{\omega} = m^2\hat{\sigma}_{Tx}^2/s_Y^2 \tag{6.24}$$

where

$$\hat{\sigma}_T^2 = [1/m(m-1)]\sum_{j \neq k}\sum s_{jk}, \tag{6.25}$$

so

$$\hat{\omega} = [m/(m-1)][\sum_{j \neq k}\sum s_{jk}/s_Y^2. \tag{6.26}$$

Recalling that

$$s_Y^2 = \sum_j\sum_k s_{jk},$$

so

$$\sum_{j \neq k}\sum s_{jk} = s_Y^2 - \sum_j s_{jj},$$

we see that

$$\hat{\omega} = [m/(m-1)][1 - \sum_j s_{jj}/s_Y^2].$$ (6.27)

For our example, Table 6.3 gives

$$\hat{\omega} = (5/4)[1 - (2.566 + 2.493 + \cdots + 3.356)/39.382]$$
$$= (5/4)(1 - 13.646/39.384)$$
$$= .8170,$$

as in the previous computation.

The estimate of reliability given in (6.27) is very well known. We can define an analogue for it in the population, namely,

$$\alpha \equiv [m/(m-1)][1 - \sum_j \sigma_{jj}/\sigma_Y^2].$$ (6.28)

The identity sign $\equiv$ draws attention to the fact that the expression on the right actually defines what is universally referred to as coefficient alpha. A number of different ways to motivate the estimation of this coefficient have been given in the literature. Coefficient alpha was first given (denoted L_3) by Louis Guttman in 1945. He showed that it is a lower bound in the population to the reliability coefficient of the test score. Coefficient alpha is often incorrectly attributed to a paper by Cronbach in 1951.[4] In view of Cronbach's contributions to our understanding of this coefficient, it is referred to here as the *Guttman–Cronbach alpha* or *G-C alpha*.

It may be shown that G-C alpha is a lower bound to coefficient omega— generally underestimating it somewhat. They are equal if and only if the population of interest can be described by the true-score equivalence model, that is, if and only if the items fit the single-factor model with equal factor loadings. That is,

$$\omega \geq \alpha,$$ (6.29)

and alpha becomes the same as omega if and only if σ_{jk} is constant for all $j \neq k$.

***Proof:

$$\omega - \alpha = (1/\sigma_Y^2)[\sum_j \lambda_j^2 - \{m/(m-1)\}\{(\sum_j \lambda_j)^2 - \sum_j \lambda_j^2\}].$$

$$\omega - \alpha = [m/(m-1)](1/\sigma_Y^2)[\sum_j \lambda_j^2 - (\sum_j \lambda_j)^2/m]$$

$$= [m/(m-1)](1/\sigma_Y^2)[\text{Var}(\lambda_j)],$$

which is positive, and zero if and only if $\lambda_j = \lambda_k$ for all j,k.[5] $$$

It is, in fact, difficult to invent a homogeneous population structure in which alpha is a very poor lower bound to omega, or to find empirical examples in which the estimate of alpha is very much lower than that of omega. Part of the case for estimating omega itself rather than bounding it—"underestimating" it—by G-C alpha is that omega comes as a by-product of the factor analysis, which checks whether the items form a homogeneous set. If they do not, at least to a good approximation, it is not appropriate to form a total test score. If the evidence shows that the items are not only homogeneous but also true-score equivalent, then G-C alpha is an estimate of omega. But at this point we can easily calculate omega anyway.

Attempts have been made to give meaning to coefficient alpha, and to its estimate from a sample, when the items are not true-score equivalent. For example, Cronbach showed that coefficient alpha gives the average of split-half reliability coefficients, computed over all possible splits, supposing they have equal probability of being chosen by the investigator. This may be of some theoretical interest. It is often referred to as the "internal consistency" reliability of a test, but no clear meaning has ever been given for the notion of "internal consistency," and the terminology is not recommended here.

In the further special case of parallel items, (a) the factor loadings are equal and (b) the unique variances are equal. In this case, all the interitem correlations (as well as the item covariances) are equal to a constant value in the population, namely,

$$\rho_1 = \sigma_{Tx}^2/(\sigma_{Tx}^2 + \sigma_{Ex}^2). \tag{6.30}$$

We can think of ρ_1 as the reliability of one item—the same for any one of them. Then in this case

$$\omega = \alpha = \rho_m, \tag{6.31}$$

where

$$\rho_m = m\sigma_{Tx}^2/(m\sigma_{Tx}^2 + \psi^2). \tag{6.32}$$

This expression shows that when every item has the same true and error variance, the reliability of a test of m items is a simple increasing function of the number of items. We can rewrite (6.32) as

$$\text{S-B} \quad \rho_m = m\rho_1/[(m-1)\rho_1 + 1]. \tag{6.33}$$

This is an expression for the reliability of a test of m parallel items or subtests, from the reliability ρ of just one, given by (6.30).

*** To see this, note that

$$\rho_m = m\sigma_{Tx}^2/[(m-1)\sigma_{Tx}^2 + \sigma_{Tx}^2 + \psi]$$

$$= \frac{m[\sigma_{Tx}^2/(\sigma_{Tx} + \psi^2)]}{(m-1)[\sigma_{Tx}^2/(\sigma_{Tx}^2 + \psi)] + 1}. \quad \text{\$\$\$}$$

The expression (6.33) is traditionally known as the *Spearman–Brown prophecy formula* (hence the added "S-B").[6] For the special case where $m = 2$, it was derived, independently, by Spearman and by Brown in 1910, as a formula to "prophesy" the increase in reliability that could be obtained if one were able to double the length of a (sub)test of known reliability ρ. If we have just one subtest, with a reliability coefficient ρ_1, then the reliability of a test of double length is

$$\rho_2 = 2\rho_1/(\rho_1 + 1). \tag{6.34}$$

This is the formula obtained by Spearman and by Brown for the obtainable reliability if we add a parallel subtest. This was then generalized to (6.33). The subscript m is attached in (6.33) to draw attention to the fact that this is the reliability coefficient of a test of m items, or, possibly, of m subtests. The expression (6.33) gives the reliability that we could get by adding $m - 1$ more (parallel) subtests to a subtest of known reliability ρ_1.

Recall from the preceding section that the SWLS data have a lower GFI if we suppose the items are parallel in the population sampled. With this assumption, (6.32) gives us

$$\hat{\omega} = \hat{\rho}_m = (25 \times 1.287)/(25 \times 1.287 + 5 \times 1.442) = .8169,$$

on substituting the ULS estimates $\hat{\sigma}_{Tx}^2 = 1.287$, $\hat{\psi}^2 = 1.442$ given in the preceding section. Alternatively, to use (6.33), we can get the average, .476, of the sample correlations of the five items, as given in Table 6.6. Then (6.37) gives

TABLE 6.6
Satisfaction With Life—SDs and Correlations

SD	1	2	3	4	5
1.602	1.	.617	.592	.448	.486
1.579	.617	1.	.518	.322	.454
1.569	.592	.518	1.	.432	.457
1.664	.448	.322	.432	1.	.434
1.832	.486	.454	.457	.434	1.

$$\hat{\omega} = \hat{\rho}_m = (5 \times .476)/(4 \times .476 + 1) = .8196.$$

[At least slight differences between estimators using sample analogues of (6.32) and (6.33) can be expected because they average the information in the data in different ways.] Generally, there is no good reason to estimate reliability using the sample S-B $\hat{\rho}_m$ instead of G-C alpha. And if the single-factor model has been fitted, as I recommend, omega may as well be used.

A common application of the S-B ρ_2 in (6.34) has been to a technique for estimating reliability known as *split-half* methods. A single test of m items—suppose m an even number—is administered, once only, and the items are split into two subtests, each of $m/2$ items, in some way. Items can be assigned at random, or odd-numbered items may be assigned to one subtest and even-numbered items assigned to the other. (Care is needed to prevent any resulting systematic pattern of assignment, such that the halves are not equivalent. In time-limited cognitive tests, for example, there must not be a split placing earlier items in one and later items in the other, because later items may be failed by not being reached.) The correlation between the half-test scores is the reliability of either. Then we can use the original Spearman–Brown prophecy formula (6.34) to approximate the reliability of the total score on the m items. This is generally not a safe, well-motivated procedure, as it does not make full use of the information in the data. It is still to be found in texts and possibly in applications, but cannot be recommended. There will certainly be variability in the reliability coefficient so estimated with the choice of split. If a split-half reliability is reported in the literature, and no better information is offered, we may reluctantly accept it, with some caution.

The reliability of the sum score of m items is given by ω if the items are homogeneous, equally by α if they are true-score equivalent, and equally by S-B ρ_m if they are parallel. From here on we reserve ω for the quantity given by (6.20), α for the quantity given by (6.28), and S-B ρ_m for the quantity given by (6.33), and similarly for the estimates obtained from the sample versions of these expressions.

It should be noted that omega and G-C alpha and their estimates from samples—but not the Spearman–Brown formula—will be altered by alteration of the scale of individual items/subtests. This is one reason why, with that one exception, we have used the covariance matrix of the items, not their correlation matrix. If we fit the single-factor model to the item correlation matrix instead of the covariance matrix, this is equivalent to standardizing each item score, substituting

$$Z_j = (X_j - \mu_{xj})/\sigma_{xj}$$

where μ_{xj} and σ_{xj} are the mean and *SD* of each item. The corresponding total score

$$S = \sum_j z_j$$

is a sum of standardized item scores. So implicitly, if we estimate omega or G-C alpha from a sample correlation matrix, we are estimating the reliability coefficient of a sum of standardized items. It would then be inconsistent to employ raw sum scores of the items. It is appropriate to mention this, because some readers may already be acquainted with common factor analysis as a psychometric technique. They would know that there is a sense in which, in general, the common factor model is independent of scale, and may be fitted to a sample correlation matrix—but not if we want coefficient omega.

The work in this chapter so far has rested on the rather restrictive model that requires all the items in the test to measure just one thing in common—to be *strictly homogeneous*, as we now call this property. In terms of item content, this requires that the items share one common attribute and that any further property is unique to each. In practice, this is a difficult ideal to attain. Fortunately, in applications, the requirement of strict homogeneity is indeed unnecessarily strict. Recall the example in Chapter 5 of two content-parallel test forms for measuring "intelligence," where it was remarked that the paired items jointly measured something they do not share with other items in their own set. Or note that the five SWLS items in Table 5.1 have been analyzed and found to be consistent with the hypothesis that they are homogeneous. But the fit is not perfect, and an examination of content suggests a division into three items measuring present satisfaction and two measuring satisfaction with the past. A set of items that share one general attribute, but form a number of small groups of items sharing further common properties, can often be treated as *essentially homogeneous*. This is because the effects of grouping are easily dominated by the general attribute shared by all items, so the groups make a negligible contribution to the common part of the variance of the total score. This kind of case is illustrated by the content-parallel example. Chapter 9 shows how to treat the possibility that the general attribute we intend to measure yields a subclassification into a few groups, as in the case of the SWLS.

BINARY DATA

In the special case of binary items, coefficient alpha can be written as

$$\alpha = [m/(m-1)][1 - \{\sum_j \pi_j(1 - \pi_j)\}/\sigma_Y^2] \tag{6.35}$$

[because $\pi_j(1 - \pi_j)$ is the variance of a binary item]. As before, we have π_j for the probability of the keyed response to item j—the proportion of examinees in the population giving it. The corresponding estimator of alpha was given by Kuder and Richardson in 1937 as their equation (20) and it is conventionally referred to as KR-20. It will be written here as

$$KR_{20} = [m/(m-1)][1 - \{\sum_j p_j(1 - p_j)\}/s_Y^2]. \tag{6.36}$$

The Guttman–Cronbach alpha, both as an estimator and as a population coefficient, was actually a later generalization on KR_{20}. The coefficient KR_{20} was developed as a good estimator of the reliability coefficient under the assumption that all items are true-score equivalent. In the case of binary items, this is the hypothesis that

$$\sigma_{jk} = \pi_{jk} - \pi_j\pi_k$$

is constant for all pairs j,k, although the difficulty level π_j may vary.[7]

If it is also assumed that the items are strictly parallel (so that $\pi_j = \pi$ for all items), then KR_{20} reduces to the computationally convenient expression

$$KR_{21} = [m/(m-1)][1 - \{\bar{Y}(m - \bar{Y})/(ms_Y^2)]. \tag{6.37}$$

This just needs the sample mean and sample variance of the total score. No item statistics are required. The computational convenience of KR_{21} may have been a motive for recommending it in the era before computers. It is now of only historical and perhaps some conceptual interest.[8]

A section of five items from the Law School Admission Test—items 11–15 of Section 6, to be referred to here as LSAT6—has been reanalyzed in a number of papers on psychometric theory. Unfortunately, the item stems are no longer available. The original data from 1,000 examinees can be summarized without any loss of information as in Table 6.7(a). The distribution of the total test scores is in Table 6.7(b). The distribution is skewed. Three examinees get a "perfect" 0, and 198 get a perfect 5.

We compute the proportions p_j passing each item, as entered in Table 6.8, and the joint proportions p_{jk} passing pairs of items, entered above the diagonal in the table. The sample item covariances are below the diagonal. The sample item variances are on the diagonal. Note that the mean of the total score is the sum of the p_j values, and is equal to 3.818. (The student is encouraged to check some of the p_j values from Table 6.7 by adding frequencies, and, similarly, to compute some joint frequencies of pairs, and a few covariances.)

From the item covariances, we have the total score variance

$$\sigma_{Ty}^2 = 1.0702,$$

from summing the 25 elements of the covariance matrix. (Or, alternatively, we may obtain this from the total test score distribution in Table 6.7.) Then G-C alpha—which is also KR_{20}—is given by

$$KR_{20} = (5/4)[1 - (.0702 + .2063 + \cdots + .1131)/1.0702] = .295.$$

Also,

$$KR_{21} = (5/4)[1 - (3.818 \times 1.182)/(5 \times 1.0702)] = .196.$$

Fitting the single-factor model to the covariance matrix in Table 6.8 is a theoretically questionable procedure, but we use a computer program to do it anyway. This gives loadings, unique variances, and the discrepancy matrix in Table 6.9. The goodness of fit index

$$GFI = 1 - (.00019002/.158238) = .9988,$$

suggesting a satisfactory fit of the items to the single-factor model. Coefficient omega, by (6.20a), is

$$\omega = (.0605 + .1345 + \cdots + .0745)^2/1.0702 = .3068,$$

TABLE 6.7
LSAT Section 6 (LSAT6)

(a) Data

Index	Test Score	Response Pattern Frequencies for Item					Observed Frequency
		1	2	3	4	5	
1	0	0	0	0	0	0	3
2	1	0	0	0	0	1	6
3	1	0	0	0	1	0	6
4	2	0	0	0	1	1	11
5	1	0	0	1	0	0	1
6	2	0	0	1	0	1	1
7	2	0	0	1	1	0	3
8	3	0	0	1	1	1	4
9	1	0	1	0	0	0	1
10	2	0	1	0	0	1	8
11	2	0	1	0	1	0	0
12	3	0	1	0	1	1	16
13	2	0	1	1	0	0	0
14	3	0	1	1	0	1	3
15	3	0	1	1	1	0	2
16	4	0	1	1	1	1	15
17	1	1	0	0	0	0	10
18	2	1	0	0	0	1	29
19	2	1	0	0	1	0	14
20	3	1	0	0	1	1	81
21	2	1	0	1	0	0	3
22	3	1	0	1	0	1	28
23	3	1	0	1	1	0	15
24	4	1	0	1	1	1	80
25	2	1	1	0	0	0	16
26	3	1	1	0	0	1	56
27	3	1	1	0	1	0	21
28	4	1	1	0	1	1	173
29	3	1	1	1	0	0	11
30	4	1	1	1	0	1	61
31	4	1	1	1	1	0	28
32	5	1	1	1	1	1	298
Total							1,000

(b) Frequency Distribution

Total Test Score	Frequency
5	298
4	357
3	237
2	85
1	20
0	3

TABLE 6.8
LSAT6—Difficulties and Covariance Matrix

		Item				
Item	p_j	1	2	3	4	5
1	.924 ~	.0702	.664	.524	.710	.806
2	.708	.0089	.2063	.418	.553	.630
3	.553	.0130	.0259	.2472	.445	.490
4	.763	.0050	.0120	.0231	.1808	.678
5	.870	.0021	.0132	.0089	.0142	.1131

TABLE 6.9
LSAT6—Spearman Analysis

	Loadings λ	Unique Variances ψ^2	Discrepancy Matrix				
			(Sample-Fitted Covariance Matrix, $\mathbf{S} - \mathbf{\Sigma}$)				
1	.0605	.0665	.0	.0008	.0017	.0021	−.0024
2	.1345	.1882	.0008	.0	.0009	.0038	.0032
3	.1861	.2126	.0017	.0009	.0	.0012	.0050
4	.1174	.1670	.0021	.0038	.0012	.0	.0054
5	.0745	.1076	−.0024	.0032	.0050	.0054	.0

which is just slightly larger than KR_{20}. Clearly the reliability is very low, and a longer test is needed. A sense of the limitations of this treatment of binary data—and the reason why it is admitted to be a "theoretically questionable procedure"—comes from the observation that the regression equations of the model are

$$\hat{x}_1 = .924 + .0605F$$
$$\hat{x}_2 = .709 + .1345F$$
$$\hat{x}_3 = .553 + .1861F$$
$$\hat{x}_4 = .763 + .1174F$$
$$\hat{x}_5 = .870 + .9745F.$$

The expected values $\hat{x}_j$ for the item scores are linear functions of the common factor F. Because the items are binary, these equations represent the probability of passing an item for an examinee with a given value of F. (Recall the introduction to Chap. 3.) One problem with the linear model is that for a small enough value of F the probability is negative, and for a large enough value it is greater than unity, which would be absurd. That is,

$$\text{if } F < -p_j/\lambda_j \quad \text{then} \quad P\{X_j = 1 | F = f\} < 0$$

and

$$\text{if } F > (1 - p_j)/\lambda_j \quad \text{then} \quad P\{X_j = 1 | F\} > 1.$$

In this data set, item 3 will have negative probabilities for $F < -.553/.186$, that is, $F < -2.97$, and item 1 will have probabilities greater than unity for $F > 1.256$. Using methods given in Chapter 7—as seen in equation (7.17)—we find that the lowest value of F in this data set is estimated as -3.795, which corresponds to the 0 total score, and the highest is 1.182, which corresponds to a total score of 5. Only the three examinees with zero total score yield an absurd probability value. We come back to this question later. A linear model is theoretically inappropriate for binary items, yet it can give an adequate overall approximation to their behavior in many applications. Note that KR_{20} assumes a linear model, and is an approximation in precisely the same way.

If we fit the true-score equivalence model to these data, from Table 6.8 we get the ULS estimate of the true score variance, as the simple average of the covariances (below the diagonal), namely,

$$\begin{aligned}
\hat{\sigma}^2 = (1/10)[&.0089 \\
&+ .0130 + .0259 \\
&+ .0050 + .0120 + .0231 \\
&+ .0021 + .0132 + .0089 + .0142] = .01263.
\end{aligned}$$

The fitted covariance and discrepancy matrices are given in Table 6.10, with a goodness of fit index

$$GFI = 1 - (.0009719/.158494) = .9939.$$

Fitting the parallel items model requires a common value of the diagonal elements of the fitted matrix. By ULS this is the average of the sample variances, $(1/5)(.0702 + .2063 + .2472 + .1808 + .1131) = .1635$, giving $.1635 - .0126 = .1509$ for the error variance. Then, by (6.32),

$$\rho_m = (5 \times .0126)/(5 \times .0126 + .1509) = .2945.$$

TABLE 6.10
LSAT6—True-Score Model

(a) Fitted Covariance Matrix

$$
\begin{bmatrix}
.0702 & .0126 & .0126 & .0126 & .0126 \\
.0126 & .2063 & .0126 & .0126 & .0126 \\
.0126 & .0126 & .2472 & .0126 & .0126 \\
.0126 & .0126 & .0126 & .1808 & .0126 \\
.0126 & .0126 & .0126 & .0126 & .1131
\end{bmatrix}
$$

(b) Discrepancies

$$
\begin{bmatrix}
.0 & -.0037 & .0004 & -.0076 & -.0105 \\
-.0037 & .0 & .0133 & -.0006 & .0006 \\
.0004 & .0133 & .0 & .0105 & -.0037 \\
-.0076 & -.0006 & .0105 & .0 & .0016 \\
-.0105 & .0006 & -.0037 & .0016 & .0
\end{bmatrix}
$$

TABLE 6.11
LSAT6—Parallel Items Model

(a) Fitted Covariance Matrix

$$
\begin{bmatrix}
.1635 & .0126 & .0126 & .0126 & .0126 \\
.0126 & .1635 & .0126 & .0126 & .0126 \\
.0126 & .0126 & .1635 & .0126 & .0126 \\
.0126 & .0126 & .0126 & .1635 & .0126 \\
.0126 & .0126 & .0126 & .0126 & .1635
\end{bmatrix}
$$

(b) Discrepancies

$$
\begin{bmatrix}
-.0933 & -.0037 & .0004 & -.0076 & -.0105 \\
-.0037 & .0428 & .0133 & -.0006 & .0006 \\
.0004 & .0133 & .0837 & .0105 & -.0037 \\
-.0076 & -.0006 & .0105 & .0173 & .0016 \\
-.0105 & .0006 & -.0037 & .0016 & -.0504
\end{bmatrix}
$$

The fitted covariance and discrepancy matrices are given in Table 6.11. The GFI = $1 - (.02135/.1584) = .8653$. This suggests that the items are not parallel, though they closely approximate true-score equivalence, as well as the more general single-factor model.

The classical factor model (6.2) is a linear model. The item scores (i.e., their expected values) are linear functions of the factor attribute. We return to the problem, noted earlier, of fitting a linear factor model to binary variables, when we consider nonlinear factor models—item response models—in Chapter 12. Meanwhile, it is enough to note that although the classical linear model (6.2) can only approximate the behavior of binary items, summation as in (6.17a) tends to cancel the effects of nonlinearity. Consequently, coefficient omega (bounded by G-C alpha, i.e., KR_{20}) still gives the reliability coefficient—defined as a ratio of common (attribute) variance to total variance. There is a more important limitation. In general the error variance (unique variance) of the total test score from a set of binary items cannot be independent of the test score. The error variance we obtain from the reliability coefficient is a general approximation to the error variances actually found along the scale of the test. An advantage of item response models is that they provide a functional relationship between the error variance and the true score (see Chaps. 12–15).

SOME PRINCIPLES OF GENERALIZABILITY

[This entire section can be omitted without loss of continuity.] As already hinted, there is a close connection between reliability and certain conceptions of *generalizability* from the items we obtain to further items that we imagine constructing. It was remarked in an earlier section that coefficient omega is the squared correlation between the total (or mean) score from m items and the mean score of items forming a test of infinite length. In effect, the true score is the mean score of the infinitely long test. Such a hypothetical limiting score is known as the *domain* score. This conforms to general mathematical usage. The domain is the set of elements—"values" in a wide sense—to which a variable is limited. In the application here, the elements of the domain are items. The domain of items is sometimes referred to as the *behavior domain* or the *universe of content*, or the *universe of admissible measurements*. Thus, the set of all items under consideration is the *item domain*, and the mean score on that set is the *item domain score*. (Note that we must now work with the mean of the item scores because the variance of the total test score will increase unboundedly as items are added.)

One generally necessary condition for the treatment of generalizability is that the items of the domain measure just one attribute in common. The entire domain should fit the single-factor model (or a corresponding unidimensional item response model—Chaps. 12 and 13). It is also necessary in some models to assume that the given set of m items has been representatively sampled from the infinite set of items that could be written and given to the respondents. Random sampling of items is generally not possible in applications. These fundamental and untestable assumptions constitute an idealization that could only be approximated in any application, and in some cases could not be realized, even approximately. Under these idealizing conditions the domain mean score both defines and determines the true score. It defines it in the sense that the set of items defines the attribute being measured by the property they have in common. It determines it in the sense that an infinite set of items measures the attribute precisely. Then the errors of measurement in using the practically available set of items are due to having a limited sample of items to represent the attribute.

The best known treatment of generalizability is based on a linear variance components model. This will be familiar to readers who are well grounded in the standard applications of analysis of variance to mixed- and random-effect models. It is appropriate to refer to it as Cronbach generalizability theory, because Cronbach and his associates have given it its most systematic development. An alternative treatment rests on the factor analysis of covariance matrices as in an earlier section of this chapter. Each of these treatments has advantages and limitations. We consider only some basic principles of Cronbach generalizability here, with a few remarks about the more extensive developments. The factor-analytic work will involve some deliberate recapitulation.

Suppose we have m measurements/item scores on n respondents, x_{ij}, $i = 1, \ldots, n; j = 1, \ldots, m$. We think of the items as coming from an infinite domain of items that would, if exhaustively tested, be homogeneous, fitting the Spearman factor model. We wish to obtain coefficients that quantify the relation between the actual m measurements and the conceivable domain measurements. In the Cronbach treatment the analysis of the data for this purpose is conventionally referred to as a *generalizability study*—commonly denoted "G-study." (In other contexts it would be a *calibration study*, and may be part of a test-development study.) For example, if we were using the factor-analytic work already covered, in the generalizability study we would compute coefficient omega or G-C alpha and would interpret it as the squared correlation between the item-sample mean score and the domain mean score. The results from the generalizability study can then be used in a *decision study*—commonly denoted "D-study"—to assess the expected measurement error in a new application. For example, having found that m items do not give a large enough G-C alpha, we may decide how many more to add to reduce measurement error sufficiently, by using the Spearman–Brown formula.

Before turning to the Cronbach treatment we review the factor-analytic treatment. To link the two we rewrite the factor model (6.2) as

$$X_{ij} = \mu_j + \lambda_j F_i + E_{ij}, \tag{6.38}$$

in which the subscript i has been added. As before, μ_j and λ_j are population parameters representing the mean (= difficulty) and the factor loading (= sensitivity, i.e., discriminating power) of item j. Attaching the subscript i

to the variables complicates the previous account, but brings it into line with the conventional treatment of analysis of variance, to be given soon. Instead of just writing X_j as the score of a randomly sampled subject, we regard the n variables X_{ij} as the scores of n respondents to be independently randomly drawn from the population. This is to be distinguished from the values x_{ij} that we have after a particular sample has been drawn. [Formally trained students of mathematical statistics will recognize that this is just to state that X_{ij}, F_i, E_{ij}, $i = 1, \ldots, n$, are n independently and identically distributed random variables. Students whose background is in applied statistics may ignore this formal statement, but should accept that (6.38) is still a model for the population, not a description of a given sample.]

Accordingly, we recall (6.17)–(6.19), and we write corresponding expressions for means instead of total test scores. These are

$$M_i = (1/m)\sum_j X_j = \sum_j \mu_j + [(1/m)\sum_j \lambda_j)F_i + (1/m)\sum_j E_{ij} \qquad (6.39)$$

or

$$M_i = \mu_\bullet + \lambda_\bullet F_i + E_{\bullet i} \qquad (6.40)$$

with

$$\sigma_M^2 = (\lambda_\bullet)^2 + \psi_\bullet^2, \qquad (6.41)$$

where the dot replacing a subscript here indicates an average over that subscript. [Note that $(\lambda_\bullet)^2$ represents the mean factor loading squared, whereas $\psi_\bullet^2$ represents the mean of the unique variances.] Recalling also (6.20b), we have for coefficient omega

$$\omega = (m\lambda_\bullet)^2 / ((m\lambda_\bullet)^2 + \psi_\bullet^2). \qquad (6.42)$$

This is the squared correlation between M_i and F_i.

The fundamental point is that F_i, the common factor defined by the homogeneous domain from which the items are taken, is a measure of the attribute that the infinity of items have in common, and that they measure precisely. The larger the number of items (with nonzero loadings) that we use, the more precisely we measure the attribute. In the limit the precision approaches perfection. Coefficient omega is the squared correlation between the observable mean score of m items and the domain mean score. It is also the proportion of variance of the mean score of the given items that is due to the domain score. Assuming homogeneity, we may call omega the *coefficient of generalizability* from the given item set to the domain.

Note that in this model we do not need to suppose that the m items are randomly or at least representatively sampled. The size of omega depends on the parameters of the items chosen. Remaining items could all have smaller or larger loadings or unique variances, without altering generalizability. As we have seen, if their required conditions on the item covariance matrix are satisfied, G-C alpha or the Spearman–Brown formula will yield the same reliability coefficient as coefficient omega, and accordingly these will serve as coefficients of generalizability. Otherwise, they are underestimates. It is not yet common practice in test development to check whether the items are true-score equivalent or parallel. It is recommended that this should always be done if possible. When their respective conditions are satisfied, these three coefficients measure generalizability, under the assumption that the item domain is homogeneous. If the given items are true-score equivalent, we can use G-C alpha without supposing that the remaining items in the domain are also true-score equivalent. It is sufficient that the given items have equal factor loadings. The remaining items need not. Similarly, it is not necessary to assume that further items in the domain are parallel if the given items are.

We can check that the items we actually construct are homogeneous, but of course we cannot know that the entire item domain is homogeneous. In applications, great care is needed in conceptualizing the attribute that is the goal of measurement, so that we have a clear prescription for the items that will be indicators of it. It is also necessary to be able to imagine writing more items of the same kind. This is the question of *content validity*, to which we turn in Chapter 10. Some accounts unnecessarily restrict generalizability theory to the addition of further parallel items.

An advantage of the factor-analytic treatment of generalizability is that it allows the selection of subsets of items from the test development—calibration or generalizability—study to make a shorter test having optimal reliability/generalizability (see Chap. 7). Attempts to extrapolate from the given items to the behavior of a longer, but still finite, test must be conjectural, because they depend on the unknown loadings—sensitivities—of the items that may be added.

A good starting point for the introduction of Cronbach generalizability theory is the point of overlap with the factor analytic treatment—namely, the model for true-score equivalent items. The true-score equivalence model is obtained, as we have seen, by equating factor loadings in (6.2) to yield

$$X_{ij} = \mu_j + T_{Xi} + E_{ij}, \tag{6.43}$$

where $T_{Xi} = \lambda F_i$ is the true score measured in the units of the (true-score equivalent) items. Recall that we allow the items to have distinct error variances σ_{Ej}^2. To move toward applications of analysis of variance, we express each item mean as

$$\mu_j = \mu + \delta_j. \tag{6.44}$$

Here δ_j represents the deviation of the difficulty of the item from μ, which is the average of the m difficulties (so $\Sigma\, \delta_j = 0$), and the model becomes

$$X_{ij} = \mu + \delta_j + T_{Xi} + E_{ij}. \tag{6.45}$$

According to (6.45), four components contribute to the score of randomly drawn respondent i on item j:

1. A parameter μ represents the fixed contribution of the average difficulty of these m items.
2. A parameter δ_j represents the difficulty of item j as a deviation, positive or negative, from the mean difficulty.
3. The true score T_i corresponds to the domain score of the respondent.
4. The response of examinee i to item j is subject to a random "error" term E_{ij}.

As before, we have the conditions that true scores and errors, and errors from different items, are uncorrelated, so we get the variance decomposition

$$\sigma_j^2 = \sigma_T^2 + \sigma_{Ej}^2,$$

and, for item covariances,

$$\sigma_{jk} = \sigma_T^2.$$

This gives us the testable structure for the covariance matrix discussed earlier. The test mean score is given by

$$M_i = \mu + \delta_{\bullet} + M_{Ti} + E_{\bullet i} \tag{6.46}$$

where $\delta_{\bullet}$ and $E_{\bullet i}$ are averages of item difficulties and errors respectively and $M_{Ti} = (1/m)\, T_i$ is the mean true score. The variance of M is

$$\sigma_M^2 = \sigma_T^2 + \sigma_{E\bullet}^2. \tag{6.47}$$

where $\sigma_{E\bullet}^2$ is the average of the error variances and $\sigma_T^2 = (1/m^2)\sigma_{Ty}^2$ is the variance of the mean true score. The covariance of M and T_x is σ_{MTx}^2, so the squared correlation between M and M_T is

$$\rho_{MTx}^2 = \sigma_{Tx}^2/\sigma_M^2 = (m\sigma_{Tx}^2)/(m\sigma_{Tx}^2 + \sigma_{E\bullet}^2). \tag{6.48}$$

This coefficient is the reliability, as before. As now reinterpreted, it is the generalizability of the test mean score—or, indeed, of the total score, because this coefficient is independent of the scale. Given sample observations x_{ij} of X_{ij}, we arrive—as in (6.24) through (6.27)—at the estimate

$$\hat{\rho}_{MTx}^2 = [m/(m-1)][1 - (\sum_j s_{jj})/s_Y^2]. \tag{6.49}$$

This is just the conventional estimate of G-C alpha in (6.28).

Consider the constructed data set in Table 6.12, with five items and 20 respondents. These data could arise as Likert scores on an attitude scale, or as ratings of the 20 subjects on five named traits by an observer, or in

TABLE 6.12
Constructed Quantitative Item Set

| Respondent | Item | | | | | $x_{i\bullet}$ |
	1	2	3	4	5	
1	3	2	3	2	3	2.6
2	5	3	3	2	2	3.0
3	2	2	1	2	2	1.8
4	5	4	3	3	2	3.4
5	2	2	2	1	2	1.8
6	3	5	4	3	3	3.6
7	1	4	3	3	3	2.8
8	3	2	4	3	2	2.8
9	4	2	3	3	3	3.0
10	3	4	3	4	3	3.4
11	4	4	3	4	4	3.8
12	4	2	3	2	3	2.8
13	6	4	4	3	4	4.2
14	3	4	3	3	3	3.2
15	5	4	3	3	2	3.4
16	2	2	2	1	2	1.8
17	3	5	4	3	3	3.6
18	1	4	3	3	3	2.8
19	3	2	4	3	2	2.8
20	4	2	3	3	3	3.0
$x_{\bullet j}$	3.3	3.15	3.05	2.7	2.7	$(x_{\bullet\bullet} = 2.98)$

a number of other ways. These data give the covariance matrix in Table 6.13. Summing the elements of the covariance matrix gives 10.516 for the variance of the sum score Y and $10.516/25 = .4206$ for the variance of the mean score. Fitting the single-factor model by ULS gives the factor loadings and unique variances in Table 6.14(a), whereas fitting the true-score equivalence model gives the corresponding results in Table 6.14(b).

Both models give an acceptable fit to the data. Summing the loadings in Table 6.14(a), squaring, and dividing by the variance of Y gives a coefficient omega equal to $2.702^2/10.516 = .694$. We can also use (6.20a) for the true-score equivalence analysis, giving $\hat{\omega} = (5 \times .538)^2/10.516 = .688$. Using the estimator for G-C alpha gives

$$\hat{\alpha} = (5/4)[1 - (1.8 + 1.292 + .576 + .642 + .432)/10.516] = .686,$$

agreeing well enough with the previous estimate.

We now reexamine the model (6.45). Readers well grounded in analysis of variance will recognize that it is, indeed, a linear model for X_{ij} with four components—the grand mean, μ, the fixed effect of item difficulty, δ_j, the random effect of respondent attribute value, T_{xi}, and a *residual*, E_{ij}. The residual consists of an interaction between the item and the respondent and anything we might further regard as "error." If we obtained repeated

TABLE 6.13
Covariance Matrix—Constructed Item Set

1.800	.163	.353	.253	.147
.163	1.292	.360	.521	.310
.353	.360	.576	.332	.174
.253	.521	.332	.642	.274
.147	.310	.174	.274	.432

TABLE 6.14
Spearman and True-Score Equivalence Analyses—
Constructed Quantitative Data Set

(a) Spearman		(b) True-Score Equivalence	
λ	ω	λ	ω
.382	1.654	.538	1.511
.688	.818	.538	.993
.541	.283	.538	.287
.694	.160	.538	.353
.397	.274	.538	.143
GFI = .990		GFI = .970	

measurements for the respondents on each item, we might separate out an error of replication from the interaction, which is thought of as the effect of the unique properties of the item on a random examinee's response.

The analysis of variance (ANOVA) can be set out as follows: Standard ANOVA algebra requires us to express each observed x_{ij} in terms of four components,

$$x_{ij} = x_{\bullet\bullet} + (x_{\bullet j} - x_{\bullet\bullet}) + (x_{i\bullet} - x_{\bullet\bullet}) + (x_{ij} - x_{\bullet j} - x_{i\bullet} + x_{\bullet\bullet}), \quad (6.50)$$

which are sample counterparts of the four components in the model. (Again we use a dot for a mean over a subscript.) From (6.50) it may be shown by the standard algebraic substitutions of analysis of variance theory that

$$SS_{Tot} = SS_\delta + SS_{Tx} + SS_E \quad (6.51)$$

where

$$SS_{Tot} = \sum_i \sum_j (x_{ij} - x_{\bullet\bullet})^2 = \sum_i \sum_j x_{ij}^2 - nmx_{\bullet\bullet}^2. \quad (6.52a)$$

$$SS_D = n\sum_j (x_{\bullet j} - x_{\bullet\bullet})^2 = n\sum_j x_{\bullet j}^2 - nmx_{\bullet\bullet}^2. \quad (6.52b)$$

$$SS_{Tx} = m\sum_i (x_{i\bullet} - x_{\bullet\bullet})^2 = m\sum_i x_{i\bullet}^2 - nmx_{\bullet\bullet}^2. \quad (6.52c)$$

$$SS_E = \sum_i \sum_j (x_{ij} - x_{\bullet j} - x_{i\bullet} + x_{\bullet\bullet})^2$$
$$= SS_{tot} - SS_\delta - SS_{Tx}. \quad (6.52d)$$

By the usual convention, SS denotes a *sum of squares* of deviations about the means that appear in the expressions. This is the fundamental analysis of sums of squares that underlies the "analysis of variance." Conventional ANOVA then defines corresponding *mean squares* (MS), which are estimates of combinations of variances, and it uses the algebra of expectations to obtain their expected values. In this case these are:

$$MS_\delta = SS_\delta/(m-1) \Rightarrow \sigma_E^2 + n[(\sum_j \delta_j^2)/(m-1)], \quad (6.53a)$$

$$\mathrm{MS}_{T_x} = \mathrm{SS}_{T_x}/(n - 1) \Rightarrow \sigma_E^2 + m\sigma_{T_x}^2, \tag{6.53b}$$

$$\mathrm{MS}_E = \mathrm{SS}_E/[(m - 1)(n - 1)] \Rightarrow \sigma_E^2. \tag{6.53c}$$

[The symbol "$\Rightarrow$" is to be read here as "is an unbiased estimate of." Note that because item difficulty has fixed effects, in (6.53) we do not have a population variance σ_δ^2 to be estimated.] This is a *mixed model*, with a random factor T_x—the random effect of respondent attribute—and a fixed factor δ_j, the fixed effect of the difficulty of each of the chosen items. We are not able to get a separate estimate of the error variance of each of the m items. But if we interpret σ_E^2 as the average of these error variances, the generalizability coefficient in (6.48) becomes

$$\rho_{MT}^2 = (m\sigma_{T_x}^2)/(m\sigma_{T_x}^2 + \sigma_E^2). \tag{6.54}$$

Then from (6.53), MS_{T_x} is an unbiased estimate of $m\sigma_{T_x}^2 + \sigma_E^2$, and $\mathrm{MS}_{T_x} - \mathrm{MS}_E$ is an unbiased estimate of $m\sigma_{T_x}^2$. So a satisfactory estimate of $\rho_{MT_x}^2$, the generalizability coefficient, is given by

$$r_{MT(A)}^2 = (\mathrm{MS}_{T_x} - \mathrm{MS}_E)/\mathrm{MS}_{T_x}. \tag{6.55}$$

[The subscript (A) is intended to denote "by ANOVA."] This is a classical formula for reliability by ANOVA, with a very long history.[9] It may be shown that $r_{MT(A)}^2$ and G-C alpha in (6.49) are algebraically equivalent, and must give the same answers. (The latter is based on a slightly more general model, as it allows the error variances of the items to be distinct.) The practical implication of this equivalence is that the researcher who has access to a computer program for ANOVA can obtain the sums of squares and mean squares as standard output, and use (6.55) instead of (6.49), as employed in specialized computer programs for G-C alpha. Whatever choice is made, it is again strongly recommended that the sample item covariances be at least examined for possible departures from the expected structure, which requires equal item covariances, with possibly unequal variances.

A conventional analysis of variance of the data in Table 6.12, set out in the standard form of presentation, is given in Table 6.15. From the mean squares for T_x and for E, we obtain $r_{MT(A)}^2 = (2.103 - .660)/2.103 = .686$, in agreement, as we expect, with G-C alpha and with omega estimated earlier under true-score equivalence.

Experienced ANOVA users may be puzzled by the absence of the usual F ratios and tests of significance. In truly doubtful cases, we could obtain these, and could test to see if there is significant variance due to the

TABLE 6.15
ANOVA—Constructed Quantitative Data Set

Source	SS	df	MS
δ	5.86	4	1.465
T_x	39.96	19	2.103
$T_x\delta$	50.14	76	0.660
Total	95.96		

attribute, or if the items vary significantly in difficulty. It is to be hoped that the first significance test will not be needed. It would be unfortunate if we have absolutely failed to measure anything. The second significance test may become of interest in an alternative model for randomly selected items.

Model (6.45) yields a coefficient of generalizability that we can now estimate in three ways, namely, as omega, as alpha, and by the ANOVA formula (6.55) if the covariances have the appropriate structure. We now ask what this tells us about the item domain. It is important to note that this coefficient is the squared correlation between the domain mean score and the score on the given items. It is not the expected squared correlation between the domain score and the mean score from a sample of m items drawn at random from the domain. It measures generalizability without the assumption that the remaining items in the domain are also true-score equivalent. It is enough that the domain is homogeneous.

An advantage of the structural (factor analysis) treatment over the ANOVA treatment of generalizability is that even when the items are true-score equivalent, we get separate estimates of the error variances of the m items. We might wish, for future applications, to choose a subset of the m items to make a shortened form of the test on the basis of the test development phase—the generalizability study. Given separate error variances, we can choose subsets with optimal generalizability (see Chap. 7).

On the other hand, if we wish to extrapolate, so to speak, from the generalizability of the given m items to the generalizability we would expect to get by adding a number of further items, we need more restrictive assumptions. This is because we cannot know the error variances or factor loadings of items we do not yet have. In practice, as we face the actual task of writing further items, we hope to have a clear enough conceptualization of the attribute to write more items measuring the same thing. But we certainly do not know how to write them to be equally sensitive to the attribute or to have equal unique variability. In applying the formulas in the direction of extrapolation to unwritten items, it is necessary to assume that the average factor loading and average unique variance of the added items equal those of the m given items. Intuitively, one sees that the larger the number of added items, the safer this assumption becomes. Even so, in applications, there could be an unpleasant surprise if, as may often be the case, the best indicators of the attribute have been written first, and writing more good items proves difficult.

*** Proof of equivalence of ANOVA formula to G-C alpha: (I cannot trace lines of proof in the original literature on this. I believe the following is necessary.)

$$\mathrm{SS}_{\mathrm{Tot}} - \mathrm{SS}_D = \sum \sum (x_{ij} - x_{..})^2 - n \sum (x_{.j} - x_{..})^2$$
$$= \sum \sum x_{ij}^2 - n \sum x_{.j}^2$$
$$= \sum \sum (x_{ij} - x_{.j})^2$$
$$= \mathrm{SS}_E + \mathrm{SS}_{Tx}.$$

It follows that

$$\sum_j s_j^2 = (m - 1)\mathrm{MS}_E + \mathrm{MS}_{Tx},$$

yielding equivalence. \$\$\$

So far we have done little more than reexamine classical reliability theory from the point of view that a true score is a domain score and therefore "the" reliability coefficient is a generalizability coefficient. Now we consider an alternative model—the *random items model* for the observations x_{ij}. The random items model requires the strong assumption that the m items are in effect randomly sampled from the item domain—that every item in the domain has an equal probability of being chosen. In this case the model for the score on the jth randomly sampled item is

$$X_{ij} = \mu + D_j + T_i + E_{ij}, \tag{6.56}$$

where D_j is the random difficulty of item j as a deviation from μ. In this model μ is the mean difficulty of the entire item domain, whereas in the fixed items model it was the mean difficulty of the m given items. Here we must suppose that the variance σ_E^2 of the error-term E_{ij} (which again includes interaction) is independent of the item sampled. The m items are drawn with independent random difficulties whose variance is σ_D^2.

Then the variance of the item score X_{ij} of a randomly drawn respondent given a randomly selected item consists of three components—one due to item difficulty, one due to respondent domain score, and one comprising error, that is,

$$\sigma_X^2 = \sigma_D^2 + \sigma_T^2 + \sigma_E^2. \tag{6.57}$$

The important consequence is that under the model of random item selection, and random item difficulty, the variance of the item difficulty is, in effect, included in the variance of the error of measurement. Part of the error with which the respondent's mean score on m items determines that person's domain mean score depends on the difficulties of the sampled items. The squared correlation between a randomly drawn item and the domain mean score is given by

$$\rho_{XT}^2 = \sigma_T^2 / [\sigma_T^2 + (\sigma_E^2 + \sigma_D^2)], \tag{6.58}$$

and the squared correlation between the mean test score M_i on a test of m items and the domain mean score is

$$\rho_{MT}^2 = (m\sigma_T^2) / [m\sigma_T^2 + (\sigma_E^2 + \sigma_D^2)]. \tag{6.59}$$

The expression (6.59) is actually for the expected squared correlation between the domain score and the score from a random sample of m items.

Standard ANOVA algebra gives the same results as in the fixed items model, (6.50) through (6.53), except that (6.53a) is replaced by

$$MS_D = SS_D / (m - 1) \Rightarrow \sigma_E^2 + n\sigma_D^2. \tag{6.60}$$

Then

$$(MS_T - MS_E) / m \Rightarrow \sigma_T^2, \tag{6.61a}$$

$$MS_E \Rightarrow \sigma_E^2, \tag{6.61b}$$

as before, and

$$(MS_D - MS_E) / N \Rightarrow \sigma_D^2. \tag{6.61c}$$

Accordingly, good estimates of the reliability/generalizability of a randomly drawn item and of the mean score of m such items are obtained by substituting these estimates in (6.58) and (6.59). In the example of Table 6.12, with the ANOVA in Table 6.15, we have $\hat{\sigma}_E^2 = .660$ and $\hat{\sigma}_T^2 = .289$ as before, and $\hat{\sigma}_D^2 = (1.465 - .660)/20 = .040$, giving $.289/(.289 + .660 + .040) = .292$ for the generalizability of a random item, and $1.443/(1.443 + .660 + .040) = .673$ for the generalizability of the mean score from m randomly drawn items. In this example, the items do not vary much in difficulty. In other cases, widely dispersed difficulties could add a great deal to the error of measurement in this model.

The application of the random items model and the resulting variances, and of the generalizability coefficients and their ANOVA estimates, would be motivated by a situation in which we actually intend to give independently drawn samples of items to different respondents. In a subpopulation of examinees having the same domain score, a set of m items with random mean difficulty D_* can take the observed mean score above or below the domain mean score, as a particularly easy or difficult set of items happens to be assigned to an examinee by chance sampling of items. In the practice of test construction and measurement, it would not be common practice to assign distinct samples of items to different examinees under the assumptions of the random items model. One may question the motivation of such a procedure. In the commonest situation, m items of known structure are given to all examinees in any population of interest. In major testing programs, a usual situation is one in which we have a large *pool* or *bank* of items, and for reasons of security of the testing process against unethical access to or use of the items, distinct subsets of items from the pool are given to examinees and they need to be comparably scored. In such a case, by methods described in Chapter 16, it will usually be possible to obtain parameters characterizing each item in the entire set, corresponding to difficulties and factor loadings. These can then be used to obtain comparable estimates of the attribute from different sets of items—a process known as *test equating*. It is also possible by these methods to assess the variance of an error of measurement that will not be inflated by the inclusion of chance effects of receiving items of varying difficulty.

A more likely application of the random items model for assessing generalizability is the case where the "items" are raters. Expert or possibly inexpert persons are employed to make judgments about a number of examinees. These are expressed in the form of, or scored as, numerical ratings. Such judgments are generally uncertain and in that sense "subjective." They might be m examiners' judgments of the quality of an expository paragraph or an essay, as written by each of n examinees. They might be ratings of a named characteristic—say, a defined personality trait—of n examinees, by m judges—professionals or peers. Raters may show, as their own stable characteristics, individual differences in the severity of their examination marks, or in the variability they are willing to allow between the essays judged best and worst. Similar remarks apply to ratings of named traits. It is hardly conceivable that we might have a large pool of raters, whose individual severities and variabilities in judgment are accurately known. If m raters in a generalizability study can be considered representatively sampled from the set of raters that might be freshly sampled in a future decision study, the random "items" model would be appropriate for describing the reliability/generalizability of one newly drawn rater's score, by (6.58) or of the mean of m of them, by (6.59). This might be well motivated if fewer raters are used in the later decision study than in the initial generalizability study. If there were more of them, the decision study could be used to assess the parameters—means and variances of ratings—characterizing the raters actually used. Then we could return to the true-score equivalence model or to the factor model for the generalizability of the ratings of the given judges to the domain of further judges. For all we then know or care, further judges might all be more or all less severe, or all more or all less sensitive to the characteristic rated. Thus, the most likely application of the random model (6.56) is in a generalizability study with multiple raters used to assess the error with which one fresh judge will approximate the mean rating that would be obtained from the available population of judges. The model does not allow the judges to vary in sensitivity or in error variance; therefore, this application will be of interest only if the absolute value of the rating is of importance. We would use this model if, for example, a new rater's essay mark is compared to a fixed criterion for a passing grade, or if a newly recruited psychiatrist's rating of psychosis is to be compared to a criterion of severity used to determine hospitalization. If ratings are used for relative judgments, the difficulty variance should not be included in the error variance, and we again return to the fixed models (6.2) or (6.45).

The remaining comments in this section are clearest to students familiar with multifactorial designs. Cronbach generalizability theory includes a wider range of measurement designs than the simple respondents by items/measurements/ratings case considered so far. In principle, one can have a generalizability design for just about every major multifactorial ANOVA design. No attempt is made to present the general form of the theory here. We briefly consider some examples, to illustrate the general nature of these developments. One possibility is that we have responses of n examinees to m objective test items, on r occasions of repeated measurement, giving item scores x_{ijk}, $i = 1, \ldots, n$; $j = 1, \ldots, m$; $k = 1, \ldots, r$. Another is that we have ratings on n individuals of m behaviors thought to be indicators of a single attribute, by r raters. Either of these cases might be represented by the model

$$X_{ijk} = \mu + T_i + \delta_j + \gamma_k + (T\delta)_{ij} + (T\gamma)_{ik} + (\delta\gamma)_{jk} + E_{ijk}. \qquad (6.62)$$

In this model, with the notation used, the effect T_i of the attribute of the examinee would be regarded as random, whereas the effects δ_j of items/rated behaviors and γ_k due to raters/occasions of measurement are fixed. But further models can be obtained by replacing δ by D, and/or replacing γ by G, to denote random sampling of items/rated behaviors and/or of occasions/raters. Note that the additional terms in parentheses are interactions, allowing effects of combinations of conditions, as well as the main effects of items and occasions/raters

Each of the resulting models yields a decomposition of the variance of X_{ijk} into components,

$$\sigma_X^2 = \sigma_T^2 + \sigma_D^2 + \sigma_G^2 + \sigma_{TD}^2 + \sigma_{TG}^2 + \sigma_{DG}^2 + \sigma_E^2, \qquad (6.63)$$

in which σ_D^2, σ_G^2, and σ_{DG}^2 are replaced by mean squares of effects if these are fixed. Students well grounded in ANOVA theory will easily see how the previous discussion can be applied to this class of design, to yield sums of squares, mean squares, and expected values of mean squares. These are combinations of the variance components in (6.63), from which they can be estimated. From these we can get generalizability coefficients in which some or all of the variance components are included with σ_E^2 in the "error term," depending on whether we regard the items/rated behaviors or the occasions/raters as random or fixed.

More generally, in these developments, we suppose that in addition to the sampled population of examinees, we have one or more distinct *facets*. In Cronbach generalizability theory this term replaces the word *factors* as used in multifactorial ANOVA designs. Facets are principles of classification of the measurements. Examples are items, rated behaviors, occasions, and raters. In Cronbach theory, the sampling units—respondents, examinees on which the measurements are made—are not regarded as forming a facet but are referred to as the *objects of measurement*. (In most applications, these units will be individual examinees. They could include other sampling units whose properties are to be measured—for example, classrooms.) The case on which the earlier discussion has been concentrated—respondents by items—is a single-facet design with respondents as objects of measurement and items as the only facet. The cases of respondents by items by occasions and of persons by ratings by raters are two-facet designs. These have, respectively, items and occasions, and ratings and raters, as their facets. A design with n persons by m ratings by r raters on t occasions is an example of a three-facet design. For example, we might have ratings of aggressive behaviors by a number of raters over a number of time intervals on preschool children in a play situation. At present, we do not seem to have more general versions of the factor theory of generalizability to analyze such data sets. (But see the model for "multitrait multimethod" data discussed in Chap 10, as an example of what might be needed).

The interested student will pursue the reference note.[10] A few more remarks must serve to guide the reader in that pursuit and to close this chapter. All of these models require stringent assumptions of representativeness. This means fair sampling, and broad exchangeability of the facet elements—raters, occasions, items—in the domain. If we feel that the first m items we write are good ones—with a medium level of difficulty, and satisfactory sensitivity to the attribute—and that it will be hard to keep finding/writing items of similar quality, it is safer to regard the items as fixed and use the factor model for generalizability, forgoing any attempt to guess the behavior of further items. The same may be true of the characteristics of readily available raters in some situations. Not all their peers know people about equally well. It is particularly difficult to imagine that occasions of measurement constitute a representative sample of an infinite domain of distinct times. Most time-dependent behavior is best analyzed for systematic trends, possibly with sophisticated probabilistic (*sto-chastic*) models for time series—autoregressive/moving average models.[11] The further apart in time repeated measurements are made, the less similar they are, and the simple ANOVA treatments of generalizability do not model this. (That is one difficulty already noted with "retest reliability.") All of the models involving a random facet—random items, random raters—are well motivated only in cases where we wish to know the error of measurement of the domain score from distinct items or distinct raters. These will mostly be cases where the decision study (a) is distinct from the generalizability study, (b) uses fresh items, raters, and so on, and (c) uses fewer items, raters, and so on than the generalizability study. Such cases would appear to be uncommon.

REVIEW GUIDE

The Spearman general factor model (6.2) for a homogeneous test is the central topic of this chapter. Its basic formulation needs close study. [The demonstration that the parameters can be determined from estimable variances and covariances, from (6.3) through (6.6), may be conceptually interesting to some students but is not essential knowledge.] The general model and its special cases, the true-score equivalence model and the parallel items model, through equations (6.3), (6.4), (6.12), and (6.14), give restrictive hypotheses to be fitted and tested for goodness of fit. Attention should concentrate on the use of both goodness of fit indices and the sizes of the discrepancies as illustrated in Tables 6.4(c), 6.5(a), and 6.5(b) to judge the fit of the model, and generally on the illustrative examples in the tables and text.

It is desirable that the student understand the decomposition of the total test score in (6.17) given by the factor model. Given the parameters of the general factor model, the student should be able to compute the reliability coefficient omega by (6.20) and, desirably, understand why it is a reliability coefficient for a homogeneous test.

The Guttman–Cronbach alpha (6.28) estimated by (6.27) and the Spearman–Brown reliability (6.33) are important special cases of omega. The student should be able to compute them and desirably should understand them as reliability coefficients when their special assumptions are satisfied and as lower bounds to the reliability of a homogeneous test. Again, close study of the examples in the tables should be helpful.

For binary data, KR_{20} and KR_{21} are of historical interest only. The numerical illustration of the application of the general factor model to a binary data set should be closely studied, and the student should simply accept the warning that we are here using the model as a possibly crude approximation to a more sophisticated model studied later.

The section on generalizability theory is regarded as an optional extra. It is probably enough to recognize (a) that coefficient omega is a coefficient measuring generalizability from a given set of items to a behavior domain, and (b) that further reading is available to the student who wishes to pursue the ANOVA treatment of generalizability to other items and conditions of observation as developed by Cronbach and his associates.

END NOTES

General: There are books on factor analysis at various levels of technicality. Most require matrix algebra. An exception is McDonald (1985). Students with a knowledge of matrix algebra will wish to consult Mulaik (1972).

Special Note: Estimation by unweighted least squares is easy to understand, but there are more sophisticated, more efficient methods of estimation, forming a class of *weighted least squares* estimators. These give differential "value" or "weight" to different discrepancies s_{jk} − σ_{jk} in forming a function of them for the computer to minimize by a search algorithm. This is a very technical topic. Note the following points: (a) Certain weights for the discrepancies, based on the sample covariances s_{jk}, give a computer program option called generalized least squares (GLS). If the item scores give a large-sample distribution of the item covariance matrix corresponding to a normal distribution—this condition may not reach the reader's intuition—GLS gives good estimators, and, if the sample size is sufficiently large—say, greater than 100—provides usable standard errors of estimate (*SEs*) of the parameters λ_j, ψ_j^2, and a chi-square test of the hypothesis (in the present case) of a single-factor model—that is, homogeneous items. (b) Certain weights for the discrepancies, based on the fitted covariances $\hat{\sigma}_{jk}$, give maximum likelihood (ML) estimators of the parameters if the unique parts of the item scores are normally distributed. ML estimators, like GLS, give *SEs* of estimate and a chi-square test of goodness of fit. (c) If the item scores, or at least their unique parts, are not normally distributed—for example, binary scores or Likert scores with few categories—special weights can be chosen to suit the case, to give good properties to the estimates. Generally these methods are limited to quite small numbers of items, and for quite good reasons have mainly been applied to item response models, and not to simple common factor models such as the single-factor model of this chapter.

1. CONFA is a simple self-contained program for confirmatory factor analysis, written by Colin Fraser and made available with this book.
2. Originally given by McDonald (1970). See McDonald (1985, Chap. 7).
3. See later section, Some Principles of Generalizability.

4. Original sources are Guttman (1945) and Cronbach (1951).

5. This proof, given by McDonald (1970), is patterned after a non-factor-analytic proof by Novick and Lewis (1967). See Lord and Novick (1968) for a conveniently accessible account of the Novick and Lewis proof.

6. See Lord and Novick (1968, pp. 112–114).

7. It is actually difficult to model binary data having this rather strange property. It seems that it has not been done, and indeed cannot be done, because it assumes a linear model. So KR_{20} is at best an approximation for binary items, which implicitly assumes the linear model.

8. This case has a simple item response model—see Chapter 13—in which every item has the same functional relation to the attribute.

9. Hoyt and, seemingly independently, Jackson and Ferguson gave this basic result in 1941. See Lord and Novick (1968).

10. Brennan (1983) is a good resource.

11. For a technical but usable source account, with references to follow up, see Cox, Hinkley, and Barndorff-Nielsen (1996).

Reliability—Applications

The object of this chapter is to describe some applications of reliability theory. The first section deals with the effect on reliability of shortening or lengthening a test—dropping or adding items. The next section contains a review of the choices of scale available for a test score and relates these to the scaling of the attribute and of the error of measurement and its variance. The following section deals with the estimation of a true score and the error of estimate. Then a section treats the problem of estimating relationships between true scores on two or more tests—"attenuation" problems. A final section deals with error in the measurement of differences.

TEST LENGTH AND RELIABILITY

Commonly in test development a set of items is given to a sample of examinees in an initial try-out study—a calibration or generalizability study. It is expected that a subset of items will be chosen for future applications. The number of items kept should be small enough to be conveniently administered in routine uses of the test, and large enough to be acceptably reliable. Clearly these considerations are in conflict. If the items give a quantitatively scored response, we are fully justified in fitting the Spearman model to the item covariance matrix, to evaluate the items in terms of their loadings and unique variances. If they are binary, we can still do this, as shown in Chapter 6, and expect to get, in most cases, a reasonable approximation to the average error behavior of these items (but see Chap. 13). If the number of items is so large that available software does not allow fitting the factor model, it is large enough to allow using classical item analysis methods to obtain approximate factor loadings (Chap. 11).

From the estimated parameters of the full set of m items, we can compute the reliability coefficient of the mean or total test score, using coefficient omega (6.20). We can also use the item parameters to calculate the reliability of any subset of r items chosen out of the m. We simply apply the formula for omega to the parameters of the chosen subset. However, it would take a lot of arithmetic to compute omega for all possible subsets of r out of m items.

As a somewhat miniaturized example (which does not exhibit the size of the arithmetic problem in larger data sets), we might consider choosing, say, four out of the five SWLS items whose properties have been examined in Chapter 6. Table 7.1 repeats their loadings and unique variances, then lists the resulting sums of loadings and sums of unique variances, and the resulting reliabilities when each item in turn is omitted to yield a four-item test. The last column contains the ratio of the square of the loading to the unique variance for each of the items. It is shown in Chapter 13 that this ratio is a measure of the amount of *information* about the attribute given by each item. The larger this information measure, the greater is the extent to which the item reduces the error of measurement of the attribute (when a good scoring method is used). The reader can accept that a satisfactory criterion for deleting items is to omit those with the smallest information measure—the smallest ratio of squared loading to unique variance. Conversely, we keep those with the largest information measures.

· From Table 7.1 we see that the items can be put in the order 1 3 2 5 4 from largest to smallest amount of information, and from most to least loss of reliability when the item is omitted to give a test of four items. Therefore it is best to omit item 4. Further calculation shows that omitting items 4 and 5, the two with the smallest information measure, gives an omega from three items of .790, whereas omitting items 1 and 3, the two with the largest information measure, gives an omega of .674.

In an application on a larger scale it is still easy to rank order the items in terms of their information measure and to choose the r of them with

TABLE 7.1
Omitting Items—SWLS

Item	λ_j	ψ_j	$\Sigma_{(j)}\lambda_j$	$\Sigma_{(j)}\psi_j^2$	ω	λ_j^2/ψ_j^2
1	1.290	.901	4.389	6.232	.756	1.847
2	1.104	1.274	4.575	5.859	.781	.957
3	1.148	1.144	4.531	5.989	.774	1.152
4	.952	1.863	4.727	5.270	.809	.486
5	1.185	1.951	4.494	5.182	.796	.720

Note. $\Sigma_{(j)}$ denotes summation with item j omitted.

the largest values of it. Without such a criterion for selection it might be necessary to calculate omega for every selection of r out of m items. This can be a very large number of omegas.

Although we may decide beforehand to keep a given number r of items, and accordingly choose the set with the smallest loss in reliability, we might instead set a criterion for the minimum acceptable reliability, and determine the number of items we need to keep. Again it helps to have the item loadings and unique variances. Once we rank order the items by their information measure, this dictates the sequence in which they would be considered for omission. It is easy to calculate the reliabilities as 1, 2, 3, . . . , items are omitted, until we reach the lowest reliability we are willing to tolerate for our purposes.

In the SWLS example, from Table 7.1 we see that (a) omitting item 4 yields $\omega = .809$, (b) omitting 4 and 5 yields $\omega = .790$, and (c) omitting 4, 5, and 2 yields $\omega = .744$. If we have set a criterion of .75 or better, we will keep items 1, 2, and 3. Of course, we may not wish to proceed mechanically in this way. Items 1, 2, and 3 appear to measure satisfaction with the present, whereas items 4 and 5 appear to measure satisfaction with the past. We might prefer to keep item 5, the better of the last two, and omit item 2, the worst of the first three, to keep the scale representative of the general concept. But the important point is that it is not necessary to compute omega for all 10 combinations of three items out of five. If we have 100 trial items and wish to make a practical test of about 20, the convenience of choosing best items by their information measures is clear when we notice that there are $_{100}C_{20} = 5.359833704 \times 10^{20}$ ways to choose 20 items from 100.

If the set of m items in the initial calibration/generalizability try-out fits the true-score equivalence model, the method for choosing a subset remains essentially the same, in spite of one simplification. In this model the squared loading—true-score variance—is a constant over the m items. So it is only the unique variance—the denominator in the information measure—that causes the measure to vary. The items with the largest unique variance give least information, and least reduction in reliability when omitted, as we would have expected intuitively.

Table 7.2 shows the computation of omega for the SWLS data, on omitting each item in turn to make a four-item test, when we accept the true-score equivalence model. We recall that the common squared loading, that is, true-score variance, was estimated as 1.287, and the unique variances are again listed in the table. In this approximating model, item 5 rather than item 4 gives the smallest loss in reliability, corresponding to its large unique variance. This is because the true-score equivalence model fails to take account of the smaller sensitivity of item 4 to the attribute.

In the parallel items model, all items are supposed to have the same loadings and the same unique variances, so they have the same information

TABLE 7.2
Computation of Omega—SWLS

Item	ψ_j	$\Sigma_{(j)}\psi_j^2$	ω
1	1.279	5.932	.776
2	1.206	6.005	.774
3	1.175	6.036	.773
4	1.482	5.729	.782
5	2.069	5.142	.800

measure. In such a case, it would not matter which items we omit, but only how many of them. In the SWLS example, we obtained estimates 1.287 for true-score variance, and 1.442 for the shared unique variance of the items. Omitting 0, 1, 2, 3, and 4 items respectively gives

$$\omega_5 = 5 \times 1.287/(5 \times 1.287 + 1.442) = .817$$
$$\omega_4 = 4 \times 1.287/(4 \times 1.287 + 1.442) = .781$$
$$\omega_3 = 3 \times 1.287/(3 \times 1.287 + 1.442) = .728$$
$$\omega_2 = 2 \times 1.287/(2 \times 1.287 + 1.442) = .641$$
$$\omega_1 = 1.287/(1.287 + 1.442) = .472$$

for the resulting tests.

The task of "prophesying" in the opposite direction to the one considered so far is much more conjectural. Given m items—perhaps not many—in a try-out study, we may be dissatisfied with the obtained reliability, and we might wish to determine how many additional items would be needed to get a specified reliability. In our SWLS example, we have $\omega = .819$ under the Spearman homogeneity model. We might wish to ask: (a) What will the reliability be if we add enough more items to make r of them? (b) How many items will make a reliability of, say, .90?

Under the rather strict assumption that the r items are parallel, each has factor loading λ^2 and unique variance ψ^2, so the reliability of any one item is

$$\rho_1 = \lambda^2/(\lambda^2 + \psi^2). \qquad (7.1)$$

(The assumption includes the m items already tested, and might already have proved false.) Then the reliability of the projected test of r items is given by the Spearman–Brown prophecy formula,

$$\rho_r = r\rho_1/[(r - 1)\rho_1 + 1]. \qquad (7.2)$$

However, we do not have to make this very strong assumption. It is enough to suppose that the additional $r - m$ items have the same average factor loading $\lambda_\bullet$ and same average unique variance $\psi_\bullet$ as the given m items. We can define an average item reliability by

$$\rho_1' = (\lambda_\bullet)^2 / [(\lambda_\bullet)^2 + \psi^2_\bullet]. \tag{7.3}$$

Then the reliability of a test of r items is again given by (7.2). Corresponding estimates are given by substituting the sample estimates of the loadings and unique variances of the m items from the trial sample.

In our SWLS example we have $\omega = .819$, and the average item reliability is estimated as .472. Assuming we can find 5 more items with the same average loadings and average unique variances, we project the reliability of the resulting 10-item test, by (7.2), as

$$\rho_{10} = 10 \times .472/(9 \times .472 + 1) = .899.$$

Alternatively, we project the total number of items that will give a specified reliability. Given the average item reliability by (7.3), and the required reliability of the lengthened test, ρ_r, say, we solve (7.2) to give

$$r = [\rho_r/(1 - \rho_r)]/[\rho_1/(1 - \rho_1)], \tag{7.4}$$

or, given the reliability of the m-item test,

$$r/m = [\rho_r/(1 - \rho_r)]/[\rho_m/(1 - \rho_m)]. \tag{7.5}$$

In the SWLS example, suppose the required reliability is .90. We have .472 for the average item reliability and .819 for the reliability of the five items. Then (7.4) gives

$$r = (.9/.1)/(.472/.528) = 10.06,$$

and (7.5) gives

$$r/5 = (.9/.1)/(.819/.181) = 1.989 \qquad r = 9.94.$$

Both answers suggest that a test of 10 items will reach a reliability of .90. The slight difference is due to rounding error.

It is intuitively obvious that the larger the number of items in the given set and the number to be added, the more reasonable the assumption about their average behavior becomes—provided that the given and the added items are representatively drawn from the item domain. In applications, however, it can easily happen that the items with the largest information measure—the "best" items—are written first, and it is difficult to augment the set with items of similar quality. Then the projected reliability of the lengthened test will be overestimated, and the number of additional items needed will be underestimated. Because these formulas are just being used as a guide, and the truth will be known in due course, this may not be a very serious problem.

SCALE AND RELIABILITY

In Chapter 3 we saw that the score on a test can be scaled in a number of ways. First, the simple sum of the m items gives the *total test score*. This is commonly referred to just as the *test score* or as the *observed test score*. If the items are binary, it is the number of keyed responses—the *number-keyed score*. If they are also cognitive items, it is the *number-right score*. Second, the mean of the item scores is the *relative score* or *relative observed score*,

$$M = (1/m) \sum_j X_j.$$

If the items are binary, this is the proportion of keyed responses, so it must lie between zero and unity. If they are also cognitive items, it is the *proportion right score*. Third, the test score can be standardized in the population of interest, to give

$$Z = (Y - \mu_y)/\sigma_y,$$

where μ_y and σ_y are the population mean and standard deviation. In practice the sample mean and standard deviation are substituted, preferably from a large random sample. Fourth, the standardized test score can be further rescaled to have some prescribed mean and standard deviation. Examples include the deviation IQ,

$$DIQ = 15Z + 100,$$

with constants chosen to match the classical age-scale based

$$IQ = 100[(\text{mental age})/(\text{chronological age})]$$

and scores such as "T-scores,"

$$S = 10Z + 50$$

or such as

$$S = 100Z + 500.$$

These last two are intended to avoid negative values. (Here I have used S, a general notation for a score based on a formula, in both of the last expressions. These are just two arbitrary choices of origin and unit, among many possible.) Both the standardized scores and their further transformations could be normalized in the population of interest, if a sufficiently large sample is available.

For any rescaling of Y there will be a corresponding rescaling of the true and error parts. From

$$Y = T + E$$

with variance decomposition

$$\sigma_Y^2 = \sigma_T^2 + \sigma_E^2$$

we get

$$M = T_m + E_m \tag{7.6}$$

with variance decomposition

$$\sigma_M^2 = \sigma_{Tm}^2 + \sigma_{Em}^2 \tag{7.7}$$

where

$$\sigma_M^2 = (1/m^2)\sigma_Y^2, \qquad \sigma_{Tm}^2 = (1/m^2)\sigma_T^2, \qquad \sigma_{Em}^2 = (1/m^2)\sigma_E^2 \tag{7.8}$$

or

$$Z = T_Z + E_Z \tag{7.9}$$

with variance decomposition

$$\sigma_Z^2 = \sigma_{Tz}^2 + \sigma_{Ez}^2 \tag{7.10}$$

where

$$\sigma_Z^2 = 1, \qquad \sigma_{Tz}^2 = \rho_r, \qquad \sigma_{Ez}^2 = 1 - \rho_r. \qquad (7.11)$$

As indicated in Chapter 5, and illustrated by the two "populations" of Table 5.1, we use (5.13), written as

$$\sigma_E^2 = \sigma_Y^2(1 - \rho_r) \qquad (7.12)$$

to get the error variance from the observed variance in a population of interest, and the reliability coefficient in that population. If two reliability studies are carried out in two distinct populations—for example, unselected adults versus college students—in general the true-score variance will be an incidental property of the population sampled and so also will be the total variance and the reliability coefficient. The wider the range of the attribute in the population, the larger the reliability coefficient is. This might tempt one to say, very loosely, the wider the range, the more "reliable" the test is, although its error variance is unchanged. Some writers avoid the consequences of this fact by speaking of the reliability coefficient as a joint property of the test and of the population of interest. The view can also be found that because the reliability coefficient is independent of scale it is a more intelligible index of the precision of measurement of the test than its error variance. The position taken here is that the true-score variance is an accident of the populations of interest, whereas the error variance, under the classical linear model, can be expected to be invariant across populations. This does require one of two conditions: (a) The test is scored without reference to the mean and variance of the population sampled, or (b) if the test score is normed—a standardized, a DIQ, or a "T" score, for example—this is done on just one recognized norming population, preferably demographically well defined. In the latter case, the reliability coefficient can possess the property that some have desired for it, and can actually be a dimensionless measure of precision. For the rest of this chapter, the work uses Y for the observed score, allowing applicability to any of the four forms just given. Any relativity to population norms should be to one agreed population of interest.

ESTIMATING AND BOUNDING A TRUE SCORE

Consider again the simple model

$$Y = T + E,$$

with E a random variable independent of T. Here Y is the test score of a randomly drawn examinee, divided into true and error parts. If we consider one individual i, we write the model as

$$Y_i = t_i + E_i, \tag{7.13}$$

where t_i is the individual's (fixed) true score, and E_i is random, with mean zero. Then the expected value—the mean—of Y_i is t_i. That is, Y_i is an unbiased estimate of t_i. A problem with the statement just made is how to define the randomness of the individual error term E_i for a fixed individual. The error term has sometimes been described as having a *propensity distribution*, corresponding to quasi-random fluctuations over time within the individual—fluctuations of mood, motivation, memory function, and so on—in short, of propensity to respond. (*Propensity* means natural inclination.) The notion of a propensity distribution might possibly be appropriate for retest reliability, especially as idealized in the coefficient of precision, but it is subject to all the limitations discussed earlier.

We rewrite the model for homogeneous items as

$$Y_i = [\sum_j \mu_j + (\sum_j \lambda_j)f_i] + [\sum_j E_{ji}] \tag{7.14}$$
$$= c_i + U_i$$
$$= t_i + E_i,$$

with a fixed examinee. It is plausible to suppose that the true score of examinee i is an attribute score, conceived as a domain score on an indefinitely large set of items of which the m given items are a subset. Essentially, the "randomness" of the respondent's unique part U_i is the sum of independent unsystematic responses to the idiosyncratic properties of the m items in the given subtest.

Under the assumption that the variance of E_i is the same for all examinees, examinee i's observed score is the unbiased estimate of that person's true score, that is,

$$\hat{t}_i = y_i, \tag{7.15}$$

and it has error variance given by

$$\sigma_E^2 = \sum_j \psi_j^2. \tag{7.16}$$

Because $E_i = \Sigma E_{ji}$, a sum of m independent random components, the distribution of E_i should approach normality for m sufficiently large.

***Here the distribution is over subsets of items, and the limiting distribution referred to is approached as the number of items becomes large. The central limit theorem is a fundamental result in statistical theory that justifies this statement. $$$

We can use percentage points from the standard normal distribution to write confidence limits/bounds on t_i. Thus we can say that with 95% probability the bounds

$$y_i + 1.96\sigma_E$$

and

$$y_i - 1.96\sigma_E$$

contain t_i.

The example from Table 6.3 gave an estimate of omega equal to .817 and a total variance of 39.382. From these quantities we get an estimated error variance of $(1 - .817) \times 39.382 = 7.206$. Then we obtain an estimated *SE* of measurement as the square root of 7.206, namely, 2.684. This yields the 95% confidence bounds on an examinee's score,

$$y + 1.96 \times 2.684 = y + 5.261$$

and

$$y - 1.96 \times 2.684 = y - 5.261.$$

Thus if an examinee gives item scores 4, 4, 4, 4, 4, and so a total score of 20, the confidence bounds are 25.261 and 14.739. Substituting a mean score simply requires dividing the score and the bounds by 5, to give, in this case, 5.05 and 2.94. Thus the examinee's modal response to the five items lies between "slightly agree" as coded and "slightly disagree" as coded, with probability 95%. Note the special usefulness of the mean score in this respect, in giving a direct meaning to the score and the confidence bounds.

The range of the test puts a restriction on the use of confidence bounds based on the normal distribution, of course. We cannot apply the upper or lower confidence limits to an examinee with an extreme high or low score—and certainly not to the "perfect" scores corresponding to 0 or m.

Clearly the distribution of errors will become skewed as these extremes are approached.

***Optional note: It may be shown that if the m items are parallel, the observed score is the best possible estimate of the true score of examinee i, in the sense of least squares. If each of the E_j is normally distributed, Y_i is also the maximum likelihood estimate of t_i. That is, $\hat{t}_i = y_i$ makes the m observed item scores of the ith examinee, $x_{1i}, \ldots, x_{mi}$, maximally probable. If the m items are homogeneous, but not parallel, better estimates (in the sense of least squares and maximum likelihood) are given by

$$\hat{t}_i = [1/\sum_j \{(\lambda_j^2/\psi_j^2)\}] \sum_j [(\lambda_j/\psi_j^2)(x_{ji} - \mu_j)] + \sum_j \mu_j \qquad (7.17)$$

with error variance

$$\sigma_E^2 = 1/\sum_j \{(\lambda_j^2/\psi_j^2)\}. \qquad (7.18)$$

(Note that this is the reciprocal of the sum of the information measures; see Chap. 13.) These expressions give more importance to items with large loadings and small uniquenesses. If the items are true-score equivalent, these best linear unbiased estimates are given by

$$\hat{t}_i = [1/\{\sum_j (\sigma_T/\psi_j^2)\}] \sum_j [(1/\psi_j^2)(x_{ji} - \mu_j)] + \sum_j \mu_j \qquad (7.19)$$

with error variance

$$\sigma_E^2 = 1/[\sigma_T^2 \sum (1/\psi_j^2)]. \qquad (7.20)$$

$$$

The observed score seems a satisfactory estimate of a given examinee's true score for three reasons:

1. It is unbiased—the mean of Y_i over possible choices of items is the true score.
2. Because it is unbiased, the standard error of measurement can be used to put confidence bounds on the true score.

3. If the items are parallel it is a "best" estimate in the sense of least squares. That is, it makes the sum of squared errors of measurement as small as possible.

A biased *regression estimator* of the true score has been described that takes account of any population to which the examinee might be thought to belong. (Note that an examinee may belong to many populations "of interest.") It can be shown by standard methods that the regression estimate of T for a given value y of Y is given by

$$\hat{T} = \rho_r y + (1 - \rho_r)\mu_y. \tag{7.21}$$

This estimate is the mean true score of all those examinees in the population of interest whose observed score is y. By (7.21), $\hat{T}$ is a simple linear function of Y. Note that the mean of $\hat{T}$ in the population of interest is μ_y. If we express $\hat{T}$ as a deviation from the mean, that is,

$$\hat{T} - \mu_y = \rho_r(y - \mu_y), \tag{7.22}$$

then $\hat{T}$ in deviation form is just Y in deviation form multiplied by the reliability coefficient (which is necessarily less than unity). The regression estimate is a "shrunken" estimate, meaning that it always gives an estimate that lies between Y and the mean of Y in the population of interest. As the reliability approaches zero, the regression estimate shrinks back to the population mean.

From one point of view, $\hat{T}$ is just T in a new set of scale units. So for most purposes it has no advantage over the simple unbiased estimate—the test score itself. Both would order examinees in the same way, and we would prefer the unbiased estimate. However, if we were using an absolute test score criterion to select examinees from some population of interest, it would change the selection rate if we use a shrunken estimator of IQ instead of the unbiased estimator given by the test score itself. For example, we might want to select children with IQs below 80 (with mean 100, *SD* 15) for special class placement. On an error-free test (of infinite length) we would select out children with $T < 80$, but in the actual test errors of measurement must cause errors of selection, in either direction. If we use Y as the unbiased estimate of T, a child with $t = 80$ has an equal probability of being over or under the criterion due to "errors of measurement"—idiosyncratic features of the items. If we use $\hat{T}$ with, say, omega equal to .8, then

$$\hat{T} = .8 \times 80 + .2 \times 100 = 84.$$

The balance is shifted so that we are selecting fewer children for special treatment. The lower the reliability, the fewer we select. Whether this is desirable or not would depend on a cost/benefit analysis of the consequences of correct versus erroneous decisions.[1]

PROBLEMS OF ATTENUATION

Historically, one of the earliest applications of true-score theory and the reliability coefficient was to correcting effects of errors on correlations between different tests. We let Y, V be scores on two tests; T_Y, T_V their true parts; ρ_Y, ρ_V their reliability coefficients; ρ_{YV} the correlation between them; $\rho_{T_Y V}$ the correlation between T_Y and V; and $\rho_{T_Y T_V}$ the correlation between T_Y and T_V. It may be shown that

$$\rho_{YV} = \rho_{T_Y V} \sqrt{\rho_Y} \qquad (7.23)$$

and

$$\rho_{YV} = \rho_{T_Y T_V} \sqrt{\rho_Y \rho_V}. \qquad (7.24)$$

***Proof: By the algebra of expectations,

$$\sigma_{YV} = \text{Cov}\{T_Y + E_Y, \ T_V + E_V\}$$
$$= \sigma_{T_Y T_V},$$

with the assumptions of the model, and

$$\rho_{YV} = \sigma_{YV} / \sqrt{\sigma_Y^2 \sigma_V^2}.$$

The results follow on using

$$\sigma_Y^2 = \sigma_{T_Y}^2 / \rho_Y \text{ and } \sigma_V^2 = \sigma_{T_V}^2 / \rho_V. \quad \$\$\$$$

By (7.23), the observed correlation between Y and V is less than the correlation between the true score T_Y and the given test score V. By (7.24), the observed correlation is less than the correlation between the true scores of both—say, if they were extended to infinite length. These reductions of the correlation between two tests below what they might be if one or both were error free are known as *attenuation* of the correlations due to errors of measurement.

As early as 1904, Spearman proposed to use these expressions in reverse, to give *correction for attenuation* formulas,

$$\rho_{T_Y V} = \rho_{YV} / \sqrt{\rho_Y} \qquad (7.25)$$

and

$$\rho_{T_Y T_V} = \rho_{YV} / \sqrt{(\rho_Y \rho_V)}. \qquad (7.26)$$

In Spearman's earliest example, Y is a measure of pitch discrimination, and V is intelligence as rated by a teacher. The correlation between them is .38 and they have reliability coefficients respectively of .25 and .55. Then (a) the correlation between a perfectly error-free measure of pitch discrimination and intelligence as rated—that is, not corrected—is projected to be

$$\rho_{T_Y V} = .38 / \sqrt{.25} = .76,$$

and (b) the correlation between perfect measures of both is projected to be

$$\rho_{T_Y T_V} = .38 / \sqrt{.25 \times .55} = 1.03.$$

Spearman's own example illustrates a danger: Underestimates of reliability coefficients may overcorrect, and give a projected gain in correlation that is quite unattainable by any practical attempts to eliminate error. With care, (7.25) and (7.26) may be used for the purpose of such a projection. A safe procedure would require the following three important conditions:

1. An unbiased and appropriate estimate of reliability should be used. G-C alpha could be used instead of omega if the items are verified to be true-score equivalent and if the projected gain in correlation is to be based on lengthening the test(s). (Test–retest reliability would not be relevant to the correlation between lengthened tests.)
2. It is theoretically feasible to augment the sets of items with further items from the same conceptual domains.
3. Estimates of the reliability coefficients are obtained from the same sample that yields the correlation to be corrected, because such coefficients typically vary with the population sampled.

***Optional note: If condition 3 cannot be satisfied, and we are forced to use reliability coefficients from previous studies—perhaps two large norming studies of the tests—we can proceed if the published account of the previous study includes test variances—say, $\sigma^2_{Y(p)}, \sigma^2_{V(p)}$—as well as the reliability coefficients—say, $\rho_{Y(p)}, \rho_{V(p)}$. (The subscript p denotes previous.) To estimate the reliabilities in the present sample we first estimate the error variances from the previous study. These are

$$\sigma^2_{Ey} = \sigma^2_{Y(p)}(1 - \rho_{Y(p)}) \tag{7.27}$$

$$\sigma^2_{Ev} = \sigma^2_{V(p)}(1 - \rho_{V(p)}). \tag{7.28}$$

We then get ρ_Y, ρ_V in the present sample by reversing these relationships, and using

$$\rho_Y = (\sigma^2_Y - \sigma^2_{Ey})/\sigma_Y \tag{7.29}$$

and

$$\rho_V = (\sigma^2_V - \sigma^2_{Ev})/\sigma^2_V. \tag{7.30}$$

$$\$\$\$ \quad - \textit{another way of estimat'g reliability}$$

    Covariances do not require correction. The derivation of the correction formulas rests on the fact that the covariance between the true scores is equal to the observed covariance. (This can be seen from the optional proof just given.) In the regression equation of V on Y,

$$V = \alpha + \beta_Y Y + E, \tag{7.31}$$

the regression coefficient is not affected by errors in the dependent variable V, but it is attenuated by errors in the independent variable Y. The regression of V on the true-score component of Y is

$$V = \beta_T T_y + E + \alpha, \tag{7.32}$$

where

$$\beta_T = \beta_Y / \sqrt{\rho_Y}. \tag{7.33}$$

In path analysis with common factors, path coefficients are systematically subjected to a kind of correction for attenuation. They require the same cautious approach as recommended for simple corrections for attenuation, but do not always receive it (see Chap. 17).

ERROR IN DIFFERENCE SCORES

Suppose we have scores from a large sample of examinees on two tests, Y_1, Y_2, and we are interested in the effects of error on the difference in scores

$$D = Y_2 - Y_1. \tag{7.34}$$

Possibly Y_2 is a nonverbal IQ, and Y_1 is a verbal IQ. The difference, D, then defines a verbal deficit score. Possibly Y_1 and Y_2 are educational achievement measures before and after an intervention. Then Y_2 is either a replication of Y_1 or an alternate form.

In the standard decomposition of the test scores into true and error parts,

$$Y_1 = T_1 + E_1,$$
$$Y_2 = T_2 + E_2,$$

we assume that E_1, E_2 are uncorrelated with each other and, of course, with the true scores T_1, T_2. Then the true difference is

$$T_D = T_2 - T_1, \tag{7.35}$$

and the error of the difference is

$$E_D = E_2 - E_1. \tag{7.36}$$

Here T_1 and T_2 are generally correlated.

The important and immediate result is that the variances of the errors are additive, because they are uncorrelated. That is,

$$\sigma^2_{E_d} = \sigma^2_{E_2} + \sigma^2_{E_1}. \tag{7.37}$$

Note that the error variance of the difference is independent of the correlation between T_1 and T_2 or between Y_1 and Y_2.

In general, Y_1 and Y_2 are correlated. Certainly they should be if the same test is repeated, or if the second is an alternate form of the first. In cases such as the difference between nonverbal and verbal IQ, again they should be (positively) correlated, because they have IQ in common, and IQ is a concept at a higher level of abstraction than either its verbal or nonverbal forms. Therefore the variance of the difference

$$\sigma_D^2 = \sigma_{Y_1}^2 + \sigma_{Y_2}^2 - 2\rho_{Y_1 Y_2}\sigma_{Y_1}\sigma_{Y_2}. \tag{7.38}$$

For given variances $\sigma_{Y_1}^2$, $\sigma_{Y_2}^2$ of Y_1 and Y_2, the variance of the difference depends on the correlation $\rho_{Y_1 Y_2}$ between them. It is smallest when the correlation is perfect and positive, so

$$\sigma_D^2 = (\sigma_{Y_1} - \sigma_{Y_2})^2. \tag{7.39}$$

It is largest when it is perfect and negative, so

$$\sigma_D^2 = (\sigma_{Y_1} + \sigma_{Y_2})^2. \tag{7.40}$$

The difference score D has a reliability coefficient

$$\rho_D = (\sigma_D^2 - \sigma_{E_D}^2)/\sigma_D^2. \tag{7.41}$$

Suppose we are choosing among pairs of tests all with fixed variances $\sigma_{Y_1}^2$, $\sigma_{Y_2}^2$ and error variances $\sigma_{E_1}^2$, $\sigma_{E_2}^2$, but different pairs have different correlations $\rho_{Y_1 Y_2}$. The reliability coefficient varies with the correlation between Y_1 and Y_2. It is smallest when this is unity, and largest when it is negative unity.

*** It is easy to show that when the correlation is unity,

$$\rho_D = [(\sigma_{Y_1} - \sigma_{Y_2})^2 - \sigma_{E_D}^2]/(\sigma_{Y_1} - \sigma_{Y_2})^2, \tag{7.42}$$

and when it is negative unity,

$$\rho_D = [(\sigma_{Y_1} + \sigma_{Y_2})^2 - \sigma_{E_D}^2]/(\sigma_{Y_1} + \sigma_{Y_2})^2. \tag{7.43}$$

$$$

Suppose we have a choice between three pairs of tests, Y_1, Y_2, all with, say,

$$\sigma_{Y_1}^2 = 16 \qquad \sigma_{Y_2}^2 = 36$$

$$(\sigma_{Y_1} = 4) \qquad (\sigma_{Y_2} = 6),$$
$$\sigma_{E_1}^2 = 2 \qquad \sigma_{E_2}^2 = 2.$$

All three have reliabilities

$$\rho_{Y_1} = 14/16 = .875$$
$$\rho_{Y_2} = 34/36 = .944.$$

Suppose one pair is correlated unity, giving

$$\rho_D = [(4 - 6)^2 - 4]/(4 - 6)^2 = 0.$$

One pair is correlated zero, giving

$$\rho_D = (16 + 36 - 4)/(16 + 36) = 48/52 = .923.$$

One pair is correlated minus unity, giving

$$\rho_D = [(4 + 6)^2 - 4]/(4 + 6)^2 = 96/100 = .96.$$

All three, however, have as error variance for the difference score

$$\sigma_{E_D}^2 = 2 + 2 = 4$$

(2 and 2 still make 4!)

Which pair would we prefer to measure a difference? There is a common belief that to get reliable differences we should choose measures that are each highly reliable but have a low correlation with each other. The line of proof leading to this conclusion includes the assumption that the choice is made between alternative Y_1, Y_2 pairs having the same error variance $\sigma_{E_D}^2$ of their difference score. It is because this error variance is independent of their correlation that the reliability coefficient is not. One might describe the dependence of the reliability coefficient of the difference on the correlation between the tests as an artifact of the coefficient. The important criterion is the error variance of the difference, and it is free of artifacts.

However, the correlation between the test scores is important. If Y_1 and Y_2 come from alternate forms in a study of gain due to an intervention, the higher the (positive) correlation between Y_1 and Y_2, the more confident we can be that we are measuring change in one attribute, not a difference between two attributes. If Y_1 and Y_2 come from, say, verbal and nonverbal IQs, the justification for being interested in the difference includes the assertion that they share, at a more abstract level, IQ—that they are not measuring unrelated or opposed properties of the examinees. For the measurement of difference, change, or gain scores, we should choose two tests with low error variance and high positive correlation.

The basic fact is that the error variances of two scores yielding a difference are additive, so the standard error (SE) of measurement of the difference is given by

$$SE(D) = \sqrt{(\sigma_{E_1}^2 + \sigma_{E_2}^2)}. \tag{7.44}$$

In the preceding example, this is given by

$$SE(D) = \sqrt{2 + 2}$$

compared with separate SEs of 1.414. In applications, the SE of measurement of the difference, $SE(D)$ can be used to put confidence limits on an individual's true difference, gain, or change score. This presents no problems.

REVIEW GUIDE

Table 7.1 should be studied as illustrating how to choose a subset of items having best reliability, given the parameters of the items in a fitted general factor model, and how to drop items until a minimum acceptable reliability is reached. The student should understand how to use the Spearman–Brown formula (7.2) as a guide to the number of items needed to reach a specified reliability. Note the necessary assumption for this.

The student needs to take the general idea of the effect of a change of scale units on total, true, and error variance, and to recognize that the reliability coefficient varies over the populations studied, whereas in general the variance of the errors does not.

The student should also be able to use (7.16) for error variance, and the material following this to compute confidence limits/bounds on a true score, estimated by the observed score. Note the problem caused by observed scores at or near the floor or ceiling of the test.

In reviewing further, it is desirable that the student should be able to use (7.25) and (7.26) to correct for attenuation. It is equally important to know the listed conditions 1–3 under which it is reasonable and safe to compute such corrections.

The central point of the final section is that the error variance of the difference between two scores is the sum of their error variances. Claims in the literature about desirable conditions for reliable differences seem to be misguided. In applications, the student should be able to compute the error variance of a difference score and obtain confidence bounds for a difference.

END NOTES

General: Lord and Novick (1968) is the primary source for the material in this chapter.

1. There is a large and technical literature on problems of selection, including problems due to measurement error. One source is Cole and Moss (1989).

Prediction and
Multiple Regression

Scores on a single test, or its item or subtest scores, or scores on a battery of tests, may be used to predict some further performance that is external to the predictor variables. The measure to be predicted might be a supervisor's rating of performance in a specific form of employment, and this could require a complex combination of aptitudes. Or items, subtests, or tests might be assembled to predict performance in undergraduate or graduate study, and students could be selected for it on the basis of their profile of predictive scores. Differential weight can be given to the scores used, to achieve optimal prediction. Tests, subtests, or items can be eliminated from an initial set when the evidence shows that they are not contributing enough to prediction.

These considerations motivate a review of multiple regression, regarded here as a way to use one or more test scores as predictors of a further variable—the *criterion*. The reader should already be familiar with the concept of regression. In the usual textbook accounts, the *independent, explanatory* variables are thought of as having their values nonrandom, under experimental control, so that only the *dependent* variable—the *response* or *outcome* variable—is random. Most of that theory carries over to the case of test scores as random predictor variables, but it is appropriate to make a fresh start and to develop the concepts a little differently. The next section reviews the regression model for a bivariate distribution, followed by a section that extends the theory to multiple regression. Subsequent sections give some specific results on estimation from samples, treat the selection of predictor variables, and give some results on partial covariance and partial correlation. A final section gives an empirical example.

BIVARIATE REGRESSION

First we consider the case of a single independent variable—a score on a single test X—which is to be used to predict a criterion variable Y. For example, X might be a score on a scholastic aptitude test, and Y a grade point average.

Suppose for the present that we know the means μ_X, μ_Y, the variances σ_X^2, σ_Y^2, and the covariance σ_{XY} of X and Y in the population. The main results of this and the next section have close analogues for a large sample of observations, and there is no great harm in thinking of them as results on samples.

We assume that the regression is linear, that is, the mean (expected value) $\hat{Y}$ for a given value x of X is given by

$$\hat{Y} = \alpha + \beta x. \tag{8.1}$$

(This assumption would follow from the assumption that the two variables have a joint normal distribution.)

The *regression coefficient* β is the expected change in Y corresponding to a unit change in X. The *regression constant* α is the intercept—the point where the graph of the function crosses the Y axis. From (8.1) we obtain the model

$$Y = \alpha + \beta X + E, \tag{8.2}$$

where E, the error of prediction of Y given X, is uncorrelated with X. We refer to E as the *residual*—literally a remainder, or unexplained residue.

***The proof that X and E are uncorrelated uses the construction:

$$\mathcal{E}\{Y|X = x\} = \alpha + \beta x,$$
$$E \equiv Y - \mathcal{E}\{Y|X = x\}$$
$$\mathcal{E}\{E\} = 0$$
$$Y = \alpha + \beta x + E \quad \text{for all } x,$$
$$\Rightarrow Y = \alpha + \beta X + E$$

with

$$\text{Cov}\{X,E\} = 0. \quad \$\$\$$$

It is convenient to rearrange the model (8.2) in deviation form, by writing

$$(Y - \mu_Y) = \beta(X - \mu_X) + E. \tag{8.3}$$

The *regression coefficient*

$$\beta = \sigma_{YX}/\sigma_X^2 \tag{8.4}$$

and the *regression constant*—the *intercept*—is

$$\alpha = \mu_Y - (\sigma_{YX}/\sigma_X^2)\mu_X. \tag{8.5}$$

***Using the fact that X and E are uncorrelated gives, from (8.2),

$$\sigma_{YX} = \beta\sigma_X^2,$$

because $\mathcal{E}\{(Y - \mu_Y)(X - \mu_X)\} = \beta\mathcal{E}\{(X - \mu_X)^2\}$.
Then from (8.3) we have

$$\alpha = \mu_Y - \beta\mu_X,$$

which gives (8.5). $\$\$\$$

The expressions (8.4) and (8.5) give the regression coefficient β and the regression constant α in terms of the means, the variances, and the covariance of X and Y.

Also, because X and E are uncorrelated,

$$\sigma_Y^2 = \beta^2\sigma_X^2 + \sigma_E^2, \tag{8.6}$$

or

$$\sigma_Y^2 = \sigma_{\hat{Y}}^2 + \sigma_E^2. \tag{8.7}$$

That is, the variance of Y is partitioned into a part due to variation in X—predictable from and explained by X—namely,

$$\sigma_{\hat{Y}}^2 = \beta^2\sigma_X^2 = \sigma_{XY}^2/\sigma_X^2, \tag{8.8}$$

and a *residual variance* σ_E^2, not due to X. The residual variance σ_E^2 is the variance of the error of prediction—the part of the variance of Y that is not explained by the variability of X. Notice also that the ratio of explained variance to the total variance of Y

$$\sigma_{\hat{Y}}^2/\sigma_Y^2 = \beta^2\sigma_X^2/\sigma_Y^2$$
$$= \sigma_{YX}^2/(\sigma_X^2\sigma_Y^2)$$
$$= \rho_{XY}^2. \qquad (8.9)$$

That is, the proportion of variance of Y predictable from X is just the square of the correlation ρ_{XY}^2. The proportion of variance of Y not predictable from X is

$$\sigma_E^2/\sigma_Y^2 = 1 - \rho_{XY}^2. \qquad (8.10)$$

***Optional note: The reader may be familiar with the regression function as a line of least squares best fit in a sample. The least squares property has a population analogue, namely

$$\sigma_E^2 \le \sigma_{(Y-Y*)}^2, \qquad (8.11)$$

the variance of the difference between Y and Y^*, where here Y^* represents any linear function

$$Y^* = \gamma X + \delta, \qquad (8.12)$$

other than (8.2) with α,β, given by (8.4) and (8.5). $$$

As a numerical example, suppose that X is a number-right score on a test of aptitude for undergraduate study, with mean $\mu_X = 50$, variance $\sigma_X^2 = 25$, and Y is a grade-point average in first year, with mean $\mu_Y = 3.0$ and variance $\sigma_Y^2 = .64$, and suppose $\sigma_{XY} = 3.5$. Then

$$\beta = 3.5/25 = .14, \qquad \alpha = 3 - .14 \times 50 = -4,$$

so

$$\hat{Y} = .14x - 4.$$

Also,

$$\sigma_{\hat{Y}}^2 = .14^2 \times 25 = .49,$$
$$\sigma_E^2 = .64 - .49 = .15,$$

and

$$\rho_{XY}^2 = .49/.64 = .766,$$

so

$$\rho_{XY} = \sqrt{.766} = .875,$$

and

$$\sigma_E^2/\sigma_Y^2 = 1 - .766 = .234.$$

Of these quantities, the most readily understandable are (a) the familiar correlation coefficient, (b) its square, which is the proportion of variance of Y determined by X, and (c) the complementary proportion of unpredictable variance. If the test score units are understandable, the gain of .14 units of grade-point average for an increase of one number-right score may be of interest, but this is generally not the case. If X were dollar expenditure per student, instead of a test score (with schools as the sampling unit, not students), we could interpret gain in performance per dollar spent, in their natural units. But mostly we cannot find this kind of interpretation.

If we rescale X and Y to be standard scores, $Z_X = (X - \mu_X)/\sigma_X$, $Z_Y = (Y - \mu_Y)/\sigma_Y$, in the population, the regression line (8.2) becomes

$$\hat{Z} = \rho_{XY}Z_X. \tag{8.13}$$

This *standardized regression coefficient* is just the correlation. It measures the (fractional) number of *SD*s by which Y changes for one *SD* change in X. Sometimes this is thought to solve the problem of interpretation, by supplying understandable and comparable units.

MULTIPLE REGRESSION

The reader will recall the basic task in school algebra of finding the solution of a set of simultaneous linear equations. A simple example is

$$2x + y = 3$$
$$4x - 4y = 7.$$

Multiple regression refers to the regression of a dependent variable on two or more independent variables. Its mathematics rests on nothing more technical than solving simultaneous equations. But when the number of equations is large it becomes too tedious, and it is best left to a computer program. The student can get a sufficient understanding of the general problem from the case of just two predictor variables, and a few more general considerations.

Suppose we have three variables, and two of them—the independent variables X_1, X_2—are test scores to be used to get predicted values of the third—the *criterion* variable Y. Suppose, again, the population values are known. We set them out as follows:

Covariance matrix

	Mean	X_1	X_2	Y
X_1	μ_1	σ_{11}	σ_{12}	σ_{1Y}
X_2	μ_2	σ_{21}	σ_{22}	σ_{2Y}
Y	μ_Y	σ_{Y1}	σ_{Y2}	σ_{YY}

(Here we use σ_{11}, etc., not σ_1^2, etc., for variance.)

An example would be:

Covariance matrix

	Mean	X_1	X_2	Y
X_1	10.0	9.0	3.6	1.8
X_2	8.0	3.6	4.0	1.2
Y	3.0	1.8	1.2	1.44

This example is artificial, but for concreteness imagine that Y is a grade-point average, on a scale of 1 to 5, and X_1 and X_2 are measures of verbal and mathematical ability, respectively.

As in the simple bivariate case, we write

$$\hat{Y} = \alpha + \beta_{Y_1} x_1 + \beta_{Y_2} x_2 \tag{8.14}$$

for the mean (expected) value $\hat{Y}$ of Y in a subpopulation of examinees for whom $X_1 = x_1$, and $X_2 = x_2$. Again we are assuming a linear model, which would be implied by the assumption that X_1, X_2, and Y are jointly normally distributed. Defining a residual or error-of-prediction E by

$$E = Y - \hat{Y},$$

gives the multiple-regression model in the form

$$Y = \hat{Y} + E. \tag{8.15}$$

That is,

$$Y = \alpha + \beta_{Y_1} X_1 + \beta_{Y_2} X_2 + E. \tag{8.16}$$

It can be shown that E is uncorrelated with X_1 and with X_2. But in general X_1 and X_2 are correlated, possibly highly correlated, with each other.

Again it is convenient to write the model in deviation form as

$$Y - \mu_Y = \beta_{Y_1}(X_1 - \mu_1) + \beta_{Y_2}(X_2 - \mu_2) + E. \tag{8.17}$$

Then in (8.16)

$$\alpha = \mu_Y - (\beta_{Y_1}\mu_1 + \beta_{Y_2}\mu_2). \tag{8.18}$$

Using the fact that E is uncorrelated with X_1 and with X_2 gives us

$$\sigma_{11}\beta_{Y_1} + \sigma_{12}\beta_{Y_2} = \sigma_{Y_1} \tag{8.19a}$$

and

$$\sigma_{21}\beta_{Y_1} + \sigma_{22}\beta_{Y_2} = \sigma_{Y_2}. \tag{8.19b}$$

Here we have two simultaneous equations in unknown βs and known variances and covariances. In the example, (8.19) gives

$$9\beta_{Y_1} + 3.6\beta_{Y_2} = 1.8 \tag{a}$$

$$3.6\beta_{Y_1} + 4\beta_{Y_2} = 1.2. \tag{b}$$

One way to solve these is as follows:

$$\text{Dividing (a) by } 3.6 \Rightarrow 2.5\beta_{Y_1} + \beta_{Y_2} = .5 \tag{a'}$$

$$\text{Dividing (b) by } 4 \Rightarrow .9\beta_{Y_1} + \beta_{Y_2} = .3. \tag{b'}$$

$$(\text{a}') - (\text{b}') \Rightarrow 1.6\beta_{Y_1} = .2 \Rightarrow \beta_{Y_1} = .125.$$

[Here we could back-substitute the value of β_{Y_1} into (a') or (b'), but instead we proceed as follows:]

$$\text{Dividing (a) by } 9 \Rightarrow \beta_{Y_1} + .4\beta_{Y_2} = .2 \tag{a''}$$

$$\text{Dividing (b) by } 3.6 \Rightarrow \beta_{Y_1} + 1.1111\beta_{Y_2} = .3333 \tag{b''}$$

$$(a'') - (b'') \Rightarrow -.71111\beta_{Y_2} = -.1333 \Rightarrow \beta_{Y_2} = .1875.$$

Then finally

$$\alpha = 3.0 - (.125 \times 10 + .1875 \times 8) = .25.$$

In the numerical example, with the evaluated coefficients, the regression equation is

$$Y = .25 + .125X_1 + .1875X_2 + E.$$

The basic operations of a computer program for multiple regression are the equivalent of these elementary operations. They may have to be carried out on a much larger scale, according to the number of independent variables. There is improved efficiency possible by using the symmetry of the covariance matrix—$\sigma_{21} = \sigma_{12}$ and so on. (It is also possible to use a very general-purpose program for path analysis, of which multiple regression is just a special case; see Chap. 17.)

We can take the algebra through from (8.19a) and (8.19b), in the same way as in the numerical example, to show how the work goes.

***Optional demonstration: Dividing (8.19a) by $\sigma_{12} \Rightarrow$

$$(\sigma_{11}/\sigma_{12})\beta_{Y_1} + \beta_{Y_2} = (\sigma_{Y_1}/\sigma_{12}). \tag{8.19a'}$$

Dividing (8.19b) by $\sigma_{22} \Rightarrow$

$$(\sigma_{21}/\sigma_{22})\beta_{Y_1} + \beta_{Y_2} = (\sigma_{Y_2}/\sigma_{22}). \tag{8.19b'}$$

$(8.21a') - (8.21b') \Rightarrow$
$$\beta_{Y_1}[(\sigma_{11}/\sigma_{12}) - (\sigma_{21}/\sigma_{22})] = [\sigma_{Y_1}/\sigma_{12} - (\sigma_{Y_2}/\sigma_{22})] \Rightarrow$$
$$\beta_{Y_1} = [(\sigma_{Y_1}/\sigma_{12}) - (\sigma_{Y_2}/\sigma_{22})]/[(\sigma_{11}/\sigma_{12}) - (\sigma_{21}/\sigma_{22})] \quad \$\$\$$$

This gives

$$\beta_{Y_1} = (\sigma_{22}\sigma_{Y_1} - \sigma_{12}\sigma_{Y_2})/(\sigma_{11}\sigma_{22} - \sigma_{12}\sigma_{21}) \tag{8.20a}$$

and similarly

$$\beta_{Y_2} = (\sigma_{21}\sigma_{Y_1} - \sigma_{11}\sigma_{Y_2})/(\sigma_{11}\sigma_{22} - \sigma_{12}\sigma_{21}). \tag{8.20b}$$

Thus, we have expressions for β_{Y_1} and β_{Y_2} in terms of the variances and covariances, and can then use these to obtain α from (8.18). The student can use these to check the solution to our example. The numerical procedure in the example generalizes to three or more independent variables, and can be described as an algorithm—a computing sequence—that can be written into a computer program. The more general algebraic expressions corresponding to (8.20) become quite complicated very quickly, and are not used as direct solutions. $\$\$\$$

Because X_1 and X_2 are both uncorrelated with E, $\hat{Y}$ in (8.15) is uncorrelated with E, so the variance of Y decomposes into two additive parts. That is,

$$\sigma_{YY} = \sigma_{\hat{Y}\hat{Y}} + \sigma_{EE}. \tag{8.21}$$

The proportion of variance of Y due to/predictable from/explained by X_1 and X_2 jointly is known as the *squared multiple correlation*. The covariance of Y with $\hat{Y}$ is also the variance of $\hat{Y}$, that is,

$$\sigma_{Y\hat{Y}} = \sigma_{\hat{Y}\hat{Y}} \tag{8.22}$$

(or $\sigma_{Y\hat{Y}} = \sigma_{\hat{Y}}^2$—in the alternative notation).

The squared multiple correlation is also the square of the correlation between actual Y and predicted $\hat{Y}$. In one notation it is symbolized by $\rho_{Y\hat{Y}}^2$. In another common notation, we represent it by

$$\rho_{Y \cdot X_1 X_2}^2 = \sigma_{Y\hat{Y}}/\sigma_{YY}. \tag{8.23}$$

In this notation, the independent variables are listed, separated by a dot from the dependent variable. The ratio of the residual variance to the total variance of Y,

$$\sigma_{EE}/\sigma_{YY} = 1 - \rho_{Y\hat{Y}}^2 \tag{8.24}$$

(or σ_E^2/σ_Y^2 in the alternative notation), is the proportion of variance of Y that is not due to the independent variables.

One expression for the variance of Y due to the independent variables is

$$\sigma_{\hat{Y}\hat{Y}} = \sigma_{Y\hat{Y}} = \beta_{Y_1}\sigma_{Y_1} + \beta_{Y_2}\sigma_{Y_2}. \tag{8.25}$$

This expression uses the regression coefficients, together with the *cross*-covariances between Y and the independent variables.

Another is

$$\sigma_{\hat{Y}\hat{Y}} = \beta_{Y_1}^2\sigma_{11} + 2\beta_{Y_1}\beta_{Y_2}\sigma_{12} + \beta_{Y_2}^2\sigma_{22}. \tag{8.26}$$

This version uses the regression coefficients together with the variances and covariances of the independent variables.

***By expectations, the first is from

$$\mathcal{E}\{[Y - \mu_Y][\beta_{Y_1}(X_1 - \mu_1) + \beta_{Y_2}(X_2 - \mu_2)]\},$$

whereas the second is from

$$\mathcal{E}\{[\beta_{Y_1}(X_1 - \mu_1) + \beta_{Y_2}(X_2 - \mu_2)]^2\}.$$

$$$

Using either of (8.25) or (8.26), with (8.23), we can compute the squared multiple correlation.

In the numerical example, using (8.25), we get

$$\sigma_{\hat{Y}\hat{Y}} = .125 \times 1.8 + .1875 \times 1.2$$
$$= .225 + .225 = .45.$$

To use (8.26) we write

$$\sigma_{\hat{Y}\hat{Y}} = .125^2 \times 9 + .125 \times .1875 \times 3.6 + .125 \times .1875 \times 3.6 + .1875^2$$
$$= .45 \quad \text{also.}$$

For the resulting squared multiple correlation, we get

$$\rho_{Y \cdot X_1 X_2}^2 = .45/\sqrt{1.44} = .3125.$$

Note that the correlations of Y with X_1 and with X_2 are

$$\rho_{YX_1} = 1.8/\sqrt{1.44 \times 9} = .5$$

$$\rho_{YX_2} = 1.2/\sqrt{1.44 \times 4} = .5,$$

and the squared correlations are each .25. Separately, each accounts for 25% of the variance of Y. Jointly they account for 31.25% of its variance. The correlation between X_1 and X_2 is

$$\rho_{X_1X_2} = 3.6/\sqrt{9 \times 4} = .6.$$

If they were uncorrelated, their separate contributions to the variance of Y would be additive, together accounting for 50% of its variance. [This can be seen from (8.26).] Because they are correlated, there is a sense in which they contain overlapping information relating to Y. Their joint contribution is less than the sum of their separate contributions, and we cannot disentangle these. Their "effects" or "predictive efficacies" respecting Y are said to be *confounded*. (The root meaning of *confounded* is "poured together"—a nice metaphor.)

If we standardize X_1, X_2, and Y in the population of interest, with

$$Z_1 = (X_1 - \mu_1)/\sigma_1, \quad Z_2 = (X_2 - \mu_2)/\sigma_2, \quad Z_Y = (Y - \mu_Y)/\sigma_Y,$$

the regression equation becomes

$$\hat{Z}_Y = \beta^*_{Y_1} Z_1 + \beta^*_{Y_2} Z_2, \tag{8.27}$$

where

$$\beta^*_{Y_1} = (\sigma_1/\sigma_Y)\beta_{Y_1} \tag{8.28a}$$

and

$$\beta^*_{Y_2} = (\sigma_2/\sigma_Y)\beta_{Y_2}. \tag{8.28b}$$

(The multipliers σ_1/σ_Y and σ_2/σ_Y just incorporate the rescaling of the units of measurement.) In our example,

$$\hat{Z}_Y = [(3/1.2) \times .125]z_1 + [(2/1.2) \times .1875]z_2$$
$$= .3125z_1 + .3125z_2,$$

and, by (8.27),

$$\sigma_{\hat{Y}\hat{Y}} = .3125 \times .5 + .3125 \times .5$$
$$= .3125.$$

This is, already, the squared multiple correlation, because Z_Y has unit variance.

If there are p predictors $X_1, \ldots, X_p$, of Y, the multiple regression equation is

$$Y = \hat{Y} + E$$

with

$$\hat{Y} = \alpha + \beta_{YX_1} X_1 + \cdots + \beta_{YX_p} X_p, \tag{8.29}$$

or

$$Y = \alpha + \beta_{YX_1} X_1 + \cdots + \beta_{YX_p} X_p + E, \tag{8.30}$$

or

$$Y - \mu_Y = \beta_{YX_1}(X_1 - \mu_1) + \cdots + \beta_{YX_p}(X_p - \mu_p) + E \tag{8.31}$$

with

$$\alpha = \mu_Y - (\beta_{YX_1}\mu_1 + \cdots + \beta_{YX_p}\mu_p). \tag{8.32}$$

The residual E is (by construction) uncorrelated with each of the independent variables, $X_1, \ldots, X_p$. We get the regression weights $\beta_{YX_1}, \ldots, \beta_{YX_p}$ where β_{YX_j} is the regression coefficient of Y on X_j—from the variances and covariances. A computer program solves p simultaneous equations like (8.19), and gets the regression constant by (8.32). The variance of Y is partitioned into

$$\sigma_{YY} = \sigma_{\hat{Y}\hat{Y}} + \sigma_{EE} \tag{8.33a}$$

where

$$\sigma_{\hat{Y}\hat{Y}} = \sum_j \beta_{YX_j} \sigma_{Y_j} \tag{8.33b}$$

or

$$\sigma_{\hat{Y}\hat{Y}} = \sum_j \sum_k \beta_{YX_j}\beta_{YX_k}\sigma_{jk}, \tag{8.34}$$

corresponding to (8.25) and (8.26). As before, the squared multiple correlation is

$$\rho^2_{Y \cdot X_1 \cdots X_p} = \sigma_{\hat{Y}\hat{Y}}/\sigma_{YY}. \tag{8.35}$$

Generally, the variance due to the independent variables cannot be further partitioned into parts due to each of them individually. The exception is the rare case where they are mutually uncorrelated, or, in applications, negligibly correlated. If they were uncorrelated, we would have

$$\sigma_{\hat{Y}\hat{Y}} = \sum_j \beta^2_{YX_j}\sigma_{jj} = \beta^2_{YX_1}\sigma_{11} + \ldots + \beta^2_{YX_p}\sigma_{pp}. \tag{8.36}$$

Then the amount of variance that is due to each source depends on two factors—β_{YX_j}, the rate of change of Y with X_j, and σ_{jj}, the population variance of X_j. Note that generally we expect the regression coefficients to be invariant over populations of interest—if the units are not based on population variances. Not surprisingly, amounts and proportions of variance accounted for, and the squared multiple correlation itself, are specific properties of the population(s) being studied, and they vary from one population to another.

Consider again the case of two independent variables. At the other extreme from the case of uncorrelated independent variables is the case where the correlation between two independent variables approaches unity. Then the denominator in (8.20) becomes very small and the regression coefficients become indeterminate.

*** If $\rho^2_{12} = 1$, then $\sigma_{11}\sigma_{22} - \sigma^2_{12} = 0$ in (8.20). Such an occurrence corresponds to lack of determination of the regression coefficients. Note that with all variables standardized, (8.20) gives, in principle,

$$\beta_{YX_1} = (\rho - \rho)/(1 - 1) = \text{``}0/0\text{''},$$

which is an indeterminate quantity, where ρ is the correlation of either X_1 or X_2 with Y. (If they are perfectly correlated, they have the same correlation with Y.) These remarks can be made more mathematically formal—and less intelligible. $\$\$\$

It is unlikely that this indeterminate situation will arise with just two independent variables, but a counterpart occurs quite often in samples when we have a large number of predictor variables. Some of the independent variables become almost perfectly predictable themselves from the other independent variables. Then even large-sample estimates of the regression coefficients—from sample analogues of the preceding equations—become extremely unstable, and they give wildly different values from one sample to another. This "pathological" condition is known as *multicollinearity* because of a geometrical picture of it that is sometimes used.

Multicollinearity has no effect on prediction as such. The best predictor, $\hat{Y}$, of Y, and also the squared multiple correlation, $\sigma^2_{\hat{Y} \bullet X_1 \dots X_p}$, are invariant quantities. They are unaltered by "miscalculations" of the regression coefficients that are due to multicollinearity. (Programs in use need to be checked for the way they handle this. Badly written software can exist.) Multicollinearity is the extreme case of the general impossibility of unconfounding—disentangling—variance due to correlated independent variables. If we simply want a set of good predictors, this does not matter. If we want to understand the relationships—perhaps through some notion of causation—it matters very much.

SOME PROPERTIES OF ESTIMATES

Discussion so far has been concerned with multiple regression as a model for the population, with a few loosely worded (though not incorrect) statements that apply to large samples. Suppose now we have a sample of n observations of p independent variables $X_1, \dots, X_p$, and a dependent variable Y. This gives a table such as

Variable	X_1	$\cdots$	X_p	Y
Individual				
1				
2				
.		x_{ji}		y_i
.				
.				
n				

with general entries x_{ji}, y_i for individual examinee i. We get sample statistics from it—means, variances, covariances—corresponding to the population values considered so far. In the classical theory for the linear model,

$$Y_i = \beta_{YX_1} x_{1i} + \cdots + \beta_{YX_p} x_{pi} + E_i, \tag{8.37}$$

the observations x_{ji} are treated as fixed, and the residuals E_i, $i = 1, \ldots, n$, are n independently and identically distributed normal random variables. Our present model shares most of the properties of the classical model, although it contains p independent and one dependent variable that are jointly random.

***This is essentially because the regression

$$Y = \alpha + \beta_{YX_1} X_1 + \cdots + \beta_{YX_p} X_p + E$$

becomes the same as (8.37) after the sample values x_{ji} of the random variables X_j have been collected. $$$

The *ordinary least squares estimates* $\hat{\beta}_{YX_j}$ of β_{YX_j} and $\hat{\alpha}$ of α minimize

$$q = \sum E_{ji}^2 = \sum_i (y_i - \sum_j \beta_{YX_j} x_i)^2.$$

They are given by sample analogues of (8.19) and (8.18). They are best unbiased estimates of the parameters in the random-independent variables model, as well as in the classical model, and their errors of estimate, ($\hat{\beta}_{yj}$ − β_{yj}), have the Student's t distribution. So we get the usual estimates, standard errors of estimate, and confidence limits as in the computer packages. (I here assume prior knowledge.)

However, r^2 given by the sample analog of (8.35) is biased upward, because resampling is over fresh values of $X_1, \ldots, X_p$, as well as Y, so to speak. An estimate[1] of $\rho_{Y \cdot X_1 X_2}^2$ that is corrected for this bias (assuming normality) is given by

$$\hat{\rho}_{Y \cdot X_1 X_2}^2 = r^2 - [(p-2)/(n-p-1)](1 - r^2)$$
$$- \{2(n-3)/[(n-p-1)(n-p+1)]\}(1 - r^2)^2. \qquad (8.38)$$

A further correction may be needed. So far, words like "prediction" and "predicted part" have been used loosely. The expression for the mean value of Y given values of the independent variables, $\hat{Y}$, is a random variable—a linear combination of random $X_1, \ldots, X_p$. It is, indeed, the best "prediction" of Y, meaning that it yields minimum error variance among all linear functions of $X_1, \ldots, X_p$. But if we estimate the coefficients of the regression from a sample of size n, we can define a *linear prediction function*

$$\tilde{Y} = \hat{\alpha} + \hat{\beta}_{Y_1} X_1 + \cdots + \hat{\beta}_{Y_p} X_p,$$

using the sample estimates. Then the squared correlation $\rho_{Y\hat{Y}}^2$ in the population is what we should really mean by the *predictive precision* of the (estimated) regression function when we use it as a predictor. An unbiased estimate of predictive precision[2] is given by

$$\hat{\rho}_{Y\hat{Y}}^2 = [(n - p - 3)\hat{\rho}_4 + \hat{\rho}_2] / [(n - 2p - 2)\hat{\rho}_2 + p], \tag{8.39a}$$

where

$$\hat{\rho}_2 = r^2 - [p(1 - r^2)] / [n - p - 1] \quad \text{if positive,} \tag{8.39b}$$
$$= 0 \quad \text{otherwise,}$$

and

$$r_4 = (\rho_2)^2 - 2p(1 - \rho_2)^2 / [(n - 1)(n - p - 1)]. \tag{8.39c}$$

These expressions may not seem aesthetically pleasing, but they are not difficult to evaluate. A numerical example of these computations is treated in detail in the last section of this chapter.

SELECTION OF PREDICTOR VARIABLES

There are at least two good reasons why we might wish to select a subset of q predictor variables out of a given set of p of them, while keeping as much predictive power as possible. First, there are certainly cases where the p independent variables in the initial set are multicollinear. If some are just linear combinations of others, they are effectively redundant measurements, and not worth getting. Second, we may want to set a limit on testing time and effort, by choosing the best q predictors available from the set.

Four purely automatic methods for predictor selection are available. In the first of these, the *exhaustive procedure*, we run the multiple regression program with every combination of q variables out of p that could be chosen, and pick the subset with the largest estimated squared multiple correlation. In many applications this is considered impractical. In the second, the *forward selection procedure*, we take the predictor that has the highest correlation with the criterion, and, at each step, we add the variable that gives the largest increase in multiple correlation. In the third, the *backward elimination procedure*, we begin with all p predictors and at each step we eliminate the variable that gives the smallest decrement in multiple correlation. Neither the forward nor the backward method is guaranteed to find the best subset. We can use either to find a prespecified number of predictors, or to stop on the basis of a criterion for the amount of change in squared multiple correlation. A common criterion is nonsignificance of the change for a chosen significance level—say, the 5% or 1% level (at the sample size that happens to be employed in the study). The variables selected and the number selected depend on the sample size and the significance level chosen. The larger the sample size, the more predictors will be retained, and for a large enough sample size, all of them must be. In the fourth, the *stepwise procedure*, we reevaluate each member of the set every time a new member is added, and we eliminate it if it is now superfluous. Again, this is usually done by a significance criterion at the given sample size.

A fundamental difficulty with the automatic methods is that their behavior in an application is strongly influenced both by sample size and by the pattern of relationships among the independent variables. It has not been common practice to examine that pattern before the selection process begins, even though the information is readily available. It is easy to invent structures in which there is no best subset, and the result of an automatic selection procedure will purely reflect sampling effects, with all subsets of q variables having comparable probabilities of being chosen. The effects of capitalization on chance in selecting predictors are usually checked by using a second sample in a technique known as *cross-validation*. The correction for bias for the regression function as a prediction function assumes no selection.

PARTIAL COVARIANCE AND CORRELATION

We may have two or more dependent variables, $Y_1, Y_2, \ldots$, for which we obtain regression functions involving the same independent variables $X_1, \ldots, X_p$. It is enough to consider just two of them, Y_1 and Y_2. Overloading notation a little, we write the two regressions with extra subscripting to distinguish Y_1 and Y_2, as

$$Y_1 = \beta_{Y_1 X_1} X_1 + \cdots + \beta_{Y_1 X_p} X_p + E_1, \tag{8.40a}$$

$$Y_2 = \beta_{Y_2 X_1} X_1 + \cdots + \beta_{Y_2 X_p} X_p + E_2. \tag{8.40b}$$

The covariance of the two residuals E_1 and E_2 is conventionally referred to as the *partial covariance* of Y_1 and Y_2. The covariance of Y_1 and Y_2 for any such fixed values is the covariance of the two residuals E_1 and E_2. We assume that the covariance of Y_1 and Y_2 in a subpopulation in which X_1

is fixed at x_1, X_2 is fixed at x_2, ..., and X_p is fixed at x_p is independent of the values at which they are fixed.

By (8.33a) and (8.34), we already have

$$\sigma_{E_1 E_1} = \sigma_{Y_1 Y_1} - \sum_j \sum_k \beta_{Y_1 X_j} \sigma_{jk} \beta_{Y_1 X_k} \qquad (8.41a)$$

and

$$\sigma_{E_2 E_2} = \sigma_{Y_2 Y_2} - \sum_j \sum_k \beta_{Y_2 X_j} \sigma_{jk} \beta_{Y_2 X_k}. \qquad (8.41b)$$

We can compute these residual variances from the covariances and regression coefficients as given earlier. The covariance of the residuals is given by an analogous expression,

$$\sigma_{E_1 E_2} = \sigma_{Y_1 Y_2} - \sum_j \sum_k \beta_{Y_1 X_j} \sigma_{jk} \beta_{Y_2 X_k}. \qquad (8.41c)$$

We can compute this in the same way.

The *partial correlation*

$$\rho_{Y_1 Y_2 \cdot X_1 \cdots X_p} = \rho_{E_1 E_2} = \sigma_{E_1 E_2} / \sqrt{\sigma_{E_1 E_1} \sigma_{E_2 E_2}}. \qquad (8.42)$$

At this point it is convenient to change notation. Let $Y_1, Y_2, \ldots, Y_p$ be p correlated variables. Any two of them can be chosen as dependent variables with respect to one or more of the others as independent variables. We write $\sigma_{12 \cdot 34 \ldots}$ for the covariance between Y_1 and Y_2 with one or more others, $Y_3, Y_4, \ldots$, as listed after the dot, held constant, and we write $\rho_{12 \cdot 34 \ldots}$ for the corresponding *partial correlation*. In the case of $\rho_{12 \cdot 3}$, say, it may be shown that

$$\rho_{12 \cdot 3} = (\rho_{12} - \rho_{13}\rho_{23}) / \sqrt{(1 - \rho_{13}^2)(1 - \rho_{23}^2)}. \qquad (8.43)$$

We can use this last expression recursively. That is, once we have the partial correlations conditional on fixing one variable, we can derive a partial correlation conditional on fixing one more, and so on, as required. The recursive process is illustrated by

$$\rho_{12 \cdot 34} = (\rho_{12 \cdot 3} - \rho_{14 \cdot 3}\rho_{24 \cdot 3}) / \sqrt{(1 - \rho_{14 \cdot 3}^2)(1 - \rho_{24 \cdot 3}^2)}. \qquad (8.44)$$

The motivation for computing partial covariances and correlations requires careful analysis of the problem to which it is to be applied. The decision to evaluate a partial correlation often rests on the notion that the variables (or variable) that we fix have a "causal" influence that is to be controlled, and they are not merely concomitantly varying quantities. The wish is to determine the relationship between the variables of current interest free from "spurious" covariation caused by uncontrolled variation of common causes. Path analysis is a way of making assumptions about directions of causal inference explicit—not necessarily safer. It can be seen as a generalized partial correlation technique (see Chap. 17). Statisticians and social science researchers have repeatedly warned that it is too easy to compute partial correlations and to misinterpret them in terms of causal inference. That warning is reissued here. Suppose we have three variables, namely, Q, an intelligence quotient, L, an achievement measure in language, and M, an achievement measure in mathematics. Is it reasonable to evaluate $\rho_{ML \cdot Q}$? Is it equally reasonable to evaluate $\rho_{MQ \cdot L}$? For what (distinct) purposes? I leave these questions for the reader.

AN EMPIRICAL EXAMPLE

To strengthen appreciation of the use of regression analysis in test construction, we consider an empirical example in some detail. The following is taken from work of Harlow, on the prediction of "purposefulness" by a number of psychosocial variables.[3] The data are from 290 college students at a northeastern university.

The variables (to be labeled by the capitalized letters in their names) are:

PURpose-in-life: This is a 20-item scale, with items such as "life to me seems always exciting" and "my life is empty, filled only with despair" (5-point Likert scale, from *strongly agree* to *strongly disagree*). (This is the dependent variable.)

self ESTeem: This is a 7-item scale, with items such as "I feel I do not have much to be proud of" and "on the whole I am satisfied with myself" (4-point Likert scale, from *rarely or none of the time* to *most or all of the time*).

meaningful RELationships: This is a single item, namely, "My life is meaningful by spending time with people I really care about including friends, family and love relationships" (5-point Likert scale, from *does not apply* to *strongly applies*).

perceived STRess: This is a 4-item scale, with 5-point Likert items asking about such things as frequency of inability to control important things, and troubles piling up too high (5-point Likert scale for frequency of problems).

SOCial support: This is a 34-item scale, with items like "I often meet or talk with family or friends" (4-point Likert scale, from *definitely true* to *definitely false*).

DEPression: This is a 20-item scale, with items reporting on the last 6 months, such as "I felt depressed" and "my sleep was restless" (4-point Likert scale from *rarely or none of the time* to *most or all of the time*).

POWerlessness: This is a 5-item scale, with items like "I feel I am not in control of my life" and "I have a hard time knowing what to do when I have a problem" (5-point Likert scale, from *strongly disagree or does not apply* to *strongly agree*).

The scores on the tests are the means of the item scores. Their means, variances and covariances, and their correlations are given in Table 8.1. Following a common convention, the variances are in the diagonal of the covariance matrix, the covariances below it, and the correlations above it.

We notice that the pattern of positive and negative correlations can be explained by the direction of scoring of the measures. If we were to reverse the scoring on the measures of STRess, DEPression, and POWerlessness, so that, like self-ESTeem, RELationship satisfaction, SOCial support, and the proposed dependent variable, PURpose(fulness), they all measure a psychosocially "positive" attribute—something like "general adjustment"— the negative correlations would all become positive. It is a good exercise to try this on the sign pattern, noticing that as we change the direction of scoring of one variable, we reverse the signs of its correlations with all the others. Then when we do the same for another variable, some of the signs change back again. So to get it right, we work on one variable at a time. We could do this now and save some trouble, but I propose to keep the "natural" polarity of these measures, to see what it will teach us.

TABLE 8.1
Data From Harlow's Study of Purposefulness

Variable	Mean	Covariances/Correlations						
PUR	3.885	.244	.679	.420	−.657	.627	−.636	−.766
EST	2.979	.157	.219	.424	−.634	.688	−.694	−.649
REL	4.571	.157	.150	.572	−.351	.516	−.345	−.338
STR	2.347	−.230	−.210	−.188	.500	−.540	.647	.625
SOC	3.364	.142	.147	.179	−.175	.210	−.608	−.557
DEP	1.854	−.169	−.175	−.141	.247	−.150	.291	.562
POW	2.098	−.254	−.203	−.171	.296	−.171	.203	.449

TABLE 8.2
Harlow Data—Regression Results

Variable	Parameter Estimate	Standard Error	95% Confidence Bounds	
			Lower	Upper
INTercept	4.147	.301	3.557	4.737
EST	0.099	.061	−0.020	0.219
REL	0.045	.026	−0.005	0.096
STR	−0.099	.035	−0.168	−0.030
SOC	0.124	.056	0.014	0.234
DEP	−0.114	.048	−0.208	−0.020
POW	−0.355	.039	−0.431	−0.279

From the description of the measures it seems reasonable to separate off the concept of purposefulness from the other measures, and treat it as a dependent variable. (Of course, in nonexperimental data a claim of a cause–effect relationship would always be debatable, but we do not have to make that claim to justify this procedure. It is enough that we may regard purposefulness as an attribute on which we are focusing interest as something to be predicted.)

There are a number of statistical computer packages available that carry out the arithmetic of multiple regression. Their generic features would include provision to nominate which variable in a data set is the dependent variable, and which are the independent variables to be included in a particular run of the program. It is easy—perhaps too easy—to run a series of explorations of subsets of the data. Output will include unstandardized parameters, the regression constant—usually labeled "intercept"—and the regression coefficients labeled by their variable names. Standard errors of estimate attached to the parameters allow us to judge the precision with which they are estimated, and to put confidence bounds on the estimates. Output may also include standardized regression coefficients, which sometimes help to indicate the relative importance of sources of variance. If the confidence bounds about the regression coefficient for a particular independent variable include zero, we may question whether that variable contributes to the regression, although judgments of this kind should not be made on purely statistical grounds. The output will also include the squared multiple correlation, and analysis of variance information that I am choosing not to consider for our purposes.

We might present the output as in Table 8.2. To obtain 95% confidence bounds I have just added/subtracted 1.96 times the standard error. The estimated regression equation may be written as

$$PUR = 4.147 + .099EST + .045REL - .099STR$$
$$+ .125SOC - .114DEP - .356POW + E.$$

TABLE 8.3
Harlow Data—Forward Selection

Step	Variable Entered	Partial Rsquared	Total Rsquared	Probability
1	POW	.586	.586	.0001
2	DEP	.062	.648	.0001
3	SOC	.022	.670	.0001
4	STR	.012	.683	.0015
5	REL	.004	.687	.0626
6	EST	.003	.690	.1073

The squared multiple correlation is .690. As in most regression analyses of behavioral data, the intercept (with its confidence bounds) is of no interest. We can judge the sizes of the regression coefficients relative to their confidence bounds, noting that POWerlessness is the only independent variable whose bounds are well away from zero. Recall that we cannot compare the sizes of these regression coefficients, as they do not share a common scale. And we cannot safely draw conclusions about the contribution of each, because their correlations with each other are too high to regard them as contributing independently to the variance of PURpose.

Results from a forward selection procedure can be reported as in Table 8.3. Recall that the stepwise procedure first selects the single variable with the largest contribution to prediction. This must be the one with the highest individual correlation—here, POWerlessness. DEPression is selected next, because it makes the largest additional contribution, then SOCial support, and so on, in the order listed in the first column. The second column lists the contribution of each added variable to the squared multiple correlation, and the third the corresponding total obtained. I have omitted the usual columns presenting analysis of variance results, but included in the last column the probability associated with the (estimated) added squared multiple correlation if in the population the corresponding addition is zero. One convention for stopping the stepwise addition of predictors, as already mentioned, is the nonsignificance of such a contribution at a chosen significance level. In the present case the sample size is quite large, so the actual contribution to prediction from STRess, and possibly even that from SOCial support, seem negligible although they are "significant" by conventional statistical standards.

At this point we face a difficult scientific question. We would wish to know what is the relative importance of the individual predictor variables in "explaining"/predicting PURpose. Strictly, the effects are confounded. It might seem safe to say that POWerlessness is the single most important explanatory variable (and we have known this in a sense from the correlations themselves). We might use the stepwise results to recast the question. We ask whether we should suppose that POWerlessness and DEPression are the two most important explanatory variables because they enter the stepwise procedure first. However, because the correlation between these two variables, .563, is not negligible, this conclusion is unsafe. We notice that the order of entry in the selection does not correspond to the order of (absolute) magnitudes of the correlations of the independent variables with the dependent variable. (Mathematically it need not, unless the independent variables are uncorrelated with each other.) The closeness of the values of these correlations suggests that the order of entry could be largely a sampling effect, and might not be replicated in a fresh sample. In fact, in another larger sample from the same study, POWerlessness is again the first variable selected, but the second is SOCial support.

One possibility is that the analysis we are attempting is too fine-grained. POWerlessness and DEPression are, one feels, conceptually distinct variables, but it might be possible to combine the six independent variables to make a general factor of—shall we say?—"adjustment," and use this as a single predictor of PURpose. Fitting the Spearman model by ULS to the six independent variables, excluding PURpose, gives the results in Table 8.4. The GFI is .963, suggesting a satisfactory fit. We see some justification in forming a total test score, for "adjustment," out of the six "subtests" in the regression equation, and using this as an "understandable" single predictor of PURpose. A simple way to do this is to take the sum of the six scores, each measured in the direction of adjustment. As an exercise, the student is encouraged to check my computations. These give the following: From the unstandardized loadings in Table 8.4, with the variance of the adjustment sum score, coefficient omega is .861. From the variances of the six tests and the sum score, G-C alpha is .858. From the covariance matrix of the six predictor measures, the variance of their sum, after changing negative correlations to positive, is 7.852, and the covariance of the sum with PURpose is 1.108. We already have the variance of PURpose, .244, in Table 8.1, so the correlation between "adjustment" and PURpose is $1.108/\sqrt{.244 \times 7.852} = .8005$, giving a squared correlation of .641. There

TABLE 8.4
Harlow Data—Spearman Analysis

Variable	Factor Loading	Uniqueness
EST	.401	.058
REL	.365	.439
STR	−.548	.200
SOC	.360	.080
DEP	−.423	.112
POW	−.503	.196

is no reason why the common factor of the six variables—or a simple sum of them—should predict nearly as effectively as the (optimal) regression, and here it is a matter of judgment whether the simple sum is nearly as good. We compare .641 with the optimal .69, and note that it matches the predictive power of the first two variables in the stepwise procedure. What is being shown is that when the effects of the independent variables are confounded, we might avoid the issue of ascribing specific roles to them as explainers of variance, and make a simple, understandable composite that explains reasonably well. This is not a general recommendation. Each regression analysis can be expected to bring its own specific problems of interpretation. In many cases the independent variables will not have a simple factor structure, and if they do, it could be that the unique parts of the tests contribute to the prediction. An example of such a kind is given in Chapters 10 and 17, taken from Hull, Lehn, and Tedlie (1991).

If we wish to use the regression equation simply as a practical predictor of an outcome variable, the problem of understanding contributions of predictors does not arise. The regression equation can then be judged purely by its predictive power—the squared multiple correlation itself. We use (8.38) to obtain the correction for bias. This gives

$$.69 - (4/283)(1 - .69) - [(2 \times 287)/283 \times 285)](1 - .69)$$
$$= .69 - .0044 - .0022$$
$$= .683.$$

Perhaps not surprisingly, the correction is negligible at this sample size.

To use the regression as a prediction equation we should also apply the estimate of predictive precision given by (8.39). We obtain

$$\rho_2 = .69 - [6 \times (1 - .69)]/283 = .69 - .0066 = .6834,$$

and

$$\hat{\rho}_4 = .6834^2 - 12(.3166)^2/(289 \times 285) = .4670 - .0001 = .4669,$$

which gives, finally, the coefficient of predictive precision

$$\hat{\rho}_{Y\hat{Y}} = (281 \times .4669 + .6834)/(276 \times .6834 + 6) = .678.$$

Again this is a negligible correction to the simple squared multiple correlation.

The stepwise procedure tells us in principle how to economize on effort in future predictive work. If we do not gain enough predictive precision from using all six tests, we will be satisfied to use just the best two, POW-erlessness and DEPression, in future work. However, this is not a simple mechanical decision. An alternative way to reduce testing for future predictive purposes is to shorten each of the six tests. Analysis of the items could show that a subset of these gives a squared multiple correlation with the criterion on the order of .64 or better after we reduce the total number of items and the total testing time to a desirable level.

REVIEW GUIDE

The material in this chapter is primarily a review of regression theory, which most readers of this book will already have learned elsewhere. The emphasis here should be on the interpretation of the regression coefficients, and the choice between unstandardized and standardized regression coefficients. The extensive account of the case of two independent variables may be of interest, and may be helpful, to some students. A computer program may be relied on to yield regression coefficients, multiple correlations, and residual variances, so the important points to understand concern the interpretation of these quantities, and the difficulties of interpretation arising from multicollinearity when the independent variables are (strongly) correlated. Some accounts of multiple regression do not stress the fact that multicollinearity does not affect prediction, but generally prevents clear interpretation of individual contributions of the independent variables by making the regression coefficients poorly determined. This is an important point for applications to test scores.

The student should give attention to the meaning of the correction for bias in (8.40), and of the estimate of predictive precision in (8.41), while taking for granted the rather clumsy-looking expressions for these. The brief account of predictor selection reflects my personal view that automatic selection methods are generally unsafe. I therefore believe that distinctions between the alternative methods are of less importance than recognizing the need for care in using any of them.

The important expression in applications of partial correlation methods is (8.47), and the student should be able to apply it. It should be understood that partial correlations have generally been used in support of causal speculations about nonexperimental data, when control of causal variables is lacking. Such speculations need caution, but cannot altogether be avoided.

END NOTES

General: There are many textbook accounts of regression. I suggest Moore and McCabe (1993) for an elementary treatment.

1. This result is due to Olkin and Pratt. See Lord and Novick (1968, pp. 285–286).
2. This result is due to Browne (1975).
3. These data and most of the analysis were very kindly supplied by Lisa Harlow, from an unpublished paper, Predicting Purpose in Life from Psychosocial Variables.

The Common Factor Model

In Chapter 6, a psychometric conception of a homogeneous set of items was introduced, based on the classical Spearman single-factor model. In this conception, the items form a homogeneous set if they measure just one attribute in common—just one common factor. We can also describe such a set of items as *unidimensional*, because they indicate variation of respondents on a single dimension. Factor analysis is an important analytic tool for test validity, as well as for other possible applications. This chapter gives a more general account of the common factor model.

The single-factor model was developed by Charles Spearman in the two decades following his paper in 1904 on the structure of intelligence. In the 1930s, Thurstone generalized the model to more than one factor. He shared with Spearman a belief that the common factor model could be used to discover the fundamental components of cognition, of personality functioning, and of other general psychological attributes.[1] On evidence to date, it may be possible to retain such a view. But it is at least equally reasonable to suggest that any dimensional structure in cognition, personality, and so on, "discovered" by using factor analysis is there to discover because it was put there by the tests psychologists choose to invent. The number of abilities or personality traits "discovered" by factor analysis depends on the specificity or breadth of the attributes the tests are designed to measure. Thus intelligence has been regarded by Spearman as a unitary, unidimensional property, by Thurstone as having 7 dimensions—named primary mental abilities—and by Guilford as having 64 dimensions.[2]

In the context of test development, the common factor model is at least a fairly safe and quite useful device for checking on the structure of the tests we choose to create. We do not need to enter the less secure and more speculative area of inquiry into the actual structure of psychological processes. Some of these may indeed reveal themselves through the dimensional analysis of individual differences. Some processes may not depend for their existence or detection on individual variability. (If all memories were equal, we could still recognize and study memory, and the general laws by which it functions.)

The common factor model has generally been applied to correlations between scores on tests, which already contain a number of items. This is partly for historical reasons, and partly because of special problems with binary items. The most important of these is failure of the assumption of a linear relation between the item scores and the common factors—the attributes or traits. Alternatives are examined in Chapters 12–16. Meanwhile, it is safe enough to regard the common factor model as applicable to relations between variables that might be: (a) scores on tests or subtests containing enough items to assume linear relations or joint normal distributions, (b) quantitative item scores for which these assumptions will hold approximately, and (c) binary item scores, for which the model is a linear approximation to the one we need. In applications to test or subtest scores, the component items should first be examined for content homogeneity. The item sums are already substituting for attributes at a first level of generality. If, in turn, their relationships are explained by common factors, these factors are at a second level of abstraction from the responses to individual items. If the items have not been grouped into tests or subtests on a reasonable basis, it is unlikely that factor analysis of the resulting composite scores will give comprehensible results.

THE MULTIPLE-FACTOR MODEL—BY EXAMPLE

Instead of proceeding immediately to the general case, let us recall the application in Chapter 6 of the single-factor model to the Satisfaction with Life (SWL) data. The model

$$X_j = \mu + \lambda_j F + E_j \quad j = 1, \ldots, m \quad (6.2)$$

with $\mathrm{Var}\{E_j\} = \psi_j^2$, was fitted to the covariance matrix of the Likert items, each measured on a 7-point scale, by unweighted least squares (ULS), yielding

$$X_1 - \mu_1 = 1.290F + E_1 \quad \psi_1^2 = 0.901$$
$$X_2 - \mu_2 = 1.104F + E_2 \quad \psi_2^2 = 1.274$$

$$X_3 - \mu_3 = 1.148F + E_3 \qquad \psi_3^2 = 1.144$$
$$X_4 - \mu_4 = 0.952F + F_4 \qquad \psi_4^2 = 1.863$$
$$X_5 - \mu_5 = 1.185F + E_5 \qquad \psi_5^2 = 1.951.$$

This model gave a reasonable fit to the sample covariance matrix; the fit indexes were satisfactory, and the discrepancies small.

It is common practice to treat the sample correlation matrix, rather than the sample covariance matrix, as the statistical summary of the data to which the common factor model is fitted.[3] It helps understanding of the structure of the data to do this. In effect, we are fitting the common factor model with each of the items or tests standardized in the population sampled, as well as the common factors, and so obtaining *standardized factor loadings*. The same general principle applies here as in regression. If both the independent variables and the dependent variables are standardized, the regression coefficient is the amount of change in standard deviation units in an item score corresponding to an increase of one *SD* in an independent variable. In the factor model the independent variables are the factors, the dependent variables are the items/tests, and the regression weights are the factor loadings. It makes no difference to the fit if we analyze the sample correlation matrix instead of the sample covariance matrix, unless we equate loadings as in the parallel forms and true-score equivalent structures. In those models, changing scale destroys the hypothesized equalities of loadings. Special restrictions should be employed if we analyze correlation matrices and wish to obtain standard errors of the estimates of the loadings, as will be shown.

For the factor analysis of items in the context of test construction, it is also useful to analyze the item covariances, perhaps accompanied by an analysis of the correlations. Some readers will recognize a parallel to computer programs for regression, which usually print out the unstandardized regression coefficients and their *SEs* for one kind of information, and then supply standardized regression coefficients as an aid to interpretation of the results. As we saw in Chapter 6 for the Spearman model, the unstandardized loadings and unique variances give coefficient omega for the test sum score. On the other hand, analysis of the sample correlation matrix allows a straightforward judgment of the sizes of discrepancies between the sample correlations and fitted correlations.

For most purposes in factor analysis it is preferable to use a discrepancy function that gives maximum likelihood estimators rather than the ULS function that was used in the work on reliability-oriented factor analysis in Chapter 6. Maximum likelihood (ML) estimation yields (a) (possibly) better criteria for goodness of fit and (b) *SEs* of estimate of the parameters. The *SEs* are particularly useful in determining if the model is behaving well, as will be explained later. ML estimates give results for G-C alpha and the Spearman–Brown reliability coefficient that may differ from the classical results given earlier, but usually the differences are slight.

Here a few further remarks about the method of maximum likelihood may be helpful to some students. Much statistical estimation is based on the simple least squares (ULS) principle: Minimize the sum of squared differences between the sample statistics and the corresponding fitted values from the model. (Note a distinction here between ULS, which minimizes differences between sample statistics and fitted parameters, and OLS in regression, which minimizes differences between actual and fitted observations over the individuals sampled.) The method of maximum likelihood has a different philosophy from ULS, and has some very good general properties in large samples. The model to be fitted will be a restrictive statistical hypothesis. In the present case, 5 factor loadings and 5 unique variances reproduce 10 covariances and 5 variances. The ML method chooses estimates of the parameters in the model that maximize the likelihood (probability) of the sample observations. Instead of simply maximizing the probability, a useful equivalent is to minimize a criterion based on the ratio of two probabilities—the probability of the sample data if the restrictive hypothesis is true, and the probability of the data if they could come from a population not subject to any restrictions.

The criterion we use is

$$L = -2n \log_e[P\{\text{data}|\text{restrictive model}\}/P\{\text{data}|\text{no restrictions}\}],$$

where n is the sample size. If the model fits perfectly in the sample,

$$P\{\text{data}|\text{restrictive model}\} = P\{\text{data}|\text{no restrictions}\},$$

so

$$L = -2n \log_e\{1\} = 0.$$

If it fits imperfectly,

$$P\{\text{data}|\text{restrictive model}\} < P\{\text{data}|\text{no restrictions}\}$$

so

$$L = -2n \log_e\{\text{number less than unity}\}$$
$$= -2n \times \{\text{negative logarithm}\}$$
$$= \text{positive quantity.}$$

This makes L a good general measure of the discrepancy between the model and the data. Under the restrictive hypothesis, L is distributed like chi-square in large samples, with degrees of freedom given by the number of free elements in the sample covariance matrix—$m(m + 1)/2$—minus the number of parameters fitted. Minimization requires a computer program that literally searches for the minimum point. When Lawley gave the mathematical theory in 1940, it could be illustrated but not seriously used, until the first computer programs by Howe and by Bargmann in 1955.

The probability of the observations given by the chi-square statistic might be used to reject or not reject the restrictive hypothesis. However, it has come to be recognized that the classical hypothesis-testing notion is not really appropriate. That is, in practice we should not simply accept or reject a factor model as a null hypothesis using the chi-square as a test of significance. Such a model can never describe a population, but can only approximate it. If the approximation is good enough, we will not consider fitting a more complicated model. The quantity

$$d = \frac{L - df}{n} \tag{9.1}$$

is a sample estimate of the *noncentrality parameter.* It is an unbiased estimate of the *error of approximation* of the model to the population. *McDonald's index of goodness of fit,*

$$m_c = e^{-(1/2)d}, \tag{9.2}$$

is scaled to lie between zero and unity, where unity represents perfect fit. (Technically, it is the geometric mean of the ratio of the probability of an observation under the hypothesized model to its probability without restriction.) An index that is coming into common use is the *root mean squared error of approximation,*

$$\text{RMSEA} = \sqrt{(d/df)} , \tag{9.3}$$

0 for perfect fit

which is zero for perfect fit.[4] A conventional "rule of thumb" is that the approximation is acceptable when RMSEA $< .05$. The basis of this rule is not clear. It is also not clear if either of these indexes is preferable to the GFI defined in Chapter 6. At the time of writing the status and utility of the goodness-of-fit indexes and any "rules of thumb" for them are still unsettled, and it may be questioned whether their use is at all desirable, but the student will certainly encounter them in research reports. In addition to these fit indexes, it is always desirable to obtain and inspect the

TABLE 9.1
SWLS—Covariances and Correlations

			Covariance Matrix		
	1	2	3	4	5
1	2.566	1.560	1.487	1.195	1.425
2	1.560	2.493	1.283	0.845	1.313
3	1.487	1.283	2.462	1.127	1.313
4	1.195	0.845	1.127	2.769	1.323
5	1.425	1.313	1.313	1.323	3.356
			Correlation Matrix		
	1	2	3	4	5
1	1.000	0.617	0.592	0.448	0.486
2	0.617	1.000	0.518	0.321	0.454
3	0.592	0.518	1.000	0.432	0.457
4	0.448	0.321	0.432	1.000	0.434
5	0.486	0.454	0.457	0.434	1.000
SDs	1.602	1.579	1.569	1.664	1.832

matrix of discrepancies between sample correlations and fitted correlations. A reasonable rule of thumb is that the fit is acceptable, because it cannot be improved on by adding parameters that are nontrivial, if the absolute discrepancies are less than .1 in an analysis of a sample correlation matrix. The pattern of the discrepancies can also be taken into account by an experienced judgment. Some parts of the model can give exact fit, whereas in other parts the fit is poor. This is one of the objections that can be made to fit indexes, which cannot reflect such details.

The correlation matrix of the SWLS data is shown, for convenient comparison, along with the covariance matrix in Table 9.1. Fitting the single-factor model by ML (a) to the covariance matrix and (b) to the correlation matrix gives the results in Table 9.2. From $\chi^2_{(5)} = 10.3085$, we have $p = .06695$, $d = (10.3085 - 5)/215 = .02469$, $m_c = \exp(-.02469/2) = .9877$, and RMSEA $= \sqrt{(.02469/5)} = .07027$. From the discrepancies and the sample correlations, we obtain GFI $= 1 - .03187/9.6587 = .9967$. All of these criteria, and the pattern of the discrepancies in Table 9.2(b), suggest acceptable fit.

The chi-square, probability value, and fit indexes based on the noncentrality parameter d are unaltered by substituting the correlation matrix for the covariance matrix. Each estimated factor loading from the correlation matrix is just the factor loading from the covariance matrix divided by the SD of the variable, and, correspondingly, each estimated unique variance is divided by the variance of the variable. For example, for item 1,

$$\hat{\lambda}_1 = 1.311/\sqrt{2.566} = .818$$
$$\hat{\psi}_2 = 0.847/2.566 = .330$$

Thus the analyses are equivalent. Rescaling the variables just rescales the parameters.

The standardized factor loadings obtained from the sample correlation matrix give the amount of difference in SD units in X_j corresponding to one SD difference in the attribute F. This is believed to aid interpretation. On this scale, we recognize certain indicators of the (factor) attribute as more sensitive to it than others. In this example, the first three items,

1. In most ways my life is close to my ideal,
2. The conditions of my life are excellent,
3. I am satisfied with my life,

TABLE 9.2
SWLS—Spearman Model by ML

	(a) Covariances				(b) Correlations		
$\hat{\lambda}$	SE	$\hat{\psi}^2$	SE	$\hat{\lambda}$	SE	$\hat{\psi}^2$	SE
1.311	(.091)	0.847	(.136)	.819	(.034)	.330	(.056)
1.135	(.101)	1.204	(.147)	.719	(.041)	.483	(.060)
1.143	(.100)	1.155	(.144)	.729	(.041)	.469	(.059)
0.924	(.113)	1.915	(.202)	.555	(.054)	.692	(.060)
1.151	(.122)	2.032	(.224)	.628	(.049)	.605	(.061)

Discrepancies for (a) Covariances

	1	2	3	4	5
1	−0.000	0.071	−0.012	−0.016	−0.083
2	0.071	−0.000	−0.015	−0.204	0.006
3	−0.012	−0.015	−0.000	0.071	−0.002
4	−0.016	−0.204	0.071	0.000	0.260
5	−0.083	0.006	−0.002	0.260	−0.000

Discrepancies for (b) Correlations

	1	2	3	4	5
1	−0.000	0.028	−0.005	−0.006	−0.028
2	0.028	−0.000	−0.006	−0.078	0.002
3	−0.005	−0.006	−0.000	0.028	−0.001
4	−0.006	−0.078	0.028	0.000	0.086
5	−0.028	0.002	−0.001	0.086	−0.000

measure the single common factor most sensitively. The last two items,

4. So far I have gotten the important things I want from life,
5. If I could live my life over, I would change almost nothing,

measure it less sensitively.

Now consider an alternative possibility. Suppose the five items measure two attributes rather than one, and the first three measure present satisfaction whereas the last two measure satisfaction with the past. The attributes, although semantically distinct, of course may be correlated. Now we consider how to model this. We write

$$
\begin{aligned}
X_1 &= \lambda_{11}F_1 + (0 \times F_2) + E_1 \\
X_2 &= \lambda_{21}F_1 + (0 \times F_2) + E_2 \\
X_3 &= \lambda_{31}F_1 + (0 \times F_2) + E_3 \\
X_4 &= (0 \times F_1) + \lambda_{42}F_2 + E_4 \\
X_5 &= (0 \times F_1) + \lambda_{52}F_2 + E_5.
\end{aligned}
\tag{9.4}
$$

The terms in parentheses can be omitted, of course. They are included to indicate a prescribed arrangement of nonzero and zero loadings in the proposed factor pattern. We call F_1 and F_2 group factors. Each is defined by a group or cluster of variables. Here F_1 is present satisfaction, and F_2 is satisfaction with the past. The loadings have two subscripts. The first identifies the item (or test) score, whereas the second identifies the common factor it measures. This example illustrates an independent clusters factor model. It should have become known as an "independent groups" model for consistency of terminology, but it did not happen that way. Each factor is defined by a cluster—a group—of variables, and no variable is an indicator of more than one factor. To distinguish factor correlations—correlations between the factors—from correlations ρ_{jk} between the test (item) scores, we use ϕ_{st} for the correlation between factor s and factor t.

From the sample covariance matrix, we obtain the estimates of the parameters given in Table 9.3(a), with SEs of estimate shown in parentheses, by minimizing the ML criterion. The sample correlation matrix gives the results in Table 9.3(b). In both analyses we obtain the correlation between the factors, $\phi_{12} = .861$ (0.061), necessarily the same (because factor correlations are unaltered by the scale of the item scores). From $\chi^2_{(4)} = 5.4775$, we have $p = .2417$, and we obtain $d = .00687$, $m_c = .9966$, and RMSEA = .04144. The correlation analysis gives GFI = $1 - .01486/9.6587 = .998$, and discrepancies in Table 9.3(b) that are all "small"—indeed, well below .1.

TABLE 9.3
SWLS—Two Independent Clusters

(a) Covariance Results

	$\hat{\Lambda}$, Matrix of Loadings				$\hat{\psi}^2$, Uniquenesses	
1	1.326	(.099)			0.808	(.139)
2	1.146	(.101)			1.180	(.147)
3	1.140	(.100)			1.161	(.145)
4			1.024	(.121)	1.720	(.212)
5			1.292	(.135)	1.688	(.265)

Discrepancies (Covariances)

0	.040	−.025	.025	−.050
.040	0	.024	−.166	.038
−.025	.024	0	.122	.045
.025	−.166	.122	0	−.000
−.050	.038	.045	−.000	0

(b) Correlation Results

	$\hat{\Lambda}$, Matrix of Loadings				$\hat{\psi}^2$, Uniquenesses	
1	.828	(.035)			.314	(.057)
2	.726	(.041)			.473	(.060)
3	.727	(.041)			.471	(.060)
4			.615	(.057)	.621	(.071)
5			.705	(.056)	.502	(.079)

Discrepancies (Correlations)

0	.016	−.010	.017	−.017
.016	0	−.010	−.063	.013
−.010	−.010	0	.047	.016
.017	−.063	.047	0	−.000
−.017	.013	.016	−.000	0

This model has one more parameter than the single-factor model to explain the relationships, and hence one less degree of freedom. All the criteria, and the actual discrepancies, suggest that it fits better than the single-factor model. It also makes substantive sense. The correlation, .861, between the factors is quite high, leaving a difficult decision whether to regard them as truly distinct. And the more complex model will certainly improve fit. The problem remains—is the set of five items a "sufficiently" homogeneous measure of SWL?

Generally the task of test construction is to develop homogeneous, essentially homogeneous, or sufficiently homogeneous tests. For this task, the following alternative, equivalent model is useful. Suppose we have three factors: G, a general factor of SWL, F_1, a group factor of present satisfaction, defined by the first three items, and F_2, a group factor of satisfaction with the past, defined by the last two. The model will be

$$X_1 = \lambda_1 G + \lambda_{11} F_1 + E_1$$
$$X_2 = \lambda_2 G + \lambda_{21} F_1 + E_2$$
$$X_3 = \lambda_3 G + \lambda_{31} F_1 + E_3$$
$$X_4 = \lambda_4 G + \lambda_{41} F_2 + E_4$$
$$X_5 = \lambda_5 G + \lambda_{51} F_2 + E_5. \tag{9.5}$$

We assume that G, F_1, and F_2 are mutually uncorrelated, because the general factor will serve to explain the relationships between variables in the distinct groups. When this model is estimated (using necessary constraints explained later), we obtain the results in Table 9.4 from the item correlations. The chi-square, the other goodness-of-fit indexes, and the discrepancies are the same as in Table 9.3. This is just a rearrangement of the previous model as a *hierarchical factor model.* It represents a hierarchical or nested classification of the variables. Each is nested within its own group factor and, at a higher level of abstraction, within the general factor. The loadings on the general factor in Table 9.4 are equal to the loadings on the two group factors in Table 9.3, multiplied by the square root of the factor correlation, $\sqrt{.861}$. The loadings on the hierarchical

TABLE 9.4
SWLS—Hierarchical Model

Correlation (Standardized) Analysis							
Hierarchical Factor Loadings							
G		F_1		F_2		Unique Variances	
.768	(.041)	0.309	(.069)			0.314	(.057)
.673	(.046)	0.271	(.060)			0.473	(.060)
.675	(.046)	0.271	(.060)			0.471	(.060)
.571	(.054)			0.230	(.057)	0.621	(.071)
.654	(.048)			0.263	(.068)	0.502	(.079)

Covariance (Unstandardized) Analysis			
Hierarchical Factor Loadings			
G	F_1	F_2	Unique Variances
1.230	0.495		0.806
1.063	0.428		1.179
1.059	0.425		1.160
0.950		0.383	1.720
1.198		0.482	1.685

group factors in Table 9.4 are the loadings on the independent cluster factors in Table 9.3 multiplied by $\sqrt{(1 - .861)}$ (see Higher Order and Hierarchical Factors section).

Rewriting the model as a hierarchical one makes our judgment take a different form. Because the standardized loadings on the general factor are large enough, we can regard the items as sufficiently homogeneous to take the total test score as, indeed, general satisfaction with life. The loadings on the hierarchical group factors are, with one bare exception, less than .3, which is a commonly accepted conventional level of standardized loadings for regarding a variable as *salient*—as an effective indicator of a factor. One way to justify this convention is to recognize that the product of two standardized loadings is the amount of correlation they "explain," so if two loadings are less than .3 they "explain" a rather negligible amount of correlation—less than .1. This is a reasonable rule of thumb. In this example we might have it both ways. We could conclude that the combination of semantic content and factor-analytic evidence justifies the more complex model, yet for applications of the test score the items are still sufficiently homogeneous. If we took the hierarchical group factors seriously, it would be possible, for some research purposes, to take two scores—not three—from the test, namely, the total or mean score, measuring Satisfaction with Life, and a difference of means in the first three and last two items, measuring a contrast between present and past satisfaction—a perceived change for the better or for the worse.

THE MULTIPLE-FACTOR MODEL—GENERAL

The common factor model for m test scores (or quantitative item scores) $X_1, \ldots, X_m$ and r common factors $F_1, \ldots, F_r$ can be written as

$$X_j = \lambda_{j1} F_1 + \cdots + \lambda_{jr} F_r + E_j. \tag{9.6}$$

Each test score enters a regression equation on the r common factors, so the residuals—unique parts—E_j are uncorrelated with the common factors. The condition that the residuals are mutually uncorrelated actually defines what we mean by common factors and unique parts. By definition, common factors are what the test scores measure in common, and the residuals are what they measure uniquely. Another way to say this is that the partial correlation between any pair of tests, conditioned on values of the r factors, is zero, that is,

$$\rho_{X_j X_k \cdot F_1 \cdots F_r} = 0 \qquad j \neq k. \tag{9.7}$$

That is, in a subpopulation in which the factor scores take fixed values $F_1 = f_1, \ldots, F_r = f_r$, the test scores are (linearly) unrelated. (This is a form of the *principle of local—conditional—independence*. A tighter version of this principle defines item response models, in Chaps. 12–14.)

Assuming that the factors are standardized, it follows by the algebra of expectations that

$$\sigma_{jk} = \sum_s \sum_t \lambda_{js} \lambda_{kt} \phi_{st} \qquad j \neq k, \tag{9.8a}$$

and

$$\sigma_{jj} = \sum_s \sum_t \lambda_{js} \lambda_{jt} \phi_{st} + \psi_j^2, \tag{9.8b}$$

where, again, ψ_j^2 is the unique variance of item j. As discussed in Chapter 6, the simple case of a single factor, where,

$$\sigma_{jk} = \lambda_j \lambda_k \qquad j \neq k,$$

gives unique solutions of the system of nonlinear equations, for the loadings and unique variances. [Recall Equations (6.5)–(6.8).] That is, in the single-factor case, the loadings and unique variances are determined by the covariances and variances. When the parameters of a model are determined by the distribution of the test scores, and here, in particular, by the covariances, we say they are *identified*. They have a unique identity; they are unique quantities to be estimated.

In the more general case of two or more common factors, the system of equations (9.8) does not have a unique solution, and it is necessary to impose some further conditions on the model, to restrict the solutions, and to make the parameters identified quantities that can be estimated. Fortunately, the needed conditions often coincide with hypotheses that reflect the design of the tests. The independent-clusters structure of the SWLS data is already an example. The model was proposed on substantive grounds—the semantic distinction between the two groups of items. The parameters of this model were in fact identified, and this property was to be expected by some general principles, as follows.

Using equations like (6.5)–(6.8), but more complex and tedious to work with, we can establish that the parameters of the common factor model are identified in the following reasonably general conditions:

1. For each factor there are at least three items (or tests), with nonzero loadings, that have zero loadings on all other factors.
2. For each factor there are at least two items/tests, with nonzero loadings, that have zero loadings on all other factors, and also, any factor having only two defining tests is correlated with other factors.

We call an item or test that indicates only one factor *factorially simple*. It measures just one attribute. If it measures two or more factors it is *factorially complex*. It is a mixture of two or more attributes. Imagine, for example, a test measuring verbal ability, a test measuring reasoning, and a test of verbal reasoning.

From conditions 1 and 2 it follows in particular that if the set of items forms independent clusters, the model is certainly identified with at least three tests per cluster, and is identified with at least two per cluster if the analysis finds that the factors are correlated. Commonly they will be. These conditions are possibly not as widely known as they should be to researchers using factor analysis, but substantive considerations in the design of a set of items often ensure that they will be approximated in applications. The conditions are very likely to be satisfied in careful test construction, as opposed to exploration of the structure of general psychological attributes. There is no accepted term in the literature for conditions 1 and 2. By a natural extension of usage, I refer to them as models possessing an *independent-clusters basis*.

More generally, a multiple-factor model in which certain factor loadings are constrained to be zero, or constrained to be equal to other loadings, as in the true-score equivalence model, is referred to as a *restricted factor model*, or as a *confirmatory factor model*, to be contrasted with *unrestricted* or *exploratory* models. There are restricted factor models in which identifiability of parameters is not guaranteed. In unrestricted multiple-factor models the parameters are certainly not identified, so devices have been invented for choosing "preferred" solutions. Thurstone's influential notion of a preferred solution rests on the concept of *simple structure*. This is often confused with independent-cluster structure. Standard methods for approximating independent clusters in computer programs are commonly misdescribed as "rotation to simple structure." Thurstone[5] gave the following five conditions for simple structure:

1. Each row of the *factor pattern*—the matrix of factor loadings—should have at least one zero element.
2. Each column should have at least r zero elements.
3. For every pair of columns there should be at least r variables with a zero loading in one column and a nonzero in the other.

4. In the case where r is greater than three, for every pair of columns there should be a large proportion of variables with zeros in both columns.

5. For every pair of columns there should be a small proportion of variables with nonzeros in both columns.

This prescription is not unambiguous, and it is not possible to prove that it serves to identify the parameters. Indeed, examples can be found—with some question whether conditions 4 and 5 are adequately met—that are not identified. Note that it is possible to have a simple structure in which no variable is factorially simple. It may then be very difficult to state what attributes are measured. It is possible that the content of a set of items could suggest a restricted factor model that follows the prescription for simple structure. Such a model can be fitted as a restrictive model, and checked for identifiability. In applications, it is likely that the simple structure will also have an independent-clusters basis that will secure identifiability. The student is warned that in published applications the researcher will often describe an independent clusters solution as a simple structure.

As the name implies, *unrestricted factor analysis* describes applications of the factor model in which the researcher does not have a priori, substantively based restrictions on the structure of the data—the pattern of nonzero/zero loadings. Possibly the investigator has no notion as to the number of factors, either, in which case considerable exploration is needed. Perhaps the investigator does not possess any prior conceptions about the data at all, in which case the analysis may properly be called *exploratory factor analysis*. Perhaps the investigator does have substantive preconceptions, but prefers not to incorporate these in the model, except, possibly, for specifying the number of factors. In this case an unrestricted model is being used to see if it discovers the expected structure. This is reasonable, because it makes it possible to discover features of the data that a specific confirmatory analysis may miss. However, it can be unsafe, as we soon see.

There are two distinct forms of lack of identifiability of the parameters of the unrestricted common factor model. One involves possible exchanges of values between the factor loadings while the unique variances are identified and unchanging. This is conventionally known as the *rotation problem* because of a geometric picture of it. It is resolved in exploratory work by finding an arbitrary set of loadings, and then transforming them into an approximation to an independent-clusters pattern (see The Rotation Problem section). The other is a more subtle and potentially worrying problem, because it involves joint indeterminacy of the factor loadings and unique variances. This second problem arises essentially from the presence of hidden *doublet factors*—factors defined by only two tests. It happens because, for just two tests, X_1, X_2, $\sigma_{12} = \lambda_1 \lambda_2$ cannot be solved uniquely for λ_1 and λ_2.

In an exploratory analysis with uncorrelated factors this indeterminacy cannot be resolved, and it is hidden by the analysis. In such a case, it is easy to get strange and unusable results. We may get a negative unique variance, because one loading—say λ_1—can become indefinitely large (as the other becomes correspondingly small) and $\psi_1^2 = \sigma_1^2 - \lambda_1^2$ becomes negative. Consequently, a common problem with unrestricted factor analysis is that of *improper solutions*—solutions containing negative estimates of variance. If the model is not identified, because of doublet factors, even if the estimates do not have negative variances, it still may not be transformable into the independent clusters solution that gives rise to the data. Approximate factor analysis methods hide these problems, but do not solve them.[6]

Most programs for unrestricted (exploratory) factor analysis are based on mathematical devices that save a little computer arithmetic but do not allow the computation of *SE*s of estimate.[7] An important use of *SE*s is to verify that the model is identified at the best-fitting parameter values. No factor model is identified at all parameter values.

***For example, in any column of factor loadings, we could set all but two equal to zero, to yield an underidentified doublet factor. But in most cases this will not be a point at or near the maximum likelihood point. $$$

A good rule is that if the model is identified, the *SE*s will be of the order of magnitude of the value of the parameter divided by $\sqrt{n}$.

The best way to do an unrestricted factor analysis is to include just enough constraints on the model to prevent exchangeability of the factor loadings. A standard way to do this is to put zero factor loadings in the upper triangle of the factor loading matrix, as in Table 9.5. This pattern is known as an *echelon matrix* because of its resemblance to the flag shape known by that name. The analysis can then be done by ML, and *SE*s obtained. If the *SE*s are on the order of $1/\sqrt{n}$ it is safe to proceed with the exploratory analysis. In the case of the SWLS data, with $n = 215$, we expect *SE*s on the order of .07. When we analyze the SWL correlation matrix with an echelon factor loading matrix, we obtain the results in

TABLE 9.5
Echelon Factor Loading Matrix

λ_{11}	0	0
λ_{21}	λ_{22}	0
λ_{31}	λ_{32}	λ_{33}
λ_{41}	λ_{42}	λ_{43}
.		
.		
.		
λ_{m1}	λ_{m2}	λ_{m3}

Table 9.6. The discrepancies are quite satisfactory, and the analysis gives chi-square = .6696 on 1 df, $d = -.00266$, $m_c = 1.001$, slightly overfitting, so RMSEA cannot be computed. However, the SEs of the parameters for item 4 are unacceptably large. This was to be expected from our previous confirmatory analysis. The model, with uncorrelated factors, is not identified, because of the doublet factor formed by variables 4 and 5. When the factors are permitted to be correlated, as in the confirmatory solution given earlier, this problem solves itself, because of the second identifiability rule above. Just from these SEs, we know that the exploratory solution is unacceptable, and it would be unsafe to use a standard program for exploratory factor analysis with transformation to approximate simple structure. Even so, we now carry the example further. Table 9.7 gives results obtained by fitting the unrestricted two-factor model to the SWLS correlation matrix with loadings transformed—"rotated"—to approximate independent-clusters structure. The correlation between the factors is .658. This can be expected to differ from the correlation in the restricted model, because the relationships between the variables are partly explained by the small loadings replacing exact zeros. A comparison with Table 9.3 might suggest that the restrictive, independent clusters model has mistreated item 5 ("If I could live my life over, I would change almost nothing"). By Table 9.7, it would appear to be factorially complex, measuring mainly present satisfaction, but also satisfaction with the past. But we know by the analysis in Table 9.6 that the unrestricted analysis gives poor estimates, so we cannot take this evidence very seriously. On balance it is safer

TABLE 9.6
SWLS—Echelon Analysis

	Factor Loadings				Unique Variances	
1	.820	(.064)			.328	(.062)
2	.749	(.068)	−.117	(.192)	.425	(.098)
3	.716	(.064)	.058	(.093)	.484	(.059)
4	.546	(.078)	.749	(.965)	.141	(1.431)
5	.612	(.068)	.133	(.168)	.608	(.085)

TABLE 9.7
SWLS—Exploratory Factor Analysis

	Factor Loadings		Unique Variances
1	.808	.016	.329
2	.857	−.158	.418
3	.650	.098	.484
4	−.068	.918	.235
5	.477	.204	.604

in this case to choose the substantively satisfying independent-clusters solution.

In the context of test theory and test construction, good test design will generally allow us to choose a restricted factor model—at least with an independent-clusters basis, if not actual independent clusters. Therefore the technical problem of "rotation" to approximate independent clusters is left to an optional extra, the later section on the rotation problem.

To close this section, we consider an example of unrestricted factor analysis that is well behaved. The correlation matrix in Table 9.8 is taken from a classic study of the "primary mental abilities" by Thurstone. Instead of items, we have subtests. The variables are believed to have approximate independent-clusters structure, with 1–3 measuring verbal ability, 4–6 measuring word fluency, and 7–9 measuring reasoning ability. These are three of Thurstone's seven primary mental abilities. We act as though either we do not know this, or we want the analysis to confirm it. Fitting three factors in echelon form, with uncorrelated factors, gives Table 9.9.

The sample size is $n = 213$, $\chi^2_{(12)} = 2.9032$, $p = .9962$, $d = -.0427$, $m_c = 1.0216$, and again the model overfits. The important point to note is that the SEs of the unique variances are acceptable, so we may trust that the model is identified with respect to those parameters. It is therefore safe to apply a procedure that finds the best approximations to independent clusters that can be obtained as linear functions of these unrestricted loadings. Table 9.10(a) gives loadings with factors (still) uncorrelated—an *orthogonal solution*, which just means "with uncorrelated factors"; Table 9.10(b) gives loadings with correlated factors—an *oblique solution*. Table 9.10(c) contains the factor correlations, and Table 9.10(d) the discrepancies.[8] The model is overfitting the data, but a two-factor solution—not given—proves clearly unacceptable.

It still seems to be common practice to compute and report the (approximate) "orthogonal simple structure" solution, such as in the example

TABLE 9.8
Thurstone Correlation Matrix

1.000	.828	.776	.439	.432	.447	.447	.541	.380
.828	1.000	.779	.493	.464	.489	.432	.537	.358
.776	.779	1.000	.460	.425	.443	.401	.534	.359
.439	.493	.460	1.000	.674	.590	.381	.350	.424
.432	.464	.425	.674	1.000	.541	.402	.367	.446
.447	.489	.443	.590	.541	1.000	.288	.320	.325
.447	.432	.401	.381	.402	.288	1.000	.555	.598
.541	.537	.534	.350	.367	.320	.555	1.000	.452
.380	.358	.359	.424	.446	.325	.598	.452	1.000

Code. 1 = sentences; 2 = vocabulary; 3 = sentence completion; 4 = first letters; 5 = four-letter words; 6 = suffixes; 7 = letter series; 8 = pedigrees; 9 = letter grouping.

TABLE 9.9
Thurstone Data—Echelon Analysis

	Loadings						Uniquenesses	
1	.908	(.054)					.175	(.030)
2	.910	(.054)	.085	(.049)			.165	(.029)
3	.854	(.056)	.059	(.055)	.009	(.049)	.268	(.033)
4	.489	(.070)	.552	(.264)	.434	(.315)	.268	(.065)
5	.470	(.070)	.449	(.276)	.454	(.257)	.372	(.058)
6	.493	(.068)	.437	(.162)	.248	(.250)	.504	(.060)
7	.492	(.070)	−.256	(.382)	.640	(.181)	.282	(.096)
8	.608	(.065)	−.157	(.208)	.332	(.125)	.496	(.058)
9	.410	(.070)	−.057	(.359)	.596	(.084)	.473	(.071)

TABLE 9.10
Thurstone Data—Exploratory Analyses

(a) Loadings— Uncorrelated Factors			(b) Loadings— Correlated Factors			(c) Factor Correlations		
.833	.243	.268	.855	−.007	.051	1	.550	.522
.827	.317	.226	.867	.093	−.014	.550	1	.512
.774	.283	.230	.811	.066	.001	.522	.512	1
.228	.792	.230	.007	.837	.028			
.213	.706	.290	−.002	.723	.124			
.315	.616	.135	.184	.621	−.064			
.229	.180	.796	.039	−.035	.844			
.444	.166	.528	.389	−.050	.476			
.151	.312	.638	−.053	.183	.645			

(d) Discrepancy Matrix								
0	.001	.001	−.005	.006	−.001	.000	−.011	.007
.001	0	−.003	.001	−.002	.003	.006	−.003	−.010
.001	−.003	0	.006	−.006	−.006	−.010	.022	.007
−.005	.001	.006	0	−.001	.000	.004	−.004	−.004
.006	−.002	−.006	−.001	0	.000	−.005	.002	.008
−.001	.003	−.006	.000	.000	0	−.002	.007	.000
.000	.006	−.010	.004	−.005	−.002	0	.003	.000
−.011	−.003	.022	−.004	.002	.007	.003	0	−.004
.007	−.010	.007	−.004	.008	.000	.000	−.004	0

of Table 9.10(a). Apart from the fact that the independent-clusters structure is not as clear as with the "oblique"—correlated-factors—solution, this
is not good practice in general. Sometimes also loadings less than a stated
criterion for salience—.3 or .4—are censored from the report. If, in addition, no information relevant to misfit is published, the analysis cannot
be evaluated by the reader, and probably not by the investigator. It is then
best to regard the investigation as not having been done at all. If the

correlation matrix is published, the reader can reanalyze it more carefully. The important point is that uncorrelated factors in general cannot approximate independent clusters or simple structures. Table 9.11(a) shows the restrictive hypothesis of independent clusters fitted with uncorrelated factors. Table 9.11(b) gives the loadings for correlated factors. The orthogonal solution—with uncorrelated factors—gives $\chi^2_{(27)} = 216.421$, $d = .8893$, and $m_c = .641$, RMSEA = .1815. By any standards, this is an extremely poor fit. The oblique solution—with correlated factors—gives $\chi^2_{(24)} = 38.1963$, $d = .0666$, and $m_c = .967$, which is clearly an acceptable approximation. Table 9.12 gives the discrepancies for the two models. The cause of the misfit by uncorrelated factors is manifest. The correlations between variables in distinct clusters are not explained at all by the orthogonal factors. It is only because the approximation to independent clusters given by uncorrelated factors is very bad that they explain the across-cluster correlations. Thus, "orthogonal simple structure" rests on an internal contradiction. Failure to obtain "orthogonal simple structure" allows the model to explain correlations of variables in distinct clusters. There is another good reason why unrestricted factor analysis with uncorrelated factors cannot in general be recommended, namely, that factors uncorrelated in one population of interest are in general correlated in other populations, so the analysis lacks generality.

A reported oblique exploratory factor analysis can be evaluated by the reader, and can be regarded as an approximation to the corresponding restricted model provided that (a) enough information about the variables is given, (b) all the loadings—both "salient" and "nonsalient"—are reported, together with the factor correlations, and (c) a criterion of good-

TABLE 9.11
Thurstone Data—Independent Clusters Results

(a) Orthogonal Factor Loadings					(b) Oblique Factor Loadings				
.908	(.054)				.905	(.054)			
.912	(.054)				.914	(.054)			
.854	(.056)				.856	(.056)			
		.857	(.064)				.836	(.061)	
		.786	(.065)				.797	(.062)	
		.688	(.066)				.703	(.064)	
				.857	(.071)				.781	(.064)
				.648	(.070)				.720	(.065)
				.698	(.070)				.703	(.066)

(c) Factor Correlations					
1.000			.643		.670
.643			1.000		.637
.670			.637		1.000

TABLE 9.12

Thurstone Data—Independent Clusters Discrepancy Matrices

0	.00	.00	.05	.03	.04	-.02	.10	-.05
.00	0	-.03	.00	-.00	.08	-.05	.10	-.07
.00	.00	0	.00	-.01	.06	-.05	.12	-.05
.44	.49	.46	0	.01	.00	-.03	-.03	.05
.43	.46	.43	.00	0	-.02	.00	.00	.09
.45	.49	.44	.00	.00	0	-.06	-.03	.01
.45	.43	.40	.38	.40	.29	0	-.01	.05
.54	.54	.53	.35	.37	.32	.00	0	-.05
.38	.36	.36	.42	.45	.32	.00	.00	0

Note. Lower triangle, uncorrelated factors. Upper triangle, correlated factors.

ness of fit is reported. If one of the older approximate methods has been employed (as in commonly used defaults in commercial computer packages), instead of ML, it remains possible that the solution is unacceptable because the data contain doublet factors, and these cannot be detected by the cruder methods of analysis.

A general strategy can be suggested for exploratory work, which would be appropriate for areas of test construction where test content does not seem a clear guide for a restricted, confirmatory model. This is as follows:

1. Fit the model to a sample correlation matrix, even when engaged in an exploratory study of items. This will aid judgment by allowing a comparison of standardized loadings.

2. Fit the model in echelon form, using "confirmatory" software, for the factor loadings, estimating SEs, for a small number of factors. If the intention was to create a homogeneous test, start with one factor.

3. If the fit seems poor, refit in echelon form with larger numbers of factors until the fit is acceptable, making sure that the SEs stay within an order of magnitude of (no more than a factor of 10 times) $1/\sqrt{n}$. It can happen that with each additional factor the fit improves, slowly and smoothly. This is a warning sign that the items are not drawn from a coherent domain, and there is no compelling answer to the question of the dimensionality of the data.

4. If echelon form gives an acceptable fit with acceptable SEs, try to get an approximation to independent clusters by a "rotation" command. Generally this will require switching to an exploratory program. There is no guarantee that such an approximation can be found. Some investigators publish a rotated solution that is clearly not forming independent clusters, and manage to misperceive it as satisfactory.

5. If there is a clear approximate independent clusters structure, submit the groups of items to a team of subject-matter experts to see if they can identify the attribute measured by each group of items, and to see if they agree in their description of the attribute. Experience suggests that individual investigators can always give post facto "interpretations" of common factors, and once these are invented, they seem plausible to others. Getting agreement between independent judges is a much more stringent test of the appropriateness of the attribute description, and it represents one ideal of scientific objectivity.

6. The solution may suggest that some items are factorially complex. Again, ask a team of experts to identify these items independently.

It is an easy but bad decision to skip steps 5 and 6. A substantively convincing account of the pattern in the factor loadings—salient and nonsalient loadings—justifies the final step of fitting the corresponding restrictive model. The fit of this model must in general be worse than that of the exploratory model. The hope is that it will not be substantially worse. Conversely, by construction we may have a clear confirmatory restrictive hypothesis to fit to the data. If the fit is poor, a follow-up exploratory analysis might serve to diagnose the failure of the design. If the fit is good, a companion exploratory analysis will still check if we have missed anything.

For test construction purposes we will then repeat the analysis with the sample covariance matrix, to get parameters that can be used for reliability calculations as in Chapters 6 and 7. A possible alternative is to compute the unstandardized loadings and unique variances from the standardized parameters obtained, by multiplying each loading by the standard deviation of the variable associated with it, and the unique variance by the variance of the variable (see later section on analysis of correlation matrices).

HIGHER ORDER AND HIERARCHICAL FACTORS

Suppose now that we have an independent-clusters model with at least three correlated factors. The three primary mental abilities in the last section provide a good example of this. Historically, Thurstone's seven primary mental abilities were "reconciled" with Spearman's single general factor of general intelligence, G, by the recognition that the correlation matrix of the primary mental abilities—*first-order factors*—could be fitted to the factor model to give a *second-order factor*. Here the second-order factor can be called *intelligence*, as it is what the first-order attributes, here *verbal ability*, *word fluency*, and *reasoning*, measure in common, leaving each also its unique property, as named. Such a higher order common factor corresponds to higher levels of abstraction from behavior.

If, indeed, we analyze the correlation matrix of the three factors, as fitted in Table 9.10(c), we get the perfectly fitting factor loadings and unique variances in Table 9.13. With modern methods of fitting, we fit the first-order and second-order parameters simultaneously, by ML, giving Table 9.14.

TABLE 9.13
Thurstone Data—Spearman Analysis of Factor Correlations

Loadings		Unique Variances	
.822	(.062)	.324	(.053)
.782	(.062)	.389	(.053)
.815	(.062)	.336	(.053)

TABLE 9.14
Thurstone Data—Second-Order Factor Model

First-Order Loadings						Second-Order Loadings	
.905	(.017)					.822	(.047)
.914	(.017)					.782	(.051)
.856	(.022)					.815	(.052)
		.836	(.032)				
		.797	(.035)				
		.703	(.042)				
				.781	(.040)		
				.720	(.044)		
				.704	(.045)		

$\chi^2_{(24)} = 38.196$, $d = .0666$, $m_c = .967$, RMSEA = .0527

In terms of equations, this model may be written

$$X_1 = \lambda_{11}F_1 + E_1$$
$$X_2 = \lambda_{21}F_1 + E_2$$
$$X_3 = \lambda_{31}F_1 + E_3$$
$$X_4 = \lambda_{42}F_2 + E_4$$
$$X_5 = \lambda_{52}F_2 + E_5$$
$$X_6 = \lambda_{62}F_2 + E_6$$
$$X_7 = \lambda_{73}F_3 + E_7$$
$$X_8 = \lambda_{83}F_3 + E_8$$
$$X_9 = \lambda_{93}F_3 + E_9 \tag{9.9a}$$

with

$$F_1 = \gamma_1 G + \varepsilon_1$$
$$F_2 = \gamma_2 G + \varepsilon_2 \tag{9.9b}$$
$$F_3 = \gamma_3 G + \varepsilon_3$$

using γ_s for the second-order loadings and ε_s for second-order unique parts.

The *second-order factor model* is one way to introduce a general factor. The other recognized way, already illustrated earlier with the SWLS, is by a *hierarchical factor model.* Substituting for F_1, F_2, and F_3 in the preceding first-order equations gives

$$X_1 = \lambda_1\gamma_1 G + \lambda_{11}\varepsilon_1 + E_1$$

$$\cdot$$
$$\cdot \tag{9.10}$$
$$\cdot$$

$$X_9 = \lambda_9\gamma_3 G + \lambda_{93}\varepsilon_3 + E_9.$$

It might seem we can just write these equations as

$$X_1 = \lambda_1^* \lambda G + \lambda_{11} \varepsilon_1 + E_1$$

$$\cdot$$
$$\cdot \hspace{6cm} (9.11)$$
$$\cdot$$

$$X_9 = \lambda_9^* \lambda G + 1_{93} \varepsilon_3 + E_9,$$

which is a model with four uncorrelated common factors—one general, and three hierarchical group factors. Unless we maintain the constraints implied in (9.10), where the coefficients of G are products of the second- and first-order loadings from the independent clusters solutions, it is not equivalent to the higher order factor model (9.9). We can, in fact, derive its parameters from the previous analysis, in Table 9.12, with

$$\lambda_1 = \lambda_{11} \gamma_1$$
$$= .905 \times .822 = .744 \text{ etc.} \hspace{2cm} (9.12)$$

Also, we can rescale the second-order unique parts to be hierarchical group factors with unit variance, instead of variances $1 - \gamma_s^2$. This requires multiplying each λ_{js} by $\sqrt{(1 - \gamma_s^2)}$ in (9.9), so that we derive the hierarchical model parameters as

$$X_1 = (\lambda_{11} \gamma_1) G + (\lambda_{11} \sqrt{1 - \gamma_1^2}) \varepsilon_1 + E_1$$
$$= .744G + .515F_1^* + E_1 \text{ etc.,}$$

where F_1^*, F_2^*, and F_3^* here represent hierarchical group factors, with unit variance. The process of deriving the hierarchical parameters from the fitted higher order model parameters is known as the Schmid–Leiman transformation.[9]

We can also fit the hierarchical model directly, as in Table 9.15. The method is computationally quite technical, and the student would need

TABLE 9.15
Thurstone Data—Hierarchical Loadings

.744	(.046)	.515	(.061)				
.751	(.046)	.520	(.062)				
.704	(.046)	.487	(.058)				
.653	(.050)			.521	(.057)		
.623	(.051)			.497	(.054)		
.529	(.051)			.438	(.050)		
.636	(.051)					.452	(.062)
.587	(.053)					.417	(.057)
.573	(.053)					.408	(.057)

advice that is specific to available computer programs. The advantage of the direct method is that it gives us the *SE*s of the hierarchical parameters.

In this case, the loadings on the general factor are large enough to justify forming a total test score for "intelligence," and, in contrast to the case of the SWLS data as in Table 9.4, the group factors do not appear to be negligible.

THE ROTATION PROBLEM

It is enough for the student to know that a number of devices have been invented whose objective is to derive a set of factor loadings from a given set, which approximate independent clusters structure. Optional extra material is presented here.

***The simple hypothesis of exploratory common factor analysis prescribes only the number of common factors. It is not detailed enough to determine factor loadings as unique quantities to be estimated (except in the unidimensional—Spearman—case). The loadings are not identified. For any set of estimates, infinitely many alternative sets exist that would fit the data equally well. The mathematician can tell us how to compute from a given set of factor loadings all the possible alternative values. These are *transformations* of the values we first happen to obtain.

Many devices have been invented for "rotation to simple structure"— actually, rotation to approximate independent clusters—by transforming a given estimated factor pattern.[10] Essentially, there are three main approaches to this problem. These are graphical and counting methods, simplicity function methods, and target methods.

Graphical and Counting Methods

The oldest method involves the drawing of graphs—pairwise plots of the columns of factor loadings against each other—by human operators and the selection by eye of new axes for the graphs. This is an extremely complicated art. Most investigators use methods that can run themselves off on a computer, thus saving human effort. The results of graphical transformations have been regarded by methodologists as the standard by which the results of other methods are judged. Perhaps some still do so. Counting methods are computer adaptations of graphical methods. The computer counts the number of variables that have a loading less than a given size (say, .3) on each factor, and it tries to find a solution that maximizes this number. Because of the geometry of the problem, originating in the graphical treatments, this count of small values is known as the *hyperplane count*—the number of points close enough to a (hyper-)plane in multidimensional space. Pure counting methods have proved unworkable, and modifications of them are not among the best methods now available.

Simplicity Function Methods

In the simplicity function methods, the basic problem put to the mathematicians is to define a quantity that is computed as a function of all mr elements of the common factor pattern. It is designed to vary, as we transform the numbers in the factor pattern, becoming a minimum (or, for some functions, a maximum) at a set of values of the factor loadings that we would regard as a reasonable approximation to simple structure—in practice, to independent clusters. Such a function is called a *simplicity function.*

On the face of it, it looks impossible to define a usable simplicity function. The function depends on the values of the "large" elements in the transformed pattern, but the independent-clusters concept has no implication at all for the sizes of elements that are thought to be nonzero. Nevertheless, a number of simplicity functions have been defined that somehow appear to work in practice. They do yield recognizably acceptable approximations to the desired structure.

A solution to the problem of defining a simplicity function can be based on the commonsense reflection that a factor pattern matrix with simple structure has an extreme distribution of the absolute sizes of its elements. It will have many large (positive or negative) values and many small values but very few values of intermediate size. Such a spread of the values to the extremes could be measured by one of the usual measures of variability in descriptive statistics. A convenient choice would be to maximize the variance of the squared loadings. This will give a contrast between absolute values—very large versus very small—rather than signed values—large positive versus large negative.

Competing variants on this idea have been developed, and claims have been made about the general relative qualities of the results obtained. It seems impossible to find a simplicity function that is "better than" other simplicity functions in the sense that it always gives results nearer to (a) the known structure of artificial test data or (b) graphical solutions. Because simplicity functions depend on the irrelevant "large" values of the factor loadings, the solution given by one simplicity function will differ from the solution given by another simplicity function, and from the "best" solution as otherwise judged, by reason of irrelevant values of factor loadings that differ from one example to another. That is, the comparative performance of these methods is example specific, depending on the particular data set to which they are applied. So it is doubtful if there could be a way to show that one simplicity function is "generally best." If we use an approximate independent clusters or simple structure only as a guide for setting up detailed restrictive hypotheses, this does not matter.

Target Methods

In target methods (also known as *Procrustean* methods), we suppose we know where the zeros would be in an exact version of a hypothesized structure. We then choose a transformation to make the loadings corresponding to the target zeros as small as possible. Usually we minimize the sum of squares of those numbers. The main advantage is that the result is independent of the large loadings. The main disadvantage is that we must first choose a target. In practice, we can use a target method to improve a result obtained by one of the other methods. This also yields an automatic decision as to the location of the exact zeros. $$$

The user of computer programs is offered the following advice: The main choice is between "orthogonal rotation" and "oblique rotation." Orthogonal rotation yields a new solution that is also in terms of uncorrelated (orthogonal) factors, and gives a common factor pattern in which the factor loadings are both regression weights and correlations (when analyzing a correlation matrix). Oblique rotation yields (a) a common factor pattern—regression weights—(b) a common factor structure—correlations between the variables and the factors—and (c) the correlation matrix of the factors. The classical argument for orthogonal transformation is that factors are principles of classification that should be as independent as possible (i.e., uncorrelated). We have already considered an effective counterargument, that uncorrelated factors and independent clusters generally contradict each other. There are further important arguments for oblique transformations. Factors that are uncorrelated in one population may well be correlated in another, and correlated factors will tend to give invariant loadings (suitably scaled) from one population to another. A good choice is VARIMAX followed by a robust target method, such as PROMAX, or followed by DIRECT OBLIMIN, a simplicity function method known to avoid a problem known as *factor collapse*—an acutely pathological outcome in which a factor disappears altogether.

THE ANALYSIS OF CORRELATION MATRICES

Theory for the statistical estimation of factor loadings, factor correlations, and unique variances by ML leads to the use of the m variances and the $m(m-1)/2$ covariances of the sample data, as sufficient statistics. If instead the analysis is based on the $m(m-1)/2$ correlations, the estimates of the factor loadings and unique variances are just rescaled by dividing by the sample SDs/variances. This is what we might guess should happen, and it can be proved mathematically. (It requires that there are no equated parameters in the model, as in parallel and true-score equivalent structures.) Also, the sample covariance matrix and the sample correlation matrix give the same chi-square and (d, RMSEA, m_c) goodness of fit indexes (but not the same GFI).

However, if we make the error of analyzing the sample correlation matrix as though it were a covariance matrix, the SEs of estimate of the parameters will be incorrect because the analysis does not take account of the sampling error in the sample SDs. Because many users do not obtain SEs, and because the SEs are generally not altered greatly by this error, it may not be of crucial importance. Nor would it matter if the SEs were being used only to check on the identifiability of the parameters at the estimated values. However, having the SEs is certainly helpful in judging salience/nonsalience of factor loadings, especially in the case of hierarchical factors.

The SEs reported earlier are the correct (large-sample) SEs for the analysis of correlations.[11] The model needed is a rearrangement of parameters, substituting for (9.8) and (9.10) the covariances

$$\sigma_{jk} = \delta_j \delta_k \left(\sum_s \sum_t \lambda_{js} \lambda_{kt} \phi_{st} \right) \quad j \neq k \tag{9.13}$$

and variances

$$\sigma_{jj} = \delta_j^2 \quad j = k, \tag{9.14}$$

where $\delta_j, j = 1, \ldots, m$, is a *scaling parameter* to be estimated instead of the unique variances. The estimate of δ_j turns out to be the sample SD of variable j, and when the correlation matrix is analyzed by this model, the estimate of each δ_j is unity, as we might expect. But the estimate itself carries a SE, and in this rearrangement of the model, the unique variances are *parametric functions*, that is, functions of the other parameters,

$$\psi_j^2 = 1 - \sum_s \sum_t \lambda_{js} \lambda_{kt} \phi_{st} \quad j = 1, \ldots, m, \tag{9.15}$$

and their SEs are functions of the SEs of the other parameters. To carry out this analysis we model the scale factors, and write *program statements* declaring values of ψ_j^2 as functions. In independent-cluster models this reduces to the simple expression

$$\psi_j^2 = 1 - \lambda_{js}^2 \qquad (9.16)$$

and is easy to implement in a computer program.

The case of a hierarchical model for a correlation matrix is more complex. This model requires m program statements of type (9.12), m statements of type (9.16), and m statements corresponding to the rescaling of the hierarchical group factor loadings. It is perhaps enough for the student to know it can be done. Advice on how to do it should be obtained in the context of an available computer program.[12] In applications, an easy strategy would be to perform two analyses. Analyzing the sample correlation matrix (without bothering to use special statements to get correct standard errors) will yield judgments of the sizes of the discrepancies, of the salience (nonnegligibility) of the loadings, and of the acceptability of the estimated unique variances. And we can ignore the (incorrect) standard errors. A parallel analysis of the covariance matrix will yield correct standard errors and suitable confidence bounds on the loadings, and parameters scaled to yield coefficients (of the type of coefficient omega) needed in work described in Chapter 10. A more sophisticated treatment would be to analyze the sample correlation matrix with correct standard errors, by the use of program statements, and compute the unstandardized parameters from these. Some computer packages include standardized discrepancies in the output of the analysis of the covariance matrix.

REVIEW GUIDE

It is my hope that a careful study of the numerical results in the section on the multiple-factor model by example will give the student an appreciation of the applicability of the method, and an understanding of other applications by analogy. The student may take for granted the chi-square statistic and the resulting fit indexes, without, perhaps, a clear conceptualization of their basis in maximum likelihood, which involves very technical considerations.

For applications in Chapter 10 and again in Chapter 14, the distinction between the alternative independent clusters and hierarchical representations of multiple factors should be carefully studied.

END NOTES

General: An elementary account of factor analysis, not requiring matrix algebra, is given by McDonald (1985). A more technical discussion is in Mulaik (1972).

1. Sources are Spearman (1927) and Thurstone (1947), but see Thorndike and Lohman (1990) for a readable history.

2. The source is Guilford (1967).

3. See McDonald (1985).

4. See Browne and Cudeck (1992).

5. The source is Thurstone (1947). See McDonald (1985) for a further elementary account, or Mulaik (1972) for an account of intermediate complexity.

6. See McDonald (1985).

7. See Mulaik (1972).

8. These analyses use COFA, a simple program for exploratory factor analysis developed by Colin Fraser from one of my own. It is included in the set of programs available from the publisher.

9. Schmid and Leiman (1957).

10. See Mulaik (1972) and Hakstian (1971).

11. McDonald, Parker, and Ishizuka (1993). The implementation of this procedure can be tedious. Efficient methods are available in PROC CALIS in the SAS package. See Hartmann (1996).

12. The analyses reported here were performed by program COSAN, written by Colin Fraser and included in the set available from the publisher (see Fraser & McDonald, 1988). PROC CALIS performs the same operations more efficiently.

Validity

The concepts of *validity* and *validation* of tests and test scores have implications that could require a survey of all possible uses of tests, because all have been considered relevant to validity. If there is a single meaning for the "validity of a test score," it is captured in the defining statement, "a test score is *valid* to the extent that it measures the attribute of the respondents that the test is employed to measure, in the population(s) for which the test is used." This can be restated in noun form: "The *validity* of a test score is the extent to which it measures . . . ." We can also say, "a test score is *validated* by evidence of the extent to which it measures . . . ." These are formal restatements of the old and often-repeated proposition: "A test is valid if it measures what it purports to measure."[1] Recall, once more, that the word *attribute* carries its natural-language meaning—a quality, which may, according to Webster, be either inherent or incidental. Thus certainly it covers traits and states, and all examples given so far. We seek evidence to validate a given use of a test score. In principle, the evidence can come both from the original design of the test and from the intention and context of its use, which may be different from the original intent of the designer.

A general account of test validation involves three broad types of consideration. First there are the relevant technical methods of test theory, such as correlation, factor analysis, regression, and path analysis. Most of these techniques have been covered already. The last, which is rather technical, is left to Chapter 17. Second, there are substantive issues, which we can only glance at, mainly to illustrate some of the ways the technology of test theory is applied to validation. Third, there are issues in the philosophy of social science that bear on the interpretation of test scores, which we cannot entirely avoid.

First, a historical sketch of the evolution of the concept of validity/validation is offered.[2] The earlier phase of development of concepts of validity—dating approximately from the late 1930s—was embedded in a behaviorist tradition in psychology and a logical positivist philosophical framework, in which judgments of "meaning" of the content of item stems and response categories were considered unacceptably "subjective" for a behavioral science. The notions prevailed that the concepts of psychology are (a) convenient, fictional, explanatory "constructs"—constructed or invented by the psychological scientist—and (b) "unobservable," but "response-inferred," that is, inferred from objective, uninterpreted, records of behavior, as they might be gathered by an interplanetary investigator with no established form of communication with the respondents.

In this philosophical climate a common view tended to prevail that the validity or validities of a test score consisted of its ability to predict observable "criterion" behaviors. Accordingly, a test would be validated for applications by relating it with some "outcome" measure external to it. Examples would include evidence from the relationship of a test score to performance in a practical training program, or from significant differences in mean score between criterion groups, such as a psychiatrically diagnosed group contrasted with an unselected group of "normals." A test could then be said to have *predictive validity* for specified criterion behaviors—possibly plural behaviors and therefore plural validities. The same positivist/behaviorist spirit led to *concurrent validation*—the use of correlations of a new test of a named trait with an existing test bearing the same name. For example, a large correlation of the Wechsler Adult Intelligence Scale (WAIS) with the preexisting form of the Stanford–Binet Intelligence Scale would be offered as evidence that the former was indeed a test of intelligence. This could yield a sequence in which a revised Stanford–Binet is correlated with the WAIS, and so on, a process metaphorically lifting the concept by its bootstraps. Yet such concurrent validation tended to be regarded as objective and hence scientific, in contrast to internal evidence that the items belong to the intelligence domain. Differences in response from groups distinguished by psychiatric diagnosis could also be regarded as a special type of concurrent validation, limited by the reliability and validity of the diagnoses.

Indeed, reasoned objections were offered to the notion of *content validity*—that item contents could serve to establish that the resulting test score was a valid measure of a specified attribute. The "subjectivity" of judgment involved in the design of the item-stem contents (and response formats) was considered unscientific and suspect. It was also recognized that it is the combined responses of examinees that constitute the test score to be

validated, and the connection of these to the item-stem contents and response formats is, certainly, somewhat indirect. Other reasoned if not
always realistic objections could be raised in applications over the relevance
and representativeness of the item contents to the attribute to be measured.
One cannot be absolutely confident that the items chosen are drawn from
the domain of the concept, and representatively cover all aspects of it.
This is not so much an objection to using content as evidence of validity
as a recognition that this task is not always a simple one.

A set of standards for test developers and users issued by the American
Psychological Association in 1954 listed predictive validity, concurrent validity, and content validity as three "types" of validity, and added a fourth.
In keeping with the positivist philosophy, this was named *construct validity*,
but actually pointed to a way beyond positivism. *Construct validity* was defined in the Standards manual as "the degree to which the individual
possesses some hypothetical trait or quality [construct] presumed to be
reflected in the test performance." The concept of validating a construct
was developed more fully in a seminal paper published in 1955, by Cronbach and Meehl, who were members of the APA committee that determined the 1954 standards. In this paper they also referred to a "construct"
as an *attribute*, which would bring us back to the definition I gave initially.
They listed as "construct" validation procedures (a) criterion-group differences, (b) factor analysis, (c) item analysis, (d) experimental studies, and
(e) studies of process.

Largely through the further work of Cronbach and through contributions from Messick,[3] the wheel has come full circle, and the common view
now seems to be that there is indeed one conception of validity, which
(out of pure habit, it seems) is still referred to as "construct" validity. That
is, the validation of an application or class of applications of a test score
can be taken to include every form of evidence that the score to some
acceptable extent measures a specified attribute—quantifiable property or
quality—of a respondent. As we see later in more detail, content validity,
concurrent validity, and validation methods initially associated with "construct" validity are all methods of investigating the extent to which a test
score measures the attribute it is used to measure.

We note that the 1966 and 1974 APA Standards manuals combined
concurrent and predictive validity, as *criterion-related* validity, but for clarity
of conceptualization it becomes necessary to keep this distinction but re-
name predictive validity the *predictive utility*[4] of a test. We then distinguish
predictive utility—using the correlation of the test with another measure
for practical prediction of the latter—from concurrent evidence—using
such a correlation as evidence that it measures the intended attribute. As
a philosophic aside, we note that the term *construct*—logical or hypothetical
construct—appears to originate in Bertrand Russell's 1929 maxim that

wherever possible, logical constructions are to be substituted for inferred entities. A widely influential paper by McCorquodale and Meehl (1948) distinguished *hypothetical constructs*, conceived as unobservable (inferred) entities, and *intervening variables*, which we can think of as abstractions from observations. (This reverses Russell's original terminology.) It is in the context chiefly of validity studies that the term *construct* lingers on, but it has become ambiguous if not contradictory in its reference.[5] So once we separate off predictive validity as predictive utility, there is no longer any reason to attach the qualifier "construct" to validity/validation, and I do so only with quotation marks or parentheses.

A convenient division for our discussion of validation methods is as follows. In the next section we examine in a general way the use of item content as evidence for validity. The following section treats internal evidence of test score validity—evidence from relations between item responses in a homogeneous set of them. A third section, under the heading "Convergent and Discriminant Validity," shows how such internal evidence can be extended to items that form subdomains of an item domain. Then we give an account of a specialized technology—the *multitrait–multimethod matrix*—that has been considered appropriate for this purpose. A final section deals with external relations—relations between a test score and other measures—both as evidence that the score measures the specified attribute—concurrent validity—and as evidence of predictive utility.

ITEM CONTENT AND TEST SCORE VALIDATION

Most tests yield scores from items that use a code shared by the test constructor with members of his or her linguistic community, including potential respondents. Commonly the code is just the shared natural language. It might also be a mathematical code, as in arithmetic, algebra, or geometric figures. Even in cases where the items test whether some part of the code has or has not been acquired by the respondent—such as first-language vocabulary or specialized linguistic usage—the code is both learnable and understandable. Self-reports or peer ratings on such traits as sociability or cheerfulness are possible because of shared language. Given a shared code, we do not have to describe content validation as a subjective matter, except in the vacuous sense in which all judgments—including all propositions in science—are "subjective," namely, that they are indeed judgments, and judgments can be true or false. This is not to say, naively, that item stems necessarily have the same meaning for the respondent as for the item writer. As we show, care is needed.

It is notable that examples given in the 1954 APA Standards document suggest that content validity is primarily applicable to an educational achievement test, such as a test in American history. The document implies that achievements are "observable." (Perhaps, although this was never made clear, the notion was that an achievement is a direct abstraction from observed performances. For example, achievement in arithmetic is abstracted from achievement in a given set of arithmetic items.) In contrast, construct validity is described in the document as applicable to such "unobservable, explanatory constructs" as intelligence, numerical ability, creativity, or need for achievement. It is not clear what conception of observable/unobservable is employed in classifying these examples. It is also notable that Cronbach and Meehl chose "cheerfulness" as their primary example of an underlying, explanatory entity—a hypothetical construct.

There are, indeed, some quite deep philosophic problems pertaining to the technical vocabulary of the social/behavioral sciences. Here we can do no more than acknowledge a few of them. First, the reader might consider the distinction between an observable attribute, exemplified by achievement measured by a subset of achievement items, and an unobservable, "underlying" entity—a "construct"—exemplified by an aptitude measured by a subset of aptitude items. My own view is that it is not helpful to speak of achievements as observable and aptitudes as unobservable, or of traits/states such as "cheerfulness" as unobservable, underlying, or in any special sense "hypothetical constructs"—to say that we can perceive that someone smiles, but cannot judge that the person is cheerful. Yet it may be helpful to distinguish between *abstractive* and *existential* concepts, although the distinction will usually demand careful analysis, and sometimes remain unclear.[6] The notion is that some concepts in scientific (and lay) psychology are abstractions from what common sense would regard as observable.[7] These include most of those quantifiable attributes measured as achievements, abilities, personality traits, interests, and attitudes—that is, most of those measured by psychological tests. And in contrast, some concepts in science have the status of postulated entities not (currently) observable. Physics, chemistry, and molecular biology, for example, seem replete with them. Generally, postulated entities belong to theories that can be described as analogues or metaphors. Bohr's model of the atom as a copy of the solar system is a good example. We might say that theories, like poetry, are created, whereas empirical laws are discovered, verified, or falsified. Psychology does not yet seem well supplied with existential concepts (or created theories), although we may have abstractive concepts masquerading as existential concepts (and just possibly conversely). Cronbach and Meehl's notion of cheerfulness as an unobservable, explanatory entity is a prototype of a common view that traits are underlying, hidden causes of their indicators, not abstractions of which the indicators are instances.[8]

An appropriate test-theoretic model for the measurement of abstractive concepts would appear to be the item-domain model already introduced. The most informative validating evidence would then come from a careful conceptual analysis of item content in combination with the use of the factor model (and its nonlinear counterpart—the multidimensional item response model in Chap. 14). This would establish homogeneity or identify subdomains. There is plenty of room for error and for disagreement between investigators in the collection and interpretation of such evidence.

I accept that there is a limitation on the account in this chapter—that I do not know how to give general advice on the application of test theory technology to the validation of measurements on existential concepts. I give one example of the difficulty. Eysenck in 1955, after considerable study of the (abstractive) trait of extraversion, postulated that high levels of reactive inhibitory neural processes in the cerebral cortex characterize extraverts and "cause" extravert behaviors. (The theory was conceived by analogy to the behavior of dogs in Pavlov's classical conditioning studies.) Here we have an example of an existential concept—an entity—namely, a set of inhibitory neural processes—with a measure on the set—level of intensity—conceived as an attribute that is quantifiable in principle. Given the inaccessibility of cortical inhibition as a measurable process/entity, Eysenck instead tested a range of deductions beyond the domain of items measuring extraversion. He predicted that extraverts and introverts should differ on persistence of sensory aftereffects, conditionability, speed–accuracy, persistence at a task, and vocabulary/intelligence ratio.[9] All of these measures are so far removed from the domain of extravert behaviors that we could not reasonably regard them as forming a subdomain of it, or as forming a neighboring domain, to be subsumed under a superordinate concept, measurable as a second-order common factor. (My concern here is not with the substantive value or correctness of the theory, but with what is measured and how the measure might be validated.) It might be tempting to regard, say, amount of aftereffect as an imperfect measure of level of cortical inhibition. (This would be analogous to measuring electric current by its effects—say, on a magnetized needle in a coil through which the current runs.) It is not obvious that this is a reasonable measure. Indeed, it is not obvious that, in attempting to confirm the theory, we need, or should look for, a validated measure of the conceptual variable "level of cortical inhibition." I take the example to suggest at least that the main forms of validating evidence dealt with in this chapter are most clearly applicable to, if not limited to, abstractive concepts defining item domains, and may or may not be capable of extension to measures on existential concepts forming parts of theories. Whether this is true more generally is open to investigation.

With this said, I take it that the conceptual analysis of content is commonly a large part of our evidence of the validity of a measure of a psychological attribute. The actual development of items as indicators of traits such as need for achievement or intelligence, or states/traits such as depression, begins with a concept of the attribute. The concept may be imprecise, but some specification is necessary. The implied content domain may have ill-defined boundaries, and may contain subdomains, corresponding to subordinate concepts. Possibly the ill-defined boundary connects the domain to a neighboring one, such that the two concepts might be "merely" correlated, or conceivably related as causes and effects. For example, depression might be conceived of as including hopelessness, or hopelessness might be a cause or an effect of depression. Similarly, depression might include, or be a cause of, suicidal tendencies (expressed in ideation).[10]

In the paradigm case of "intelligence," there is Spearman's classic 1904 definition of it as the eduction of relations and correlates. This is recognizable as the basis of generalization and of propositional thought. Spearman's concept of intelligence fairly clearly includes such examples as analogies (black is to white as night is to ___?___), number series (1 3 5 7 ___?___), and letter series, which are still the basis of tests of fluid intelligence.[11] Other conceptions of intelligence may guide the construction of other sets of indicators. However, it is surely impossible to write items in the first place without a conceptualization of the attribute of which they are to be indicators. Similarly, an analysis of the concept of need for achievement by Jackson, Ahmad, and Heapy[12] suggested that its content domain includes six subdomains: (a1) concern for excellence, (a2) achievement via independence, (b1) status with experts, (b2) status with peers, (c1) competitiveness, and (c2) acquisitiveness. Items were then written as exemplars of these six (sub)concepts.

One way to look at this is to regard content design as guided in the first place by a conceptual system held by the test constructor(s) that constitutes a low-order classificatory theory. An independent content analysis by others of the written items is one test of the conceptual system, and constitutes a form of (content) validation. In some cases—such as a scale for attitude to gun control—the conceptual attribute may have such an indisputable character that the separate task of content analysis seems redundant. (I have seen an apparently serious discussion of an index of the validity of the item "I intend to vote in the next election" as a measure of intention to vote in the next election.)[13] When validation is attempted by statistical analysis of internal and external relations of item responses or test scores, the concepts and the content may in many cases have the final word, as well as the crucial role in the test design. Suppose we find high correlations between scores for (a) quantitative ability, (b) knowledge of mathematical facts, and (c) interest in mathematics. This finding may not compel us to override the conceptual distinction between ability, knowledge, and interest, and declare that these attributes of the respondent are not distinct. On the other hand, content analysis is certainly not the whole of validation. By definition, validity is the extent to which the test score measures a property of the respondents in the population(s) sampled, so it is not simply a property of the test as such. For example, a time-limited test containing elementary arithmetic items may indeed measure achievement in arithmetic, when given to children of appropriate age. If given to college students, presumably it measures speed of cognitive functioning. Note that this last conjecture rests on a conceptual analysis that takes account of the respondents and thereby goes beyond a rational analysis of item content.

Although the view can be found that content validity is not applicable to aptitude and personality tests, this is not consistently accepted, and the grounds for the claim are not clear. Content analysis is, of course, primarily a substantive matter, not a test-theoretic one. Most of the work on it has been in the context of measuring educational achievement. For this purpose, it is possible to describe a content domain in terms of educational objectives. Then items in the achievement test can be matched to the domain of objectives and their representativeness subjected to mild forms of quantification. We might compute the percentage of items matched to objectives, or percentage of objectives not matched to items.[14] Educational achievement is synonymous with attainment of the objectives of the teaching/learning process. It may be assessed on a content basis that is independent of the cognitive processes involved. Commonly, the objectives will be hierarchically classified or cross-classified in some way. Such classification schemes as Bloom's well-known taxonomy[15]—knowledge, comprehension, application, analysis, synthesis, and evaluation—suggest that some attempt is made to take account of cognitive processes. Yet a peculiar feature of achievement domains follows from the fact that they are curriculum based rather than trait based. They are generally cognitively complex, invoking many mental processes. Any psychometric structure they show may just reflect the fact that cognitive performances are generally nonnegatively correlated. It is enough for a set of performances to be positively correlated for a dominant dimension of achievement to emerge in any achievement domain.[16]

As soon as we begin a conceptual analysis, we can expect any content domain, of whatever degree of breadth or specificity, to reveal a conceptual structure, corresponding to a classification scheme. Such a "narrow" domain as elementary addition problems in arithmetic has facets such as "single-digit numbers vs. two-digit numbers" crossed with "requires vs. does not require place-value." Need for achievement, as mentioned earlier, has been subdivided into (a1) concern for excellence, (a2) achievement through independence, (b1) status with experts, (b2) status with peers, (c1) competitiveness, and (c2) acquisitiveness. On being told that factor analysis suggests a splitting of the domain into (a) autonomous striving for excellence with concern for excellence and achievement through independence nested within it, (b) need for status—with experts or peers, and (c) entrepreneurial competitiveness—including competitiveness and acquisitiveness—we recognize that such a classification might have been offered a priori. And further discussion might suggest that only the first of these can properly be called need for achievement itself, with the others being extrinsic motives.

In the original item design, the objects of classification into subconcepts are (a) to ensure that all aspects—all *facets*—of the general attribute have been identified, and (b) to write items to obtain a balanced, comprehensive representation of them, as far as possible. This depends on circumstances. For example, clinical psychologists recognize lack of empathy as a facet of sociopathy, yet it could be very difficult to design self-report items so that a sociopath reveals such a lack.

In a corresponding, independent, confirmatory content validation, a panel of judges can be chosen for the expected relevance and competence of their judgments. They are asked to sort the items, under varying degrees of information governing the sorting task. They could receive a complete disclosure of the test constructor's conceptual system, or they could be requested to construct their own conceptual system. A variety of indices of interpanelist agreement and panelist–constructor agreement might be computed.[17]

If the account of validity evidence from item content were left at this point, it could be described as overly optimistic and naive. The substantive literature on the development and application of psychological tests contains many instances that would serve as correctives to naivete and optimism. Readers will seek these out in their fields of specialization. Here we note again that the connection between the item stems and formats and the test score is quite indirect, and there is plenty of room for slippage in the conceptualization.

Some conceptual problems constitute disagreements—as, for example, between the psychiatric view that includes anxiety in the depression syndrome and the view that does not. Both internal and external relations can in principle yield evidence bearing on such disagreements. Errors within a conceptualization of an attribute or in item design, again in principle are open to correction.

It is not obvious where the limits of "content" analysis are located. Behavioral scientists are members of the species they study, and members of our species, whether scientists, poets, or parents, understand a great deal of human behavior, verbal or nonverbal, by empathy—a form of understanding given scientific legitimacy under the label *Verstehen*.[18] For example, parents and psychologists alike would interpret, in an infant of 12 months, seeking contact, smiling, approaching, vocalizing, and waving, as signifying *attachment* to the parent. The rating of such behaviors in the standard experimental setup known as the *Strange situation* has been used to measure *security attachment*. This measure has been subject to a considerable amount of work directed at validating it, but it would appear that none of this has involved questioning the significance of the smiling and so on.[19]

Another example that perhaps stretches the limits of the notion of content analysis is work on the "Hassles Scale." In the context of the observation that lack of social supports interacts with stressful life events to cause a variety of psychological and physical health problems, Kanner, Coyne, Schaefer, and Lazarus (1981) developed a self-report scale measuring "hassles"—minor but common stressors, that is, everyday life events that can be described as irritating, frustrating, and distressing to the respondent—traffic jams, problems preparing meals, and so on. Dohrenwend, Dohrenwend, Dodson, and Shrout (1984) tested the possibility that what the individual reports as (i.e. counts as) a stressor is itself a measure of (and perhaps a consequence rather than cause of) psychological health problems. To do this they obtained ratings of the items from a large sample of clinical psychologists in terms of the likelihood that they are symptoms of a psychological disorder. In response to a reply to this critique from Lazarus, DeLongis, Folkman, and Gruen (1985), Dohrenwend and Shrout (1985) further observed that the use of the header for the items, "there are a number of ways in which a person can *feel* hassled" [italics added], and the use of a response format limited to judgments of the "hassle" as (1) somewhat severe, (2) moderately severe, and (3) extremely severe, pushed the measure in the direction of failure to cope, rather than reportage of events. In turn, a conceivable source of contamination in the study by Dohrenwend et al. is the possibility that clinical psychologists will, by the habits of their profession, interpret the "objective" report of a stressful life event as a pathological symptom.[20] We are not here concerned with the substantive conclusions to be drawn in this example. It is offered to indicate how sophisticated content analysis can become, and to serve as a general warning against naiveté and optimism on the part of the test constructor.

As a way of leading into the next section, we recall that the five items of the SWLS were subclassified into Present Satisfaction and Satisfaction with the Past in Chapter 2, and a corresponding psychometric model was tested in Chapter 9. Generally, given a conceptual structure for the content domain, the next question is whether the conceptual structure elicits a corresponding structure in the responses of examinees in a population of interest.

INTERNAL PSYCHOMETRIC ANALYSIS

We wish to see how the analysis of item or subtest relationships can serve to validate the measurements. Chapters 6 and 9 have already given much of the technology needed here for what we may call the internal analysis of item or subtest relationships as it bears on (construct) validity—the structure of a conceptual domain. This is because evidence of reliability and generalizability, as already treated, and evidence of validity based on internal analysis are virtually identical.

The simplest case is that of a homogeneous test. The m items of a test may have been written so that they approximate a content-homogeneous set. This requires that they are indicators of just one conceptual attribute, and that each measures something unique to itself. That is, the items are written so that there are no subdomains in the domain. This is a difficult objective to aim for, and it is not necessarily the ideal target in test construction. As already discussed in Chapter 6, the psychometric test of homogeneity is whether the item covariance/correlation matrix fits a Spearman single-factor model in the population of interest. Confirmation that the test is psychometrically homogeneous, together with a convincing conceptual analysis, jointly constitute evidence of validity. That the examinees respond to the items as though indeed they measure just one attribute of the examinees is evidence that the test measures the one attribute—the one construct—that the conceptual analysis indicates it should measure. But note that there remains room for error in the conceptual analysis that cannot be corrected by the factor-analytic check on homogeneity. A homogeneous test can measure the wrong thing.

In Chapter 6, the SWLS data were shown to approximate a unidimensional test, perhaps closely enough to validate the total score as simply measuring the one attribute intended. The marginal nature of that possible decision makes the data set useful for the illustration of further possibilities. The five items were considered, alternatively, in Chapter 9, as drawn from the content domain with two subdomains, namely, Present Satisfaction—items 1–3—and Satisfaction with the Past—items 4–5. Accordingly, the data set was reanalyzed in Table 9.3. It is a matter of empirical fact, not a matter of rational content analysis, how far these content domains correspond to distinct behavior domains—distinct clusters exhibited in the structure of the responses of examinees in the population sampled. If we are not surprised at finding the correlation of .861 between the independent-cluster factors in Table 9.3, this is because such a correlation falls within a range of expectation based on experience, not mere logic. We would be surprised by a perfect correlation, because there must be people who recognize that their life has radically changed, for better or for worse. We would also be surprised by a zero or negative correlation, because there must be some degree of experiential consistency between past and present. In this example, the structure of relationships between the responses reflects the structure of the content domain. Therefore the independent-clusters analysis of Table 9.3 gives validating evidence that the five items do measure the two distinct but closely related subdomains we have identified on the basis of item content.

The hierarchical model in Table 9.4 provides even more useful evidence. When we rearrange the model in terms of three uncorrelated factors—the general (domain) factor of satisfaction with life and the two hierarchical group (subdomain) factors—we can see that the loadings on the general factor are acceptably high, whereas the loadings on the hierarchical group factors barely reach the accepted criterion for salience, and so would jointly account for very little of the item relationships. This evidence convincingly shows that we can use the sum score on the five items to measure the superordinate attribute they were designed to measure.

We turn next to the notion of treating the validity of a test score as an indexable quantity. It has long been accepted that the "criterion" validity of a test is measured by the correlation between the test score and the criterion measure. It is perhaps not immediately obvious how to quantify validity in the absence of a criterion. Yet in fact we already know how. In Chapter 6, reliability was treated as the precision with which a homogeneous test of m items measures the attribute of which the items are indicators. When the attribute is identified with the domain score—the score on a test of infinite length—reliability is measured by coefficient omega, given by (6.20), to which G-C alpha, given by (6.25), is a generally very good lower bound.

We recall that coefficient omega is the square of the correlation between the test score and the domain score. We are logically impelled to say that in a homogeneous test, omega is both a reliability coefficient and a (construct) validity coefficient. The test score is valid to the extent that it is related to the domain score defined by the attribute.

If our m items are multidimensional, and fit the independent-clusters factor model, we should not form the total score, but instead should form a cluster total score for each attribute. In the case of the SWLS data, we have for Present Satisfaction

$$Y_1 = X_1 + X_2 + X_3,$$

with variance, from Table 9.1,

$$2.566 + 1.560 + 1.487$$
$$+ 1.560 + 2.493 + 1.283$$
$$+ 1.487 + 1.283 + 2.462 = 16.181.$$

Then from Table 9.3, by (6.20b),

$$\omega(Y_1) = (1.326 + 1.146 + 1.140)^2/16.181 = .806.$$

Similarly, for Satisfaction with the Past,

$$Y_2 = X_4 + X_5,$$

with variance, from Table 9.1,

$$2.769 + 1.323 + 1.323 + 3.356 = 8.771.$$

Then from Table 9.3,

$$\omega(Y_2) = (1.024 + 1.292)^2/8.771 = .612.$$

The two sum scores, Y_1 and Y_2, are, of course, correlated. As discussed in Chapter 3, the covariance of the sums of two disjoint sets of item scores is just the sum of their item covariances. Their correlation is then obtained by dividing by the square root of the product of their variances, given by the sum of the elements of the covariance matrix of each set. Here, by Table 9.1,

$$\rho_{Y_1 Y_2} = (1.195 + 0.845 + 1.127$$
$$+ 1.425 + 1.313 + 1.313)/\sqrt{16.181 \times 8.771}$$
$$= .606.$$

(The fact that the correlation between the cluster sums is less than that of their common factors, .861, is an example of attenuation due to the unique parts included in these sums.)

The independent-clusters solution gives separate values of omega, one for each cluster. These are (construct) validity coefficients for the subtest scores as measuring the subdomains. The rearranged hierarchical solution in Table 9.4 restores the general attribute and yields an index of the construct validity of the total score. The total score

$$Y = X_1 + X_2 + X_3 + X_4 + X_5$$

has, from Table 9.1, variance 39.388, so (6.20b) gives

$$\omega(Y) = (1.230 + 1.063 + 1.059 + 0.950 + 1.198)^2/39.388$$
$$= .768.$$

This is the squared correlation between Y and G in equation (9.5), so the correlation itself is given by

$$\rho_{YG} = \sqrt{\omega} = \sqrt{.769} = .877.$$

*** Proof:

$$X_j = \lambda_j G + \lambda_{j1} F_1 + \lambda_{j2} F_2 + U_j,$$

so

$$Y = (\Sigma\lambda_j) G + (\Sigma\lambda_{j1}) F_1 + (\Sigma\lambda_{j2}) F_2 + \Sigma U_j,$$

so

$$Cov(Y,G) = (\Sigma\lambda_j),$$
$$\rho_{YG} = (\Sigma\lambda_j)/\sigma_Y = \sqrt{\omega} . \quad \$\$\$$$

In this section, discussion has focused on the one example, but the points illustrated are general. Fitting a single-factor model to the item covariance matrix tests whether items constructed to be content homogeneous are psychometrically homogeneous—whether the responses mirror the content structure. Fitting a multiple-factor model tests whether the items form subdomains. These might be expected by construction, and a confirmatory factor model fitted, or might be found by exploratory factor analysis. A hierarchical factor model allows a judgment of the relative importance of the general attribute of the domain and the subdomain attributes.

The alert reader will have noticed that the value of omega—.769—obtained for the hierarchical general factor of the Satisfaction with Life Scale is less than G-C alpha. It was shown in Chapter 6 that alpha is a lower bound to omega in a homogeneous test, and omega can be computed equivalently by (6.20), as a function of the general factor loadings, or by (6.21), as a function of the unique variances. However, it is not a lower bound to omega if—as in the hierarchical model—the test or subtest contains factorially complex items. In such cases, (6.21) does not give us the value of omega, which is the squared correlation between the test score and the general factor. Instead, (6.21) would give the proportion of variance due to all the factors, which is not the desired reliability/validity coefficient. This is one reason why Chapter 6 defined omega by (6.20), and not by (6.21). McDonald (1970) showed that the quantity given by (6.21) is bounded below by G-C alpha, in both homogeneous and nonhomogeneous—multiple-factor—tests, but the calculation of this quantity does not seem well motivated, and is not recommended. For the same reason, the calculation of G-C alpha cannot be recommended unless it has been verified that the set of items is homogeneous, because in the general case it has no particular relationship to omega. (It does seem to have been common practice for researchers to obtain alpha as a—lower bound—estimate of reliability in sets of items that may be, or are known to be, nonhomogeneous. The practice is not recommended.)

Accordingly, in correspondence to the factor model we have used, we may compute validity coefficients as follows:

1. A single-factor analysis gives the squared correlation of the total test score with the general factor—the domain score—by (6.20) or (6.21).
2. An independent-cluster analysis gives the squared correlation of each cluster score with its cluster/group factor, again by (6.20) or (6.21).
3. A hierarchical solution gives the squared correlation of the total test score with the hierarchical general factor, by (6.20), but not by (6.21).

Although we could also compute the proportion of variance of the total test score due to all of the factors—general and group—for comparison, by (6.21), this is not a well-motivated index.

These procedures can be applied as an approximation to binary data, but a more rigorous extension of this work to binary items requires multidimensional item response theory, treated in Chapter 14.

CONVERGENT AND DISCRIMINANT VALIDITY

The concepts and principles to be discussed in this section overlap with those of the preceding one, but they belong to a line of development that deserves a separate and appropriate treatment. They also supply an introduction to structural models for crossed, as opposed to hierarchical designs.

In what has become regarded as a classic paper on construct validity, Campbell and Fiske in 1959 suggested that multiple measures of a construct could be said to have *convergent validity* if they are sufficiently highly correlated, and they could be said to have *discriminant validity* if they have sufficiently low correlations with tests of other, distinct constructs.[21] The natural explication of these somewhat intuitive conceptions is through the independent-clusters factor model. In the SWLS data we ask whether the two clusters are sufficiently discriminable to treat them as separate attributes. Similarly, the analysis of the Thurstone Primary Mental Ability subtests in Table 9.10 confirms that the three groups of subtests indeed measure separate attributes. The correlations within and between groups in Table 9.7 directly suggest that the subtests exhibit convergent and discriminant validity in the sense of Campbell and Fiske. The factor model then accounts for those relative sizes.

We wish to quantify convergent and discriminant validity—that is, we wish to compute coefficients of convergent and discriminant validity. To do this, we can compute (a) the correlation between the cluster sums and their own factor, and (b) the correlation between the cluster sums and the other factors. We already have, in the last section, for the Satisfaction with Life data, the correlations

$$\rho_{Y_1 F_1} = \sqrt{.806} = .898,$$
$$\rho_{Y_2 F_2} = \sqrt{.608} = .780.$$

These are, respectively, the correlations between the cluster sums of Present Satisfaction and of Satisfaction with the Past, and their own attributes (factors). It is easily shown that the correlations of each cluster sum with the factor of the other cluster sum are obtained by multiplying their correlation with their own cluster sum by the correlation between the factors. Thus,

$$\rho_{Y_1 F_2} = \rho_{Y_1 F_1}\rho_{F_1 F_2} = .898 \times .861 = .773,$$
$$\rho_{Y_2 F_1} = \rho_{Y_2 F_2}\rho_{F_1 F_2} = .780 \times .861 = .672.$$

These correlations can be arranged in a *convergent-discriminant validity matrix*

$$
\begin{array}{c}
 \\
Y_1 \\
Y_2
\end{array}
\begin{array}{cc}
F_1 & F_2 \\
\left[\begin{array}{cc}
.898 & .773 \\
.672 & .780
\end{array}\right].
\end{array}
$$

This matrix shows that the Y_1 cluster score is nearly as good a measure of the attribute F_2 of the Y_2 cluster score as the Y_2 score itself.

Similarly, from Table 9.7, we define three cluster sums:

Y_1, the sum of the three verbal tests.

Y_2, the sum of the three word-fluency tests.

Y_3, the sum of the three reasoning tests.

We refer to the corresponding factors in the independent-clusters solution of Table 9.10 as V, W, and R. Then from the information in these two tables we obtain the three values of omega, by (6.20b), for the clusters. We obtain

$$\omega(Y_1) = (.905 + .914 + .856)^2/(3 + 2 \times 2.383) = .921,$$

giving

$$\rho_{Y_1 V} = \sqrt{.921} = .960,$$

and similarly we get

$$\rho_{Y_2 W} = .909,$$

and

$$\rho_{Y_3 R} = .884.$$

We combine these with the factor intercorrelations of Table 9.10(c) by multiplying by the factor correlations. Thus, $\rho_{Y_1 W} = \rho_{Y_1 V}\lambda_{VW}$, $\rho_{Y_2 V} = \rho_{Y_2 W}\rho_{VW}$, and so on. This gives the convergent/discriminant validity coefficients in Table 10.1. In this case, each cluster sum is highly correlated with its own factor, but has sufficiently low correlations with other factors to justify the judgment that the three sets of subtests have convergent and discriminant validity.

*** MULTITRAIT–MULTIMETHOD MATRICES

This is an optional, technical extra section.

The main contribution of Campbell and Fiske was to suggest that any test can be regarded as a "*trait–method unit,* a union of a particular trait content with measurement procedures not specific to that content" (1959). The covariation of scores might be due to irrelevant method effects as well as (or perhaps even rather than) to a common trait or construct. In the SWLS example, all the items are worded positively and share a 7-point response format as detailed in Chapter 5, Table 5.1. Some of the covariation of the items could be due to a form of *response set.* Response sets are

TABLE 10.1
Thurstone Data—Convergent/Discriminant Validity Coefficients

	V	W	R
Y_1	.960	.617	.643
Y_2	.584	.909	.579
Y_3	.592	.563	.884

individual differences in a general response tendency, such as a tendency to acquiesce, or to give a socially desirable response. More generally, the idea is that measurements of the construct can be contaminated by effects of the method of measurement. To segregate this contamination, Campbell and Fiske recommended a *crossed design*: Each of two or more distinct "traits" is measured by each of two or more distinct "methods," yielding a *multitrait–multimethod (covariance or correlation) matrix*. They suggested that by studying such a matrix we can get evidence of convergence of the alternative methods measuring each trait, and discrimination of distinct traits measured by the same methods. Their original proposal was to study the pattern of correlations directly.

A number of structural models, mainly using confirmatory factor analysis, have since been proposed for the analysis of such crossed designs. These have generally been applied to correlation matrices rather than to covariance matrices. This creates some problems because in a crossed design we expect to have equated parameters, and therefore need a model for variances and covariances (and possibly for means). This area of research seems quite active, and not yet ready for a general survey.[22] It may suffice to focus discussion on a single illustration and then to make some general remarks.

Table 10.2 gives a correlation matrix rearranged from one discussed in Campbell and Fiske (1959). The 15 measures are ratings (on an 8-point scale) for the five named traits, of 124 clinical psychologists in training, by the training staff, their teammates, and themselves. Unfortunately, the means and variances have not been recorded. The common task is rating, which is not here considered a "method." Rather, "method" corresponds to the rater. The matrix contains three types of correlation. The blocks of 3×3 matrices marked down the diagonal contain correlations between ratings of the same trait by different raters (*monotrait–heteromethod* correlations). The underscored coefficients are between ratings of different traits by the same rater (*heterotrait–monomethod* correlations). The remaining coefficients are between ratings of different traits by distinct raters (*heterotrait–heteromethod* correlations).

As in the case of the Primary Mental Abilities correlation matrix of Table 9.7, the three ratings, regarded as multiple indicators of each of the named traits, show convergent validity if they have high intercorrelations in each of the diagonal, marked blocks (monotrait–heteromethod). Also, as in the Primary Mental Abilities matrix, they show discriminant validity if these correlations are higher than the unmarked correlations outside the diagonal blocks (heterotrait–heteromethod). However, because of the crossed design, as further evidence of discriminant validity, the correlations of distinct ratings of the same trait—monotrait–heteromethod correlations—should be higher than the correlations of any rater's ratings of

TABLE 10.2
Campbell and Fiske Correlation Matrix:

Assertiveness
Cheerfulness   Staff ratings
Seriousness   ×   Teammate ratings
Unshakable poise   Self-ratings
Broad interests

	A.St	A.T	A.Se	C.St	C.T	C.Se	S.St	S.T	S.Se	U.St	U.T	U.Se	B.St	B.T	B.Se
A.St	1.00														
A.T	.71	1.00													
A.Se	.48	.46	1.00												
C.St	.37	.35	.31	1.00											
C.T	.39	.37	.36	.51	1.00										
C.Se	.17	.09	.23	.42	.24	1.00									
S.St	-.24	-.18	-.22	-.14	-.15	-.10	1.00								
S.T	-.27	-.15	-.15	-.31	-.19	-.25	.43	1.00							
S.Se	-.04	-.40	-.05	-.13	-.11	-.12	.22	.31	1.00						
U.St	.25	.26	.19	.46	.38	.10	.08	-.06	-.13	1.00					
U.T	.03	.11	.12	-.05	.23	-.11	.03	.19	.06	.20	1.00				
U.Se	.13	.10	.16	.27	.15	.26	-.03	.00	.11	.22	.14	1.00			
B.St	.35	.41	.12	.19	.29	-.03	.09	.03	-.05	.31	.07	-.04	1.00		
B.T	.19	.33	.23	.05	.22	-.03	.19	.19	.06	.29	.29	-.03	.47	1.00	
B.Se	.37	.27	.21	.15	.12	.15	-.07	.17	.09	.05	.31	.26	.35	.35	1.00

Note. A, assertiveness; C, cheerfulness; S, seriousness; U, unshakable poise; B, broad interests; St, staff ratings; T, teammate ratings; Se, self-ratings. Underscored coefficients are between ratings of different traits by same rater.

distinct traits—heterotrait–monomethod correlations. Simple inspection of the correlations suggests that these properties generally hold, except in the case of "unshakable poise"—which is possibly an ill-defined trait.

There are now a large number of structural models for crossed designs. It is not a settled question whether any of them is an improvement on inspecting correlations. If a number of named traits are rated by several raters, as in the example, presumably the named traits are the attributes that the ratings measure in common, and whose validity is in question. (This point is not clear in discussions of such methods.)

A linear, additive model for the example could be written as

$$Y_{tr} = \lambda_{tr}F_t + \gamma_{tr}F_r + E_{tr}. \tag{10.1}$$

In this model, Y_{tr} is trait t judged by rater r; F_t is the "true" rating of the tth trait, as measured by the three ratings; λ_{tr} is the loading associated with the rth rater rating trait t; F_r is the random effect of the rth rater on the trait ratings, and γ_{tr} the loading associated with it. For example, the assertiveness rating by staff can be represented as

$$Y_{A.St} = \lambda_{A.St}F_A + \gamma_{A.St}F_{St} + E_{A.St}.$$

It would actually be better to fit such a model as this to a covariance matrix, and to the means of the ratings, but all work in the literature to the time of writing seems to (mis)apply this type of model to a sample correlation matrix. (I follow custom, knowingly doing the wrong thing, because the data set is almost regarded as a paradigm case, and means and variances are unrecorded.) The model is easier to define and fit than to explain, so further explanation is postponed until we consider the output of the analysis. With some apparent arbitrariness, we suppose (a) the five trait factors F_t are correlated, (b) the correlations between trait factors F_t and rater factors F_r are zero, and (c) the three rater factors F_r are mutually uncorrelated. The consequence of these assumptions is that the trait factors account for heterotrait–heteromethod correlations—correlations between distinct ratings of distinct traits—whereas the rater factors account only for heterotrait–monomethod correlations—correlation between ratings of different traits by one rater, but not for ratings of different traits by different raters.

This model gives an acceptable fit, by maximum likelihood, with a chi-square of 86.521 on 70 df, $p = .088$, $d = .133$, $m_c = .936$, and RMSEA = .044. The factor loadings and unique variances, with their standard errors in parentheses, are given in Table 10.3.

The three loadings associated with each of the five trait factors represent the (standardized) effect of the subject (ratee) on the rating from staff,

TABLE 10.3
Campbell and Fiske Data—Analysis

	A	C	S	U	B	St	T	Se	ψ^2
A.St	.874 (.047)					-.0541 (.099)			.533 (.084)
A.T	.813 (.050)						.174 (.087)		.509 (.079)
A.Sc	.556 (.074)							.079 (.109)	.685 (.083)
C.St		.791 (.068)				.193 (.112)			.338 (.104)
C.T		.685 (.072)					.267 (.101)		.460 (.099)
C.Se		.444 (.090)						.202 (.115)	.762 (.087)
S.St			.589 (.102)			.445 (.162)			.455 (.176)
S.T			.659 (.103)				.369 (.110)		.429 (.146)
S.Sc			.410 (.103)					.307 (.117)	.737 (.103)
U.St				.760 (.175)		.484 (.160)			.187 (.278)
U.T				.192 (.110)			.547 (.122)		.664 (.133)
U.Sc				.312 (.112)				.534 (.141)	.618 (.185)
B.St					.630 (.090)	.276 (.121)			.527 (.116)
B.T					.616 (.088)		.498 (.111)		.373 (.129)
B.Sc					.575 (.089)			.576 (.145)	.338 (.172)

Note. Symbols as in Table 10.2.

217

team, and self. If we think of F_t as the "true" level of trait t (in standard score units) in a random ratee, the factor loading λ_{tr} represents the response of each rater to a unit difference in F_t. The relative magnitudes of these across the raters seem to require, for their interpretation, a correspondence to the clarity of the trait name and/or to the ability of each rater type to make the necessary judgment. Thus, staff, teammates, and the rater him- or herself would be clear what assertiveness is, and would have opportunity to assess it. Hence it has a large loading for all three rater types. And we might indulge in some amount of post facto rationalization to explain why staff and teammates are more responsive to the ratee's cheerfulness than the actual ratee.

The rater effect, F_r, in the model is, in a sense, an error due to the rater, also random over ratees. The assumption that the errors of distinct raters are uncorrelated is motivated (a) by a wish to obtain the consequence that these error effects will account only for within-rater covariation of ratings, not covariation of different raters' ratings of the traits, and (b) by the fact that without it, I get unacceptable parameter values—correlations greater than unity between the rater errors. It may seem plausible that errors of judgment of the ratees by distinct raters could be correlated. Thus, all could be subject to the same general "halo effect," rating subjects under the influence of one trait by an assumed consistency of trait constellation. But such an effect, although it can be imagined, could not be segregated by any analysis of a multitrait–multimethod matrix. For this reason, a possibly overrestrictive model has been adopted, for clarity of separation. Indeed, there is a quite general lack of theory relating multitrait–multimethod matrices to method effects.

Somewhat symmetrically with the loadings of the raters on the traits, the loadings of the traits on the rater error factor represent the extent to which each trait generates error in the individual rating. Well-defined, readily observable traits such as assertiveness and cheerfulness generate very little rater error, in contrast to "unshakable poise" and "broad interests." The fact that the three sets of loadings for staff, teammates, and self are similar fits this notion. They do not seem to be governed by distinct implicit notions about what traits should belong together in the ratees.

From the model (10.1), with zero correlation between any trait factor and any rater error factor, we have a partition of the unit variance of each (standardized) rating into three components,

$$\text{Var}\{Y_{tr}\} = 1 = \lambda_{tr}^2 + \gamma_{tr}^2 + \psi_{tr}^2. \tag{10.2}$$

These are, respectively, trait variance, rater variance, and unique (error?) variance. For example,

$$\mathrm{Var}\{Y_{\mathrm{A.St}}\} = 1 = .874^2 + (-.054)^2 + .233.$$

Table 10.4 gives the proportion of variance due to these three sources, fulfilling one of the objectives of multitrait–multimethod analysis: segregating variance due to "method contamination"—here, rater error—from "true" trait variation. For example, we can see that the smallest contribution of "method"/rater error is to ratings of assertiveness by staff, whereas the largest is to ratings of broad interests by self.

We compute a convergent/discriminant validity coefficient matrix for the five traits, as in the examples in the previous section. The correlations between the five trait factors are given in Table 10.5. From the correlations of the ratings in Table 10.2 (giving the variances of the five sum scores over raters) and the loadings on the trait factors in Table 10.3, we obtain the five omega values:

$$\omega(A) = .801 \quad \omega(C) = .698 \quad \omega(S) = .551$$
$$\omega(U) = .385 \quad \omega(B) = .645.$$

We combine these with the trait correlations in Table 10.5 as before to get the validity coefficient matrix in Table 10.6.

A further aspect of the analysis has been left undisclosed to this point. The model I used included a further restriction. The correlations between the five trait factors were restricted to fit a single higher order common factor, a construct tentatively named "positive affect." The object was to

TABLE 10.4
Campbell and Fiske Data—Variances

	Trait Variance	Rater Variance	Unique Variance
A.St.	.764	.003	.233
A.T	.661	.030	.309
A.Se	.309	.006	.685
C.St	.626	.037	.338
C.T	.469	.071	.460
C.Se	.197	.041	.762
S.St	.346	.198	.455
S.T	.434	.136	.429
S.Se	.168	.094	.737
U.St	.578	.234	.187
U.T	.037	.299	.664
U.Se	.097	.285	.618
B.St	.397	.076	.527
B.T	.379	.248	.373
B.Se	.331	.332	.338

Note. Symbols as in Table 10.2.

TABLE 10.5
Campbell and Fiske Data—Trait Correlations

A	1	.613	−.407	.481	.400
C	.613	1	−.429	.506	.421
S	−.407	−.429	1	−.336	−.280
U	.481	.506	−.336	1	.330
B	.400	.421	−.280	.330	1

Note. Symbols as in Table 10.2.

TABLE 10.6
Campbell and Fiske Data—Validity Coefficients

	A	C	S	U	B
Y_1	.895	.549	−.364	.430	.358
Y_2	.512	.835	−.358	.423	.352
Y_3	−.302	−.318	.742	−.249	−.208
Y_4	.298	.314	−.208	.620	.205
Y_5	.321	.338	−.225	.265	.803

see if the 15 ratings could reasonably be summed to give a measure of a global attribute, and to illustrate the further use of omega as a validity coefficient for the total score. The loadings of the five trait factors on the general factor are:

A   .763 (.087)
C   .804 (.089)
S   −.534 (.137)
U   .630 (.157)
B   .524 (.116)

These were combined with the first-order trait loadings in Table 10.3 to obtain loadings of the 15 ratings on the general factor, in the equivalent hierarchical model. From Table 10.2, the variance of the sum of the (standardized) ratings is 42.40. This gives, for the general factor,

$$\omega(G) = (.763 \times .874 + .763 \times .813 + .763 \times .556 + .804 \times .791 \ldots)^2/42.40 = .404,$$

or $\rho_{YG} = \sqrt{.404} = .636$ for the correlation between the total score and the general factor of "positive affect." It is, of course, very unlikely that such a study would be followed up by the routine use and combination of ratings from three such sources for the evaluation of further individuals. A more likely use of the information would be as a basis for choices of rater (subject to considerations of cost and convenience) and of traits to be rated, to maximize trait validity and minimize contamination due to rater error.

A final disclosure about the analysis of the example is necessary. When the model is fitted without imposing a Spearman model on the trait correlations, a better fit is obtained, as shown by a chi-square of 67.693 on 65 df, $d = .02172$, RMSEA = .018, and $m_c = .989$. However, standard errors are unacceptably large, so the restriction to the Spearman model is partly motivated by the desire to obtain identified parameters.

A few general remarks can be offered about multitrait–multimethod matrices. No doubt these remarks will rapidly become out of date. The typical pattern of the factor loading matrix in a crossed design does not satisfy identifiability conditions, so a common problem with linear models for these matrices is underidentifiability, or at least unacceptably large errors of estimate of the parameters. This would have happened in the example treated here, without the Spearman model for the trait correlations. This problem needs further research. When we consider the class of multitrait–multimethod matrices, another unsettled question we notice is the denotation of "methods." In the example considered, the "methods" were distinct raters. Examples in the literature include (a) different raters, as already considered, (b) repeated occasions, and (c) different scaling methods, at least. The actual diversity of crossed designs suggests a need for specific models following the logic of each design. For example, a design with variables crossed with repeated occasions would require an analysis of means and covariances (not correlations) in terms of time series, as mentioned in Chapter 6 with reference to Cronbach generalizability theory. This would be quite a different model from the one for trait–rater combinations. Further, it is possible to lose sight of the fact that these crossed designs were motivated by a desire to segregate and measure variance (as in Table 10.4) due to "method error." Known types of method error include halo effect, social desirability, acquiescence sets, evaluation apprehension, demand artifacts, and key informant biases in ratings.[23] We have already noted that the multitrait–multirater design of the example is not able to segregate halo effect, unless it is not shared by staff, teammates, and self. Possibly what is needed is a search for designs specific to "halo effect, social desirability, . . .", bearing in mind that perhaps some of these cannot be separated by means of any design whatsoever.

Multitrait–multimethod matrices typically contain variables that are not indicators of "constructs," in the sense of abstract attributes corresponding to a domain of possible indicators. One limitation of the treatment of the example just given is that it is hard to define a population of rater types, of which staff, teammates, and self are examples. So it is not clear that we may regard the trait factors as well defined or regard them as common factors in the sense in which positive affect is the common factor of the traits.

Multitrait–multimethod matrices do not appear to have the special association with convergent/discriminant validity that has traditionally been accepted following Campbell and Fiske's original association of them. The independent-clusters common factor model seems to provide a much more straightforward treatment of convergent/discriminant validity. $$$

CONCURRENT VALIDITY AND PREDICTIVE UTILITY

Before going into more practical matters, it is necessary to glance, if superficially, at yet another problem in the philosophy of social science. This is the question of whether or not the relations of a concept to other concepts are constitutive of its meaning. In their seminal 1955 paper on "construct" validity, Cronbach and Meehl took the position that the meaning of a test score is not known until it has been embedded in a *nomological net*—a comprehensive network of laws relating it to other variables. In this view, the meaning, for example, of *depression* as measured by the set of items in the Beck Depression Inventory will not be known until we have a comprehensive set of laws relating the depression measure to antecedents such as stressful life events or perhaps a physiological constitutional determiner, and laws relating depression in turn to suicidal impulses or acts, and so on. The alternative view is that the meaning of some (most?) concepts measured by test scores is already constituted by internal content analysis and homogeneity analysis. Relationships of a depression measure to life stress or to suicidal tendencies would not then be needed to tell us what the score "means," but would rather provide independent information of scientific and possibly practical value. My own view is that the conceptual autonomy of the measure—the independence of its meaning from the empirical relations into which it enters—assures clear understanding of those relations. If we say that suicidal tendencies or life stresses are part of the meaning of depression, we are not free to regard its relations to these as in some sense causal.[24] This is not to deny that external relationships of a test score to other variables may serve as evidence correcting a misconceptualization of an attribute. One reason why an expected relationship may fail to be confirmed is invalidity of measurement of variables in the relationship.

It has already been noted that the correlation of a total test score with an external measure can be used in two ways. First, it can be used as an index of its predictive utility—its usefulness as a predictor of that performance. Second, it can be collateral evidence of its validity—that it measures an attribute expected from theory to influence or be influenced by the external measure.

A test score, or a score profile from a battery of subtests, is often used to predict an external "criterion" using regression methods as described in Chapter 8, or the simple correlation of the test score with the outcome measure. Cognitive applications include prediction (and selection of examinees) with reference to attainment in college or graduate school, or to performance in complexly skilled vocations, such as performance as a motor mechanic, nurse, or air traffic controller. Noncognitive applications include prediction of recidivism, or response to therapy, or breakdown under stress. A test score or test-score profile used in this way can be said to have criterion-related validity, and some writers, understandably enough, will continue to do so. I have chosen to regard this as a matter of the predictive utility of the test score, for reasons already given. At one time, as already noted, predictive validity/utility was believed to be the primary sense of validity, because contents and "constructs" were subject to suspicion from behaviorists. Indeed, it has sometimes been said that a test has as many validities as there are external measures that it is correlated with.[25] To stay within the compass of the general definition of validity, we would have to say that the possibly complex set of attributes measured by the test is a *disposition* or *tendency* to behave in the ways expressed in the external, predicted criterion. Such "dispositions" would include the notion of "aptitudes" for cognitive/vocational performances. The concept of *aptitude* represents a suitability to a specific situation or purpose—an aptness or fittingness of the task to the person and the person to the task. I therefore choose the simpler option of referring to *predictive utility*.

The distinction between the use of an external criterion measure for predictive utility—just as a performance that requires predicting—and its use as concurrent evidence of validity—evidence from concurrent measures that the test score measures the conceptual attribute it was designed for—depends on context, not on any test-theoretic technicalities. Thus, an intelligence test might be given as a useful predictor of academic attainment, and used as a selection device. Alternatively, the size of the correlation between the intelligence test and academic attainment might be interpreted as evidence that the test measures intelligence, where intelligence is considered distinct from academic attainment, but as one factor that influences it. For this purpose, the correlation should not be too low—this will suggest the test does not measure cognition at all—and not too high—this will suggest the intelligence test is really just another academic attainment measure. More complex and systematic studies of the relation of test scores to external measures can be used for validation. Path analysis—Chapter 17—seems to cover a large part of what Cronbach and Meehl originally meant by a nomological net—a network of laws, possibly causal, possibly merely correlational—connecting the measures.

The use of external relationships for validation points toward an unending mode of inquiry into all possible contexts for the variable whose validity is still in question—if it is not settled by evidence from content and structure as already discussed. A simple and crude illustration may help to make this point. Further confirmation that a test measures anxiety could—ethics permitting—be obtained experimentally by demonstrating significant changes in anxiety score through manipulation of anxiety-provoking situations. Given the ethical considerations, a permissible alternative is to postulate a network of relations of the anxiety measure with uncontrolled environmental measures and to study the network by means of path analysis (Chap. 17). Confirmation of the predicted relationships can be taken as evidence for the composite hypothesis that both (a) the test measures anxiety and (b) anxiety is related to environmental factors as the theory states. (Competing explanations of the confirming evidence would need to be examined also.) Failure to find predicted relationships or effects would be weighed against the evidence of content and structure, to allow the possibility either that the test does not "really" measure anxiety, in spite of evidence from content, or that the theory of the effects of environment on anxiety is incorrect.

It is possible to investigate discriminant validity, and possibly also convergent validity, at the level of the test score. One would obtain scores on the test in the context of scores from other tests that are thought to measure different attributes—hoping to find correlations that are not too high. One might include scores from tests thought to measure the same attribute—hoping to find correlations that are not too low. It does not seem possible to describe a general strategy for setting up such a design in applications.[26] Generally, if it were not for limitations due to computer software, it would be more informative to analyze the joint factor structure of the items, or at least of appropriately formed subtests.

The use of external relationships as further evidence of (construct) validity is appropriate when the test has indeed been designed to be a content-homogeneous, approximately unidimensional measure of an attribute, preferably with a high value of omega or G-C alpha. Its purpose is then to verify—given doubt—that the attribute has been correctly conceptualized. When the test is used simply as a practical predictor (and selection device) of some important nontest outcome—for example, of success in therapy or of being admitted to jail or graduate school—predictive utility is most efficient if the m items or subtests of the test are selected in such a way that they are each highly correlated with the criterion, and are mutually uncorrelated. Such a set of items will have zero omega and G-C alpha. The reader will see the truth of this statement on reviewing the material on multiple regression in Chapter 8. There is nothing strange about the observation that we maximize the predictive utility of a set of items or subtests by minimizing their validity. When both are regarded as types of validity, this fact can appear paradoxical.

In applications, it may be difficult to find uncorrelated items each highly correlated with an outcome variable. The predictors of excellence in graduate school or of successful therapy outcome are hardly likely to be unrelated. There is a continuum connecting alternative treatments of item correlations for predictive utility. At one extreme, items may be chosen from a large initial pool by stepwise regression. Hopefully, this will simultaneously minimize correlations between predictors and keep a large squared multiple correlation with the outcome variable. If this approach is taken, the multiple-regression weights will be used to make a weighted total test score. The careful investigator will use cross-validation (Chap. 8) and will estimate the predictive precision of the regression by (8.41). At the other extreme, a very small number—perhaps two or three—of homogeneous (sub)tests may be chosen for their theoretical relevance to components of the outcome. For example, the three components of the Graduate Record Examination could be combined to predict performance in a specific graduate school, in suitable weighted proportions. Similarly, a complex skill requiring both intelligence and motor coordination could be predicted by using two corresponding component tests. Clearly, there are strategic choices lying between the two extremes.

Given a test whose items group into two or more subtests, prediction of an external variable from the subtest scores will in general be better than from the overall test score. At least in the calibration sample, by definition the multiple regression maximizes the relationship with the criterion. Of course, this may not hold up in cross-validation with a fresh sample. If the subtests fit a Spearman factor model, and the unique components of the subtests are not only uncorrelated with each other (by definition) but are also uncorrelated with the criterion, it will suffice to use the total test score as predictor. If, as is quite possible, one or more unique components are correlated with the criterion, they add information to the prediction. A technical account of this possibility requires a *structural equation model.*

The topic of structural equation modeling is deliberately postponed to Chapter 17, regarded as an optional extra for some readers. But as a foretaste of that material, and as a way to point to the problems and challenges implied by a general program of validation by fitting models representing a network of laws—a nomological net—we consider some interpretations of a simple empirical example. Until Chapter 17 is reached, the reader can think of a structural equation model as like a common factor model, with causal relations replacing some of the relations between common factors and their indicators. Hull, Lehn, and Tedlie (1991) obtained measurements of "self-criticism" (SC), "high personal standards" (HPS), and "overgeneralization of failure" (OGF). These had been treated in previous work by Carver and Ganellan (1983) as components of a "self-punitive attitude" (SPA). Hull et al. also obtained a measure of "depression" (D). (The sample size was 138.) These terms have sufficient natural-language meaning for it to seem plausible that the measures SC, HPS, and OGF do indeed belong to subdomains of SPA. A carefully trained psychologist, who knows that causal relations cannot be safely inferred from correlations, might nevertheless entertain the following causal conjectures:

1. A self-punitive attitude causes depression. (And accordingly, psychotherapy directed at self-punitiveness should reduce depression.)
2. Depression causes a self-punitive attitude. (And accordingly, an antidepressant should reduce self-punitiveness by reducing depression.)
3. Depression is a subdomain contained within the domain of self-punitive attitude.

Perhaps not surprisingly, the models implied by 1 through 3 are indistinguishable, all three yielding a chi-square of 45.7563 on 2 df, $d = .317$, RMSEA $= .398$, $m_c = .853$. We then consider three further hypotheses, namely:

4. Depression is caused by self-punitive attitude, plus a special causal contribution to it from the overgeneralization-of-failure component.
5. All four variables are subdomains of self-punitive attitude, with a special correlational link between overgeneralization and depression.
6. All four have self-punitive attitude as one common factor, but depression and overgeneralization have an additional factor in common.

Models 4 through 6 again are indistinguishable, all yielding a chi-square of 2.1303 on 1 df, $d = .00819$, RMSEA $= .091$, $m_c = .996$.[27] Details of this example are given in Chapter 17. All analyses lead to the unequivocal conclusion that overgeneralization of failure has a special correlation with depression over and above the correlation of self-punitive attitude with it. However, because of the equivalence of the alternative explanatory models, it seems impossible to use these relationships as external evidence of the conceptual structure of each of the four tests, beyond any evidence that would be available from the item-score relations within and between them. It is difficult to say how general this conclusion would prove to be.

As the final topic of this section, we consider the effects of error of measurement. In both concurrent validity and predictive utility studies, both the predictor variables and the criterion are subject to "error," so it might seem natural to consider using reliability theory to correct the correlations between predictors and criteria for errors of measurement. The mathematical principle is simple, but care is needed about the motivation for such corrections in applications. Suppose we have reliability coefficients (a) for the predictor Y, (b) for the criterion V, say, or (c) for both. Chapter 7 gave formulas (7.25) and (7.26) for correction for attenuation, here repeated for case (a),

$$\rho_{T_Y V} = \rho_{YV} / \sqrt{\rho_Y} \,,$$

for case (b),

$$\rho_{Y T_V} = \rho_{YV} / \sqrt{\rho_V} \,,$$

and for case (c),

$$\rho_{T_Y T_V} = \rho_{YV} / \sqrt{\rho_Y \rho_V} \,.$$

As before, T_Y and T_V are the true parts of Y and V, and ρ_Y and ρ_V are their reliability coefficients.

In applications, the motivation of any of these corrections needs careful examination. If the predictor test is a set of unrelated items selected for their correlation with V, certainly it would be a mistake to correct for "error" due to lack of a common attribute. (The equivalent of this error can occur in the use of path analysis.) Even if the predictor is a homogeneous test, correction for attenuation will be well motivated if either (a) we wish to know by how much prediction can be improved by lengthening the test (and that supposes we would know in theory at least how to do so), or (b) we believe the evidence of (construct) validity of the predictor is better exhibited by the correlation of its true score/attribute with the external measure. In many applications, we wish to know how well the given test predicts, in spite of its measurement properties, which might be poor.

Correction for errors in the outcome variable alone would seem reasonable in certain applications. The motive is to see how well the predictor would have performed if the criterion were not defective. Care is needed. If we are fortunate enough to have multiple measures of outcome—and not just one supervisor's rating of performance, or one psychiatrist's rating of therapeutic outcome—these may reflect components of the outcome, all of which are necessary to the indexing of "success." In such a case, their combination, not their common attribute, is then the desired criterion, and correction for attenuation is inappropriate.

*** The reader who is already familiar with a multivariate method known as *canonical variate analysis*, which finds a weighted combination of predictors to maximize prediction of a weighted combination of criteria, will recognize its applicability to this problem. That topic is outside the scope of the present account.[28] \$\$\$

It seems that it would be an unusual circumstance in which (7.26) should be used to correct for "errors" in both the predictor and the outcome variable. The referents of the corrected correlation are, in effect, scores on tests of infinite length measuring the two attributes. The purely theoretical purposes of such corrections may be left to Chapter 17 on path analysis with latent variables—structural equation models.

REVIEW GUIDE

The discussion of the general concept of validity should be studied in detail. The section on internal analysis should be straightforward reading, at this stage. Its central point is that construct validity can be measured by coefficient omega, which gives the squared correlation between the test score and the attribute defined by the item domain.

The treatment of convergent–discriminant validity as correlations between subtest scores and the factors of the subtests departs from the original notion of Campbell and Fiske (1959). The student should both understand the concept and be able to compute a convergent–discriminant validity matrix from the factor model parameters.

The student should already, from Chapter 7, be able to apply the formulas for correction for attenuation. It is important to understand the conditions under which corrections are justified.

END NOTES

General: A primary resource—and recommended further reading—for this chapter is Messick (1989). See also Wainer and Braun (1988).

1. Angoff (1988) described this as the "traditional formula" before the 1950s.
2. This account is mainly an interpretation of Angoff (1988).
3. Messick (1980, 1989) in particular.
4. Angoff (1988).

5. A paper by Feigl (1950) gave a still readable account of the problem of theories that postulate the existence of unobservable entities, as seen in the framework of positivist empiricism. In McCorquodale and Meehl's (1948) account an "intervening variable" was close to Russell's notion of a "logical construction," and a "hypothetical construct" was close to the "inferred entity" that Russell wished to eliminate from science.

6. This is a variant on the basic conceptions of McCorquodale and Meehl (1948) and Feigl (1950).

7. A sophisticated discussion of what can be firmly declared to be "observable" leads into a philosophical tangle. For once I cut the knot by appealing to "common sense."

8. An excellent account of a realist treatment of theory in social science, focusing on identity and the emotions, was given by Greenwood (1994).

9. Eysenck (1955). For an account of the more recent substantive status of the theory see Claridge (1986). An early defense of the theory is to be found in a paper by McDonald and Yates (1960).

10. For an interesting example of this problem the reader is referred to Abramson, Metalsky, and Alloy (1989), who discussed a subspecies of depression, named *hopelessness depression*, of which hopelessness is conceived as a cause, not as directly characterizing the subspecies.

11. See Spearman (1927) and Cattell (1971).

12. Cited by Messick (1989).

13. Saris and Van Meurs (1990).

14. See, for example, Hambleton (1980).

15. See Bloom, Hastings, and Madaus (1971).

16. McDonald (1988) discussed Guttman's "first law of intelligence."

17. Haynes, Richard, and Kubany (1995) gave a fairly systematic account of content validation, which can be recommended for follow-up reading.

18. A classical discussion of *Verstehen* by Abel (1948), understandably taking a positivist/behaviorist position, significantly conceded that empathic understanding serves as an aid in preliminary explorations and in generating hypotheses.

19. See Lamb, Thompson, Gardner, Charnov, and Estes (1984).

20. This sequence of articles is recommended for further reading.

21. Campbell and Fiske (1959) is the source reference.

22. For discussion of models for MTMM, see Widaman (1985) and Browne (1984a).

23. Bagozzi (1993) gave a useful discussion.

24. The interested reader is referred again to Abramson et al. (1989) for the details behind these remarks.

25. See, for example, Lord and Novick (1968, Chap. 12).

26. Reynolds and Kobak (1995) described a validation study of a self-report depression scale, the Hamilton Depression Inventory (HDI). They gave as concurrent evidence a high correlation between the HDI and a clinical interview from which it was derived, and as evidence of convergent validity correlations with self-esteem (negative), hopelessness, suicidal ideation, and anxiety. A low correlation with a social desirability scale was described as evidence of discriminant validity. An interesting example of the combination of a number of lines of validation evidence is to be found in Block, Block, and Harrington (1974). These authors examined the validity of a score on the Matching Familiar Figures Test as a measure of "reflection–impulsivity." The study combines careful analysis of alternative conceptualizations of content, with generalizability to other tests that should also measure the attribute, and expected relations to other measures. This could be regarded as checking convergent/discriminant validity at the level of the test score.

27. Hull et al. (1991) were careful to indicate that they avoided characterizing their models in "causal" terms, and that they made their data available so that others—as here—can test alternative models. See Carver and Ganellen (1983) for the concept of self-punitive attitude and its components.

28. For an account of canonical variate analysis see Johnson and Wichern (1992).

Classical Item Analysis

In a sense, this chapter takes up where Chapter 3 left off, but its topics find a more natural place here, because they use material in Chapters 6 and 9 and because they prepare for topics following shortly—item factor analysis and item response theory in Chapters 12 and 13.

A number of devices have been developed in classical test theory that constitute the topic of *item analysis*. Classical item analysis uses conventional parameters of general statistical theory to characterize (a) items, (b) relations between items and test scores, and (c) relations between pairs of items. The usual intention is to use these as aids in making a choice of best subsets of items. Given an initial pool of items, we may wish to choose a subset that gives a test of suitable length for general application. We will want it to be homogeneous, and have satisfactory reliability, validity, or predictive utility.

The first section deals with relations between the items and the test score of which they are components, with some reference to the comparable problem of relations between the items and an external criterion variable. The next section deals with statistics of test scores in relation to the item parameters, and the use of these for item selection. The final section treats item correlations.

ITEM–TEST RELATIONS

Traditionally, the correlation between the item score and the total test score has been regarded as an index of *item discriminating power*. The term lacks a precise definition, and the item–test correlation is at best a rough index of it. The intuitive notion is that if this correlation is high, the item discriminates between examinees with low total score and examinees with high total score. If the total score is a reliable measure of just one attribute, the item–test correlation ρ_{X_jY} should give at least a rough indication of the correlation between X_j and the attribute the items are designed to measure. This at least appears to be the motivation.

It is no longer necessary to take the traditional treatment for granted. Before taking up the more precise conception of item discrimination provided by item response theory, we can critically evaluate the classical item–test coefficients in terms of the factor model. In applications, we would hope to have a large item pool from which we will select a much smaller set for a final test. If the item pool contains a small enough number of items to allow fitting a factor model or item response model (say 200 or less),[1] those models will provide the appropriate methods. If the pool is too large, the traditional item parameters can be effective substitutes. Here we illustrate classical item analysis with our ubiquitous LSAT6 and SWLS data. The expected effects of having larger numbers of items can be indicated easily enough.

There are two plausible alternatives in computing covariances or correlations between an item and a test score. If we compute the covariance/correlation between X_j and $Y = \Sigma\ X_k$—the *item–total-score* relationship—because Y includes X_j itself, the coefficient obtained will be spuriously increased, but the same quantity Y is the criterion for "discriminating power" for every item. If we compute the covariance/correlation between X_j and $Y - X_j$—the *item remainder score*, omitting X_j from the item sum with which it is correlated—this eliminates the spurious increase of the obtained parameter, but the criterion is different for each item. For a sufficiently large number of items, the effect of omitting or not omitting the item score will become negligible.

Table 11.1 contains a listing of parameter estimates for the five items of the LSAT6 data, and Table 11.2 contains parameter estimates for the five items of the SWLS data. These collect together the computations to be described, and they are referred to as needed, to illustrate the general points to be made. The necessary information for computing the estimates in Tables 11.1 and 11.2 is contained, respectively, in Tables 6.8 and 6.3.

By (3.27) the variance of the test score, $Y = X_1 + \cdots + X_m$, is given by the sum of the m^2 elements of the covariance matrix of the items. Table 6.8 gives the estimate 1.0702 for the variance of the LSAT6 score. Table 6.3 gives 39.383 for the SWLS variance. We now list a number of possible measures of item discriminating power.

1. The first measure of item discriminating power to consider is the covariance between the jth item score and the test score. This is the sum of the elements in the jth row or column of the covariance matrix. That is,

TABLE 11.1
LSAT6 Item Parameter Estimates

		X_1	X_2	X_3	X_4	X_5
(1)	p_j	.924	.709	.553	.763	.870
(2)	$\hat{\sigma}_{jj}$	.0702	.2063	.2472	.1808	.1131
(3)	$SD(X_j)$	.2650	.4520	.4972	.4252	.3363
(4)	$\hat{\sigma}_{XY_j}$	.0992	.2663	.3181	.2351	.1515
(5)	$\hat{\sigma}_{XZ_j}$	.0960	.2574	.3290	.2273	.1464
(6)	$\hat{\rho}_{XY_j}$	.3619	.5695	.6617	.5346	.4353
(7)	$N^{-1}(p_j)$	1.4325	.5505	.1132	.7160	1.1264
(8)	$n\{N^{-1}(p_j)\}$	.1430	.3429	.3954	.3087	.2115
(9)	$\rho_{XY}^{(b)}$	.6706	.7507	.8321	.7363	.6922
(10)	$\hat{\sigma}_{XZ}^{(f)}$	.101	.265	.319	.234	.150
(11)	$\hat{\sigma}_{(Y-X_j)}^2$	.9421	.7439	.6810	.7808	.8803
(12)	$\hat{\sigma}_{X_j(Y-X_j)}$	.0297	.0600	.0709	.0543	.0384
(13)	$\hat{\sigma}_{XZ_j(Y-X_j)}$	.0303	.0696	.0859	.0615	.0409
(14)	$\hat{\rho}_{X_j(Y-X_j)}$	.1143	.1540	.1728	.1446	.1216
(15)	$\hat{\rho}X_{(Y-X_j)}^{(b)}$	.2119	.2030	.2172	.1992	.1934
(16)	$\hat{\sigma}_{XZ_j}^{(f)}$	.1012	.2653	.3192	.2342	.1503
(17)	$\hat{\sigma}_{XZ_j(Y-X_j)}^{(f)}$	.0316	.0684	.0872	.0605	.0396
(18)	λ_j	.0605	.1345	.1861	.1174	.0745
(19)	ψ_j^2	.0665	.1882	.2126	.1670	.1076

TABLE 11.2
SWLS Item Parameter Estimates

		X_1	X_2	X_3	X_4	X_5
(1)	$SD(X_j)$	1.6019	1.5789	1.5690	1.6640	1.8319
(2)	$\hat{\sigma}_{XY_j}$	8.233	7.494	7.672	7.259	8.730
(3)	$\hat{\sigma}_{XZ_j}$	1.312	1.194	1.222	1.157	1.391
(4)	$\hat{\rho}_{XY_j}$	0.819	0.756	0.779	0.695	0.759
(5)	$\hat{\sigma}_{(Y-X_j)}^2$	25.483	26.888	26.501	27.654	25.279
(6)	$SD_{(Y-X_j)}$	5.0481	5.1854	5.1479	5.2587	5.0278
(7)	$\hat{\sigma}_{X_j(Y-X_j)}$	5.667	5.001	5.210	4.490	5.374
(8)	$\hat{\sigma}_{XZ_j(Y-X_j)}$	1.123	0.964	1.012	0.853	1.069
(9)	$\rho_{X_j(Y-X_j)}$	0.701	0.611	0.645	0.513	0.584
(10)	$\hat{\sigma}_{XZ_j}^{(f)}$	1.311	1.202	1.221	1.158	1.383
(11)	$\hat{\sigma}_{XZ_j(Y-X_j)}^{(f)}$	1.122	0.974	1.010	0.856	1.059
(12)	λ_j	1.290	1.104	1.148	0.952	1.185
(13)	ψ_j^2	0.901	1.274	1.144	1.863	1.951

$$\sigma_{X_jY} = \sum \sigma_{jk} \qquad j = 1, \ldots, m, \tag{11.1}$$

where the summation is over k. For example, the covariance of item 1 with total score in the LSAT6 data is

$$.0702 + \cdots + .0021 = .0992.$$

Similarly, we obtain the remaining entries in rows 4 and 2, respectively, of Tables 11.1 and 11.2. [Alternatively, these covariances can be obtained from raw data by forming the sum score as an $(m + 1)$-th variable and computing the m covariances by the standard formula (3.2.13).]

2. Next, we compute the covariance of each item (unstandardized) with the standardized test score, σ_{XZ}, where $Z = (Y - \mu_y)/\sigma_Y$. These *semistandardized covariances*—with the test score standardized whereas the item scores are not—are estimated by

$$\hat{\sigma}_{X_jZ} = \hat{\sigma}_{X_jY}/\hat{\sigma}_Y. \tag{11.2}$$

For example, for item 1 of the SWLS data, we have in line 2,

$$\hat{\sigma}_{X_1Y} = 8.233 \qquad \sigma_Y = \sqrt{39.383} = 6.2756,$$

yielding

$$\hat{\sigma}_{X_1Z} = 8.233/6.2756 = 1.312.$$

We get the remaining entries in row 5 of Table 11.1 and row 3 of Table 11.2 in the same way.

3. Next we get the item–test correlations ρ_{X_jY} in turn by dividing each semistandardized covariance by $\hat{\sigma}_{X_j}$. [Or, directly, we compute them by the standard formula (3.2.11) from raw data.] In the examples, the required *SD*s are in Table 11.1, row 3, and Table 11.2, row 1. In the LSAT6, the correlation between item 1 and the total,

$$\rho_{X_1Y} = .096/.265 = .362$$

and for SWLS

$$\rho_{X_1Y} = 1.312/1.6019 = .819.$$

The remaining values, in row 6, Table 11.1, and row 4, Table 11.2, follow similarly.

Of these first three, the product–moment correlation between the item score and the total test score has most commonly been singled out as a measure of the "discriminating power" of the item. In the case of a binary item, the ordinary product–moment correlation, as defined by (3.2.11), can be given an alternative expression suitable for hand computation, namely,

$$\rho_{XY} = [(\mu_+ - \mu_Y)/\sigma_Y]/\sqrt{[pi_j/(1 - \pi_j)]} \,, \tag{11.3}$$

where μ_+ is the mean total score for those who give the keyed response to item j, and μ_Y is the test-score mean. It is traditional to refer to the product–moment correlation between a binary variable and a quantitative variable as a *point-biserial correlation.*

4. An alternative to the product–moment coefficient for the correlation of a binary variable and a quantitative variable is known as the *biserial correlation.* Suppose that in place of a binary item score X (temporarily omitting a subscript) we might have had a quantitative variable X^* (a "response tendency," so to speak), and suppose X^* and Y have a joint normal distribution. However, some process cuts the values of X^* into values below a certain *threshold* τ and values above that threshold. If a random respondent's X^* value is above τ, the response coded unity occurs, and if X^* is below τ the response coded zero occurs. The biserial correlation is the product–moment correlation between X^* and Y. It is given by

$$\rho_{XY}^{(b)} = \sigma_{XZ}/n\{N^{-1}(\pi)\} \tag{11.4}$$

where σ_{XZ}, as before, is the population semistandardized covariance, the covariance of X with $Z = (Y - \mu_Y)/\sigma_Y$, and π is the proportion of the population giving the response coded $X = 1$. The notation $n\{N^{-1}(\pi)\}$ is used here to represent the following two-step operation, using a table of the normal curve: Given π, we can obtain the standardized deviate value Z_π that has an area π to the left of it. This is an inverse—$N^{-1}\{\ \}$—of the usual operation of finding the area $N\{Z\}$ to the left of a deviate Z. Having found Z_π, we find the ordinate $n(\pi)$—the height of the normal curve at the normal deviate value Z_π. Compactly, this is written as $n\{N^{-1}(\pi)\}$—the ordinate at the point corresponding to area π. A consistent estimate of $\rho^{(b)}$ is given by

$$\hat{\rho}^{(b)} = \hat{\sigma}_{XZ}/n\{N^{-1}(p)\}, \tag{11.5}$$

(where p is the sample proportion giving $X = 1$). This is just the sample analogue of (11.4). In Table 11.1, row 7 contains the standard normal deviate corresponding to an area p_j to the left of it, and row 8 contains the corresponding ordinate. This gives the resulting biserial correlations in row 9.

There is a direct relationship between the "point biserial" correlation—that is, the ordinary product–moment coefficient—and the biserial coefficient, which depends only on item difficulty, namely,

$$\rho_{XY}^{(b)} = K\rho_{XY}, \tag{11.6a}$$

where K is given by

$$K = [\sqrt{\pi(1 - \pi)}]/[n\{N^{-1}(\pi)\}]. \tag{11.6b}$$

The multiplying factor K is easily calculated. The point biserial correlation is never greater than $.798 \times$ biserial, and it has this ratio at $\pi = .5$. For binary item scores, the biserial correlation is a traditional alternative to the point biserial/product–moment correlation, as a measure of "discriminating power."

It can be said that the item–test covariances and correlations considered so far are spuriously high because they contain a term in the total due to the item itself. Each of these quantities has a counterpart in which the total test score is replaced by the remainder score.

1. It is easily seen that the covariance of X_j with $Y - X_j$ is estimated by

$$\hat{\sigma}_{X_j(Y-X_j)} = \hat{\sigma}_{XY} - \hat{\sigma}_{jj}. \tag{11.7}$$

For example, in Table 11.1,

$$\hat{\sigma}_{X_j(Y-X_j)} = .099 - .0702 = .0089 + \cdots + .0021,$$

and we get the quantities in row 12, Table 11.1, and row 9, Table 11.2, in the same way.

2. Correspondingly, in row 13, Table 11.1, we obtain the semistandardized covariances with the remainder score

$$\hat{\sigma}_{X_j(Y-X_j)} = \hat{\sigma}_{X_j(Y-X_j)}/\hat{\sigma}_{(Y-X_j)} \tag{11.8}$$

and in Table 11.2, rows 6 and 7 give row 8.

3. Likewise, the correlations are obtained as

$$\rho_{X_j(Y-X_j)} = \hat{\sigma}_{X_jZ(Y-X_j)}/\hat{\sigma}_{X_j} \qquad (11.9)$$

or

$$\rho_{X_j(Y-X_j)} = \hat{\sigma}_{X_j(Y-X_j)}/(\hat{\sigma}_{X_j}\hat{\sigma}_{(Y-X_j)}). \qquad (11.10)$$

In the examples, given the computations already completed, it is easiest to complete lines 14, Table 11.1, and 9, Table 11.2, by (11.9).

4. For binary items we compute the corresponding biserial correlations in row 15, Table 11.1, as before, dividing the semistandardized covariances in row 5 by the quantities in row 8.

Before we examine this plethora of possible coefficients describing the relationship between an item and a test score, a few more rows of the table need explanation. We would like to know which of these coefficients might be best criteria for choosing between "good" and "bad" items in an item pool. The implicit assumption behind the traditional device of measuring the "discriminating power" of an item by its correlation with test score is that the test is approximately unidimensional and is sufficiently reliable for the test score to serve as a good approximation to the general attribute measured by most of the items if not all of them. Here, the test is the initial item pool, before selection of "good" items.

If the item set actually fits the single-factor model (here repeated as $X_j = \lambda_j F + E_j + \mu_j$, with unique variances $\text{Var}\{E_j\} = \psi_j^2$), then as the number of items becomes large, the semistandardized covariances—the covariance σ_{X_jZ} of item j with the standardized test score and the covariance $\sigma_{X_jZ(Y-X_j)}$ of item j with the standardized remainder score—will both converge on the factor loadings of the unstandardized items. That is, in a large set of items, the loading—the expected increase in item score corresponding to a unit increase in the (standardized) true score/factor attribute—is closely approximated by σ_{X_jZ}, the covariance of the unstandardized item score with the standardized test score.[2] In the case of a binary item, this is the increase in probability of the keyed response per unit factor-score increase. In a small set of items, the approximation can be poor. This can be seen in Table 11.1 by comparing row 18, the LSAT6 loadings taken from Table 6.9, with row 5, which is too high, and row 14, which is too low. Similarly, in Table 11.2, compare row 12, the SWLS loadings, with rows 3 and 8. The form of the expressions for the semistandardized covariances σ_{X_jZ} and

$\sigma_{X_jZ(Y-X_j)}$ suggests they will respectively overestimate and underestimate the item loadings in small item sets. This is what we see in the example.

*** Proof:

$$\sigma_{X_jY} = \lambda_j(\sum_j \lambda_k) + \psi_j^2 \tag{11.11}$$

with

$$\sigma_Y^2 = (\sum \lambda_k)^2 + \sum \psi_j^2, \tag{11.12}$$

so

$$\sigma_{X_jZ} = [\lambda_j(\sum_j \lambda_k) + \psi_j^2]/\sqrt{(\sum \lambda_k)^2 + \sum \psi_k^2}. \tag{11.13}$$

where the summations are over k.
    Also,

$$\sigma_{X_j(Y-X_j)} = \lambda_j(\sum \lambda_k), \tag{11.14}$$

with

$$\sigma_{(Y-X_j)}^2 = (\sum \lambda_k)^2 + \sum \psi_k^2, \tag{11.15}$$

so

$$\sigma_{X_jZ(Y-X_j)} = [\lambda_j(\sum_j \lambda_k)]/\sqrt{(\sum \lambda_k)^2 + \sum \psi_k^2}, \tag{11.16}$$

where the summations are over $k \neq j$.
    From the form of these expressions, it follows that as the number of items becomes large, the semistandardized covariances—the covariance σ_{X_jZ} of item j with the standardized test score and the covariance $\sigma_{X_jZ(Y-X_j)}$ of item j with the standardized remainder score—will both converge on the factor loadings of the unstandardized items. $$$$$

    Similarly, as the number of items becomes large, the item–test correlations ρ_{X_jY} converge on the factor loadings of the standardized items. But these no longer have the property in the binary case of representing a change in probability of the coded response as a function of the change in factor score. These traditional measures of item discriminating power might be appropriate if standardized items were used to form the total

test score, but as we know, it has not been general practice to sum standardized item scores

***   We can alternatively estimate the semistandardized covariances from
the loadings and unique variances of the items using (11.13) and (11.16).
These are given in rows 16 and 17, Table 11.1, and rows 10 and 11, Table
11.2, labeled with a superscript (f) to indicate their factor-analytic basis.
For example, in the LSAT6 data,

$$\sigma^{(f)}_{X_1 z(Y-X_1)} = \frac{.0605(.1345 + \cdots + .0745)}{\sqrt{[(.1345 + \cdots + .0745)^2 + (.1882 + \cdots + .1076)]}} \ . \qquad \$\$\$$$

The final topic of this section is motivated by criterion-related validity.
Given an external criterion measure V, we might compute the covariances
and correlations of the items in an initial item pool with V, in order to
choose items to make a good predictive final test. Very little needs to be
added about this. The standard formulas (3.2.13) and (3.2.11) give the
covariance and correlation of any item with V. (For binary items, the
specialized point biserial correlation can be applied, but regular computer
data entry will lead to the ordinary product–moment calculation, so the
specialized expression is not needed in practice.) In the case of binary
data, the corresponding biserial coefficient can be computed by (11.6) or
directly by (11.5). If V consists of, say, q items, $V_1, \ldots, V_q$, we can compute
the joint covariance matrix of $X_1, \ldots, X_M, V_1, \ldots, V_q$. The correlation between $Y = X_1 + \cdots + X_M$ and $V = V_1 + \cdots + V_q$ is

$$\rho_{YV} = \sum \sum \sigma_{X_j V_l} / \sqrt{(\sum \sum \sigma_{X_j X_k})(\sum \sum \sigma_{V_l V_m})} \ . \qquad (11.17)$$

(This has already been illustrated in Chap. 10.) Inspection of the covariances can detect items that do not contribute to the correlation. This
could extend to possible revision of the criterion measure.

TEST STATISTICS

Recall that the mean of the total test score Y in the population of interest
is just the sum of the item means,

$$\mu_y = \sum \mu_{X_j}.$$

In the case of binary items these are also the probabilities of the keyed
positive responses. From Table 6.8, the estimated mean of the LSAT6 test
score is

$$\hat{\mu}_Y = \frac{.924 + \cdots + .870}{5}$$

$$= 3.819,$$

and for the SWLS it is 22.25.

Recall that the variance of the total test score is given by the sum of the m^2 elements of the item covariance matrix. An alternative expression for the variance of the test score is

$$\sigma_Y^2 = \sum \sigma_{X_j Y}. \tag{11.18}$$

Thus, from row 4, Table 11.1, we have for LSAT6

$$\hat{\sigma}_Y^2 = .099 + \cdots + .151 = 1.069.$$

(This is within rounding error of the sum of the covariances, 1.0702.) From row 2 of Table 11.2, we have for SWLS

$$\hat{\sigma}_Y^2 = 8.233 + \ldots + 8.730$$

$$= 39.388 \quad (\text{close to } 39.383).$$

From (11.18) we get an alternative and interesting expression for the *SD* of *Y*, namely,

$$\sigma_Y = \sum \sigma_{X_j Z}. \tag{11.19}$$

*** Dividing (11.18) left and right by σ_Y creates the *SD* of *Y* and the semistandardized covariances $\sigma_{X_j Z}$. $$$

For example, from row 5, Table 11.1, we obtain

$$\hat{\sigma}_Y = 0.96 + \cdots + .146 = 1.055.$$

Similarly, from row 3, Table 11.2, we obtain

$$\hat{\sigma}_Y = 1.312 + \cdots + 1.391 = 6.276$$

(compare $\sqrt{39.38} = 6.275$).

A more conventionally accepted form of (11.19) in the literature replaces the semistandardized covariances by functions of the item–test product–moment correlations and the item *SD*s. That is, the expression becomes

$$\sigma_Y = \sum \sigma_{X_j} \rho_{X_j Y}. \tag{11.20}$$

As mentioned in Chapter 3, one intuitive criterion for choosing items to make a "good" test is to maximize total test variance. More precisely, we try to maximize the ratio of the variance of the test score to the sum of the variances of the item scores of the m items (chosen out of an initial larger pool). Because G-C alpha is of the form

$$\alpha = [m/(m-1)][1 - (\sum \sigma_{X_j}^2)/\sigma_T^2],$$

such a choice of items will maximize alpha also. G-C alpha can be alternatively written as

$$\alpha = [m/(m-1)][1 - (\sum \sigma_{X_j}^2)/(\sum \sigma_{X_j}^2 + \sum \sigma_{X_j(Y-X_j)})]. \qquad (11.21)$$

At least approximately, the best m items to keep, by this criterion, would be those with the largest $\sigma_{X_j(Y-X_j)}$ values. In the LSAT6 data, if we wished to keep four items we would eliminate item 1. In the case of the SWLS we would eliminate item 4.

These devices for item selection are needed when the item pool is too large for factor analysis, but they rest on the assumption that the item pool fits the single-factor model. The procedure can be unsafe because this assumption may fail. If the item pool is hierarchically structured, it will correspond to a general factor and a number of hierarchical group factors. Mechanically selecting items to maximize alpha may eliminate all but one of the group factors, with loss of generality of the attribute. A judicious combination of content and psychometric considerations is desirable in selecting items.

If the item pool is small enough to allow factor analysis—say, 200 or less according to the available program—we could keep, as the best m items, those that maximize coefficient omega, given by

$$\omega = (\sum \lambda_j)^2 / [(\sum \lambda_j)^2 + \sum \psi_j^2].$$

Generally, by this criterion, we would keep the items with the largest information values, λ_j^2/ψ_j^2. (See Chap. 13.)

G-C alpha may also be written

$$\alpha = [m/(m-1)][1 - (\sum \sigma_j^2)/(\sum \sigma_{X_j}\rho_{X_jY})^2], \qquad (11.22)$$

so there is some justification for a common belief that choosing items with the largest correlation with the item sum will tend to make alpha a maximum. Such a procedure is perhaps not as safe as using the covariance.

There does not seem to be any clear, direct justification for using biserial correlations for these purposes.

The final topic of this section is the analogous problem of the effect of item selection on the predictive utility/concurrent validity of the test score. The object is to choose items $X_1, \ldots, X_m$ out of a pool, to maximize the correlation of their simple sum Y with a criterion V. Here we do not, as in Chapter 8, consider a multiple regression of the external criterion variable, on the m items or subtests. It may be shown that the correlation of Y with V is a simple ratio of sums of the semistandardized covariances $\sigma_{X_j Z_V}$ and $\sigma_{X_j Z_Y}$, where

$$Z_V = (V - \mu_V)/\sigma_V \qquad Z_Y = (Y - \mu_Y)/\sigma_Y,$$

namely,

$$\rho_{YV} = \left(\sum \sigma_{X_j Z_V} \right) / \left(\sum \sigma_{X_j Z_Y} \right). \tag{11.23}$$

If m items are to be selected from a larger pool of items to maximize predictive validity, this can be done approximately by choosing items with the best ratios of $\sigma_{X_j Z_V}$ to $\sigma_{X_j Z_Y}$.

*** To explain why "approximately": If we have an initial set of M pairs of positive values, $\sigma_{X_j Z_V}$ and $\sigma_{X_j Z_Y}$, it is likely, but not assured, that successively choosing items with the largest possible ratio will give m items with the largest possible ratio of the simple sums of these quantities. The sum of the ratios is not, of course, the ratio of the sums. $$$

For a given set of m chosen items, the predictive utility coefficient ρ_{YV} is bounded above by the multiple correlation of the m item scores X_1, $\ldots, X_m$ with Y. We can think of the simple sum as using equal weights in place of regression coefficients—as though these were each unity. This commonly gives a correlation not much less than the optimized multiple correlation, and not subject to attenuation in cross-validation. This assumes a homogeneous test with items scored in the same direction, having positive correlations.

A classical result from true-score theory, in Chapter 7, produces an apparent paradox concerning the relation between reliability and validity. We recall the expression (7.23),

$$\rho_{YV} = \rho_{T_Y V} \sqrt{\rho_Y}.$$

This gives a relation between the predictive utility/concurrent validity ρ_{YV} of Y and its reliability coefficient ρ_Y. It follows, or at least appears to follow, from (7.18), that "the validity of a test with respect to any criterion cannot exceed the index of reliability."[3] That is,

$$\rho_{YV} \leq \rho_{T_Y Y}$$

It might then seem that (a) reliability is maximized by choosing items with high $\sigma_{X_j Z_Y}$, (b) concurrent validity is maximized by choosing items with high $\sigma_{X_j Z_V}$, and (c) these choices conflict with each other, to the point of contradiction. To see the apparent contradiction clearly, imagine finding m items that are mutually uncorrelated, and therefore have zero omega and zero G-C alpha. Then by (7.23) their sum cannot have a correlation greater than zero with any other variable.

The apparent paradox is resolved, in effect, by denying that (7.23) is generally true. Here, Y is a sum of item scores that fit a common factor model and their "error terms" are their unique parts. By definition, these m terms $E_1, \ldots, E_m$ are mutually uncorrelated, but the truth of (7.23) rests on the additional assumption that they are uncorrelated with all other variables. Such an assumption is extremely strong, generally falsifiable, and generally false. We already have the example in Chapter 10 of the failure of this assumption, from Hull et al., where overgeneralization of failure, as an indicator of self-punitive attitude, has a specific relationship to depression. Thus, to make a good practical predictor, it is appropriate to choose an item set with good predictive utility, with no concern for its reliability/construct validity as measured by omega or bounded by alpha. In effect, this uses the relations of the unique parts of the items to the criterion to maximize predictive ability.

Selecting items for a test to have good (construct) validity is quite different from selecting to give predictive utility. For this we might consider combining selection for high omega or alpha with selection that increases or at least does not decrease a specified concurrent relationship—a correlation with a criterion that should be related to the attribute, according to theory. These selection procedures are indeed in direct conflict, so it is probably better to select the items on the internal criterion only—to increase omega or G-C alpha—and then check the resulting test for its convergent validity, and also, if appropriate, its discriminant validity, by the methods of Chapter 10.

ITEM CORRELATIONS

Pairwise item relationships—item covariances and correlations—are not, of course, parameters that serve to describe a single item. But certainly they are parameters of importance in the construction and analysis of tests.

In preceding chapters we used covariance matrices for some purposes and correlation matrices for others.

Partly because they are independent of the units of measurement of the variables, there is a strong traditional tendency in psychometric theory to treat correlations as somehow the fundamental quantities. The approach taken in these pages includes deliberate attempts to counter this tendency when necessary. In particular, we saw that the covariance of two binary items, j and k,

$$\sigma_{jk} = \pi_{jk} - \pi_j \pi_k,$$

directly measures the association between them—the departure of the joint probability of getting both keyed responses from the product of their separate probabilities. We also saw that the ordinary product–moment correlation (phi) between two binary items is not a suitable measure of association between them, in part because it cannot attain the value of unity unless the items have equal difficulty parameters. For a number of our objectives—those most closely associated with classical test theory—we have been fitting the common factor model to the item covariance matrix. This gives unstandardized factor loadings and unique variances, from which we get further quantities of interest.

In the early history of factor theory, an unfortunate tendency developed to think of factor analysis as something the investigator "does to" a correlation matrix in order to "extract" common factors, that is, to obtain factor loadings. This notion arose out of approximate devices for fitting the model, invented before the computer revolution. Again, as a corrective to this tendency, discussion in Chapters 6 and 9 deliberately treated the factor model as a model for the item or subtest scores. The notion that one "factor analyzes" a correlation matrix gave rise to a largely misdirected search for appropriate correlations between binary items for such purposes as factor analysis, with no conception of a corresponding model for the item scores. One mistaken suggestion, made and abandoned early, was to use "phi over maximum phi," that is, to create a pseudo-correlation matrix whose elements are the correlations given by (3.2.15) divided by their maximum attainable value, given by (3.2.21).

An alternative that eventually found a very strong post facto justification is the *tetrachoric correlation.* (*Tetrachoric* means fourfold, from *tetra* meaning four and *choris* meaning apart.) As we have seen, the biserial correlation between a binary item X and a quantitative variable Y can be described as the correlation of Y with a quantitative underlying "response tendency" X^*, such that if X^* exceeds a certain threshold value, the keyed response occurs. The tetrachoric correlation rests on the same principle. If X_j, X_k are two binary item scores, associated with each is a quantitative "response tendency" X_j^*, X_k^* and two thresholds τ_j, τ_k (corresponding, in fact, to item difficulties). If

$$X_j^* > \tau_j \quad \text{then} \quad X_j = 1,$$
$$X_j^* \leq \tau_j \quad \text{then} \quad X_j = 0,$$

and if

$$X_k^* > \tau_k \quad \text{then} \quad X_k = 1$$
$$X_k^* \leq \tau_k \quad \text{then} \quad X_k = 0.$$

It is assumed that X_j^*, X_k^* are standardized variables—mean zero, variance unity—with a bivariate normal distribution. In 1900, just 4 years after he developed the product–moment coefficient, Karl Pearson gave a mathematical result from which the tetrachoric correlation can be computed, given the population proportions in the usual two by two table, as discussed in Chapter 3. This is difficult to do without a computer program.

*** The mathematical basis of the tetrachoric correlation, and its accurate computation, is very technical. The following brief remarks are offered in case they help the reader to a sense of the technical difficulties and the necessity of leaving computation to a computer program.

Under the operative assumption that X_j^* and X_k^* are each normally distributed, the probabilities of the keyed response to each are the areas to the right of τ_j and of τ_k in the standard normal curve, that is, to the left of $-\tau_j$ and $-\tau_k$. Thus, given π_j, π_k, we have

$$\tau_j = -N^{-1}\{\pi_j\} \qquad \tau_k = -N^{-1}\{\pi_k\},$$

where, as for the biserial correlation, $N^{-1}\{\pi\}$ means: Find the standardized deviate with area π to the left of it. Pearson gave a polynomial series that expresses the product–moment correlation coefficient of X_j, X_k (phi) in terms of the tetrachoric correlation coefficient. From this expression, it is easy to evaluate the phi coefficient from the tetrachoric coefficient. The reverse numerical problem, given the phi coefficient and the item difficulties, is to keep a number of terms in the series and solve the polynomial equation for the unknown tetrachoric coefficient. The more terms we keep, the more accurate is the approximation, and the more numerically demanding are the computations. Substituting sample proportions for population probabilities gives a consistent estimate of the population tetrachoric coefficient. It is fortunate that this work can be given to a computer program. $$$

Unlike the product–moment correlation, the tetrachoric correlation can attain values of unity or minus unity when the items have different difficulty parameters. A necessary and sufficient condition that the tetrachoric correlation equals unity is that either

$$P\{X_j = 1, X_k = 0\} = 0 \quad \text{or} \quad P\{X_j = 0, X_k = 1\} = 0.$$

A necessary and sufficient condition that the tetrachoric equals minus unity is that either

$$P\{X_j = 1, X_k = 1\} = 0 \quad \text{or} \quad P\{X_j = 0, X_k = 0\} = 0.$$

These conditions are satisfied if all pairs of values $\{X_j^*, X_k^*\}$ lie on a straight line, with positive slope for unity or negative slope for minus unity.

There is no simple relation between the tetrachoric correlations and the item statistics discussed in the previous section. The assumption of a bivariate normal distribution of X_j^*, X_k^* defines a tetrachoric correlation in a sense. But it is a strong and possibly false assumption when applied to selected examinees. If we select a subpopulation of, say, college students from a more general population, it seems unlikely that the "underlying response tendencies" will have a joint normal distribution in both the original and the selected populations.

Tetrachoric correlations can be used in item factor analysis as an estimation device for item response theory (see Chap. 12). To complete this section, we compare the matrix of tetrachoric correlations for the LSAT6 data, in Table 11.3(a), with the matrix of product–moment (phi) coefficients in Table 11.3(b). Note that the tetrachoric correlations are larger

TABLE 11.3
LSAT6 Correlation Matrices

(a) Tetrachoric Correlations

1	1	.1724	.2268	.1052	.0647
2	.1724	1	.1890	.1104	.1709
3	.2268	.1890	1	.1864	.1038
4	.1052	.1104	.1864	1	.1997
5	.0647	.1709	.1038	.1997	1

(b) Product–Moment Correlations

1	1	.0743	.0987	.0444	.0236
2	.0743	1	.1152	.0624	.0868
3	.0987	.1152	1	.1093	.0532
4	.0444	.0624	.1093	1	.0993
5	.0236	.0868	.0532	.0993	1

than their product–moment counterparts. It is known that for items of middle difficulty, the tetrachoric coefficient will be approximately $1\frac{1}{2}$ times phi. The closest items to this condition, items 2 and 3, give a ratio of 1.64, and the furthest from it, items 1 and 5, give a ratio of 2.74. Generally, we might draw different conclusions about the relative degree of "association" between the items from tetrachoric and phi coefficients, and different again from inspection of covariances. More sophisticated analyses are needed.

REVIEW GUIDE

Let it be admitted that there is a large collection of unexciting formulas in this chapter, most of which are no longer of importance in test construction work. It is good exercise for the student, on a first reading, to see how these variant expressions arise. In review, it is enough to recognize that in very large item pools that may be assumed homogeneous, the semistandardized covariances of the items with the total scores can substitute for factor loadings in choosing good subsets of items. Other item statistics are less useful, but the student should be able in principle to compute the point biserial and biserial correlations, as these are still in common use. The account of biserial and tetrachoric correlations in terms of underlying response tendencies and a threshold for the binary response is conceptually important, providing a lead into the work on item response theory. In review, the student will probably find it most useful to gather together and summarize the remarks on methods of item selection.

The student should be able to follow the discussion of the reliability– "validity" paradox sufficiently to see that it is not in fact paradoxical, and should recognize the fundamental difference between selecting items for predictive utility and selecting for validity.

END NOTES

A general reference for the material in this chapter is Lord and Novick (1968). The treatment of semistandardized covariances is from first principles.

1. The NOHARM program in its standard PC configuration fits the (unidimensional) normal ogive model up to about 200 items. Some computer programs are limited to smaller numbers because they use more sophisticated (and efficient) methods.
2. The notion of "semistandardized" covariances is, I believe, my own. It is introduced because of these minor theoretical results, which I have not been able to find in the literature. Perhaps they have been missed, although they are very obvious, because most researchers in test theory have not recognized the key role played by the factor model.
3. Lord and Novick (1968, p. 72).

Item Response Models

In Chapter 6 it was pointed out that if we fit the single-factor model to binary items, the equation of the regression

$$\hat{X}_j = \lambda_j f + \mu_j$$

represents the probability of the correct (or keyed) response for an examinee with a given value f of the common factor F. That is, the regression function is the conditional probability function

$$P\{X_j = 1 | F = f\} = \lambda_j f + \mu_j. \qquad (12.1a)$$

For a binary item, the item mean μ_j is the (unconditional) probability π_j of the correct/keyed response. The linear conditional probability function

$$P\{X = 1 | F = f\} = \lambda_j f + \pi_j \qquad (12.1b)$$

is the implicit foundation of classical true-score theory for binary items. It is the model used to give coefficient omega and its lower bound, KR_{20}—the special case of G-C alpha—as previously shown, to provide a basis for assessing errors of measurement of the attribute. However, the linear function is at best an approximation, and it must become a bad approximation if the range of values of the factor score is sufficiently wide.

There are three major limitations of the common factor model as applied to binary data in Chapter 6. First, the function gives a negative probability if

f is small enough, and a probability greater than one if f is large enough. And this is not acceptable. In the LSAT6 example, it was noted that item 3 has a negative probability of passing for respondents with $F < -2.972$, and item 1 has a probability of passing greater than unity for respondents with $F > 1.256$. The lower and upper bounds on the factor score correspond to the floor—all responses are incorrect/nonkeyed—and the ceiling—all responses are correct/keyed—of the test. These can include absurd probability values. Second, the linear common factor model assumes that the unique parts E_j of the items have variances independent of F, which cannot be true for binary items. Third, it assumes that the error of estimate of the factor score is constant over all values of F, which again cannot be true for binary items. Thus, the linear model is an approximation, representing average behavior of the items over the range of the test.

There are two main ways to look at the work that has been developed to overcome these limitations. One is an extension of the theory underlying biserial and tetrachoric correlation coefficients, and we refer to it as *item factor analysis*. The other is a direct treatment of nonlinear functions suitable for conditional probabilities. This makes up a more general class of *item response models*, and is now usually referred to as *item response theory*. (Actually, the older name, *latent trait theory*, is much more appropriate, because the defining property of this class of models is that one or more latent traits—an alternative name for common factors—explain associations between the item responses.) Unfortunately, item response theory has been developed somewhat in isolation from common factor theory. Also, work on it has mostly concentrated on the very special case of items measuring a single cognitive ability. Consequently, the essential unity of true-score theory, common factor theory for test scores or item scores, and item response theory has sometimes not been noticed.

In the next section we consider the choice of appropriate regression curves for binary responses—*item response curves*. Then these are applied to define item response models—latent trait or nonlinear common factor models—by a principle of conditional independence. Under the heading of Item Factor Analysis, we show how one item response model can be obtained from a linear model for quantitative underlying variables, as employed in the derivation of biserial and tetrachoric correlations. The final section is concerned with methods for estimating and testing the fit of item response models.

ITEM RESPONSE FUNCTIONS

Suppose we have X, a binary response variable, and F, a quantitative independent variable. The independent variable might be (a) a controlled experimental variable, (b) an uncontrolled, measurable property of the respondents, or (c) an attribute measured in common by the binary response X and a set of further responses. The problem of a suitable regression function of X on F is the same for any of these three possibilities. Recall that the regression—the conditional mean of X for a given value of F—is the conditional probability of the response scored $X = 1$. As a function of F, this regression can be referred to as an *item response function*, an *item response curve*, or an *item characteristic curve*. (All three terms are in common use.) To represent a probability, it must be bounded above by unity and below by zero, so it cannot be a straight line. It must indeed be curvilinear.

Classical illustrative examples in the literature, in which F is a controlled experimental treatment, include experiments on the effectiveness of insect sprays. Increasing doses, f_1, f_2, ..., of spray are applied to a controlled space containing flies, and the response scored $X = 1$ is the death of a fly. We require three properties for a function representing the conditional probability $\text{Prob}\{X = 1 | F = f\}$:

1. It should be bounded above by unity, and below by zero.
2. It should be smooth and monotone-increasing.
3. It should approach horizontal asymptotes at each extreme value of F. (This follows from 1 and 2.)

That is, the function should resemble that shown in Fig. 12.1. In almost all applications, when F becomes sufficiently large, the probability should

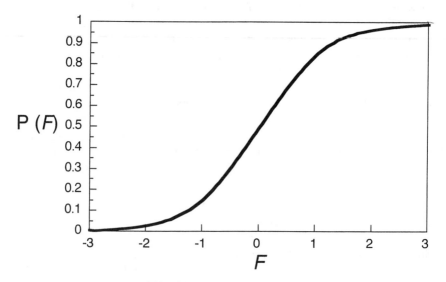

FIG. 12.1. Item response curve.

approach unity. In some applications, when F becomes sufficiently small, we want the probability to approach zero. In some cases, the lower asymptote could be above zero. This would correspond, in the insect example, to base-rate "natural" mortality. In item response theory, where F is a latent trait or common factor, it will correspond to "chance" success in multiple-choice cognitive items.

Two commonly used item response functions are the *logistic function* and the *normal-ogive function*. A good way to think about these is to regard them as *link functions*. That is, they are functions linking the probability of the keyed response to a linear function of the independent variable. The logistic function $L(Z)$ is given by

$$L(Z) = 1/(1 + e^{-Z}), \qquad (12.2a)$$

or

$$L(Z) = 1/[1 + \exp(-Z)], \qquad (12.2b)$$

by use of the conventional exponential function $\exp(\ )$. The normal-ogive function is just the cumulative normal distribution function. Formally, it is the integral

$$N(Z) = \int_{-\infty}^{Z} (1/\sqrt{2}\pi) \exp(-\tfrac{1}{2}t^2) \, dt. \qquad (12.3)$$

Informally, it is the area to the left of Z in the standard table of the normal curve. In the applications that follow, we introduce the constant $D = 1.701$ into the logistic function, writing it as

$$L(Z) = 1/(1 + e^{-Dz}). \qquad (12.4)$$

Just using a pocket calculator with an "exp" key for the logistic function, and a table of the areas under the normal curve for the normal ogive, the reader will easily verify the listing of values in Table 12.1.

With the choice of the multiplier $D = 1.701$ in (12.4), the logistic function and the normal-ogive are virtually indistinguishable.[1] They differ by less than .01 over the entire set of values of Z. This is the function graphed in Fig. 12.1.

Now we define a family of curves by choosing parameters a,b in the linear function

$$Z = bF + a. \qquad (12.5)$$

TABLE 12.1
Logistic and Normal-Ogive Functions

z	$-\infty$	...	-3	-2	-1	0	1	2	3	...	∞
$L(Z)$	0		.0061	.0323	.1545	.5	.8455	.9677	.9939		1
$N(Z)$	0		.0014	.0228	.1587	.5	.8413	.9772	.9986		1

Combining this with the link functions $L(Z)$ or $N(Z)$ gives the desired logistic or normal-ogive item response functions,

$$\text{Prob}\{X = 1|F = f\} = L(bf + a)$$
$$= 1/\{1 + \exp[D(bf + a)]\}, \qquad (12.6)$$

or

$$\text{Prob}\{X = 1|F = f\} = N(bf + a), \qquad (12.7)$$

where $N(\ )$ is the integral in (12.3) as given in normal curve tables. The constant a and the slope parameter b in (12.5) determine a set of straight lines, which are then "squeezed" by the link functions into the required range, zero to unity. From here on, it is convenient to use the link functions just as $L(Z)$ and $N(Z)$.

To get a sense of how the parameters control and create a family of curves (to define models and fit data), consider first the five logistic curves obtained by setting $b = 1$, and choosing $a = -2, -1, 0, 1, 2$, graphed in Fig. 12.2. Clearly, varying a moves the graph of the function along the F axis. The value of a (for fixed b) controls the position of the point of inflexion of the curve—the point where it changes its direction of curvature—which is also the point corresponding to a probability of .5. (More precisely, the position of the point of inflexion is $-a/b$.) Next consider the curves obtained by setting $a = 0$, and choosing $b = .5, 1, 2, 4$, and also $b = -1$, graphed in Fig. 12.3. Clearly, varying b controls and corresponds to the steepness of the slope of the curve at its point of inflexion. Note that the item with negative b follows a course opposite to the others. In cognitive tests, with proper scoring—credit for the correct answer—we would not expect to find items with negative slope parameters. In personality and attitude items, this would correspond to an item scored in the opposite direction to the others. It is always possible to reverse the scoring and eliminate the negative coefficient, in a unidimensional item response model. In the following sections, F is standardized in a population of interest. Accordingly, the origin in Figs. 12.2 and 12.3 is the mean of F, and the unit is its standard deviation. This locates the curves relative to the scale of F. Just from inspecting these curves, we see that the larger the

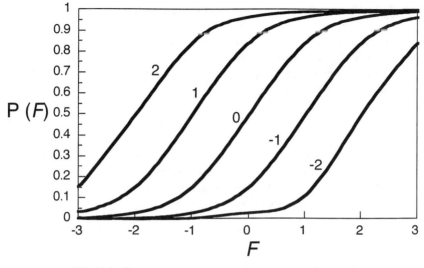

FIG. 12.2. Item response curves, varying constant parameter.

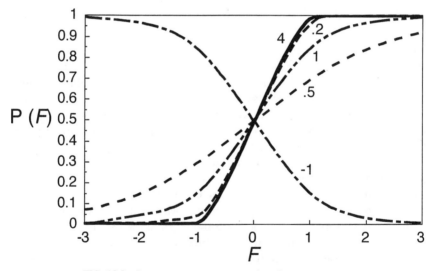

FIG. 12.3. Item response curves, varying slope parameter.

value of a, the easier the item is. A smaller value of F corresponds to a given probability of passing the item (with the usual extension of meaning to noncognitive items). Thus, a can be regarded as a parameter determining item difficulty—as an *item difficulty parameter*. We also recognize that b orders the items in respect of the maximum rate of change of probability of the keyed response as a function of F, so it can be crudely identified as an *item discrimination parameter*. (The representation of the model in terms of item factor analysis—in a later section of this chapter—gives other parameters that have a more familiar interpretation.)

Note for later reference (Chap. 14) that the link functions $L(Z)$ and $N(Z)$ can be used to link the item response probability to multiple independent variables—including multiple common factors, $F_1, \ldots, F_r$—by writing a linear combination

$$Z = a + b_1 F_1 + \cdots + b_r F_r \tag{12.8}$$

in place of (12.5). Partly for this reason, the form (12.5) is used in the present account. This follows a common representation in regression theory, with a for the intercept/constant, and b for the slope. A traditional alternative in item response theory is

$$Z = b(F - d) = bF - bd, \tag{12.9a}$$

or, in the almost universally accepted notation for this parameterization,

$$Z = a(F - b). \tag{12.9b}$$

This parameterization does not permit generalization to multiple factors/latent traits, and will not be used here. Readers already habituated to the notation in (12.9b), with, further, the use of θ for an "ability," where here we have F for what will generally be a common factor, are asked to be tolerant of a notation change whose aim is to underline the generality and unity of concepts from regression, factor theory, and item response theory.

The family of item response functions obtained by varying values of the parameters a and b in (12.5)–(12.7) is known, for obvious reasons, as a two-parameter family. A restricted, one-parameter family is given by fixing b to a common value for all items and allowing only a to vary from item to item. In multiple-choice cognitive items, to allow for responses coded unity to occur by "chance," we introduce a *pseudo-guessing parameter* c to the item response function, writing it as

$$P\{X = 1|F = f\} = c + (1 - c)L(Z) \tag{12.10a}$$

or

$$P\{X = 1|F = f\} = c + (1 - c)N(Z). \tag{12.10b}$$

As Z becomes a large negative number and $L(Z)$ or $N(Z)$ become zero, the curve will approach the nonzero lower asymptote c. The qualifier *pseudo* draws attention to the fact that the parameter models the possibility of giving a correct answer "as though by chance," without supposing an actual process in the examinee describable as pure guessing. This extension yields a three-parameter family of item response functions, with varying values of a, b, and c.

What we now have is a set of mathematical functions with acceptable properties for describing conditional probabilities. In the next section we combine these with a principle of conditional independence to obtain item response models containing common factors. In the literature of item response theory these have been renamed *latent traits*. (The older terminology is more expressive of the concept, so I occasionally use both.)

THE PRINCIPLE OF LOCAL INDEPENDENCE

Recall that common factors are defined by the property that they explain the covariation of item or subtest scores. To the extent that the linear approximation holds, the factor or factors will explain the covariance of all pairs of binary item scores X_j, X_k, as in Chapter 6, meaning that these covariances are zero in a subpopulation that has a fixed value of the factor score(s). It is the common factor—interpreted as their common attribute—that ties the items together, so to speak.

In item response theory, it is customary to make a stronger assumption than pairwise conditional independence, as follows: The *strong* or *full principle of local independence* states: In a subpopulation in which r *latent traits* $F_1, \ldots, F_r$ take fixed values $f_1, \ldots, f_r$, the responses are (conditionally) independent. The principle of local independence states what is meant by latent traits. That is, $F_1, \ldots, F_r$ are latent traits if the item responses are independent in a subpopulation in which $F_1, \ldots, F_r$ are fixed. The strong principle of local independence implies the *weak* or *bivariate principle of local independence*, which states that pairs of items j,k are uncorrelated in a subpopulation in which the r latent traits are fixed.

Each item score X_j is either zero or unity. We write $X_j = x_j$ to represent either of these possibilities. Then any response pattern, such as $X_1 = 1$; $X_2 = 0$; $X_3 = 0$; $X_4 = 1$; $X_5 = \cdots$ can be represented generally by

$$X_1 = x_1 \quad X_2 = x_2 \quad X_3 = x_3 \quad X_4 = x_4 \quad X_5 = x_5 \ldots$$

where we imagine each x_j to be set at one of the two values of X_j. In the strong principle,

$$\text{Prob}\{X_1 = x_1; X_2 = x_2; \ldots ; X_m = x_m | F_1 = f_1, \ldots, F_r = f_r\}$$
$$= \text{Prob}\{X_1 = x_1 | F_1 = f_1, \ldots, F_r = f_r\}$$

$$\times \text{Prob}\{X_2 = x_2 | F_1 = f_1, \ldots, F_r = f_r\}$$
$$\times \cdots$$
$$\times \text{Prob}\{X_m = x_m | F_1 = f_1, \ldots, F_r = f_r\}. \qquad (12.11)$$

In words, the conditional probability of any pattern of (zero/unit) responses is the product of the conditional probabilities of those responses. (The tradition of referring to this principle of conditional independence as a principle of "local" independence arises from the notion that fixed values of $F_1, \ldots, F_r$ correspond to a point or location in the r-dimensional space of their possible values.) In the weak principle,

$$\text{Prob}\{X_j = x_j \text{ and } X_k = x_k | F_1 = f_1, \ldots, F_r = f_r\}$$
$$= \text{Prob}\{X_j = x_j | F_1 = f_1, \ldots, F_r = f_r\}$$
$$\times \text{Prob}\{X_k = x_k | F_1 = f_1, \ldots, F_r = f_r\}, \qquad (12.12)$$

so their covariances are zero. In words, the weak principle of local independence states that the covariance of all pairs of items is zero in a subpopulation in which the factors or latent traits are fixed. This is the same as the principle we have used to define common factors.

Some treatments of item response models use the distribution of the item responses, that is, the population probabilities and sample frequencies of the 2^m response patterns, as in, for example, Table 6.7(a). These methods apply the strong principle of local independence and are known as *full information methods*. Others use just the probabilities/sample frequencies of the keyed response to each item and the joint probabilities/proportions of keyed responses to pairs of items, or the equivalent information as in Table 6.8. These methods apply the weak principle of local independence and may be referred to as *bivariate information methods*. Comparisons of full information methods and bivariate information methods[2] suggest that there is as yet nothing to choose between them. There appears to be no study of the case where the strong principle of local independence requires more latent traits than the weak principle, to fit a binary data set. Also, nothing is known about the appropriate interpretation of such a case if it were to happen.

The reader who finds that the strong principle of local independence places too strong a demand on intuition should accept that latent traits are the precise counterparts in nonlinear models for common factors, as dealt with already in the linear models. They are defined by the property that they account for association between item responses, and they are interpreted—again—as the attributes the items measure in common. Methods currently available for fitting multiple latent traits, with suitable methods for yielding interpretable, exploratory or confirmatory, independent clusters, use bivariate information only. Thus the important extension of theory is from a linear to a nonlinear common factor model by the "squeezing" action of the link functions $L(Z)$ and $N(Z)$.

Just as in linear common factor models, item response theory provides a set of restrictive models for the structure of the data. The assumption that the item response functions all have the same mathematical form is not tested in most methods of fitting the model. Some methods assume also that the latent trait(s) is (are) normally distributed. This assumption (which may be incompatible with the assumption of the form of the curves) is also generally not tested. The simplest model supposes that all items have identical response functions. This corresponds exactly to parallel items. There is no exact counterpart of the true-score equivalence model in item response theory. The one-parameter model—sometimes known as "the" Rasch model (discussed in Chap. 13)—is the closest analogue. The assumption that there is just one latent trait explaining relationships between the items corresponds to the simple Spearman common factor model, and it gives us the appropriate test for a homogeneous set of binary items. Usable methods for fitting multiple-trait—*multidimensional*—item response models, with all the properties of exploratory and confirmatory common factor models, have been available for some time but they are not yet in common use (see Chap. 14). The principle of local independence is not itself a testable assumption. It actually states what is meant by latent traits or common factors. Because most work on item response theory has been confined to simple *unidimensional* cases (i.e., models with just one latent trait), the hypothesis of unidimensionality—that just one attribute explains the item relationships—has sometimes been confused with the "hypothesis" of local independence. This is implicitly contrasted with an alternative hypothesis that local independence in some sense fails, whereas the data are still, in some undefined meaning of the word, "unidimensional."

Once we get estimates of the parameters of an item response model, and evidence that the model fits the data, we can use the parameters, together with the item responses of an individual examinee, to obtain good estimates of the respondent's latent traits, and to put confidence bounds on them. They also serve a variety of more specialized purposes (see Chaps. 13, 15, and 16). Before we turn to such matters, we consider an alternative representation of the model in terms of underlying quantitative "response tendencies." This both enriches the account of the model and points to one class of estimation methods.

ITEM FACTOR ANALYSIS

As mentioned in Chapter 11, in the earlier literature it was sometimes supposed that factor analysis is something we "do" to a sample correlation matrix, and this supposition led to a badly posed question about the appropriate correlation matrix to factor analyze if we have binary data. In Chapter 6, with some hesitation, we fitted the linear factor model to a binary-item covariance matrix—not a correlation matrix. This gave a linear approximation to the item response functions.

Lord, in 1952, showed that if a single latent trait F has a normal distribution, then fitting the linear factor model to the tetrachoric correlations of the items yields a unidimensional normal-ogive model. Christoffersson in 1975 and Muthen in 1978 generalized Lord's result to multiple factors, with improved methods of estimation. To see how this was established, suppose (as in the derivation of biserial and tetrachoric correlations) that each binary item has associated with it an "underlying" quantitative response tendency X_j^* and a threshold value τ_j, such that

$$\text{if} \quad X_j^* > \tau_j \quad \text{then} \quad X_j = 1$$

and

$$\text{if} \quad X_j^* \leq \tau_j \quad \text{then} \quad X_j = 0.$$

Now suppose also that the underlying response tendencies $X_1^*, \ldots, X_m^*$ fit the Spearman single-factor model

$$X_j^* = \lambda_j F + E_j^* \tag{12.13}$$

with uncorrelated unique parts E_j^*. We impose a scale on each X_j^* so that it is standardized, with mean zero, and variance unity [hence no μ_j in (12.13)], and

$$\lambda_j^2 + \psi_j^2 = 1.$$

Accordingly we have

$$\psi_j^2 = 1 - \lambda_j^2. \tag{12.14}$$

We now assume that F and each E_j^* has a normal distribution, so that each X_j^* also has a normal distribution. It is then easy to show that

$$P\{X_j = 1 | F = f\} = P\{X_j^* > \tau_j | F = f\} = N(z) \tag{12.15a}$$

where

$$z = [\lambda_j / \sqrt{1 - \lambda_j^2}]f - [1 / \sqrt{1 - \lambda_j^2}]\tau_j. \tag{12.15b}$$

***

$$P\{X_j = 1|F = f\} = P\{\lambda_j f + E_j^* > \tau_j|F = f\}$$
$$= P\{E_j^* > \tau_j - \lambda_j f\}$$
$$= N\{(\lambda_j f - \tau_j)/\sqrt{1 - \lambda_j^2}\}. \qquad \$\$\$$$

It is enough for the student to accept that the factor model (12.13) gives the normal-ogive model, except that we have a new pair of parameters λ_j, τ_j, defining the family of item response curves in (12.15). These are in correspondence with the parameters a_j, b_j in (12.5). Given one set of parameters we can easily compute the other set. From (12.15b),

$$b_j = \lambda_j/\sqrt{1 - \lambda_j^2} \qquad (12.16a)$$

$$a_j = -\tau_j/\sqrt{1 - \lambda_j^2} \qquad (12.16b)$$

so given λ_j, τ_j we can compute a_j, b_j. Conversely,

$$\lambda_j = b_j/\sqrt{1 + b_j^2} \qquad (12.17a)$$

$$\tau_j = -a_j/\sqrt{1 + b_j^2} \qquad (12.17b)$$

so given a_j, b_j, we can compute λ_j, τ_j. We refer to the parameters λ_j, τ_j as the *common factor* parameters, and to the use of them as the *common factor parameterization* of the normal ogive model; we refer to the parameters b_j, a_j as the *response function* parameters and to the use of them as the *response function parameterization* of the model. Each has its merits. The common factor parameters are most useful in a preliminary examination of the structure of the data, because we can use established factor-analytic criteria for judging the sizes of the factor loadings. The response function parameters are useful in applications of a fitted model because they generally simplify computations.

By the principles from which tetrachoric correlations are derived, the matrix of item tetrachoric correlations fits the Spearman single-factor model, with loadings λ_j and unique variances $1 - \lambda_j^2$. Further, it may be shown/seen that the probability of the keyed response to each item, π_j, is related to the threshold τ_j simply by

$$\pi_j = N(-\tau_j). \qquad (12.18)$$

This gives a particularly simple interpretation of the threshold parameter. The factor loading λ_j of the item is the product–moment correlation between X_j^* and F. The product–moment correlation between X_j^* and F is the biserial correlation between binary X_j and F, that is,

$$\lambda_j = \rho_{X_jF}^{(b)}. \tag{12.19}$$

These last two results complete a connection between classical item analysis and item response theory. In the discussion of Table 11.1 the interpretation of the biserial correlations between the items and the total score or the remainder score was left in suspense. We saw that the point biserial coefficients with total and remainder score in Table 11.1 put bounds on the factor loadings in the linear model, and they converge on it as the number of items increases. We now see that the corresponding biserial coefficients—with total and with remainder score—put bounds on the item factor loadings of the tetrachoric correlation matrix and converge on them in sufficiently large item sets. The reader will naturally conjecture at this point that one way to fit the normal-ogive model is to use sample analogues of these results. That is the first device considered in the next section.

ESTIMATING ITEM PARAMETERS

A natural "heuristic" estimate of the normal-ogive model follows from the results of the preceding section. By substituting sample tetrachoric correlations for population tetrachorics, and sample proportions giving keyed responses for population probabilities, we can get consistent estimates of the threshold and loading parameters τ_j, λ_j of the item factor model, fitting the linear common factor model to the tetrachoric coefficients by ULS, and applying (12.18) to the sample proportions to give estimates of τ_j.

Resuming work on the LSAT6 example, we have the sample tetrachoric coefficients in Table 11.3 and the item difficulty parameters p_j in Table 6.8. The latter give the estimates of τ_j in Table 12.2, by applying (12.18). That is, each simply corresponds to an area p_j to the right of it in the standard normal curve table. The ULS estimates of the loadings λ_j are given also in Table 12.2. These give the matrix of discrepancies between the sample and the fitted tetrachoric coefficients in Table 12.2, and a GFI of .993. Using (12.16) we can express the parameters in the alternative response curve parameterization, $\hat{a}_j, \hat{b}_j$ shown also in Table 12.2. The quantities $-a_j/b_j$ in the table give the position on the graph of the point of inflection of the curves. These are d_j values in the traditional representation (12.9a).

TABLE 12.2
LSAT6—Item Factor Analysis Results

Item	$\hat{\tau}_j$	$\hat{\lambda}_j$	$\hat{a}_j$	$\hat{b}_j$	$-\hat{a}_j/\hat{b}_j$
1	−1.4325	.3738	1.5444	.4030	−3.832
2	−0.5505	.4100	0.6035	.4495	−1.343
3	−0.1132	.4823	0.1292	.5506	−0.2355
4	−0.7160	.3708	0.7710	.3993	−1.931
5	−1.1264	.3221	1.1897	.3402	−3.497

This method of estimation is generally referred to as a *heuristic* method, meaning that it is not quite statistically respectable. Its main deficiencies are as follows:

1. It does not give SEs for the parameter estimates.
2. It does not give a statistical basis for judging goodness of fit.
3. It cannot handle the three-parameter model with a pseudo-guessing parameter.

It has the advantage for an introductory account that it connects item response theory closely to linear factor analysis and to other concepts dealt with earlier.

The remaining methods to be described are very technical, and the following remarks will merely identify them and indicate a few distinctive features. Three further methods for fitting a two-parameter normal-ogive model (and, later, a multiple-factor normal-ogive) are fairly close in conception to the heuristic method. These share the property that they are all bivariate information methods, and assume that the latent trait has a normal distribution.

Christoffersson in 1975 gave a weighted least squares method. He showed how to fit an item factor model to proportions passing and joint proportions passing. His method gives thresholds and factor loadings, together with SEs of estimate and a chi-square for goodness of fit. Muthen in 1978 gave a weighted least squares method of estimation using the threshold estimates

$$\tau_j = N^{-1}\{p_j\},$$

and the sample tetrachoric correlations. His method also gives SEs of estimate of the parameters and an asymptotic chi-square for judging goodness of fit.

McDonald (1980) obtained yet another variant, the NOHARM method (for normal ogive harmonic analysis robust method) whose primary objective was to supply a generally reliable procedure for large sets of items.[3] For this purpose, ULS estimation has been chosen. Instead of fitting the normal-ogive model, as in the three methods so far, it fits a polynomial to the data that is close to the normal-ogive (in the sense of least squares) and is determined by normal-ogive parameters. A distinctive feature of the method is that it yields a fitted item covariance matrix, created by the approximated normal-ogive. As in the linear model fitted in Chapter 6, the fitted matrix can be subtracted from the sample item covariance matrix, to yield a discrepancy matrix directly representing departures from pairwise independence of the items after their associations are accounted for by the model. The user of the program can read in pseudo-guessing parameters for multiple-choice cognitive items, chosen on the basis of the number of options or other prior information. All illustrations in this book use NOHARM.

Fitting the two-parameter normal ogive model by NOHARM gives the parameter estimates in Table 12.3. The GFI is .9988. The discrepancies are given later in Table 12.6.

From a table of the normal curve, or by an equivalent computer program, we can compute the response function for each item over a suitable range of values of the latent trait. For the LSAT6 data, I prefer to tabulate these at a number of values, rather than draw a graph, which will not discriminate between small differences. The reader may choose to sketch the corresponding graph. Table 12.4 gives values of the item response functions with the parameter values from Table 12.3. Corresponding values from the linear approximation in Chapter 6 are given in parentheses. For example, to get the value for item 1 at $f = -3$, we compute $z_1 = 1.549 + .412(-3) = .31$, and find the corresponding value of the normal ogive function, .62, from the normal curve table. The linear approximations are just points on the lines

$$\hat{X}_1 = .924 + .0605f,$$

$$\vdots$$

$$\hat{X}_5 = .870 + .0745f,$$

TABLE 12.3
LSAT6—NOHARM Analysis

Item	$\hat{\tau}_j$	$\hat{\lambda}_j$	a_j	b_j
1	−1.433	.381	1.549	.412
2	−0.550	.379	0.595	.410
3	−0.133	.478	0.152	.544
4	−0.716	.377	0.773	.406
5	−1.126	.345	1.200	.368

TABLE 12.4
LSAT6—Normal-Ogive Item Response Functions

Item	−3		−2		−1		0		1		2	
1	.62	(.74)	.76	(.80)	.87	(.86)	.94	(.92)	.97	(.98)	.99	(1.04)
2	.26	(.30)	.41	(.44)	.57	(.57)	.77	(.71)	.84	(.84)	.92	(0.98)
3	.07	(.01)	.17	(.18)	.35	(.37)	.56	(.55)	.76	(.74)	.89	(0.93)
4	.33	(.41)	.48	(.53)	.64	(.65)	.78	(.76)	.88	(.88)	.94	(1.00)
5	.54	(.65)	.68	(.72)	.80	(.80)	.88	(.87)	.94	(.94)	.97	(1.02)

from Chapter 6. The reader may check further values.

In this example, the linear approximation is remarkably good up to f = 2. This is partly because the items are not sharply discriminating—that is, they do not have high b_j values. It is not known how representative the example is. Generally, the linear approximation is suitable for representing "average" behavior over the range of the test, but is not a good basis for most of the purposes of item response theory.

Full information methods are based on the strong principle of local independence, and use the frequencies of all the response patterns, as in Table 6.7(a). These are limited in applications because the total number of response patterns—2^m—grows very rapidly with the number of items. As remarked already, it has yet to be shown that these methods have any advantages over methods employing just information from proportions and pairwise proportions, based on the weak principle of local independence. The most promising of the full information methods is the method of "marginal maximum likelihood" given by Bock and Aitkin (1981).[4] Like the methods of Christoffersson and Muthen, this gives SEs of estimate and a chi-square for goodness of fit.

One way to distinguish full information methods from bivariate information methods is to note that the former use a chi-square based on $(2^m − 1) − 2m$ degrees of freedom. This is because they use 2^m response pattern frequencies (of which one is redundant because it is the total sample size minus the sum of the remaining frequencies) to estimate $2m$ parameters. (In applications, with m large, a number of the response patterns may not occur at all.) The bivariate methods yield a chi-square based on $m(m − 1)/2 − m$ degrees of freedom. This is because they use m p_j values and $m(m − 1)/2$ p_{jk} values to estimate the $2m$ parameters—λ_j, τ_j. A comparison between a full information method and a bivariate information method must take account of this, as we now see.

It happens that the LSAT6 data have been analyzed by all of the methods mentioned. Of course we cannot generalize too far from the following comparison, but it is at least suggestive. Table 12.5 repeats the heuristic estimates of the common factor parameters, and gives those from NOHARM,

TABLE 12.5
LSAT6—Comparison of Models

	Thresholds					Loadings				
	Heuristic	NOHARM	C	M	B&A	Heuristic	NOHARM	C	M	B&A
1	-1.432	-1.433	-1.448	-1.440	-1.005	.374	.381	.380	.385	.381
2	-0.551	-0.550	-0.549	-0.547	-0.731	.410	.379	.412	.414	.395
3	-0.113	-0.133	-0.138	-0.137	-0.650	.482	.478	.457	.454	.470
4	-0.716	-0.716	-0.718	-0.714	-0.772	.371	.377	.381	.388	.370
5	-1.126	-1.126	-1.139	-1.129	-0.900	.322	.345	.344	.355	.350

Note. Models: C, Christoffersson; M, Muthen; B&A, Bock and Aitkin.

Christoffersson, Muthen, and Bock and Aitkin (the only full information method represented here). Bock and Aitkin used an idiosyncratic parameterization. They rescaled so that what they call threshold parameters sum to zero and the product of all "slope" parameters is unity. Factor loadings and thresholds have been calculated (possibly not accurately) from their parameters. Except for the calculation of the Bock and Aitkin threshold estimates, there is very little variation between these methods.

Table 12.6 gives the discrepancy matrices (a) for the item covariance matrix fitted by NOHARM and (b) for the tetrachoric correlations fitted by the heuristic method. (The others would give negligibly different results if they were available.) The GFI for the item covariance discrepancies is .9988, and for the tetrachoric correlations .9930. The second set of discrepancies, and GFI, corresponds to the sample and fitted correlations of underlying variables. The first corresponds to covariances of the binary variables themselves.

Christoffersson's, Muthen's, and Bock and Aitkin's methods give chi-squares from which the noncentrality parameter d, McDonald's index m_c, and the RMSEA can be computed. These are given in Table 12.7. The three methods give comparable probability values for the data and comparable goodness of fit indexes. The full information method does not give a worse fit than the bivariate methods, so in this application there is no inconsistency in the dimensionality indicated by the weak and the strong forms of the principle of local independence. It is not known how representative this case is.

Of all the material in this volume, the topic of this section seems the most likely to become out of date quite soon. Item response theory is currently in a curious situation. Methodology for applications of the models given the item parameters seems to have outstripped methodology for estimating those item parameters. We can use item parameters to design tests and to estimate latent traits from sets or alternative subsets of items, but we still seem to need better estimates of item parameters for these applications. The problem of estimation seems to remain acute in the case of the three-parameter model (12.10). In this model, it may not be reasonable to suppose that the parameter controlling the lower asymptote is just the reciprocal of the number of response options. This would suppose that the respondent with "no knowledge" chooses an option "at random." But it is known that errors of estimate of the three item parameters jointly are commonly unacceptably large. The primary problem seems to be that they are jointly almost underidentified. It is easy to show that if the item response curve is close to a straight line, the pseudo-guessing parameter can be absorbed into the intercept term, so the three parameters are jointly underidentified. In many applications, the linear model is a close approximation.

TABLE 12.6
LSAT6—Discrepancy Matrices From NOHARM and Tetrachorics

(a) Covariance Discrepancies

$$
\begin{bmatrix}
0 & .000 & -.003 & .002 & .002 \\
.000 & 0 & .001 & .004 & -.003 \\
-.003 & -.001 & 0 & .004 & -.003 \\
.002 & .004 & .000 & 0 & -.005 \\
.002 & -.003 & .005 & -.005 & 0
\end{bmatrix}
$$

(b) Tetrachoric Discrepancies

$$
\begin{bmatrix}
0 & .019 & .047 & -.033 & -.056 \\
.019 & 0 & .009 & .042 & .039 \\
.047 & .009 & 0 & .008 & .051 \\
-.033 & .042 & .008 & 0 & .080 \\
-.056 & .039 & .051 & .080 & 0
\end{bmatrix}
$$

TABLE 12.7
LSAT6—Fit Measures

	Chi-Square	df	p	d	m_c	RMSEA
Christoffersson	5.02	5	.413	.00002	.99999	.002
Muthen	5.08	5	.406	.00008	.99996	.004
Bock and Aitkin	21.28	21	.442	.00028	.99986	.0036

Attention has been concentrated on the normal-ogive in this section because it gives simple practical methods of item parameter estimation, and because it links to classical theory through item factor analysis, as in the preceding section. The logistic model is commonly preferred to the normal-ogive in many applications because it provides a simple sufficient statistic for estimating the latent trait in the one- and two-parameter models. This at least saves arithmetic. Whether it has greater importance than this is open to debate. For purposes of illustration, we capitalize on the numerical near equivalence of the two curves and use the fitted parameters from NOHARM as though they are the parameters of the logistic model.

We refer to the population from which a sample gives the estimated item parameters as the *calibration* or *reference* population. This population determines the origin and unit of measurement. The mean of F is zero and the variance of F is unity in this population. We refer to the estimation of the item parameters as item *calibration*. The estimated parameters are used, with the item responses, to estimate the latent traits of new examinees. These may be from the same population, or from another population of interest, with the calibration/reference population still providing the origin and unit of measurement. The item difficulty parameter a_j will be very poorly estimated if an item is very difficult—that is, the proportion giving the keyed response in the calibration population is close to zero. An item with no examinees passing it cannot be calibrated at all. Respondents with higher values of F are needed. The item difficulty parameter will also be very poorly estimated if an item is very easy—that is, the proportion giving the keyed response in the calibration population is very low. If it is a multiple choice cognitive item, with a proportion of the calibration population passing it as though by guessing, the parameters of the appropriate three-parameter model will be hard to estimate, and will be particularly poorly estimated if all the items are "easy"—that is, there are very few respondents whose trait values lie on the part of the scale corresponding to the lower asymptote, or if the item response curves are well approximated by straight lines. Both of these conditions apply to the LSAT6 data. The pseudo-guessing parameter can best be estimated for supremely difficult items that everyone passes by "chance," but such an item is not usable.

TABLE 12.8
LSAT6—One-, Two-, and Three-Parameter Models

Item	1P		2P		3P (c_j = .2)	
	a_j	b_j	a_j	b_j	a_j	b_j
1	1.565	.440	1.549	.412	1.437	.449
2	0.601	.440	0.595	.410	0.387	.482
3	0.146	.440	0.152	.544	−0.185	.756
4	0.782	.440	0.773	.406	0.591	.468
5	1.230	.440	1.200	.368	1.063	.408
GFI	.9984		.9988		.9988	

In this text, it suffices to use the NOHARM program to fit item parameters. If a one-parameter model is desired, we equate the slope parameters b_j in the NOHARM program. If a three-parameter model is desired, we arbitrarily choose values of the pseudo-guessing parameter according to the number of response options. For example, because the LSAT6 data are from five-choice cognitive items, we suppose each has a lower asymptote of .2. This suffices for illustrations. Table 12.8 gives the item parameters for the one-parameter model, the two-parameter model, and the three-parameter model for the LSAT6 data from NOHARM.

Perhaps the most notable difference between these results shows when we graph the functions. The pseudo-guessing parameter lifts the curves for the three-parameter model at the lower end of the scale, as it must, but the curves are very close for higher values. This is probably not atypical. The parameters in Table 12.8 are the basis of most calculations in Chapter 13.

REVIEW GUIDE

A careful study of the item response functions, their equations, and their graphs is fundamental to what follows. It is desirable but not essential to have a full appreciation of the principle of local independence. It is enough to recognize that it makes the latent trait an explanatory variable, like a common factor, explaining relations between the item responses. The derivation of item response theory from a factor model for underlying response tendencies provides one way to understand these models. Equations (12.13) through (12.19) need close attention for such an understanding. The methods of estimation can be taken for granted, and the parameters thus estimated will carry more significance for the reader after they are put to work in Chapter 13.

END NOTES

General. A primary source for this chapter is Lord and Novick (1968).

1. The constant 1.701 is due to Haley (1952).
2. Knol and Berger (1991).
3. For a relatively nontechnical, but more detailed, account of NOHARM, see McDonald (1997a).
4. Bock and Aitkin (1981).

Properties of Item
Response Models

From one point of view, as we have seen, item response theory is an extension of factor analysis for binary items. The first phase of work on an item response model—fitting the model, estimating the item parameters, and assessing goodness of fit—parallels the concerns of factor analysis. In this phase, (a) we determine whether or not the data are unidimensional/homogeneous, and if not, how many latent traits are needed (see Chap. 14), and (b) we assess the items as relatively good or bad indicators of the factor attribute/latent trait they measure in common. Most applications of the common factor model have been multidimensional, that is, with multiple common factors, and the work is commonly considered to be finished when the factor structure is confirmed or discovered. Usually, the factor analysis of test- or Likert-item scores is followed up by grouping the variables into independent clusters—homogeneous subtests—and taking raw sum scores from these as simple measures of the factors. We seldom choose to obtain a better estimate of the factor score, partly because the simple sum is in practice nearly optimal anyway.

In contrast, in item response theory there is a second phase, usually discussed in the context of a homogeneous test of "ability." Its objects have generally been seen as (a) the efficient estimation of the ability of any given examinee, (b) estimation of measurement error, and (c) the employment of certain general invariance properties of common factor/latent trait models to get comparable results out of subsets of respondents (distinct populations of interest) or subsets of items (equivalent or equated tests). These objectives motivate the substance of this chapter, and form the substance of Chapters 15 and 16.

The present topic requires the introduction of a technical meaning for the word *information*—which is not to be confused with the use of it in Chapter 12, in distinguishing "full information" and "bivariate information" methods for estimating item parameters. An attempt is made to introduce this to the general reader of this book, at a level that should meet intuitive understanding. The reader is free to accept the material on information as a set of devices for estimating or controlling standard errors. Perhaps more than in other chapters, a large amount of the material in this one is marked off as optional because of its technical character. Some students will prefer to skip the technicalities at first reading, and possibly entirely.

In the first section, some preliminary matters concerning scores are introduced. The next section uses the linear Spearman factor model, treated as a linear item response model, to introduce the information concept, and, once again, to show the essential unity of classical (linear) test theory and modern (nonlinear) item response theory. Then we introduce the counterpart theory for a nonlinear item response model, followed by a section that treats some special properties of the logistic models. The final section deals with the effect of changing the metric of the latent trait.

THE CONCEPT OF A SCORE

We are interested in obtaining a good estimate of the latent trait/common factor f of a respondent, given the values $x_1, \ldots, x_m$, of the respondent's item scores. First we must be more precise about what is being estimated. This requires an idealization. For the respondent's value of a trait to be a unique quantity to be estimated from the given set of m item scores, we must be willing to suppose that the m items we use are a subset from an indefinitely large number of such items that we might have written, and, given time, administered. That is, idealizing the question, we imagine an infinity of items, fitting an item response model, of which F is uniquely the common factor.

The reader who is troubled by this idealized conception may take comfort from the fact that given, say, the 5 items of the short SWLS scale—items A–E in Table 5.1—we can choose to add just one more, from the long scale in the table. Given the 14 items in the long scale, we can see how to write at least one more, to make a 15-item, reasonably homogeneous set. And so on. A practical limit will be reached in any application, but for any abstract attribute, we ought to be able to conceive of writing further indicators—further instances of the concept. Idealizing, we imagine the latent trait to be the limit of such a process, continued indefinitely. If we cannot add instances, we do not have a concept.

Another preliminary consideration is as follows: Throughout the preceding chapters, we have concentrated on just two "test scores" formed from the m item scores of a test, namely, the test score—the simple sum of the item scores—and the relative test score—the mean of the item scores. Any estimate of a latent trait will be calculated from the pattern of responses represented by the item scores, and the test score and relative test score are just two of many functions of the item scores that we could consider using for this or other purposes. At this point we widen our conceptions and describe any quantity calculated from the item scores as a *formula test score*. We might for some purposes (see next section) obtain, as a formula test score, a *weighted sum* of the item scores,

$$s = w_1 x_1 + \cdots + w_m x_m, \tag{13.1}$$

where the weights, $w_1, \ldots, w_m$, give different degrees of importance to the component items. We could take a nonlinear function of the items, such as

$$s = \phi(x_1 + \cdots + x_m). \tag{13.2}$$

A natural choice of ϕ would be, for example, the log-odds function of the mean of the item scores, as used in Table 4.1. This transforms a score confined between 0 and 1 to a measurement that, like a common factor/latent trait, may be unbounded. Because a formula score includes the simple sum score, we add the word *formula* to emphasize the generality of the concept. Where necessary to avoid confusion, henceforward we refer to the ordinary test score as the *sum score*. Any estimator of the factor attribute/latent trait from an examinee's response pattern is a formula score, and in the last section of this chapter we see how to understand the nonlinear relation given by the test characteristic curve between the sum score measure of the trait in its bounded metric, and an estimator of the trait in the unbounded metric imposed by the choice of a (nonlinear) item response model.

Yet another technical consideration concerning test scores can be tacked on to this section before proceeding to our main concern. An item response function/curve represents the mean of the item score as a function of the latent trait, and can be represented generally by

$$\hat{X}_j(f) = \mathcal{E}\{X_j | F = f\} = \phi_j(f), \tag{13.3}$$

where $\phi_j(\ )$ is the normal-ogive, the logistic, or possibly some other link function. The expected value of the test score for a given value of the respondent's latent trait is what we earlier called the true score. This is just the sum of the means of the item scores for a given value f of F. We write the true score t as a function of f, namely,

$$t(f) = \hat{Y}(f) = \mathcal{E}\{Y|F = f\} = \Sigma \; \phi_j(f), \tag{13.4}$$

and by a natural extension of terminology we call this relationship between true score and latent trait the *test characteristic function/curve.*

In the linear model the test characteristic function is the familiar expression—recalling (6.22)—in the sum of the item loadings and the sum of the item means,

$$
\begin{aligned}
t = \mathcal{E}\{Y|F = f\} &= \Sigma \; \lambda_j f + \Sigma \; \mu_j, \\
&= kf + c,
\end{aligned}
\tag{13.5}
$$

where $k = \Sigma \; \lambda_j$ and $c = \Sigma \; \mu_j$. This just represents a change of scale from that of F, with its mean zero and variance unity, to the scale of the sum score, with mean $c = \Sigma \; \mu_j$ and variance $k^2 = (\Sigma \; \lambda_j)^2$. In cases with nonlinear link functions, we sum the item response functions (not their parameters, of course). In the LSAT6 example, from the item parameters in Table 12.3 and the approximating linear model, we calculated values of the item response functions for the two-parameter normal-ogive (and linear approximation) at $F = -3, -2, -1, 0, 1, 2$, as given in Table 12.4. Summing these gives the test characteristic function at the six points for the normal-ogive and the linear approximation in Table 13.1. Or, for the linear model, we just write, from Table 6.9,

$$
\begin{aligned}
\mathcal{E}\{Y|F = f\} &= (.0605 + .1345 + \cdots + .0745)f + (.924 + \cdots + .870) \\
&= .573f + 3.818.
\end{aligned}
$$

These functions are also graphed in Fig. 13.1.

In this example, the linear approximation does seem remarkably good. (Other examples can be found in Chap. 16.) The expected value of the test score for a given value of the latent trait is, to repeat, what we earlier called the true score, and the test characteristic function gives the relation between the true score and the latent trait. The final section of this chapter, which is regarded as an optional extra, discusses the relationship between the true score and the latent trait as a possible transformation of the scale

TABLE 13.1
LSAT6—Test Characteristic Functions

f	-3	-2	-1	0	1	2
NO	1.82	2.51	3.27	3.88	4.39	4.72
Lin	2.10	2.67	3.24	3.82	4.39	4.96

Note. NO, normal-ogive; Lin, linear.

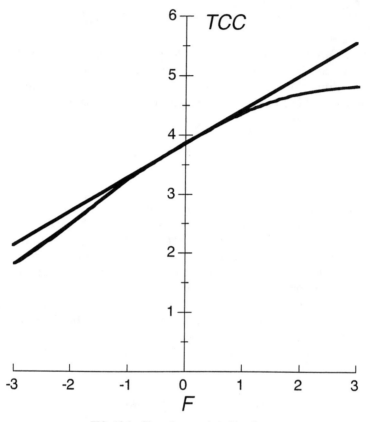

FIG. 13.1. Test characteristic functions.

on which we measure the attribute, and examines the effects of such a transformation on the error of measurement.

INFORMATION AND THE LINEAR ITEM RESPONSE MODEL

The object of this section is to give a simple account of the information concept, by applying it to the linear factor model. (Readers with prior knowledge of this topic may find this a little surprising, but should quickly recognize that it is a natural consequence of a unified treatment of linear and nonlinear factor/latent-trait models.)[1]

Recall the expression (6.2) for the simple Spearman common factor model,

$$X_j = \lambda_j F + \mu_j + E_j, \tag{13.6}$$

with the properties and consequences developed in Chapter 6 (and the use of ψ_j^2 for the variance of E_j). We expect this model to be a good approximation to the behavior of Likert items such as the SWLS data, and a crude yet acceptable approximation to some sets of binary items. Now we suppose that we know the values of the item parameters, at least to a close approximation by estimation from a large sample.

In the (linear) common factor model, it may be shown that if f is the value of the latent trait of a given respondent, defined by an infinite behavior domain from which the m items are drawn, the best possible unbiased estimator of f from the values of the respondent's item scores is

$$\tilde{f} = \Sigma \ w_j(x_j - \mu_j), \tag{13.7a}$$

where

$$w_j = [1/\{\Sigma \ (\lambda_j^2/\psi_j^2)\}](\lambda_j/\psi_j^2). \tag{13.7b}$$

This estimator has the following four important properties:

1. It maximizes the likelihood of the item scores, $x_1, \ldots, x_m$, of the respondent (assuming the unique parts are normally distributed). Loosely speaking, it makes the observed scores more probable than any other value of f.

2. It minimizes the weighted least-squares function

$$q = \Sigma \ (e_j^2/\psi_j^2) = \Sigma \ [(x_j - \mu_j - \lambda_j f)^2/\psi_j^2], \tag{13.8}$$

that is, it minimizes the sum of squares of the differences between the item scores and their common parts, divided by their unique variances to give most weight to the best indicators.

3. It is a *sufficient statistic*; that is, it uses all the information in the data that can be used for the estimation of f.

4. It is *asymptotically efficient*; that is, in sufficiently large sets of items it has a smaller error of estimate than any other weighted sum of item-scores.

Because of property 1 we refer to it as the maximum likelihood (ML) estimator.

*** Optional extra: If the unique part E_j of each item score X_j is normally distributed, the probability that E_j lies in the infinitesimal interval $[e_j, e_j + \Delta]$ is

$$\text{Prob}\{e_j \le E_j < e_j + \Delta | F = f\} = (2\pi\psi_j^2)^{-1/2} \exp\{-\frac{1}{2}(e_j^2/\psi_j^2)\}\Delta,$$

$$j = 1, \ldots, m$$

By local independence, the joint probability

$$P(f) = \text{Prob}\{e_1 \le E_1 < e_1 + \Delta, \ldots, e_m \le E_m < e_m + \Delta | F = f\}$$

is the product of these probabilities. This joint probability is the probability that simultaneously $X_j = \lambda_j f + \mu_j + E_j$ lie in the intervals $x_j \le X_j < x_j + \Delta$, $j = 1, \ldots, m$. When the respondent's item scores are known, and f is not, the function

$$L(f) = P(f)/\Delta^m,$$

namely

$$P = \Pi(2\pi\psi_j^2)^{-1/2} \exp\{-\frac{1}{2}[(x_j - \mu_j - \lambda_j f)^2/\psi_j^2]\},$$

is the *likelihood* of the observations, treated as a function of f. Because the logarithm of the likelihood

$$\mathcal{L}(f) = \ln L(f) = \Sigma \ln(2\pi\psi_j^2)^{-1/2} - \frac{1}{2} \Sigma [(x_j - \mu_j - \lambda_j f/\psi_j^2)^2]\},$$

choosing f to maximize the likelihood is, in this simple linear model, equivalent to minimizing the weighted least squares function

$$q = \Sigma[(x_j - \mu_j - \lambda_j f)^2/\psi_j^2].$$

The student who understands this much will know that by well-known methods, the minimum of q, and maximum of the likelihood, are given by (13.7), and that (13.10) follows. Properties 3 and 4 hold by well-known general results in statistical theory. $\$\$\$$

It is appropriate to think of the m items, drawn from a behavior domain, as yielding a random $\tilde{F}$ from (13.7) that differs from the value f of the respondent's attribute by a random error of estimate ε. This is due to the responses of the examinee to specific properties of the items chosen—an interaction of the random examinee and the item. (As discussed in Chap. 6 on generalizability theory by analysis of variance, there may be other sources of "error" within the examinee, but in the absence of replicated measurements these are confounded with—cannot be distinguished from—the interaction term.) The error of measurement of the ML estimator is defined as the difference

$$\tilde{\varepsilon} = \tilde{F} - f, \tag{13.9a}$$

so

$$\tilde{F} = f + \tilde{\varepsilon}. \tag{13.9}$$

Note that in item response theory (and factor analysis) we have parameters belonging to the items that we estimate from samples, and the sampling error is referred to, naturally, as error of estimate. We also have parameters belonging to the examinees—abilities, attributes, true scores, which we estimate from samples of items. The error in estimating the value of a respondent's attribute due to sampling of items—that is, generally, to the random interaction between the examinee and the items—is referred to as *measurement error.*

The variance of this error of estimate, using the best (ML) estimator, is

$$\text{Var}\{\tilde{\varepsilon}\} = 1/[\Sigma(\lambda_j^2/\psi_j^2)]. \tag{13.10}$$

We notice that the reciprocal of the variance of the error of estimate,

$$1/\text{Var}\{\tilde{\varepsilon}\} = \Sigma(\lambda_j^2/\psi_j^2), \tag{13.11}$$

is a sum of m separate terms, one for each item. (This is because of local independence.) Accordingly, each item makes a separate contribution to the reduction of the error of estimate.

Consider, for example, the five SWLS items, treated as a homogeneous set, with the Spearman model fitted. The factor loadings and unique variances from Table 6.1(a) give the further results in Table 13.2. The weights, in the last column of the table, are obtained by dividing the quantities λ_j/ψ_j^2 by the sum of the λ_j^2/ψ_j^2 values.

The best (maximum likelihood/weighted least squares) estimate of f, given by (13.7), for a respondent with scores $x_1, \ldots, x_m$ is then

$$\tilde{f} = .277(x_1 - 4.22) + .168(x_2 - 4.52) + .194(x_3 - 4.69)$$
$$+ .099(x_4 - 4.88) + .118(x_5 - 3.92).$$

TABLE 13.2
SWLS—Parameters for Information and Weights: Linear Model

Item	λ_j	ψ_j^2	λ_j^2/ψ_j^2	λ_j/ψ_j^2	w_j
1	1.29	0.901	1.847	1.432	.277
2	1.104	1.274	0.957	0.867	.168
3	1.148	1.144	1.152	1.003	.194
4	0.952	1.863	0.486	0.511	.099
5	1.185	1.951	0.720	0.607	.118

For example, a respondent with scores 5, 4, 5, 3, 4 gets an estimated latent trait value of .012. From the sum of the values in the third column in this table, the error variance is

$$\text{Var}\{\tilde{\varepsilon}\} = 1/5.162 = .1937.$$

The standard error of estimate is the square root of this, namely .440, from which we can get confidence limits for an estimated latent trait.

We return to the point made earlier that the reciprocal of the error variance is a sum of m contributions from the separate items. An intuitively understandable first notion of the *information* in the test—consistent with its precise technical meaning—is as the reciprocal of the error variance of our sufficient and efficient estimator. The smaller the error variance, the greater is the information given by the estimator about the location of the respondent's attribute value. As further items from the behavior domain are added, each contributes a further term λ_j^2/ψ_j^2 toward the reciprocal of the error variance—further information about the value of f—until it is precisely determined by the observations.

We write

$$I\{f\} = 1/\text{Var}\{\tilde{\varepsilon}\} \tag{13.12}$$

to indicate that the reciprocal of the variance of the error of measurement is the amount of information I in the test about f, given by the item scores $x_1, \ldots, x_m$, through the sufficient and efficient statistic $\tilde{f}$. In the SWLS example, $I\{f\} = 5.1626$. We also write

$$\begin{aligned}
I\{f\} &= I(f, x_1) + \cdots + I(f, x_m) \\
&= \lambda_1^2/\psi_1^2 + \cdots + \lambda_m^2/\psi_m^2,
\end{aligned} \tag{13.13}$$

to indicate that each item contributes a separate, independent piece of information toward the goal of determining f as precisely as possible. Note that the item with the largest ratio of the squared factor loading to the unique variance makes the largest contribution to error reduction, and so gives most information. An item with a zero loading, unsurprisingly, contributes no information, that is, no error reduction. As we (in imagination) add indefinitely more items with nonzero information, the error variance reduces to zero. In the example, item 1 contributes most to error reduction—most information—followed by 3, 2, 5, and 4. The reader will note a slight correction to the account of the factor model in Chapter 6. Earlier we judged an item to be a good indicator of an attribute if its loading was large and its unique variance small. These properties are now combined as a ratio in the information term.

The *relative efficiency* of two tests, A and B, say, measuring the same attribute, is defined by the ratio of their error variances, or, equivalently, the ratio of their information functions. Conventionally we write

$$RE\{f,A,B\} = I_A\{f\}/I_B\{f\} = Var\{\varepsilon_B\}/Var\{\varepsilon_A\}, \qquad (13.14)$$

so that the ratio is less than one if the first test named is less efficient—giving less information, or, equivalently, having a larger error of measurement. As an extremely miniaturized example, from Table 13.2 we see that the information in a "test-A" containing items 1–3 is $1.847 + .957 + 1.152 = 3.956$ (and its error variance is $1/3.956 = .253$). Similarly, a "test-B" containing items 4 and 5 has information 1.206 (and error variance .829). The relative efficiency of "test-A" to "test-B" is then $3.956/1.206 = .829/.253 = 3.280$. For a more general treatment of efficiency, see the optional section at the end of this chapter.

To complete this section, and as a link to the next, we need the counterpart results from an application of the simple linear model to the binary items of the LSAT6. The means p_j—which are proportions passing—the loadings λ_j, and the unique variances ψ_j, obtained in Chapter 6, are repeated in Table 13.3, with the further quantities needed. From Table 13.3, as in the previous example, we obtain

$$I\{f\} = .4481,$$

and

$$Var\{\bar{\varepsilon}\} = 1/.4481 = 2.232.$$

In making the transition from this model—thought of as a possibly crude approximation to the behavior of binary items—to an appropriate nonlinear item response model, it will be of interest to recognize the item information in column 3 of Table 13.3, and the test information and error

TABLE 13.3
LSAT6—Parameters for Information and More: Linear Model

Item	p_j	λ_j	ψ_j^2	λ_j^2/ψ_j^2	λ_j/ψ_j^2	w_j
1	.924	.0605	.0665	.0550	.910	2.031
2	.709	.1345	.1882	.0961	.715	1.596
3	.553	.1861	.2126	.1629	.875	1.953
4	.763	.1174	.1670	.0825	.703	1.569
5	.870	.0745	.1076	.0516	.692	1.544
Sum	3.819	.5730	.7419	.4481		

variances, as approximations to quantities that all become functions of F. In the linear model, the item supplies the same information at every value of the attribute. The important feature of the nonlinear item response models is that the information from each item, and hence the error variance, becomes a function of the attribute.

INFORMATION AND MEASUREMENT ERROR
IN ITEM RESPONSE MODELS

We now consider estimating the value of a respondent's latent trait f, given the respondent's scores $x_1, \ldots, x_m$, on m binary items, under a nonlinear model for the probability of the keyed response as a function of f. The link function

$$P_j(f) = \text{Prob}\{X_j = 1|f\} = P(z_j),$$

relates the probability of the keyed response to the linear function $z_j = a_j + b_j f$, as in the normal-ogive and logistic functions. In this section we use the two-parameter logistic model for numerical illustrations. Its parameters are in the 2P columns of Table 12.8. In the next section we give further results for one-parameter, two-parameter, and three-parameter logistic models. The logistic and normal-ogive response curves are virtually interchangeable, but the logistic function is slightly more convenient mathematically. Most of the results in this section are general, applying equally to a logistic, to a normal-ogive, or to other possible item response functions.

Given the examinee's response pattern, and regarding f as to be estimated, we need an expression for the likelihood function—the likelihood of the data for varying values of the person-parameter f. Given such an expression, the method of maximum likelihood logically leads us to choose as an estimate of f the point at which this function has its maximum value—the value of f that makes the observed response pattern most probable.

The logarithm of the likelihood has its maximum at the same point f = $\bar{f}$ that maximizes the likelihood itself (because it is a monotone function of the likelihood), and it is convenient, instead, both for arithmetic and for theory, to work with the log-likelihood. This is given by

$$\mathcal{L}(f) = \ln \text{Prob}\{X_1 = x_1, \ldots, X_m = x_m\}$$
$$= \Sigma [x_j \ln P_j + (1 - x_j) \ln Q_j]. \tag{13.15}$$

With the aid of a simple computer program, or tediously by hand calculation, we can plot a graph of the log-likelihood and choose the maximum point. For example, in the LSAT6 example, suppose a respondent yields, in Table 6.7(a), the response pattern 10110, that is, $x_1 = 1$, $x_2 = 0$, $x_3 = 1$, $x_4 = 1$, $x_5 = 0$. Then, using the two-parameter logistic model, with parameters from Table 12.8, we have

$$\mathcal{L}(f) = \ln L(1.549 + .412f)$$
$$+ \ln[1 - L(.595 + .410f)]$$
$$+ \ln L(.152 + .544f)$$
$$+ \ln L(.773 + .406f)$$
$$+ \ln[1 - L(1.200 + .368f)],$$

where $L(z) = 1/[1 + \exp(-1.701z)]$. We can easily, if tediously, use a pocket calculator to give

$$\mathcal{L}(-3) = -5.268$$
$$\mathcal{L}(-2) = -4.443$$
$$\mathcal{L}(-1) = -4.140$$
$$\mathcal{L}(0) \ = -4.360$$
$$\mathcal{L}(1) \ = -5.037$$
$$\mathcal{L}(2) \ = -6.369$$
$$\mathcal{L}(3) \ = -7.172.$$

From just these six values we can see that the maximum is between zero and −2, and the graph in Fig. 13.2 shows that it is close to −1. By interpolating further values in the range around −1 we can determine the maximum point as closely as we please. (It is −.936, in fact.) For most readers of this book it may suffice to think of any computer program for finding the maximum likelihood estimate as searching along the line for the point f that gives the maximum value of $\mathcal{L}(f)$, using algorithms for choosing points at which to evaluate the function that save arithmetic. For every response pattern except the one giving the keyed response to all items, and the one giving a nonkeyed response to every item—the two *perfect*

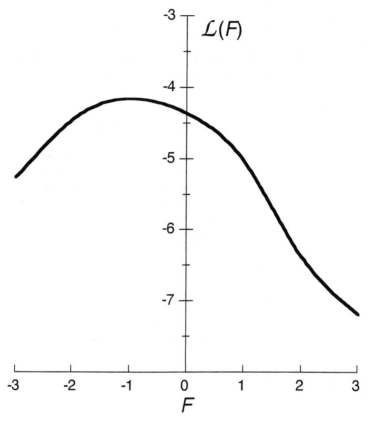

FIG. 13.2. Log-likelihood function.

patterns, that is, perfect "pass" and perfect "fail" scores, say—the log-likelihood function has a maximum point and value. (But see remarks later referring to the three-parameter logistic model.) For the perfect scores, the log-likelihood is an increasing or decreasing function of F, and a maximum point cannot be obtained. This is not to say that such examinees have a (positively or negatively) infinite amount of the attribute, but merely that the test is too easy or too difficult to measure their ability, as could be shown by adding more items—easier or more difficult, as needed. Technical devices (based on Bayesian probability concepts) have been described for estimation that give finite estimates of ability corresponding to perfect scores. This is philosophically controversial and is not described here.

*** Optional extra: A rather neat expression is available for the probability of $X_j = 1$, or $X_j = 0$, in a single formula that leads to an expression for the probability of any response pattern and thus to (13.15). We write

$$\text{Prob}\{X_j = x_j | F = f\} = P_j^{x_j} Q_j^{(1-x_j)}, \tag{13.16}$$

where $Q_j = 1 - P_j$, the probability that $X_j = 0$. If $X_j = 1$, this gives

$$P_j^1 Q_j^0 = P_j.$$

If $X_j = 0$, it gives

$$P_j^0 Q_j^1 = Q_j.$$

By the principle of local independence, the probability of any specified response pattern for m items—$x_1, \ldots, x_m$—is then

$$\text{Prob}\{X_1 = x_1, \ldots, X_m = x_m\} = (P_1^{x_1} Q_1^{(1-x_1)})$$

$$\cdot (P_2^{x_2} Q_2^{(1-x_2)}) \cdot \cdots \cdot (P_m^{x_m} Q_m^{(1-x_m)}). \tag{13.17}$$

Thus, for example,

$$\text{Prob}\{X_1 = 1, X_2 = 0, X_3 = 1, X_4 = 1, X_5 = 0\}$$
$$= P_1^1 Q_1^0 P_2^0 Q_2^1 P_3^1 Q_3^0 P_4^1 Q_4^0 P_5^0 Q_5^1$$
$$= P_1 Q_2 P_3 P_4 Q_5,$$

as we would write directly from elementary probability theory for this combination of five independent events. $\$\$\$$

For a good understanding of the information/error-of-measurement functions in nonlinear item response models, it is desirable that the student lacking even elementary calculus should at least have an intuitive grasp of the concept of the *gradient*—slope—of a function. In the case of a straight line, the student of this book certainly possesses already the concept of the slope—and *gradient* is a synonym for slope—of the line $z = a + bf$. The coefficient b is the change in z corresponding to a unit increase in f. A nonlinear item response function $P(a + bf)$ has a local slope that also varies along the f dimension and can itself be plotted as a function of f. It can be thought of as the slope of a tangent to the curve at each point on it, or as the relative change dP in $P(f)$ when f is increased by such an infinitesimal amount df that in the range of the increase the function is locally linear. (That is, the slope/gradient of $P(f)$, which we will denote by $P'(f)$, at the point f is the limit of $[P(f+df) - P(f)]/df$, as df becomes very small.) If we choose $P_j(f) = N(a_j + b_j f)$, the two-parameter normal-ogive, the gradient is given by

$$N'(a_j + b_j f) = b_j n(a_j + b_j f), \qquad (13.18a)$$

where

$$n(a_j + b_j f) = (1/\sqrt{2\pi}) \exp[-(a_j + b_j f)^2/2] \qquad (13.18b)$$

is the ordinate of the normal curve at the point f. Because the normal-ogive and logistic functions are indistinguishable, we find it more convenient to choose $P_j(f) = L(a_j + b_j f)$ in the following illustrations. In the logistic model the gradient of the function is given by

$$L'(a_j + b_j f) = b_j l(a_j + b_j f), \qquad (13.19a)$$

where

$$l(a_j + b_j f) = -Db_j[L(b_j f + a_j)]^2. \qquad (13.19b)$$

****By a standard application of the calculus chain rule, it can be shown that the gradient of the log-likelihood function $\mathcal{L}(f)$ in (13.15) is

$$\mathcal{L}'(f) = \Sigma \; [P_j'(f)/\{P_j(f)Q_j(f)\}][x_j - P_j(f)]. \qquad (13.20)$$

At the point where $\mathcal{L}(f)$ is a maximum—the value of f that is the ML estimate—the gradient $\mathcal{L}'(f)$ is zero. However, setting this expression to zero does not give an equation that can be solved explicitly for the ML estimator, essentially because the response functions are not linear. It is intuitively plausible that the error of measurement of the maximum likelihood estimator depends on how quickly the value of the (log)likelihood changes as f moves away from the maximum point. Very general (and heavily mathematical) theory gives a measure of the variance of the error of measurement as $\mathrm{Var}\{\mathcal{L}'(f)\}$. $$$

As in the linear case, we call the reciprocal of the error of measurement the *information* about f in the response pattern—the *test information function*. It can be shown that this *information function* is given by

$$I\{f\} = 1/\mathrm{Var}\{\bar{\varepsilon}\} = \sum_j \{[P_j'(f)]^2/[P_j(f)Q_j(f)]\}. \qquad (13.21)$$

This expression is actually very similar in form to (13.13) for the linear case. The numerator corresponds to the square of factor loadings, which are the slopes in $\lambda_j f + \mu_j$. The denominator—the variance of each item score at f—corresponds to unique variance. But now both numerator and denominator vary as functions of f.

Given the item parameters in a chosen model—normal-ogive, or one-, two-, or three-parameter logistic model—we can use this expression to tabulate or graph the test information function. As before, because of the principle of local independence, each item makes a separate and independent contribution to the information about f, that is, to reduction of measurement error, so we write for the *test information function*

$$I\{f\} = \Sigma \ I\{f,x_j\}, \tag{13.22a}$$

where

$$I\{f,x_j\} = [P_j'(f)]^2/[P_j(f)Q_j(f)], \tag{13.22b}$$

which is the *item information function* for each item. Again [as in (13.9)], we write

$$\tilde{F} = f + \tilde{\varepsilon}$$

to represent the estimate as the sum of the true value of the latent trait, plus an error of measurement (estimation) that is due to the specific properties of the items. Then, in sufficiently large samples of items, as in (13.11a),

$$\mathrm{Var}\{\tilde{\varepsilon}\} = 1/I\{f\}.$$

As in the linear model, the ML estimator is efficient in sufficiently large samples of items—has the smallest error variance of any estimator.

For purposes of illustration, the parameters in the 2P columns of Table 12.8 have been used as logistic model parameters for the LSAT6, to compute the item response functions in Table 13.4(a) and the item information functions and test information function, in Table 13.4(b), at the seven points $f = -3, -2, -1, 0, 1, 2, 3$. The response functions in Table 13.4(a) are virtually indistinguishable from those for the equivalent normal-ogive model in Table 12.4.

We notice that at $f = -3$, the order of the information values of the items is 1 4 5 2 3 from most to least. That is, item 1 makes the largest contribution to error reduction, and so on. For $f = -2$ the order is 3 4 2 1 5. For $F = 0$ 1 2 3, the order is, consistently, 3 2 4 5 1. In the linear approximation in Table 13.2 the order was 3 2 4 1 5. Generally, items will make different relative contributions to the precision of measurement at different points along the latent trait dimension. Table 13.5 sums up the various computations described, and should repay careful study.

Figure 13.3a graphs the information function for the two-parameter logistic model for the LSAT6, and Fig. 13.3b graphs the corresponding error variance.

TABLE 13.4
LSAT6—Item Response and Information Functions, 2PL

(a) Item Response Functions

Item	f						
	−3	−2	−1	0	1	2	3
1	.630	.774	.874	.933	.956	.983	.991
2	.254	.406	.578	.733	.847	.917	.957
3	.075	.169	.339	.564	.766	.892	.954
4	.319	.483	.651	.788	.881	.937	.967
5	.541	.688	.805	.884	.935	.964	.981

(b) Item Information Functions

Item	f						
	−3	−2	−1	0	1	2	3
1	.114	.086	.054	.031	.016	.008	.004
2	.092	.117	.118	.095	.063	.037	.020
3	.059	.120	.192	.210	.154	.083	.038
4	.104	.119	.108	.080	.050	.028	.015
5	.097	.084	.062	.040	.024	.013	.008

The test information function values $I\{f\}$ at the chosen points, their reciprocals, which are the corresponding error variances, and their square roots, the standard error of measurement of f by $\tilde{f}$, express the same trend in different ways; because all the items are easy for this population, as was established much earlier, we have more information/lower standard errors for low-ability examinees than for high-ability examinees. For some purposes, this might be what is desired. For others, it would be a defect of the test. The results for the linear approximation are also shown. We notice, as

TABLE 13.5
LSAT6—Summary of 2PL Results

	f						
	−3	−2	−1	0	1	2	3
TCC	1.82	2.52	3.25	3.90	4.39	4.69	4.85
$I\{f\}$	0.466	0.526	0.534	0.455	0.307	0.170	0.084
$\mathrm{Var}\{\tilde{f}\}$	2.146	1.901	1.873	2.198	3.257	5.882	11.904
$SE\{\tilde{f}\}$	1.47	1.38	1.37	1.48	1.81	2.43	3.44
Linear approximation							
TCC	2.10	2.67	3.24	3.82	4.39	4.96	5.59
$\mathrm{Var}\{\tilde{\varepsilon}\}$	2.23	2.23	2.23	2.23	2.23	2.23	2.23

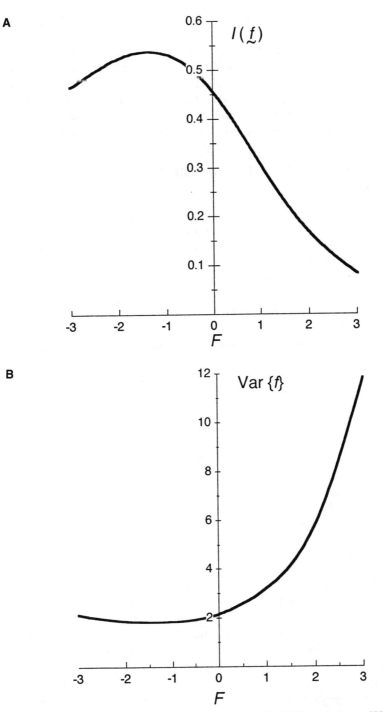

FIG. 13.3.   (a) Information function: 2PL, LSAT6. (b) Error variance: 2PL, LSAT6.

we might intuitively expect, that the error variances in the approximating linear model are close to the values in the normal-ogive model at $f = 0$, as though it was a reasonable single approximate value for the error variances across the distribution of F. The approximation is worst at the high end of the ability scale in this example. Notice also that the item information values in the linear approximation are close to those in Table 13.5 for $f = 0$.

THE ONE-, TWO-, AND THREE-PARAMETER LOGISTIC MODELS

The general principles developed in the preceding section were illustrated by the two-parameter logistic model. In this section we set out some further basic results for information/standard errors of measurement for the one-parameter logistic (1PL), two parameter logistic (2PL), and three-parameter logistic (3PL) models. To avoid overloading the expressions, we write

$$P_{1j}(f) = 1/[1 + \exp(a_j + bf)], \tag{13.23}$$

for the 1PL item response function, with parameters b_j set to a common value b;

$$P_{2j}(f) = 1/[1 + \exp(a_j + b_j f)], \tag{13.24}$$

for the 2PL function, as before; and

$$P_{3j}(f) = c_j + (1 - c_j)/[1 + \exp(a_j + b_j f)], \tag{13.25}$$

for the 3PL function with lower asymptote—pseudo-guessing parameter— c_j. We write $Q_{1j}(f)$, $Q_{2j}(f)$, $Q_{3j}(f)$, for the complementary probabilities of the nonkeyed response.

The 1PL Model

In the 1PL model it is assumed that the items have a common parameter b determining discriminating power, and a zero lower asymptote, so the item response functions are of the form (13.23). This gives the 1PL model a number of special properties. In this model, the probability of a response pattern and the corresponding likelihood function, for given f, take a very simple form.

Consequently, in the 1PL model, the estimate of f—the maximum likelihood point—depends only on the test score, not on the particular form of the response pattern. This is because the probability of the response pattern depends on the parameter f only through the sum score, which contains all the information in the pattern relevant to the value of f. That is, the sum score is a sufficient statistic for f. The actual value of the log-likelihood, and, correspondingly, of the probability of the response pattern at any value of f, depends on the particular form of the pattern, but only through a term in the log-likelihood function that is independent of f.

**** The probability of a response pattern, for an examinee with $F = f$, is

$$P\{x_1, \ldots, x_m | f\} = \exp(DbfY) \cdot \{\Pi_j Q_{1j}(f)]\} \cdot \exp(\Sigma \, a_j x_j), \quad (13.26a)$$

where Y, as before, is the sum score. If the response pattern for an examinee is given, and f is to be estimated, (13.26a) is the likelihood function, whose maximum gives the maximum likelihood estimator.

Equivalently, we maximize the log-likelihood, which is

$$\mathcal{L}(f) = DbfY + \Sigma \ln Q_{1j}(f)] + D\Sigma \, a_j x_j. \quad (13.26b)$$

The form of this expression is interesting. The first term depends on both Y and f, and it increases linearly with f. The second depends only on f, not on the data, and it decreases (nonlinearly) as f increases. The third term is a constant in the function of f that depends on the particular response pattern. An example follows shortly. $$$$

The item information functions are given by

$$I\{f, x_j\} = (Db)^2 P_{1j}(f) Q_{1j}(f) \quad (13.27)$$

and the test information function is given by

$$I\{f\} = I\{f, Y\} = (Db)^2 \Sigma \, P_{1j}(f) Q_{1j}(f) \quad (13.28)$$

yielding, again, the error variance function as the reciprocal of this. Illustrating with the LSAT6 data, from Table 12.8, we take the estimates $b = .440$, $a_1, \ldots, a_5$ as 1.565, .601, .146, .782, 1.230, and compute the desired quantities at $f = -3, -2, -1, 1, 2, 3$ as before. Table 13.6 gives values at these points of the item response functions, the test characteristic function, the item information functions, the test information function, and error variances. The table also contains the log-likelihood function for our imagined examinee with score pattern 10110. [***It also includes the terms in (13.26b) that make it up. $$$]

In this example, the item response functions show broad similarities and differences relative to those of the 2PL model in Table 13.5. These similarities and differences carry into the test information function. The examinee with response pattern 10110 gives an ML estimate of ability equal

TABLE 13.6
LSAT6—Summary of 1PL Results

Item	f						
	-3	-2	-1	0	1	2	3
P_{11}	.603	.762	.871	.935	.968	.985	.993
P_{12}	.228	.384	.568	.735	.854	.925	.963
P_{13}	.120	.223	.378	.562	.730	.851	.924
P_{14}	.286	.458	.641	.791	.889	.944	.973
P_{15}	.462	.644	.793	.890	.945	.973	.987
TCC	1.698	2.472	3.251	3.913	4.386	4.678	4.839
$I\{f,X_1\}$	.134	.101	.063	.034	.017	.009	.004
$I\{f,X_2\}$	.098	.132	.137	.109	.070	.039	.020
$I\{f,X_3\}$	.059	.097	.131	.138	.110	.071	.040
$I\{f,X_4\}$	.114	.139	.129	.093	.055	.030	.015
$I\{f,X_5\}$	.139	.128	.092	.055	.029	.015	.007
TIF	.545	.598	.552	.428	.282	.162	.085
Var$\{\varepsilon\}$	1.834	1.671	1.810	2.334	3.548	6.165	11.71
$DbfY$	-6.736	-4.491	-2.245	0	2.245	4.491	6.736
$\Sigma \ln Q$	-2.265	-3.820	-5.966	-8.658	-11.768	-15.176	-18.790
$D\Sigma a_j X_j$	4.135	4.135	4.135	4.135	4.135	4.135	4.135
LLIK	-4.795	-4.070	-3.970	-4.416	-5.288	-6.444	-7.766

Note. LLIK, log-likelihood function.

to -1.332, with *SE* 1.315. The reader may choose to ignore the three lines giving components of the loglikelihood.

***If you choose to examine them, note how—as shown by the form of (13.26b)—a linear increase with f in the first term is overtaken by the nonlinear decrease in the second to yield a maximum point and value, whereas the third term enters only as a term independent of f, whose value depends on the particular response pattern giving the test score *Y*. $$$$

A basic property of the 1PL model has been believed to give it unique scaling characteristics. This may be arrived at by the following line of thought: From the response function of any item, we can obtain a comparative measure that is independent of it. We derive the *odds ratio*

$$P_j(f)/Q_j(f) = \exp[D(bf + a_j)]$$ (13.29a)

and the log of this, the *log-odds*,

$$\ln\{P_j(f)/Q_j(f)\} = D(bf + a_j). \tag{13.29b}$$

ᵘᵘᵘWe are just inverting the function $\text{Prob}\{X_j|z\} = P_j(z)$. $$$

Given a set of m items that fit the 1PL model, consider two subpopulations of examinees whose trait values are, respectively, f_1 and f_2. Any item X_j from the set gives (on dividing by Db), a difference in log-odds between the subpopulations of the form

$$[\ln\{P_j(f_1)/Q_j(f_1)\} - \ln\{P_j(f_2)/Q_j(f_2)\}]/Db = f_1 - f_2. \tag{13.30}$$

That is, for any item, if we compare the log-odds value of two subpopulations, it is equal to the difference in their trait-values, on division by Db, which just corresponds to a choice of scale unit. Such a comparison is said to have the property of *specific objectivity*. It is objective because the difference is independent of the item used in the comparison, and specifically so because it depends on the entire set of items measuring the trait. The property of specific objectivity defines a class of models that we call *Rasch-type* models, after Georg Rasch, who first introduced them and studied their properties.

It may be shown that any one-parameter model for binary data is specifically objective—that is, any model of the general type

$$\text{Prob}\{X_j|f\} = P(a_j + bf), \tag{13.31}$$

in which $P(\ )$ is any (strictly) increasing link function has this property.

*** This is because $a_j + bf = P^{-1}[\text{Prob}\{X_j = 1|f\}]$, so

$$P^{-1}[\text{Prob}\{X_j = 1|f_1\}] - P^{-1}[\text{Prob}\{X_j = 1|f_2\}] = f_1 - f_2. \quad \$\$\$$$

But the 1PL model, using the logistic function, is unique among all item response models for binary data, in possessing two of the basic properties we have considered, namely, that (a) the sum score is a sufficient statistic for f, and (b) comparisons of subpopulations are specifically objective—independent of the item or items used for the comparison. The combination of these properties (or just the second, regarded, incorrectly, as a special property of the 1PL model) has caused some psychometric theorists to prefer it to any other item response model, to the point of recommending selection of items that jointly fit the model, and eliminating items that would require a more complex model. (The problem of "guessing" in multiple-choice cognitive items would still remain.) The model is sometimes described as providing "item-free" measurement. It has also been claimed that the 1PL model provides special scale properties in the measurement of the trait. We consider this claim more closely in Chapter 18 on scaling theory.[2]

It might seem that the property of specific objectivity gives a warrant for regarding the items that fit the 1PL model as interchangeable indicators of their latent trait, as needed—see Chapter 16—for equating tests. It is important to recognize straight away that even when different items or sets of items yield specifically objective comparisons—so that estimates of differences are independent of the items chosen—the error variances will not in general be independent of the items chosen. A comparison of the item information functions for item 1, the easiest item, and for item 3, the most difficult item, shows that item 1 gives more information at low levels of f, but the relationship reverses at higher levels, and the items are interchangeable only about the point $f = -2$, where they have equal information value. More generally, distinct subsets of items that have been jointly calibrated can be given to different respondents to estimate their latent trait values on a common scale, but the equivalence of the measurements does not give equal precision of measurement. See Chapter 16 for applications of this kind. It there becomes clear that to make interchangeable items (and equivalent tests) it would generally be a bad strategy to reduce available choices of items by retaining only those with equal loadings/slope parameters.

A notable feature of the 1PL model (and also the 2PL, discussed later) might at first sight seem counterintuitive. The estimate of the examinee's attribute is independent of the parameter a_j controlling item difficulty. In a cognitive task such as the LSAT6, it could seem that an examinee who passes the three most difficult items and fails the easiest two demonstrates greater ability than one who passes the three easiest items and fails the two most difficult ones. (We might think we should give greater weight in a formula score to more difficult items—an extra credit for difficulty. One suspects that instructors occasionally do this.) Note from Table 6.7(a) that $81/1,000$ respondents pass the three easiest items and fail the other two, while only $2/1,000$ pass the most difficult three and fail the two easiest. On second thoughts, we recognize that the model behaves as it should. To explain the behavior of the examinee who passes difficult items and fails easy ones, we would need to build a more complex model that takes account of an attribute of "carelessness" as well as the attribute of "ability."

***The item difficulty parameter does enter the likelihood function itself, in the form of the third term in (13.26b), which does not depend on f. The particular pattern used so far to illustrate estimation, 10110, given by $15/1,000$ examinees, corresponds to passing item 1, easiest, item 3, most difficult, and item 4, in between. For this pattern, with a sum score of 3, we have at $f = -1$, say,

$$\mathcal{L}\{-1\} = DbYx(-1) + \Sigma \ln Q_j(-1) + D\Sigma\, a_j x_j$$
$$= -5.966 + (-2.243) + 4.135$$

$$= -8.209 + 4.135$$
$$= -4.075,$$

The corresponding probability of this specific response pattern, at that point, is the likelihood given by (13.26a), or, using our computations so far, $\text{Prob}\{10110|F = -1\} = \exp[\mathcal{L}(-1)] = \exp(-4.075) = .0170$. For the response pattern 10011, which corresponds to passing the three easiest items, the third term in the log-likelihood is $1.701(1.565 + .782 + 1.230) = 6.084$, so $\text{Prob}\{10011|F = -1\} = \exp(-8.209 + 6.084) = .1192$. For the response pattern 01110, which corresponds to passing the three most difficult items, the third term is $1.701(.601 + .146 + .782) = 2.601$, so $\text{Prob}\{01110|F = -1\} = \exp(-8.209 + 2.601) = .0037$. $\$\$\$\$$

Table 13.7 gives the probabilities for all the response patterns that give a total score $Y = 3$, at $f = -1$. A study of this table shows that the two most likely patterns correspond to passing the two easiest items, 1 and 5, but the next most likely pattern, 11010, corresponds to failing item 5. The pattern 01110, passing the three most difficult items and failing the two easiest, is the least likely of all the patterns giving $Y = 3$. Generally, the greater the spread of item difficulties, and/or the steeper the item response curves, the greater will be the dominance in probability of one response pattern giving each sum score. (See Chap. 18 on the "perfect scale.") Without building a model for "carelessness," it is possible to consider the occurrence of an unlikely response pattern, such as 01110 in our example, as "anomalous," suggesting that the examinee has in some sense been careless in responding to the items.

The 2PL Model

A few remarks can be added beyond the discussion of this case already given in the last section. From the form of the likelihood function, whereas

TABLE 13.7
LSAT6 Response Pattern Probabilities

Pattern	Prob{pattern|f = −1}
00111	.0107
01011	.0232
01101	.0078
01110	.0037
10011	.1192
10101	.0105
10110	.0170
11001	.0878
11010	.0409
11100	.0139

in the 1PL model the simple sum score is a sufficient statistic, in the 2PL model all the information in the response pattern relevant to estimation of f is in a weighted sum score $\Sigma \, b_j x_j$, with the slope parameters b_j as weights.

****In the 2PL model (13.24), the probability of a response pattern for given f is

$$\text{Prob}\{X_1 = x_1, \ldots X_m = x_m | F = f\}$$
$$= \exp(Df\Sigma \, b_j x_j) \cdot \Pi_j Q_{2j}(f) \cdot \exp(D\Sigma a_j x_j), \tag{13.32}$$

with corresponding log-likelihood function, from (13.15),

$$\mathcal{L}(f) = Df\Sigma \, b_j x_j + \Sigma \ln Q_{2j}(f) + D\Sigma \, a_j x_j. \tag{13.33}$$

These expressions differ from the corresponding ones for the 1PL model just by the substitution of the weighted sum $\Sigma \, b_j x_j$ for b times the simple sum Y in the first term of (13.26a) and (13.26b). In the 2PL model, this weighted sum is a sufficient statistic for f, containing all the information in the response pattern that is relevant to f. $$$

The item information function is

$$I\{f,X_j\} = (Db_j)^2 P_{2j}(f) Q_{2j}(f), \tag{13.34}$$

and the test information function is, again, $\Sigma \, I\{f,X_j\}$, as in (13.22a). For the LSAT6 data we already have the various functions tabulated in Table 13.5. These can be reviewed at this point, for comparison with the 1PL results. Not surprisingly, in this example the item response functions are close to the 1PL results except for item 3, which has a higher discrimination parameter than the others in the 2PL model.

Figure 13.4 graphs the item information functions, from which we can see that the higher the value of b_j, the sharper the peak in the information function. It is not necessarily a good thing to have very high b_j values and sharply peaked information functions. Such items contribute strongly to error reduction at their optimum—peak information—point, but contribute less away from there. The information functions of the 2PL and 3PL models give the test developer a great deal of flexibility in designing a test to have a preferred spread of measurement error along the dimension. By summing information functions of selected items, it is possible to distribute error variance evenly over a desired range, or to concentrate precise measurement at the low, high, or middle part of the range, or at both extremes, as desired.

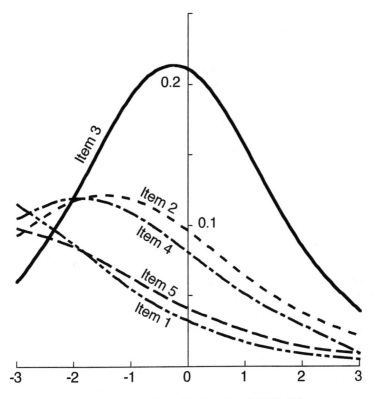

FIG. 13.4. Item information functions: LSAT6, 2PL.

The 3PL Model

The three-parameter model was designed specifically for multiple-choice cognitive items, so in discussing this model it is appropriate to refer to the latent trait as the ability common to the m items in the test. With the introduction of the pseudo-guessing parameter, there is no quantity calculated from the response pattern that serves as a sufficient statistic for ability. This is still true if we equate the discrimination parameters in an attempt to get a Rasch-type model that allows guessing, or if we also equate the pseudo-guessing parameters to give an even simpler model. In the latter case, with all $b_j = b$, and all $c_j = c$, we regain specific objectivity. But this is a property of any three-parameter model with equated slope and pseudo-guessing parameters, that is, any model of the form

$$\text{Prob}\{X_j = 1 | F = f\} = c + (1 - c)\phi(bf + a_j).$$

[This is because any such function can be inverted to give item-free comparisons as in (13.30).]

In terms of modern computer arithmetic, the absence of a sufficient statistic is a trivial defect. We still have the general likelihood function (13.15), whose values allow the plotting of a graph or a search by a computer algorithm for the maximum point. The general expressions for the item and test information functions give us

$$I\{f,X\} = [D(1 - c_j)b_j]^2 P_{3j}(f)Q_{3j}(f) \tag{13.35}$$

for the 3PL item information function, and

$$I\{f\} = D^2\Sigma\ [(1 - c_j)b_j]^2 P_{3j}(f)Q_{3j}(f) \tag{13.36}$$

for the 3PL test information function.

*** In contrast to the 1PL and 2PL models, the 3PL model does not give a weighted sum of item scores with weights for efficient estimation of f that are independent of f. At high values of f, P_j approaches one, and the weights become independent of the pseudo-guessing parameter, but at low levels they are dependent on c_j. Only easy items are of use in measuring low levels of f, as we would have expected. If, impossibly, we could use a weighted sum $Y_w = \Sigma\ w_j x_j$ of the item scores using weights that depended on f (but if we knew f we would not need to estimate it), the best weights to use would be

$$w_j = P'_{3j}(f)/[P_{3j}(f)Q_{3j}(f)] = Db_j[P_{3j}(f) - c_j]/[1 - c_j]. \quad \$\$\$\$$$

Using the parameter estimates $a_j = 1.437, .387, -.185, .591,$ and $1.063,$ and $b_j = .449, .482, .756, .468,$ and $.408,$ from Table (12.8), and the common value .2 for the pseudo-guessing parameter, gives the item response/characteristic functions in Table 13.8. The unsurprising feature of these is that the curves stay above .2 at the low end of ability, and move toward agreement with the 2PL curves at the high end. (Because the items are easy, only item 3 goes below expected guessing level in the 1PL and 2PL models, as may be seen in Tables 13.6 and 13.4.) The notable feature of the item, test, and sum-score information functions in Table 13.8 is that at the low-ability end there is an increase in error variance—a loss of information when we allow for guessing based on the number of response categories. This is more realistic than the 1PL and 2PL models, which assume that an examinee with sufficiently low ability prefers wrong options almost certainly. The log-likelihood function for our examinee with response pattern 10110 is given by

$$\mathscr{L}(f) = \ln P_{31}(f) + \ln\ Q_{32}(f) + \ln P_{33}(f) + \ln P_{34}(f) + \ln\ Q_{35}(f).$$

TABLE 13.8
LSAT6—Summary of 3PL Results

	f						
	-3	-2	-1	0	1	2	3
P_{31}	.63	.77	.87	.94	.97	.99	.99
P_{32}	.31	.42	.57	.73	.85	.93	.97
P_{33}	.21	.24	.33	.54	.78	.92	.98
P_{34}	.36	.49	.64	.79	.89	.94	.97
P_{35}	.55	.68	.80	.89	.94	.97	.98
TCC	2.063	2.601	3.221	3.874	4.427	4.749	4.895
$I\{f,X_1\}$	.099	.088	.059	.034	.017	.008	.004
$I\{f,X_2\}$	.030	.069	.108	.109	.078	.044	.022
$I\{f,X_3\}$	.001	.014	.093	.253	.245	.111	.036
$I\{f,X_4\}$	.045	.086	.108	.093	.060	.032	.016
$I\{f,X_5\}$	.075	.081	.067	.045	.026	.014	.008
TIF	.250	.339	.436	.534	.426	.210	.085
Var{ε}	3.998	2.948	2.246	1.872	2.346	4.764	11.77
SE	2.00	1.72	1.52	1.37	1.53	2.18	3.43
$\mathcal{L}'(f)$	-4.197	-4.089	-4.133	-4.410	-5.111	-6.227	-7.573

Its values shown in Table 13.8 suggest a shift toward the lower ability when we allow for guessing. The ML estimate of this examinee's ability is -1.78, with 1.67 for the SE of measurement at that point on the ability scale. In the 3PL model, as in the 1PL and 2PL models, the likelihood does not have a maximum for examinees with "perfect" response patterns—all pass or all fail. Unlike the 2PL and 3PL models, it can also fail to have a maximum for other patterns—generally for those "careless" examinees who pass the difficult items and fail the easy ones. For example, the pattern 01110 in the LSAT6 data gives a strictly decreasing series of values of the loglikelihood from -5.374 at $f = -5$ to -12.002 at $f = 5$, and a search algorithm does not find a maximum.

In the LSAT6 example, the 3PL model—or rather, the equivalent normal-ogive—gave the same fit as the 2PL, measured by the GFI, and was hardly an improvement on the 1PL. As remarked earlier, the 3PL model would be underidentified, and equivalent to the 2PL model, except for departures from linearity. The main reason why we might choose the 3PL model over the other two is that it gives a more conservative estimate of the error variance, logically allowing for error due to guessing. For the purpose of estimating ability it may suffice to take the estimate of c as $1/k$. It is unlikely that the ability estimate will be nonnegligibly improved by

TABLE 13.9
Information Functions and Relative Efficiencies, Tests A and B

		f						
		−3	−2	−1	0	1	2	3
1PL	A	.273	.229	.155	.089	.046	.024	.011
	B	.157	.229	.268	.247	.180	.110	.060
	RE	1.74	1.00	.58	.36	.26	.22	.18
2PL	A	.211	.170	.116	.071	.040	.021	.012
	B	.151	.237	.310	.305	.217	.120	.058
	RE	1.40	.72	.37	.23	.18	.17	.21
3PL	A	.174	.169	.126	.079	.042	.022	.012
	B	.031	.083	.201	.362	.323	.155	.058
	RE	5.61	2.04	.63	.22	.13	.14	.21

more precise estimates of the pseudo-guessing parameters, if these are available, given a reasonable number of items.

In the earlier section on information and the linear item response model, the relative efficiency of two test scores was defined as the ratio of their test information functions, and illustrated, using the linear model, with two subtests of just two items each, taken from the five SWLS items. I have left to this point the corresponding results for nonlinear item response models for binary data. In these, the test information functions, and therefore the relative efficiency of two tests, will be a function of the latent trait. As a miniature illustration, let us take the two easiest items—1 and 5—for "test A" and the two most difficult—2 and 3—for "test B" from the LSAT6. Summing item information functions for these pairs of items, from Tables 13.6, 13.4, and 13.8, respectively, gives the test information functions for the 1PL, 2PL, and 3PL models. These are listed in Table 13.9, together with their relative efficiencies. We see what is otherwise obvious. The easy test is more efficient—yielding more information and a smaller measurement error—at the lowest level of ability, and the difficult test is more efficient at higher levels.

FORMULA SCORES AND TRANSFORMATIONS

In addition to the information in the efficient estimator and the information contributed separately by each item, we can, for any (formula) score based on the items, define the information about f available from that score. I take a relatively simple approach to this concept and treat only one alternative to the "best" (ML) estimator, namely, an estimate from the sum score—which is a simple formula score. (The ML estimator is also a formula score, of course.)

First we reconsider the simple linear (Spearman) model. The sum score gives the test characteristic function as in (13.5), This is a regression equation, with the sum of the loadings as its regression coefficient—the expected change in Y corresponding to a unit increase in F. It is also the function relating true score T to F. We can rescale the test score Y to give

$$\hat{F} = (Y - c)/k = (Y - \Sigma\, \mu_j)/(\Sigma\, \lambda_j). \tag{13.37}$$

This is an unbiased (but not fully efficient) estimator of f—different from, and simpler than, $\tilde{f} = \Sigma\, w_j x_j$ in (13.7). Again there is an error of measurement by $\hat{F}$, say $\varepsilon = \hat{F} - f$, obtained by rescaling $E = Y - t$. In the scale of the true score,

$$\mathrm{Var}\{E\} = \Sigma\, \psi_j^2, \tag{13.38}$$

and it follows that

$$\mathrm{Var}\{\hat{\varepsilon}\} = \Sigma\, \psi_j^2/(\Sigma\, \lambda_j)^2. \tag{13.39}$$

Equation (13.39) represents the variance of the error of measurement of f from the rescaled sum score Y—error due to random variation of Y for given f. In the SWLS example, from Table 13.2, the sum of the loadings is 5.679, and the error variance of Y, the sum of the unique variances, is 7.733, so

$$\mathrm{Var}\{\hat{\varepsilon}\} = 7.733/5.679^2 = .2212.$$

As must happen, this is larger than .1937, the minimum error variance we found from (13.11) by using the efficient ML estimator of f. The information in any formula score is equivalent to the reciprocal of the error of measurement of f from the given formula score after rescaling the score, as illustrated by (13.37), to be an unbiased estimator of it. (In nonlinear models, the rescaling varies along the attribute dimension.) Conventional accounts tend not to emphasize this natural basis of the concept. Thus, in the linear model, the information about f in the simple sum score can be denoted by

$$
\begin{aligned}
I\{f, Y\} &= 1/\mathrm{Var}\{\hat{\varepsilon}\} \\
&= (\Sigma\, \lambda_j)^2/(\Sigma\, \psi_j^2).
\end{aligned} \tag{13.40}
$$

In the SWLS example,

$$I(f,Y) = 1/.2212 = 4.521,$$

to be compared with the maximum information in the data, 5.1626, from (13.13) applied to quantities in Table 13.2.

The reader will note the difference between (13.40) and (13.13). It can be shown algebraically that the information in the sum score is less than or equal to that in the test, as given by the ML estimator, with equality if and only if the items all have the same information value.

We now extend the notion of *relative efficiency* from the comparison of two test information functions to the comparison of two formula scores, possibly from the same items, defined, generally, as the ratio of their information functions or, equivalently, the ratio of their error variances, when they are rescaled to be estimators of f. Conventionally, we write $RE\{f,S_1,S_2\}$ for the relative efficiency of two formula scores, S_1 and S_2, in estimating f, with

$$RE\{f,S_1,S_2\} = I\{f,S_1\}/I\{f,S_2\}, \qquad (13.41a)$$

where the expression is written so that if the first score, S_1, is less efficient (gives less information) than the second, S_2, the ratio is less than one, and conversely. This corresponds directly to the notion that if both are scaled to become unbiased estimators, f_1, f_2, say, of f, whose errors of measurement are denoted by $\varepsilon_1, \varepsilon_2$, the relative efficiency is

$$RE\{f,f_1,f_2\} = Var\{\varepsilon_2\}/Var\{\varepsilon_1\}, \qquad (13.41b)$$

which is less than one if f_1 has greater error variance than f_2, and thus is less efficient. If a single formula score S is compared with the full information in the set of items, we write, for the *efficiency* of the score, no longer considered relative,

$$Eff\{f,S\} = I\{f,S\}/I\{f\} = Var[\tilde{\varepsilon}]/Var[\varepsilon_S], \qquad (13.42)$$

where $\varepsilon_S = F_S - f$, and F_S is S rescaled to be an unbiased estimator of f. In the SWLS example, the efficiency of the sum score $Eff\{f,Y\} = 4.521/5.1626 = .1937/.2212 = .876$. In the approximating linear model for the LSAT6, from Table 13.3, the error variance of the sum score Y is .742, the sum of the unique variances. Rescaling, by dividing by the sum of the loadings, gives the information in the sum score,

$$I\{f,Y\} = 1/Var\{\hat{\varepsilon}\} = .573^2/.742 = .4426,$$

to be compared with previously obtained $I\{f\} = .4481$, so its efficiency is

$$\text{Eff}\{f,Y\} = .4426/.4481 = .988.$$

That is, using the ordinary test score (rescaled) gives an error variance $1/.988 = 1.012$ times that of the efficient estimate—a clearly negligible loss in this example.

As a further link back to classical theory, we notice that the squared correlation between $\tilde{F}$ and F, over the population of interest, is

$$\rho^2\{\tilde{F},F\} = I\{f\}/[I\{f\} + 1], \tag{13.43}$$

This is because, from (13.9),

$$\begin{aligned}
\text{Var}\{\tilde{F}\} &= \text{Var}\{F\} + \text{Var}\{\tilde{\epsilon}\} \\
&= 1 + \text{Var}\{\tilde{\epsilon}\} \\
&= 1 + \{1/[\Sigma \ (\lambda_j^2/\psi_j^2)]\},
\end{aligned} \tag{13.44}$$

and

$$\text{Cov}\{\tilde{F},F\} = \text{Var}\{F\} = 1.$$

In the SWLS example, this gives us

$$\rho^2\{\tilde{F},F\} = 5.162/6.162 = .838.$$

We also notice—as should be no surprise—that coefficient omega is

$$\omega = \rho^2\{F,Y\} = I\{F,Y\}/(I\{F,Y\} + 1) \tag{13.45}$$

which gives $4.521/5.521 = .819$ for the SWLS data, in agreement with its value as calculated in Chapter 6. For the LSAT6,

$$\rho^2\{\tilde{F},F\} = .4481/1.4481 = .309,$$

which is very little larger than coefficient omega, which we found to be .307, in Chapter 6, and which is also given by (13.45).

We turn now to the information and efficiency functions for sum scores in the logistic models. In the 1PL model the test information function $I\{f\}$ and the sum-score information function, $I\{f,Y\}$, where $Y = \Sigma \ x_j$, are the same. Accordingly, the efficiency of the sum score Y is unity at every point. This is because the sum score contains all the information in the item scores, so both are given by the sum of the item information functions (by local independence).

In the 2PL model, the sum-score information function is

$$I\{f,Y\} = D[\Sigma \ b_j P_{2j}(f) Q_{2j}(f)]^2/[\Sigma \ P_{2j}(f) Q_j(f)], \tag{13.46}$$

which is not the same as the test information function. It can be shown, not surprisingly, that the efficiency of the sum score

$$\text{Eff}\{f,Y\} = I\{f,Y\}/I\{f\} \leq 1 \qquad (13.47)$$

everywhere along the f dimension. In the 3PL model it is

$$I\{f,Y\} = D^2[\Sigma(1 - c_j)b_jP_{3j}(f)Q_{3j}(f)]^2/[\Sigma\ P_{3j}(f)Q_{3j}(f)]. \qquad (13.48)$$

It should suffice for us to examine these results for the 2PL model, given in Table 13.10. The values of the sum-score information function $I\{f,Y\}$ are necessarily lower than those of the test information function $I\{f\}$, but not very much, and the corresponding error variances $\text{Var}\{\hat{\epsilon}\}$ larger, also not very much. This comparison is reflected in the efficiency values $\text{Eff}(f,Y)$.

Table 13.10 also contains the variance of E, the error in the true score, which follows a quite different trend from the variances of the errors in the estimates of the latent trait f. The nonlinear test characteristic function relates these two metrics and also gives the relationship between the corresponding error variances.

The scale of measurement—the *metric*—of latent trait models (including the classical common factor model) is not determined or tested by data. It is determined by the assumptions we make about the functional form of the item response curve—of the regression of the items/observed variables on the latent variables [or, possibly, the assumption we might make about the distribution of the latent trait(s)]. It is as though we were to mark off the units, $\cdots$ −3 −2 −1 0 1 2 3 $\cdots$ on a plastic, deformable substance that can be compressed or stretched to any extent at various places along the axis at will, with a resulting change in the shape of the item characteristic curves. In other words, the latent trait values have only ordinal properties—merely placing the respondents in order along the axis. Any monotone function—any order-preserving transformation—of a given set of numbers describing the level of each respondent's attribute gives a new scale as acceptable as the original one. The assumption that

TABLE 13.10
Information, Error Variance, and Efficiency for Formula Scores—2PL

$I\{f\}$	.466	.526	.534	.455	.307	.170	.084
$\text{Var}\{\tilde{f}\}$	2.146	1.901	1.873	2.198	3.257	5.882	11.904
$I\{f,Y\}$	.462	.519	.524	.455	.300	.166	.082
$\text{Var}\{\hat{\epsilon}\}$	2.16	1.93	1.91	2.20	3.33	6.02	12.19
$SE\{\hat{f}\}$	1.47	1.39	1.38	1.48	1.82	2.45	3.49
$\text{Eff}\{Y\}$	.861	.944	.998	.974	.949	.943	.976
$\text{Var}\{E\}$	.958	1.021	.962	.773	.517	.283	.128

one of the items has a specified item response function—for example, the logistic—imposes a spacing on the values of the attribute; that is, it determines a mathematically convenient scale of measurement. (The assumption that the remaining $m-1$ items also have logistic curves is then possibly false, but is not separately tested.)

The scale on which the latent trait is measured can be subjected to any transformation that preserves the order assigned to the respondents. The bounded true-score scale is just one of these—certainly the most common. The information function and its reciprocal—error variance—change quite radically under these transformations. For example, at the extreme values—the floor and ceiling of the test—the error variance of the latent trait f becomes infinite, but the error variance of the true score becomes zero. On the other hand, the efficiency of a scoring formula and the relative efficiency of two formulas are invariant under choices of scale.

In the true-score metric, the estimate of the true score is "squeezed" at the extremes, and its error variance in that metric is reduced, whereas in the unbounded latent trait metric, the error variance becomes indefinitely large toward the extremes. The unbounded metric shows clearly that we cannot get good estimates of the attribute for examinees for whom the test is too easy or too difficult. The bounded raw score metric invites the false conclusion that at the floor and ceiling we measure perfectly, but this merely reflects what can be called a distortion of measurement at the extremes.

Now we look at these matters in some detail. As implied already in the discussion of the linear model, the information in a formula score S is the reciprocal of the variance of the error of estimate of f from the formula score when it is rescaled to be an unbiased estimate of f. If the regression of S on f—the expected value of the formula score as a function of the trait,

$$\hat{S} = \mathcal{E}\{S|F = f\} = \Phi(f), \tag{13.49}$$

—is nonlinear, rescaling S to be (locally) an estimate of f requires a possible change of origin (which need not concern us), and division by the gradient $\Phi'(f)$ at the point f, so that a change in f corresponds to an equal change in $S/\Phi'(f)$. Accordingly, the (local) error variance of the formula score as an estimator—which we will denote by $\text{Var}(\varepsilon_S)$—due to interaction of the respondent with the items used is the variance of $S/\Phi'(f)$ at fixed f, that is,

$$\text{Var}\{\varepsilon_S\} = \text{Var}\{S/\Phi'(f)|f\} = \text{Var}\{S|f\}/[\Phi'(f)]^2. \tag{13.50}$$

The *formula-score information function* is by definition the reciprocal of the error variance, that is,

$$I\{f,S\} = [\Phi'(f)]^2/\text{Var}\{S|f\}, \tag{13.51}$$

and the relative efficiency of two formula scores, S_1, S_2, denoted by $\text{RE}\{f, S_1, S_2\}$, and the efficiency of formula score S, denoted by $\text{Eff}\{f, S\}$, as defined in (13.41) and (13.42), are also functions of f. At one point on the latent trait dimension, S_1 could be more efficient—give smaller error variance—than S_2, and at another point be less efficient.

The test characteristic function, which expresses the true score T as a function of F, is given by

$$t = \Sigma\, P_j(f), \tag{13.52}$$

and is the expected value of Y for a given value of F. [Compare (13.4).] From the classical true-score model, $Y = t + E$, we have $E = Y - t$. It can be shown that

$$\text{Var}\{E\} = \Sigma\, P_j(f)\, Q_j(f). \tag{13.53}$$

[For any binary item X_j, $\mathcal{E}\{X_j^2|f\} = \mathcal{E}\{X_j|f\} = P_j(f)$,

$$\text{Var}\{E_j\} = \mathcal{E}\{[X_j - P_j(f)]^2\} = P_j(f) - P_j^2(f) = P_j(f)\, Q_j(f),$$

and these variances sum to give $\text{Var}\{E\}$ by the principle of local independence.] This is a counterpart of (13.38) in the linear model, but now it varies as a function of f. An expression can be obtained for the variance of the unbiased estimator of f obtained by rescaling Y. This is given by

$$\text{Var}\{\hat{\varepsilon}\} = \Sigma\, P_j(f)\, Q_j(f)/(\Sigma\, P'(f))^2. \tag{13.54a}$$

We can substitute the normal-ogive or 1-, 2-, or 3PL item response functions and their slopes to tabulate or graph this function. Correspondingly we can define, as in (13.39), an information function for the sum score as the reciprocal of this, that is, as

$$I(f, Y) = 1/\text{Var}\{\hat{\varepsilon}\}. \tag{13.54b}$$

The test information function (13.21) is the information in the entire response pattern, and corresponds to the precision of the maximum likelihood estimator. The test score information function is the information in the (sum or mean) test score, and corresponds to the (generally reduced) precision we get when we summarize the data by the test score, and transform it to estimate f.

If, more generally, we wish to transform the metric of the latent trait, we need to know how this affects errors of measurement. If S is any formula score, its expected value, say T_S, is a function of the latent trait F, say

$$T_S = g(F),$$

with local slope dT_S/dF. We write $S = T_S + E_S$, where T_S, the "true part" of the formula score, is its expected value at $F = f$, and $F_S = f + \varepsilon_S$ for the corresponding score when T_S is rescaled locally to be an unbiased estimator of f. It can then be shown (by Taylor series expansion) that

$$\text{Var}\{\varepsilon_S\} = \text{Var}\{E_S\}/(dT_S/dF)^2, \tag{13.55a}$$

or, taking the reciprocal,

$$I(f,S) = I(T_S,S)(dT_S/dF)^2. \tag{13.55b}$$

Conversely,

$$\text{Var}\{E_S\} = (dT_S/dF)^2\text{Var}\{\varepsilon_S\}, \tag{13.56a}$$

and

$$I(T,S) = I(f,S)/(dT_S/dF)^2. \tag{13.56b}$$

This relationship can be applied quite generally, to formula scores that are not functions of the sum score Y, and, in a common type of application, to formula scores that are metric transformations of the sum score. Here we apply it just to study the relationship between the latent trait in the 3PL model and the sum score itself. In the special case of the sum score,

$$dT/dF = D\Sigma\, b_j(1 - c_j)[P_j(f) - c_j]Q_j(f). \tag{13.57}$$

Table 13.11, which adds values for f at positive and negative infinity, repeats the test characteristic function, test information function, and its reciprocal, the error variance in estimating f efficiently by maximum likelihood from Table 13.8. It then gives the information function $I(T,Y)$ for the sum score in the metric of the true score, and its reciprocal, $\text{Var}\{E\}$. The squared slope from (13.54) and the error variance in true-score metric then give the information function for the sum score in the metric of the latent trait, and its reciprocal, the error variance in that metric. The lines of the table to concentrate on are the error variances in the two metrics and the

TABLE 13.11
LSAT6—Formula Score Results

f	TCC	TIF	$Var\{\bar{\varepsilon}\}$	$I\{T,Y\}$	$Var\{E\}$	$(\Delta T/\Delta F)^2$	$I(f,Y)$	$Var\{\varepsilon_S\}$
$-\infty$	1	0	∞	1.25	.8	0	0	∞
.								
.								
.								
-3	2.06	.250	3.40	0.914	1.094	.236	.216	4.63
-2	2.60	.339	2.95	0.935	1.070	.343	.321	3.12
-1	3.22	.436	2.25	1.035	.966	.420	.435	2.30
0	3.87	.534	1.87	1.290	.775	.404	.521	1.92
1	4.43	.426	2.35	2.060	.485	.196	.404	2.48
2	4.75	.210	4.76	4.249	.235	.047	.200	5.00
.								
.								
.								
∞	5	0	∞	∞	0	0	0	∞

gradients that provide the relation between them. Here $Var\{\varepsilon_S\}$ is the variance of the sum score, transformed to be in the metric of the latent trait. $Var\{E\}$ is the variance of the sum score itself—it is in sum-score/true-score metric. $Var\{\hat{\varepsilon}\}$ is the variance of the ML estimator in the metric of the latent trait. The object here is to illustrate the transformation principle. For the practical objective of obtaining $Var\{E\}$ we already have (13.53).

Recall that in Chapter 6 we obtained for LSAT6 a coefficient omega of .307, which with total variance of 1.070 gives a true score variance of .328 and error variance of .742. Comparing with the values for $Var\{E\}$ in Table 13.9 we note again that this crude general estimate of error variance in the classical true-score model has been replaced by a function of true score. Unsurprisingly, the classical estimate .742 is close to .775, the value in the table at the mean of the latent trait. We see how the unbounded latent trait is squeezed between zero and five when transformed into a true score, with smaller changes in true score corresponding to unit changes in F toward the extreme values—as must happen more generally. The error variances for the latent trait and the true score therefore follow opposite trends. The error variance in estimating the latent trait tends to become very large at the extremes, whereas the error variance of the true score moves toward the expected chance variability at the bottom end of the scale, and zero variability at the top end. These observations are not paradoxical. They are two opposed ways of describing the same basic fact—that the test cannot be used for an examinee who performs at its floor or ceiling. At the ceiling, the true score is constrained from changing in response to the attribute and conveys no information about it. At the floor, the observed score has the mean and variance of the number of chance successes out of five trials, with

.2 chance of success at each. These results illustrate a general principle that information functions—hence error variance—change radically with the choice of metric, which is essentially arbitrary.

Recall the general results:

$$I\{f\} = \Sigma \ [P_j'^2/P_jQ_j]$$
$$I\{f,Y\} = [\Sigma \ P_j']^2/[\Sigma \ P_jQ_j].$$

With

$$T = \Sigma \ P_j,$$
$$dT/dF = \Sigma \ P_j',$$

so

$$I\{T,Y\} = I\{f\}/(dT/dF)^2 = 1/[\Sigma \ P_jQ_j].$$

Because

$$\lim_{f \to \infty} P_jQ_j = 0,$$

it follows that

$$\lim_{f \to \infty} \ [1/I\{T,Y\}] \ = 0.$$

Next we write

$$\lim \ I\{f,Y\} = \lim [(\Sigma \ P_j')^2/(\Sigma \ P_jQ_j)),$$
$$= \lim (\Sigma \ D(1 - c_j) b_j P_jQ_j)^2/(\Sigma \ P_jQ_j)),$$
$$\leq \lim \ D^2 s \Sigma \ P_jQ_j,$$
$$= 0,$$

[writing s for the largest $b_j(1 - c_j)$].

Again generally, because $I\{T,Y\} = I\{f,Y\}/(dT/dF)^2$ for any score Y, it follows that the efficiency of a formula score and the relative efficiency of two formula scores are unaffected by transformations of the scale. $$$

REVIEW GUIDE

A general sense of the maximum likelihood estimator of a latent trait in the linear model for quantitative responses and in the nonlinear models for binary responses would include an understanding of its four good properties as listed.

The test characteristic curve as a relation between the true score and the trait is a central concept.

The student should accept the general concept of information as a reciprocal of error variance—constant in the linear model for quantitative responses, and a function of the trait in the nonlinear models for binary responses. The central use of the information concept is to provide independent, additive contributions of the separate items to the reduction of error. This is most useful in test construction by selecting items from a pool with known item parameters.

The central points in the discussion of the 1PL–3PL models can be reduced, virtually, to the statement that in the 1PL and 2PL models, an unweighted or a weighted sum score, respectively, is sufficient for estimation of the latent trait. My discussion of the property of specific objectivity takes a position on a controversial matter. The student may be content to accept that there are contrary opinions as to whether the special properties of the 1PL model—both sufficiency of the unweighted sum and specific objectivity—justify eliminating items from a set if they have unequal discrimination parameters.

My central recommendation for this chapter for all students, whatever their level of mathematical skill, is to study the tables, row by row, to recognize the principles and applicabilities they illustrate. It is possible to understand item response theory mathematically without a commonsense appreciation of what it does for us.

For those who read the final section, the most practical point concerns the relation between the true score and the latent trait and their very different error-variance functions. It is possible to bypass the mathematical exposition wrapped around (13.52)–(13.57), and study the illustration in Table 13.9 to grasp the seeming paradox that at the ceiling of a test the true score has zero error variance and the latent trait has infinite error variance.

END NOTES

Most of the material in this chapter is based on chapters by Birnbaum in Lord and Novick (1968), which are very technical, and on material in Lord (1980), which is a useful follow-up reference. A major and rapidly developing field based on the properties of item response models is known as *computer adaptive testing*. A computer program can tailor the choice of items to give each examinee according to the responses given to items already presented. The interested reader is referred to Wainer et al. (1990).

1. The treatment in the section on information and the linear response model is based on work by McDonald (1982a), with further developments by Mellenburgh (1994).
2. See Andrich (1988) for a further discussion of Rasch models (and a point of view different from that given here).

Multidimensional Item Response Models

In Chapter 6 we considered the Spearman single-factor model as a simple model for a homogeneous test—a test whose items measure just one attribute in common. We saw that the Spearman model is a good approximation to the behavior of quantitative items such as Likert items, and may be an acceptable approximation to the behavior of binary items. The model, with its special cases, was used to answer the primary question whether the test is indeed unidimensional, and to assess the error of measurement of the attribute by the test score. Chapter 12 extended this work to give item response models that should more precisely fit a homogeneous set of binary items. Then Chapter 13 applied these to assess the error of measurement of the attribute by sufficient statistics from the response patterns. In these nonlinear models, the error variance is a function of the latent trait/common factor. Chapter 9 introduced the multiple-factor model, in which the item responses are multidimensional, depending on two or more common factor attributes. So instead of asking if the items form a homogeneous set, with just one attribute constituting a common dimension of variation of the respondents, we could ask how many attributes are measured by the items, that is, on how many dimensions do the respondents vary. In the context of careful test design, we could also ask whether the items group into independent clusters, each making a separate homogeneous subtest, or, in a partly exploratory study, if some of them are complex, measuring two or more common attributes simultaneously. The hierarchical model was used as a way to see if a multidimensional test is nevertheless sufficiently dominated by a general factor to be treated as unidimensional. Chapter 10 used the multiple factor model as a way to measure construct validity.

The objectives of this chapter, quite predictably, are (a) to define and fit a multidimensional item response model that is suitable for binary data, by extension of Chapter 12, with properties parallel to those of the linear multiple factor model in Chapter 9, (b) to use it to answer questions about measurement error as in Chapter 13, and (c) to use it to answer questions about validity as in Chapter 10. First, we introduce a multidimensional item response model. Then we extend the treatment of measurement error in Chapter 13. The final section shows how the model can be used to obtain an index of validity.

A MULTIDIMENSIONAL ITEM RESPONSE MODEL

Table 14.1 lists 15 multiple-choice items from the ACT Mathematics Usage Test.[1] Each item has five options, and hence would have a pseudo-guessing parameter in the order of .2. It seems reasonable to describe items 1–5 as measuring geometry achievement and items 6–10 as measuring algebra achievement, two subdomains of mathematics achievement. Items 11–15 (which have given reason to suspect them of complexity in previous analyses) are not as readily classified. Table 14.2 gives the proportion passing each item (in the diagonal) and the item joint proportions.

We might consider a confirmatory factor model for these data of the form

$$X_j = \mu_j + \lambda_{j1}F_1 + \lambda_{j2}F_2 + E_j, \qquad (14.1)$$

TABLE 14.1
Fifteen ACT Mathematics Items

Item	Item Stem Description
1	Angles in a right triangle
2	Areas of bisected triangles
3	Length hypotenuse—right triangle
4	Length adjacent—right triangle
5	Area trapezoid
6	$2\sqrt{28} + 3\sqrt{175}$
7	$1/(\sqrt{2} - 1)$
8	$(-3)^2 + 3^{-2}$
9	x for which $[x(x - 2)]/[(x - 1)(x - 2)]$ undefined
10	$2^2 + 2^0 + 2^{-2}$
11	Application of $7\frac{3}{4} + 17.85 + 6\frac{1}{2}$
12	Slope of line $2x + 3y + 6 = 0$
13	Radius of circle given circumference
14	Speed given distance and time
15	Longest diagonal in box

TABLE 14.2
ACT Sample Raw Product Moments

.49	.44	.38	.30	.29	.13	.23	.16	.16	.23	.21	.31	.31	.25	.09
.44	.77	.56	.41	.41	.17	.30	.22	.21	.32	.27	.40	.43	.32	.12
.38	.56	.68	.35	.35	.15	.27	.19	.18	.28	.23	.36	.37	.29	.12
.30	.41	.35	.46	.27	.11	.21	.14	.15	.21	.19	.27	.28	.22	.08
.29	.41	.35	.27	.48	.11	.21	.13	.14	.22	.19	.27	.29	.22	.08
.13	.17	.15	.11	.11	.20	.09	.08	.08	.10	.09	.13	.12	.10	.05
.23	.30	.27	.21	.21	.09	.36	.13	.13	.17	.15	.22	.23	.19	.07
.16	.22	.19	.14	.13	.08	.13	.26	.09	.12	.11	.14	.16	.13	.06
.16	.21	.18	.15	.14	.08	.13	.09	.24	.12	.12	.16	.17	.14	.05
.23	.32	.28	.21	.22	.10	.17	.12	.12	.40	.15	.24	.23	.18	.07
.21	.27	.23	.19	.19	.09	.15	.11	.12	.15	.30	.20	.22	.16	.06
.31	.40	.36	.27	.27	.13	.22	.14	.16	.24	.20	.47	.30	.25	.08
.31	.43	.37	.28	.29	.12	.23	.16	.17	.23	.22	.30	.49	.26	.09
.25	.32	.29	.22	.22	.10	.19	.13	.14	.18	.16	.25	.26	.38	.07
.09	.12	.12	.08	.08	.05	.07	.06	.05	.07	.06	.08	.09	.07	.16

which is the same as model (9.4) for the SWLS data. Here we would allow
nonzero loadings for items 1–5 on factor 1, identifying it as a geometry
factor, nonzero loadings of items 6–10 on factor 2, identifying it as an
algebra factor, and nonzero loadings on both factors for items 11–15. We
would allow the factors to be correlated, representing their common membership in the mathematics item domain. The notion is that items 11–15
are complex—combining geometry and algebra—and do not require further types of mathematics knowledge. We can apply the linear model, by
the methods of Chapter 9, as an approximate model, but it is more appropriate to apply a link function as in Chapter 12, or—an equivalent—to
extend the concept of item factor analysis to multiple factors. In the latter
approach to the problem, we suppose, as in Chapter 12, that an underlying
response tendency X_j^* fits the two-factor model (14.1) and suppose that X_j
= 1 if X_j^* exceeds a threshold value τ_j, and zero if not. Assuming F_1, F_2,
normally distributed with variance unity and E_j normally distributed with
variance ψ_j^2 gives a two-dimensional item response model with common-
factor parameters,

$$\text{Prob}\{X_j = 1 | F_1 = f_1, F_2 = f_2\} = N\{(\lambda_{j1}/\psi_j)f_1 + (\lambda_{j2}/\psi_j)f_2 - (\tau/\psi_j)\}. \quad (14.2)$$

Its equivalent with item response function parameters is

$$\text{Prob}\{X_j = 1 | F_1 = f_1, F_2 = f_2\} = N\{b_{j1}f_1 + b_{j2}f_2 + a_j\} \quad (14.3)$$

where

$$b_{j1} = \lambda_{j1}/\psi_j, \qquad b_{j2} = \lambda_{j2}/\psi_j, \qquad a_j = -\tau_j/\psi_j. \qquad (14.4)$$

We suppose the factors are correlated, and write

$$\text{Cor}\{F_1, F_2\} = \phi_{12}. \qquad (14.5)$$

We can directly regard $N(\ )$ in (14.3) as a suitable link function to make a nonlinear model for binary items.

*** Note that we think of the underlying variable as scaled so that ψ_j is calculated from the loadings and the correlation between the factors, by $\psi_j = \sqrt{(1 - \lambda_j^2 - \lambda_k^2 - 2\lambda_j\lambda_k\phi_{12})}$. $$$

The concepts in Chapter 9 concerning (a) identified, confirmatory models with independent clusters, or at least with an independent-clusters basis, as in the present example, (b) hierarchical solutions, or (c) rotation of the loadings carry over unaltered to the multidimensional item response model. Indeed, without such concepts, we could not resolve the underidentifiability problem or understand the results of the analysis. Independent clusters, or the equivalent hierarchical solution, are very appropriate representations for testing the success of the process of test construction, because the competent test developer typically writes items belonging to subdomains of a behavior domain. Once we have the two-dimensional item response model, it is easy to see how to write it for three or more dimensions, so for simplicity we continue with just the two-dimensional case.

As in Chapter 12, we assume the latent traits are normally distributed, so the probability of the keyed response to each item, π_j, is related to the threshold τ_j by

$$\pi_j = N(-\tau_j) \qquad (14.6)$$

and the matrix of tetrachoric correlations fits the prescribed confirmatory or exploratory structure—number of factors and pattern of their loadings. Alternatively, we can use the NOHARM program for these analyses. Applying NOHARM to this data set gives the exploratory solution in Table 14.3, the independent clusters solution in Table 14.4, and the hierarchical solution in Table 14.5.[2] (The threshold values in Table 14.3 apply in all analyses.) The item response function parameters a_j, b_j are not listed, but are easily computed by the reader if desired, by (14.4).

The independent-clusters solution in Table 14.4 gives a GFI of .995, suggesting acceptance of the model with items 1–5 and 6–10 forming homogeneous subtests measuring geometry and algebra, and items 11–16

TABLE 14.3
ACT Exploratory Solution

Item	Threshold	Promax Loadings		Uniqueness
1	−0.031	.596	.209	.458
2	0.731	.775	−.102	.481
3	0.470	.365	.092	.819
4	−0.103	.576	.062	.623
5	−0.050	.432	.081	.767
6	−0.840	−.042	.501	.772
7	−0.367	.152	.463	.681
8	−0.631	−.066	.468	.812
9	−0.722	.134	.558	.583
10	−0.260	.006	.400	.837
11	−0.536	.374	.395	.533
12	−0.074	.342	.414	.548
13	−0.019	.392	.348	.567
14	−0.317	.249	.442	.614
15	−1.001	−.257	.476	.849

Factor correlation .579
GFI .996

TABLE 14.4
ACT Independent Clusters Basis Solution

Item	Loadings		Uniqueness	Structure Coefficients		Item–Trait Covariances	
	I	II		I	II	I	II
1	.766		.413	.766	.566	.306	.226
2	.642		.588	.642	.474	.196	.145
3	.431		.814	.431	.318	.154	.114
4	.604		.636	.604	.496	.240	.177
5	.485		.765	.485	.358	.193	.143
6		.439	.809	.324	.439	.090	.122
7		.592	.650	.437	.592	.163	.221
8		.386	.851	.285	.386	.093	.126
9		.666	.556	.492	.666	.152	.205
10		.388	.849	.287	.388	.111	.150
11	.365	.367	.534	.636	.637	.220	.220
12	.355	.363	.551	.623	.625	.248	.249
13	.358	.349	.567	.616	.614	.246	.245
14	.223	.436	.615	.545	.601	.207	.228
15	−.335	.548	.859	.070	.300	.017	.073

Factor correlation .739
GFI .995

TABLE 14.5
ACT Hierarchical Solution

Item	Loadings			Item–Trait Covariances		
	G	I′	II′	G	I′	II′
1	.658	.287		.263	.115	
2	.552	.241		.169	.074	
3	.371	.162		.132	.058	
4	.519	.226		.206	.090	
5	.417	.182		.166	.072	
6	.377		.164	.105		.046
7	.509		.222	.190		.083
8	.332		.145	.109		.047
9	.573		.250	.176		.077
10	.334		.145	.129		.056
11	.629	.137	.138	.217	.047	.047
12	.617	.133	.136	.246	.053	.054
13	.608	.134	.131	.243	.054	.052
14	.566	.084	.163	.215	.032	.062
15	.183	−.126	.205	.044	−.030	.050

complex items drawing on both. The exploratory solution in Table 14.3 assures us that we have not missed anything important. That is, it resembles the independent clusters solution closely, with items 1–5 and 6–10 still involving one factor, and items 11–15 still complex, although this pattern was not imposed. The GFI for the exploratory solution, .996, is remarkably close to that for the confirmatory solution, although the latter is a much more restrictive model, with only 20 factor loadings estimated instead of 30. This also indicates that the solution is satisfactory. We note that the correlation between geometry achievement and algebra achievement is .739 in the confirmatory solution and .579 in the exploratory solution. Generally, these can be expected to differ, although not radically. The threshold parameters are directly understood as functions of item difficulty in the calibration population. We can again make a broad judgment of the factor loadings by classical criteria, regarding those greater than .3 as salient. However, attempts to make a more fine-grained interpretation of the results should take account of the thresholds as well as the sizes of the loadings, and, indeed, of the item response functions and information functions, to be considered in the next section. For example, an outstanding anomaly is the behavior of item 15. On the face of it, this is very much a geometry item, yet it is negatively related to F_1, geometry achievement. This anomaly can be explained by the fact that the proportion of respondents passing item 15—.16—is on the order of chance level. That is, the item is too difficult for the examinees in the calibration group, so the estimate of its factor loadings cannot be relied on.

Again, as in Chapter 9, we can rearrange the parameters in the independent-clusters-basis model to give the parameters of the hierarchical model, with three uncorrelated factors,

$$\text{Prob}\{X_j = 1 | G = g, F_1^* = f_1^*, F_2^* = f_2^*\}$$
$$= \lambda_j g + \lambda_{j1}^* f_1^* + j_2^* f_2^*, \tag{14.7}$$

as in Table 14.5, where G is a general domain—mathematics achievement—factor/latent trait, and F_1^*, F_2^* are hierarchical subdomain factors for geometry and algebra.

The Schmid–Leiman transformation gives us

$$\lambda_j^* = \lambda_{j1}\sqrt{\phi_{12}} \qquad \text{items 1–5}$$
$$\lambda_j^* = \lambda_{j2}\sqrt{\phi_{12}} \qquad \text{items 6–10}$$
$$\lambda_j^* = (\lambda_{j1} + \lambda_{j2})\sqrt{\phi_{12}} \qquad \text{items 11–15}$$
$$\lambda_{j1}^* = \lambda_{j1}\sqrt{1 - \phi_{12}}$$
$$\lambda_{j2}^* = \lambda_{j2}\sqrt{1 - \phi_{12}}$$

because with just two factors we rather trivially explain the correlation ϕ_{12} in terms of the general factor by writing

$$F_1 = \sqrt{\phi_{12}}\, G + \varepsilon_1,$$
$$F_2 = \sqrt{\phi_{12}}\, G + \varepsilon_2,$$

where

$$\text{Var}\{\varepsilon_1\} = \text{Var}\{\varepsilon_2\} = \sqrt{1 - \phi_{12}}\ .$$

INFORMATION FUNCTIONS AND MEASUREMENT ERROR

An independent clusters solution seems generally desirable in multidimensional item response models. When we put the items we have calibrated into use, it will be natural to form subtest scores for each homogeneous subset of items, giving a *profile* of subtest scores for the respondent, as well as, possibly, a total score. For such purposes we would be inclined to eliminate complex items. Another reason is that we ourselves inhabit a three-dimensional space, and consequently find it easy to draw two-dimensional graphs, difficult to draw three-dimensional graphs, and impossible to draw graphs in four or more dimensions. Just the simple case of two attributes would require a representation of the item response functions as curved surfaces in three-dimensional space. The independent clusters solution avoids these complexities.

We recognize the problem of visualization as soon as we consider the expressions for item and test characteristic functions. The item characteristic function for an item with a nonzero loading on just one latent trait can be thought of as the ordinary curve for the unidimensional case. Considered as functions of both latent traits, we can if we wish imagine a graph such as those in the figures in Chapter 12 as a slice through a "wave," representing the fact that

$$\text{Prob}\{X_j = 1 | F_1 = f_1, F_2 = f_2\} = N\{(\lambda_{j1}/\psi_j)f_1 - (1/\psi_j)\tau_j\}$$

is independent of, and constant over, all values of f_2. (And similarly for items in the other cluster.) For an item loading on both latent traits, the "wave" rises in a direction determined by the relative sizes of λ_1 and λ_2, representing the fact that

$$\text{Prob}\{X_j = 1 | F_1 = f_1, F_2 = f_2\} = N\{[(\lambda_{j1}f_1 + \lambda_{j2}f_2)/\psi_j] - (\tau_j/\psi_j)\},$$

is constant over all combinations of f_1 and f_2 that make $\lambda_{j1}f_1 + \lambda_{j2}f_2$ constant. We can avoid a problem of visualization that is difficult for two latent traits and impossible for more than two, by invoking independent-cluster concepts and thinking, as in Chapter 12, of the model as a linear model for underlying response tendencies.[3]

As before, the test characteristic function is the sum of the item characteristic functions. It is natural, in an independent clusters model, to form subtest characteristic functions and subtest information functions, one for each homogeneous subtest. In an independent-clusters-basis model, we would, again, form the subtest functions for the homogeneous subtests, and we might choose to treat the complex items as forming a subtest of interest. We need a special notation to represent choices of subtests, which need not group items in their given order, as in the mathematics example, 1–5, 6–10, 11–15. We can use set theory notation, writing $\{s\}$ to represent a chosen subset of items. For example, we write $\{s\} = \{1 \ 2 \ 3 \ 4 \ 5\}$ for the selection of items 1–5, or $\{s\} = \{1 \ 3 \ 6 \ 15\}$ for the selection of items 1 3 6 15 to form a subset. We use s without the braces to mean the number of items in the subset $\{s\}$. Then we can write

$$Y_{\{s\}} = \sum_{\{s\}} X_j \tag{14.8}$$

to represent the subtest sum score from the subset of items $\{s\}$, and

$$M_{\{s\}} = (1/s)\sum_{\{s\}}X_j \qquad (14.9)$$

for the mean. For example, if $\{s\}$ is the subset $\{1\ 3\ 6\ 15\}$,

$$Y_{\{s\}} = X_1 + X_3 + X_6 + X_{15},$$
$$M_{\{s\}} = (1/4)(X_1 + X_3 + X_6 + X_{15}).$$

So far we have considered only the multidimensional normal-ogive. For any link function $P(\ )$—that is, any monotone function bounded by zero and unity—we write, using common factor parameters,

$$\text{Prob}\{X_j = 1 | F_1 = f_1, F_2 = f_2\} = P(z_j) \qquad (14.10)$$

where

$$z_j = (\lambda_{j1}/\psi_j)f_1 + (\lambda_{j2}/\psi_j)f_2 - (1/\psi_j)\tau_j. \qquad (14.11)$$

The two-dimensional counterpart of the 3PL model is

$$\text{Prob}\{X_j = 1 | F_1 = f_1, F_2 = f_2\} = c_j + (1 - c_j)L(z_j), \qquad (14.12)$$

with $L(\ )$ the logistic function and z_j given by (14.11). The counterpart of the 2PL model is, of course, given by (14.12) with all pseudo-guessing parameters set to zero. Analogues of the 1PL model are given by setting the pseudo-guessing parameters to zero and equating loadings within clusters, and possibly also equating them between clusters. The standard terminology—1PL, 2PL, 3PL—was developed for simple unidimensional cases, with the models named for the number of parameters belonging to each item. Strictly, this nomenclature is unsuitable for multidimensional models, but we can keep it, although no longer with the same meaning, and speak of a two-dimensional 3PL model to mean a two-dimensional logistic model with a pseudo-guessing parameter, and so on. Note that each item has just one threshold parameter, or equivalent a_j parameter, and just one pseudo-guessing parameter, if allowed, but the number of factor loadings—or equivalent slope parameters—depends on the number of dimensions and the prescribed cluster structure.

Given the item response functions for any subset $\{s\}$ of items, we can obtain the subtest-sum characteristic function—the expected value of the subtest score $Y_{\{s\}}$ for given f_1, f_2, as the sum of the item response functions of the items in the subset, and similarly for the subtest-mean characteristic function as the mean of the item characteristic functions. This includes, of course, the test characteristic function as the expected value of the sum or mean of all of the items.

Naturally, if a subtest is homogeneous, the subtest characteristic function, like the item characteristic functions of which it is the sum, reduces to a simple curve as in the unidimensional model, and the subtest sum is a subtest true score, in one-to-one correspondence with the trait defined by the subtest. If any items in the subtest are complex, the subtest characteristic function requires a three-dimensional—or, more generally, a (p + 1)-dimensional—representation. Alternatively, we can tabulate the subtest characteristic function for combinations of values of the latent traits.

Given the threshold values, loadings, and unique variances for the mathematics example in Table 14.4, treated as parameters of the two-dimensional 2PL model, it is straightforward to compute the item response functions with a very simple computer program, or tediously by pocket calculator, and then form the needed sums or means of these for subtest or test characteristic functions. Table 14.6 lists the simple subtest mean characteristic functions for items 1–5—geometry—and items 6–10—algebra—for values −2 −1 0 1 2 of the respective traits. A cross-tabulation is given for the values of the subtest-mean characteristic function for the complex items 11–15. It would be possible to present a corresponding tabulation for each item in the subtest, but this becomes too complex to be usefully informative. We can also think about the surface in terms of the direction of steepest ascent of the "wave" that can be intuitively pictured in the cross-tabulation. Such a geometric picture may suit the intuition of some readers but not all, perhaps. It is not necessary for a good understanding of the model.

Given the item parameters, as estimated from a large calibration sample, the log-likelihood function has the same expression as in a unidimensional item response model, namely,

$$\mathcal{L}(f_1,f_2) = \Sigma \ [X_j \ln P(z_j) + (1 - X_j) \ln Q(z_j)], \qquad (14.13)$$

as in (13.15), but with z_j given by (14.11). If the items have an independent cluster structure, the log-likelihood can be written as a sum of terms, one

TABLE 14.6
ACT Test Characteristic Curves

s_1		s_2		s_3					
θ_1	TCC	θ_2	TCC	θ_1/θ_2	−2	−1	0	1	2
−2	.149	−2	.051	−2	.026	.076	.175	.325	.507
−1	.326	−1	.121	−1	.042	.110	.236	.415	.614
0	.586	0	.260	0	.085	.182	.333	.521	.708
1	.821	1	.471	1	.162	.289	.452	.622	.770
2	.938	2	.679	2	.271	.418	.580	.698	.795

for each cluster. Each term corresponds to a unidimensional model for the cluster, and we can independently search for the maximum likelihood estimates of f_1, f_2 by graphing each function along its own line, or using a computerized search method. Thus, at the stage of estimating latent traits, the multidimensional independent clusters model behaves just like a collection of unidimensional models, even though the traits are correlated. A necessary condition for each term of the log-likelihood to have a maximum is that the examinee does not give a perfect subtest score—all unities or all zeros. If any item in the set is complex, we must search for the maximum of $\mathcal{L}$ with respect to both—or, more generally, all—latent traits.

As stated earlier in reference to the unidimensional case, the sharpness of curvature of the loglikelihood function near the maximum point determines the error of measurement. The test information function is the variance of the slope of the loglikelihood function, and its reciprocal is the variance of measurement error. In multidimensional models, as here represented by the two-dimensional case, the measurement errors of f_1, f_2 are generally correlated, so it is not enough to consider their variances, as reciprocals of their information functions—variances of the slopes of the log-likelihood function with respect to f_1 and f_2. Also, to take advantage of independent clusters, to the extent to which they have been successfully designed into the items, we need expressions for the information and measurement error from subsets of the items.

We write

$$\bar{F}_{1\{s_k\}} = f_1 + \varepsilon_{1\{s_k\}}, \tag{14.14a}$$

$$\bar{F}_{2\{s_k\}} = f_2 + \varepsilon_{2\{s_k\}}, \tag{14.14b}$$

to represent maximum likelihood estimates of f_1, f_2 from subset $\{s_k\}$ as a sum of the true values and errors of measurement due to specific properties of items in that subset. Consider, and generalize from, our mathematics example. The subsets $\{s_1\}, \{s_2\}$ are homogeneous, and these, as we would expect, give expressions that are the same as the previous unidimensional results, namely,

$$\text{Var}\{\varepsilon_{1\{s_1\}}\} = 1/[\sum_{\{s\}} (\lambda_{j1}^2/\psi_1^2)(P'(z_j)^2/P(z_j)Q(z_j))], \tag{14.15a}$$

$$\text{Var}\{\varepsilon_{2\{s_2\}}\} = 1/[\sum_{\{s\}} (\lambda_{j2}^2/\psi_2^2)(P'(z_j)^2/P(z_j)Q(z_j))], \tag{14.15b}$$

and the errors of measurement are uncorrelated. Also, of course, such a subset gives no information about—and no error reduction for—the latent trait on which its items all have zero loadings. If a subset contains complex items, as in $\{s_3\}$ of the mathematics example, it can be used to estimate both f_1 and f_2, but the errors of measurement are correlated—possibly very highly correlated. Similarly, the errors will be correlated if we use the entire set to estimate the traits. In applications it will often be wise to eliminate such items from the test. For researchers determined to use them, expressions for the variances and covariances of their measurement errors are given in the following optional extra material. Results for formula score information and error variances are the same as in the unidimensional case in independent clusters. We do not consider them here for the case of complex items.

*** Optional extra, requiring elementary calculus, elementary matrix algebra, and set-theory notation: We suppose r factors/latent traits $F_1, \ldots,$ F_r. We write

$$\mathcal{L}_{\{s_k\}} = \sum_{\{s_k\}}[X_j \ln P(z_j) + (1 - X_j) \ln Q(z_j)]. \qquad (a14.1)$$

By a standard application of calculus,

$$d\mathcal{L}_{\{s_k\}}/df_t = \sum_{\{s_k\}} X_j(\lambda_{jt}/\psi_j)[P'(z_j)/P(z_j)] \qquad (a14.2)$$
$$- (1 - X_j)(\lambda_{jt}/\psi_j)[P'(z_j)/Q(z_j)]$$

which can be rearranged as

$$d\mathcal{L}_{\{s_k\}}/df_t = \sum_{\{s_k\}}(\lambda_{jt}/\psi_j)P'(z_j)/[P(z_j)Q(z_j)][X_j - P(z_j)]. \qquad (a14.3)$$

(Note that $\mathcal{E}\{d\mathcal{L}_{\{s_k\}}/df_t\} = 0$ for all t.)

By the algebra of expectations, for two subsets, $\{s_k\},\{s_l\}$, not necessarily disjoint,

$$\text{Cov}\{d\mathcal{L}_{\{sk\}}/df_t, \ d\mathcal{L}_{\{sl\}}/df_{t'}\}$$
$$= \sum_{j\varepsilon\{s_k\}}\sum_{j'\varepsilon\{s_l\}}[\lambda_{jt}\lambda_{j't'}/(\psi_j\psi_{j'})]\,\mathcal{E}\{(X_j - P_j)(X_{j'} - P_{j'}\}.$$
$$\cdot[P'(z_j)P'(z_{j'})]/[P(z_j)Q(z_j)P(z_{j'})Q(z_{j'})],$$
$$= \sum_{j\varepsilon\{s_k\cap s_l\}}[\lambda_{jt}\lambda_{jt'}/(\psi_j^2)][P'(z_j)^2/(P(z_j)Q(z_j))], \qquad (a14.4)$$

by local independence. We note that this covariance is zero for disjoint sets, and for $\{s_k\} = \{s_l\}$ it is zero if and only if

$$\sum_{\{s_k\}} \lambda_{jt}\lambda_{jt'} = 0. \tag{a14.5}$$

If all loadings are nonnegative, the last condition requires that $\{s_k\}$ has independent cluster structure.

We write

$$I_{tt'} = \text{Cov}\{d\mathcal{L}_{\{s_k\}}/df_{t'},\ d\mathcal{L}_{\{s_k\}}/df_t, \tag{a14.6}$$

and form the $r \times r$ matrix

$$\mathbf{J} = [I_{tt'}]. \tag{a14.7}$$

Then defining the $r \times 1$ vector of estimates of the r latent traits,

$$\tilde{\mathbf{F}}_{\{s_k\}} = \mathbf{f} + \boldsymbol{\varepsilon}_{\{s_k\}}, \tag{a14.8}$$

yields

$$\text{Cov}\{\boldsymbol{\varepsilon}_{\{s_k\}}\} = \mathbf{J}^{-1}, \tag{a14.9}$$

by general asymptotic theory of maximum likelihood estimators. $\$\$\$$

MEASURING VALIDITY OF BINARY ITEMS

In Chapter 10 we saw how to obtain validity coefficients, as correlations between cluster sums—sums of item scores in independent clusters—and common factors. In an independent clusters solution, a convergent validity coefficient is the correlation between a cluster sum and the factor defined by that cluster; discriminant validity coefficients are the correlations between a cluster sum and the factors defined by the other clusters. The formulas used for these coefficients rested on a linear factor model for the items. All we need to do in this section is to add a slight further development of the mathematics to adapt this treatment to binary items fitting a multidimensional item response model.

In the linear model with independent clusters, the correlation between any cluster sum and its own factor is given by the square root of coefficient omega, and the correlation between the cluster sum and another factor is the square root of omega multiplied by the correlation of its own factor with the other factor. We interpret the common factors as attributes defined by an indefinitely large number of items in the behavior domain from which our items are drawn. Then these coefficients are convergent/discriminant validity coefficients because they measure the extent to which each cluster sum relates to the attribute its items measure in common, and the extent to which it relates to the other attributes measured by the item set.

If we use the normal-ogive link function without a pseudo-guessing parameter, to fit a multidimensional item response model, we can use the classical theory of biserial correlations, as discussed in Chapter 11, to extend the treatment in Chapter 10 to binary items. The biserial correlation between a standardized variable Z and a binary variable X is the correlation between Z and the underlying "response tendency" X^*, such that $X = 1$ if X^* exceeds a threshold value τ), and $X = 0$ if it does not. We have used this way of thinking to derive the normal-ogive model as an item factor model. This correlation is given by

$$\rho_{(b)}\{X,Z\} = \text{Cor}\{X^*,Z\} = \text{Cov}\{X,Z\}/n(\tau),\qquad(14.16)$$

where, as before, $n(\tau)$ is the ordinate of the normal curve at τ.

We use the mathematics example as a paradigm case, from which it is easy to generalize. In this example, we have been considering three cluster sums, $\{s_1\} = \{1\ 2\ 3\ 4\ 5\}$, $\{s_2\} = \{6\ 7\ 8\ 9\ 10\}$, $\{s_3\} = \{11\ 12\ 13\ 14\ 15\}$, of which the first two are homogeneous. In the underlying factor model,

$$X_j^* = \mu_j + \lambda_{j1}F_1 + \lambda_{j2} + F_2 + E_j,$$

so the covariances between X_j^* and F_1, F_2 are—by the algebra of expectations—

$$\text{Cov}\{X_j^*,F_1\} = \lambda_{j1} + \lambda_{j2}\phi_{12},\qquad(14.17a)$$

$$\text{Cov}\{X_j^*,F_2\} = \lambda_{j1}\phi_{12} + \lambda_{j2}.\qquad(14.17b)$$

These reduce to

$$\text{Cov}\{X_j^*,F_1\} = \lambda_{j1},\qquad \text{Cov}\{X_j^*,F_2\} = \lambda_{j2}\qquad(14.18)$$

in the homogeneous sets $\{s_1\},\{s_2\}$. Then

$$\text{Cov}\{X_j,F_1\} = (\lambda_{j1} + \lambda_{j2}\phi_{12})\,n(\tau_j),\qquad(14.19a)$$

$$\text{Cov}\{X_j, F_2\} = (\lambda_{j1}\phi_{12} + \lambda_{j2})\, n(\tau_j), \tag{14.19b}$$

and the desired validity coefficients are of the form

$$\text{Cor}\{Y_{\{s_k\}}, F_p\} = [\sum_{\{s_k\}} n(\tau_j)\text{Cov}\{X_j, F_p\}]/\sqrt{\text{Var}\{Y_{\{s_k\}}\}}\,. \tag{14.20}$$

In the mathematics example, the variances are: $\text{Var}\{Y_{\{s_1\}}\} = 2.106$, $\text{Var}\{Y_{\{s_2\}}\}$ = 1.549, and $\text{Var}\{Y_{\{s_3\}}\} = 1.940$. It is easy to calculate the validity coefficients given in Table 14.7 from these, with the loadings in Table 14.4, and the factor correlation $\phi_{12} = .739$, using a table of the normal curve.

As we would hope, the cluster sums $Y_{\{s_1\}}$ and $Y_{\{s_2\}}$ from the homogeneous sets yield the necessary condition for convergent and discriminant validity, each having a higher correlation with its own construct than with the other. It is an intriguing discovery that the sum of the "mixed" items, $Y_{\{s_3\}}$, has a higher correlation with the algebra achievement factor than the algebra cluster sum, and is not far short of the geometry cluster sum in its correlation with the geometry achievement factor. This might seem a motive for keeping these items—except perhaps item 15—but the test developer needs to take account of the complex behavior of measurement error that results from the complexity of the items.

REVIEW GUIDE

A sufficient sense of the potential of multidimensional item response theory as a natural extension to binary data of confirmatory and exploratory common factor models, will come from careful study of the example. The mathematics of the model will interest some but not all readers of this text.

I have stressed the importance of independent clusters here as in factor analysis, for the interpretability of the multidimensional model. In most applications subtests will be formed and the unidimensional theory of Chapter 13 applied for the test characteristic functions, information func-

TABLE 14.7
ACT Subtest–Trait Correlations

	Independent Clusters		Hierarchical		
	I	II	G	I'	II'
s_1	.751	.555	.645	.283	
s_2	.486	.658	.565		.246
s_3	.673	.728	.692	.111	.191

tions, error variances, and so on, avoiding the technicalities needed for complex items. In the final section it would be minimally sufficient for the student to accept (14.20) as the expression for subtest convergent and discriminant validities, as illustrated in Table 14.6.

END NOTES

The material in this chapter is based on McDonald (1982b). A very similar account is in McDonald (1997a). Other approaches to multidimensional item response theory are to be found in the literature. A treatment based on direction vectors has been given by Reckase (1985). See Reckase (1997) for a relatively nontechnical account. It is my belief, as should be clear, that independent clusters provide the best basis for applications, but further work could change the picture.

1. These data are used by kind permission of the American College Testing program.
2. The NOHARM program, included in the set on diskette available from Lawrence Erlbaum Associates, was designed to fit multidimensional item response models with confirmatory or exploratory independent cluster structures.
3. See Reckase (1997).

Comparing Populations

Throughout the earlier chapters the phrase *populations of interest* has been used to point to the fact that many of the indices and parameters dealt with are accidental parameters of the population sampled. Every respondent can be classified as belonging to an indefinite number of populations. There is that most obvious identification of individuals by gender. There are less obvious but commonly employed classifications (by self or imposed by others) in terms of "ethnic group"—those complex results of some thousands of years of cultural and political history marked by expansion, invasion, infiltration, conflict, and conquest across the surface of our planet that may give different citizens of a modern nation-state a chosen or imposed identity distinct from their citizenship. There are attempted classifications by "race," from the infamous imposed classifications that have marked segregationist societies to identities chosen by members of a disempowered group for whom racial pride may function positively in a movement toward empowerment. There are possible classifications on such cultural bases as religion, and classifications by socioeconomic status or educational level. Ever finer classifications can be obtained if we select groups by their score on one test to study their responses to others, until the individual is the intersection of so many properties that the individual is a population containing just one member.

Test theory, developed primarily in the context of cognitive tests, has been centrally motivated by educational applications. Because a major use of tests of abilities/aptitudes has been the selection of individuals for admission to college and university programs, and, in some countries, to selective high schools, the most obvious populations of interest are those whose existence has been given recognition in laws concerning discrimination. Although tests alone cannot be used to redress the wrongs created by discrimination and by the enormous inequalities of educational and economic opportunity that characterize most modern states, there is a plain duty on the part of test developers to ensure that the tests themselves are not sources of discrimination and inequity. Accordingly, there has been a considerable amount of effort in work on test theory to study the conditions under which a test score on individuals from distinct populations (a) measures the same attribute and (b) gives an unbiased estimate of the relative standing of the individuals on that attribute. Research applications of noncognitive tests—measures of values and attitudes, for example—also require a technology to check whether the test measures the same attribute in populations of interest to the investigation, and, if so, whether it gives an unbiased estimate of it. Thus, it is possible for men and women to perceive the same set of attitude items sufficiently differently to raise the question whether "the same" attribute is being measured in both genders. The main illustration in this chapter is a study of just this possibility.

In classical test theory, as we have seen, indexes such as reliability coefficients, and item parameters such as item difficulty measured by proportion passing, or item–test correlations, are incidental properties of the population sampled. It is considered to be an axiom of item response theory that, in contrast, the item parameters are invariant across populations of interest, provided that an appropriate common scale of the latent traits is adopted. This *axiom of invariance* is a mathematical tautology. It has sometimes been misunderstood to imply that if, say, a unidimensional item response model fits two populations of interest, the parameters must be the same in both populations (when the latent trait is measured on a common scale). What the axiom of invariance actually means is that if the item parameters from the two groups cannot be rescaled so as to coincide, we can always introduce further latent traits so that they do. This is trivially true, because we can always use population membership as a "latent trait"[1] and make a model whose parameters are tautologically invariant. In applications, it is not mathematically guaranteed—for a model with a fixed number of latent traits—that the item parameters can agree across populations. If they do not, we cannot strictly claim that the items measure the same attribute in these populations; what they have in common may be at least slightly different.

In a comparison of two populations, it has become an accepted convention to identify one population as the *reference group*, and the other as a *focal group*. "Reference group" is a synonym for what we have called the calibration group. As before, it determines the metric of the latent traits. In the sociopolitical context of the United States, for gender studies it is customary to choose males as the reference group; for education, it is common to find comparisons of European Americans with African Americans, Hispanic Americans, Asian Americans, and/or Native Americans, with the European Americans as the reference group. It is perhaps futile to discuss here the possible biases that may determine such a choice, because a reference group generally must be chosen to determine the metric on which the item parameters are calibrated. It is enough to recognize that the choice is arbitrary, and is inconsequential from a measurement perspective.

In most treatments of this type of problem, initially each latent trait is scaled to be standardized—separately—in both reference and focal groups. If in fact the items will fit the same model with the same item parameters when the scale of the focal group is changed to standard score units taken from the reference group, then there are simple linear relationships between the sets of item parameters from which the change of scale can be determined. Corresponding approximate relationships will be revealed in estimates of these parameters from samples. If the two sets of item parameters cannot be made to agree by a change of scale, this fact will be revealed in departures of the item parameters from the expected linear relationships. *Coefficients of congruence* (agreement) between the sets of item parameters can be computed. As we show later, if the departures from a linear correspondence are sufficiently great and, accordingly, the coefficients of congruence are not large enough, we should not suppose that the items measure the same attribute in both groups.

In applications it may happen that a number of the items have parameters that are linearly related, and can be supposed to measure the same latent trait or traits, whereas some do not. It has become customary to say (somewhat redundantly) that if a binary item gives a different probability of its keyed response for subjects of the same ability in the reference and focal groups, the item shows *differential item functioning* (DIF). ("DIF" is more pronounceable than "DF"). For a more general definition of DIF, we say that a (quantitative or binary) item shows DIF if it gives a different mean response for examinees in different groups with the same value of the attribute (ability, attitude, personality trait, etc.). The concept of differential item functioning requires enough items to determine "the" attribute—that is, enough items that do not exhibit DIF—but this is probably not a very restrictive condition in applications. A necessary and sufficient condition for an item not to show DIF is that its item response function should be the same in the relevant populations. Recent research has provided a number of nonparametric devices intended to detect and evaluate DIF, using the score on a subset of the items as a substitute for the attribute.[2] Partly because these methods are rather technical, and have not yet been carefully evaluated, and partly because they do not easily fit our framework, we consider a direct method that applies classical factor-analytic concepts to the problem. This is the natural extension of the treatment of factor and item response models in previous chapters. The direct method also has a number of advantages that the nonparametric devices lack.

The next sections, accordingly, describe methods based on the classical treatment of factorial congruence that have the following properties:

1. They are applicable, in essentially the same way, to both quantitative and binary responses.

2. They can be applied equally to unidimensional and multidimensional data.

3. They provide a direct assessment of the amount of DIF in one or more items, and, more generally, of the agreement (congruence) of the parameters of all the items.

4. The analysis distinguishes three distinct types of DIF, namely, (a) differential item difficulty (known in the DIF literature as *uniform DIF*), (b) differential item discriminating power (referred to as *nonuniform DIF*), and (c) the effect of differential item dimensionality on an approximating model of lower dimensionality. (At the time of writing, researchers using item response models commonly fit unidimensional models to multidimensional data, although there is no good reason for this practice.)

5. Given the nature of the DIF, as in the previous point, we may hope to examine the item for the substantive cause of differential functioning.

6. The analysis yields an understandable assessment of the effect of one or more differentially functioning items in the set on the relative test score obtained when we exclude/include those items. That is, we can estimate the extent to which the test score may give a statistically biased estimate of the attribute, and therefore a judgment that is biased in a number of sociopolitical or legal senses.

7. The method provides an estimate of the mean and variance of the trait for the focal group in the metric of the reference group.

Taken together, these seven properties allow the test developer to make rational, substantively based decisions as to how to deal with the differentially functioning items, and how to develop further items.[3]

It is convenient to develop the procedure by example, carrying through a fairly detailed analysis of a paradigm case. In the next section we consider a unidimensional and a multidimensional linear model for quantitative responses, and the following section covers counterpart nonlinear unidimensional and multidimensional models for binary responses. A single data set is used to illustrate these developments. It is easily seen how these procedures may be applied more generally. For definiteness, and in line with the example to be used, we suppose that the populations of interest are identified by gender, with males as the reference group and females as the focal group, and accordingly use m and f as identifying subscripts.

QUANTITATIVE RESPONSES

Suppose we have m items yielding quantitative item scores $X_1, \ldots, X_m$ from a random respondent. A likely source is (integer) Likert scores for ordered-category responses. We assume we may fit a linear common factor model to sampled values by normal theory, to a sufficiently good approximation. To identify the populations we attach a superscript m or f, writing $X_j^{(m)}$ and $X_j^{(f)}$ for the jth item score from the male and female populations, respectively. Suppose for the present that the items form a unidimensional/homogeneous set, fitting the simple Spearman single-factor model in each population. We write the model as

$$X_j^{(m)} = \mu^{(m)} + \lambda_j^{(m)}F_m + E_j^{(m)}, \tag{15.1a}$$

and

$$X_j^{(f)} = \mu^{(f)} + \lambda_j^{(f)}F_f + E_j^{(f)}. \tag{15.1b}$$

Here $\mu^{(m)}$ and $\mu^{(f)}$ are the item means in each group—counterparts of item "difficulty"—and $\lambda_j^{(m)}$ and $\lambda_j^{(f)}$ are item factor loadings—counterparts of item "discrimination," whereas F_m and F_f are the common factor/latent trait in each population, and $E_j^{(m)}$ and $E_j^{(f)}$ is the unique part of each item response, corresponding to the idiosyncratic property of the item. As before, we assume that the unique parts of the item responses are mutually uncorrelated.

The linear item response functions are the regression functions, given by

$$\mathcal{E}\{X_j^{(m)}|F_m = f_m\} = \mu^{(m)} + \lambda_j^{(m)}f_m, \tag{15.2a}$$

and

$$\mathcal{E}\{X_j^{(f)}|F_f = f_f\} = \mu^{(f)} + \lambda_j^{(f)}f_f. \tag{15.2b}$$

These functions are separately identified if we fix the scale by fixing the mean and variance of F_m and of F_f in their respective populations. Ordinarily we standardize both, setting means to zero and variances to unity.

Consider the items of the Illinois Rape Myth Acceptance Scale, listed in Table 15.1.[4] The responses are on a 7-point Likert scale, from *strongly*

TABLE 15.1
Illinois Rape Myth Acceptance Scale (Items Reordered)

1. When women talk and act sexy, they are inviting rape.
2. When a woman is raped, she usually did something careless to put herself in that situation.
3. Any woman who teases a man sexually and doesn't finish what she started realistically deserves anything she gets.
4. Many rapes happen because women lead men on.
6. In some rape cases, the woman actually wanted it to happen.
7. Even though the woman may call it rape, she probably enjoyed it.
10. When a woman allows petting to get to a certain point, she is implicitly agreeing to have sex.
11. If a woman is raped, often it's because she didn't say "no" clearly enough.
12. Women tend to exaggerate how rape affects them.
16. In any rape case one would have to question whether the victim is promiscuous or has a bad reputation.
18. Many so-called rape victims are actually women who had sex and "changed their minds" afterward.

5. Men don't usually intend to force sex on a woman, but sometimes they get too sexually carried away.
13. When men rape, it is because of their strong desire for sex.
14. It is just part of human nature for men to take sex from women who let their guard down.

8. If a woman doesn't physically fight back, you can't really say that it was a rape.
9. A rape probably didn't happen if the woman has no bruises or marks.
19. If a husband pays all the bills, he has a right to sex with his wife whenever he wants.

15. A rapist is more likely to be Black or Hispanic than White.
17. Rape mainly occurs on the "bad" side of town.

disagree = 1 to *strongly agree* = 7. The items have the character of beliefs that can be regarded as myths, in the sense that they may be widely held, but not on rational/evidential grounds, and they represent the cognitive/perceptual component of an attitude. It is possible[5] that acceptance of these statements serves distinct psychological functions for men and women—for the former, rationalizing/legitimating offensive behavior, and for the latter, denying vulnerability. Apart from conventional considerations, there is here an additional substantive reason for making the male population the reference group, namely, that a primary concern of research on rape myths is their specific predictive function for the behavior of males. The 19 items in the scale were selected to represent 19 subscales, each of five items, which had been very carefully constructed to reflect recognizably distinct facets of this false-belief/attitude complex. An examination of the item contents suggests a multidimensional structure, but for the first analysis we treat the data as unidimensional.

Data are available from $N = 368$ men and $N = 368$ women. Analyses in this and the next section employ the COSAN program. Table 15.2 gives means and variances of the item scores, and maximum likelihood (ML) factor loadings from the item covariance matrices. The Spearman model gives chi-squares (152 df) respectively of 344.05 for the male and 350.17 for the female samples, with RMSEAs both .059.

If the item parameters differ between groups only because of the choice of metric, then f_m and f_f in (15.2) are related by the scale transformation

$$f_f = kf_m + c, \tag{15.3a}$$

with inverse transformation

$$f_m = (1/k)f_f - (c/k). \tag{15.3b}$$

It then follows that

$$k\lambda_j^{(f)} = \lambda_j^{(m)}, \tag{15.4a}$$

and

$$\mu_j^{(f)} + c\lambda_j^{(f)} = \mu_j^{(m)}, \qquad j = 1, \ldots, p. \tag{15.4b}$$

TABLE 15.2
Unidimensional Quantitative Responses

Item	$\mu^{(m)}$	σ_m^2	$\mu^{(f)}$	σ_f^2	λ_m	λ_f	μ_f^*	λ_f^*	$\mu_m - \mu_f^*$	$\lambda_m - \lambda_f^*$
1	2.88	3.01	1.87	1.87	1.13	0.88	2.96	1.10	−.08	.13
2	3.12	2.77	2.32	2.27	0.85	0.77	3.28	0.98	−.16	−.13
3	2.13	1.91	1.43	0.86	0.79	0.55	2.11	0.69	.02	.10
4	3.79	2.92	2.60	2.69	1.12	1.01	3.86	1.28	−.07	−.16
6	3.01	2.51	2.11	2.91	0.99	0.79	3.10	1.00	−.09	−.01
7	1.69	2.74	1.22	2.08	0.62	0.30	1.59	0.37	.10	.24
10	2.97	1.23	1.86	0.42	1.14	0.86	2.93	1.08	.04	.05
11	2.52	2.08	1.77	1.02	0.91	0.68	2.62	0.86	−.10	.05
12	2.25	1.15	1.53	0.33	0.88	0.58	2.26	0.74	−.01	.15
16	3.63	2.99	2.34	1.89	0.95	0.86	3.42	1.09	.21	−.14
18	3.40	2.32	2.50	1.58	1.03	0.89	3.61	1.12	−.21	−.09
5	4.24	2.28	3.47	1.37	0.67	0.74	4.39	0.93	−.15	−.26
13	3.91	3.52	2.79	3.21	0.85	0.60	3.54	0.76	.37	.09
14	2.39	2.35	1.89	1.81	0.76	0.44	2.44	0.55	−.05	.21
8	2.13	2.32	1.46	1.89	0.73	0.50	2.08	0.63	.05	.11
9	1.72	3.40	1.25	2.54	0.47	0.22	1.52	0.28	.20	.19
19	1.92	1.92	1.13	1.23	0.73	0.15	1.32	0.19	.60	.54
15	2.36	2.31	1.89	2.22	0.51	0.15	2.08	0.19	.28	.31
17	2.24	1.92	1.67	0.23	0.35	0.32	2.06	0.40	.18	−.05

By (15.4a), if the item parameters differ only because they are referred to the origin and unit determined by their own group, then in a graph of the loadings for the female group against the loadings for the male group, the points should lie on a straight line through the origin whose slope is k. Similarly, by (15.4b), in a graph of the differences in the means, $\mu_j^{(m)} - \mu_j^{(f)}$, against the loadings in the female group, the points should lie on a straight line through the origin whose slope is c. In graphs from sample data, there will be departures from the straight line due to sampling errors, and possibly departures due to differential functioning of some of the items. In the extreme, we might find a scatter of points about the lines suggesting actual overall failure of congruence—failure of agreement of at least a reasonable number of the item parameters. Without any more sophisticated technology, but with experience, we could identify differentially functioning items fairly successfully as points lying too far from a best-fitting straight line. As an exercise, the student is advised to plot these graphs, and make tentative judgments as to which items depart most from the expected straight line.

For a more careful procedure than mere inspection, we can carry out the following calculations: An estimate of the multiplier k from sample factor loadings given by

$$k = [\Sigma \ \lambda_j^{(m)}\lambda_j^{(f)}]/[\Sigma \ \lambda_j^{(f)2}] \tag{15.5}$$

minimizes the quantity

$$q_\lambda = \Sigma \ (\lambda_j^{(m)} - k\lambda_j^{(f)})^2 \tag{15.6}$$

and an estimate of the additive constant c given by

$$c = [\Sigma \ (\mu_j^{(m)} - \mu_j^{(f)})\lambda_j^{(f)}]/(\Sigma \ \lambda_j^{(f)2}) \tag{15.7}$$

minimizes the quantity

$$q_\mu = \Sigma \ (\mu_j^{(m)} - \mu_j^{(f)} - c\lambda_j^{(f)})^2. \tag{15.8}$$

This chooses a rescaling that makes the parameters as close as possible, when measured by a sum of squares of differences. The summation can be taken over all the items or over a subset believed to be free from DIF. They are easily if tediously computed by hand, or simple computer programs can be applied. In the example, the estimate of k is 1.261, and that of c is 1.246.

We note that relative to the zero mean and unit variance assigned to the male group as reference population, the mean and variance of the trait in the female group are, respectively, $-c/k$ and $1/k^2$. In our example, the mean of the latent trait in the female group is $-1.246/1.261 = -.988$, and its variance is $1/k^2 = .629$. That is, the female group is both well below the male group on the average, and less diverse in their rape myth acceptance, in (male) standard score units. This is to be expected on substantive grounds.

The rescaled parameters from the female population, given by

$$\lambda_j^{(f)*} = k\lambda_j^{(f)} \tag{15.9a}$$

and

$$\mu_j^{(f)*} = \mu_j^{(f)} + c\lambda_j^{(f)}, \tag{15.9b}$$

may be compared to $\lambda_j^{(m)}$ and $\mu_j^{(m)}$, respectively. In our example, these and the resulting differences are given in the last four columns of Table 15.2. Simple inspection of the listed differences suggests that relative to the remainder of the items, item 19 has large differences in both loading and item mean, and the same is true, although less clearly, for item 15. Item 13 shows a notable difference in mean but not in loadings. Note also the positions of these items on the graphs.

The analysis gives standard errors for the item parameters, from which we can obtain approximate confidence bounds on the differences between them. We might regard confidence bounds that do not include zero as indicating significant DIF. But note that for a sufficiently small sample size, no item will show significant DIF, whereas for a sufficiently large sample size all items will; that is, no subset of items could be thought of as related by a scale change. The important question is the amount of the difference, not its technical "significance." The *SE*s of the loadings are all very close to .05 in both groups, and the *SE*s of the mean parameters are given by the item *SD*s divided by root sample size. These *SD*s, for the male group, range from 1.07 to 1.84, giving a mean *SE* on the order of .07. It should be an acceptable heuristic device to take a common set of approximate confidence bounds of $\pm.14$ ($\approx 2 \times .05 \times 2^{1/2}$) for the difference in loadings between the groups after rescaling, and $\pm.2$ ($\approx 2 \times .07 \times 2^{1/2}$), for the difference in means. From Table 15.2 we see that four items appear to have nonnegligible and "significant" differential slope parameters—in order, 19, with difference $.735 - .194 = .561$; 15, with difference .314; 7, with difference .244; and 5, with difference $-.226$. Three appear to have nonnegligible and "significant" differential mean parameters—in order, 19, with difference .60; 13, with difference .37; and 15, with difference .28—also possibly 16 and 18. (Tabulated values have been rounded.)

Burt's *coefficient of factorial congruence*

$$g_\lambda = (\Sigma\ \lambda_j^{(m)}\lambda_j^{(f)})/[(\Sigma\ \lambda_j^{(m)2}(\Sigma\ \lambda_j^{(f)2})]^{1/2} \qquad (15.10a)$$

(a "correlation coefficient not corrected for means") here measures the closeness of the loadings to agreement, without rescaling, and equals unity if and only if $q_\lambda = 0$ exactly. It is natural to define a corresponding coefficient of congruence for the difference in mean parameters $\mu_j^{(m)} - \mu_j^{(f)}$ by

$$g_\mu = [\Sigma\ (\mu_j^{(m)} - \mu_j^{(f)})\lambda_j^{(f)}]/[\{\Sigma\ (\mu_j^{(m)} - \mu_j^{(f)})^2\}\{\Sigma\ \lambda_j^{(f)2}]^{1/2}. \qquad (15.10b)$$

This measures the closeness of the item means to agreement, without rescaling, and equals unity if and only if $q_\mu = 0$. Again the summation can be over all the items or over a subset thought to be free of DIF. In our example, the congruence coefficients are $g_\lambda = .973$, $g_\mu = .968$, for all the items, and $g_\lambda = .991$, $g_\mu = .990$, with the suspect items, 19, 15, 13, 7, and 5, omitted.

If a number of the items are judged to have nonnegligible DIF, the effect of excluding/including these items can be assessed by comparing the relative test score characteristic curves for the retained items with that for the full set. Let $\{X_1, \ldots, X_r\}$ be any subset of the item scores. The relative test-score characteristic functions for the two groups are given in the metric of the male group, by

$$\mathcal{E}\{M_r \mid F_m = f_m\} = \mu_{rm} + \lambda_{rm}f_m \qquad (15.11a)$$

and

$$\mathcal{E}\{M_r \mid F_f = f_f\} = \mu_{rf}^* + \lambda_{rf}^*f_f \qquad (15.11b)$$

where M_r is the mean score on the selected items, μ_{rm} and λ_{rm} are means of the parameters for the male group over the r selected items, and μ_{rf}^*, λ_{rf}^* are means of the rescaled parameters for the female group. Noncoincidence of these functions is a precise specification of what we call (in the linear model) *differential test score functioning* (DTF). In our example we examine the effect of omitting versus retaining items 5, 7, 13, 15, and 19 on the relative test-score information functions. The expected values of the means of the item scores, as a function of the latent trait, for the full set, are

$$\mathcal{E}\{M_m \mid f\} = 2.753 + .815f$$

for the male group, and

$$\mathcal{E}\{M_m \mid f\} = 2.693 + .749f,$$

tor the temale group, whereas for the reduced set they are

$$\mathcal{E}\{M_r \mid f\} = 2.727 + .864f$$

for the male group, and

$$\mathcal{E}\{M_r \mid f\} = 2.732 + .840f$$

for the female group. In the range -3 to 3, the differences appear negligible. In sociopolitically significant applications it might nevertheless not be a sufficient reason to retain differentially functioning items that they have a negligible effect on the relationship between the test score and the attribute being measured. There is a cogent argument that justice should not only be done but should be clearly seen to be done.

We have seen that there is no mathematical reason why a unidimensional item response model—or model of fixed dimensionality—must have invariant item parameters. It is perfectly possible to find items with either loadings or means that cannot be brought into coincidence by rescaling the focal group to the units of the reference group. It might be conjectured, loosely speaking, that if an item shows DIF it must be because the item measures something in addition to the intended attribute in one of the populations but not the other.

Such conjectures require care in interpreting them. Using the methods of Chapters 9 and 14, it should be possible to determine whether in fact two populations require distinct models with different numbers of latent traits. If the mistake is made of fitting a unidimensional model to data that are in fact multidimensional, the parameters in the appropriate multidimensional models may be invariant with appropriate scaling, whereas the unidimensional approximation shows DIF. Thus DIF can consist of actual differences in loadings or item means in a unidimensional model or of apparent differences that result from the use of a unidimensional approximation to multidimensional data.

If the conjecture is that DIF is due to additional "dimensions" measured by the aberrant items, in general such "dimensions" cannot be interpreted strictly as latent traits. In the case of a single item, if we postulate that it measures "something in addition" to the recognized latent trait in one of the groups, the "something in addition" has the character of an item-specific component in that group. This is included in the item's unique component, and is not an additional dimension as ordinarily understood; that is, it is not a common factor/latent trait.

In the case of quantitative responses, a population-specific component produces a difference between populations in the unique variance of the item. But it will not induce, and hence cannot explain, a change in the slope parameter—the common factor loading. (In a standardized factor model, the unique variance is the unit complement of the communality and a change in unique variance changes the loadings, but not, as here, when the response is unstandardized.) If the conjecture is that there is a difference between populations in the mean of the unique component of the item, this is merely a tautological account of the irreducible difference—not removed by rescaling—in the mean parameter. The same is true for more than one item, if each is postulated to measure "something in addition" that is specific to itself. (There has been considerable confusion on this point in the literature on differential item functioning, on the part of researchers who are possibly not familiar with the formal properties of the common factor model.)

On the other hand, one way—although not the only one—in which differences in slopes could arise is indeed by fitting an approximating unidimensional model to data in which there is either a difference in dimensionality—in the number of latent traits—between groups, or distinct correlations between the traits. (And, to repeat, it still seems to be a common, although unfortunate practice, to approximate multidimensional data with a unidimensional model in applications of nonlinear item response models.) If, for example, items 19, 15, 13, 7, and 5 happen to define a separate factor in the female group, but not in the male group, or if there is such a factor in both groups, with a lower correlation for females between it and the factor defined by the complementary subset, this might account for the reduction in their loadings in the unidimensional approximation. It could also account for differences in the item means if these were related appropriately to the loadings. Such an analysis would give a nonvacuous account of DIF in terms of additional dimensions, that is, additional latent traits.

We note, however, that it would be inappropriate and usually ineffective to ignore substantive considerations, choosing to fit a two-dimensional structure with a second latent trait defined by the differentially functioning items. Thus, in the present example, items 19, 15, 13, 7, and 5 do not have mean differences proportional to their loadings. And they should, if they correspond to a second factor. Also, an examination of their item stems does not suggest that they share a distinct conceptual basis. It turns out that fitting this model (a) does not improve fit and (b) does not reduce the differences between parameters of these items.

When irreducible differences are found between item parameters, the possibility remains that (some) differences are due to fitting the unidimensional approximation to data whose substantive character requires a multidimensional structure, and that the differences may vanish or at least change their pattern when an appropriate model is used. Besides, on general grounds we need methods for comparing populations and checking for DIF that apply to a multidimensional structure.

It is a very straightforward mathematical task to write down analogues of equations (15.1) through (15.11) for the case of two groups having r common factors, replacing (15.3) by a more general transformation. (It is also possible in principle to apply and slightly extend classical treatments of factorial congruence transformations to cases with unequal numbers of latent traits). However, such generality does not seem well motivated in the present applications. Rather, it is reasonable to restrict the transformation of metric to separate scale transformations, one for each trait. Consequently, we do not require a more general formulation, but simply apply (15.1) through (15.11) to each latent trait in turn. Note that such transformations will not alter the correlations between the traits.

A careful study of the nineteen item stems in Table 15.1 suggests the application of a more general model for the function of these myths, based on well-known mechanisms of blame, rationalization, and denial, to yield a four-factor model, namely:

I.   Blame the victim: items 1, 2, 3, 4, 6, 7, 10, 11, 12, 16, 18.

II. Excuse the offender: items 5, 13, 14.

III. Deny it is an offense: items 8, 9, 19.

IV. Deny it happens "here" (the respondent's usual location): items 15, 17.

(Note that the items in Table 15.1 have been reordered in the tables to group as shown.) The results from fitting this model to the two groups are given in Table 15.3. Because the model contains no factorially complex items, it is convenient to write the parameters in single columns, rather than setting them out in the form of conventional 19 × 4 factor patterns. The four-factor model gives chi-squares (146 df) respectively of 241.17 and 296.32 for male and female groups, clearly fitting better than the unidimensional results. The improvement is greater in the male group. Applying (15.5) and (15.7) separately for each factor gives the scaling coefficients, coefficients of congruence, and relative means and variances of the trait in the female group shown in Table 15.4. It is of interest to note that the female group gives its smallest mean difference for factor IV, its smallest relative variance for factor III, and its largest mean difference and relative variance for factor II. These differences make substantive sense. Note also that all factor correlations are lower for the female group than the male group, suggesting clearer distinctions between these dimensions of rape myth acceptance, particularly between "blame the

TABLE 15.3
Multidimensional Quantitative Responses

	μ_m	μ_f^*	λ_m	λ_f	λ_f^*	$\mu_m - \mu_f^*$	$\lambda_m - \lambda_f^*$
1	2.88	2.92	1.14	.88	1.09	−.04	.05
2	3.12	3.24	.86	.77	.96	−.12	−.10
3	2.13	2.08	.79	.54	.68	.05	.11
4	3.79	3.82	1.14	1.02	1.27	−.03	−.13
6	3.01	3.06	1.00	.80	1.00	−.05	.00
7	1.69	1.57	.61	.30	.38	.12	.31
10	2.97	2.88	1.13	.86	1.06	.11	.07
11	2.52	2.58	.92	.68	.85	−.06	.07
12	2.25	2.22	.88	.58	.72	.03	.16
16	3.63	3.37	.96	.86	1.07	.26	−.11
18	3.40	3.57	1.05	.90	1.11	−.17	−.06
5	4.24	4.56	.73	.93	.95	−.32	−.22
13	3.91	3.61	.88	.77	.79	.30	.09
14	2.39	2.44	.80	.52	.53	−.05	.27
8	2.13	2.32	.94	.61	1.13	−.19	−.17
9	1.72	1.66	.63	.29	.54	.06	.09
19	1.92	1.38	.83	.18	.33	.54	.50
15	2.36	2.44	1.04	.46	.56	−.08	.48
17	2.24	2.73	.83	.89	1.08	−.49	−.25

Factor Correlations

$$\begin{bmatrix} 1. & .801 & .773 & .329 \\ .962 & 1. & .494 & .236 \\ .756 & .637 & 1. & .432 \\ .419 & .283 & .540 & 1. \end{bmatrix}$$

Note. In matrix, male results below the diagonal, female results above it.

TABLE 15.4
Scaling Constants and Female Means/Variances

	I	II	III	IV
k	1.240	1.026	1.849	1.211
c	1.188	1.064	1.399	0.718
$1/k^2$	0.650	0.950	0.293	0.682
$-c/k$	−0.958	−1.037	−0.757	−0.592

victim" and "excuse the offender," which for the male group appear to function as virtually the same concept.

However, we come next to the observation that on rescaling the loadings and mean parameters for each dimension separately, as in Table 15.3, we still appear to have nonnegligibly different loadings for items 5, 7, 15, and 19, and now also for item 14, and also different means for items 13 and

19, but no longer for item 15. The hypothesis that rape myth acceptance functions for men as a rationalization for offensive behavior and functions for women as a denial of vulnerability suggests the unidimensional analysis should indicate differences in slopes that are ultimately explained by distinct correlations of factor I, the most well-represented dimension, with factor IV, and possibly also with factors II and III. This does not seem to be the case. The functional type of explanation has an important general role in accounting for general levels and group differences in nonrational beliefs and attitudes, but a more fine-grained analysis would be needed generally to account for the behavior of individual items. Thus the notable behavior of item 15 fits a conception that by identifying rapists as "other" than themselves, men can avoid recognizing themselves as potential rapists, whereas women are less likely to identify rapists as "other" than the men they know. As another kind of "explanation," the even more notable behavior of item 19 might be "explained" by saying that for the male group this is integrated into a more general system of sexist beliefs that would not be shared by the female group. The other instances of DIF might similarly allow a specific account, rather than an account in terms of additional dimensions. Note in particular that the difference in mean for item 13 persists from the unidimensional analysis in Table 15.2. But in the context of the other two items, 5 and 14, defining factor II, "excuse the offender," it becomes possible to see that item 13 specifically refers to "rape" whereas the other variables defining this factor refer to forced sex/taking sex. Gender differences on this item are then at least intuitively understandable. These tentative suggestions are offered just to show the kind of inquiry that opens up when differentially functioning items are detected and studied.

BINARY ITEMS

The task in this section is to carry over the diagnostic devices in the previous section to binary items. The treatment here is limited to normal-ogive models without a pseudo-guessing parameter. Because a pseudo-guessing parameter is unaltered by scale transformations, the treatment applies equally to cases including such parameters. The normal-ogive is here preferred to a logistic model, for reasons that we demonstrate.

In Chapters 12 and 14 we found a direct connection between an item response model for binary data and the linear common factor model for quantitative item scores through item factor analysis. We assumed that a set of "underlying" quantitative response "tendencies" $X_1^*, \ldots, X_m^*$ follows the common factor model as in (15.1), and that the m binary variables X_1, $\ldots, X_m$ result from dichotomizations at threshold values $\tau_1, \ldots, \tau_m$ of the response tendencies. We then have, under normality assumptions,

$$P_j(f) = E\{X_j|F = f\} = P\{X_j = 1|F = f\}$$
$$= N\{(\lambda_j f - \tau_j)/(1 - \lambda^2)^{1/2}\} \tag{15.12}$$

where $N\{\cdot\}$ is the normal-ogive function. We recall also the two alternative parameterizations of this model in common use. These are

$$P_j(f) = N\{\alpha_j + \beta_j f\}, \tag{15.13}$$

and

$$P_j(f) = N\{\beta_j(f - \delta_j)\}, \tag{15.14}$$

in which δ_j is the item difficulty parameter as most commonly defined. In principle, any of these three parameterizations might be employed to rescale the focal group—here female—to the metric of the reference group—here male. In the example to be considered shortly, measures of congruence suggest that the parameterization (15.12) from item factor analysis gives a closer correspondence between parameters than the other two, and is to be preferred for this purpose. It is conjectured that this will generally be the case. The common factor loadings should generally be more stable than the slope coefficients in (15.13) and (15.14), as well as being interpretable by factor-analytic standards, and the threshold parameters are simply inverse normal-ogive transformations of the proportion of respondents giving the keyed response. In any case, the relative stability of the coefficients in the different parameterizations can be compared in each application.

For the purpose of illustration, the Likert responses to the Rape Myth Scale have been dichotomized, with values greater than 3 replaced by 1, and 0 otherwise. Again the NOHARM program is used. Table 15.5 gives the fitted values of the loadings and thresholds for the dichotomized data from the two groups.

Applying (15.5) and (15.7) to these yields $k = .9704$ and $c = 1.0563$, and hence the loadings and thresholds for the female group rescaled to the metric of the male group by using (15.9). The largest differences in loadings are: item 17, .220; item 14, .207; item 19, .200; item 15, .195; item 3, .179. The largest differences in thresholds are: item 19, .739; item 16, .220; item 15, .205; item 3, .190; item 18, .157. A heuristic estimate of the SE used in applications of NOHARM is the reciprocal of the root sample size. We might thus take common bounds $\pm.15$ for the differences, as the basis for a judgment of "significance" as well as for the precision of estimation of these. Again we may use the tabulated results to check the effect of

TABLE 15.5
Unidimensional Binary Responses

Item	τ_m	τ_f	λ_m	λ_f	τ_f^*	λ_f^*	$\lambda_m - \lambda_f^*$	$\tau_m - \tau_f^*$
1	−0.43	−1.19	.62	.69	−0.46	.67	−.04	.03
2	−0.32	−0.83	.56	.55	−0.25	.53	.03	−.07
3	−1.03	−1.66	.56	.76	−0.85	.74	−.18	−.19
4	0.16	−0.67	.80	.69	0.15	.67	−.13	.00
6	−0.18	−0.76	.64	.67	−0.06	.65	.00	.13
7	−1.36	−1.92	.60	.65	−1.23	.63	−.03	−.12
10	−0.35	−1.12	.64	.64	−0.45	.62	.00	.09
11	−0.70	−1.23	.68	.63	−0.56	.61	.07	−.14
12	−0.77	−1.41	.64	.63	−0.74	.62	.03	−.03
16	0.10	−0.71	.58	.56	−0.12	.75	.04	.22
18	0.04	−0.62	.75	.77	0.20	.75	.00	−.16
5	0.50	0.01	.52	.59	0.63	.58	−.06	−.13
13	0.18	−0.43	.48	.48	0.08	.47	.01	.09
14	−0.69	−1.05	.55	.36	−0.67	.35	.21	−.02
8	−0.97	−1.63	.51	.62	−0.98	.60	−.09	.00
9	−1.58	−2.29	.52	.56	−1.71	.54	−.02	.13
19	−1.10	−2.29	.63	.43	−1.84	.42	.21	.74
15	−0.58	−0.93	.33	.14	−0.78	.14	.19	.19
17	−0.97	−1.41	.22	.46	−0.93	.44	−.22	−.04

including/omitting items suspected of DIF on the mean test score characteristic function.

***Optional extra: The reader might have noticed that the scaling parameter k, in the dichotomized data, is no longer greater than unity and has not been interpreted as yielding the relative variance of the trait for the women, as $1/k^2$. One way to obtain information as to relative scale and relative variance is to expand the item response functions as polynomial series. The basis of the NOHARM program is the mathematical result[6] that the two-parameter normal ogive model can be expanded as a rapidly converging infinite polynomial series

$$p_j(f) = \gamma_{j0} + \gamma_{j1} x + \gamma_{j2} x^2 \cdots \cdot \qquad (15.15)$$

The constant and the coefficient of the linear term are given by

$$\gamma_{j0} = N(\tau_j) \qquad (15.16a)$$

and

$$\gamma_{j1} = \lambda_j n(\tau_j), \tag{15.16b}$$

where $n(\cdot)$ is the normal ordinate. Rescaling by applying (15.5) and (15.7) to γ_{j1} and γ_{j0} to match the linear part of this series will again yield scaling coefficients corresponding to changes both of mean and variance.

Table 15.6 gives the constant and the coefficient of the linear term for the two groups, as computed from the loadings and thresholds in Table 15.5. Applying (15.5) and (15.7) to these coefficients yields $k = 1.248$, hence $1/k^2 = .642$, and $c = 1.200$, hence $-c/k = -.962$. These are close to the values obtained before dichotomizing the Likert responses. A conventional alternative is to use the means and variances of the difficulty parameters δ_j in (15.14) to obtain both scaling factors. However, we note that these quantities appear to be somewhat unstable—at least in our example—compared with either the thresholds in Table 15.5 or the polynomial constants in Table 15.6. From the tabulated results, we find that the correlation across genders (a) between the threshold parameters (τ_j) is .952, (b) between the constants in the polynomial (γ_{j0}) is .951, and (c) between the difficulty parameters (δ_j) is .676. (Note that these quantities are expected to be linearly related but not proportional.) The coefficients of congruence, given by (15.10), are (a) .981 for the loadings, (b) .967 for the coefficients β_j in parameterizations (15.13) and (15.14), and (c) .934 for the coefficient of the linear term (γ_{j1}) in the polynomial expansion

TABLE 15.6
Unidimensional Binary—Polynomial Coefficients

Item	γ_{0m}	γ_{0f}	γ_{1m}	γ_{1f}	γ_{0f}^*	γ_{1f}^*
1	.33	.12	.23	.14	.28	.17
2	.37	.20	.21	.15	.39	.19
3	.15	.05	.13	.08	.14	.10
4	.56	.28	.32	.23	.57	.29
6	.43	.22	.25	.20	.46	.25
7	.09	.03	.09	.04	.08	.05
10	.36	.13	.24	.14	.29	.17
11	.24	.11	.21	.12	.25	.15
12	.22	.08	.19	.09	.19	.12
16	.54	.24	.23	.17	.45	.22
18	.52	.27	.30	.25	.57	.32
5	.69	.50	.09	.24	.79	.30
13	.57	.33	.19	.18	.54	.22
14	.24	.15	.14	.08	.24	.10
8	.17	.05	.13	.07	.13	.08
9	.06	.01	.06	.02	.03	.02
19	.14	.01	.14	.01	.03	.02
15	.28	.18	.11	.04	.22	.05
17	.17	.08	.07	.07	.16	.08

(15.15). These results possibly account for problems that have been reported in using the means and variances of the difficulty parameters to obtain the two scaling constants k and c. It is reasonable to recommend (a) using the item factor analysis parameterization for rescaling and comparison of parameters, and (b) using the linear section of the polynomial expansion if a comparison of the distributions of the latent trait is desired. Table 15.7, added for completeness, contains the estimates of the coefficients in the parameterizations (15.13) and (15.14). $$$

For the case of multidimensional normal-ogives, there remains very little to add, other than a report of illustrative results. The simple devices described earlier combine to yield scaling constants and rescaled loadings and thresholds in a confirmatory multidimensional normal-ogive

$$p_j(f_1, \ldots ,f_m) = N\{(\tau_j + \lambda_{j1}f_1 + \cdots + \lambda_{jm}f_m)/\psi_j\}, \quad j = 1, \ldots ,p, \quad (15.17)$$

where τ_j is the threshold as before, $\lambda_{j1}, \ldots ,\lambda_{jm}$ are the factor loadings of the jth response tendency on m factors, and ψ_j^2 is the unique variance. (In the application here it is assumed that each item loads on only one factor.)

Table 15.8 gives the thresholds and loadings for the dichotomized data sets, applying the four-dimensional model as given earlier. I have chosen

TABLE 15.7
Unidimensional Binary—Alternative Parameters

Item	β_m	β_f	δ_m	δ_f
1	0.80	0.95	0.68	1.72
2	0.68	0.65	0.57	1.51
3	0.68	1.18	1.85	2.16
4	1.34	0.96	−0.20	0.83
6	0.84	0.90	0.29	1.14
7	0.75	0.86	2.27	2.95
10	0.82	0.84	0.56	1.75
11	0.94	0.82	1.02	1.95
12	0.84	0.82	1.20	2.22
16	0.71	0.67	−0.18	1.27
18	1.13	1.21	−0.05	0.80
5	0.61	0.74	−0.97	−0.01
13	0.55	0.55	−0.37	0.88
14	0.66	0.38	1.25	2.94
8	0.59	0.79	1.90	2.64
9	0.60	0.67	3.06	4.13
19	0.80	0.48	1.76	5.30
15	0.35	0.14	1.75	6.53
17	0.32	0.51	4.37	3.10

TABLE 15.8
Multidimensional Binary Responses

	τ_m	λ_m	λ_f	τ_f^*	$\tau_m - \tau_f^*$	$\lambda_m - \lambda_f^*$
1	−0.43	.63	.69	−0.52	−.09	−.06
2	−0.32	.56	.55	−0.29	.03	.01
3	−1.03	.57	.77	−0.91	−.13	−.20
4	0.16	.80	.70	0.11	.06	.10
6	−0.18	.64	.67	−0.11	−.08	−.03
7	−1.36	.60	.65	−1.29	−.07	−.05
10	−0.35	.64	.65	−0.49	.14	−.01
11	−0.70	.68	.64	−0.61	.09	.05
12	−0.77	.64	.64	−0.79	.02	.01
16	0.10	.58	.57	−0.16	.26	.01
18	0.04	.75	.77	0.14	−.10	−.02
5	0.50	.54	.68	0.61	−.10	−.13
13	0.16	.50	.54	0.05	.12	−.04
14	−0.69	.58	.40	−0.70	.01	.18
8	−0.97	.64	.77	−0.73	.24	−.13
9	−1.58	.66	.75	−1.42	−.16	−.09
19	−1.10	.79	.48	−1.73	.63	.30
15	−0.58	.74	.32	−0.76	.15	.42
17	−0.97	.51	.98	−0.91	−.06	−.47

to assume that $k = 1$ for each factor in this case, because the factor loadings are standardized in both groups, and for three of them there are few indicators. The values of c for the four factors are, respectively, .975, .884, 1.163, and .512, corresponding in order of size to those in the four-factor analysis of the quantitative responses. Table 15.9 gives the constant and linear terms for the four polynomial expansions. These yield meaningful scaling constants k, respectively 1.394, .968, 2.363, and 1.362, and of c, respectively 1.232, .999, 2.108, and 1.658. These are very roughly in line with the values in the quantitative analysis, given the degradation of information that follows from dichotomization. Conclusions as to differentially functioning items follow as before. The congruence coefficients for the constants γ_{0m} and γ_{0f} are, respectively, .889, .968, .839, and .931, and for the coefficients of the linear terms, γ_{1m} and γ_{1f}, .986, .941, .837, and .812.

REVIEW GUIDE

Minimally, the student can take for granted the expressions (15.5) and (15.7) for the rescaling constants, on which the rest of the work in this

TABLE 15.9
Multidimensional Binary—Polynomial Coefficients

	γ_{0m}	γ_{1m}	γ_{0f}	γ_{1f}	γ^*_{0f}	γ^*_{1f}
1	.33	.23	.12	.14	.28	.19
2	.37	.21	.20	.16	.40	.22
3	.15	.13	.05	.08	.14	.11
4	.56	.32	.28	.24	.58	.33
6	.43	.25	.22	.20	.47	.28
7	.09	.09	.03	.04	.08	.06
10	.36	.24	.13	.14	.30	.19
11	.24	.21	.11	.12	.26	.17
12	.22	.19	.08	.09	.19	.13
16	.54	.23	.24	.17	.45	.24
18	.52	.30	.27	.25	.58	.35
5	.69	.18	.50	.24	.74	.23
13	.57	.19	.33	.18	.51	.17
14	.24	.17	.15	.08	.23	.08
8	.17	.13	.05	.07	.10	.16
9	.06	.06	.01	.02	.04	.04
19	.14	.14	.01	.02	.04	.04
15	.28	.12	.18	.04	.24	.05
17	.17	.05	.08	.07	.19	.09

chapter depends. A close study of the numerical example will show both the possibilities for applications and the general principles of this technology.

END NOTES

General references are Lord (1980) and Holland and Wainer (1993). The method that is central to this chapter is a modification of Lord's (1980) method. The use of (15.5) and (15.6) applied to factor loadings and thresholds is the main departure from Lord's procedure.

1. See McDonald (1982a).
2. See Holland and Wainer (1993) for a relatively nontechnical discussion of these methods. Holland applied a technique due to Mantel and Haenzel to this problem, and accordingly the procedure is most commonly described as the *Mantel–Haenzel* method. Stout was the originator of what is referred to as the *SIBTEST* method.
3. The method described is an update and minor modification of Lord (1980). The main modification is the method of rescaling the parameters.

4. See Lonsway and Fitzgerald (1995). I am grateful to Louise Fitzgerald, Diane Payne, and Kim Lonsway for permission to use these data, and for helpful discussions of substantive aspects of their research.

5. Kim Lonsway (private communication).

6. The original very technical account is in McDonald (1967).

Chapter 16

Alternate Forms and the Problem of Equating

There are a number of situations in which we would like to measure a given attribute using two different tests, that is, two different sets of items. It is conventional to refer to two tests measuring "the same" attribute as *alternate forms of a test*. The need for alternate forms arises most commonly and with greatest urgency in cognitive testing. Tests of general scholastic aptitude or of specific scholastic aptitudes are commonly used to select students into institutions for further learning. The development of alternate forms is motivated by the need for test security, and the contradictory need for freedom of information. The latter need includes the right of an examinee to verify some aspect of the testing process, either as a legal right or as an ethically acknowledged one. It may be necessary to produce a large set of items—an *item bank*—from which subsets of items can be drawn and used for the measurement of a given aptitude. If the item bank contains enough items, there is no possibility that an examinee having access to it could adopt a strategy of memorizing correct answers. Another situation motivating the development of alternate test forms is one where an educational achievement test, defined by an educational curriculum, is administered at the beginning and end (and possibly at intermediate points) of a course of instruction, to track the learning process. We do not then want to contaminate the measurements by the reuse of items already seen. We note immediately that curricular domains are typically rather complex, and the notion that "the same" knowledge is measured by distinct sets of items can be more problematic, in terms of substantive considerations of content validity, than in the case of some, at least, of the aptitudes.

There is an immense literature on the possibility and extent of a distinction between achievements and aptitudes. The notion is, at least, that in aptitude testing an attempt is made to assess a candidate's (current) "aptness" or suitability for a course of study or a type of work, whereas in achievement testing an attempt is made to assess acquired knowledge of an educational curriculum. Items written to measure an aptitude may be approximately unidimensional by design, whereas items designed to cover the content of an educational curriculum may be multidimensional, reflecting the complexity of cognitive processes demanded by the curriculum. A dominant dimension in any achievement test can be expected, however, simply as a general reflection of a tendency for achievements to be positively correlated.

In measurements of attitude, of personality traits by self-report, or of mood-states, by ordered-category items for which the linear models of Chapters 6 and 9 are most appropriate, the need for alternate forms would hardly seem to arise. Some personality tests have been designed to conceal or obscure the nature of the clinical information being sought. Setting aside the ethical questions that would arise in at least some applications of these, their security resides in the success with which the nature of the intended attribute is concealed from the respondent, and is lost when their purpose is admitted. There will seldom be a problem in the reuse of items measuring an attitude, in order to track changes in it, for example, as a consequence of a program designed to counter sexism, racism, or xenophobia. Similarly, one could hope to reuse items measuring personality adjustment or mood to track changes through time or evaluate treatments, without causing measurement problems. Nevertheless, to keep this account unified and general, allowance is made for the possibility of using linear models, as well as the nonlinear models of Chapters 12–15, in the construction or evaluation of alternative test forms. The linear model, as we have seen, can be a satisfactory general approximation to the item response model for binary data. It would also be appropriate if alternate forms were made by choosing distinct groups of questions from a large set of such groups. For example, we might have subtests consisting of passages of literature with a number of questions about each passage, yielding a number-right score measuring knowledge/understanding/evaluation for each passage—testlets or item bundles.

The construction, evaluation, and use of alternate forms gives rise to a number of problems in test theory. First it is necessary to examine the properties two forms should have that would qualify them for use as "alternates." This examination, which includes a review of the concept of parallel tests, occupies the next section. It sets the ground for a discussion of the practical problem of constructing two alternate forms that we are willing to regard as interchangeable. Then we discuss the problem of *equating* two existing test forms—of obtaining directly comparable scores from them. The topic of test equating covers techniques intended to transform one test score so that it is measured on the scale of the other test. Perhaps more important, it should also cover techniques for determining the extent to which the attempt to equate scores is successful, and for determining the region of the attribute scale in which the test scores can be considered comparable. This will almost certainly not be the entire range.

EQUIVALENCES OF TEST FORMS

After preliminaries in Chapters 1–4, we began what could properly be called test theory in Chapter 5, with the classical true-score model—the deceptively simple representation of an observed score as the sum of true-score and error-of-measurement components. This led naturally to the notion of parallel measurements, Y and Y', scores on tests (which can also be described as "test Y" and "test Y'," respectively) that yield a shared true score T, and errors of measurement E and E', assumed to be uncorrelated with the true score and with each other, and to have equal variances. As we saw, statistics based on just the test scores put very little constraint on two test forms to qualify the resulting measurements as "parallel." We require only that their means and variances should be equal. Three or more test forms, to be parallel, must fit the same (restrictive) model as the one that was developed in Chapter 6 for parallel items.

There is a further requirement on two parallel measurements, Y, Y', that is restrictive and falsifiable, but is not commonly examined. It can be shown that if Y and Y' are correlated with any other tests, say $V_1, V_2, \ldots$, their covariances (and their correlations) with these further tests must be equal.[1] This result is theoretically interesting, but it does not provide guidance for the construction of two sets of items yielding parallel test scores. Also, given two supposedly parallel test forms, we might correlate them with all other tests currently under consideration, and find that the correlations agree, but this finding is subject to being overturned at any time by a check with further external variables. So we could in principle use external correlations to show that two test forms are not parallel, but not as evidence that they are.

We note that nothing in the conditions for parallel measurements constitutes a mathematical requirement that the items in parallel tests themselves have matched item parameters—equal item means and loadings in the linear model or equal item parameters in a suitable item response model. Indeed, nothing so far requires that the items in parallel tests jointly form a homogeneous set, measuring just one attribute. (It is at least implicit that the two total test scores measure the same attribute.) It is conventionally recommended that to construct two tests as nearly parallel as possible, the constituent items should be paired to match as closely as possible in item parameters, subject matter, and item type (e.g., multiple choice with the same number of response options).

It is a reasonable intuition that two test forms containing paired items with equal item parameters in a jointly unidimensional model will give parallel measurements, in the sense so far required—equal means and variances. In fact, it may be shown that this is true. Two test forms satisfying the conditions that their items are paired to have equal parameters in a joint unidimensional model have been called *strictly parallel*.[2] I call two such test forms *item-parallel*, which is a little more self-explanatory than *strictly parallel*. It can be shown,[3] but the proof is very technical, that a necessary and sufficient condition for the scores Y and Y' on two alternate forms to have the same distribution for a given ability (or level of the attribute measured) is that the forms be item-parallel. This is a very strong condition—very difficult to satisfy—with a very important resulting property. It is a condition for the complete interchangeability of the test forms. In applications it is a condition for equity. *Equity* is the requirement that it cannot matter to the examinee which form of the test is administered.

It follows from results in Chapter 13 that if two forms are item-parallel, they consequently have:

1. Equal test characteristic curves—obtained by summing the equated item characteristic curves.
2. Equal test information functions—obtained by summing equated item information functions.
3. Equal test-score information functions (and, more generally, equal formula-score information functions).
4. Hence they also have (a) matched true scores and (b) matched error variances at every point on the measurement scale.

It is possible in theory for two test forms to have equal test characteristic functions and equal test score information functions (or formula-score information functions, for some scoring formula) without being item-parallel. If two test forms have the properties that (4a) true scores are matched and (4b) error variances are matched everywhere on the score range, this will also imply an acceptable level of equitable interchangeability of the test forms. The condition is still not one of perfect interchangeability, because at the extremes of the observed-score scale the distributions of the errors are squeezed by the floor and ceiling of the tests. Then confidence bounds based on the error variances may be inadequate, and conclusions from the forms could systematically disagree. Such effects should be very slight, and would occur at the ends of the test scale where conclusions are unsafe anyway.

The literature has not settled terminology, so I refer to test forms having the same test characteristic curve (TCC) as *TCC-parallel*, and tests that have the same test characteristic curve and the same test score information function (TSIF) as *TCC/TSIF-parallel*. Thus we can now recognize four distinct degrees of parallelism or equivalence between "parallel" test forms made up of items out of a homogeneous domain, namely: (a) *item-parallel* (or strictly parallel), with items paired to have equal parameters, (b) *TCC/TSIF-parallel*, with matched true scores and measurement error variances at every point of the scale, (c) *TCC-parallel*, with matched true scores but possibly different measurement-error variances, and (d) *classically parallel*, in which case any matching of true scores is purely by assumption. Only the first two of these can be considered (equitably) interchangeable in any strict sense. If two TCC-parallel forms differ sufficiently in error variance at points on the scale, chance can operate to systematically advantage/disadvantage subjects of different abilities in a manner that can be called "unfair."

Note that if two alternate forms are item-parallel, it does not follow from theory that they will have equal correlations with every other test we might construct. It is possible that further tests will contain items that share specific properties of the given items, so that the "error" components become correlated, to different extents in the alternate forms. It may reasonably be conjectured that this situation will seldom arise in applications unless there is some systematic pattern of item content differentiating the test forms. For example, in the ACT mathematics example of Chapter 14, if the items can be classified as algebra, geometry, or mixed, although fitting a unidimensional model to a good approximation, differential content might be enough to yield distinct correlations with further tests of quantitative ability.

MATCHING TEST FORMS

Suppose now that a large set of items has been developed that are intended to serve as a "bank" from which we will draw subsets to serve as alternate forms of a test for an aptitude. The initial problem is that of calibrating the items—estimating their item parameters and in the process verifying that the full set is homogeneous, that is, fits a unidimensional item response model. This can be a demanding problem in data analysis. Suppose that a large sample of examinees is available for the initial study of the items. We recognize that it is generally not possible to give the entire set to each examinee, because of limitations of testing time, fatigue, and declining motivation. Various designs have been employed to overcome this problem. A common device is to give overlapping subsets of items to different samples of examinees so as to estimate the item parameters. The items common to subsets serve to put the nonoverlapping items on a common scale.[4] It is hoped that by careful linking of nonoverlapping items through the overlapping ones, items not given to the same examinees nevertheless will have parameters on a common scale, and they would be jointly unidimensional. The assumption of joint unidimensionality is not tested in these designs, and might fail, particularly if the items are of different difficulties and the more difficult items demand a distinct cognitive process.

Given that the items in the bank have been cocalibrated with acceptable precision, the next problem is that of selecting items from it to make two alternate forms—or more, but we consider the case of just two. The problem is one of selecting items to meet some criterion of equivalence, at least to a good approximation. The complexity of the matching task will depend in part on whether a one-, two-, or three-parameter model is used. This, however, is not a good reason for preferring a one-parameter model unless it does happen to fit the items of the bank.

If it is indeed reasonable to suppose that the item bank is unidimensional, so the items essentially measure just one attribute as their common property, there is no good reason to consider item content in making the alternate forms. If there is any reason to think that the items may group into subdomains, one might try to ensure that these are represented in the alternate forms, given enough latitude—number of available items, and ranges of parameter values.

The complexity of the process of selecting a subset of items from a given set is shown by a consideration of combinatorics—the branch of mathematics that answers questions such as the number of distinct ways in which r elements can be chosen out of a set of n of them. Those readers who know the expression for the answer to this question will be able to verify the statement that there are, rounding somewhat, 2.715×10^{66} [$_{400}C_{20} \times {}_{380}C_{20}$] ways to choose 20 items out of 400, and then choose 20 more out of the remaining 380. Those readers who do not, will be content to accept that the number of distinct selections that can be made to create alternate forms is typically very large. Any attempt to computerize the optimal selection of items for alternate forms would therefore be computationally very demanding.

Let us consider an example. Table 16.1 gives the item parameters from the 60 items of the ACT mathematics test, as estimated by NOHARM. A subset of these was used in Chapter 14. These are all five-choice items—a correct answer and four distractors—but some have an overall proportion of passes at or below the chance level, so in the preliminary sorting process the pseudo-guessing parameters were set to zero. The GFI for the entire set is .982.

We wish to choose two sets of 10 items, to be denoted test Y and test V, that are approximately item-parallel. We need to pair the items to have

TABLE 16.1
Parameters—60 ACT Mathematics Items

Item	τ	λ	Item	τ	λ	Item	τ	λ
1	−.031	.724	21	−.038	.629	41	−.631	.373
2	−.536	.708	22	−.054	.309	42	−.722	.606
3	−.225	.658	23	−.103	.588	43	−1.149	.353
4	.744	.397	24	−.291	.698	44	.782	.582
5	.837	.484	25	−.426	.193	45	.461	.551
6	.428	.435	26	−1.028	.597	46	−.093	.438
7	.318	.440	27	.629	.558	47	.065	.453
8	.268	.526	28	.020	.595	48	−.050	.477
9	.155	.419	29	−.022	.382	49	−.496	.493
10	.255	.555	30	.152	.536	50	−.216	.315
11	.277	.625	31	−.060	.542	51	−.260	.342
12	−.074	.681	32	−.083	.472	52	−.448	.533
13	−.070	.552	33	−.019	.641	53	−.402	.615
14	−.478	.444	34	−.076	.556	54	−.691	.546
15	−.569	.368	35	−.180	.370	55	−.706	.461
16	−.840	.405	36	−.363	.647	56	−1.001	.152
17	.731	.602	37	−.367	.521	57	.047	.464
18	.470	.393	38	−.317	.638	58	−.267	.478
19	.173	.715	39	−.663	.621	59	−.238	.474
20	.152	.640	40	−.455	.442	60	−.946	.425

approximately matching thresholds and factor loadings. (The same procedure can be applied using any parameterization of the model.) To give an idea of the nature and complexity of the problem, I describe a search without computer assistance for best-matched pairs. We draw up a "frequency distribution" of the threshold values, as in Table 16.2, with the actual item numbers replacing frequency counts. We then examine the factor loadings of the items as grouped in Table 16.2 and choose pairs from the same row in the table—for example, 8 versus 10 from the interval .2–.29. Inspection of these suggests—the reader is free to disagree—that the sets of items chosen in Table 16.3 are reasonably well matched, and it might be difficult to do better. The matching was based on the analysis with pseudo-guessing parameters zero. The 20 selected items have been reanalyzed with pseudo-guessing parameters all .2, and hence the thresholds and loadings are altered from those in Table 16.1.

Table 16.4 gives values of the test characteristic curves and the error variances at intervals from −3 to 3. These appear to be virtually indistinguishable.

Table 16.5 gives the item contents. From these it can be seen that the paired items do not bear any particular relation to each other in terms of their specific properties. The additional demand to match item contents would reduce the available choices, and we may guess that it would yield

TABLE 16.2
Distribution of Parameters—ACT Items

τ Range		Items
0.8	0.89	5
0.7	0.79	4 17 44
0.6	0.69	27
0.5	0.59	
0.4	0.49	6 18 46
0.3	0.39	7
0.2	0.29	8 10 11
0.1	0.19	9 19 15 10
0.0	0.09	47 57
−0.1	−0.01	1 12 13 21 22 23 29 32 33 34 46 48
−0.2	−0.11	35
−0.3	−0.21	3 24 50 51 58 59
−0.4	−0.31	36 37 38 53
−0.5	−0.41	14 25 40 49 52
−0.6	−0.51	2 15
−0.7	−0.61	39 41 54
−0.8	−0.71	42 55
−0.9	−0.81	16
−1.0	−0.91	56 60
−1.1	−1.01	26
−1.2	−1.11	43

TABLE 16.3
Parameters—Matched ACT Items

Test Y			Test V		
Item	τ	λ	Item	τ	λ
8	0.018	.610	10	0.003	.694
6	0.207	.543	18	0.256	.462
14	−1.056	.833	40	−1.013	.766
58	−0.695	.696	59	−0.651	.663
13	−0.412	.738	34	−0.421	.742
32	−0.430	.637	46	−0.447	.618
47	−0.234	.600	57	−0.257	.604
21	−0.369	.812	33	−0.344	.813
50	−0.619	.481	51	−0.684	.486
22	−0.391	.450	29	−0.348	.498

TABLE 16.4
Test Characteristic Curves—Matched ACT Item Sets

F	TCC-Y	TCC-V	Var{E_y}	Var{E_v}
−3.0	2.12	2.14	1.67	1.68
−2.5	2.20	2.22	1.71	1.72
−2.0	2.40	2.36	1.78	1.78
−1.5	2.57	2.58	1.88	1.87
−1.0	2.95	2.95	2.02	2.01
−0.5	3.54	3.55	2.18	2.18
0	4.43	4.46	2.31	2.32
0.5	5.63	5.69	2.28	2.28
1.0	6.95	6.98	1.96	1.94
1.5	8.10	8.07	1.44	1.45
2.0	8.89	8.84	0.93	0.96
2.5	9.35	9.32	0.57	0.60
3.0	9.61	9.60	0.35	0.36

TABLE 16.5
Content of Matched ACT Items

Test Y		Test V	
50	tan from sin and cot	51	$2^2 + 2^0 + 2^{-2}$
32	radius from arc and angle	46	$8^{-2/3}$
13	intersecting forms	34	volume of boxes
21	graph of inequality	33	radius from circumference
47	radical expressions	57	roots of a polynomial
58	combine means	59	trigonometric expression
8	income and costs	10	quadratic expression
22	radical computation	29	$4X + 2 = 12 − 6X$ (in words)
6	Cartesian coordinates	18	lengths in right triangle
14	quadratic expression	40	solution of quadratic

a worse match. The attempt to make item-parallel forms by pairing on content, without taking account of parameter values, also seems unlikely to yield an optimal match.

It is interesting to note that if the object is to obtain alternate forms that are TCC/TSIF-parallel, this does not impose the requirement that they be item-parallel. Yet an examination of Table 16.1 points up the extraordinary difficulty of the selection task if we attempt to select alternate forms matched on both test characteristic curves and error variance functions, and it would seem pointless, if a little easier, to match the forms only on one of these properties. Even so, either of these tasks alone seems more demanding than finding matched pairs of items.

THE PROBLEM OF TEST EQUATING

The need to equate two test forms arises when we already have two forms of a test, that is, two tests intended to measure the same attribute. After discussion of the general problem, we consider (a) true-score equating, (b) linear equating, and (c) equipercentile equating.

Test form Y may be given to one examinee and test form V to another, and we wish to place the scores on a common scale. A very reasonable common scale would be that of the latent trait in an item response model, but it seems to be the common convention in practical applications of tests to accept the sum score on one test—say, Y from test form Y—as providing the scale and to find a transformation of the sum score V that can be directly compared to Y.

There is a sense in which the task of equating is unnecessary if it is possible and impossible if it is necessary—at least if the objective is to obtain equitable interchangeability of the forms. If we have been in a position to construct item-parallel tests, they are already fully comparable, and no equating is needed. It can be shown that if a transformation is needed, the measurement-error behavior of the two test scores cannot also be matched on the entire range of the scores.

A distinction has been made in the literature between the problem of equating for tests of equal difficulty—*horizontal equating*—and for tests of unequal difficulty—*vertical equating*. This distinction might better be represented as a continuum of degree of difference in difficulty. The motivation for finding a common scale for tests of quite different difficulty can be somewhat different from that of tests of comparable difficulty. In the latter case, there is likely to be a concern for equity. In the former, it may be that we wish to study growth in an ability/achievement over time, and over a range of growth for which a single test is not suitable. It is possible in such a case to be less concerned to match error properties, except in a limited range where the tests overlap. It would still seem desirable, given the technology of item response theory, that the error variances should be studied, although this does not yet seem to be a common practice in equating studies, or a common recommendation in the literature.

For simplicity, discussion here will be confined to tests containing binary items yielding number-right integer scores. The material that follows on linear equating methods naturally extends to tests containing subtests in the form of "testlets" or "item bundles" as their basic components. A limitation on the treatment here is that there will be no discussion of methods used for cases where we have not been able to calibrate the item parameters on a common scale, and different items are given to distinct populations.

There is a possible confusion about the nature and objectives of equating that must first be examined. It can be said that the object of equating test scores is to find a function that maps the scores from one test form onto the scale of the test scores from the other. On the face of it the mapping may appear to be one of raw scores onto raw scores. This statement needs careful formulation, however, as can be seen from the following considerations:

1. The raw scores on the tests are integers. In general integers cannot be mapped into integers—as the examples that follow make clear.

2. Because of errors of measurement, the raw scores on two tests actually obtained from a common group of examinees are not, of course, in one-on-one correspondence and therefore cannot possibly be mapped into each other.

3. If the items of the tests are jointly homogeneous—at least approximately measuring just one attribute in common—the true scores from both tests are functions of the attribute. They are therefore in one-on-one correspondence, so it is possible to map true scores into true scores. If they are not jointly homogeneous, a fundamental motive for equating is lacking.

It has commonly been claimed in the literature on equating that a transformation based on true scores cannot be applied to the raw scores that are all we obtain in practice, or at least that such applications lack mathematical justification, and are made heuristically, with some misgivings.[5] The reader is warned that the position to be described here includes a denial of that claim.

Consider, again, the case where we have succeeded in constructing two item-parallel tests, Y and V, as in the previous section. If one examinee is given test Y and another given test V, the test scores are equated (by construction of the tests) in the sense that examinees of the same ability have the same true score and the same test-score error variance. The raw scores—which in general will disagree—are not equated except in the sense that each is an unbiased estimate of the same true score. (Because the error variance is a function of the true score, an examinee who by chance scores below his or her true level may receive a different estimate of error variance from that at the true point, and similarly for an examinee who by chance scores above his or her true level. But this is not a denial of equitable exchangeability, which can only concern long-run expectations.)

Suppose now we have two test forms Y and V, and we know or assume that the items of each test measure one and the same attribute—aptitude, curricular achievement—in common. Thus their true scores are in one-to-one correspondence with the attribute, and therefore with each other. The scores on form V are equated to those on form Y at a point on the ability continuum to the extent that a transformation of true scores on form V gives a measure of ability on the true-score scale of form Y at this point, with the same error variance. This statement may become clearer after discussion of the technique that directly follows from the definition. This is known in the literature as *true-score IRT equating.*

True-Score IRT Equating

From Chapter 13 we already have the essential concepts that enable a brief and simple account of this method.

Step 1: From a prior analysis of a large item set that includes the items of the two tests, or from a joint analysis of just these items, we have or obtain their item parameters on a common scale for the attribute. Consider, for example, the item sets in Table 16.6. These were chosen from the set of 60 math items in Table 16.1, to yield tests of distinct difficulty, with test Y as—relatively—the easy test and test V the difficult test.

Step 2: From these we compute values of the test characteristic functions for each test sum score at intervals along the attribute continuum—T_Y, T_V as functions of f, and also the error variance functions. Thus we have the true score on each as a function of f and the corresponding measurement error variance. Table 16.7 gives the test characteristic curves, labeled respectively TCC$_Y$ and TCC$_V$, and the error variance functions for the example, labeled Var$\{E_Y\}$ and Var$\{E_V\}$. (For the moment we ignore the last column.)

Step 3: At this point we have a one-to-one mapping of true scores on one test into true scores on the other. The paired true scores correspond to the chosen series of values of the attribute, and of course neither consists of integers. The relationship is perfectly symmetric. In the example, if an examinee's expected score on the easier test Y is 6.67, the person's expected score on the more difficult test V is 3.31, both corresponding to $F = 0$. An unimportant asymmetry is introduced when we choose to read off from

TABLE 16.6
Item Parameters—Easy and Difficult ACT Items

	Test Y			Test V	
Item	τ	λ	*Item*	τ	λ
5	0.830	0.731	3	−1.729	2.544
4	0.650	0.561	14	−1.798	1.378
27	0.575	0.855	15	−2.177	1.429
6	0.247	0.655	25	−1.018	0.359
7	0.094	0.675	40	−1.554	1.164
8	0.023	0.860	46	−0.547	0.705
9	−0.145	0.669	49	−4.514	4.012
57	−0.331	0.810	52	−3.647	3.513
10	0.004	1.014	58	0.974	0.982
18	0.286	0.500	59	−0.912	0.981

this relationship the expected scores on test V that correspond to integer expected scores on test Y (or conversely, but we choose just one direction for this process—usually an arbitrary choice). This does not destroy the reversibility of the correspondence, but merely represents a choice of the test that becomes the basis of the scale of measurement. Here we are choosing to equate test V to test Y, meaning that we specify (noninteger) values on the scale of test Y in correspondence with integer true scores on test V, so that integer scores on test V can be reported as noninteger scores in the metric of test Y. This can be done to a quite good approximation from a well-drawn graph of T_V on T_Y. From the illustrative graph in Fig. 16.1 the possibility can be seen of reading T_Y values to the first decimal place for each integer value of T_V, given the greater precision that would be provided by regular graph paper. Table 16.8 gives values obtained in this way. Here $Y(T_V)$ represents the noninteger value in the metric of test Y corresponding to integer true scores on test V. A variety of interpolation methods could be employed to obtain more precise values of $Y(T_v)$ corresponding to each integer score on test V. It should suffice for the student needing just a general account of this topic to recognize that in true-score IRT equating, the test characteristic functions are directly used to obtain a list of the transformed (noninteger) values $Y(T_V)$ of integer true scores on test V. These can then be compared to test Y scores in the sense that an examinee who gets a score of V on test V would be expected to get a score of $Y(V)$ on test Y. In the example, consider an examinee

TABLE 16.7
Test Characteristic Curves and Error Variance
Functions—Easy and Difficult ACT Items

F	TCC_Y	$Var\{E_Y\}$	TCC_V	$Var\{E_V\}$	$V\{E\}$
−4.0	2.15	1.69	2.02	1.61	—
−3.5	2.25	1.74	2.03	1.62	10.92
−3.0	2.42	1.82	2.06	1.63	9.36
−2.5	2.68	1.93	2.11	1.66	7.88
−2.0	3.09	2.08	2.20	1.70	6.82
−1.5	3.69	2.23	2.36	1.75	6.32
−1.0	4.52	2.34	2.60	1.79	6.16
−0.5	5.55	2.32	2.90	1.80	5.47
0	6.67	2.10	3.31	1.84	3.40
0.5	7.74	1.68	4.08	2.00	1.52
1.0	8.57	1.19	5.79	2.09	0.79
1.5	9.14	0.77	7.79	1.41	0.44
2.0	9.50	0.47	8.73	0.90	0.36
2.5	9.71	0.28	9.23	0.55	0.25
3.0	9.83	0.16	9.48	0.37	0.16
3.5	9.90	0.10	9.62	0.28	0.08
4.0	9.94	0.06	9.71	0.22	—

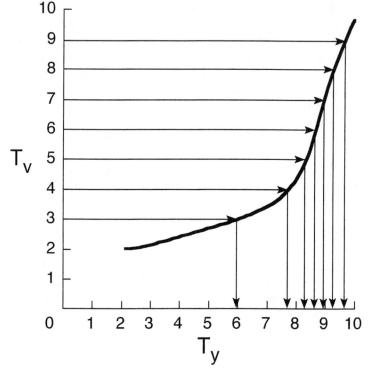

FIG. 16.1. Graph of T_v on T_y.

TABLE 16.8
True-Score IRT Equating—ACT Items

T_V	3	4	5	6	7	8	9
$Y(T_V)$	6.0	7.6	8.2	8.6	8.9	9.2	9.6

who gets a test score of 4 on test V. Taking this to be an unbiased estimate of the examinee's true score, we use the tabulation to assign a score of 7.6 on test Y—the test we have chosen to provide our conventional scale of measurement for this ability.

It will be noticed that Table 16.8 omits the perfect score 10 and scores— 0, 1, 2—up to and including the score expected "by chance" in 10 five-category items. This omission reflects a realistic recognition that true-score IRT equating cannot be applied at the ceiling of the difficult test or in the region of chance response. It is not, from the point of view adopted here, a defect of the method.

When the equating process has been completed, there remains the important task of examining the error properties of the equated forms.

We already have the result that the variance of the error of estimate of a true score from the observed score is given by

$$\text{Var}\{E|f\} = \sum_j \text{P}_j(f)\,Q_j(f).$$

The values of these functions for the example are given in Table 16.7, with the test characteristic functions. Inspection suggests a general tendency for the error variance on the easy test to exceed those of the difficult test below $f = 0$, with a reverse tendency above $f = 0$, but the differences would appear negligible. However, it is necessary to determine the effect of the scale transformation $V \rightarrow Y(V)$ on the error variance of $Y(V)$. At any point on the scale we can regard the relationship between T_V and T_Y as approximately linear, and the slope of the function, as seen from Fig. 16.1, is the ratio of the change in each for a given change in f. From the graph of T_Y on T_V we can see that at the low end of the scale T_Y changes very rapidly with T_V, and the rate of change declines through most of the rest of the range.

***Technically, it may be shown that the error variance of $Y(V)$ is given by

$$\text{Var}\{E\} = (dT_Y/dT_V)^2\text{Var}\{E_V\}. \qquad (16.1) \qquad \$\$\$$$

The last column of Table 16.7 gives the error variance of the transformed $Y(V)$. It is easily seen that the error variance of the more difficult test, as referred to the scale of the easy test, is very much larger in the low-ability region than that of the easy test—as we intuitively expect—and smaller, except near the test ceiling, in the high-ability region. There is a small interval around $f = -.5$ to $.5$ where one might regard the forms as equitably interchangeable. Generally, we can expect to find very different error variances between tests of different difficulty in parts of the scale. Therefore we cannot, as noted at the beginning of this section, expect to regard such tests as exchangeable if the interest is in measuring individual examinees.

An important and valuable feature of true-score IRT equating that has just been illustrated is that it contains a complete set of diagnostics for the extent of success or failure of the equating enterprise. Given the plot of the test characteristic functions against each other, we can recognize the ranges of the score on each test where they can be well enough equated. From the error variance functions we can recognize the score ranges where equitable interchangeability is possible, at least approximately. Other methods of equating lack these important features.

Linear Equating Methods

We turn now to an examination of three methods based on linear approximations. These would have their best application in cases where the item scores are already quantitative, capable of being fitted by the Spearman model, as in the unlikely case where we wish to equate Likert items, or in the case of item bundles giving sum scores for a common stimulus. Because linear methods are occasionally used with binary data, and it is of interest to see how they compare with true-score IRT, we use the same example as illustration.

The simplest linear equating method assumes that a linear transformation—a change of origin and unit—of one set of scores puts it on the same scale as the other. This corresponds to the assumption that standardized scores on the two tests are equal in the calibration population, so

$$(Y - \mu_Y)/\sigma_Y = (V - \mu_V)/\sigma_V. \tag{16.2}$$

Then the linear function of V,

$$L(V) = (\sigma_Y/\sigma_V) V + \mu_Y - (\sigma_Y/\sigma_V)_{\mu V} \tag{16.3}$$

is on the scale of test Y. In applications we substitute sample estimates.

In our example we find from the raw data file that

$$\hat{\mu}_Y = 6.566 \quad \hat{\mu}_V = 3.570,$$
$$\hat{\sigma}_Y = 2.208 \quad \hat{\sigma}_V = 2.186,$$

so substituting these estimates in (16.3) gives

$$L(V) = 1.01V + 2.96.$$

This gives the values in Table 16.9. This may be compared to the listing in Table 16.8. It is interesting to note that the agreement is not unacceptable over the range 3 to 6, failing badly where expected—that is, where high scores on the difficult test yield equivalent, rescaled scores beyond the ceiling of the easy test.

The method just described is conventionally known as *observed score linear equating*. This is appropriate terminology in the sense that the method uses only observed characteristics of the raw scores—their means and standard deviations. It may also be implied, somewhat less appropriately, that because it uses only observable features of the score distributions it in some sense equates raw scores. To the extent that the approximation gives an acceptable reference of scores on test V to the scale of test Y, it is best

TABLE 16.9
Observed Score Linear Equating—ACT Items

V	0	1	2	3	4	5	6	7	8	9	10
L(V)	2.96	3.97	4.98	5.99	7.0	8.01	9.02	10.03	11.04	12.05	13.06

thought of as having the same purpose as true-score IRT—providing a mapping of the expected values of V at the integer points onto the scale of Y.

A classical linear equating procedure, *Levine's true-score method*,[6] takes account of the true score basis of test equating by substituting true scores for observed scores and true-score standard deviations for observed standard deviations in (16.2). The true-score means are, of course, the observed score means. This yields

$$L(T_V) = (\sigma_{TY}/\sigma_{TV}) T_V + \mu_Y - (\sigma_{TY}/\sigma_{TV})\mu_V \qquad (16.4)$$

in place of (16.3). For this purpose we require estimates of the true-score variances of the tests. It would generally be safe to get these from the observed variances through the lower bound estimates of reliability given by G-C alpha, because any underestimation will be somewhat compensated for by the fact that it will affect both the numerator and denominator of the ratio of standard deviations. But in keeping with the unifying principles used in this book, we may use a Spearman factor analysis of the item covariance matrix of each test form to obtain the true-score variances of the sum scores as the square of the sum of their item factor loadings, rather than go through the reliability coefficients—coefficient omega. Table 16.10 gives the item means, loadings, and unique variances for tests Y

TABLE 16.10
Spearman Parameters—ACT Items

	Test Y				Test V		
Item	p_j	λ_j	ψ_j	Item	p_j	λ_j	ψ_j
5	.80	.14	.14	3	.41	.25	.18
4	.77	.13	.16	14	.32	.16	.19
27	.73	.18	.16	15	.28	.13	.19
6	.67	.17	.19	25	.33	.07	.22
7	.62	.18	.20	40	.32	.15	.20
8	.61	.21	.20	46	.46	.17	.22
9	.56	.18	.21	49	.31	.19	.18
57	.52	.20	.21	52	.33	.20	.18
10	.60	.23	.19	58	.39	.18	.21
18	.68	.13	.20	59	.41	.19	.21

and V in our example, yielding $\sigma_{TY} = 1.733$ and $\sigma_{TV} = 1.678$, and test means $\mu_Y = 6.566$ and $\mu_V = 3.571$. Then (16.4) gives

$$L(V) = 1.033 T_V + 2.878,$$

which is hardly different from the observed score function, and yields the similar tabulation in Table 16.11.

At this point we note what might appear to be a third linear method, based directly on the Spearman factor model. Essentially, we suppose that the item characteristic functions can be approximated by the linear factor model, giving

$$T_Y = \mu_Y + \lambda_{Y \bullet f} \tag{16.5a}$$

and

$$T_V = \mu_V + \lambda_{V \bullet f}, \tag{16.5b}$$

where $\lambda_{Y \bullet}$ and $\lambda_{V \bullet}$ are the mean loadings for the two tests. In the example these are estimated by

$$T_Y = 6.566 + 1.733 f,$$

and

$$T_V = 3.571 + 1.678 f.$$

Eliminating f from these equations gives

$$L(T_V) = (\lambda_{Y \bullet}/\lambda_{V \bullet}) T_V + \mu_Y - (\lambda_{Y \bullet}/\lambda_{V \bullet})\mu_V. \tag{16.6}$$

However, assuming we use the Spearman model, and not G-C alpha, to estimate true-score variances, this is just the same as Levine's true-score method. The point is that Levine's true-score method will be applicable to binary data to the extent that a linear factor model approximates the item characteristic functions of the individual items, or, at least, that non-linearities in these mutually cancel in forming the test characteristic func-

TABLE 16.11
True-Score Linear Equating—ACT Items

V	0	1	2	3	4	5	6	7	8	9	10
$L(T_V)$	2.88	3.91	4.94	5.98	7.01	8.04	9.08	10.01	11.14	12.17	13.20

tions. In our example, it is clear that this does not happen, and the linear approximation is good only over a rather restricted range.

Because we are now dealing with a true-score model, it is possible to examine the error behavior of the equated test scores, at least as an average. From the results in Table 16.10, we have, respectively, $\omega_Y = .616$ and $\omega_v = .590$, so the tests have closely comparable reliabilities, true-score variances, and (average) error variances. However, we know from the true-score IRT analysis that this average behavior conceals very different relative error variances along the ability continuum. Thus, although it is an improvement on simple observed score equating, linear true-score equating is generally deficient, because of likely failure of the linear approximation toward the ends of the scale, and corresponding failure of the error variance to reflect the extent of equitable interchangeability.

Equipercentile Equating

As a final note to this chapter, it should be mentioned that another commonly used equating method simply draws up the empirical cumulative frequency distribution of total scores on the two tests from a large sample of examinees. Scores on the two tests corresponding to a given percentile—proportion of examinees attaining that score—are taken to correspond to the same level of ability. Pairs of equivalent scores can then be listed in correspondence to a series of percentile points—much as we listed them in correspondence to values of the latent trait—and interpolation methods are used to get the transformed values of the integer points for V. This method is not subject to the severe problems attaching to the linear methods, but it shares with them a lack of information about the error behavior of the equated scores. It is therefore not competitive with the true-score IRT method, which on current evidence is the method of choice.

A limitation of the present introductory account is that no attempt has been made to discuss the complexities arising when calibration designs are used—as briefly mentioned in the preceding section—with subsets of items given to different examinees, distinct populations, and so on. Indeed, one assumption that needs to be checked is that there is no differential item functioning between populations to which the tests may be applied Accordingly, the methods of the last chapter would be needed before the equating step.

REVIEW GUIDE

The distinctions between item-parallel, TCC/TSIF-parallel, TCC-parallel, and classically parallel tests are of central importance. The matching procedure in the next section illustrates the possibility of creating item-parallel tests, and a simple strategy for doing so.

The central points illustrated in the final section are:

1. Equating tests that are not item-parallel is not, strictly speaking, an achievable goal.
2. IRT true-score equating is the most precise and the most informative method. The illustration of this method—including the predicted failure to match error variances—will repay close study.
3. The alternative equating methods, some of which appear to be in use, cannot be recommended.

END NOTES

General: for further reading, see Holland and Rubin (1982).

1. See Lord and Novick (1968)
2. Lord (1980, Section 13.3)
3. Lord (1980, Section 13.3)
4. Lord (1980, Section 13.9)
5. Lord (1980, Section 13.7)
6. See Holland and Rubin (1982).

Introduction to Structural Equation Modeling

Structural equation modeling (SEM), also known as *path analysis with latent variables,* is a general system for the analysis of dependencies/independencies in a set of measured variables and/or common factors of subsets of variables. It is rapidly gaining in popularity as a way to investigate "causal" relations in nonexperimental data. This is primarily because of the ease with which an investigator can draw a path diagram to express a conjecture about cause–effect relations, and "confirm" it with increasingly user-friendly commercial software. Given the usual caveats about drawing causal inferences from "mere" correlations, and for other reasons that appear later in this chapter, we might characterize it as a dangerously conjectural technique for asking essential research questions which otherwise are impossible to consider. Properly understood, and carefully used, it does have the advantage over less systematic modes of analysis intended to support causal theories that it makes its own assumptions and limitations explicit. Superficially applied, it is an easy way to give an impressive and plausible but possibly totally incorrect account of a set of measurements in the social and behavioral sciences. Applications of the second kind are possibly in the majority.

The topic of SEM is admittedly somewhat marginal to this book. There are two main reasons for giving at least a brief introduction here. First, there is such a close connection between models and computer software for common factor analysis and for SEM that the student needs to be made aware of the points of overlap, the similarities, and the differences between them. Second, a possible application of it is to (construct) validation. It supplies a natural technology for Cronbach and Meehl's conception of a nomological net as discussed in Chapter 10. One line of evidence as to what is measured by a test—perhaps in the widest sense of an observational device for recording behavior—could be evidence that it can be affected by, or have an effect on, other variables whose nature is well understood. For example, to decide what is signified by a score on a rating schedule measuring the extent to which an infant clings to its mother in a strange situation—strength of maternal bond, fearfulness, and so on—we might manipulate, if possible, or observe, otherwise, the conditions that appear to control the behavior to confirm a theory as to what state or trait of the infant is being measured. Already in Chapter 10 we considered an example—depression and self-punitive attitude—that assumed the methods of this chapter, and whose formal analysis is given here.

First we give a preliminary discussion of the philosophically complex concept of a causal relation between quantitative variables. Next is an account of the basic methods of representing structural equation models (a) as a set of equations and (b) as a path diagram. The following section describes the case of path analysis without common factors, and the choice of assumptions available for their application. The final section extends the discussion to cases with common factors.

MEASURING CAUSE–EFFECT RELATIONS

If we are to develop methods for assessing the size of the effect of one variable on another, first we must consider what we mean by a cause and an effect. For brevity, it is necessary to skim lightly over, and almost bypass, what is really a deep question in the philosophy of science. The reader will almost certainly have already been trained or persuaded to believe that correlations—"mere" associations—do not provide evidence of causation. The observation that Y_1 and Y_2 are correlated in a population of interest does not give evidence that Y_1 (partly) determines Y_2—partly, among possibly other determiners—or conversely. The relation is symmetric in Y_1 and Y_2. The reader will also, almost certainly, have been trained or persuaded to accept that in an experiment in which we control values of the "experimental variable" Y_1 and observe values of the "response" variable Y_2, a demonstrated relation between them is interpreted as a causal dependence of Y_2 on Y_1. If a manipulated change in Y_1 yields a change in Y_2, we may properly say that Y_1 is a *cause* of (change in) Y_2, although not in general the only cause. That is, when values of one variable can be manipulated, set, or controlled by a human investigator, changes in another are consequent effects. Our willingness to accept that the experiment gives convincing evidence of a cause–effect relation points to a formalization of what we mean by *cause*. When we assign subjects at random to an experimental and a control condition, and by a test of significance we conclude that the treatment has an effect, or, better, when we estimate the size of the effect and decide that it is nonnegligibly large, we are attempting to approximate a factual claim about a counterfactual state of the world. We would like to say, for any subject, that if the treatment had not been given, the subject's response would have been different by, approximately, the estimated mean treatment effect. Thus, a causal statement goes beyond concomitance by declaring that if the treatment variable Y_1 is set at value y_1, and the response variable Y_2 takes a certain value, then if, contrary to fact for a given subject, Y_1 had been set to a different value, Y_2 would have been different by a value equal to the treatment effect.

On the face of it, one might suppose that only conditions that (human) investigators can in principle manipulate can be causes. It is possible to take this view, but it is also reasonable to allow more general counterfactual conjectures to be recognized as causal statements. For example, the theory that the solar system was created by a near collision of our sun with a passing star is not an assertion of concomitance—when planets happen to form, stars happen to pass—but a conjecture that if a star had not passed, the planets would not have formed.

Because of the rapid growth of SEM applications, it is possibly a good discipline to impose on our use of this technique the test of imagining control/manipulation of an alleged causal variable, always asking the question: In what sense can we imagine an intervention by some agency that creates the contrary-to-fact conditions? For this to be imaginable, it is axiomatic that the cause is defined and measured independently of its effects, as otherwise it could not be independently manipulable. It is also axiomatic that a change in a causal variable cannot occur later in time than its effect—the consequent change in another variable. In applications in behavioral science, a careful theoretical analysis will commonly be needed that is directed at the nature of a hypothetical intervention whereby a given individual might be re-equipped with different abilities, attitudes, affective states, intentions, and so on, yet still conceived of as "the same" person. A safe but limited model of the behaving person would represent the person as a unitary organism on which environmental events—summarized in controllable values of variables—are externally impressed. (Newton's first law of motion represents the paradigm: A body continues in a state of rest or uniform motion in a straight line, unless acted on by external, impressed force.) We then measure consequent changes in the properties/attributes/behavior of the organism, or consequent effects on the environment of the organism's behavior. This model is relatively safe because it emphasizes the externality to the individual of the causal force "impressed on" the person.

If we wish to make causal conjectures about relations between events that are in some sense "inside" the organism, diagnosed and measured by such observations as we can make, we need a less safe model of broader scope. This represents the organism as a set of linked but distinct subsystems, such that events in one subsystem are external to another, and can legitimately be treated as impacting externally on it. Much theorizing in social psychology, personality research, and cognitive science amounts to postulating subsystems and causal interactions internal to the organism. The problem, which is an acute and difficult one in applications of SEM, is then to get nonexperimental evidence justifying (a) the choice of one model of the subsystems over another and (b) one model of causal sequencing over another. For example, on some models of attitude, it is an integrated cognitive–affective–value complex stimulated by and directed toward the object of the attitude. On another model, the cognitive, affective, and conative facets of attitude are separated into postulated subsystems, and we can conjecture (a) that affect is dependent on (caused by) cognitions, and value is determined by both, or (b) that affect influences cognition, or (c). . . . Causal analysis then requires imagined or actual control directed at one of these components.

On the face of it, the axiom that causes are external to the systems on which they act—that they are external impressed forces—suggests that nonexperimental studies of relations between environmental variables and organismic variables are safer for causal inferences than studies relating two or more organismic variables measured on individuals in a population of interest. This would put a severe limitation on applications of SEM. The axiom that causes temporally precede their effects, or at least do not follow them, suggests that *longitudinal* studies, with measures of conjectured causes taken earlier than conjectural response variables, will be safer than *cross-sectional* studies, with all measurements taken essentially simultaneously. This would also set an unfortunate limitation on SEM work. And longitudinal studies are still open to the objection that an apparently causal relation between an earlier and a later measure may just represent a relation of temporally stable traits of the person, or perhaps aspects of an unfolding developmental sequence that does not allow conceptual manipulation of the earlier measured attribute.

Perhaps because it is well known that although a causal relation implies correlation, a correlation does not imply a cause–effect relation, many writers on structural equation models stop short of describing the asymmetric relation in a directed path $Y_k \to Y_j$ as modeling a conjectural counterfactual situation, with human or natural agencies resetting Y_k to a different value. The use of alternative terms, such as paths of "influence," seems at best ambiguous.[1] In my view, attempts to identify such a directed relationship with functional or statistical dependence—Y_j is a mathematical function of Y_k, or predictable from it—fail to deal with the fact that generally the relationship can be inverted.[2] The reader is encouraged to examine other views. I have chosen to state mine as explicitly as possible.

Perhaps enough has been said to point up the difficulties attending causal inference from nonexperimental data. We must also face the fact that if investigators took the view that such inferences should never be attempted, many of the most important questions in the behavioral and social sciences would remain entirely out of the bounds of ethical and otherwise practical modes of research.

THE CONVENTIONS OF STRUCTURAL EQUATION MODELING

The topic now known alternatively as SEM or as path analysis with latent variables had its historical roots in econometrics under the first of these labels and in work on genetics by Sewell Wright under the label of path analysis. Some writers restrict the phrase *path analysis* to models without *latent variables*—where *latent variables* most usually correspond to common factors or latent traits. Others treat SEM and path analysis (possibly with latent variables) as coextensive. That is the choice I make here.

As a paradigm case, we start by considering a simple causal chain connecting three variables, with a specific example that is elaborated later. Suppose we have Y_1, a measure of Physical Health (PH), Y_2, a score on Constructive Thinking (CT), and Y_3, a measure of Subjective Well-Being (SWB). For the moment, these phrases are taken to be understandable. Details are given later. We postulate (a) that Y_1, measured as reported health problems, has a negative effect on Y_2—that health problems reduce one's ability to engage in constructive thinking; (b) that Y_2 has a positive effect on Y_3—that constructive thinking improves one's subjective well-being; and (c) that Y_1 affects Y_3 only through the mediation of Y_2. This set of hypotheses can be represented by two linear structural equations:

$$Y_2 = \beta_{21} Y_1 + E_2 \qquad (17.1a)$$

$$Y_3 = \beta_{32} Y_2 + E_3. \qquad (17.1b)$$

Neglecting the "error terms" E_2 and E_3, we regard (17.1a) and (17.1b) as representing the notion that a controlled unit increase in Y_1 would yield a change β_{21} in Y_2 and a controlled unit increase in Y_2 would yield a change β_{32} in Y_3. To save unnecessary complications, we assume for the rest of this chapter that each variable is measured from its mean, so constants corresponding to means can be omitted from these equations. Whenever we wish, we can also suppose all variables are standardized.

If we had written

$$Y_2 = \beta_{21} Y_1 + E_2 \tag{17.2a}$$

$$Y_3 = \beta_{32} Y_2 + \beta_{31} Y_1 + E_3, \tag{17.2b}$$

this would be an alternative hypothesis that Y_1 does not just have an indirect effect on Y_3 through its action on Y_2, but can directly influence Y_3. Under the causal chain hypothesis (17.1), if we were to intervene, fixing the value of Y_2, a controlled change in Y_1 would not cause a change in Y_3. Under the alternative model (17.2), an unrestricted recursive model as defined shortly, if we control Y_2, a change in Y_1 will still cause a change in Y_3.

On the face of it, the causal chain hypothesis implies that the partial correlation, given by (8.43), between Y_1 and Y_3, conditional on Y_2, should be zero. Conditioning on (observations of) Y_2 is taken to simulate controlling Y_2. This is, in fact, an accepted test in the earlier work on path analysis, and it points to the fact that SEM can be regarded as an elaboration of partial correlation methods. Most commonly, the testable implications of a structural equation model correspond to a set of partial correlations that are required to be zero.[3]

Suppose we know the population values of the *path coefficients* β_{jk} in the models (17.1) or (17.2) or have estimates of them from a large sample. A path coefficient is a measure of effect size—the size of the *direct effect* of Y_k on Y_j. In the unrestrictive model (17.2), β_{21} is the change (positive or negative) in Y_2 that would result from a unit controlled increase in Y_1; β_{32} gives the change in Y_3 that would result from a unit increase in Y_2; and β_{31} is the change that would result from a unit change in Y_1 while Y_2 is held constant. Thus the model quantifies the notion of a direct effect of one variable on another.

Our simple causal chain model also points toward the idea of measuring the *indirect effect* of one variable on another through a sequence of direct effects. Suppose, in the chain model, we apply a controlled unit increase to Y_1 and allow Y_2 to change by β_{21} as a direct consequence, with Y_3 changing in turn as a direct consequence of the change in Y_2. If a unit increase in Y_2 would cause a change β_{32} in Y_3, then a change β_{21} in Y_2 would cause a change $\beta_{32}\beta_{21}$ in Y_3. This is the indirect effect of a unit increase in Y_1. In the alternative, unrestricted model (17.2), a unit increase in Y_1 will have an effect on Y_3 consisting of the indirect effect through Y_2 and the direct effect β_{31}. This *total effect* $\tau_{31} = \beta_{31} + \beta_{32}\beta_{21}$ is the sum of the direct and indirect effects. That is, a unit increase of Y_1 with Y_2 allowed to change as a consequence yields a sum of direct and indirect effects in the unrestricted model. Note that these could act in opposition, possibly canceling.

These remarks illustrate two major objectives of SEM:

1. We wish to obtain estimates of the direct effect of one variable Y_k on another variable Y_j, defined as the (positive or negative) change β_{jk} in

Y_j, conjectured to result if Y_k were subjected to a controlled unit increase while all other variables in the system were held constant.

2. We may wish also to obtain estimates of the total effect of one variable Y_k on another, Y_j, defined as the conjectured change τ_{jk} in Y_j, if Y_k were given a unit increase, and all other variables in the system were left free to change as a consequence of the controlled increase in Y_k.

The needed technology includes (a) a more general system of equations like (17.1) and (17.2)—usually accompanied by a graphical method of representing them, for convenience of thought; (b) some assumptions yielding expressions for covariances of the variables in the system which give a restricted model with identified parameters to be estimated—a very similar technology to factor analysis; (c) methods of estimation from a sample, and measures of goodness of fit—again parallel to factor analysis; (d) tests on individual path coefficients; and (e) a general analysis of direct and indirect effects.

We begin with a given set of random variables $Y_1, \ldots, Y_m$ in a population of interest, which by sampling yields a covariance matrix to which the structural equation model is to be fitted. The model is intended to give a restrictive, testable model for the covariance matrix of the given variables, much as the common factor model does. The equations of the model introduce additional random variables. Some of these are error terms, as in (17.1) and (17.2), accounting for the failure of the modeled relations to be completely deterministic. Others, as would be expected, and as will be seen in the final section of the chapter, have the character of common factors/latent traits/true scores, accounting for the covariances of their indicators by the principle of local independence. It appears to be possible also to create structural equation models in which further random variables are added to the given set that are neither error terms nor common factors. These are not considered in this introductory account.

Unfortunately, there is considerable confusion and contradiction in the terminology of structural equation modeling, and a general lack of formal definition where it seems most needed. Some writers distinguish (a) *manifest* variables—the given variables whose covariances are to be explained; (b) *latent* variables—in some sense "unobservable," "underlying," conceptual variables, although not necessarily common factors; and (c) error terms. Others describe all further variables added to the given (sampled) set—including error terms—as "latent variables." There is, however, no agreed meaning for the manifest/latent variable distinction. There are also a number of variant conventions for the representation of a structural equation model by a *path* diagram, partly, but not entirely, corresponding to variant terminology.

The general role of the path diagram in structural equation models is to provide a convenient way—perhaps too convenient, as it encourages superficial research—to develop a model for a network of causal processes. The specific role of the path diagram is to enable an analysis in terms of direct and indirect effects without using rather complex (matrix) algebra. It is now an almost universally accepted convention to represent a given variable—a variable we have measured on sampled subjects and included in the data matrix to be analyzed—as a square or rectangle containing the variable name (see figures). A common factor in the model is represented by a circle or ellipse containing its name. There are three main conventions in the literature for entering an error term in the path diagram. Many writers follow the convention of writing its name into the diagram without an enclosing boundary, to distinguish it from both given (manifest) variables and common factors (and possibly other variables added to complete the model equations). Others enclose all added variables in a circle, including the error terms. It is then common to refer to the given variables as *manifest*, expressing an intuitive notion that they are in some sense "observable," and all added variables as *latent*, expressing the notion that they are in some sense "unobservable." We refer to each representation of a variable in the path diagram as a *vertex* (adopting desirable terminology from graph theory[4] that is not yet in wide use in path analysis). Two vertices may be connected (a) by a *directed path*, represented by a single-headed arrow, or (b) by a *nondirected path*, represented by a line with an arrowhead at both ends. It has been a common although redundant convention to use a straight line for a directed path and a curve for a nondirected path. Although not necessary, this can aid in distinguishing them.

In the terminology of graph theory, the word *arc* is used for a single path connecting two vertices, and a *directed path* is a sequence of unidirectional arcs—connected arcs all pointing the same way, as in

$$Y_1 \rightarrow Y_2 \rightarrow Y_3 \rightarrow Y_4.$$

Conventional path analysis/SEM does not currently possess words for the useful distinction between an arc and a path, so where necessary I use the phrase *chain of unidirectional paths* to maintain the distinction.

We define a correspondence between a set of structural equations and a path diagram. For directed paths there is a single accepted rule, namely: If there is a term β_{jk} in the equation for Y_j, then there is a directed path from the Y_k vertex to the Y_j vertex. See the directed paths in models (17.1) and (17.2) as represented by Figs. 17.1 and 17.2. Note the paths with unit coefficients connecting variables with their error terms. This corresponds to terms in the equations of type $+(1)E$.

Some further definitions can now be introduced. An *exogenous variable*—also known as a *root variable*—has no directed path ending on it. It is, we could say, purely causal, taken for granted as a source of the system of

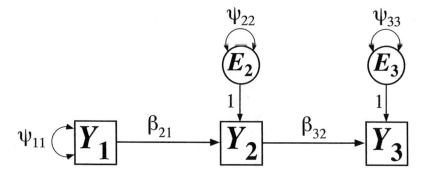

FIG. 17.1. Simple chain model.

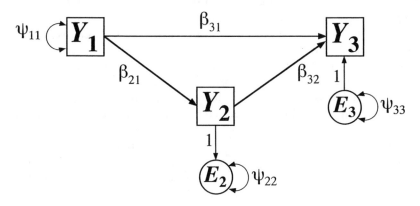

FIG. 17.2. Simple recursive model.

relations. It is thought of as outside (*exo*) the kind of (*genus*) variables in the system, and its own causal origins remain unexplained. In the diagrams so far, Y_1 is the *exogenous variable*. An *endogenous variable* has at least one directed path ending on it—for example, variables Y_2 and Y_3 in the figures so far.

The second rule of correspondence, for nondirected paths, takes a number of variant forms. I adopt two conventions. First, we can have a nondirected path between vertices representing two error terms, between two exogenous variables, or between an exogenous variable and an error term associated with an endogenous variable. These represent covariance between the given variables that is not explained by the directed paths. (Generally, the covariance of two exogenous variables, which is not explained within the system of variables—given or added—is assumed nonzero. Other nondirected paths are included or omitted by specific assumption.) Second, we draw closed loops beginning and ending on each exogenous variable, and on each error term, to represent its variance. This is a less common convention than the first, but it provides a complete correspondence between the parameters in the model—those to be estimated plus the fixed unit coefficients of the error terms—and the paths drawn in the diagram. Partly because of the second convention adopted, I enclose all additional vertices, including those for error terms, in circles, as it is awkward to attach a closed nondirected path to an unenclosed vertex.[5]

A further distinction is needed. A path model is *recursive* if no chain of unidirectional paths forms a closed loop. A closed loop would imply some form of mutual or reciprocal determination of variables by each other. It is *nonrecursive* if there is at least one closed loop. The term *recursive* derives from *cursum,* the past participle of the verb *currere* (to run), and *re* (back). The notion is that in a recursive model all the paths run back to their source in the exogenous variables. This usage may seem counterintuitive. In the terminology of graph theory, a recursive model has a *directed acyclic graph,* where *acyclic* means no cycles, that is, no loops. Figure 17.3 schematically illustrates recursive versus nonrecursive path diagrams (omitting nondirected paths). Some writers include an assumption about covariances of error terms in the definition of recursive models. This does violence to the origin and intention of the distinction, and is not adopted here.

The concept of mutual or reciprocal causation presents some deep problems in philosophy of science. It is very difficult to conceive a sense in which two variables simultaneously determine each other's values. A closed loop can represent either a system of dynamic processes that have come into equilibrium with each other at the time the measurements are taken, or a cross section of what should better have been observed as a recursive system changing over intervals of time.[6] Nonrecursive models are

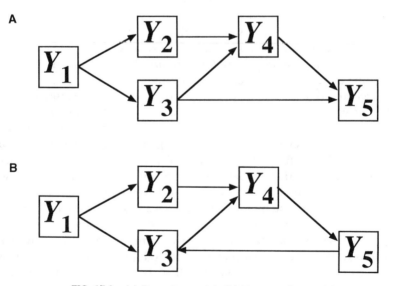

FIG. 17.3. (a) Recursive model. (b) Nonrecursive model.

too technical to be discussed in this brief introduction, and are not considered further here. The student is warned that it is easy to draw a diagram containing closed loops, but much care and understanding is needed over the assumptions appropriate to such a model, and even more over the real meaning of it.

PATH ANALYSIS WITHOUT COMMON FACTORS

We have p given variables, $Y_1, \ldots, Y_p$, of which at least one must be exogenous. In the simplest possible model for path analysis, the *reticular action model* (RAM)[7] (reticular = network), we do not distinguish by notation between exogenous and endogenous variables, but because an exogenous variable has no preceding, determining variables, we include it in the system of equations by regarding it as consisting purely of its error term. In the model in Fig. 17.4 there are two exogenous variables, Y_1 and Y_2, and we write the equations of the model as

$$Y_1 = E_1$$
$$Y_2 = E_2$$
$$Y_3 = \beta_{31} Y_1 + E_3$$
$$Y_4 = \beta_{42} Y_2 + E_4$$

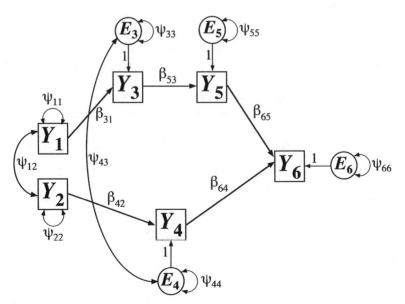

FIG. 17.4. Model with two exogenous variables.

$$Y_5 = \beta_{53}Y_3 + E_5$$
$$Y_6 = \beta_{65}Y_5 + \beta_{64}Y_4 + E_6. \qquad (17.3)$$

The status of Y_1 and Y_2 as exogenous is sufficiently expressed in the lack of causal variables in their equations. We write

$$Cov\{E_j, E_k\} = \psi_{jk}$$

for the covariance of two error terms, including the covariance of an error term with an exogenous variable, the covariance of two exogenous variables, and the corresponding variances when $j = k$. The parameters of the model are (a) the specified path coefficients, (b) the error-term variances, and (c) any specified covariances. We have yet to consider what assumptions we make about error covariances. It is assumed in this example that the exogenous variables and (arbitrarily) the error terms of Y_3 and Y_4 are correlated. I recommend that the vertices in a path diagram should be ordered, left–right or top-down, as close as possible to the causal order of the variables, for clarity of interpretation. Clarity takes priority over aesthetic considerations. Path diagrams with effects radiating out in various directions are easily misunderstood. An example is given below.

In addition to the representation of a SEM/path model by a diagram, as in Fig. 17.4, or equations, as in (17.3), we can present the parameters of the model in two matrices. Consider the matrices **B** and **Ψ** in Table 17.1. The element entered as β_{jk}—in row j and column k—in the matrix **B** is understood to represent a directed path coefficient from the column variable to the row variable. In the matrix **Ψ** the element $\psi_{jk} = \psi_{kj}$ is the covariance of the error terms of Y_j and Y_k. Some structural equation models use three or more matrices to represent a path model. This is unnecessary.[8]

Much as in the closely parallel case of the factor model, it is possible to express the $p(p-1)/2$ covariances of the observed variables, and their p variances, as functions of the path coefficients and the error-term variances and covariances. Without using more advanced methods (matrix

TABLE 17.1
SEM Parameter Matrices

		B						Ψ			
0	0	0	0	0	0	Ψ_{11}	Ψ_{12}	0	0	0	0
0	0	0	0	0	0	Ψ_{21}	Ψ_{22}	0	0	0	0
β_{31}	0	0	0	0	0	0	0	Ψ_{33}	Ψ_{34}	0	0
0	β_{42}	0	0	0	0	0	0	Ψ_{43}	Ψ_{44}	0	0
0	0	β_{53}	0	0	0	0	0	0	0	Ψ_{55}	0
0	0	0	β_{64}	β_{65}	0	0	0	0	0	0	Ψ_{66}

algebra) I cannot set out these equations in general form. As a simple demonstration, the case of the three-variable recursive model (17.2) gives the expressions

$$\sigma_{11} = \psi_{11}$$
$$\sigma_{22} = \beta_{21}{}^2\psi_{11} + \psi_{22}$$
$$\sigma_{33} = \beta_{32}{}^2\beta_{21}{}^2\psi_{11} + \beta_{32}{}^2\psi_{22} + \beta_{31}{}^2\psi_{11} + \psi_{33}$$
$$\sigma_{21} = \beta_{21}\psi_{11}$$
$$\sigma_{31} = \beta_{32}\beta_{21}\psi_{11} + \beta_{31}\psi_{11}$$
$$\sigma_{32} = (\beta_{32}\beta_{21}{}^2 + \beta_{31})\psi_{11} + \beta_{32}\psi_{22}. \tag{17.4}$$

And this is just a simple case. However, the user of path analysis never needs to obtain and evaluate such expressions. It is enough to know that simple programmable matrix expressions exist for these, and under certain assumptions the parameters are identified—unique quantities to be estimated. From a sample covariance matrix a computer program can find ULS, ML, or GLS estimates of the parameters, indexes of goodness of fit, and large-sample standard errors, as in Chapter 9. For this purpose, depending on the available computer program, the user supplies either the equations, as in (17.3), or the path diagram, as in Fig. 17.4, or, as in the COSAN program used in this book, the two matrices **B** and **Ψ** as in Table 17.1, containing the parameters to be estimated, and fixed zeros.

As has been remarked already, it is now very easy to draw a path diagram representing a "theory" of causal influences operating through a set of variables, obtaining and effortlessly confirming a causal account of non-experimental data. It has been noted, early in this chapter, that causal inferences generally represent conjectures as to what would happen if certain variables were brought under control, or at least imagined to take other values. Care is always needed in the interpretation of a path model. This requires a clear conceptualization of just what it would mean to achieve controlled, counterfactual values. In thought, we can set aside ethical barriers and some practical barriers, but must pause over the conceivability of the kind of counterfactual state of the system that is being considered. This is particularly important when the imagined control is applied to one measurable state of the individual, to yield a consequent change in another measurable state. In the example at the beginning of this section, we can imagine that an environmental intervention might improve the individual's health status with a consequent improvement in constructive thinking and subjective well-being. Perhaps we can also imagine an intervention in the form of psychotherapy, or merely an educational program that improves constructive thinking without changing health status, with a consequent change in subjective well-being. (I think of Dr.

Pangloss, in Voltaire's satire, "proving" to Candide that all is for the best in the best of all possible worlds.) It is, however, very easy to put counter-proposals such as (a) that constructive thinking and subjective well-being are correlated effects of the common cause, physical health, (b) that constructive thinking is part of the subjective well-being behavior domain, and so forth. Thus an important task in any application is to ask whether alternative models can be distinguished from each other by fitting them to data.

Indeed, there are two major problems—one might say, weaknesses—pertaining to path analysis, that have perhaps not received as much attention in the literature as they deserve. These are the problem of equivalent models and the problem of assumptions about error-term covariances.

The problem of equivalent models can be outlined as follows: For any proposed model, expressed as a system of directed paths and (implicitly at least) nondirected paths, there are virtually always one or more distinct models that are equivalent to it in the sense that they give precisely equal fit and are indistinguishable from it by any statistical analysis. Thus, under the usual assumptions, the chain model $Y_1 \rightarrow Y_2 \rightarrow Y_3$ cannot be distinguished from the reverse model $Y_3 \rightarrow Y_2 \rightarrow Y_1$. In our example, no data analysis can distinguish the hypothesis that health affects constructive thinking, which then affects subjective well-being, from the reversed causal sequence. Only a substantive consideration suggests a choice between these models, namely, that if health is not psychogenically determined, and is objectively recorded, it does not seem plausible that it could be an effect of well-being. No fully general rule has been found for writing down all the path models that cannot be distinguished from a given model. The most general rule given to the time of writing is too complex in application to be appropriate for brief discussion here.[9] The user should at least fit the theoretically competitive models and watch out for those that give exactly the same chi-square and discrepancy matrix. It is then virtually certain that these are equivalent models, and only substantive considerations, with luck, can enable a choice between them.

We turn now to the second major problem of path analysis, the set of assumptions to be made about the error-term covariances. First we need to recognize a basic difference between the regression of a dependent variable on one or more independent variables and an equation representing a causal dependency. Following a common convention, we use the same notation as previously for a regression equation to represent the notion that controlled variables on the right hand side of the equation produce changes in the variable on the left, writing, say,

$$Y = \beta_1 X_1 + \cdots + \beta_p X_p + E.$$

Here, the *error term E* is thought of as containing, possibly, an *error of measurement*, in the sense used throughout this book, and also, generally, an *error in the equation*, due to failure to measure and include in it all causal variables that would, if known and controlled, jointly determine the true value of *Y*. Until further notice we ignore errors of measurement. A commonly accepted alternative name for error terms is *disturbances*, indicating that they represent a disturbance of the value of the effect variable from what it would have been if the unknown causes could be held constant. The fundamental difference between a regression equation and a *structural equation* is this: In a regression equation, by definition, the regression residual—the error term—is uncorrelated with the independent variables. In a structural equation, it cannot be known that the error term, a disturbance—the effect of unknown omitted variables—is uncorrelated with causal variables in the equation. As we show later, very stringent assumptions are necessary if we are to obtain path equations containing identified, estimable parameters.

There does not seem to be any comprehensive discussion in the literature, whether in textbooks or specialized articles, about the assumptions an investigator "should" make about nondirected paths, and the basis of these in mathematical, scientific, or philosophical analysis of causal models. A set of inconsistent habits appears to have grown up, without comprehensive and critical review. The following treatment must be brief, and therefore superficial.[10]

If we assume (until the next section) that all variables are measured with negligible error, then the error terms—errors in variables—are generally supposed to be the composite effects of omitted variables. They are sometimes referred to as *disturbances*, randomly altering endogenous variables from the values determined by the variables in the system. It is commonly assumed that if the given *p* variables were to be embedded in what would almost certainly be a very much larger set of variables, forming an augmented system, each endogenous variable in the given system would be completely determined by the given variables and the many more. There is already a fairy-tale quality about this assumption, if it includes the belief that determinacy of the endogenous variables can be attained while the original exogenous variables remain exogenous. This would require a rather curious form of cooperation of the unknown with the known, such that any added variable that is a cause of one or more endogenous variables cannot also be a cause of an exogenous variable. Yet this assumption is one general element in the somewhat casual basis for treatments of error terms as effects of omitted variables.

In recursive models, the most commonly employed assumption is that the error-term covariances are all zero, except for the covariances between the exogenous variables, which, of course, are not accounted for by the model. Exceptions to this rule are sometimes permitted. A nondirected path between two variables might represent the action of a specified variable that theory requires to be included in the model, but that happens to be unavailable. For example, the theory of the example relating health to constructive thinking to subjective well-being might include a common cause of CT and SWB in the form of, say, socioeconomic status, but a measure of it could not be obtained. A nondirected path between Y_2 and Y_3 in the chain model shown later in Fig. 17.6, that is, an estimated covariance ψ_{32}, then acts as a "placekeeper" for the action of the specified but unmeasured variable. And note that in such a case, if the nondirected path is omitted, the model is misspecified and its parameters are incorrectly estimated. I label this common assumption the *uncorrelated-error-terms assumption*, and its permitted exception, *specified placekeepers*. The uncorrelated-errors assumption is a strong sufficient condition that all parameters in a recursive model are identified. Some specified placekeepers yield identifiability, whereas others do not. The uncorrelated-errors assumption implies a very strong form of cooperation of the unknown with the known. It requires that all omitted variables are neatly grouped into subsets, each belonging to just one endogenous variable, ready to explain further variance, but, unlike the variables we already have, augmenting variables are not capable of being common causes of two or more variables. For example, given the directed paths of Fig. 17.5, there must be omitted variables accounting for further variance of Y_2 and Y_3, but there cannot be an omitted variable accounting for the covariance of Y_2 with Y_3, so on this

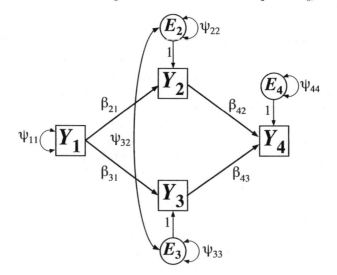

FIG. 17.5. Double chain model.

assumption we would delete the nondirected path between them. The known Y_1 is then supposed their only possible common cause. In applications, this may be an extremely strong assumption.

An alternative assumption has been motivated by the consideration that exogenous variables have their values determined, in some sense prior to the values of the endogenous variables, by causes outside the system, and hence, it is claimed, they should not be correlated with the error-terms of the endogenous variables. We call this the *exogenous variables assumption*. In some accounts this is given as the assumption that must be made so that path coefficients will be correctly estimated. It is, however, neither a necessary nor a sufficient condition for the correct estimation of path coefficients, and again it requires cooperative behavior on the part of the unknown, omitted variables. (In some cases, but not in general, the exogenous variables assumption is used in nonrecursive models.)

A further assumption to be found in the literature has a similar motivation to the exogenous variables assumption. The *precedence assumption* is the supposition that if there is a chain of unidirectional paths from Y_k to Y_j—that is, Y_k causally precedes Y_j—the value of Y_k is determined before that of Y_j, so Y_k should be uncorrelated with E_j. It can be shown algebraically that this is the same as assuming that if Y_k causally precedes Y_j, E_k and E_j are uncorrelated. On this assumption we may have the nondirected path in Fig. 17.5, because Y_2 does not precede Y_3 or conversely. The precedence assumption is a sufficient condition that all parameters in a recursive model are identified.

So far it has been insisted that structural equations are not in general regression equations. Because each equation purports to represent conjectural changes in the variable on the left with controlled changes in variables on the right, and the error term is a composite effect of omitted variables, there is no mathematical reason why the error term should behave like a regression residual. The *regression assumption* is the assumption that each error term in a structural equation model does indeed behave like a regression residual, although it is not one. The regression assumption is a sufficient condition that all parameters are identified, but without further assumptions it does not yield a restrictive model. Its important consequence is that those omitted variables whose effects are contained in the error term will not alter the estimates of the path coefficients when they are added to make an augmented system.

The regression assumption is not generally made explicit as such, in modern work. (In early work it gave the only technology—fitting each equation as a regression.) In recursive models, the uncorrelated-errors assumption implies the precedence assumption and in turn the precedence assumption implies the regression assumption. Accordingly, under any of these three assumptions the model is identified, and the path coefficients will be unaltered in an augmented system that is *well behaved*, in the sense that the added variables happen to satisfy the regression assumption. (In nonrecursive models, mathematical contradictions arise between the regression assumption and the other two, and the belief seems widely held that the contradiction is avoided rather than resolved by adopting the exogenous variables assumption instead. The basis of this belief is unclear.)

A path model is, quite generally, a composite hypothesis consisting of (a) omitted directed paths, expressing a hypothesis that causal influence is restricted to mediation through specified pathways, and (b) omitted nondirected paths, expressing a conjecture as to the nonexistence of further common causes. The omission of enough paths of both types yields a restrictive hypothesis that can be fitted to a sample covariance matrix and tested for goodness of fit. The omission of directed paths expresses a substantively based causal hypothesis. The omission of nondirected paths expresses a hope that we have not left out anything that will substantially alter the estimates of the directed path coefficients. In the nondirected path specification, the uncorrelated errors assumption is a very restrictive model nested within the precedence assumption, which in turn is nested within the regression assumption. A model for the directed paths may give a very poor fit with uncorrelated error terms, an improved fit with correlated errors for unordered variables (the precedence assumption), and a further improvement under the regression assumption. Although both the uncorrelated errors assumption and the precedence assumption imply no nondirected paths between ordered variables, placekeepers for specified unmeasured variables can be added between ordered or unordered variables, and will yield identified models in some cases but not others. For example, in Fig. 17.6 the chain model (17.1) is identified in cases a–c, but not in case d.[11]

As in the case of the common factor model, except in rather unusual circumstances where we wish to equate two or more coefficients, it is generally reasonable to fit a path model to a sample correlation matrix, although again it is necessary to use rather technical methods to obtain correct standard errors.[12] If we fit the model to a correlation matrix, each path coefficient represents the change in SD units in Y_j that would result from one SD increase in Y_k, so we say that the path coefficients are standardized.

A correlation matrix taken from a study by Feist et al.[13] illustrates a number of the general principles and problems associated with SEM, and serves as a good example of its general use. It is easy to adapt the published information to give path analyses without latent variables/common factors—this section—and with them—next section. For the purpose of this exposition, a certain amount of empirical detail is needed. We wish to consider two alternative models linking the following five attributes:

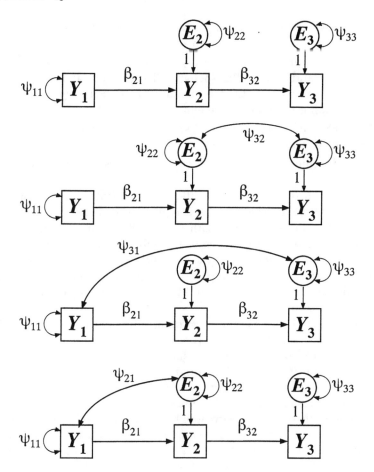

FIG. 17.6. Chain model with alternative assumptions.

SWB: subjective well-being.
WA: world assumptions.
CT: constructive thinking.
PH: subjective physical health symptoms.
DH: daily "hassles."

Each of these is measured by two or three subscales, all with Likert items.

SWB: PIL (purpose in life) = extent to which one possesses goals and
      direction; EM (environmental mastery) = extent to which one
      uses opportunities matching one's goals and talents; SA (self-ac-
      ceptance) = extent of satisfaction with self.

WA: BWP (benevolence of world and people); SW (self as worthy) = extent of satisfaction with self.

CT: GCT (global constructive thinking) = optimism/acceptance of self and others; BC (behavioral coping) = ability to focus on effective action; EC (emotional coping) = ability to avoid self-defeating thoughts and feelings.

PH: FS (frequency of symptoms); MS (muscular symptoms); GS (gastrointestinal symptoms).

DH: TP (time pressures); MW (money worries); IC (inner concerns).

It is hoped that these labels are sufficiently descriptive for our purpose.

These multiple indicators of the five primary attributes can be used—as in the next section—to give a path model relating five common factors, or summed to give composite measures. Table 17.2 reproduces correlations among these 14 variables (sample size 149). The SWB measures are obtained 1 month after the rest, as part of a longitudinal study, but because the SWB scale has a retest reliability of .92, we treat the data as cross-sectional for expository purposes.

By the methods of Chapter 3, we obtain the correlation matrix of five composite scores in Table 17.3. (Because we are summing correlations, this matrix corresponds to sums of standard scores, not raw scores, from the components. Generally this would affect results very little.)

We consider two opposed path models for the five attributes, following the original investigation, but with minor changes. Figure 17.7(a) expresses a "bottom-up" theory of subjective well-being, that health problems and daily hassles (negatively) affect world assumptions and constructive thinking, and these in turn jointly determine SWB. Figure 17.7(b) expresses a "top-down" theory of SWB, treating it as a trait that determines WA and CT, and these in turn determine what the individual regards as, and so reports as, health problems and hassles, or, possibly, psychogenically causes actual health problems and conflicts/frustrations. Clearly, these are substantively very different accounts of subjective well-being. Yet it turns out that the two models are mathematically equivalent. Both yield $\chi^2_{(2)} = 10.6108$, noncentrality $d = .0579$, and $m_c = .972$, a satisfactory fit. The fitted parameters and their standard errors are given in Table 17.4 and are also shown on the path diagrams in Fig. 17.7. Both of these methods of presenting results, with coefficients on the path diagram, or in tables, are acceptable. It is not common to present the equations. Table 17.5 gives the discrepancy matrix, the same for both models—further evidence of equivalence.

We notice that only two discrepancies are nonzero—the one for the covariance between SWB and PH, and the one between SWB and DH. This corresponds to the fact that the two actual restrictions in both these models consist of the omission of directed paths between these variables. (Discrep-

TABLE 17.2
SWB—Correlation Matrix of Measures

	FS	GI	MS	TP	MW	IC	BWP	SW	GCT	BC	EC	PIL	EM	SA
FS	1.00	.59	.50	.32	.24	.29	-.32	-.36	-.31	-.27	-.24	-.19	-.22	-.12
GI	.59	1.00	.34	.23	.14	.18	-.17	-.21	-.22	-.13	-.26	-.12	-.10	-.01
MS	.50	.34	1.00	.26	.29	.24	-.27	-.33	-.26	-.24	-.26	-.29	-.20	-.17
TP	.32	.23	.26	1.00	.52	.50	-.11	-.14	-.27	-.24	-.25	-.20	-.35	-.18
MW	.24	.14	.29	.52	1.00	.52	-.25	-.21	-.33	-.20	-.28	-.26	-.38	-.30
IC	.29	.18	.24	.50	.52	1.00	-.24	-.27	-.50	-.42	-.43	-.30	-.38	-.41
BWP	-.32	-.17	-.27	-.11	-.25	-.24	1.00	.50	.38	.37	.36	.48	.35	.48
SW	-.36	-.21	-.33	-.14	-.21	-.27	.50	1.00	.53	.56	.50	.56	.50	.62
GCT	-.31	-.22	-.26	-.27	-.33	-.50	.38	.53	1.00	.82	.90	.64	.61	.69
BC	-.27	-.13	-.24	-.24	-.20	-.42	.37	.56	.82	1.00	.73	.68	.62	.68
EC	-.24	-.26	-.26	-.25	-.28	-.43	.36	.50	.90	.73	1.00	.55	.50	.65
PIL	-.19	-.12	-.29	-.20	-.26	-.30	.48	.56	.64	.68	.55	1.00	.73	.81
EM	-.22	-.10	-.20	-.35	-.38	-.38	.35	.50	.61	.62	.50	.73	1.00	.73
SA	-.10	-.01	-.17	-.18	-.30	-.41	.48	.62	.69	.68	.65	.81	.73	1.00

TABLE 17.3
SWB—Correlation Matrix of Composites

	PH	DH	WA	CT	SWB
PH	1.00	.37	−.40	−.32	−.21
DH	.37	1.00	−.29	−.42	−.41
WA	−.40	−.29	1.00	.55	.63
CT	−.32	−.42	.55	1.00	.73
SWB	−.21	−.41	.63	.73	1.00

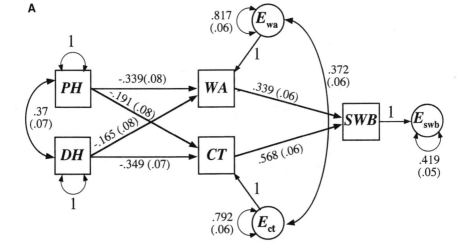

FIG. 17.7. (a) Bottom-up model. (b) Top-down model.

TABLE 17.4
Fitted Parameters—SWB Composites

	PH	DH	WA	CT	SWB
(a) Bottom-Up Model					
Matrix **B**					
PH					
DH					
WA	−.339(.08)	−.165(.08)			
CT	−.191(.08)	−.349(.07)			
SWB				.339(.06)	.568(.06)
Matrix **Ψ**					
PH	1.00	.37			
DH	.37(.07)	1.00			
WA			.817(.06)	.372	
CT			.372(.06)	.792(.06)	
SWB					.419(.05)
(b) Top-Down Model					
Matrix **B**					
PH			−.328(.09)		−.147(.09)
DH			−.086(.09)		−.379(.08)
WA					.630(.05)
CT					.730(.04)
SWB					
Matrix **Ψ**					
PH	.862(.05)	.225			
DH	.225(.07)	.843(.05)			
WA			.603(.06)	.090	
CT			.090(.04)	.467(.06)	
SWB					1.000

TABLE 17.5
Discrepancy Matrix—SWB Composites

	PH	DH	WA	CT	SWB
PH	0	0	0	0	.097
DH	0	0	0	0	−.084
WA	0	0	0	0	0
CT	0	0	0	0	0
SWB	.097	−.084	0	0	0

ancies do not always align in this way to omitted paths, but quite commonly will be observed to do so.) Note that generally, indexes of fit are not informative in path analysis, because large parts of the model can be unrestrictive, with only a few discrepancies capable of being nonzero. Here we are testing only for the absence of a direct effect—one direction or the other—between SWB and PH and between SWB and DH. The rest of the model is unrestrictive. In current practice—at the time of writing—researchers appear to rely too much on goodness-of-fit indexes, when the actual discrepancies are much more informative. It is here recommended that these—at least a summary of the nonzero ones—should be part of any published report.

Note that the equivalence of the bottom-up and top-down models of SWB does not, as might be supposed, imply that SWB and PH/DH mutually cause each other, in an alternative nonrecursive model with both sets of paths. Given the equivalence, we are forced back on thought experiments, which are, in any case, necessary before a path analysis, as the basis for formulating it, and in many cases are unavoidable after the analysis, when the investigator is faced with a choice between substantively distinct but algebraically equivalent alternative models.

What we need to do is to consider how, in principle, an intervention could be designed—medical treatments, psychotherapy, educational programs—to alter the level of one of the attributes while holding others constant, experimentally obtaining direct effects, or altering the level of one and allowing others to change as a consequence, to get indirect effects. I leave this exercise to the reader. But again I emphasize, as the central problem and most exciting challenge of structural equation modeling, that it requires and invites thought experiments concerning counterfactual conjectures, based on a rich theoretical framework for the observations. The fact that SWB in these data is measured 1 month after the other variables might seem to establish that it cannot be a cause, but because it appears to be a very stable trait (retest reliability .92), we cannot rule out the possibility that SWB 1 month later is a good substitute for a measure of SWB obtained before or at the same time as the other measures.

Another problem illustrated by this data set concerns the externality of definition of the attributes. We notice that SWB, WA, and CT all contain one indicator that can be labeled "self-acceptance." In principle, therefore, the (therapeutic) manipulation of self-acceptance in one of these composite variables would imply manipulation of that component in the others. Thus they lack the independence in definition/measurement that is necessary if we are to treat them as having cause–effect relations.

Finally, note that the two equivalent models of Fig. 17.7 comply with the precedence assumption, because WA and CT are not causally ordered and their error terms are allowed to be correlated, corresponding to some omitted common cause. (I might justify this nondirected path substantively, by noting that world assumptions and constructive thinking are two abstractive concepts that appear to have considerable semantic overlap, and so can easily be imagined to have a specific cognitive common cause beyond those allowed in the top-down and bottom-up models.) In the bottom-up model, the correlation between their error terms is $.372/\sqrt{.817 \times .792}$ = .462. In the top-down model it is .170. If these error terms are required to be uncorrelated, the bottom-up model gives $\chi^2_{(3)}$ = 46.313 and the top-down model gives $\chi^2_{(3)}$ = 14.938, no longer equivalent models. The original model of Feist et al. includes paths between SWB and PH, and between SWB and DH, and has neither a directed nor a nondirected path between WA and CT. The absence of a (directed or nondirected) path between WA and CT is the only restriction tested in their model. (In their top-down model they do include a nondirected path between PH and DH, as the precedence rule would require, but not between WA and CT. No reasons are given for these two choices. Their practice in this matter is not unrepresentative of the literature and possibly reflects the prevailing inattention in SEM applications to the problem of nondirected paths.) Using their model gives $\chi^2_{(1)}$ = 35.702 for the bottom-up model, and $\chi^2_{(1)}$ = 4.3276 for the top-down model, also not equivalent, and the parameters shown in Fig. 17.8.

As a second example, closer to the specific motive of applying a structural equation model in a validity study, we consider a data set already briefly discussed in Chapter 10. Hull et al. (1991) discussed the problem of relating a *multifaceted construct*—an attribute whose item domain consists of two or more recognized subdomains—to an outcome or causal variable. This can be regarded as a problem in concurrent validity or predictive utility, depending on whether the concern is with the nature of the item domain or the effectiveness of prediction.

As mentioned already in Chapter 10, Hull et al. obtained self-report measures from 138 respondents of (a) self-criticism (SC), (b) (tendency to) high standards (HS), (c) overgeneralization of failure (OGF), (d) and depression (D). In previous work, Carver and Ganellan (1983) had treated SC, HS, and OGF as subdomains of a concept called self-punitive attitude (SPA). The reader can accept the natural-language meaning of these terms or consult the original. On the face of it, there is a range of possible ambiguity about the connections between these test scores and the (sub)domains they represent, which might seem to bear on the question of what they measure. At least the following possibilities suggest themselves: (a) SPA (psychogenically?) causes D; (b) D (constitutionally?) causes SPA; or (c) HS, SC, OGF, and D are four subdomains of a single attribute—that is, D is a fourth indicator of the factor defined by the other three—depression more widely conceived, perhaps.[14] The correlation matrix is given in Table 17.6.

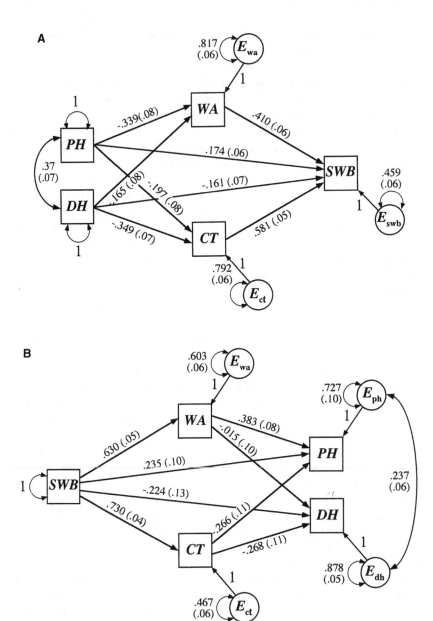

FIG. 17.8. Further models for subjective well-being: (a) Bottom-up. (b) Top-down.

TABLE 17.6
Depression Example—Correlation Matrix

	D	OGF	SC	HS
D	1	.551	.184	.034
OGF	.551	1	.388	.252
SC	.184	.388	1	.579
Hs	.034	.252	.579	1

The path diagrams for models (a), (b), and (c) and parameters fitted by maximum likelihood (using COSAN), are given in Figs. 17.9 in parts (a), (b), and (c), respectively. All three parts of the figure give a chi-square on 2 df of 45.756, m_c = .853, and RMSEA = .398. They are equivalent models, and cannot be distinguished on the basis of any data. In fact, model (c) is not merely equivalent to model (a), it is the same as model (a). An appearance of difference arises from the effect to perception of moving the path to D away from the paths for the other indicators in the path diagram of Fig. 17.9(a), and close to them in the diagram of Fig. 17.9(c). Thus, the models for the total test scores for these sets of items are unable to determine whether their items belong to subdomains of a single domain [model (c)] or belong to two domains, in cause-to-effect or in effect-to-cause relationship.

The fit of this set of equivalent models is poor, and following Hull et al. we note that there may be a special relationship between OGF and D over and above the relation of D to the common factor of OGF, SC, and HS. Accordingly, we fit as model (d) the Hull et al. model for these data, given in Fig. 17.9(d), in which D is an effect both of SPA and of the OGF indicator of SPA. We add, further, model (e)—Fig. 17.9(e)—in which SPA is the common factor of all four indicators, but there is a special correlational link between OGF and D, and model (f)—Fig. 17.9(f)—in which a second factor (negative affect?) accounts for that link. (The loadings on the second factor are equated to make an identified model.) Again, models (d), (e), and (f) are equivalent, giving a chi-square on 1 df of 2.130, m_c = .996, and RMSEA = .090.

On the face of it, these models imply quite different interpretations of the relationships between the attributes measured by the test scores, and in turn suggest quite different "meanings" for those attributes. To say that depression is an indicator of self-punitive attitude seems very different from saying it is a cause of it, and different again to say it is an effect. The one unambiguous conclusion might seem to be that there is a special link of some kind between D and OGF over and above its relation to the common factor of OGF, SC, and HS, but this observation does not seem to contribute to our understanding of what is measured. It is hard to say how far we may generalize from this case.

A

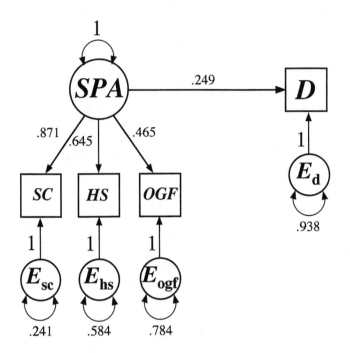

B

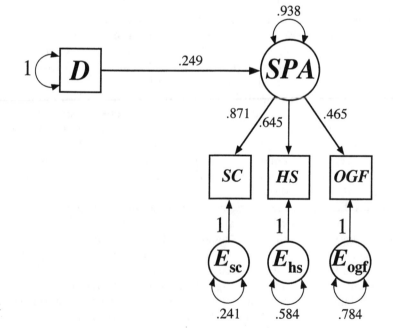

FIG. 17.9. *(Continued)*

C

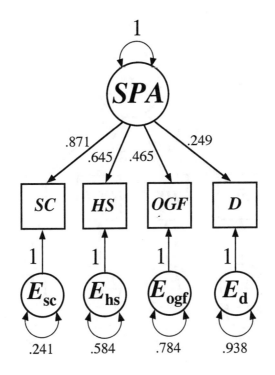

D

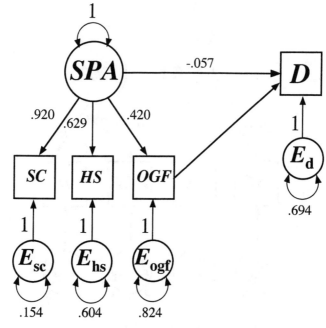

FIG. 17.9. *(Continued)*

E

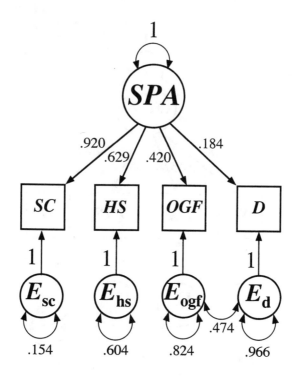

F

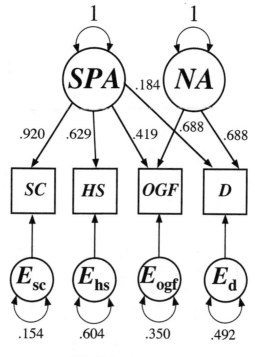

FIG. 17.9. *(Continued)*

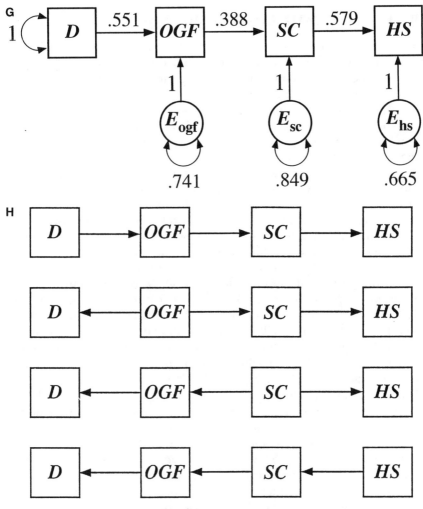

FIG. 17.9. *(Continued)*

Inspection of the correlations in Table 17.6 suggests that a further path model for the four measures is also conceptually plausible. A simple causal chain, with D determining OGF, OGF determining SC, and SC determining HS, is modeled in Fig. 17.9(g). (A well-known aphorism, "if you torture a data set long enough it will confess to anything," is here ignored, for expository purposes.) This model overfits the data, giving a chi-square of 2.7037 on 3 *df*, $m_c = 1.001$. (RMSEA cannot be computed.) Alternative, equivalent models whose directed paths are given in Fig. 17.9(h) allow alternative interpretations of varying plausibility, and it is only the degree of theoretical plausibility that provides for any choice between them, because they cannot be distinguished on the basis of observations.

PATH ANALYSIS WITH COMMON FACTORS

So far we have considered models for the given variables with just the addition of error terms to account for the covariance matrix of the given set. Now we consider embedding common factors, with multiple indicator variables, in the network of paths.[15]

I am taking the position, consistent with all of our usage so far, that the common factor of a set of items/variables/indicators is interpreted in applications as the common attribute of which each indicator is a specific measure, with its own unique, idiosyncratic property. With this view, common factors cannot be causes of their defining indicators, because a cause must be defined independently of its effects. Confusion on this point can arise in the absence of a clear concept of unobservable variables, with the substitution of the term *latent variable* for *common factor*, because the conceptual distinction between a common factor and a common cause is not expressed algebraically in the equations of the model, or in the directed paths of a model for path analysis with latent variables.

For the purpose of this introductory sketch, it is convenient to proceed by example, doing further work on the subjective well-being data. Table 17.2 contains the correlations between 14 variables—3 indicators of PH, 3 of DH, 2 of WA, 3 of CT, and 3 of SWB. Setting aside the question of a causal model linking the five attributes, we expect to find that the 14 variables fit an independent-clusters factor model, with the given grouping of the indicators. This gives $\chi^2_{(67)} = 138.081$. Table 17.7 gives the factor loadings and unique variances. The factor correlations are in Table 17.8.

If we could add enough further indicators from the behavior domain of each attribute, the correlations of the composites as in Table 17.3 and the correlations of the common factors as in Table 17.8 would be the same. In effect, the reliability, omega, of each composite would approach unity, and the sum score for each attribute would become a perfect measure of the factor attribute, that is, the true score. If we apply the bottom-up and top-down models in Fig. 17.7 to the factor correlations, we obtain the directed path coefficients in Table 17.9, to be compared with those in Table 17.4. Such disagreements as we see come from the imperfection of the measures obtained from using such a small number of indicators. This is not the regular procedure. It is done to show the similarities and differences between path analysis with and without latent variables.

From the factor loadings and unique variances, by (6.26b), we obtain coefficient omega for the five composite scores, namely: PH, .753; DH, .757; WA, .676; CT, .936; and SWB, .901. Correcting the correlations of the composites in Table 17.3 for attenuation by (7.26) gives the correlations of the true scores in Table 17.10. The correspondence between the results in Table 17.10 and Table 17.8 is close though imperfect. One possible way to perform a path analysis is just this two-step procedure, fitting an inde-

TABLE 17.7
Factor Loadings and Unique Variances—SWB Measures

| | Loadings | | | | | Unique Variances |
	PH	DH	WA	CT	SWB	
FS	.896					.197
GI	.647					.582
MS	.566					.679
TP		.674				.546
MW		.692				.521
IC		.773				.403
BWP			.630			.604
SW			.794			.369
GCT				.990		.020
BC				.830		.312
EC				.907		.177
PIL					.867	.248
EM					.793	.371
SA					.938	.120

TABLE 17.8
Factor Correlations—SWB Measures

	PH	DH	WA	CT	SWB
PH	1.000	.450	−.527	−.357	−.186
DH	.450	1.000	−.399	−.537	−.478
WA	−.527	−.399	1.000	.664	.820
CT	−.357	−.537	.664	1.000	.754
SWB	−.186	−.478	.820	.754	1.000

TABLE 17.9
SEM Parameters—SWB Factors

	PH	DH	WA	CT	SWB
Matrix **B**, bottom-up model					
PH					
DH					
WA	−.436	−.203			
CT	−.145	−.472			
SWB			.607	.398	
Matrix **B**, top-down model					
PH			−.521	−.013	
DH			−.078	−.498	
WA					.820
CT					.754
SWB					

TABLE 17.10
SWB—True-Score Correlations of Composites

	PH	DH	WA	CT	SWB
PH	1.00	.490	−.561	−.381	−.255
DH	.490	1.000	−.405	−.499	−.496
WA	−.561	−.405	1.000	.691	.807
CT	−.381	−.499	.691	1.000	.795
SWB	−.255	−.496	.807	.795	1.000

pendent-clusters factor model, and obtaining either the directly estimated factor correlations or (through omega) the disattenuated correlation matrix of the factors/true scores by the attenuation formulae. In a second step, one would fit the path model to these correlations. An advantage of this procedure would be its clear separation of the path model from the common factor model.

However, the generally accepted procedure is to fit a single model, in one step, that contains both causal paths and common factor loadings, to the sample correlation matrix (possibly to the covariance matrix) of the indicator variables. In our example, the bottom-up and top-down models with common factors are represented respectively by the path diagrams in Fig. 17.10, parts (a) and (b). These, again, are equivalent models, giving $\chi^2_{(69)} = 159.57$, $d = .607$, and $m_c = .738$.

The graphic distinction between common factors and their indicator variables is the convention of representing a vertex as a square for an indicator and a circle for a common factor. The relation between a common factor and an indicator of it is diagramed as a directed path, the same as for a cause–effect relation between independently defined and (hypothetically) separately controllable variables. The RAM model for a case with latent variables is the same as for one without. The computer creates a fitted covariance/correlation matrix of all the variables, common factors and given variables together, then selects out the matrix containing just the fitted correlations of the given variables. Then the discrepancy matrix and fit indexes are calculated for these. In the example both the bottom-up and top-down models give the same discrepancy matrix, as given in Table 17.11.

A problem in path analysis with latent variables concerns the scale of measurement to be assigned to an endogenous latent variable. Standard procedures for fitting such models do not give correct standard errors, and sometimes they give parameters on a scale that is hard to interpret. Here, as before, the scale is arbitrary. For exogenous latent variables we can fix their variances to be unity. But the total variance of an endogenous latent variable is not a parameter in the model, and we do not wish to set its error-term variance—which is itself a parameter—equal to unity. This is just the variance remaining when some has been accounted for by the direct and indirect effects of preceding variables. We would like to give unit (total) variance to all common factors, especially in analyzing a correlation matrix, so that all factor loadings and path coefficients are standardized. A number of devices have been used in computer programs to solve this problem.[16] The older programs do not give correct standard errors. Special commands have been used here in COSAN to give a fully standardized analysis with correct large-sample standard errors. The two-step procedure illustrated earlier sidesteps the problem of standardizing the latent variables, by obtaining their correlation matrix in the first step from a factor analysis or a correction for attenuation, but again these analyses do not give correct standard errors.

It is generally good to perform both a confirmatory factor analysis and a path analysis as in our example. The path analysis gives a more restricted submodel nested within the factor analysis. The difference in chi-square tests the two separate parts of the model, the common factor specification and the path model specification. Here, the difference is $\chi^2_{(2)} = 21.49$, giving $d = .131$ and $m_c = .937$, for the path model. In one accepted terminology the common factor model is referred to as the *measurement model* and the causal path model as the *structural model.* (The entire model is also a "structural model," giving the structure of the covariance matrix.)

The failure of the RAM model to make a direct distinction between the factor and the path aspects of the full model carries the advantage that it easily handles cases with a mixture of manifest and latent variables in the path model. (Suppose, for example, we had only one measure of WA instead of two.) In the literature, this situation is sometimes redundantly and perhaps confusingly represented by the notion that a measured variable in the causal path model is a single indicator of an exactly corresponding latent variable that is not a common factor—with a unit path coefficient and zero error-term variance making up the redundancy. This can cause technical difficulties, and is otherwise unnecessary.

Finally, given (estimated) path coefficients and their standard errors (which should always be reported), we can evaluate these individually. We put, say, a 95% confidence interval on an estimated path coefficient, adding and subtracting 1.96 times its *SE.* If the confidence interval does not contain zero, the path coefficient is technically significant at the ubiquitous 5% level—for those who believe in tests of significance. For example, in the bottom-up model in Fig. 17.7(a), the 95% confidence interval for the smallest path coefficient, from PH to CT, is $-.191 \pm 1.96 \times .08$, that is, $-.191 \pm .157$, which is to say, between $-.348$ and $.034$. If the computer program employed does not give indirect/total effects as part of its out-

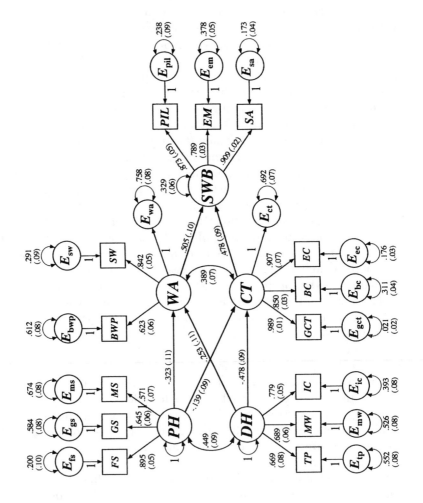

A

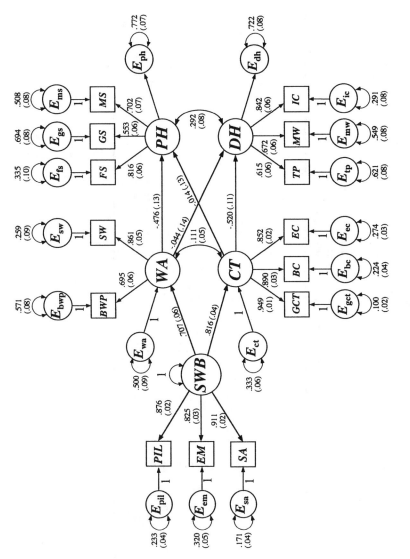

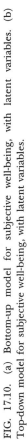

FIG. 17.10. (a) Bottom-up model for subjective well-being, with latent variables. (b) Top-down model for subjective well-being, with latent variables.

B

403

TABLE 17.11
Discrepancy Matrix—SWB Measures

0													
.013	0												
-.010	-.028	0											
.051	.036	.088	0										
-.037	-.059	.113	.059	0									
-.023	-.046	.040	-.021	-.017	0								
-.077	.005	-.115	.056	-.079	-.047	0							
-.031	.027	-.120	.084	.021	-.009	-.025	0						
.003	.006	-.060	.088	.038	-.083	-.015	-.003	0					
-.007	.059	-.072	.060	.109	-.070	.039	.112	-.001	0				
.047	-.053	-.077	.078	.058	-.048	-.002	.011	.002	-.023	0			
.101	.090	-.104	.057	.004	-.001	.058	-.010	-.002	.124	-.057	0		
.045	.091	-.031	-.116	-.139	-.108	-.034	-.019	.007	.114	-.053	.018	0	
.202	.208	.023	.086	-.026	-.100	.042	.028	.003	.103	.020	-.002	-.009	0

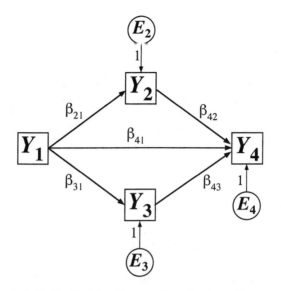

FIG. 17.11. Model to illustrate direct/indirect effects.

put—COSAN does not—generally we can obtain them by pocket calculator. The principle is that the effect of Y_k on Y_j through any particular chain of unidirectional paths is the product of the path coefficients in that chain. The total effect is the sum of these products over all distinct paths (parts of which may coincide). If there is a direct path from Y_k to Y_j and also other chains of unidirectional paths, we can, if desired, separate that direct effect from the indirect effects in the other paths. A careful thought experiment is needed for such a refined interpretation of nonexperimental data. We ask which direct, indirect, or total effects correspond to a conceivable manipulation or counterfactual state of the respondents.

In our example, from the bottom-up model, Fig. 17.7(a), the indirect effect of DH on SWB is $-.349 \times .568 = -.198$. An intervention to increase daily hassles by one SD is conjectured to reduce subjective well-being by .198 SDs. (A more kindly intervention, designed to reduce daily hassles, should give the corresponding increase in SWB.) This example does not illustrate the distinctions available. The model in Fig. 17.11 is more interesting in this respect. It gives $\beta_{41} + \beta_{42}\beta_{21} + \beta_{43}\beta_{31}$ as the total effect of Y_1 on Y_4, and $\beta_{42}\beta_{21} + \beta_{43}\beta_{31}$ for the indirect effect. Because any of these coefficients can be positive or negative, it is quite possible for the contributions of the separate pathways to augment or tend to cancel each other.

Perhaps enough has been said to direct the student to the possibilities and the problems of path analysis. It is to be hoped that further critical work on this technology will improve its potential and reduce the dangers of its simplistic misapplication.

REVIEW GUIDE

This is no more than an introduction to a large and rapidly developing technology. A careful study of the relationship between the path diagrams and the parameters and equations of the model is needed. The technical aspects can be left to a computer program, with the conceptions about fit carried over from the treatment of the factor model. Warnings about equivalent models and assumptions, especially with respect to nondirected paths, may help the student take a critical attitude toward a technique that has possibly been applied so far with more enthusiasm than care.

END NOTES

General: There is a fairly technical, fairly comprehensive account of this topic, using the rather complex LISREL model and notation, by Bollen (1989). McDonald (1985, Chapter 4) is a nontechnical supplement. James, Mulaik, and Brett (1982) gave a different perspective. Other texts on SEM tend not to examine critical questions about the assumptions and their consequences. The earliest developments of path analysis were by Sewell Wright. The application of modern methods of fitting is due to work by Keesling and Wiley, which was further developed by Jöreskog as the LISREL model, for which, again, see Bollen.

1. The reader is advised to observe carefully the terminology used by writers in this field, and to try to draw an explicit sense in which they conceptualize the asymmetric relations between variables that are the foundation of structural equation models. It would be invidious to review examples in the literature that offer possibly causal statements in a variety of noncausal terminologies. One reference the reader might wish to pursue for its account of "dependency relations" and cautious recognition of the possibility of a counterfactual account such as adopted here is Cox and Wermuth (1996).
2. James, Mulaik, and Brett (1982) treat the causal relationship as a functional relation, and use a nonmonotone, therefore noninvertible, function to illustrate an asymmetry in the terms of the function. It is not clear how they would carry the discussion to an invertible function.
3. See Pearl (1998).
4. The path diagrams of SEM have come into use rather casually and unsystematically. Graph theory is a systematic, rather more formal mode of representation of relationships, whose terminology could have been employed for SEM. I have ventured to introduce the term *vertex* from it. It would also be good to substitute *directed arc* for *directed path*, and then reserve the term *directed path* for a chain of unidirectional arcs, giving a simple, consistent terminology. The interested student will find a straightforward introduction to graph theory in Wasserman and Faust (1994).
5. This follows McArdle (1978).
6. For a further account, see McDonald (1997b). In part this is based on primary work by Strotz and Wold (1960), who were clear about systems in equilibrium, and problems in "reciprocal causation."
7. McArdle (1979) and McArdle and McDonald (1984).

8. See Bollen (1989). The earliest model in wide use for structural equation modeling, due to Keesling and Wiley—see Keesling (1972) and Wiley (1973)—and extensively developed by Jöreskog—see Jöreskog and Sörbom (1979)—contains eight parameter matrices, and can appear to impose unnecessary restrictions. A variant—EQS—on the RAM model developed by Bentler (1985) contains three. Currently available commercial software includes LISREL, EQS, and PROC CALIS (Hartmann, 1996), which simulates COSAN, EQS, and the RAM model.

9. For a relatively nontechnical account of the problem, with illustrations from the literature, see MacCallum, Wegener, Uchino, and Fabrigar (1993). A precise rule given by Verma and Pearl (1990) covers the class of all models without equated parameters.

10. See McDonald (1997b) for a relatively nontechnical account of the basis of this discussion of error, and necessary references.

11. An account of identifiability conditions is given by Pearl (1998).

12. McDonald, Parker, and Ishizuka (1993).

13. Feist et al. (1995). I am grateful to Gregory Feist both for his permission to use this example and for his generous tolerance of my choice to reinterpret it for expository purposes.

14. As noted already in Chapter 10, Hull et al. were well aware that there may be plausible alternative models for these data and indeed invited researchers to offer them.

15. The problem of the meaning of the manifest/latent or observable/unobservable distinction can be looked at in the following way. Formally, an *observable/manifest variable* is a random variable whose values can be obtained from sample measurements. A random variable is observable in principle if its values can be obtained from sample measurements given the parameters of the model. At least any given variable is observable in this sense. An *unobservable/latent variable* is one whose values cannot be so obtained. An *error term* is the complementary variable expressing uncertainty in the determination of one variable by others. The error terms are random variables that carry the distribution of the given variables when their source variables—the variables on which they directly depend—are fixed. In a model without common factors, given the parameters, we can in principle obtain the values of an error term from sampled measurements. Given the path coefficients and values $y_{1i}, \ldots, y_{pi}$, of the variables in the system, for individual i, we can obtain the corresponding error terms

$$e_{ji} = y_{ji} - \sum_k \beta_{jk} y_{ki}, \qquad (17.5)$$

where the summation is over the source variables of Y_j. On the face of it, this appears to limit latent (unobservable) variables to what we have previously called common factors or latent traits, although there may be unobservable variables not of this kind. But in a model with common factors/latent traits we cannot obtain the values of any latent trait (given less than an infinite number of observable variables from a behavior domain) from sample measurements, so I prefer not to speak of error terms as latent variables, which would tend to confuse them with common factors. We do not then regard error terms (in an equation containing no common factors) as unobservable. I have therefore compromised by avoiding the conventional, undefined distinction between manifest and latent variables.

16. Again, McDonald, Parker, and Ishizuka (1993).

Some Scaling Theory

Chapter 4 gives a brief sketch of notions about measurement, deliberately designed to allow the main developments of theory to go through, without too much conceptual trouble due to lack of foundations. The main points of that chapter are that (a) measurement is the assignment of numbers to quantifiable attributes according to a rule, (b) the rule can be arbitrary, allowing more than one assignment, and (c) distinct assignments can be nonlinearly related.

The word *scale* has generally been used in two ways in psychological measurement. It is sometimes used as a synonym for a test, as in "the Wechsler Adult Intelligence Scale." We acknowledge but avoid that usage here. The other sense of scale is contained in the description of *scaling* as the process of setting up the rule of correspondence between observations and the numbers assigned. The resulting *scale* is—implicitly at least—the established correspondence. Simple examples already are the Likert scale—assigning integers in correspondence to ordered categories—and the basic binary scoring scheme for dichotomous and multiple-choice items. A nice terminology for the scaling process distinguishes *observations* of an attribute from *data*—assigned numerical values. Scaling is then mapping observations into data. Generally, we have been content to accept that the scales we have considered have arbitrary origins and units, and merely ordinal properties.

Much research in psychometric theory, influenced by paradigms in physical measurement, has been directed at finding models and methods for scaling attributes of persons or perceived attributes of stimuli that possess desirable scale properties. Relatively few of these developments have become part of the practical technology of test construction and use, but it is desirable that the student should have a general awareness of them, and a sense of poooibilitiet to be followed up,

In this chapter we first give an introduction to some basic concepts related to properties of physical and psychological measurements. The next section outlines a useful classification of types of observation due to Coombs. The final section sketches a handful of the models and devices that have been recognized as some form of scaling process.

FUNDAMENTAL PROPERTIES OF MEASUREMENTS

We wish to study possible correspondences between observations of attributes of objects—persons or stimuli—and assignable numerical values—numbers from the number system. We recognize first that numbers have the following axiomatic characteristics.

For any numbers a, b, c, d:

(A1) Either $a = b$ or $a \neq b$.

(A2) If $a = b$ then $b = a$.

(A3) If $a = b$ and $b = c$ then $a = c$.

(A4) If $a > b$ then $a \leq b$.

(A5) If $a > b$ and $b > c$ then $a > c$.

(A6) $a + b = b + a$.

(A7) If $a = c$ and $b = d$ then $a + b = c + d$.

(A8) $(a + b) + c = a + (b + c)$.

(A9) $a + 0 = a$

(A10) If $a = c$ and $b > 0$ then $a + b > c$.

(A1)–(A3) concern identity relations between numbers. (A4) and (A5) concern order relations. (A6)–(A8) concern additivity. (A9) and (A10) introduce the number zero.

In constructing a scale for a quantifiable attribute—setting up a correspondence with numbers—we may or may not be able to set all these characteristics of numbers to match observable features of the attribute. We hope to find empirical properties of observations that are in correspondence with these.

We begin with some scaling paradigms in the context of physical measurement. The measurement of length seems the most obvious, natural, and inevitable of all scaling procedures because its properties and procedures are historically well established and learned early by users of existing scales. That makes it interesting. Our task is to make the familiar unfamiliar, in order to understand it more deeply. The following material is organized under headings corresponding to four widely recognized "levels" of achievable measurement—nominal, ordinal, interval, and ratio scales.[1] A nominal scale requires only the existence of an *equivalence rule*, parallel to axioms (A1)–(A3). An ordinal scale corresponds to the existence of a *dominance rule*, parallel to axioms (A4) and (A5). An interval scale, on one view, corresponds to the existence of a *combination rule*, parallel to (A6)–(A8). Later we give alternative treatments of "equality of intervals." A ratio scale corresponds to having also a *null object*, giving parallels to axioms (A9) and (A10).

Nominal Scales

Mere classification can be regarded as the most primitive form of measurement, or, indeed, as not yet amounting to measurement. (The second is my own preference.) An object can be placed in one of a set of mutually exclusive and exhaustive categories—such as gender, with values M versus F, blood type, with values A, B, AB, and O, or perhaps height, with values short versus tall. The categories are equivalence classes, with the objects in a category being equivalent with respect to the property thus categorized. If, instead of assigning alphabetic or verbal codes—M/F, A/B/AB/O, short/tall—numbers are assigned as numerical codes—0/1, 1/2/3/4, 1/2—some writers refer to the resulting coding scheme as a *nominal scale*. We introduce the following special notation.

A $\ominus$ B means that object A is in the same category as object B. The student may read this as "A is equivalent to B." As would then be noted, the only properties of the categorical observation scheme in correspondence to those of numbers are the rather obvious;

(E1) Either A $\ominus$ B or it is not.

(E2) If A $\ominus$ B, then B $\ominus$ A.

(E3) If A $\ominus$ B and B $\ominus$ C then A $\ominus$ C.

We may then use a mapping rule for assigning numbers, namely, that

$$n(A) = n(B) \quad \text{if and only if} \quad A \ominus B, \tag{18.1}$$

that is, assign the same number to A and to B if and only if they are in the same equivalence class.

As hinted by the questionable example of height with values short/tall, a categorization is often a precursor of a more sophisticated system of numerical measures. In the case of quantifiable attributes—in contrast to inherently qualitative properties—we will also have equivalence relations, but it is convenient for this account to discuss these in the context of order properties.

Ordinal Scales

Given two straight sticks, A and B, we can lay them side by side and parallel, as here:

A

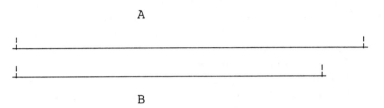

B

and observe that stick A overlaps stick B. We use the symbol ⊗ to generalize on this relationship, which we describe as "A *dominates* B," following a convention in measurement theory. In the case of the property of length, we say that A dominates B if A overlaps B. The dominance relationship is particularized in different ways for different types of observation. Further intuitively understandable examples include: With respect to physical mass, A dominates B if, in a laboratory balance, the scale pan containing A drops and the pan containing B rises. For temperature, A dominates B if heat flows from A to B. For hardness, mineral A dominates mineral B if A scratches B.

Given an empirical dominance relationship, we can check whether:

(E4) If A ⊗ B, then it is not true that B ⊗ A.

(E5) If A ⊗ B and B ⊗ C then A ⊗ C.

In the case of minerals, we might suppose it could happen that A scratches B and B scratches A, or that A scratches B scratches C scratches A. Empirically, it turns out that this does not occur. Given (E4) and (E5) in correspondence to (A4) and (A5), we can use the mapping rule

$$n(A) > n(B) \quad \text{if and only if} \quad A \otimes B, \tag{18.2}$$

—that is, assign numbers to the attribute such that the number assigned to A is larger than that assigned to B if A dominates B—overlaps it, overbalances it, scratches it, and so on. A crude yet quite usable scale of length can be constructed by selecting a sequence of N sticks such that each is dominated by the next in the sequence, and then assigning to them, say, the integers 1 to N or, in fact, any ordered sequence of numbers. The length of an object is then the number assigned to the stick that barely overlaps it. In the case of length and mass we certainly can do better than this. In the case of hardness, it seems that we cannot, and the Mohs scale of hardness is, indeed, an assignment of the integers from 1 to 10 to a standard ordered set of minerals, ordered by their scratching relationship. Much psychological measurement rests on no more than an empirical dominance relation and (E5). For this we may allow (E5) to be a matter of probability, to allow for error and instability in the relationship, requiring that each dominance relationship hold with probability greater than .5. Along with the dominance relationship, generally we will have, at least approximately, an equivalence relationship. If, of two sticks A and B, neither overlaps the other (to a limit of observation), we say they are equivalent, and similarly for balance, for heat flow, and so on. Thus, given empirical properties (E1)–(E5) in correspondence to (A1)–(A5), we use (18.2) to give an ordinal scale, recognizing that any ordered sequence of numbers can be used. Accordingly, given an ordinal scale, the numbers in the scale can be replaced by any other set of order-preserving numbers. That is, they can be subjected to any monotone transformation.

Interval Scales

Given a set of sticks, we choose two, A and B, place them end-to-end, and find a stick C that is equivalent to the joined sticks A and B.

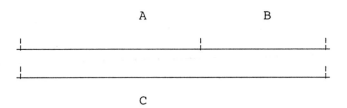

Similarly, with masses, we find a mass C that balances A and B when placed together in the same scale pan. These examples suggest the concept of a *combining operation* (also known as *concatenation*), potentially corresponding to arithmetic addition for numbers. We here write A ⊕ B for "A combined with B," and for length and mass at least we have

$$A \oplus B \ominus C$$

with respect to the property named. The problem—and it is a commonly unsolvable problem in any science—is to find usable combination operations of the type exemplified, in further applications. In physical measurement, to my knowledge, there are only a handful of these—length and mass, as noted, and electrical resistance (joining resistances in series)—but their existence has strongly influenced much thinking in measurement theory. (Note that in the examples, bodies—sticks, masses—are combined in such a way that their properties combine. In psychological testing we certainly do not expect to combine examinees in such a way that their scholastic abilities combine in a way parallel to addition.)

Given, as in the two examples, a combination rule A ⊕ B ⊖ C, it might seem inevitable, and certainly natural, that we map the property measured into numbers by the rule of correspondence

$$n(A) + n(B) = n(C) \quad \text{if and only if} \quad A \oplus B \ominus C. \quad (18.3)$$

That is, the scale values add to give the scale value of the combination if and only if A combined with B is equivalent to C. It turns out that this is not inevitable. If this is in fact the appropriate rule, then we have empirical counterparts of the axiomatic properties (A6)–(A9), namely,

(E6)   A ⊕ B ⊖ B ⊕ A.
(E7)   If A ⊖ C and B ⊖ C then A ⊕ B = C ⊕ D.
(E8)   (A ⊕ B) ⊕ C = A ⊕ (B ⊕ C).

Note that these are "obvious" yet not tautological properties, and they are matters of empirical observation. For example, (E6) holds for length, as illustrated by

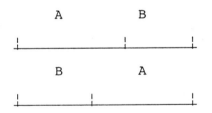

because we live in an empirical space in which this is what we observe as a matter of fact. Possession of the empirical characteristics (E6)–(E8) certainly presupposes (E1)–(E3), and generally will be accompanied by (E4) and (E5). But note that we do not yet have an empirical counterpart of (A9) and (A10), which invokes the number zero. To see what the lack of these last two counterpart properties means, we consider temperature.

The case of temperature is often cited in the measurement literature as a paradigm case of an *interval scale*. This is yet to be defined, and for the moment we loosely imagine it as a scale on which differences in the scaled attributes can be equated. We have already noted that temperature allows equivalence and dominance operations—A is hotter than B if heat flows from A to B when they are united, and they are of equivalent levels of temperature if heat flows neither way. These operations suggest a combination rule. If we mix A and B (under a number of restrictive and controlled conditions—e.g., A and B inert fluids, same density, volume, constant pressure) and heat does not flow between the mixture and a third body C, then

$$A \oplus B \ominus C.$$

That is, the temperature of A mixed with B is equivalent to the temperature of C. Given this relation, we may then verify that empirically, (E6)–(E8) hold. It will then seem "natural," for a mixture, to adopt the mapping rule

$$t(C) = \tfrac{1}{2}[t(A) + t(B)] \quad \text{if and only if} \quad A \oplus B \ominus C. \qquad (18.4)$$

That is, the temperature, the scaled measure $t(C)$ assigned to the mixture $A \oplus B$ under the prescribed conditions, is the average of the initial temperatures $t(A)$ and $t(B)$. (A more complex and general rule could be given, invoking relevant physical laws, but we are not here doing physics.)

We can consider obtaining equivalent mixtures

$$A \oplus X \ominus B \oplus Y,$$

—that is, mixing two mixtures and observing no heat flow. Then from

$$t(A \oplus X) = t(B \oplus Y),$$

the mapping rule gives

$$[t(A) + t(X)]/2 = [t(B) + t(Y)]/2,$$

so

$$t(A) - t(B) = t(Y) - t(X). \qquad (18.5)$$

As the notation suggests, we might think of A and B as two bodies whose temperatures we wish to compare, and X, Y as all pairs of bodies that combine with A and B by (18.4) to give equivalent mixtures. Then the mapping rule (18.4) gives the testable empirical relation (18.5), which states that the temperature *interval* $t(A)–t(B)$ equals the interval $t(Y)–t(X)$ for all bodies X,Y that give equivalent mixtures. We say that the equivalence relation and the mapping rule jointly provide temperature measurement on an *interval scale*. To restate the concept, scale values can be assigned in such a way that the numerical difference in temperature between two bodies A and B is equal to the numerical difference in temperature of any two bodies Y and X that combine with A and B to give equivalence. The student new to this concept may feel that this is a complicated way to state the obvious. We might say loosely that we have "given meaning" to the statement that the difference between 10° Celsius and 0° Celsius equals the difference between 100° and 90°. But this is not to say, trivially, that $10 - 0 = 100 - 90$, and so on, a statement about numbers. It is to say that once we have assigned temperatures, say 10° to body A and 0° to body B, then for any bodies Y,X such that $t(Y) - t(X) = 10°$, heat will not flow between A mixed with X and B mixed with Y. Note that even in this rather oversimplified account, it requires a fairly sophisticated theoretical model for heat (and temperature) to reach an interval scale.

Generally, the highest ambition of theorists working on scaling has been to find empirical relationships and a mapping rule yielding a recognizable form of interval scale, "giving meaning" in some specified way, to the statement that

$$n(A) - n(B) = n(Y) - n(X), \tag{18.6}$$

where $n(\cdot)$ means a scale value assigned to a property. That is, we look for a theoretical model that implies an empirical check of whether the mapping rule gives consistent differences. In applications to psychological attributes in the final section of this chapter we look for theoretical models that circumvent the problem that we cannot combine respondents, so to speak.

Given one assignment of numbers that satisfy the conditions for an interval scale, it follows that the only alternative assignments using the same model are linear functions of it. Thus, in temperature, an arbitrary origin and arbitrary unit are fixed in the Celsius scale by taking 0°C as the freezing point of water, and 100° as its boiling point. The alternative Fahrenheit scale is then related to the Celsius scale by

$$F = 1.8C + 32,$$

and, conversely,

$$C = (1/1.8)F - (32/1.8).$$

A nonlinear relation would give inconsistent differences in applications of (18.4). The unit in Celsius is given in terms of boiling point and freezing point as

$$(\text{B.P.} - \text{F.P.})/100$$

of course. The equality of these units over the range of the temperature scale is established by applications of (18.4). (Practical temperature—a *derived scale*—measured over the most familiar range by the height of a column of mercury in a hopefully uniform tube, inherits its equal-interval property, in theory, by checking it against the equivalence operations afforded by fluid mixing, which gives the *fundamental scale.*)

Note that when we choose (a) a set of empirical operations and (b) a mapping rule, yielding verifiable equal-interval properties, we have not yet shown that no distinct combinations of empirical operations and mapping rules could yield equal-interval properties for the measurement of selected objects. The "naturalness" of the first choice can blind investigators to alternative possibilities. It is not impossible in theory to find sets of objects that conform to distinct and incompatible interval scales.

Ratio Scales

The paradigm case of length (as also mass, and resistance, but not temperature) yields a further property, parallel to axioms (A9) and (A10). We may imagine choosing shorter and shorter sticks until in the limit we have one of vanishing length—a *null object* $\emptyset$ with respect to the length attribute, such that

(E9) $A \oplus \emptyset \ominus A$,

and

(E10) if $A \ominus C$ and $B \oslash \emptyset$, then $A \oplus B \oslash C$.

Assigning the scale value zero to the null object,

$$n(\emptyset) = 0, \tag{18.7}$$

representing absence of the attribute, gives a "natural" origin to the scale of measurement. Generally, together with (E1)–(E8), this gives a correspondence between the attribute and the axiomatic properties of the number system (A1)–(A10) that constitutes the ideal of *fundamental measurement.* The full set of empirical operations, with the mapping rules, gives a *ratio scale.* In the case of length, for example, we can combine stick A with itself p times, to give $C \ominus A \oplus A \ldots \oplus A$, and by the mapping rule the ratio of the length of C to the length of A is p. We can properly say that one stick is p times as long as the other. Given a set of rules yielding a ratio scale, only the unit of the scale is arbitrary, so alternative assignments of numbers are proportional. For example, lengths (L) in centimeters and in inches are related by

$$L_{inches} = 2.54 L_{cm},$$

and

$$L_{cm} = (1/2.54) L_{inches}.$$

This rather long excursus into measurement theory, illustrated by physical applications, is summarized in Table 18.1.

In one view, Table 18.1 could appear incomplete. Some writers on this topic would add a fifth column headed "permissible statistics," claiming that these levels of scale properties determine the appropriateness of statistical operations—testing mean differences, fitting regressions, and so on. That is not the view taken here, although there are certainly relevant questions to be asked about the fitting of statistical models.[2] Given a "nominal scale"—a coding of equivalence classes for which we have used numbers, where alphabetic or verbal coding would serve equally—it would certainly be a mistake to perform computations on these numbers as though they corresponded to ordinal, interval, or ratio properties. On the other hand, given an ordinal scale, it may equally be a mistake to limit statistical operations to rank-correlation and nonparametric methods, as has been suggested in claims about "permissible statistics," and a mistake to require interval-scale properties before applying a simple *t*-test for a mean difference in the measure due to contrasting experimental conditions. It is easy, it seems, to forget that an ordinal scale is not just a ranking. Ordered categories have an absolute character as well as a relativity to each other, and the assignment of

TABLE 18.1
Types of Scale

Scale Level	Empirical Relations	Empirical Properties	Permissible Transformations
Nominal	$\ominus$	(E1)–(E3)	Any one-to-one
Ordinal	$\oslash$	(E1)–(E5)	Any monotone
Interval	$\oplus$	(E1)–(E8)	Any linear
Ratio	$\oslash$	(E1)–(E10)	Any ratio

numbers follows a rule that yields a degree of reproducibility. As already noted in Chapter 4, there are two main considerations about scaling that are relevant to statistical applications, namely, whether the required statistical assumptions are satisfied, and whether the statistical hypothesis is itself invariant under changes of scale.

In the case of a *t*-test on mean differences, we require that the response measure should be normally distributed in the population, and the within-group variances should be equal. If one or both assumptions are not satisfied, we may transform the response scale—whatever its level of measurement—to satisfy the assumptions, and perform the test. If, more usefully than a conventional test of significance, we estimate the size of the difference, and use the *SE* either directly or indirectly to obtain confidence limits, to assess precision of estimation, with the consequent advantage of judging the theoretical or practical importance of the effect size, then again we can transform the scale to satisfy statistical assumptions. If the original scale is the accepted conventional measure of the attribute, the confidence limits can be transformed back to that scale. And nowhere do these operations depend on permission derived from measurement properties. These remarks generalize fairly obviously to analysis of variance in experimental designs with qualitative experimental conditions and so on.

A second statistical consideration enters as soon as we consider a quantitative relationship between two or more variables. The hypothesis that the relationship between two attributes, each measured on an ordinal scale, has a particular functional form is not itself invariant under permissible transformations of scale. If, say, the regression of one variable on the other is linear with the given scales, we can choose a transformation of one or both scales that makes it nonlinear. If the original relationship is monotone but nonlinear, we can find a transformation that makes it linear. Hypotheses specifying the form of a relationship are not themselves invariant under possible scale changes.

Given a measure of an attribute with ordinal properties, we may find it convenient to choose a scale that makes its distribution normal in one population of interest. Given two such measures, we may find it convenient to choose a scale or two scales that simplify the relation between the two variables—by making it linear or by removing an interaction term. Neither of these procedures endows an ordinal scale with interval scale properties. Scale values for an attribute having ordinal properties (a) can be accepted as a conventional, agreed assignment—for example, the total or mean test score used throughout previous chapters, (b) can be defined by a model— for example, the latent trait in an item response model, whose scale is determined by the choice of the item response function, (c) can be determined by a convenient choice of distribution in the population of interest—for example, the normal distribution, or, possibly, the use of percentiles, (d) can be chosen to simplify the mathematical relationship with other variables, and (e) can possibly be shown to possess equal-interval properties under a chosen model. If statistical assumptions fail for measures on an interval scale, it is still possible to transform the data to satisfy the statistical assumptions, either foregoing the interval property or transforming back for further purposes.

COOMBS'S THEORY OF DATA

A useful classification of types of observation in psychological measurement and of appropriate methods of mapping them into numerical data was given by Clyde Coombs.[3] In all types, there is a response of individuals to "stimuli," and the data represent distances between individuals, between stimuli, or between individuals and stimuli. In some cases, the relations concern perceptions of stimuli—their perceived properties or values from the point of view of the individual respondent. In applications, the stimuli can be items such as cognitive items or attitude statements, objects of preference, such as icecreams, or laboratory stimuli such as auditory tones or simple optical presentations. In short, a stimulus is anything to which a subject may respond.

Coombs's classification of observations gives four types (in the original work referred to as *quadrants*, a terminology we do not need for our purpose). It is possible, but technically more demanding, to define types of data, and discuss appropriate observations. I prefer to consider four types of observation, and some ways to model them.

Type I. Preferential Choice Observations

Members of a set of m stimuli are presented in pairs to an individual, who responds by choosing the preferred stimulus. For example, four named ice creams—say vanilla, strawberry, walnut, pistachio—might yield a preference table for an individual as in Table 18.2. Here $\otimes$ is to be read as "is preferred to," and represents preference of the row stimulus to the column stimulus. In the example, the ordering is consistent, with $P \otimes W \otimes S \otimes V$. Alternatively, the individual may be asked simply to rank-order the stimuli directly. This is less informative because it forces consistency, but may be more convenient in some applications.

The fundamental point is that a preferential choice observation represents a relation between an individual and a pair of stimuli, a fact that has implications for finding a rule for mapping the observations into data. The response of preferential choice sets a boundary on the class of stimuli to which it is appropriate. We might identify this approximately as the

TABLE 18.2
Preferential Choice Matrix

	V	S	W	P
V				
S	⊘			
W	⊘	⊘		
P	⊘	⊘	⊘	

class of stimuli having value for the respondent. This can be an affective value, and specifically an appetitive value (foods, drinks) or a wide-sense aesthetic value (art objects, books, and television programs), interests (job satisfactions, hobby activities), and attitudes. We here ignore a further subclassification of preferential choice observations on a basis of dominance versus proximity, made by Coombs for all four types, but virtually inapplicable to this one.

Type II. Single-Stimulus Observations

This is the type that has been the central topic of this book. A single stimulus—an item—is presented to the individual and a dichotomous response obtained. Examples include, of course, pass/fail, for a cognitive item, yes/no, for a clinical self-report item, and agree/disagree, for an attitude item. In the psychophysical laboratory, typical examples would constitute detecting/not detecting a faint signal, such as an auditory stimulus, possibly for the practical purpose of recording an audiogram.

Fundamentally, these observations are named for the fact that they represent a relationship between an individual and a single stimulus. The class of stimuli open to single-stimulus observations is quite wide, and includes both items possessing value and items—for example, cognitive items and signal-detection stimuli—that do not.

Type III. Stimulus-Comparison Observations

The individual is asked to judge the stimuli in pairs, as to which possesses more of a specified (perceived) attribute—for example, heaviness of weights, loudness of sounds, "conservatism" of political statements. A complete set of such *pair comparisons* from one individual could be represented exactly as in Table 18.2, but with the relationship ⊘ interpreted as "judged to be more X than" (where X is the specified attribute), replacing "preferred to." Again, given such a complete set of pair comparisons, we can check the consistency of the ordering of the stimuli with respect to the attribute.

Fundamentally, we have a relation between two stimuli as perceived by a judge with respect to a specified attribute. We may be able to get a number of repeated observations of the pair comparisons from a single judge, especially in the context of psychophysical laboratory studies. The task of repeatedly comparing two attitude items could rapidly become fatiguing and yield stereotyped responses. We might instead replicate the comparisons over a number of judges. Both these procedures give a table of the relative frequencies with which S_j is judged to have more of a named attribute than S_k. Models are then used to scale the perceptions of the stimuli with respect to the attribute, either from the point of view of a single judge, or averaged over the sample of judges. Type III observations are not to be confused with Type I. In Type III cases, the individual is judging the attribute of the stimuli, not preferring one. If, for example, the stimuli are attitude items, say on a scale for "conservatism," the judgment that one item represents a greater degree of conservatism than another can be independent of the degree of conservatism of the judge.

Type IV. Similarities Observations

Pairs of stimuli are compared by an individual, yielding a judgment that members of one pair are more similar than members of another. For example, color chips could be presented, such as a red–orange pair and a green–yellow pair, and the first pair declared more similar than the second. Fundamentally, similarities observations yield a relationship between pairs of pairs of stimuli, as perceived by an individual judge.

These are the four basic types of observation recognized by Coombs. In his theory, they map most naturally into four types of data. I have departed from the original account, in which it is the data types that are classified.

In Type I data, the stimuli and the individuals are represented together as points in what is then called a *joint space*. The point representing an individual actually is an ideal stimulus, not included among those presented, that would be preferred over all other stimuli—the absolutely most preferable ice cream, for example. Stimuli are then ordered by their distances from the individual's ideal choice (see next section).

In Type II data, again the stimuli and the individuals are represented as points in a joint space. In the simple case of homogeneous cognitive items, the items are ordered on a line with respect to their difficulty, and the examinee is represented by a hypothetical item that would be the most difficult the examinee could pass—the easiest the examinee could fail—in a deterministic model that does not allow "error."

In Type III data, the (perceived) stimuli are represented by points on a line. If S_j is to the right of S_k, S_j dominates S_k, that is, is judged to have more of the named attribute than S_k.

In Type IV data, again the stimuli are represented by points in a space, and the dissimilarity of two stimuli is mapped into the distance between the points. If the S_j–S_k pair is judged more similar—less dissimilar—than the S_l–S_m pair, the distance between the S_j and S_k points will be smaller than the distance between the S_l and S_m points.

This has been the merest sketch of Coombs's system, but it should suffice as a basis for the handful of models and methods in the next section, and as a guide to further reading.[4]

SOME SCALING MODELS AND METHODS

As an introductory sampling of this topic, I choose to sketch an account of six topics: two treatments of Type II data—(a) the Walker–Guttman scale and (b) (again) the Rasch model—then (c) Coombs's model for Type I observations, (d) the application of models for pair comparison frequency data to Type I and Type III observations, (e) basic principles of multidimensional scaling, connected to Type IV observations and to wider applications, and (f) basic principles of optimal scaling. This last "scaling" method does not fall into a Coombsian category.

The Walker–Guttman Scale

We have noted that a set of m binary items yields 2^m possible response patterns [recall Table 6.7(a)]. Walker (1931) described, as an *ideal answer pattern* for cognitive items, an observation set in which only $m + 1$ of these occur, such that if the examinees are ordered with respect to their ability and the items are ordered with respect to their difficulty, the allowable patterns will be as illustrated in Table 18.3, with the keyed response coded 1, and the nonkeyed response coded 0.

Guttman (1950) made an extensive study of such patterns, mainly in the context of attitude items, so the literature generally refers to an ob-

TABLE 18.3
Ideal Answer Pattern

	Item				
Examinee	*A*	*B*	*C*	*D*	*Frequency*
5	1	1	1	1	n_5
4	1	1	1	0	n_4
3	1	1	0	0	n_3
2	1	0	0	0	n_2
1	0	0	0	0	n_1

servation matrix of this type as a Guttman scale or perfect scale. I refer to a table of this kind as a *Walker–Guttman observation matrix*, and the resulting order of respondents and of items as a *perfect scale*.[5]

As Coombs pointed out, such an observation matrix allows us to map the items and the respondents onto the number line to form a joint scale, as in

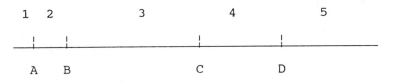

by the rule that respondents to the right of the item endorse it (for attitudes), pass it (for cognitive items), and so on. More generally, examinee G is placed to the right of item *j* if by some dominance rule G dominates *j*. In the case of cognitive items, the line is simultaneously a scale of item difficulty and examinee ability. In terms of difficulty, the person is represented by an ideal item that the person just manages to pass. In terms of ability, the item is represented by the ability of the person who just manages to pass it. Clearly, the spacing between the item points (or, alternatively, between examinee points) is arbitrary, so both ability and difficulty are measured on an ordinal scale. Similarly, with attitude items, the respondents and the items are ordered on the attitude scale, which simultaneously represents the strength of the attitude of the respondent and the strength of the attitude reflected in the item as perceived by the respondents.[6]

Generally in Type II cases the relation between the respondent and the item can be treated as a dominance relation. It is possible to have attitude items at both ends of the scale that a respondent would not endorse because one is too weak and the other too strong to be accepted. Such items are said to have a *proximity* relation to the respondent instead of a dominance relation, obtaining endorsement if sufficiently close to the respondent's position.[7]

Note that we could have labelled the five person types in Table 18.3 by the number of items passed/endorsed. The nice feature of the Walker–Guttman matrix and resulting perfect scale is that it supplies a one-to-one correspondence between the response patterns and the total scores of the respondents. From the total score, we know all about the behavior. In theory, the precision of measurement of the attribute increases directly with the number of items, but in practice it is very difficult to find/write items that give only $m + 1$ allowable response patterns. As we add more items from the behavior domain to increase precision of measurement, the method breaks down. This is a fundamental dilemma for the perfect scale.

Failure of an attempt to obtain a perfect Walker–Guttman response matrix can be due to unique variation/"error," or to multidimensionality, or to both. Attempts have been made to develop multidimensional joint-space representations of response matrices that give nonallowable patterns in one dimension.[8] The main problem with these is that they place a strong requirement of freedom from any form of "error" in the responses.

Rasch-Type Models

It should be intuitively recognizable that the Walker–Guttman response matrix results as a limiting case of an item response model. In the 1PL model of Chapter 13, or, indeed, any unidimensional item response model without a pseudo-guessing parameter, if the slopes of the item response curves are allowed to become indefinitely steep, eventually each becomes what is known, for good descriptive reasons, as a *step* or *jump* function, moving discontinuously from zero to unit probability at some point on the attribute scale, as in Fig. 18.1(a). A set of such step functions, as in Fig. 18.1(b), yields the $m + 1$ response patterns allowed in the Walker–Guttman response matrix. In this limiting case the principle of local independence is satisfied, but in a degenerate fashion, because the conditional probability of any response pattern—allowable or not—is zero, except for the two perfect patterns—all zero or all unity. This fact, and the dilemma noted, imply that a researcher contemplating fitting a perfect scale should be advised to fit an item response model instead. If the approximation to the

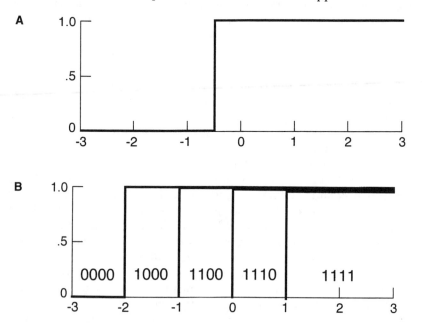

FIG. 18.1.   (a) Step function. (b) Set of step functions.

ideal response matrix is close, this will be shown in the steepness of the item response functions. Similarly, it is a better strategy to fit a multidimensional item response model, by the straightforward methods of Chapter 14, than to attempt to fit a multidimensional joint scale that does not admit error/unique components.

Among the item response models for Type II observations, the 1PL model—sometimes loosely referred to as "the" Rasch model—has often been singled out as having special, indeed unique, scaling properties. Changing notation slightly from the treatment in Chapter 13, we recall and further consider the class of item response models defined by the property of specific objectivity. As explained there, these models yield a comparison of abilities independent of the items chosen out of a specified set of them, and a comparison of item difficulties independent of the examinees chosen (also from a specific population). With, as before, f_i for the ability of examinee i and δ_j for the difficulty of item j, all models of the type

$$P\{X_j = 1 | F = f_i\} = \phi(f_i - \delta_j), \tag{18.8}$$

where $\phi(\cdot)$ is any (invertible) monotone function, give specific objectivity. This is because (18.8) allows us to obtain

$$f_i - \delta_j = \phi^{-1}(P\{X_j = 1 | F = f_i\}) \tag{18.9}$$

where $\phi^{-1}(\cdot)$ represents the inverse of the function $\phi(\cdot)$. Then the difference in ability between two subpopulations i' and i is

$$f_{i'} - f_i = \phi^{-1}(P\{X_j = 1 | F = f_{i'}\}) - \phi^{-1}(P\{X_j = 1 | F = f_i\}), \tag{18.10}$$

which is the same for all items. The difference in difficulty between two items is likewise the same for all examinee subpopulations. (Recall that this does not mean the items are interchangeable, as their error properties are not equivalent.) We call any model having specific objectivity a Rasch-type model. As mentioned in Chapter 13, the 1PL model is unique in the class of all Rasch-type models in possessing the property that the item sum (or mean) score is a sufficient statistic for an examinee's ability, and the proportion passing each item is a sufficient statistic for the item difficulty parameter. These further properties have led to a great deal of concentration on the 1PL model, and a tendency to fall into the mistaken belief that specific objectivity is unique to the 1PL model, and that it is unique among item response models in giving measurements on an interval scale.

Specific objectivity is, we see, a general property of all Rasch-type models. There is a sense in which any Rasch-type model also yields an interval scale for sets of items chosen for their conformity to it. However, for any distinct choices of the function ϕ in (18.8), we can in theory choose distinct sets of items conforming to these chosen models and yielding distinct and mutually contradictory interval scales.[9] Recall that it is not generally expected that the items in a homogeneous behavior domain will fit the 1PL model, so it is necessary, in seeking specific objectivity, to pick out some specific subset of items that does so. Similarly, we might choose another subset giving specific objectivity with a distinct Rasch-type model. When we put two such sets of items together, it will be found that the resulting scales are not linearly related, and neither model fits all items, although a more general unidimensional model will. It is the choice of the item response function that determines the metric of the ability.

Coombs's Preference Model

We turn next to models for Type I—preferential choice—observations. Given m items—ice creams, attitude statements—n respondents either rank the items in the order of their preference, or possibly give a set of pairwise preferences, from which ranks can be obtained, and consistency of choice checked. Here *preference* has a wide sense, including proximity to the respondent's own beliefs. By permutation theory, there are $m! = m(m - 1)$ $\cdots 3 \times 2 \times 1$ distinct possible rank orders for m items. For example, four items A, B, C, D, give the 24 rank orders

```
A A A A A A B B B B B B C C C C C C D D D D D D
B B C C D D A A C C D D A A B B D D A A B B C C
C D B D C B C D A D A C B D A D A B C A C A B
D C D B B C D C D A C A D B D A B A C B C A B A.
```

We obtain a unidimensional deterministic model of preference—with no allowance for imperfections due to "error"—as in the following illustration. Suppose that four stimuli, A, B, C, D, can be placed on a line as shown in Fig. 18.2. We add division points marked AB, AC, AD, BC, BD, and CD to the figure, corresponding to midpoints, halfway between the points representing the specified items. These division points mark off seven segments of the line corresponding to distinct rank orders, as also indicated in the figure. The principle is that a respondent in any segment, represented by the respondent's ideal stimulus value—his or her absolutely preferable stimulus—ranks the items according to their nearness to that ideal point. Thus, for any person whose ideal is a point in segment 2, the stimuli B, A, C, D, are ranked in nearness to that ideal point. The midpoints mark a switch of two stimuli in the order of their closeness to the ideal point. The student should understand this principle on a careful exami-

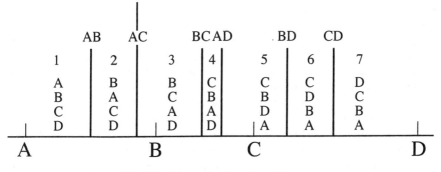

FIG. 18.2. Joint scale of preferential choice.

nation of the figure. More generally, if there is a single scale line on which stimuli and ideal points can be mapped, there are just $[m(m-1)/2] + 1$ allowable rank orders out of the $m!$ possible, so the model is very restrictive. Here, for four items, there are just 7 allowable rankings out of 24 possible.

The demonstration in Fig. 18.2 shows how, given an ordering and spacing on the line, the allowable ranks are derived. I do not describe the algorithm necessary in applications for going from given rankings to the order and spacing on the line. The reader may find it an interesting game to try to solve this problem for the example by "commonsense" reasoning. But it suffices to know that such methods exist.[10]

Like the deterministic, ordinal perfect scale for Type II observations, the joint scale for preferential choice suffers the dilemma that the precision of the scale increases with the number of stimuli, and so does the likelihood of obtaining rank-orders not allowed by the simple unidimensional model. Again it is possible to ascribe such failures to "error" or to multidimensionality. Thus, it might be that the stimuli and the respondent's ideals can be graphed in two dimensions, and allowable orders are determined by relative distances in various directions of the stimulus points from a respondent's ideal point. The geometry of such multidimensional models rapidly becomes very complicated, and is not considered in this introductory account.

Pair Comparison Data

We recall that in Type III observations either one judge makes replicated comparisons of pairs chosen out of m stimuli, or n judges perform that task, usually just once for each pair. If the judgments are consistent, they yield a rank order of the stimuli and almost trivially they are placed on an ordinal scale. The judgment that A is heavier than B is clearly quite different from the judgment that A is preferable to B, and this difference marks off Type III from Type I observations. Yet it turns out that the same models—Thurstone scaling models—can be used for either, provided we allow for "error" in the judgment or choice. Both lead to forms of Thurstone's *law of comparative judgment.*[11]

Just as we can derive an item response model from a linear model for underlying continuous variables, or directly from a normal ogive or logistic item regression curve, so it is possible to derive a Thurstone scaling model from an underlying process, or directly by use of the normal ogive as a transformation. (And using the logistic function in the following yields an indistinguishable model—the Bradley–Terry–Luce model.)[12]

We first examine Thurstone scaling as a practical technology, and then consider its meaning more carefully. Suppose we collect some pair comparison data from preferential choice of ice creams—vanilla, strawberry, walnut, pistachio. A table of raw observations would take the form

			Comparison			
Individual	$V \otimes S$	$V \otimes W$	$V \otimes P$	$S \otimes W$	$S \otimes P$	$W \otimes P$
1						
2						
.						
.						
.						
n						

recording, say, 1 in the appropriate column of the table if an individual prefers S_j to S_k, and 0 otherwise. Such information can be summarized as in Table 18.4, but with loss of information about consistency of individual choices. Each entry is the proportion of respondents preferring the column stimulus to the row stimulus. Thus, 81% prefer strawberry to vanilla, 73% prefer pistachio to strawberry, and so on. (My own tastes are reflected in these figures.) The same data could equally represent judgments, comparing the stimuli on a named attribute—conservatism of statements, loudness of auditory stimuli. They could also, in cases where replication of an uncertain judgment seems possible, represent repeated judgments of a single judge, as in loudness comparisons, rather than a proportion of judges.

Two obvious but important features seen in Table 18.4 are that (a) we have arbitrarily but reasonably entered .5 in the diagonal to represent the omitted choice between a stimulus and itself and (b) the entries P_{jk} for $S_j \otimes S_k$ and P_{kj} for $S_k \otimes S_j$ sum to unity. For the moment, as a practical device, we choose to derive a table of numbers

$$Z_{jk} = N^{-1}(P_{jk}), \tag{18.11}$$

where Z_{jk} is the standardized normal deviate corresponding to a cumulative probability P_{jk}. This is the inverse of a scaling rule by which

TABLE 18.4
Preferential Choice Proportions

	V	S	W	P
V	(.5)	.81	.90	.93
S	.19	(.5)	.68	.73
W	.10	.32	(.5)	.64
P	.07	.27	.36	(.5)

$$P_{jk} = N(Z_{jk}). \qquad (18.12)$$

This gives Table 18.5. Note that entry $Z_{jk} = -Z_{kj}$. Included in the table are sums and means of the columns. In simple Thurstone scaling the means are estimated scale values, say δ_j, of the perceived preferability of the stimuli. They are determined up to an arbitrary additive constant. According to the model we are implicitly using, each Z_{jk} should equal the difference in scale value of S_j and S_k, estimated by the column means. Table 18.6 contains fitted Z_{jk} values, given by differences of the column means.

Comparing with Table 18.5, we see that these are certainly close to the actual values. Basically, to the extent that the scale value differences fit the transformed proportions Z_{jk}, the Z_{jk} have consistent additive properties. If

$$Z_{jk} = \delta_j - \delta_k \qquad (18.13)$$

for all j and k, then

$$Z_{jk} = \delta_j - \delta_k = (\delta_j - \delta_l) + (\delta_l - \delta_k) = Z_{jl} + Z_{lk}. \qquad (18.14)$$

Note that an arbitrary constant can be added to the scale values. It is common practice to assign zero to the stimulus with the lowest value in a given set. The observed proportions are consistent with the hypothesis that

TABLE 18.5
Normal Deviates Matrix

	V	S	W	P
V	0	.88	1.28	1.45
S	−0.88	0	0.46	0.61
W	−1.28	−.46	0	0.36
P	−1.45	−.61	−0.36	0
Sum	−3.61	−.19	1.38	2.42
Mean	−0.90	−.05	0.44	.60

TABLE 18.6
Thurstone Model—Fitted Values

	V	S	W	P
V	0	.85	1.34	1.50
S	−0.85	0	0.49	0.65
W	−1.34	−.49	0	0.16
P	−1.50	−.65	−0.16	0

the given stimuli can be assigned scale values by the transformation (18.11), which has interval scale properties.

We have not yet, perhaps, recognized a plausible motive for adopting this rule for assigning scale values to the stimuli. A direct way to arrive at it comes from the general observation that a normal-ogive (or logistic) is a reasonable choice for a regression of a binary item on any independent variable. Indeed, historically, in early work on psychophysics (briefly noted in Chapter 1) on detecting the difference between two physical stimuli, it was observed that the probability of correct detection was a normal-ogive function of the difference in physical units between the stimuli. This was known in the classical literature as the phi–gamma law, where it did describe the relationship between two measured quantities—the observable physical stimulus difference and the probability of detection. It was transferred by Thurstone to the case where there is no independent (physical) scale for the stimulus as such, so we use the normal-ogive as a transformation, not an empirical law, to obtain scale values from proportions. We then test the resulting transformed differences for consistency with additivity. Looked at in this way, we are just saying that the scaling model for probability of the judgment or preferential choice $S_j \odot S_k$ is

$$P\{S_j \odot S_k\} = N(\delta_j - \delta_k), \qquad (18.15)$$

where δ_j, δ_k represent the (scaled) level of the judged attribute, including that of preferability for Type I observations. This seems a natural extension of item response function concepts (but note that we are not using the principle of local independence, and not defining a latent trait).

A more complex account, leading to this model, postulates a random quantitative *discriminal process*, D_j, underlying the act of comparative judgment or choice between stimuli, that is associated with each stimulus, so that

$$S_j \odot S_k \text{ if and only if } D_j > D_k, \text{ that is, } D_j - D_k > 0. \quad (18.16)$$

If we suppose that (a) D_j has a mean δ_j, (b) it has variance σ^2, the same for all stimuli, and (c) discriminal processes for distinct stimuli are uncorrelated (or all correlations are equal), then we can choose a scale unit so that (18.16) gives (18.11) and the rest of the practical technology of Thurstone scaling as already described.

There is an ambiguity in the last paragraph that needs to be resolved. If the data are collected over a sample of n judges and the proportion of judges forms the entries in such a table as Table 18.3, then the discriminal process D_j is a random quantity associated with the perception of stimulus j by individuals. If the data are n replications of the judgment task, then the discriminal process is associated with the perception of the stimuli by just one judge. In the first case, D_j varies with the randomly chosen judges. For any chosen judge, i, there will be a set of fixed values d_{ji} of the discriminal processes, and there should be a single ranking of the stimuli, with no inconsistencies in the pair comparisons, which are perfectly determined for that judge by the d_{ji}–d_{ki} differences.

In the case of replications on the pair comparisons by a single judge, scaling requires that there be considerable inconsistency—otherwise the method breaks down—and the randomness of the discriminal process D_j for each of the m stimuli is intraindividual (necessarily). Then the notion is that inside the "head"/sensorium/central nervous system of the individual judge there are m unobservable random processes fluctuating through time, with underlying momentary differences yielding the choice of S_j or of S_k according as the difference is positive or negative at the moment of judgment. The principle of correspondence is (18.16), applied at the moment of response. This could make good sense in detection of faint stimuli, where the sensory system could be subject to neural "noise."

For the case of a Thurstone model for preferential choice, with no within-individual replication, in the basic model there is just one random variable, the location of a random subject's ideal point. The principle of correspondence is

$$S_j \oslash S_k \quad \text{if and only if} \quad |D - \delta_j| < |D - \delta_k|. \tag{18.17}$$

This principle is quite different from (18.6), which is really for intraindividual replications. Here the stimuli are fixed points on the number line, and the individual—represented by that person's ideal—is a random point on the line, so the random individual chooses the stimuli in the order of their absolute distances from the ideal point. The only difference between this and the basic Coombsian model described ealier is that the assumption that the individuals' ideal points have a normal distribution defines a metric for the scale values and leads to the Thurstone scaling procedure. (The assumption that the random respondent's ideal points have a logistic distribution similarly yields the Bradley–Terry–Luce metric and scaling procedure. Other distribution assumptions would define possibly distinguishable and contradictory scales.) If, when applying this scaling procedure, we also test the pair comparisons for each subject for consistency, failure of consistency implies either that the preferences need a multidimensional model, or that we need to add m intraindividual "error" terms, random within judges, specific to the stimuli, representing uncertainty in the decision. It would be necessary to abandon the simple scaling procedure based on the summary of observations in frequencies as in Table 18.4, and to obtain replications of pair comparisons for each judge, to separate the sources of variability.

The student will have noticed enough features common to the Thurstone (and Bradley–Terry–Luce) scaling procedures and to the models of Chapters 12–14 to cause curiosity as to whether these scaling models can be called item response models for comparative responses. Recall that an item response model is the commonly accepted term for what is better described as a latent trait model, the defining property of which is that associations between responses are explained by the principle of local independence. That principle requires that in a subpopulation with fixed values of one or more latent traits, the responses are independent. The latent traits are then common properties of the items that yield the responses. The Thurstone scaling model—whether for intraindividual judgments of paired stimuli, or for choices in a sample of respondents—shares the item response functions with item response models, and has a similar accounting of choice in terms of underlying continuous variables. However, the model for judgments certainly does not account for response patterns by the principle of local independence, and the model for choice does so only in a rather degenerate sense.

Multidimensional Scaling

The student will not be surprised to learn that models for Type IV observations in Coombs's scheme—similarity observations—are rather complex. Just a sketch of this area will suffice here, pointing the interested reader to further reading.[13] Unlike the other three types, Type IV observations do not seem to have been given a basic deterministic treatment. The more usual approach to similarities divides the task into two phases. The first is the production, from the observations, of numerical data representing dissimilarities of pairs of stimuli. There are a number of ways to collect similarity observations and map them into dissimilarity data. I take just one, which suffices to show that it can be done, namely, a Thurstone scaling in which the objects of judgment are pairs of stimuli, and the attribute judged is similarity. Using either a single judge or a sample of judges we obtain pair comparisons of similarities of pairs—the judgment that S_j–S_k are more/less similar than S_l–S_m. Thurstone scaling of the obtained frequencies gives a scale value δ_{jk} of dissimilarity of each pair.

For the second task, suppose now that for m stimuli we have their $m(m - 1)/2$ judged dissimilarities δ_{jk}, by Thurstone scaling as described or possibly by some other device. Given a set of numbers representing pairwise dissimilarities, we would like to find that we can place the m stimuli as points in a space so that the dissimilarities correspond to distances between them. Suppose, again taking four stimuli, A, B, C, D, we have completed a Thurstone scaling of dissimilarities, yielding

$$\delta_{AB} = 1.5 \quad \delta_{AC} = 2.0 \quad \delta_{AD} = 3.0 \quad \delta_{BC} = .5 \quad \delta_{BD} = 1.5 \quad \delta_{CD} = 1.0.$$

If we mark A as a point on a line and B, C, and D as points 1.5, 2.0, and 3.0 units from A, we see immediately that the remaining intervals B–C = .5, B–D = 1.5, and C–D = 1.0, so the stimuli may be mapped as points on a straight line as in Fig. 18.3. This can be interpreted to mean that the judges are indeed recognizing (dis)similarity between the stimuli in terms of just one attribute.

Suppose instead that the similarities are

$$\delta_{AB} = 2.5 \quad \delta_{AC} = 2.5 \quad \delta_{AD} = 3.0 \quad \delta_{BC} = 2.0 \quad \delta_{BD} = 2.5 \quad \delta_{CD} = 2.5.$$

It happens, by my choice of these numbers, that although A, B, C, and D cannot consistently be represented as points on a line yielding these distances, they can be represented by the four points in two-dimensional space shown in Fig. 18.4. I used Pythagoras' theorem—that the square on the hypotenuse of a rightangled triangle is the sum of the squares on the

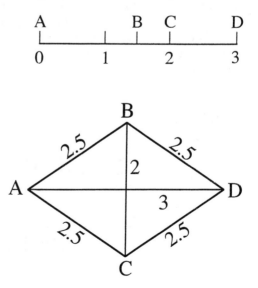

FIG. 18.3.   Unidimensional model
for dissimilarities.

FIG. 18.4.   Two-dimensional model
for dissimilarities.

other two sides—with the numbers 1.5, 2.0, and 2.5, making up four tri-angles with $1.5^2 + 2.0^2 = 2.5^2$, to invent this simple figure. Real data will not be so simple, and we actually need a technology to get from dissimi-larities to the coordinates of points in a space, rather than to get from a given configuration of points to the implied distances.

The technical problem is, indeed, to get an r-dimensional configuration of points that yields a set of interpoint distances d_{jk} corresponding to the dissimilarities δ_{jk}. This is the general problem of *multidimensional scaling*. It exists in two main varieties. In *metric multidimensional scaling* we try to find a configuration of points giving interpoint distances as close as possible to the numerical dissimilarities. In *nonmetric multidimensional scaling* we try to find a configuration of points giving interpoint distances whose rank order is as close as possible to the rank order of the dissimilarities. Non-metric multidimensional scaling seems to be the dominant approach to the scaling of dissimilarities, because it does not require the dissimilarities to have better than ordinal properties.

No attempt is made here to describe the algorithms that have been developed for this purpose, except to note that the most widely accepted algorithm rests on plotting tentatively determined distances against the given dissimilarities, as in Fig. 18.5, and finding a sequence of line segments that make a *monotone polygon*, that is, that always go up (or stay horizontal) but never go down. The coordinates in r-space of the m stimuli are guessed, then iteratively improved, to make the squared differences between the distances and the points on the best-fitting monotone polygon as small as possible. Indeed, a curious feature of nonmetric multidimensional scaling is that, virtually uniquely among data-analytic techniques, we regress the stimulus values on the data, instead of regressing the data on the stimulus values. By this unusual proceeding, we avoid doing arithmetic on the dis-similarities, which are thought of as having only ordinal properties.

Taking this technology for granted, suppose we find that the stimuli can be represented as points on a line as in the first case illustrated. It is

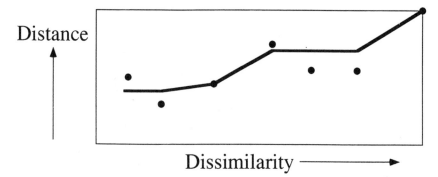

FIG. 18.5. Monotone polygon.

then hoped that we can interpret the dimension on which the stimuli are dispersed as the attribute that appears to contrast the most widely separated stimuli. If we require two or more dimensions to represent the stimuli, as in Fig. 18.4, the idea is that the judges are implicitly responding to two or more attributes with respect to which the stimuli are dissimilar. The task of naming these attributes then becomes a rather subtle one. With just two dimensions, it may be possible to make sense of the entire configuration and recognize two main directions of dispersion of the stimuli corresponding to identifiable attributes. Higher dimensional nonmetric multidimensional scaling analyses sometimes invoke factor-analytic criteria, using rotation methods such as VARIMAX to give a kind of "simple structure" to the coordinates, although the custom does not seem to have been given any conceptual foundation.

Nonmetric multidimensional scaling has been rather creatively misapplied by some researchers to correlation matrices, converted into measures of dissimilarity between tests or items.[14] At the time of writing, this approach to the structure of multivariate test data does not seem to have been subjected to critical evaluation. Because correlation coefficients measure the extent to which variables are linearly related, it may seem contradictory to convert them into measures of dissimilarity for nonmetric, ordinal forms of analysis. Users of nonmetric multidimensional scaling need to accept a rather crude level of fit to avoid high-dimensional solutions, because it is hard to find a suitable representation of the configuration without design principles such as we have in confirmatory structural models, as a basis (axis set) for the presentation of the data. It is possible that with further work, nonmetric multidimensional scaling may eventually be sufficiently refined to provide an alternative treatment of items and test scores.

Optimal Scaling

Finally, we briefly take note of yet another technology that is sometimes regarded as a scaling method, at least according to the main labels—*optimal scaling* and *dual scaling*—under which it is most commonly known. (An alternative name is *correspondence analysis*.) Actually, optimal scaling is very closely related to factor analysis and item response theory. For a brief sketch of possibilities, it suffices to outline the method in terms of its aims, illustrated by a simple application.

Consider a data set arising from m multicategory items. These may be ordered or unordered, but if they are ordered, the analysis does not make use of this fact. Although there need not be the same number of categories in each item, it will simplify discussion if we suppose, as in the example to follow, that we have four items each with three categories, and an observation matrix of the type in Table 18.7. (For the moment we ignore the last column.)

TABLE 18.7
Nishisato Multicategory Data Matrix

Res	Item 1			Item 2			Item 3			Item 4			Optimal Score
	C1	C2	C3	C1	C2	C3	C1	C2	C3	C1	C2	C3	
1	0	0	1	1	0	0	0	0	1	1	0	0	-0.95
2	0	1	0	1	0	0	0	1	0	0	0	1	-0.05
3	0	1	0	1	0	0	0	0	1	0	0	1	-0.62
4	1	0	0	0	0	1	0	0	1	0	1	0	1.41
5	0	0	1	1	0	0	0	0	1	0	0	1	-0.83
6	1	0	0	0	1	0	1	0	0	0	0	1	0.86
7	0	1	0	1	0	0	0	0	1	0	0	1	-0.62
8	0	1	0	1	0	0	0	0	1	0	0	1	-0.62
9	1	0	0	0	0	1	0	1	0	1	0	0	1.21
10	0	0	1	1	0	0	0	0	1	1	0	0	-0.95
11	1	0	0	0	0	1	0	0	1	0	1	0	1.41
12	0	1	0	1	0	0	1	0	0	1	0	0	-0.63
13	0	1	0	1	0	0	0	1	0	0	1	0	0.60
14	0	0	1	1	0	0	0	0	1	1	0	0	-0.95
15	1	0	0	1	0	0	0	0	1	0	1	0	0.72
16	0	0	1	1	0	0	0	0	1	1	0	0	-0.95
17	0	0	1	1	0	0	1	0	0	1	0	0	-0.84
18	0	1	0	0	1	0	0	0	1	0	0	1	0.06
19	0	0	1	1	0	0	0	0	1	1	0	0	-0.95
20	0	1	0	1	0	0	0	0	1	0	0	1	-0.62
21	1	0	0	0	1	0	0	1	0	0	1	0	1.97
22	0	1	0	1	0	0	0	0	1	0	0	1	-0.62
23	1	0	0	0	1	0	0	1	0	0	1	0	1.97
Sum	7	9	7	16	4	3	3	5	15	8	6	9	

The respondent chooses, or is recorded as belonging to, one and only one category, C1, C2, or C3, and the category checked for each item is coded as 1, with zeros elsewhere. We would like to make a scoring scheme for each item so that the m (here $m = 4$) scores given to each respondent have some desirable property. We give a *weight*—or value—w_{jk} to the kth category of the jth item so that a respondent gets a score s_j equal to the weight or value given to the category checked. That is, a respondent who checks category k of item j gets score $s_j = w_{jk}$ for that item. The optimal weighting problem is to choose weights that are "best"/optimal in some mathematically definite sense. Of several equivalent definitions of optimal weights, I name just two. We choose weights so that the ratio of the variance of the total score

$$S = \Sigma_j s_j$$

to the sum of the variances of the m item scores $s_1, \ldots, s_m$ is maximized. Recalling the material of Chapter 6, the student will recognize that this means choosing a weighting scheme for the categories that maximizes G-C alpha for the resulting weighted (formula) test score. This will also maximize the ratio of the sum of the covariances of the item scores to the sum of their variances and will tend to have the effect of maximizing the sum of the item correlations.[15]

The technical solution to the problem just stated invokes some classical results in matrix algebra—the eigenvalues and eigenvectors of a matrix—which are beyond the scope of this text.[16] It must suffice to give a simple example of the kind of results obtained by optimal weighting methods. Table 18.7 actually gives responses to four three-category items by 23 respondents.[17] The items are as listed in Table 18.8. Because each of these items can be considered to be ordered, we might just assign Likert scale values 1, 2, 3, to the successive categories. If we do this, we obtain the item correlations in Table 18.9.

Suppose that we sum the four Likert item scores to obtain a total score, after changing signs so they measure in the same direction—measuring, we guess, a form of conservatism marked by aging and nostalgia/dogmatism. G-C alpha from Table 18.9 is then .505.

Using one technology for optimal weighting gives the set of category weights w_1 in Table 18.10. Using another yields the weights w_2 in the table. Using either of these to score respondents on the four items gives the correlation matrix in Table 18.11, with a G-C alpha equal to .817. It also gives the standardized optimal scores for the 23 respondents in the last column of Table 18.6.

TABLE 18.8
Nishisato Multicategory Items

Item 1: How old are you? C1, 20–29; C2, 30–39; C3, 40 or over.
Item 2: Children today are not as disciplined as when I was a child. C1, Agree; C2, I cannot tell; C3, Disagree.
Item 3: Children today are not as fortunate as when I was a child. C1, Agree; C2, I cannot tell; C3, Disagree.
Item 4: Religion should not be taught at school. C1, Agree; C2, Indifferent; C3, Disagree.

TABLE 18.9
Nishisato Item Correlations—Likert Scaling

	1	2	3	4
1	1	−.705	.234	−.325
2	−.705	1	−.104	−.031
3	.234	−.104	1	.176
4	−.325	−.031	.176	1

TABLE 18.10
Nishisato Items—Optimal Scaling

Item	Category	δ	w_1	w_2	l	λ^*
1	C1	.314	.863	1.448	.466	.427
	C2	.391	−.245	0.340	−.161	−.147
	C3	.304	−.585	0.000	−.305	−.280
2	C1	.696	−.532	0.000	−.363	−.375
	C2	.174	.561	1.093	.191	.212
	C3	.130	.580	1.112	.172	.163
3	C1	.130	−.126	0.173	−.019	−.010
	C2	.217	.615	0.911	.184	.242
	C3	.652	−.299	0.000	−.165	−.232
4	C1	.348	−.430	0.000	−.178	−.219
	C2	.261	.798	1.228	.299	.350
	C3	.391	−.246	0.184	−.121	−.131

TABLE 18.11
Nishisato Item Correlations—Optimal Scaling

Item	1	2	3	4
1	1	.797	.392	.703
2	.797	1	.348	.477
3	.392	.348	1	.368
4	.703	.477	.368	1

Although the weights obtained in this procedure are not themselves unique, the resulting item correlation matrix is. One way to explain this is to think of the optimal score S as a dependent variable in a regression on the category scores—in the example, 12 of them. Because of the categorical structure, the category scores are not independent—recall Chapter 8 on multicollinearity—so the weights are indeterminate, although the resulting scores are unique except for a choice of scale. It is therefore not a safe procedure in general to make judgments of the comparative sizes of category weights. Yet it appears to have become customary to regard them as interpretable quantities, although a principle underlying the interpretation does not seem to have been found.

One way to think of optimal scaling is as a way to approximate a linear item response model for multicategory responses. Suppose the data in Table 18.7 arise from a latent trait—representing a form of "conservativism." We suppose that the probability of each response to the items is a linear function of the latent trait, that is,

$$P\{Y_{jk} = 1 | F = f\} = \delta_{jk} + \lambda_{jk}f. \tag{18.8}$$

Because the respondent must choose one category, these probabilities must sum to unity for each item. Then (18.8) requires that the loadings λ_{jk} sum to zero and the parameters δ_{jk} are overall probabilities of each category and sum to unity for each item. This is a crude but usable approximate model for the factor analysis of multicategory observations,[18] and optimal weighting in turn provides a crude approximation to it. Table 18.12 gives the covariance matrix of the 12 categories.

Applying COSAN to this covariance matrix, with devices to keep the sums of loadings zero for each item, gives the estimates of δ_{jk} and λ_{jk} in Table 18.10. This table also gives the coefficients of the regression of the optimal score S on the 12 category scores, denoted λ^* because they are approximations to the factor loadings as obtained by COSAN. The standardized optimal scores in the last column of Table 18.6 range between −1 and 2. Figure 18.6 graphs the item response functions, using the δ_{jk} and λ_{jk}^* values in Table 18.10. (The use of COSAN factor loadings would in this case be very similar.)

The probability values at the two extremes repay careful examination. At the extreme optimal score of −1, the respondents (a) are almost certainly over 29, with about equal probability of being under or over 39, (b) almost certainly agree that children are not as disciplined as [formerly], (c) almost certainly disagree that children are not as fortunate as [formerly], and (d) agree or disagree with about equal probability that religion should be taught in schools, with about zero probability of being indifferent. At the extreme optimal score of 2, the respondents (a) are almost certainly below 29, (b) with about equal probability "cannot tell" or disagree that children today are not as disciplined as [formerly], (c) almost certainly "cannot tell" if children are not as fortunate as [formerly], and (d) almost certainly are indifferent as to whether religion should be taught in schools. The reader is invited to consider whether these observations are consistent with

TABLE 18.12
Nishisato Item-Category Covariance Matrix

.212	−.119	−.093	−.168	.077	.091	.004	.064	−.068	−.062	.138	−.076
−.119	.238	−.119	.075	−.025	−.051	−.008	.002	.006	−.093	−.059	.151
−.093	−.119	.211	.093	−.053	−.040	.004	−.066	.062	.155	−.079	−.076
−.168	.075	.093	.213	−.121	−.091	−.004	−.064	.068	.062	−.095	.032
.077	−.025	−.053	−.121	.144	−.023	.021	.049	−.070	−.061	.042	.019
.091	−.051	−.040	−.091	−.023	.113	−.017	.015	.002	−.002	.052	−.051
.004	−.008	.004	−.004	.021	−.017	.113	−.028	−.085	.042	−.034	−.008
.064	.002	−.066	−.064	.049	.015	−.028	.170	−.142	−.032	.074	−.042
−.068	.006	.062	.068	−.070	.002	−.085	−.142	.227	−.009	−.040	.049
−.062	−.093	.155	.062	−.061	−.002	.042	−.032	−.009	.227	−.091	−.136
.138	−.059	−.079	−.095	.042	.052	−.034	.074	−.040	−.091	.193	−.102
−.076	.151	−.076	.032	.019	−.051	−.008	−.042	.049	−.136	−.102	.238

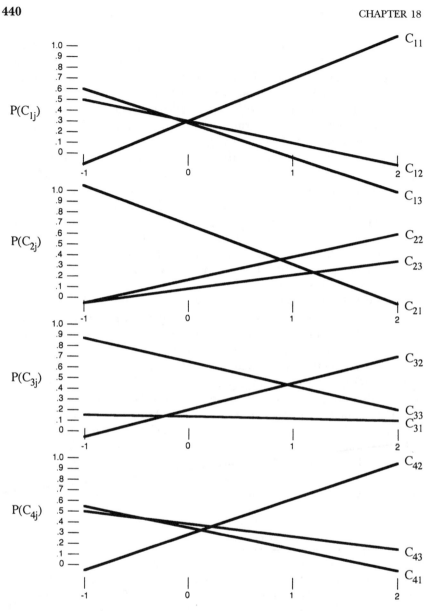

FIG. 18.6. Multicategory item response functions.

the conjecture that what is measured is a form of conservatism marked by nostalgia and dogmatism.

Note that some category probabilities are outside the permissible range of zero to unity within the range of standardized optimal scores. Effectively, we are using a linear model to approximate an undefined item response model with monotone item response functions. Optimal scaling is in turn an approximation to the approximation. At the time of writing, the only rigorously developed item response model for multicategory data—due to Bock—assumes that the categories have a natural order, and does not allow the item response functions to be monotone.[19] The application of this model to the present data set would—perhaps inappropriately—force one category to go from zero probability to unit probability, one to go from unit probability to zero, and one to go from zero to zero, with an intermediate nonzero maximum. It is to be hoped that better models for unordered category data will be developed in the future.

REVIEW GUIDE

It is not obvious how to give general guidance on this chapter. Readers will vary greatly in what they would wish to take from it. The account of scale properties in the section leading to Table 18.1 should matter to all students, as should the discussion of "permissible statistics." Not everyone will share my admiration for Coombsian data theory, sketched in the middle section. I hope some will be stimulated to read further on it. The final section is a sampling of models and methods whose main intent, again, is to stimulate some, although perhaps not all, readers to pursue some of these further.

END NOTES

1. This classification is due to Stevens (1946).
2. See Stevens (1946) and Guttman (1977).
3. The source is Coombs (1964).
4. Coombs (1964), although somewhat technical, is recommended reading.
5. Walker (1931) discussed the notion of choosing cognitive items giving an "ideal" answer pattern, in which a person who passes a given item passes all easier items. Guttman (1950) applied the corresponding notion to attitude items.
6. Coombs (1964).
7. Coombs (1964).
8. See, for example, Shye (1985).
9. An informal proof should suffice here. If two sets of items follow detectably different one-parameter families of item response models, such as a linear model and a logistic model, inverting the item response function for each set gives distinct measures of differences between groups of examinees, and the scales so defined will be nonlinearly related when the items are joined together.
10. Coombs (1964).
11. A classic, readable account of Thurstone's law of comparative judgment is given by Guilford (1954).
12. Sources are Bradley and Terry (1952) and Luce (1959). For a review see Bradley (1984).

13. See Young and Hamer (1987).
14. See, for example, Tziner (1987).
15. The primary source is Guttman (1941).
16. See, for example, Johnson and Wichern (1992).
17. Taken with permission from Nishisato (1996). See Nishisato (1994) for a nontechnical introduction to this technique and further references to the field.
18. McDonald (1969, 1983).
19. Bock (1972) is the source, but see Bock (1997) for an introductory account.

Chapter 19

Retrospective

This final chapter is not intended to summarize the text. The intention is to consider selected aspects of the topics from the particular viewpoint that provides what has been claimed to be a unified treatment. We should now be in a position to take a broad view of the field, to see the relationships between the topics, and also to acknowledge some limitations created by the choice of a unifying principle. More particularly, we should also be able to consider some of the choices between methods that we face in applications.

A rereading of the questions in the introduction to Chapter 1 will show how far the need has been met to provide an answer, or, in some cases, a choice of answers, to these. And at this stage the brief and broad history of some concepts in test theory in Chapter 1 should be more fully intelligible than at first reading. We recall at this point the claim made in Chapter 1 that common factor analysis and item response theory, applied to items selected from an item domain, provide a unifying principle and yield a unified account of test theory. We have seen that for binary item scores the (linear) common factor model is, in theory and in applications (as to the LSAT6 data), an approximation, sometimes crude, sometimes quite acceptable, to the nonlinear (logistic or normal ogive) item response models. The closeness of the approximation will depend essentially on the item factor loadings. If these are not too high—say, on the order of .6—the approximation will be good. If they are intermediate—say, .7 to .8—it will be reasonable. If they are high—say, greater than .9—the approximation will likely be unacceptable.

Some readers will be aware that a very general principle in pure and applied mathematics, used in physics and other sciences, represents a strictly nonlinear function as a series expansion in powers (a convergent polynomial series) of the argument, or as a sine/cosine series. This principle gives us a technique known as *harmonic analysis* or *Fourier analysis*.

***Some readers will be familiar with Taylor series. In harmonic analysis, the polynomial expansion is weighted by the distribution—in the present applications—of the common factor/latent trait, giving best fit where there are most examinees, and is therefore preferred to Taylor series, which give a locally best approximation. $$$

McDonald in 1967 gave polynomial series representations of the normal-ogive item response function and the step function.[1] (Other functions can in principle be similarly treated.) Further work leading to the NOHARM theory and computer program essentially showed that when we take account of the distribution of examinee abilities/trait values, the polynomial series representing the normal-ogive model is so rapidly convergent that terms beyond the cubic can safely be neglected, and just the linear approximation is remarkably good. That is, changes in the parameter estimates and discrepancy matrix from adding more terms tend to be negligible. More generally, it can be conjectured that any monotone response function—any function that is always increasing or always decreasing—will be fairly well approximated by a best-fitting straight line in the region where the main part of the population is concentrated. This very general mathematical principle is implicit in virtually the whole of the treatment of test theory adopted in this text.

In Chapter 2, partly to fix ideas, partly because of their central importance, our work focused on the items of an objective test—items yielding responses that can be scored without the need for judgment on the part of the examiners. The reader should be able to determine, without specific advice, how far the material in the remaining chapters can apply to marks, scores, ratings, and so on given by examiners/judges that do not meet the definition of objectivity. As we saw both in Chapter 6 and in Chapter 10, ratings of named traits by multiple raters do raise some problematic issues with respect to inter-rater agreement—the exchangeability of raters, or the sense in which raters can be treated as drawn at random from a specifiable population. But in many cases it is safe enough to apply the methods given for estimating error of measurement and so on to scores in which some of the error is due to examiner/rater judgment.

The nine item types summarized in Table 2.1 gave two main forms of scorable item response, namely, binary responses and quantitative responses, scored over a limited range of integer values. (A few item types were left to Chapter 18.) We rarely have responses to items or subtests that can be considered essentially continuous variables. In the chapters—primarily Chapters 6 and 7—in which linear models have been applied, the assumption of linearity and the assumption that the unique variances are constant over the range of the trait are both approximations to reality. The use of ML estimation in these linear models assumes normality, which adds a third approximation. Very technical alternatives to the estimation methods of Chapter 6 and Chapter 9 are now available.[2] Some of these have been incorporated in computer packages for factor analysis and path analysis, to cover applications to what we have regarded as "quantitative" item scores, measured over a limited number of integer values. These methods are regarded as beyond the scope of an introductory text. At the time of writing they still need further evaluation. The interested reader will watch developments and obtain advice about the contents and use of accessible computer packages. A sketch of the logical basis of these developments must suffice here.

Many integer-scored item responses arise, of course, from Likert scoring of ordered categories. Those which do not—such as scores on item bundles and checklist counts—can be treated as though the integer scores arise from ordered categories. By a further extension of the conception of "underlying response tendencies" used to obtain biserial and tetrachoric correlations in Chapter 11, and to give a form of item factor analysis in Chapter 12, we can define *polychoric correlations*—correlations between response tendencies underlying two sets of ordered categories. We can then apply structural models—factor analysis or path analysis—to sample versions of these correlations. It is also possible to mix binary responses, ordered-category responses, and quantitatively scored tests, in a factor model or path model, by using tetrachoric correlations (binary with binary), polychoric correlations (ordered-category with ordered-category, including binary), biserial (ordered-category with quantitative), or *polyserial* (ordered-category with quantitative). Although it would be possible to use unweighted least squares estimation, the more sophisticated methods of analysis use appropriate weight matrices in a *weighted least squares*—WLS—estimation. This gives a chi-square and the usual derived goodness-of-fit indexes in sufficiently large samples. Currently, it appears that weight matrices based on sample observations may not give statistics that can be relied on until the sample size becomes extremely large. It is here conjectured that the use of both the linear approximation and the normal approximation may seldom yield unacceptably inferior results compared with the more sophisticated methods in the range of sample sizes generally available to researchers. But any remarks on this issue will date very rapidly, and the reader of this book is encouraged to check the available procedures as their utility and limitations become better understood.

From the point of vantage we have reached, the classical item and test statistics developed in Chapter 3 can be seen as basic statistical ingredients for the models and methods of later chapters. Those models and methods enable us to go beyond the population specificity of item and test means, variances and covariances, to models whose parameters, suitably scaled, serve as scientific invariants in the comparison of examinees from distinct populations. A general principle governs population-specific versus invariant statistics as follows: The parameters of a regression function are unaltered by selection on the basis of independent variables, because the regression represents the conditional mean of the response variable for selected values of the independent variables. Except for choice of scale, we therefore expect parameters describing the common factor equations and item response functions to be invariant, whereas means, factor correlations, unique variances, and so on are accidents of the population. Some writers describe this, imprecisely, as a contrast between the population specificity of classical test theory and the scale-free properties of modern item response theory.

The brief and undeveloped remarks in Chapter 4 serve merely to establish that measurement in the behavioral/social sciences requires some degree of reproducibility in the assignment of numbers to attributes according to a rule. But it does not generally yield or require better than ordinal properties. As discussed in more detail in Chapter 18, the numbers assigned generally reflect only ordinal relations between the amounts of the attribute, and differences between the numbers assigned generally do not reflect intervals in the attribute measured. Even those models—such as the 1PL "Rasch" model as in Chapters 13 and 18, or the Thurstone and Bradley–Terry–Luce models for pair comparisons as in Chapter 18—that allow testing for interval properties leave open the possibility that subsets of items give distinct and contradictory interval scales. The contradiction would be revealed when the items are put together. Thus the discussion in Chapter 18 merely elaborates the position stated in Chapter 4, that we may choose a metric—a set of units spread out along the number line—in any convenient way. We may also, for some purposes, further choose any monotone transformation of an initially chosen metric. Care is needed over statistical hypotheses—for example, about distributions or linearity of relationships—that are themselves not invariant over the choice of sets of units. Generally, the metric is conveniently chosen to fix the form of a set of item response functions, to linearize a relationship, or to simplify a distribution. In retrospect, we note that care is also needed over the effect of the choice of metric on error of measurement/information. As Chapter 13 showed, error variance, as a function of the scaled attribute, can follow entirely different courses for different metrics. Thus it goes from zero to zero through larger values for true-score metric, and from infinity to infinity through smaller values for the usual latent trait metric.

We have noted that classical true-score theory, as in Chapters 5 and 7, with its basic Spearman factor model, as in Chapter 6, assumes not only that the item scores (and hence the test score) are linear functions of the attribute, but also that the item unique variance (hence the test-score error variance) is constant over the range of the attribute (and of the true score). This assumption is, of course, inherently unrealistic for binary item responses, and it inevitably fails at points close to the floor or ceiling of the test.

The theory as given in Chapter 6 brings the common factor model and item response models together, with the former an approximation to the latter. It bases classical reliability theory on the linear common factor model and its special cases. One advantage of this treatment is that it makes the assumptions of classical reliability theory explicit. Readers familiar with accounts of KR_{20} for the reliability of binary items might easily have failed to notice that implicitly KR_{20} as an equality assumes a one-parameter linear item response function, and as a lower bound requires a two-parameter linear function. This is already at best an approximation, for the reasons given in Chapter 12.

Another general consideration central to the material of Chapters 5–7 concerned the population-specific character of the reliability coefficient— the ratio of true score to total variance—and the expected population invariance of the error variance. The general principle was suggested earlier that means, variances, and covariances are generally population specific whereas regression parameters, properly scaled, are generally population invariant. We think of the invariance of the error of measurement of a test as a special, exceptional case, reflecting properties of the measuring instrument, not accidents of the population.

The emphasis in this text has been on the *SE* of measurement as the important end product. The reliability coefficients—omega, alpha, the Spearman–Brown formula, and in particular KR_{20} for binary item scores— are devices for estimating this end product. This does not rule out the possibility of evaluating the test in terms of the size of its reliability coefficient in the population on which the test is calibrated, but an emphasis on the *SE* of measurement (a) points up its invariance property, (b) warns against regarding the reliability coefficient as invariant, and (c) enables the direct link to item response models, where we do not have a reliability coefficient, except perhaps as a kind of average.

This is a suitable place to consider a question that must have occurred to the reader in progressing from classical reliability theory to item response theory. For binary item responses, the theory of Chapter 13 is more refined and clearly appropriate than that of Chapter 7. Does it follow that the test developer and user should always adopt the more refined theory, now that it is available, and regard the classical treatment as an out-of-date device to be discarded? Similarly, should we ever use the Spearman–Brown prophecy formula, and other devices as in Chapter 7, to make decisions about the length of a test when we have the possibilities of using the item information functions to create a test with a prespecified *SE* of measurement at each point of the attribute continuum?

These are questions requiring a program of comparisons of results from the classical true-score model and item response models applied to empirical and constructed data sets. In the absence of sufficient evidence of this kind, a few conjectural remarks must suffice. In the nearly two decades since the technology described in Chapter 13 has become available, almost all applications of tests and measurements have still used scores that are simple linear functions of raw sum scores, together with classical reliability estimates—usually of coefficient alpha. This would partly be due to the inertia of old practice, and the situation can be expected to change. Meanwhile, the conjecture offered here is that away from the floor and ceiling of the test—regions where no models can save us—the classical linear, constant error-variance treatment will give a sufficiently good, average-error approximation for most small-scale research and testing programs, both in noncognitive and cognitive applications of tests with binary responses. The most common research applications merely require correlating the test score with other measures, with no interest in the precision of measurement of any one examinee. The refined methods of Chapter 13 may, at least for some time, be reserved for large-scale cognitive testing programs, including computer adaptive testing, based on large item banks.

Item response theory, in Chapters 12–16, has primarily assumed the logistic item response function, and to a less extent the indistinguishable normal-ogive. Some interesting research developments show the possibilities of working with *nonparametric* item response models that require only monotone item response functions, not prescribed functions with parameters to be estimated.[3] Eventually these may yield methods of estimating abilities/attributes and obtaining *SEs* of measurement. Meanwhile, for the reasons already given, the assumption of the logistic function form does not seem a troubling restriction on the practical task of measurement.

It might be claimed that the 1PL "Rasch" model, as discussed in Chapters 13 and 18, fills the gap between large-scale normative testing programs and smaller scale cognitive testing—for example, school-based programs—or noncognitive studies. There may be some merit to this claim, but note that (a) precisely because the 1PL model has the raw sum score as a sufficient statistic for the attribute, the choice between the test score and the 1PL estimate of the attribute is just a choice of metric, and (b) the items are not exchangeable with respect to their information/error properties. Under either choice of metric the ideal of "person-free" and "item-free" measurement is most certainly not attainable, at least in a population yielding scores near the floor or ceiling of the test.

From the perspective given by the account of the unidimensional linear or nonlinear models in Chapters 6 and 12, and of the multidimensional linear and nonlinear models given in Chapters 9 and 14, we can see more clcarly the central role of the (wide-sense) factor model in test theory. Through most of the history of this field it has tended to be seen as mapped into two main regions, namely, classical test theory—primarily true-scorc theory—and item analysis/item response theory, both of which are supposed applied to content-homogeneous tests, and the common factor model (usually in its exploratory form) was occasionally invoked as an ancillary, unrelated technology. There is a more than coincidental closeness of the multidimensional results provided by independent-cluster factor analysis (Chapter 9) and independent-cluster item response theory (Chapter 14). Again, the relation between these serves to reunify "classical" and "modern" test theory.

The treatment of validity in Chapters 10 and 14 rests primarily on unidimensional or independent-cluster factor and item response models. It may be admitted that this gives the treatment a rather narrow focus. It identifies (construct) validity with the extent to which the score on a homogeneous test correlates with the corresponding latent trait—the factor common to the items. This presupposes both content validity and a conceptualized item domain. Suitable warnings have been given about these limitations. (My own impressions of the field of validity studies lead me to the opinion that the aspirations of validity theory to the use of a more widely based technology are not mirrored in applications.)

The possibility is left open that (further) evidence of (construct) validity can be obtained by embedding the test score in a theoretical network of relationships. Specifically, this is likely to be a network expressed as a (causal) path model, the technology of which was sketched and illustrated in Chapter 17. It is my current belief that path analysis is not yet an entirely safe procedure for these purposes, primarily because of the problem of equivalent models. It remains to be shown how such wider inquiries can add to—or subtract from—evidence from Spearman or independent-cluster analyses of the items. Thus, a set of items may appear homogeneous, embodying a nameable abstract concept (thus having content validity) and measuring its latent trait well, yet we may reject a hypothesized path model in which the test score is included. The choice between invalidating the construct and "invalidating"—rejecting—the postulated causal relations might be a difficult one, but a balance of probabilities could well favor retaining the factor-analytic evidence and rejecting the causal model.

The interpretation of convergent and discriminant validity given in Chapters 9 and 14 in terms of independent-cluster factors departs from the dominant convention in the literature, which links it to multitrait–multimethod matrices, following Campbell and Fiske. The interested reader will of course examine the alternative views available.

Similarly, I have adopted the concept of predictive utility, and treated "concurrent" validation as one form of validating evidence, although possibly a rather weak form. Again, the reader is encouraged to examine alternative views. The extreme position that a test has as many validities as there are measures with which it has nonzero correlations surely strains our notion of reasonable usage. On the other hand, the reader may feel that my treatment of content/construct validity in terms of explicitly denoted item domains, is too idealistic. Let me make two concessions:

1. In developing our understanding of a behavioral domain it may be necessary to lift ourselves up by our bootstraps, refining an initially crude conception with the help of any relevant evidence. This could include concurrent measures of associated attributes, and might correspond to an informally conceived causal model, already covered as construct validity, which is the better for formalization as a path model.

2. Predictive utility studies, in which we bring together a set of items giving a high squared multiple correlation with an educationally important, or, more generally, socially important outcome, have their own undeniable value. It is my prejudice that good theory will be a better guide than trial-and-error empiricism in such cases, and in applications a combination of theory and empirical evidence may justify itself after the facts.

Much of the account in this text rests, explicitly or implicitly, on the idealization represented by an infinite domain of items. The position taken is that the measurement of any abstractive psychological attribute inescapably demands a conceptual quasi-infinity of possible indicators, if it is to be a defined quantity that can be estimated with known error variance. It is my belief that without the concept of an item domain, we cannot give a rational and coherent account of error of measurement, together with the possibility of reducing error by adding further items to a test. Alternative accounts of error in test theory have been given, and the reader is encouraged to examine these.[4]

There has been a recurring controversy with implications for the foundations of test theory, known as the "factor indeterminacy" issue. It can be shown that the basic equations of factor models, true-score models, and all item response models using the principle of local independence have arbitrary alternative solutions for the latent trait values. This is essentially because there are more "unknowns"—common factors plus unique components—than knowns—test/item scores in the equations of these models. For some writers, this mathematical result implies that a common factor score is not a determinate quantity to be estimated in the first place. It is not obvious what this means in applications to real data. In applications, on one interpretation, if further items are added to an item set that are not drawn from a prespecified, conceptualized item domain, different investigators could arrive at different sets of items measuring distinct attributes whose correlations are quite low.[5] Only if we follow Guttman's classical account of behavior domains, requiring these applications to rest on a preconceived behavior domain, do we have a determinate factor score/true score/latent trait for which a finite set of item scores can give an unbiased estimate and *SE* of measurement.

The idealization involved in the notion of an infinite item domain does not give a general warrant for just any use of these methods. Rather, it provides a critical framework for judging the success or failure of applications. It is possible to point to sets of items—for example, a specialized knowledge test of the keys of the Beethoven symphonies—that by their denotation do not allow augmentation with further items "of the same kind." Reflecting on the possibility of such augmentation tells us if we are indeed identifying an abstract attribute that can be regarded as having a true value, and an error of measurement due to the choice of a limited number of exemplifying items. In applications the idealization can and must be loosened to some extent. It should suffice that further items can be conceived that will make a "large" set measuring a "dominant" dimension with "negligible" error. Thus *large* replaces *infinite, dominant dimension* replaces *single dimension*, and *negligible* replaces *zero*. It is then a matter for the test constructor whether this state of affairs can be conceived.

Under mild conditions, for a sufficiently large number of items/indicator variables, the common factor/true score/latent trait will be in perfect correspondence to the sum score or any rationally weighted score from the items. Some discussions of the "factor indeterminacy" issue fail to address the central importance in a finite set of items of having a means to obtain an unbiased estimate of the attribute, as scaled, and an *SE* of measurement. For this purpose, generally the models treated in this text and the ML estimators of the attribute are necessary. Alternative composites of item scores, such as principal components, do not yield these needed statistical properties. Again, the reader is invited to consider alternative positions on this matter.[6]

Chapter 15 focused on a minor modification of the treatment by Lord of the relationship between item scores in distinct populations, and of the detection and assessment of differentially functioning items. The three main motives for this choice of method were:

1. It conforms to the central intention of this text to make the wide-sense factor model the key to a unified account of test theory.
2. Lord's treatment, as adapted, seems the most natural and fundamental approach to these problems.
3. It has not yet been shown that other devices, such as the Mantel–Haenszel or Stout's SIBTEST method, can usefully replace or improve on the classical method in detecting DIF or making diagnoses of its various causes.

Again, this is an area that can be expected to show rapid developments, and the interested reader will watch for these.

Similarly, the treatment here of alternate forms and of equating in Chapter 16 has rested on item response theory, for the same three reasons as in the last paragraph with respect to DIF. The treatment of alternatives to item response theory true-score equating may seem unduly dismissive to some readers. I believe the evidence is clear that IRT true-score equating is the method of choice (a) for its superior scaling properties, compared to linear methods, (b) for its superior information properties, compared to the equipercentile method, and (c) (probably) for its superior efficiency, compared to any other method. Again, developments in the literature should be watched.

In retrospect and in summary, it is here claimed that the major part of the collection of topics, methods, devices, and so forth that make up the field of test theory can be treated as applications of a generally nonlinear common factor model to items drawn from a domain of indicators of an abstract psychological attribute.[7] It is left to the reader of this text and of the wider literature to judge the limitations and the further potential of this treatment.

END NOTES

1. McDonald (1967).
2. Browne (1984b) was the originator of *asymptotically distribution free* estimation methods. Muthen (1984) gave a general model with mixed binary, ordered category, and continuous variables. A good account of these developments, of intermediate technical level, is in Bollen (1989), pp. 415–447.
3. These developments have primarily been directed at testing for unidimensionality. See, for example, Ellis and Wollenberg (1993).
4. See Lord and Novick (1968) for the concept of a propensity distribution. Again, see Ellis and Wollenberg (1993) for further developments of this notion.
5. See McDonald (1977) and McDonald and Mulaik (1979).
6. A recent round of debate on factor indeterminacy can be found in Maraun (1996a, 1996b, 1996c), Steiger (1996a, 1996b), Bartholomew (1996a, 1996b), Rozeboom (1996a, 1996b), Schonemann (1996a, 1996b), Mulaik (1996a, 1996b), and McDonald (1996a, 1996b). Although this group of papers is not clearly an advance on previous accounts in the literature, the interested reader will at least see how this question tends to generate heat, if not light.
7. See McDonald (1986).

Appendix A
Some Rules for Expected Values

A number of the optional proofs in this book are simple applications of the algebra of expected values—of population means. The student who chooses to follow these proofs needs to review or accept the following basic statistical principles.

Consider a set of random variables, $X_1, \ldots, X_m$. We write $\mathcal{E}\{\cdot\}$ for an expected value—a population mean. We write

$$\mu_j = \mathcal{E}\{X_j\},$$
$$\sigma_{jj} = \mathrm{Var}\{X_j\} = \mathcal{E}\{(X_j - \mu_j)^2\},$$

and

$$\sigma_{jk} = \mathrm{Cov}\{X_j, X_k\} = \mathcal{E}\{(X_j - \mu_j)(X_k - \mu_k)\}.$$

Let

$$Y = a + b_1 X_1 + \ldots + b_m X_m = a + \Sigma\, b_j X_j.$$

We use two fairly general principles from the algebra of expectations:

$$\mathcal{E}\{Y\} = a + \Sigma\, b_j \mu_j, \tag{A1}$$

and

$$\mathrm{Var}\{Y\} = \Sigma\,\Sigma\, b_j b_k \sigma_{jk}. \tag{A2}$$

If $a = 0$ and all the coefficients $b_j = 1$, so that

$$Y = X_1 + \cdots + X_m,$$

then

$$\mathcal{E}\{Y\} = \Sigma\,\mu_j \tag{A3}$$

and

$$\mathrm{Var}\{Y\} = \Sigma\,\Sigma\,\sigma_{jk}. \tag{A4}$$

Commonly in the applications in this book we have just two variables, X_1 and X_2, giving

$$Y = a + b_1 X_1 + b_2 X_2,$$

so that (A1) reduces to

$$\mathcal{E}\{Y\} = a + b_1\mu_1 + b_2\mu_2, \tag{A5}$$

and, if $\mu_2 = 0$, to

$$\mathcal{E}\{Y\} = a + b_1\mu_1. \tag{A6}$$

Similarly, in the case of just two variables, we have

$$\mathrm{Var}\{Y\} = b_1{}^2\sigma_{11} + 2b_1 b_2\sigma_{12} + b_2{}^2\sigma_{22}. \tag{A7}$$

If $\sigma_{12} = 0$, that is, X_1 and X_2 are uncorrelated, then

$$\mathrm{Var}\{Y\} = b_1{}^2\sigma_{11} + b_2{}^2\sigma_{22}, \tag{A8}$$

and if Y is just the simple sum of X_1 and X_2, this becomes

$$\mathrm{Var}\{Y\} = \sigma_{11} + \sigma_{22}, \tag{A9}$$

representing a simple analysis of the variance of Y into its two parts.

Glossary

Achievement test—a test designed to measure formal learning.

Alpha—see *Guttman–Cronbach alpha.*

Alternate forms of a test—two or more tests designed to measure the same *attribute.*

Alternate-form reliability—the correlation between the *total scores* on two *alternate forms* of a test. Syn., *coefficient of equivalence.*

Aptitude test—a test designed to select examinees for a course of instruction or to predict their performance in it.

Attenuation—the change in a correlation or *regression coefficient* due to *error of measurement* in one or more test scores.

Attribute—general term for a property or quality. Used to cover *traits* and *states* or other properties that tests are designed to measure.

Axiom of invariance—states that an *item response model* exists such that the *item parameters* are invariant over populations if a common *metric* is applied. Sometimes mistakenly supposed to imply that any item response model yields invariant parameters.

Behavior domain—a set of possible observations/measurements, usually thought to be (countably) infinite, from which a realizable subset is drawn. Syns., *universe of content, universe of admissible measurements.*

Binary item score—a score for an item that takes just two values, usually 0 or 1.

Binary item—an item yielding a *binary score.*

Binary response—a response to a *binary item.*

Bipolar attribute—an *attribute* of respondents defined by a contrast of opposite extremes. Hence can be scored in either direction.

Biserial correlation—the correlation of a continuous variable with a postulated (normally distributed) response tendency underlying a *binary response.*

Bivariate information methods—methods of estimation of *item parameters* in *item response theory* that use only individual and pairwise proportions of responses.

Bivariate regression—the *regression* of a dependent/response variable on just one independent/explanatory variable.

Calibration population—the population on which the parameters of a set of items are determined.

Category score—the score given to a chosen response category in an item giving three or more, commonly unordered, response categories.

Category weight—the weight given to each response category in an item with three or more response categories, from which a *category score* can be formed.

Ceiling of a test—highest score obtainable on the test.

Checklist—an item allowing multiple, not mutually exclusive, responses. Commonly used also for an observation schedule for use by an observer to record specified behaviors.

Coefficient alpha—see *Guttman–Cronbach alpha.*

Coefficient of congruence—a coefficient measuring the degree of correspondence between item or test parameters (usually in a *common factor* or *item response model*) in two *populations of interest.*

Coefficient of equivalence—see *alternate form reliability.*

Coefficient of generalizability—a measure of the generalizability of a score based on a given set of observations to a corresponding infinite *behavior domain.*

Coefficient omega—the *reliability coefficient* of a set of items fitting the *general factor model.*

Coefficient of precision—an ideal *reliability coefficient,* the ratio of true score variance to observed score variance obtained in ideal conditions. (The conditions are not well defined.)

Coefficient of stability—see *retest reliability.*

Combination operation—an empirical operation on objects or an attribute of objects that yields scale values of the attribute having *interval* properties. Syn., *concatenation operation.*

Common factor—a variable (*general-factor* case) or one of a set of variables (*multiple-factor* case) such that, in a subpopulation in which they are fixed, their *indicators* are uncorrelated. In applications, common factors are interpreted as the common properties of tests/items.

Common factor parameterization—the representation of an *item response model* in terms of a linear *common factor model* for response tendencies underlying the *binary item scores.* Contrast *response function parameterization.*

Completion/constructed-response item—one that requires the examinee to supply an answer.

Composite score—a score obtained by combining (commonly as a weighted or unweighted sum), two or more item subtest or test scores.

Computer adaptive test—a test administered by computer in which each item attempted is determined by the response to the preceding item.

Concatenation operation—see *combination operation.*

Confirmatory model—(in *common factor analysis* and *multidimensional item response theory*), a model with restrictions on the parameters, usually the *factor loadings,* corresponding to the design of the variables, and commonly yielding an *identified model.* Syn., *restricted model.*

Confounding—impossibility of separating amounts of variance of a dependent/response variable due to each independent/explanatory variable when the latter are correlated. See *multicollinearity*.

Construct validity—The extent to which a test measures the attribute, thought of as a theoretical concept, that it is designed or used to measure. In one specific treatment it is given by the squared correlation between the test score and the *common factor* of the items. More generally a test has construct validity if the evidence suggests that it measures the theoretical concept it is designed to measure. *Path analysis* can be used for this purpose.

Content equivalent forms—two tests whose items, taken jointly, have a common content.

Content-parallel forms—two tests whose items are paired to have a common content.

Content validity—a test has content validity if the item contents/stems are indicators of the attribute it is designed or used to measure.

Convergent validity—the extent to which the test measures the *attribute* it was designed to measure, as contrasted with its measurement of other attributes. Compare *discriminant validity*. Note that there is no current agreement on how this should be assessed.

Correction for attenuation—correction yielding the hypothetical statistics—correlations, regression coefficients—associated with two or more measures, if free from *error of measurement*.

Correspondence analysis—see *optimal scaling*.

Criterion—any measure external to a test used to judge its *validity*.

Criterion-referenced test—term adopted for a test whose metric is not referred to a *calibration population*. (Contrast *norm-referenced test*.) The notion motivating criterion-referenced tests, and this terminology for them, is that they measure the attribute of an examinee—usually an educational achievement—against some absolute criterion of "mastery."

Criterion-related validity—the extent of relationship (usually squared multiple correlation) of a test score to an external *criterion*, either measuring *predictive validity* or used as external evidence of *construct validity*.

Cronbach generalizability theory—a family of models for generalizability based on analysis of variance. Its development is largely due to the work of Lee J. Cronbach.

Decision study—term adopted in *Cronbach generalizability theory* for the use of previously calibrated measures to estimate performance of (usually) further respondents in (possibly) further test conditions.

Dependent variable—the response variable in a regression on one or more *independent variables*.

Dichotomous item—an item with just two response options.

Difference score—the score obtained by subtracting one test score from another (a signed difference). Commonly, either a difference between repeated/replicated measures or a difference between scores on *alternate forms*.

Differential item functioning (DIF)—term (and ubiquitous acronym) adopted to describe the finding that an item has distinct probabilities of yielding a given item score for examinees in two populations that have the same value of the *attribute* measured by other items in the test. This implies that the item has distinct *item response functions* in the populations.

Differential test functioning—term adopted to describe the observation that a test has a distinct *test characteristic curve* in two *populations of interest.*

Difficulty parameter (of an item or test)—in classical test theory, the mean/expected value of the item or test score in a *calibration population.* For a *binary item* this is the probability of giving the *keyed response.* Actually, an inverse measure of difficulty.

Direct effect—(in *structural equation/path models*) the change in one variable due to a unit controlled increase, actual or conjectured, in one on which it directly depends, when all other variables on which it directly depends are held constant.

Directed path—(in the graph of a *structural equation model*) a single-headed arrow from a causal variable to one it directly affects.

Discrepancy—(in models for covariance matrices) the difference between a sample covariance and the corresponding estimated covariance calculated from the estimated model parameter(s).

Discrepancy function—a function of the *discrepancies* in a model for a covariance matrix, used to measure the *goodness of fit* of the model and to decide if the fit is acceptable.

Discriminant validity—a term introduced to describe the intuitive requirement that a test score should not have "high" correlations with *attributes* it is not designed to measure.

Discriminating power—see *discrimination parameter.*

Discrimination parameter—a measure of the extent to which an item discriminates between extreme values of an *attribute*, by giving distinct means at those values. A number of parameters, such as the item factor loading, the item information in a linear model, or the covariance of the item score and the test score, can be considered to fit this definition. Syn., *discriminating power.*

Dissimilarities—numbers representing degrees of dissimilarity between pairs of entities.

Distractors—options in multiple choice cognitive items believed by the test constructor to correspond to incorrect answers. (Examples could be found where the belief is not justified.)

Dominance relationship—an empirical relation between *attributes* of objects giving a natural order to the amount of the attribute, so yielding a scale for the attribute with ordinal properties.

Doublet factor—a *common factor* having only two tests or items with nonzero *loadings* on it in a *confirmatory factor/item response model*, or only two nonnegligible loadings in an *exploratory model.*

Dual scaling—see *optimal scaling.*

Efficiency/relative efficiency—the ratio of the *information* in a *formula test score* to the information in an alternative formula score. If the alternative is the ML estimator, the efficiency is not regarded as relative.

Endogenous variable—(in *path analysis/structural equation modeling*) a variable that is directly dependent on at least one other variable in the system.

Equating—finding a transformation of the scores on one test form to the *metric* of another.

Equity—the requirement that it is a matter of indifference to an examinee which of two or more tests is administered for the measurement of an *attribute*—almost always an ability/achievement.

Equivalence (coefficient)—see *coefficient of equivalence*.

Equivalence relationship—(in scaling theory) describes the relationship between two objects that are the same in respect of an *attribute*.

Equivalent models—alternative *structural models* that give the same distribution of the *observable variables* and in particular the same covariance matrix.

Error of measurement—the error of estimation of the value of an *attribute* of an examinee, possibly scaled to be a *true score*.

Essentially homogeneous test—one whose items fit a *factor/item response model* with a *general factor* and negligible *hierarchical group factors*.

Exogenous variable—(in *structural equation/path models*) a variable that is not dependent, directly or indirectly, on other variables in the system.

Exploratory model—a *common factor/item response model* with no constraints on the pattern of *factor loadings* or slope parameters.

Facets—(in *Cronbach generalizability theory*) term used for principles of classification of a set of measurements, other than the *objects of measurement*—such as items, rated behaviors, raters.

Factor analysis—general term in use for the practical application of a *common factor* model to empirical data.

Factor correlations—correlations between the factors in a *confirmatory* or *obliquely rotated multiple factor* or *multidimensional item response model*.

Factor loadings—the coefficients in a *common factor model* representing the difference in an *indicator variable* (item or test score) corresponding to a unit difference in a *factor score*.

Factor pattern—a matrix of *factor loadings*.

Factor score(s)—in the mathematical model of factor analysis, the variable(s) accounting for the covariances of the *indicator variables* by the *principle of local independence*. In applications, interpreted as their common *attribute(s)*.

Factorial congruence—the agreement of the *factor loadings* in two *populations of interest*.

Factorially complex variables—variables having nonzero, or nonnegligible, *loadings* on more than one *common factor*.

Factorially simple variables—variables having nonzero, or nonnegligible, *loadings* on only one *common factor*.

First-order factors—(in a *higher order factor model*) factors explaining relationships between observed *indicator variables*—usually *item scores/test scores*.

Floor of a test—lowest score obtainable on the test.

Focal group—a *population of interest* to be compared to a *reference group/calibration group*.

Formula score information function—the *information* in a *formula test score*.

Formula test score—any function of the *item scores* chosen to measure an *attribute*.

Frequency count—(for items) a score for a *check list item*, consisting of the number of *keyed responses*.

Full information methods—methods of estimation of *item parameters* in *item response models* that use the entire sample distribution of the *item scores*. (Not to be confused with *information* in the estimation of latent traits of examinees.)

Fundamental measurement—a correspondence between the *attribute* being scaled and the axiomatic properties of the [real] number system.

G-C alpha—see *Guttman–Cronbach alpha.*

General factor—a *common factor* on which all the *observed variables* in a set have nonzero *loadings.*

General-factor model—see *single-factor model.*

Generalizability coefficient—see *coefficient of generalizability.*

Generalizability study—(in *Cronbach generalizability theory*) data collection for the purpose of obtaining coefficients that quantify the relationship between the obtained measurements and corresponding domain measurements.

Goodness of fit index—an index—commonly a function of the *discrepancies* in a *structural model*—measuring how well the model fits the data.

Group factors—*common factors* defined by groups or clusters of *observed/indicator variables*—*item or test scores.*

Guttman–Cronbach alpha—the *reliability coefficient* of a test whose items fit the *true-score equivalence model.* In more general conditions it is a lower bound to reliability.

Hierarchical model—a *factor* or *item response model* with a *general factor* and two or more uncorrelated group factors.

Homogeneous test—a test measuring just one *attribute.*

Higher order factors—*common factors* explaining the covariation of common factors of lower order.

Horizontal equating—equating two tests of approximately equal *difficulty.*

Ideal answer pattern—(for binary items) a pattern of *item responses* such that if the *keyed response* is given to an item, the keyed response is given to all items with higher *difficulty parameters.* (A more general treatment and definition for the categories of an unordered category item is not covered in this text.)

Identified model—a model in which the parameters are uniquely determined by the distribution of *observable variables.*

Improper solution—(in *structural models*) an estimated set of parameters yielding impossible statistical properties, such as negative variances or impossible correlations between factors.

Independent clusters basis—a *factor pattern* in a *confirmatory factor/multidimensional item response model* in which each common factor is identified by two or more *factorially simple variables* (for correlated factors) or by three or more factorially simple variables (for uncorrelated factors).

Independent clusters model—in a *confirmatory factor/item response model*, a model in which each variable loads on just one factor. In an *exploratory factor model*, each variable has a nonnegligible loading on just one factor.

Indicators—variables, generally scores on tests or items, whose common contents identify a *common factor/latent variable/latent trait* as an empirical attribute of the examinees.

Indirect effect—*total effect* minus *direct effect.*

Information—(in a test or in a *formula test score*) the extent to which it determines the value of the *attribute* being measured (in the *metric* chosen). It can be defined as the reciprocal of the variance of the *error of measurement* in a locally unbiased estimator of the attribute.

Information function—the *information* in a score as a function of the *attribute.*

Internal consistency—a term traditionally used for the extent to which the items of a test measure the *attribute* "consistently"—in particular having positive and "high" correlations. The term is in common use but does not seem to have a clear definition. *Coefficient alpha* (and its special cases, the *Kuder–Richardson* coefficients) is sometimes regarded in the literature as an "internal consistency" *reliability*.

Interval scale—a scale in which equal intervals in scale value correspond to equal differences in amount of the *attribute* measured.

Item analysis—a term used to refer to devices for assessing the properties of the items of a tests by computing conventional statistics.

Item bank—a set of items, usually large, from which subsets are drawn to form *alternate forms*, or used for *computer adaptive testing*. Syn., *item pool*.

Item bias—*differential item functioning* that yields the possibility of unfair comparisons between members of different populations.

Item bundles—a term seemingly coming into use for subtests generally consisting of items with a common "topic," such as a passage for reading with multiple questions about it.

Item calibration—estimating item parameters in a *calibration group, reference group,* or *generalizability study* for later use on possibly further examinees.

Item characteristic curve/function—the mean/expected value of an *item score* as a function of the *attribute*(s) measured by the test. For *binary items* it is the conditional probability of the *keyed response* as a function of the *attribute*.

Item code—any identifying symbol, possibly a number, used to record a response to an item.

Item difficulty parameter—see *difficulty*.

Item discrimination parameter—see *discrimination parameter*.

Item discriminating power—see *discriminating power*.

Item domain—an indefinitely large set of items whose common content defines a concept or class of concepts.

Item factor loading—factor loading in the *common factor parameterization* of an *item response model*.

Item factor analysis—a model and method that yields a *normal-ogive item response model* by combining a linear *factor model* for underlying variables with a threshold for a *binary response*, and a normal distribution for the *unique part*.

Item information—the *information* in a single item.

Item information function—(in a nonlinear *item response model*) the *information* in a single item as a function of the *attribute*.

Item-parallel tests—tests whose items are paired to have identical *item response functions*.

Item parameters—parameters determining each *item response function*.

Item pool—see *item bank*.

Item remainder score—*total/sum score* on a test minus the score on a specified item.

Item response function/curve—see *item characteristic curve*.

Item response model—a structural model for item scores based on the *principle of local independence*.

Item response theory—the theory governing a family of models defined by the *principle of local independence*.

Item score—the numerical value assigned to an item response.

Item stem—the invariant part of an item.

Joint space—a geometrical representation on a line or in a space of two or more dimensions, for measures representing both stimuli and responses to them.

Keyed response—(in *dichotomous* or *multiple choice* items) the response option giving an *item score* of unity, contrasting with the alternative responses scored zero, in the commonest form of item scoring.

Kuder–Richardson formula 20 (KR$_{20}$)—estimator of the *reliability coefficient* of a test score from a set of *binary items* under the assumption that the items are *true-score equivalent.*

Kuder–Richardson formula 21—estimator of the *reliability coefficient* of a test score from a set of *binary items* under the assumption that the items are *strictly parallel.*

Latent trait(s)—variables accounting for dependence in probability in a set of items, by the *principle of local independence* (strong or weak form). Interpreted in applications as common attributes of the items. Syn., *latent variable, common factor.*

Latent trait theory—see *item response theory.*

Latent variable—term most commonly used in *structural equation/path modeling* for a *common factor* or *latent trait.* Also used in the recent literature for a general notion of an *unobservable variable.*

Law of comparative judgment—model given by Thurstone for *pair comparison* and *ranking* observations based on normally distributed underlying response tendencies.

Likert scaling—assigning integer values to ordered *response options.* (Terminology is due to a virtually universal misreading of Likert's work on sophisticated scaling methods for ordered category items.)

Linear prediction function—a fitted linear *regression* used to predict the value of the response of a new examinee.

Link function—a nonlinear function used to relate the probability of a response to a linear function of *latent traits.*

Logistic function—the function $1/[1 + \exp(-z)]$ as used for the *regression* of a *binary* variable on a quantitative variable.

Manifest variable—term sometimes used in *structural equation/path analysis* for an *observable variable.*

Matching item—an item requiring the examinee to match a set of responses to a list of stimuli.

Measurement—the assignment of numbers to observations according to a rule. Also used for an outcome of the assignment process.

Metric—a chosen set of numbers to be assigned as measures of an *attribute.* Includes choice of origin and unit of measurement.

Metric scaling—term in *multidimensional scaling* for techniques that treat quantities representing *dissimilarities* as measures of *distances.*

Multicollinearity—(in *multiple regression*) interdependency of two or more independent/explanatory variables that tends to prevent accurate estimation of *regression coefficients* and causes *confounding.*

Multidimensional models—(in *factor/item response models* and other scaling models) a model requiring more than one dimension to represent the stimuli or responses being measured.

Multidimensional scaling—refers to a class of models for the representation of *dissimilarities* by *distances* in a space of two or more dimensions.

Multidimensional item response models—models in *item response theory* with more than one *latent trait*.

Multiple-choice item—an item allowing choice of one option out of more than two unordered response options.

Multiple correlation—the correlation between a response/dependent variable and its regression estimator.

Multiple-factor models—*common factor models* allowing more than one *common factor*.

Multiple regression—a model giving the mean/expected value of a dependent/response variable as a function of two or more independent/explanatory variables.

Multitrait–multimethod matrix—a term used to describe a not well defined set of measurements in which all combinations of two *facets* are employed.

Nominal scale—a set of scale values assigned to objects so that the same value is given to *equivalent* objects with respect to an *attribute*, but the values do not possess *ordinal, interval*, or *ratio* properties.

Nondirected path—(in *structural equation/path* models) a path (graphed as a two-headed arrow) representing a nonzero covariance of error terms. Possibly includes an error-term variance.

Nonmetric scaling—term used in *multidimensional scaling* for techniques in which *distances* are ordinally related to *dissimilarities*.

Nonrecursive model—(in *structural equation/path* models) a model containing at least one closed sequence of unidirectional paths. (Some writers add "or at least one pair of correlated error-terms.")

Nonuniform DIF—a term used to describe the observation that an item gives distinct *slope/discrimination parameters* in two *populations of interest*.

Normal-ogive function—the normal cumulative distribution function, used as a *regression* of a *binary score* on a quantitative variable. Used in particular as a *link function* in *item response models*.

Norm-referenced test—a test with *metric* referred to a chosen *population of interest*—the *calibration population*.

Null object—an entity possessing a zero amount of an *attribute*.

Number keyed score—a test score given by the number of *keyed responses*.

Number right score—a cognitive test score given by the number of answers that are accepted to be correct.

Objective test—a test that can be scored without the use of judgment by the examiner.

Objects of measurement—term introduced in *generalizability theory* for the units—examinees, classrooms—whose *attribute* is to be measured. (The concept is somewhat informal.)

Oblique factors—correlated *common factors/latent traits*.

Observable variable—a variable whose values can be obtained from sampled observations.

Observed-score linear equating—method of equating based on a linear approximation to the relationship between observed scores.

Observed score—used for a *test* or *item score* when contrasted with a *true score*.

Omega—see *coefficient omega*.

Optimal scaling—a method of assigning *weights* to alternative responses to each of a set of items to maximize G-C *alpha*, or a mathematical equivalent of this.

Ordered category item—an item with more than two *response options* that have a natural order.

Ordinal scale—a measurement scale in which natural order properties of the attribute are mapped into the number system, but *interval* and *ratio* properties are lacking.

Orthogonal factors—uncorrelated *common factors*.

Pair comparison observations—observations of choices between two alternatives—either preferences or judgments of the amount of an *attribute* they possess. Sometimes referred to as "paired comparisons," as though it is comparisons, not stimuli, that are paired.

Parallel items—items having identical *item characteristic functions*.

Parallel tests/forms—(in classical true score theory) tests having identical true scores and error variances. This implies that they have the same means and variances, and the same pairwise covariances (for more than two), and, in theory, the same covariances with every other test score. In item response models, we may define parallel tests as tests having identical *test characteristic curves*. See *strictly parallel tests*.

Partial correlation—the correlation between two (dependent) variables, conditioned on fixed values of one or more (independent) variables.

Partial covariance—the covariance between two variables conditioned on fixed values of one or more other variables.

Path analysis with/without *latent variables*—see *structural equation modeling*. Some writers reserve *path analysis for* structural equation modeling without *latent variables*.

Path coefficient—a coefficient representing a *direct effect*.

Percentile equating—a method of *equating* based on the cumulative distributions of scores from the *test forms*.

Perfect scale—the order of respondents and the order of items obtained from a *Walker–Guttman observation matrix*.

Phi–gamma law—traditional term for the *normal-ogive* relationship between the probability of detection of a physical stimulus and its intensity.

Population of interest—any population to which a test might be given.

Predictive validity—the extent to which a test score can predict the value of a criterion measure.

Predictor selection—the process of choosing a subset of predictor variables, usually from multiple regression analyses. Devices for this include the *exhaustive method*, in which regressions on all subsets are computed, the *forward method*, in which variables are added that contribute most to prediction, the *backward method*, in which variables are removed that contribute least, and the *stepwise method*, in which each member of a set is reevaluated when a new one is added, and eliminated if superfluous.

Preferential choice observations—a set of observations in which the respondent records preferences between stimuli.

Principle of local independence—the defining principle of *item response theory*, it states that conditionally (i.e., for any fixed value of one or more *latent traits*), the responses to a set of items are independent in probability. That is the *strong form* of the principle. The *weak* form requires only that the responses are conditionally uncorrelated.

Proportion keyed score—see *relative score.*

Proportion right score—see *relative score.*

Proximity relationship—(between a respondent and a stimulus/item category) a relation such that the respondent chooses the stimulus/category if it is sufficiently close to the respondent's ideal.

Pseudo-guessing parameter—a parameter allowing a nonzero lower asymptote to the *item response function* corresponding to the possibility of obtaining a correct answer by guessing.

Quantitative item score—a score ranging over more than two values, as distinct from a *binary item score.*

Random items model—(most commonly in *generalizability theory*) a model in which the items are supposed randomly selected from an *item domain.*

Ranking item—requires the respondent to place the *response options* in order.

Rasch-type models—a class of *item response models* defined by the property of *specific objectivity.*

Ratio scale—a scale such that ratios of scale values correspond to ratios of values of the attribute.

Raw score—see *sum score.*

Recursive model—(in *structural equation/path models*) a model in which there are no closed sequences of unidirectional paths.

Reference group—term used in the context of population comparisons for the *calibration population* that determines the *metric* of an *item response model.*

Regression/regression equation—the mean/expected value of a dependent/response variable expressed as a function of one or more independent/explanatory variables.

Regression constant—the constant term in a *regression.*

Regression coefficient—a multiplier representing the expected difference in a response/dependent variable corresponding to a unit difference in an independent/explanatory variable.

Relative score—the ratio of the number of *keyed responses* given by an examinee to the total number of items. Syn., *proportion keyed score.* In cognitive items, it is the *proportion right score.*

Reliability coefficient—the ratio of *true-score* variance to *observed-score* variance of a test.

Reliability index—the correlation between the *true score* and the *observed score* of a test.

Residual—term generally reserved for difference between a dependent/response variable and its regression on one or more independent/explanatory variables. Sometimes applied more widely to differences between observations/sample statistics and fitted values, including *discrepancies.*

Residual variance—variance of a *residual* in—commonly—a *regression.* This may include *factor/item response* models.

Response function parameterization—term adopted here for the representation of an *item response function* by a link function whose argument is a linear function of the *latent traits.*

Response option—a choice available to an examinee of the response to an *objective test* item.

Restricted model—see *confirmatory model.*

Retest reliability—(in classical treatments of true-score theory) a *reliability coefficient* computed from the correlation between repeated measures from a single test. Sometimes conceived as a *coefficient of stability.*

Rotation—term for the transformation of a matrix of *loadings* in a *common factor model* or *multidimensional item response model* to yield a preferred solution—commonly to approximate *independent clusters,* possibly to approximate *simple structure.*

Scaling—broadly, the assignment of numerical values to observations or some aspect of observations.

Schmid–Leiman transformation—a reparameterization of an *independent clusters factor/item response model,* as a *hierarchical model.*

Semistandardized covariance—the covariance between an *item score* and a standardized test score.

Similarities observations—judgments of the similarity of stimuli (possibly of stimulus pairs).

Simple structure—a classical set of conditions given by Thurstone for a restricted matrix of loadings to be fitted in a *confirmatory model* or approximated by *rotation* devices in an *exploratory model.* Not as restrictive as *independent clusters structure.*

Single factor model—see *general factor model.*

Single stimulus observations—observations of a *dichotomous response* to a single stimulus or *binary response* to a single item.

Spearman–Brown (prophecy) formula—reliability of a set of *parallel items.* Commonly used to conjecture the reliability of a lengthened test.

Spearman factor model—see *general factor model.*

Specific objectivity—(in *item response models*) providing a comparison of *attributes/*abilities independent of the items chosen from a specified set of them, and a comparison of item *difficulties* independent of the examinees chosen from a specified population.

Split-half reliability—a coefficient of reliability obtained by applying the *Spearman–Brown* formula to the correlation between two complementary subsets of items of a test, of equal size.

Stability (coefficient)—see *coefficient of stability.*

Standard error of measurement—the standard deviation of *errors of measurement.*

Standard error of estimate—the standard deviation of the estimate of any parameter in a statistical model. This includes in particular the *standard error of measurement.*

State (of an examinee)—an attribute of an examinee that is quite unstable over time. Contrast *trait.*

Step/jump function—a function that is constant up to a certain value of its argument, then moves discontinuously to a distinct constant value.

Stimulus comparison observations—observations such that the respondent judges stimuli in pairs, as to which possesses more of a specified *attribute.*

Strictly parallel items—items having identical *item response curves.*

Strictly parallel tests—tests having paired items with identical *item response functions.* Syn., *item parallel tests.*

Structural equation modeling—the representation of relationships between *observable variables* and, possibly, *latent variables*, by a set of equations representing the dependency of some on one or more others.

Structural model—a model for the interrelationships in a set of variables. Includes *factor/item response models* and *structural equation models*.

Sum score—unweighted sum of *item scores*.

TCC/TSIF-parallel tests—tests with identical *test characteristic curves* and *test score information functions*.

TCC-parallel tests—tests with identical *test characteristic curves*.

Test battery—a set of tests giving a profile of test scores.

Test score information function—the *information* in a (formula) test score as a function of the *attribute* measured. Can be thought of as the reciprocal of the variance of the estimator, scaled locally to be unbiased.

Test characteristic curve/function—the mean/expected value of a test score as a function of a latent trait.

Test equating—see *equating*.

Test information function—the *information* in a set of items as a function of the *common factor/latent trait*. May be defined as the reciprocal of the variance of the *error of measurement* of the efficient estimator.

Testlet—a subtest consisting of a "small" number of items. Includes *item bundles*.

Total effect—the change in a given variable in a *structural equation/path model* resulting from a (conceptual or actual) unit increase in a specified other, whereas remaining variables are allowed to change only as a consequence of the change in that other.

Total score—see *sum score*.

Trait—an attribute of an examinee that can be regarded as stable over a considerable length of time. Contrast *state*.

True score—(in classical test theory) a part of a random examinee's *observed score* thought to be free from *error of measurement*. It can be interpreted as a measure of the *attribute* in the *metric* of the *observed score*.

True-score equivalence model—a classical linear model in which the items have the same *true-score variance*—or equivalently, the same *factor loading*—and possibly different *error variances*—or, equivalently, possibly different *unique variances*.

True-score equivalent items—items in a *true-score equivalence model*.

True-score IRT equating—expressing the scores on one test form in the *metric* of another by using the relationship between their *test characteristic functions*.

True-score linear equating—expressing the scores on one test form in the *metric* of another by using an approximating linear model for the relationship of their *test characteristic functions*.

True-score model—Spearman's classical representation of an *observed score* as the sum of a *true score* and an *error of measurement*.

True-score theory—the theory governing the *true-score model* and its applications.

Unidimensional models—(in *common factor/item response models*) models with just one *factor/latent trait*.

Unidimensional test—a test whose items fit a *unidimensional model*.

Uniform DIF—term used to describe the observation that an item gives distinct *difficulty parameters*, but identical *discrimination parameters*, in two *populations of interest*.

Unique part—the *residual* in a *common factor model*, corresponding to specific characteristics of a variable, and possibly errors such as instability over time of the response.

Unique variance—variance of the *unique part* of a variable.

Uniqueness—see *unique variance*.

Universe of admissible measurements—see *behavior domain*.

Universe of content—see *behavior domain*.

Unobservable variable—a variable in a *structural model* that cannot be measured as a function of (a finite number of) observable variables.

Unordered category item—an item with more than two response categories, lacking a natural order. Includes *multiple-choice items* and *checklists*.

Unrestricted model—see *exploratory model*.

Validity—(of a test) the extent to which a test measures the *attribute* it is used to measure.

Vertical equating—equating two tests whose *difficulty* is nonnegligibly different.

Walker–Guttman observation matrix—(in binary data) a matrix of responses such that if the respondent gives the *keyed response* to an item, the respondent gives the *keyed response* to all items with a higher proportion of keyed responses.

References

Abel, T. (1948). The operation called *Verstehen*. *American Journal of Sociology*, *54*, 211–218.

Abramson, L. Y., Metalsky, G. I., & Alloy, L. B. (1989). Hopelessness depression: a theory-based subtype of depression. *Psychological Review*, *96*, 358–372.

Anastasi, A. (1982). *Psychological testing* (5th ed.). New York: Macmillan.

Andrich, D. (1988). *Rasch models for measurement*. Newbury Park, CA: Sage.

Angoff, W. H. (1988). Validity: an evolving concept. In H. Wainer & H. I. Braun (Eds.), *Test validity* (pp. 19–32). Hillsdale, NJ: Lawrence Erlbaum Associates.

Bagozzi, R. P. (1993). Assessing construct validity in personality research: Applications to measures of self-esteem. *Journal of Research in Personality*, *27*, 49–87.

Bartholomew, D. J. (1996a). Comment on: Metaphor taken as math: Indeterminacy in the factor model, *Multivariate Behavioral Research*, *31*, 551–554.

Bartholomew, D. J. (1996b). Response to Dr. Maraun's first reply to discussion of his paper. *Multivariate Behavioral Research*, *31*, 631–636.

Bentler, P. M. (1985). *Theory and implementation of EQS, A structural equations program, Manual for Program Version 2.0*. Los Angeles: BMDP Statistical Software, Inc.

Berk, R. A. (Ed.). (1980). *Criterion-referenced measurement: The state of the art*. Baltimore, MD: Johns Hopkins University Press.

Binet, A., & Henri, V. (1895). La psychologie individuelle. *Annee Psychologique*, *2*, 411–463.

Block, J., Block, J. H., & Harrington, D. M. (1974). Some misgivings about the Matching Familiar Figures Test as a measure of reflection-impulsivity. *Developmental Psychology*, *10*, 611–632.

Bloom, B. S., Hastings, J. T., & Madeus, G. F. (1971). *Handbook on formative and summative evaluation of student learning*. New York: McGraw-Hill.

Bock, R. D. (1972). Estimating item parameters and latent ability when responses are scored in two or more nominal categories. *Psychometrika*, *37*, 29–51.

Bock, R. D. (1997). The nominal categories model. In W. J. van der Linden & R. K. Hambleton (Eds.), *Handbook of item response theory* (pp. 33–49). New York: Springer.

Bock, R. D., & Aitkin, M. A. (1981). Marginal maximum likelihood estimation of item parameters: An application of the EM algorithm. *Psychometrika*, *46*, 443–459.

Bollen, K. A. (1989). *Structural equations with latent variables*. New York: Wiley.

469

Bradley, R. A. (1984). Paired comparisons: Some basic procedures and examples. In P. R. Krishnaiah & P. K. Sen (Eds.), *Handbook of statistics* (Vol. 4, pp. 299–326). New York: North-Holland.

Bradley, R. A., & Terry, M. E. (1952). The rank analysis of incomplete block designs. I. The method of paired comparisons. *Biometrika, 39,* 324–345.

Brennan, R. L. (1983). *Elements of generalizability theory.* Iowa City, IA: American College Testing Program.

Browne, M. W. (1975). Predictive validity of a linear regression equation. *British Journal of Mathematical and Statistical Psychology, 28,* 79–87.

Browne, M. W. (1984a). The decomposition of multitrait–multimethod matrices. *British Journal of Mathematical and Statistical Psychology, 37,* 1–21.

Browne, M. W. (1984b). Asymptotically distribution free methods in the analysis of covariance structures. *British Journal of Mathematical and Statistical Psychology, 37,* 62–83.

Browne, M. W., & Cudeck, R. (1992). Alternative ways of assessing fit. *Sociological Methods and Research, 21,* 230–258.

Campbell, D. T., & Fiske, D. W. (1959). Convergent and discriminant validity by the multitrait–multimethod matrix. *Psychological Bulletin, 56,* 81–105.

Carver, C. S., & Ganellan, R. J. (1983). Depression and components of self-punitiveness: High standards, self-criticism, and overgeneralization. *Journal of Abnormal Psychology, 92,* 330–337.

Cattell, R. B. (1971). *Abilities: Their structure, growth and action.* Boston: Houghton Mifflin.

Christoffersson, A. (1975). Factor analysis of dichotomized variables. *Psychometrika, 40,* 5–32.

Claridge, G. (1986). Eysenck's contributions to the psychology of personality. In S. Modgil & C. Modgil (Eds.), *Hans Eysenck: Consensus and controversy* (pp. 73–85). Philadelphia: Falmer.

Cohen, R. J., Swerdlik, M. E., & Smith, D. K. (1992). *Psychological testing and assessment: An introduction to tests and measurement.* Mountain View, CA: Mayfield.

Cole, N. S., & Moss, P. A. (1989). Bias in test use. In R. L. Linn (Ed.), *Educational measurement* (3rd ed., pp. 201–219). New York: Macmillan.

Coombs, C. H. (1964). *A theory of data.* New York: Wiley.

Cox, D. R., Hinkley, D. V., & Barndorff-Nielsen, O. E. (Eds.). (1996). *Time series models in econometrics, finance and other fields.* London: Chapman & Hall.

Cox, D. R., & Wermuth, N. (1996). *Multivariate dependencies: models, analysis and interpretation.* Monographs on statistics and probability 67. London: Chapman and Hall.

Cronbach, L. J. (1951). Coefficient alpha and the internal structure of tests. *Psychometrika, 16,* 297–334.

Cronbach, L. J., & Meehl, P. E. (1955). Construct validity in psychological tests. *Psychological Bulletin, 52,* 281–302.

Diener, E., Emmons, R. A., Larsen, R. J., & Griffin, S. (1985). The satisfaction with life scale. *Journal of Personality Assessment, 49,* 71–75.

Dohrenwend, B. S., Dohrenwend, B. P., Dodson, M., & Shrout, P. E. (1984). Symptoms, hassles, social support, and life events: Problem of confounded measures. *Journal of Abnormal Psychology, 93,* 222–230.

Dohrenwend, B. C., & Shrout, P. E. (1985). "Hassles" in the conceptualization and measurement of life stress variables. *American Psychologist, 40,* 780–785.

Ellis, J. L., & Wollenberg, A. L. (1993). Local homogeneity in latent trait models: A characterization of the homogeneous monotone item response model. *Psychometrika, 58,* 417–429.

Eysenck, H. J. (1955). A dynamic theory of anxiety and hysteria. *Journal of Mental Science, 101,* 28–51.

Feigl, H. (1950). Existential hypotheses. *Philosophy of Science, 17,* 35–62.

Feist, G. J., Bodner, T. E., Jacobs, J. F., Miles, M., & Tan, V. (1995). Integrating top-down and bottom-up structural models of subjective well-being: A longitudinal investigation. *Journal of Personality and Social Psychology, 68,* 138–150.

Feldt, L. S., & Brennan, R. L. (1989). Reliability. In R. L. Linn (Ed.), *Educational measurement* (3rd ed., pp. 105–146). New York: Macmillan.

Fraser, C., & McDonald, R. P. (1988). COSAN: Covariance structure analysis. *Multivariate Behavioral Research, 23,* 263–265.

Glaser, R. (1963). Instrumentation, technology, and the measurement of learning outcomes. *American Psychologist, 18,* 519–521.

Greenwood, J. D. (1994). *Realism, identity and emotion: Reclaiming social psychology.* London: Sage.

Guilford, J. P. (1954). *Psychometric methods.* New York: McGraw-Hill.

Guilford, J. P. (1967). *The nature of human intelligence.* New York: McGraw-Hill.

Guttman, L. (1941). The quantification of a class of attributes. In P. Horst (Ed.), *The prediction of personal adjustment* (pp. 321–348). New York: Social Science Research Council.

Guttman, L. (1945). A basis for analyzing test–retest reliability. *Psychometrika, 10,* 255–282.

Guttman, L. (1950). Chapters 2, 3, 6, 8, 9. In S. Stouffer et al. (Eds.), *Measurement and prediction.* Princeton, NJ: Princeton University Press.

Guttman, L. (1957). Simple proofs of relations between the communality problem and multiple correlation. *Psychometrika, 22,* 147–157.

Guttman, L. (1977). What is not what in statistics. *Statistician, 26,* 81–107.

Hakstian, A. R. (1971). A comparative evaluation of several prominent methods of oblique factor transformation. *Psychometrika, 36,* 175–193.

Haley, D. C. (1952). *Estimation of the dosage mortality relationship when the dosage is subject to error* (Tech. Rep. No. 15). Stanford, CA: Applied Mathematics and Statistics Laboratory, Stanford University.

Hambleton, R. K. (1980). Test score validity and standard setting methods. In R. A. Berk (Ed.), *Criterion-referenced measurement: The state of the art* (pp. 45–123). Baltimore: Johns Hopkins University Press.

Hartmann, W. (1996). *Proc Calis: Extended user's guide.* Cary, NC: SAS Institute, Inc.

Haynes, S. N., Richard, D. C. S., & Kubany, E. S. (1995). Content validity in psychological assessment: A functional approach to concepts and methods. *Psychological Assessment, 7,* 238–247.

Holland, P. W., & Rubin, D. B. (1982). *Test equating.* New York: Academic Press.

Holland, P. W., & Wainer, H. (Eds.). (1993). *Differential item functioning.* Hillsdale, NJ: Lawrence Erlbaum Associates.

Hull, J. G., Lehn, D. A., & Tedlie, J. C. (1991). A general approach to testing multifaceted personality constructs. *Journal of Personality and Social Psychology, 61,* 932–945.

James, L. R., Mulaik, S. A., & Brett, J. M. (1982). *Causal analysis: Assumptions, models, and data.* Beverly Hills, CA: Sage.

Johnson, R. A., & Wichern, D. W. (1992). *Applied multivariate statistical analysis* (3rd ed.). Englewood Cliffs, NJ: Prentice-Hall.

Joreskog, K. G., & Sorbom, D. (1979). *LISREL VI: Analysis of linear structural relationships by maximum likelihood, instrumental variables and least squares.* Uppsala: University of Uppsala.

Kanner, A. D., Coyne, J. C., Schaefer, C., & Lazarus, R. S. (1981). Comparison of two modes of stress measurement: Daily hassles and uplifts versus major life events. *Journal of Behavioral Medicine, 4,* 1–39.

Kaufman, A. S. (1990). *Assessing adolescent and adult intelligence.* Boston: Allyn & Bacon.

Keesling, J. W. (1972). *Maximum likelihood approaches to causal analysis.* Unpublished doctoral dissertation, University of Chicago.

Knol, D. L., & Berger, M. P. F. (1991). Empirical comparison between factor analysis and multidimensional item response models. *Multivariate Behavioral Research, 26,* 457–477.

Kuder, G. F., & Richardson, M. W. (1937). The theory of the estimation of test reliability. *Psychometrika, 2,* 151–160.

Lamb, M. E., Thompson, R. A., Gardner, W. P., Charnov, E. L., & Estes, D. (1984). Security of infantile attachment as assessed in the "strange situation": Its study and biological interpretation. *Behavioral and Brain Sciences, 7,* 127–171.

Lazarsfeld, P. F. (1960). Latent structure analysis and test theory. In H. Gulliksen & S. Messick (Eds.), *Psychological scaling: theory and applications* (pp. 83–96). New York: Wiley.

Lazarus, R. S., DeLongis, A., Folkman, S., & Gruen, R. (1985). Stress and adaptational outcomes: The problem of confounded measures. *American Psychologist, 40,* 770–779.

Lonsway, K. A., & Fitzgerald, L. F. (1995). Attitudinal antecedents of rape myth acceptance: A theoretical and empirical reexamination. *Journal of Personality and Social Psychology, 68,* 704–711.

Lord, F. M. (1952). A theory of test scores. *Psychometric Monograph,* No. 7.

Lord, F. M. (1980). *Applications of item response theory to practical testing problems.* Hillsdale, NJ: Lawrence Erlbaum Associates.

Lord, F. M., & Novick, M. R. (1968). *Statistical theories of mental test scores, with contributions by Alan Birnbaum.* Reading, MA: Addison-Wesley.

Luce, R. D. (1959). *Individual choice behavior.* New York: Wiley.

MacCallum, R. C., Wegener, D. T., Uchino, B. N., & Fabrigar, L. R. (1993). The problem of equivalent models in applications of covariance structure models. *Psychological Bulletin, 114,* 185–199.

MacCorquodale, K., & Meehl, P. E. (1948). On a distinction between hypothetical constructs and intervening variables. *Psychological Review, 55,* 95–107.

Maloney, M. P., & Ward, M. P. (1976). *Psychological assessment: A conceptual approach.* New York: Oxford University Press.

Maraun, M. D. (1996a). Metaphor taken as math: Indeterminacy in the factor analysis model. *Multivariate Behavioral Research, 31,* 517–538.

Maraun, M. D. (1996b). Meaning and mythology in the factor analysis model. *Multivariate Behavioral Research, 31,* 603–616.

Maraun, M. D. (1996c). The claims of factor analysis. *Multivariate Behavioral Research, 31,* 673–689.

McArdle, J. J. (1978, December). *A structural view of structural models.* Paper presented at the Winter Workshop on Latent Structure Models Applied to Developmental Data, Department of Psychology, University of Denver.

McArdle, J. J. (1979, September). *Reticular Analysis Modeling (RAM) theory; The simplicity and generality of structural equations.* Paper presented at the American Psychological Association Annual Meeting, New York.

McArdle, J. J., & McDonald, R. P. (1984). Some algebraic properties of the Reticular Action Model for moment structures. *British Journal of Mathematical and Statistical Psychology, 37,* 234–251.

McCrae, R. R., & Costa, D. T., Jr. (1985). Updating Norman's "adequate taxonomy": Intelligence and personality dimensions in natural languages and in questionnaires. *Journal of Personality and Social Psychology, 49,* 710–721.

McDonald, R. P. (1967). Nonlinear factor analysis. *Psychometric Monograph,* No. 15.

McDonald, R. P. (1969). The common factor analysis of multicategory data. *British Journal of Mathematical and Statistical Psychology, 22,* 165–175.

McDonald, R. P. (1970). The theoretical foundations of common factor analysis, principal factor analysis, and alpha factor analysis. *British Journal of Mathematical and Statistical Psychology, 23,* 1–21.

McDonald, R. P. (1977). The indeterminacy of components and the definition of common factors. *British Journal of Mathematical and Statistical Psychology, 30*, 165–176.

McDonald, R. P. (1982a). Linear versus nonlinear models in item response theory. *Applied Psychological Measurement, 6*, 379–396.

McDonald, R. P. (1982b, July). *Unidimensional and multidimensional models for item response theory.* IRT/CAT Conference, Minneapolis, MN.

McDonald, R. P. (1983). Alternative weights and invariant parameters in optimal scaling. *Psychometrika, 48*, 377–392.

McDonald, R. P. (1985). *Factor analysis and related methods.* Hillsdale, NJ: Lawrence Erlbaum Associates.

McDonald, R. P. (1986). Describing the elephant: Structure and function in multivariate data. *Psychometrika, 51*, 513–534.

McDonald, R. P. (1988). The first and second laws of intelligence. In A. Watson (Ed.), *Intelligence: Controversy and change* (pp. 78–85). Melbourne: Australian Council for Educational Research.

McDonald, R. P. (1996a). Latent traits and the possibility of motion. *Multivariate Behavioral Research, 31*, 593–601.

McDonald, R. P. (1996b). Consensus emergens: A matter of interpretation. *Multivariate Behavioral Research, 31*, 663–672.

McDonald, R. P. (1997a). Normal ogive multidimensional model. In W. J. Van der Linden & R. K. Hambleton (Eds.), *Handbook of item response theory* (pp. 258–269). New York: Springer-Verlag.

McDonald, R. P. (1997b). Haldane's lungs: A case study in path analysis. *Multivariate Behavioral Research, 32*, 1–38.

McDonald, R. P., & Mulaik, S. A. (1979). Determinacy of common factors: A non-technical review. *Psychological Bulletin, 86*, 297–306.

McDonald, R. P., Parker, P. M., & Ishizuka, T. (1993). A scale-invariant treatment for recursive path models. *Psychometrika, 58*, 431–443.

McDonald, R. P., & Yates, A. J. (1960). Hammer's critique of Eysenck's dimensional psychology. *Australian Journal of Psychology, 12*, 212–218.

Mellenburgh, G. J. (1994). Generalized linear item response theory. *Psychological Bulletin, 115*, 300–307.

Messick, S. (1980). Test validity and the ethics of measurement. *American Psychologist, 30*, 955–966.

Messick, S. (1989). Validity. In R. L. Linn (Ed.), *Educational measurement* (3rd ed., pp. 13–103). New York: Macmillan.

Moore, D. S., & McCabe, G. P. (1993). *Introduction to the practice of statistics* (2nd ed.). New York: Freeman.

Mulaik, S. A. (1972). *Foundations of factor analysis.* New York: McGraw-Hill.

Mulaik, S. A. (1996a). On Maraun's deconstructing of factor indeterminacy with constructed factors. *Multivariate Behavioral Research, 31*, 579–592.

Mulaik, S. A. (1996b). Factor analysis is not just a model in pure mathematics. *Multivariate Behavioral Research, 31*, 655–661.

Muthen, B. (1978). Contributions to factor analysis of dichotomous variables. *Psychometrika, 43*, 551–560.

Muthen, B. (1984). A general structural equation model with dichotomous, ordered category, and continuous latent variable indicators. *Psychometrika, 49*, 115–132.

Nishisato, S. (1994). *Elements of dual scaling: An introduction to practical data analysis.* Hillsdale, NJ: Lawrence Erlbaum Associates.

Nishisato, S. (1996). Gleaning in the field of dual scaling. *Psychometrika, 61*, 559–599.

Novick, M. R., & Lewis, C. (1967). Coefficient alpha and the reliability of composite measurements. *Psychometrika, 32*, 1–13.

Pearl, J. (1998). Graphs, causality and structural equation models. *Sociological Methods and Research, 27,* 226–284.

Reckase, M. D. (1985). The difficulty of test items that measure more than one ability. *Applied Psychological Measurement, 9,* 401–412.

Reckase, M. D. (1997). A linear logistic multidimensional model. In W. J. Van der Linden & R. K. Hambleton (Eds.), *Handbook of item response theory* (pp. 271–286). New York: Springer-Verlag.

Reynolds, W. M., & Kobak, K. A. (1995). Reliability and validity of the Hamilton Depression Inventory: A paper-and-pencil version of the Hamilton Depression Rating Scale Clinical Interview. *Psychological Assessment, 7,* 472–483.

Rozeboom, W. W. (1996a). What might common factors be? *Multivariate Behavioral Research, 31,* 555–570.

Rozeboom, W. W. (1996b). Factor-indeterminacy issues are not linguistic confusions. *Multivariate Behavioral Research, 31,* 637–650.

Saris, W. E., & Van Meurs, A. (1990). *Evaluation of measurement instruments by meta-analysis of MTMM studies.* Amsterdam: North Holland.

Sax, G. (1980). *Principles of educational and psychological measurement and evaluation* (2nd ed.). Belmont, CA: Wadsworth.

Schmid, J., & Leiman, J. M. (1957). The development of hierarchical factor solutions. *Psychometrika, 22,* 53–62.

Schonemann, P. H. (1996a). The psychopathology of factor indeterminacy. *Multivariate Behavioral Research, 31,* 571–577.

Schonemann, P. H. (1996b). Syllogisms of factor indeterminacy. *Multivariate Behavioral Research, 31,* 651–654.

Shye, S. (1985). *Multiple scaling: The theory and application of partial order scalogram analysis.* New York: Elsevier.

Spearman, C. (1927). *The abilities of man: Their nature and measurement.* New York: Macmillan.

Steiger, J. H. (1996a). Dispelling some myths about factor indeterminacy. *Multivariate Behavioral Research, 31,* 539–550.

Steiger, J. H. (1996b). Coming full circle in the history of factor indeterminacy. *Multivariate Behavioral Research, 31,* 617–630.

Stevens, S. S. (1946). On the theory of scales of measurement. *Science, 105,* 677–680.

Strotz, R. H., & Wold, H. O. A. (1960). Recursive versus nonrecursive systems: An attempt at synthesis. *Econometrika, 28,* 417–427.

Thorndike, R. M., & Lohman, D. F. (1990). *A century of ability testing.* Chicago: Riverside.

Thurstone, L. L. (1947). *Multiple factor analysis.* Chicago: University of Chicago Press.

Tziner, A. E. (1987). *The facet analytic approach to research and data processing.* New York: Peter Lang.

Verma, T., & Pearl, J. (1990). Equivalence and synthesis of causal models. In *Uncertainty in artificial intelligence* (pp. 255–268). Cambridge, MA: Elsevier.

Wainer, H., Dorans, N. J., Flaugher, R., Green, B. F., Mislevy, R. J., Steinberg, L., & Thissen, D. (1990). *Computerized adaptive testing: A primer.* Hillsdale, NJ: Lawrence Erlbaum Associates.

Wainer, H., & Braun, H. I. (Eds.). (1988). *Test validity.* Hillsdale, NJ: Lawrence Erlbaum Associates.

Walker, D. A. (1931). Answer pattern and score scatter in tests and examinations. *British Journal of Psychology, 22,* 73–86.

Wasserman, S., & Faust, K. (1994). *Social network analysis: Methods and applications.* New York: Cambridge University Press.

Widaman, K. F. (1985). Hierarchically nested covariance structure models for multitrait-multimethod data. *Applied Psychological Methods, 9,* 1–26.

Wiley, D. E. (1973). The identification problem for structural equation models with unmeasured variables. In A. S. Goldberger & O. D. Duncan (Eds.), *Structural equation models in the social sciences* (pp. 69–83). New York: Academic Press.

Young, F. W., & Hamer, R. M. (Eds.). (1987). *Multidimensional scaling: History, theory, and applications.* Hillsdale, NJ: Lawrence Erlbaum Associates.

Author Index

Note: Numbers in bold indicate pages with complete bibliographic information.

Subject Index

Note: Numbers in bold indicate primary accounts or definitions.